Decades of Deceit
The Stalker Affair and its Legacy

Paddy Hillyard

First published 2024

Beyond the Pale Books
Teach Basil
2 Hannahstown Hill
Belfast BT17 0LT

www.beyondthepalebooks.com

ISBN 978-1-914318-27-6 (paperback)

Printed in Ireland by Walsh Colour Print, Castleisland, Co. Kerry

Front cover photo courtesy Pacemaker. It shows the hayshed where Michael Tighe was shot dead and Martin McCauley wounded. Back cover photo shows the car in which Sean Burns, Gervaise McKerr and Eugene Toman were shot dead by the RUC. (See Chapter 2)

In memory of

Fintan Ward Hillyard 1985-2014

And for my grandsons:

Rory, Finn and Rowan

'Oh, what a tangled web we weave
When first we practise to deceive!'
Marmion by Sir Walter Scott, 1808.

'But if history offers any lesson here, it may be that the real "outposts of
tyranny" are the institutions left behind by the colonial and military
strategists in Britain's twentieth-century empire.'
Caroline Elkins, 2005.

'And in the dirt lay justice like an acorn in the winter.'
The Road to Derry, Séamus Heaney, 1972.

Contents

List of Abbreviations

ACC	Assistant Chief Constable
ACPO	Association of Chief Police Officers
AG	Attorney General
ASP	Assistant Secretary Political
ASU	Active Service Unit
CAJ	Committee on the Administration of Justice
CC	Chief Constable
CCF	Criminal Compensation Fund
CCRC	Criminal Cases Review Commission
CDIU	Central Drugs Intelligence Unit
CHIS	Covert Human Intelligence Sources
CID	Criminal Investigation Department
CIU	Criminal Intelligence Unit
CME	Correct Methods of Entry
CPS	Crown Prosecution Service
CS	Chief Superintendent
DC	Detective Constable
DCC	Deputy Chief Constable
DCI	Detective Chief Inspector
DCInt	Director and Co-ordinator of Intelligence
DCS	Detective Chief Superintendent
DIS	Defence Intelligence Staff
DIU	Drugs Intelligence Unit
DPP	Director of Public Prosecutions
DPPNI	Director of Public Prosecutions in Northern Ireland
DRC	Data Reference Centre
DS	Detective Superintendent
DSgt	Detective Sergeant
DUS	Deputy Under Secretary
DVLA	Driver and Vehicle Licensing Agency
ECHR	European Convention on Human Rights
ECtHR	European Court of Human Rights.
FIG	Fraud Investigation Group
FOI	Freedom of Information
FOIA	Freedom of Information Act 2000
FRU	Force Research Unit
GCHQ	Government Communications Headquarters
GMP	Greater Manchester Police
GMPA	Greater Manchester Police Authority
HAI	Historical Abuse Inquiry
HET	Historical Enquiries Team.
HMIC	Her Majesty's Inspectorate of Constabulary
HMSU	Headquarters Mobile Support Unit
IBA	Independent Broadcasting Authority
ICRIR	Independent Commission for Reconciliation and Information Recovery
IJS	Irish Joint Section
INLA	Irish National Liberation Army

IPC   Investigatory Powers Commissioner
IPT   Investigatory Powers Tribunal
IRA   Irish Republican Army
ISC   Intelligence Services Commissioner
ISU   Internal Security Unit
JIC   Joint Intelligence Committee
JFF   Justice for the Forgotten
JSG   Joint Support Group, the successor to FRU
LFF   Long Firm Fraud
MI5   The Security Service
MCA   Manchester Conservative Association
MMI   Municipal Mutual Insurance
NCCL   National Council for Civil Liberties
NDNA   New Decade, New Approach
NIO   Northern Ireland Office
NIPA   Northern Ireland Police Authority
NISC   Northern Ireland Security Coordinator
OIRA   Official Irish Republican Army
PACE   Police and Criminal Evidence Act 1984
PCA   Police Complaints Authority
PFC   Pat Finucane Centre
PIIC   Public Interest Immunity Certificate
PIRA   Provisional IRA
PNC   Police National Computer
PPS   Public Prosecution Service
PRC   Policy Review Committee
PS   Permanent Secretary
PSNI   Police Service of Northern Ireland
PUS   Permanent Under Secretary
QSG   Quality Street Gang
RHD   Red Hand Defenders
RCS   Regional Crime Squad
RIPA   Regulation of Investigatory Powers Act 2000
RUC   Royal Ulster Constabulary
SAS   Special Air Service
SB   Special Branch
SDLP   Social Democratic and Labour Party
SHA   Stormont House Agreement
SIS   Secret Intelligence Service
SOI   Senior Investigating Officer
SOP   Static Observation Post
SoS   Secretary of State
TCG   Tasking and Coordination Group
TSU   Tactical Support Unit
UDA   Ulster Defence Association
UDR   Ulster Defence Regiment
UVF   Ulster Volunteer Force
WEIU   Weapons and Explosives Intelligence Unit

Dramatis Personae

The controversial shootings

Burns, Sean; **Toman, Eugene**; and **McKerr, Gervaise.** Members of the IRA, shot dead by members of the RUC HMSU, 11 November 1982.

Carroll, Roddy and **Grew, Seamus**. Members of the INLA, shot dead by members of the RUC HMSU, 12 December 1982.

McCauley, Martin and **Tighe, Michael** shot by members of the RUC HMSU in a hayshed, 24 November 1982. McCauley was seriously wounded and Tighe killed. McCauley was prosecuted for possession of firearms found in the hayshed, convicted and given a two-year suspended prison sentence, which was subsequently overturned.

The key figures

Stalker, John. Deputy Chief Constable of Greater Manchester Police (GMP), 1984-1987. Married Stella 1961, two daughters. Met Kevin Taylor when their children attended the same school. Appointed to head investigation into the killing of six men by the police in Northern Ireland, May 1984. Suspended and removed from Northern Ireland inquiry, May 1986. Faced disciplinary charges. Allegations of a conspiracy to remove him. Reinstated by Police Authority, August 1986. Resigned from GMP, March 1987. Died 15 February 2019, aged 79.

Taylor, Kevin. Born during the great depression. In 1961, became a full-time professional gambler in London and later a property developer. Married Beryl, 1964, two daughters. Developed an inner-city site in Manchester, 1967. Sold site for £2.75 million and bought further sites from proceeds, 1984. Arrested and prosecuted for conspiracy to obtain pecuniary advantage from Co-operative Bank by deception, September 1987. Made bankrupt. Trial collapsed after police committed perjury, 1990. Began civil action for malicious prosecution against GMP. Settled with a payment of £2.4m in compensation, 1995. Died 26 October 2001, aged 69.

The Security Service – MI5

Deverell, John. MI5 officer and Director and Co-ordinator of Intelligence. Dates unknown.

Sheldon, Bernard. Head of Legal Services, MI5. Dates unknown.

Ranson, David. Director and Co-ordinator of Intelligence in Northern Ireland. Dates unknown.

Walker, Patrick. Thought to have been assistant to David Ranson, precise dates unknown but probably 1979-1980 before becoming Director and Co-ordinator of Intelligence around 1981. Devised the counter-insurgency strategy (herein: MI5/Walker strategy) introduced in 1981. Appointed Director General of the Security Service in 1987.

Her Majesty's Inspector of Constabulary

Byford, Sir Lawrence. Chief Constable of the Lincolnshire Police, 1973-1977. Regional Inspector, HMIC, 1978, and Chief Inspector, HMIC, 1983. Chaired Scarborough meeting at which decisions appear to have been taken to suspend Stalker from duty and remove him from the Northern Ireland inquiry, May 1986. Knighted in 1984. Died 10 February 2018.

Myers, Sir Philip. Chief Constable of North Wales Police, 1974-1986. Regional Inspector, HMIC, responsible for the RUC and GMP, 1981. Selected Stalker for the Northern Ireland inquiry, May 1984. Attended Scarborough meeting, May 1986. Knighted in 1985. Died 21 June 2014.

West Yorkshire Police

Sampson, Sir Colin. Chief Constable of West Yorkshire, 1983-1989. HMIC 1989-1990. Appointed to investigate the disciplinary charge against Stalker and to complete the investigation begun by Stalker into the killing by the RUC of six men in Northern Ireland in 1982, May 1986. Knighted in 1992. Died 15 October 2018.

Greater Manchester Police and No 1. Regional Crime Squad

Anderton, Sir Cyril James. Chief Constable of GMP, 1976-1991. Chair of Association of Chief Police Officers, 1990. Recommended Stalker to carry out investigation in Northern Ireland, May 1984. An outspoken and highly controversial Chief Constable. Knighted in 1990. Died 5 May 2022.

Grant, James. Detective Superintendent. Head of Operational Support Services, 1985, which included Drugs Intelligence Unit (DIU) and Surveillance Unit. Both units played central role in the investigation into Taylor. Previously, second-in-command under Topping in Discipline and Complaints Department. Alleged mason.

Lees, Ralph. Assistant Chief Constable. Responsible for CID, 1984-1989. According to Stalker, he was a very capable uniformed officer but had no detective experience. Queen's Police Medal, 1986. Retired 1989.

McGourlay, Bernard. Chief Superintendent. Deputy Head, No. 1 RCS, 1983-1985. Central figure in the Taylor/Stalker story. Reported golf conversation to Topping in 1984 which allegedly, together with information from David Burton, a police informer, triggered the investigation into Stalker and Taylor.

Simons, John. Detective Superintendent. Head of the Commercial Fraud Squad, which investigated Taylor. A member of Stalker's inquiry team in Northern Ireland. Alleged mason.

Thorburn, John. Chief Superintendent. Following the reorganisation of the command structure of the CID in 1985, side-lined and appointed head of policy and administration rather than operations. Second-in-command of Stalker's investigation in Northern Ireland. Retired in 1989.

Topping, Peter. Chief Superintendent. Head of Discipline and Complaints Department, 1984. Instigated investigation into Stalker and Taylor. Promoted Head of CID (Operations), January 1985. Organised search of bodies in the Moors Murders case, December 1986. Retired on medical grounds and wrote a book, published 1989, Queen's Police Medal, 1989. Alleged mason.

Drugs Intelligence Unit (DIU)

Born, Norman. Detective Chief Inspector. Head of DIU, 1985-1989.

Caldwell, Kenneth. Detective Sergeant. Joined DIU, June 1986.

Corfield, Alan. Detective Sergeant. Joined DIU, June 1986.

Fiddler, Frank. Detective Sergeant. Joined DIU, February 1985. Headed the Surveillance Unit, which observed Taylor's offices for 114 days.

Hogg, Peter. Detective Constable. Joined DIU, June 1986.

Knowles, David. Detective Constable. Joined DIU, June 1986.

Murray, Rodney. Detective Inspector. Joined DIU, February 1985.

Richardson, John. Detective Inspector. Joined DIU, February 1985.

Stephenson, Anthony. Detective Inspector. Joined DIU as a fraud officer, November 1985.

Ware, Keith. Sergeant. Joined DIU, February 1985.

Waterworth, John. Detective Inspector. Joined DIU, February 1985.

Royal Ulster Constabulary

Hermon, Sir John. Chief Constable, 1980-1989. Agreed to an outside investigation into the three shooting incidents in Northern Ireland, May 1984. Received Stalker's interim report, September 1985. Forwarded report to the DPPNI, February 1986. Stalker had planned to interview him under caution but was removed beforehand. Published autobiography, 1997. Knighted 1982. Died 6 November 2008.

McAtamney, Michael. Deputy Chief Constable, 1980. Hermon asked him to review the three events which led to the death of the six men by the RUC and to work directly with the DPPNI over the matter. Stalker had planned to interview him under caution but was removed beforehand.

Forbes, Trevor. Assistant Chief Constable, 1981. Head of Special Branch. Stalker had planned to interview him under caution but was removed beforehand.

Hamilton, Paul, Constable; **Quinn, Sean**, Sergeant; and **McCloy, Alan**, Constable. Killed by the IRA in land-mine explosion on Kinnego Embankment, Armagh, 27 October 1982.

Robinson, John, Constable. Appeared in court charged with the murder of Seamus Grew, 20 March 1984. Acquitted.

Brannigan, David, Constable; **Montgomery, William**, Sergeant; and **Robinson, Frederick**, Constable. Charged with the murder of Eugene Toman, 20 May 1984. All acquitted.

Co-operative Bank officials

Bowley, Terence. Joined the Co-operative Bank in Manchester, 1979. Headed-up the Corporate Business Department, 1984. Oversaw loans to Taylor. Arrested and charged with Taylor and others with conspiracy to defraud the Co-operative Bank, September 1987. The trial collapsed after the police committed perjury.

Chadwick, Lewis. Advances Department member.

Cowburn, John. Corporate Business manager.

Davenport, David. Associate Corporate Business Manager and assistant to Terence Bowley.

Gorvin, Roger. Director.

Sheppard, Hylie. Assistant general manager. Chief inspector in its fraud department.

Wood, Stephen. Security clerk.

The accused

Bowley, Terence. See above.

Britton, Derek. Taylor's accountant. Arrested and charged with Taylor and others, with conspiracy to defraud the Co-operative Bank, September 1987. The trial collapsed after the police committed perjury.

McCann, Vincent. A quantity surveyor and business associate of Taylor. Advised him on some of his property purchases. Arrested, October 1987, and charged with Taylor and others with conspiracy to defraud the Co-operative Bank. The trial collapsed after the police committed perjury.

Lawyers

Buckley, Charles. Practising licence revoked by the Law Society when he was bankrupted after a business venture failed, 1980. Offered his services to Taylor and used the law to uncover the abuses in the investigation of Taylor.

Corkery, Michael, QC. Chief prosecutor in the trial of Taylor and his three co-defendants.

Farley, Roger, QC. Taylor's counsel in the civil action brought against GMP.

Ferguson, Richard, QC. Represented Taylor in his criminal trial. Originally from Northern Ireland where he stood as an Ulster Unionist MP for South Antrim, 1968. Taylor considered that he would bring an understanding of the Northern Ireland dimension to the case. However, the Taylor defence team became unhappy with his lack of intervention in the cross-examination and he resigned.

Hood, David. Initially, junior to Ferguson in Taylor's criminal trial. When Ferguson resigned, Hood replaced him. His cross-examination exposed how the police constructed a crime against Taylor through lies and other abuses. Led to the Judge dismissing all charges against Taylor and his co-defendants.

Morrow, Graham, QC. Anderton's defence counsel in the civil action brought by Taylor.

Tabachnik, Eldred, QC. Anderton's defence counsel in the civil action brought by Taylor.

Quality Street Gang

Considerable controversy over whether it was a criminal gang, in the sense that its members conspired together to commit crimes, or a loose collection of known criminals who were blamed for major unsolved crimes in the Manchester area.

Burton, David. Career criminal, narcissist, inveterate and pathological liar, and master of deception. Police informer to various organisations. 'Blowerman' in a Long Firm Fraud in Belfast and Manchester organised by Mark Klapish, 1980-1981. Told GMP that Klapish had contracted IRA to blow-up his warehouse in

Belfast, late 1981. GMP claim he provided information to police that Stalker was corrupt and Taylor a major criminal, 1981, 1983 and 1984.

Donnelly, Jimmy. An alleged member.

Monaghan, James Patrick. An alleged member.

Klapish, Mark. A Manchester businessman and an alleged member of the QSG. He organised the LFF in Belfast and arranged for the IRA or UDA to blow up his premises in Kent Street, 1980-1981.

Schiavo, Louis. An alleged member.

Schiavo, Vincent. An alleged member.

Trickett, Jack. An alleged member.

Drug smugglers

Brooks, Alan. Used Taylor's yacht, *Diogenes*, when up for sale, to smuggle drugs into Dartmouth, England with the help of William Whittaker, a professional yacht skipper, 3 February 1985.

O'Connor, Maurice. Trafficked cannabis from farms in North Africa to the United Kingdom and Ireland. Passenger on *Sherama*, with several wanted criminals when it docked in Gibraltar, 11 June 1984.

Whittaker, William Allie. A professional yacht skipper involved in the importation of drugs into the United Kingdom. Skippered *Sherama* when it arrived in Gibraltar, 11 June 1984.

Worswick, Eric. Arrested for handling stolen goods, 1985. Also involved in drug smuggling. Agreed to become a 'participating informer' to provide information, *inter alia*, on *Diogenes*.

Preface

THIS BOOK is about a journey to unravel the truth in one of the most notorious events in British and Northern Irish policing history: the sacking of John Stalker, Deputy Chief Constable of the Greater Manchester Police, from a highly sensitive police inquiry in Northern Ireland. He was asked to investigate the fatal shooting of six young men by the Royal Ulster Constabulary, in three separate incidents in November and December 1982. A year earlier, the Security Service, MI5, had introduced a new secret policing strategy – without any legal framework or parliamentary approval – which relied heavily on the use of informers and state agents to provide intelligence, while placing less priority on the detection and prosecution of crime. Stalker started his inquiry in May 1984 and submitted only an interim report in September 1985. This was incomplete because he had been denied access to crucial information by both the RUC and MI5. In May 1986, before completing a final report, he was instructed to take extended leave and was removed 'forever' from the Northern Ireland inquiry, while facing a disciplinary charge of associating with 'known criminals in a manner likely to bring discredit upon Greater Manchester Police'.

It was widely believed that there had been a conspiracy to remove Stalker. The speculation was that his report would do enormous damage to the reputation of the RUC at a time it was struggling to deal with widespread political violence from both the Provisional IRA and loyalist armed groups – a situation bordering on a civil war between the two main communities in Northern Ireland. It was further argued that criticism would be disastrous at the very moment the force was required to police loyalist and unionist protests following the introduction of the Anglo-Irish Agreement, signed by the British and Irish governments in November 1985.

I have had a long-standing interest in the rule of law in Northern Ireland. It began following what has now become known as Bloody Sunday. On 30 January 1972, the Parachute Regiment opened fire on an anti-internment demonstration killing thirteen people and injuring many others, one of whom later died. I did not go on the demonstration because of the violence the week before by the British army during an anti-internment protest on Magilligan Strand. Many of my friends, colleagues, and students from the then New University of Ulster in Coleraine did go on the demonstration. That evening everyone assembled around the communal television in the main entrance hall of the University to watch the BBC news. Colonel Wilford, commander of 1st

Battalion Parachute Regiment, was interviewed and said: 'We were fired upon, and we returned fire.' There was uproar as those present had witnessed the deliberate, organised, and indiscriminate firing on a peaceful demonstration. The following day, several of us drove to Derry and took statements from eyewitnesses for the National Council for Civil Liberties.

A Tribunal of Inquiry was set up in February 1972, chaired by the Rt. Hon. Lord Justice Widgery, to investigate the circumstances of the events on Bloody Sunday. It was not held in Derry but in Coleraine, a predominantly Protestant town which was perceived as a hostile environment for Catholics. The location deterred many from giving evidence. I attended some of the hearings. The atmosphere was intimidating with several English public school-educated barristers, representing the army, showing total disdain for the shocked and traumatised citizens of Derry. Several had considerable difficulty understanding the local accents.

Lord Widgery's report was a whitewash. He ignored most of the eyewitness statements, exonerated the army and laid the blame on those who had organised the march. Many years later, it emerged that Prime Minister Edward Heath had made it clear to Lord Widgery, on the occasion of his appointment, that the government was fighting not only a military war but also a propaganda war. Widgery, who had served in the British army, understood the comment. It was not until the publication of the Saville Inquiry report in 2010 – some 38 years later – that the truth emerged. All those shot were totally innocent of any wrongdoing. Prime Minister David Cameron apologised in the House of Commons: 'There is no doubt, there is nothing equivocal, there are no ambiguities. What happened on Bloody Sunday was both unjustified and unjustifiable. It was wrong.'

My understanding of what happened on Bloody Sunday from taking witness statements, attending some of the Tribunal of Inquiry hearings and reading the Widgery report, had a profound impact on my thinking about the rule of law. Naively, I had assumed that a Lord Chief Justice, trained to examine the facts of a case and to make an impartial and objective judgment, would have reached the conclusion that the Parachute Regiment had indiscriminately opened fire on a demonstration without any justification. The fact that he ignored the evidence and reached such a perverse and biased conclusion was profoundly disturbing. It illustrated for me the vulnerability of the rule of law to political pressure and how a state can abuse the law to construct 'truth'.

In subsequent years, I carried out, either alone or with colleagues, several studies into the rule of law in Northern Ireland. Following Stalker's removal from the Northern Ireland inquiry in 1986, I was naturally sceptical of what I will call the 'official narrative', which was that his removal had nothing to do with Northern Ireland and was solely related to events in Manchester. I decided that I would carefully monitor developments. Shortly after Stalker's suspension, there were rumours that Stalker's friend, Kevin Taylor, a well-known property developer and ex-chair of the Manchester Conservative Association, was involved in organised crime and drug smuggling. Subsequently, it was revealed that the basis of a disciplinary charge against Stalker was his friendship with Taylor. When Taylor was charged, not with any drug offence but with fraud, and the trial collapsed, I became even more sceptical of the official narrative that there was no connection to Stalker's Northern Ireland inquiry.

In order to clear his name, Taylor began a civil action in 1993 against Greater Manchester Police for malicious prosecution. At the time, I was lecturing at the University of Bristol. When the case started two years later, I drove up to Liverpool to attend the trial. I met Taylor and introduced myself. We went for a coffee in the basement of the court. He complained that despite the widespread rumours about him, he still had not had his day in court. He said that he was looking forward to being called and was determined to clear his name. He introduced me briefly to John Stalker before the civil action hearing began.

Stalker was the first witness. He constantly challenged the police 'intelligence' on Taylor, pointing out irregularities in the documentation, the lack of professionalism in the collection of information, and laying bare the absurdity of some of the interpretations being put on the evidence. It added to my concerns about the official narrative that there was no conspiracy to remove Stalker, but simply a coincidence of events in Manchester and Northern Ireland. I decided to research the events more deeply.

Following the civil action, I contacted Kevin Taylor. He and Beryl, his wife, were extremely generous with their time. Kevin subsequently granted me access to his personal papers. The book is based on these papers and a detailed analysis of the transcripts of his criminal trial and the civil action. In addition, over the years I have carried out numerous interviews with journalists, lawyers, police officers, officials in various law enforcement agencies, and with a few people who made a living from crime.

The research also benefited from the mass of published sources. Many millions of words have been written about the Taylor/Stalker affair. The two targets of the police investigation, Stalker and Taylor, have themselves written books. Stalker's book was simply called *Stalker*. Kevin Taylor's was entitled: *The Poisoned Tree: The untold truth about the police conspiracy to discredit John Stalker and destroy me.*

Peter Taylor, a highly respected journalist and an expert on Northern Ireland, followed developments from the start and produced two BBC Panorama programmes on the story before publishing his own book called *Stalker: The Search for the Truth*. Exceptionally, he argued that there was no conspiracy, simply a coincidence of parallel events in Northern Ireland and Manchester. David Murphy, an academic, published an excellent and detailed analysis of the press reporting of the story under the title: *The Stalker Affair and the Press*, in 1991.

Seeking the truth in any set of events is never easy, but the very documents which might shed some light on what happened are in the hands of those suspected of malpractice – the police, the government, and their servants. Under the Public Records Act 1958, government papers must be deposited in the National Archives after 20 years. Files, however, may be retained after this time if they are 'required for administrative purposes or ought to be retained for any other special reason'. There are also various exemptions under the Freedom of Information Act, 2000. After a four-year struggle and a complaint to the Information Commissioner, some files concerning the Stalker Affair were eventually deposited in the National Archives at the end of December 2023 – some 39 years after Stalker's removal. The paucity of documents, however, made it impossible to cross check information given in the criminal trial and civil action with government sources. For example, it is impossible to ascertain the simple fact as to when precisely the Home Secretary was informed that Stalker was to be suspended pending the investigation of disciplinary offences. Many documents appear to have been either destroyed or retained, further adding to the suspicion that there was a conspiracy to remove Stalker.

Inquests potentially provide another avenue for seeking the truth. Incredibly, the inquests into the six deaths investigated by Stalker and Sampson have still not been heard, over 40 years later. Following various aborted attempts, they were abandoned in September 1994 because the government refused to disclose to the coroner the contents of Stalker's report or the report by Sampson who took over Stalker's investigation. The Secretary of State for Northern Ireland had signed a Public Interest Immunity Certificate protecting the reports from disclosure – a technique used in various trials and legal actions, including the civil action brought by Taylor against GMP.

Kevin Taylor and his family endured years of rumour and malicious gossip, principally about him being involved in financing drug deals and organised crime, before he was made bankrupt by an intensive police investigation. He and his family lost everything, including their home. They were forced to rely on social security benefits and the generosity of friends. The stress of it all had an untold impact on his health and he died at the age of 69 in October 2001, seven weeks after bypass surgery.

The impact of the events on Stalker and his family was equally profound. The media attention was relentless and rumour and speculation endless. Although reinstated to his post, Stalker's high-flying police career was halted in its tracks, and he was forced to retire from the career he loved. He could have served as a police officer for another nineteen years. He died in 2019, aged 79.

How to deal with legacy cases remains a matter of considerable contention. In 2022, the government introduced legislation designed to stop all police and ombudsmen investigations, judicial inquiries, and inquests concerning Troubles-related killings. It will close the door on any further police investigations in relation to the six deaths investigated by Stalker, cancel their outstanding inquests planned to occur in 2024, and stop all the currently available democratic legal actions into the hundreds of other unsolved deaths. It will prevent most families from ever knowing the truth about who killed their loved ones and whether a state agent or informer was involved in their murder. Crucially, the legislation will grant impunity to those employed by the state to gather intelligence and who were allowed to commit crimes, including murder, their handlers, and civil servants and politicians who devised the illegal and secret system of intelligence gathering without a legal framework.

The violent conflict in Northern Ireland lasted for the best part of thirty years until the Belfast or Good Friday Agreement was approved by referendums in 1998. Over three and a half thousand people were killed. Terrible atrocities were committed by republican and loyalist armed groups. Many thousands were tried and convicted in the courts and sent to prison. The focus of this book, however, is not on these actors but on the state and its employees – the police, the army, intelligence services and civil servants. This focus is justified because the state has a duty to uphold the law. All of its actions must be lawful and accountable to the law. Without this, the state lacks legitimacy.

Truth is so often hidden and commonly delayed. It is always ambiguous, contradictory, paradoxical, and complex. It emerges in dribs and drabs but is then denied or distorted. Differentiating between possibilities and certainties, between fact and fiction, is no easy task. Falsehoods abound when a state wishes to cover-up the behaviour of its officers and servants. My intention in this book is to get as close to the truth about the Stalker/Taylor affair as possible. This in turn reveals much about the intelligence-led policing strategy that prevails to this day.

Paddy Hillyard
Belfast, January 2024

Chapter 1

Introduction

ONE DAY IN LATE MAY 1984, James Anderton, Chief Constable of Greater Manchester Police (GMP), entered the office of John Stalker, his Deputy, to ask him if he would be prepared to head an investigation into the conduct of the police in Northern Ireland. The Director of Public Prosecutions in Northern Ireland (DPPNI) had put pressure on John Hermon, Chief Constable of the Royal Ulster Constabulary (RUC), for an outside police force to investigate three shooting incidents in which six young men had been shot dead by special police units. The first incident involved the killing of three men in a car which, according to the police, refused to stop. The second involved a shooting in a hayshed a few weeks later, in which one man was killed and another badly injured. The third, again only a matter of weeks later, involved another car incident leading to the death of two more men. This car also refused to stop, claimed the police. The three incidents led to a widespread belief that the police were operating a shoot-to-kill policy.

Stalker was an obvious choice. He was a high-flyer with considerable experience in criminal investigations. He had become Deputy Chief Constable (DCC) at the young age of 45 and was considered by most of his colleagues to be the quintessential honest cop. He responded with little hesitation and agreed to head up the inquiry. He selected a small team of officers from GMP and set up a secure office in a former hotel in Knocknagoney, Belfast. After a few months, in November 1984, his team discovered that, in the second of the incidents, the hayshed had been bugged at the time of the shooting. They suspected that someone had supplied the police with intelligence about explosives which had been stored in the barn.[1] Stalker demanded access to the tape and details of those who had supplied the intelligence. His requests were continually denied with a range of excuses, including the catch-all reason – national security. In the absence of this crucial information, Stalker submitted

1

an interim report in September 1985 with the expectation of completing the inquiry once he received the requested information. It was not to be.

On 19 May 1986, an extraordinary meeting took place in the North Yorkshire town of Scarborough. Stalker was the only item on the agenda. Several of the most senior police officers in England assembled in the Queen Alexandra Room of the Royal Hotel during the annual conference of the Police Federation. The meeting was chaired by Sir Lawrence Byford, Her Majesty's Chief Inspector of Constabulary (HMIC) – a Home Office body tasked with the oversight of policing. It was attended by Sir Philip Myers, who was responsible in HMIC for the oversight of GMP and the RUC. Also present were James Anderton, Colin Sampson, head of West Yorkshire Police, and Ralph Lees, ACC of GMP. Mr Steve Vessey, a staff officer in HMIC, took notes.[2]

It was rumoured that Hermon also attended the meeting.[3] In early 1988, the Home Secretary, Douglas Hurd, in a somewhat guarded parliamentary written answer, denied the rumour. He said: 'I understand that Sir John Hermon was in Northern Ireland throughout that day and that he had no prior knowledge of the meeting.'[4] No evidence, however, has ever been produced to support Hurd's statement. It would, of course, have been totally inappropriate for Hermon to have attended the meeting which discussed Stalker's future, as he himself was due to be interviewed by Stalker under caution.

Byford produced a file note of the meeting based on Vessey's notes. It was a mysterious document and began:

> The meeting had been called to consider the action which was necessary to take in connection with intelligence which had been gathered in the Greater Manchester Police area which indicated that the Deputy Chief Constable of Greater Manchester, Mr Stalker, was closely associated with Kevin Taylor the subject of investigation by the Greater Manchester Police Commercial Branch, and an associate of the Quality Street Gang of Manchester criminals. The situation was rendered more difficult because of links between the Quality Street Gang and the IRA and because Mr Stalker had for some years been conducting an inquiry about misconduct within the Royal Ulster Constabulary in close liaison with the DPP for Northern Ireland.[5]

Kevin Taylor was a property developer, an ex-Chair of the Manchester Conservative Association (MCA), and a man with no criminal record who by that stage had been investigated for over a year and a half by a secret unit within GMP. The 'gang' referred to by Byford was a loose collection of individuals, some of whom had criminal records. They got the title – the Quality Street Gang (QSG) – when a few of them, with their smart suits and gold chains, walked into the bar run by a colourful character in the group, Jimmy Donnelly – a.k.a. 'Jimmy the Weed'. Someone shouted: 'Here comes the Quality Street Gang.' It was a reference to a popular advert, which depicted a group of men of similar appearance walking into a bank, and rather than pulling out a gun, one of the robbers draws out a box of Quality Street chocolates.

Ever since, there has been considerable debate about the QSG. Was it a criminal gang in the sense that they all conspired together to commit specific crimes, or simply a group of suspected criminals who knew each other?[6] Many people, including Stalker, considered the gang to be a myth. Nevertheless, unsolved serious crime in Manchester was often attributed to the QSG. It certainly gained a glamorous notoriety immortalised in songs by *Thin Lizzy* singer, Phil Lynott.[7] More recently, there has been a proposal to name a Manchester hotel after it![8]

The file note confirmed two actions. The first was that Stalker should be removed from the Northern Ireland inquiry. This was before Stalker had been challenged by anyone, including his own CC, about his 17-year friendship with Kevin Taylor. The second was that Sampson should complete not only the Northern Ireland inquiry but also investigate disciplinary charges against Stalker. Sampson's presence at the meeting strongly suggested that it had been agreed in advance that he should conduct both inquiries.

Vessey's notes recorded an astonishing remark that Byford made to the meeting. He said there was a need '*for the record of the meeting to demonstrate action without malice and the duty to report* (emphasis added)'.[9] Significantly, Byford's own report excluded these references as to the seemingly real purpose of the meeting which was to give the impression that proper procedures were being adhered to.

On 30 May 1986, the Greater Manchester Police Authority (GMPA) held a scheduled meeting. Half an hour before the meeting, the Labour Group met to discuss the agenda. At the very end of this meeting, Councillor Briggs, chair of GMPA, told those present that he intended to issue a press statement after the main meeting, a copy of which was circulated. It read:

> Information has been received in relation to the conduct of a Senior Police Officer which discloses the possibility of a disciplinary offence. To maintain public confidence, the Chairman of the Police Authority, Councillor Norman Briggs, J.P., has requested the Chief Constable of West Yorkshire, C. Sampson, Esq., Q.P.M., to investigate this matter under the appropriate Statutory Provisions and the Police Complaints Authority, an independent Statutory Body, has agreed to supervise the investigation through its Deputy Chairman, Roland Moyle, Esq., who has approved the appointment of Mr Sampson. The Deputy Chief Constable is on temporary leave of absence whilst the matter is being investigated.[10]

The statement caused astonishment and left everyone totally mystified, but there was no time to raise questions. The GMPA assembled at 2.30 p.m. and supported the action that the Chair had taken on behalf of the Authority, that Stalker should take leave of absence and that Colin Sampson, CC of West Yorkshire Police, should investigate a possible disciplinary offence. This was the beginning of the end of Stalker's distinguished and unblemished police career.

Following the announcement, two conflicting theories about Stalker's removal quickly developed. The most popular one was that there had been a conspiracy to remove him. Councillor Tony McCardell, chair of the Greater Manchester Council's Police Monitoring Committee, told a meeting that he believed that Stalker had to be taken off the Northern Ireland investigation when he started to reveal what he had found.[11] This view was shared by a large section of the Irish, British and foreign press.[12] *The Observer* ran the headline, 'High-level order to silence Stalker', reporting that senior government officials in the Northern Ireland Office (NIO) in London and Belfast were concerned about his discoveries and asked him 'to whitewash' the RUC in his inquiry.[13] The article finished by quoting a very senior Home Office official who said, 'Please do not press me on the way Mr Stalker is not to be allowed to resume the RUC inquiry.'[14] The Boston Globe's William Shannon, wrote in the *Manchester Evening News* that: 'Only a conspiracy could explain it.'[15]

Several papers and journalists accused MI5 of direct involvement in Stalker's downfall.[16] *Private Eye* was the first to advance the idea that the government 'reached for old friends' in MI5, who were worried that Stalker had stumbled on their own involvement in the 'hit squads'. MI5 was brought in, it argued, to 'rubbish Stalker and get rid of him before his report was published'.[17] A few weeks later, *The Star* ran a front-page headline suggesting that MI5 was involved in a smear campaign against Stalker.[18]

Dublin-based journalist, Frank Doherty, argued in the *Sunday News* that Stalker was getting to know too much about the presence of a British security mole in An Garda Síochána (the Irish police) and numerous illegal operations by British intelligence and forces in cross-border activities. According to Doherty, Stalker had to be removed before his investigation did irreparable damage to these activities, concluding that MI5 played a key role in Stalker's removal.[19]

The two central characters in the saga, Stalker and Taylor, have never been in doubt that there was a conspiracy. Taylor argued that there was a police plan, initiated from the highest echelons of government, to destroy him in order to discredit his friend, John Stalker. He wrote:

There can be no doubt that those in Whitehall played their part. The unmistakable stamp of power is there in the profligate excesses of the enquiry. Yes, I believe that MI5 was involved but, in that sense, they too were probably no more than tools. What happened to Stalker and myself was nothing less than oppressive government; a gross abuse of power invested in our leaders, for the furtherance of their own ends.[20]

Stalker also believed that there was a conspiracy to remove him:

The decision that resulted in my removal was, I think, a political one, based on the coming together of common interests that were threatened by what, in June 1986, I was about to do. In September 1985, and in the five months that followed, my interim report was read with anger and fear at senior levels within the RUC … In April 1986 a government decision was made to end my involvement in the enquiry. A decision of this importance I feel sure would be unlikely to have been made at anything less than the highest levels. The advantages of my report were now outweighed by the disadvantages, and I had in short become an embarrassment.[21]

He continued:

It is not an overstatement to say that the Anglo-Irish negotiations hung at that time by a thread – and the main strand in that thread was the willingness or otherwise of the RUC to crush Loyalist provocation and to ban or divert their marches through sensitive Catholic areas. Dublin – and America – watched carefully, and the Catholic community in the North sensed that this was a very special year; half-hearted efforts on the part of the RUC, or apparent acquiescence to Loyalist demands, would have resulted in violent counter-attacks and political upheaval …[22]

While the Anglo-Irish negotiations may have played a part in Stalker's downfall, it is also the case that his investigation posed a threat to the security strategies used in Northern Ireland at the time. In 1988, he is reported as saying: 'I was getting too close to the truth about policemen operating under cover without proper control.'[23]

Contrary to the above views of a conspiracy, the official account of the Taylor/Stalker affair has been that there was no connection whatsoever between events in Northern Ireland and those in Manchester. Shortly after Stalker's suspension, the RUC issued a strong statement to this effect:

Allegations or inferences have been made concerning Mr Stalker in connection with the RUC and his investigations here. The RUC emphatically reject these allegations and inferences and deeply resents any completely unjustified statements which have been made. The Greater Manchester Police team which conducted the investigations led by Mr Stalker will continue under the direction of Mr Sampson.[24]

Yet in appointing Sampson to continue both the Northern Ireland inquiry *and* to examine any possible disciplinary charges against Stalker, a link was inevitably created in the public mind between both police investigations. Sampson's dual appointment was described as 'a monumental blunder' by Chris Ryder, a security expert on Northern Ireland.[25] The authorities have always insisted, however, that it was pure coincidence that information about Stalker and his possible corruption came to the notice of the police in Manchester around the time he was appointed to conduct the Northern Ireland inquiry. As he had only just started the shoot-to-kill investigation and the direction of his inquiry was unknown, there was, it was argued, no connection between the Northern Ireland inquiry and developments in Manchester, and certainly no conspiracy.[26]

Support for this official narrative came from one dissenting voice within the media, BBC reporter and presenter, Peter Taylor – an expert on Northern Ireland.[27] In 2014, he was awarded a Royal Television Society lifetime achievement award and a BAFTA special award for his career-long contribution to factual and current affairs television.[28] In 1977, he produced a programme documenting how prisoners were being ill-treated during interrogation by the RUC.[29] There was a storm of protest. Roy Mason, the Secretary of State (SoS) for Northern Ireland, accused the programme of being 'insensitive' and 'riddled with unsubstantiated allegations'.[30] No-one in Westminster, however, seemed concerned about Peter Taylor's evidence of ill-treatment.

Following Stalker's removal, Peter Taylor produced two Panorama programmes.[31] The first, entitled *Stalker: Conspiracy or Coincidence?* was broadcast on 16 June 1986, but failed to reach a conclusion on the question posed. The second reached the definite conclusion that there was no conspiracy, only a coincidence of events. *Stalker & Company*, was broadcast on 19 August. It began with Peter Taylor boldly stating: 'We investigate his [Stalker's] association with Kevin Taylor and the connection between Taylor's yacht, *Diogenes*, and an international drug smuggling ring', information which could only have come from the police.[32] The implication was obvious: Taylor was involved in drug smuggling and the police were only doing their job investigating him and his friend Stalker.

In 1987, Peter Taylor also published a book on the Stalker affair, *Stalker: the Search for the Truth*, in which he goes into the idea that there was no conspiracy in greater detail. He argues that the seeds of Stalker's downfall were sown between June 1984 and March 1985, but that it was not easy to pin down exactly what happened in this period. He wrote:

> The main difficulty has been to tie down the precise nature of the intelligence, the channels through which it came – and whether there has been any corroboration of it, without which Chief Constable James Anderton ought not to have taken such an extraordinary course of action which led to the

investigation of the Deputy Chief Constable by his own men. The timing of the events is also critical.[33]

This 'difficulty' did not prevent him reaching a definite conclusion about what happened. He accepted that '*all the circumstantial* (emphasis added) evidence seemed to point to a conspiracy and the hand of MI5'[34] and that there were certainly several very good political reasons for a conspiracy. The revelation of MI5's activities would cause a major political scandal and the airing of Stalker's findings through the courts would send shockwaves through the RUC at the very moment their morale needed to be preserved in the context of the Anglo-Irish Agreement. However, he concluded that 'there was no conspiracy – at least involving Northern Ireland'.[35] He wrote this despite never managing to tie down '*the precise nature of the intelligence*' (emphasis added) or '*the channels through which it came*' (emphasis added)[36] in the crucial eight-month period, June 1984 to March 1985. What happened instead, Peter Taylor argued, was a coincidence of 'two largely unconnected chains of events' over the entire period from May 1984 to May 1986.[37] One set of events involved Stalker running into problems in Northern Ireland, while the other took place in Manchester and involved the investigation into Kevin Taylor.

Peter Murtagh, voted Journalist of the Year for his coverage of the Stalker affair, reviewed Stalker's book for *The Guardian*. He wrote: 'The whole business has been a monstrous scandal. And in any other democracy that valued principles of accountability, those responsible would be forced to explain their actions.'[38] He went on to say that all we get is 'cover-up and subterfuge' and government lawyers claiming that Watergate could not happen in Britain because of the wonderful system of parliamentary accountability.[39]

Murtagh also reviewed Peter Taylor's book in the Belfast magazine, *Fortnight*, challenging the idea that there was no conspiracy.[40] Taylor responded by letter,[41] denying that he had been sought out by mandarins and their masters to reproduce the official storyline. On the contrary, his conclusion was based on 'a painful examination of the detail of the story'.[42] He further argued that the great thing about conspiracies is that you do not have to prove them.

While circumstantial evidence may be enough to satisfy some conspiracists, most people would wish to see corroborating evidence. This is certainly the case in a criminal trial, in which conspiracy charges are often used in the prosecution of fraud and other criminal activity. Ironically, fraud was the offence for which Kevin Taylor and his co-accused were eventually charged. Outside of the criminal justice process, the main problem is that, in many instances, the evidence to prove a conspiracy theory is held by those in power.

Peter Taylor's letter went on to criticise Murtagh for taking as his starting point January 1985 and ignoring the flow of information into GMP which he says started eight months earlier. This was a fair point, making it essential to examine the chronology of events in both Manchester and Northern Ireland carefully. To strengthen his view that there was no conspiracy, Peter Taylor pointed to the fact that Colin Sampson, who took over Stalker's Northern Ireland inquiry, produced a tougher report recommending that additional RUC officers should be charged with offences along with MI5 officers. 'If there had been a "Brit" conspiracy to get rid of Stalker', as he put it, 'then appointing Colin Sampson was a mistake because he failed to collude in a cover-up.'[43] Although Peter Taylor was adamant that this was the main reason why the conspiracy theory fails, it does not necessarily follow that there was no 'Brit' conspiracy. There could still have been a conspiracy to remove Stalker once the implications of his inquiry became known, notwithstanding Sampson's seemingly tougher recommendations.

In 1987, Kevin Taylor was eventually arrested along with three others. Contrary to the impression left by the Panorama programme that he was involved in drug smuggling, Taylor was charged with conspiring to defraud the Co-operative Bank, a charge originating with the police, as the bank had no concerns with their client. In December 1989, Taylor, and three co-defendants, came to trial. The case against them collapsed after all the evidence was rendered inadmissible because the Recorder had been 'misled' in the GMP's application for access orders and all four were acquitted. It was a considerable embarrassment for GMP and only added to the view that there was a conspiracy to remove Stalker.

Following the collapse of the fraud trial, Taylor brought a civil action against GMP for malicious prosecution which began in Liverpool High Court in May 1995. After 21 days of court hearings, the two sides reached a settlement with an award to Taylor of £2.4 million. He reluctantly accepted this because he feared his legal aid would be withdrawn if he did not do so. GMP made it clear that its agreement to settle did not imply any wrongdoing on its part and that it had been forced to settle because of the rising costs of defending the action. Nevertheless, the size of the award further strengthened the view that there was a conspiracy and Taylor had been the fall-guy. He had been maligned and prosecuted to suggest that Stalker, at best, had dubious friends and, at worst, was corrupt.

In late 1989, Peter Kosminsky produced a drama-documentary on the Stalker affair entitled *Shoot to kill*. It was based on information supplied by Chief Superintendent John Thorburn, Stalker's second-in-command for the

Northern Ireland investigation, who had by then retired from the police. As the topic of the film was politically very sensitive, the IBA demanded to see it prior to broadcast. Unusually, the entire board of the IBA watched the film. This was unprecedented at the time. Other highly controversial dramas, such as *Death on the Rock* or ITV programmes on the Guildford Four or the Birmingham Six, had not received the same treatment.[44] The IBA board wanted a change in the title, which was rejected, but it did obtain a weaker version of the final caption concerning the Attorney General's decision that no one should be prosecuted in relation to the killings investigated by Stalker (Chapter 19).[45] Kosminsky's film was broadcast over two nights in June 1990.[46] It left the audience in no doubt that there was a conspiracy to remove Stalker.

In 1991, Peter Taylor made a third documentary about the Taylor/Stalker affair.[47] It began with a clip from David Hood, Kevin Taylor's defence barrister in the criminal trial, saying that the investigation into his client: 'had one purpose, one purpose only, and that was to drum up a case against him and to use the case against him to discredit John Stalker and to remove him from the Northern Ireland inquiry'.[48] Peter Taylor challenged this and said that there were some events around which a 'powerful mythology grows', in this case, that Stalker was a victim of a conspiracy. He then presented what he described as 'new evidence' to challenge the conspiracy theory. He failed, however, to interrogate critically some of the 'new evidence' which he claimed GMP possessed when Stalker's inquiry in Northern Ireland was barely out of the starting blocks. He concluded the programme by stating confidently that when history judges the Stalker saga it will be based on facts, not on some 'seductive mythology'.[49]

This book attempts to establish all the facts, based on a forensic analysis of the information presented in Kevin Taylor's criminal trial and civil action, supplemented by his personal papers and numerous interviews. It has been no easy task. Although police forces have a standard set of procedures for recording information and intelligence, these were extensively ignored by GMP in their investigation of Taylor and Stalker. There were no contemporaneous reports of key meetings and interviews, and police pocketbooks were incomplete. Numerous documents were unsigned, undated, and contained no stamp to indicate when they were sent or received, making it impossible to know if and when a claimed event took place.

Several documents appear to have been created at a date later than claimed and one document was confirmed to be a forgery. As a consequence, considerable doubt is cast on the official story that there was evidence as early as June 1984 to justify an investigation into Stalker. Further doubt that Stalker's removal was a mere coincidence, stems from the intensity of the investigation into Taylor. GMP devoted huge resources to ruining his reputation and constructing a crime against him, with the purpose of justifying disciplinary charges against Stalker.

In Northern Ireland, the Taylor/Stalker affair takes place against the backdrop of a 'dirty war' in which MI5 introduced a secret counter-insurgency strategy in 1981 to defeat the IRA. It further consolidated the extensive use of spies – a traditional strategy used in the past to quell insurrections against British rule in Ireland.[50] Informers and state agents were allowed to commit crimes, including murder, with impunity.[51] Their protection and the intelligence they provided was prioritised over and above the detection and prosecution of crime, undermining the criminal justice system and police investigations in Northern Ireland. As a consequence, despite constant demands from Stalker and his team, the RUC and MI5 refused to reveal details about any state agents involved in the killings he was investigating.

In Manchester, the story takes place against a backdrop of a belief that there was widespread police corruption, deep concerns about the role of the Brotherhood of Freemasons in determining advancement in GMP, an above-the-law approach to policing among some officers, and the lack of detective experience by those in charge of the CID. Of considerable significance, as we shall see, is the part played by a police informer, David Bertlestein, who had connections in Belfast and Manchester. Bertlestein later changed his surname by deed poll to 'Burton'.

In 1981, David Burton reported that QSG had arranged for the IRA to firebomb a warehouse in Belfast, as part of a 'long firm fraud' in which he was heavily involved. While awaiting trial, Burton told police that Taylor was financing drug smuggling and Taylor's friend Stalker was corrupt. According to GMP, it was *this* information that triggered the investigation into the two men. Informer Burton is, therefore, central to the Taylor/Stalker affair.

Chapter 2

Conspiracies in Death

THE BALLYNERY NORTH ROAD runs south of Lough Neagh and north of the M1 motorway in county Armagh.[1] Near the westerly end of the road stood a run-down building. It was slightly behind the right-hand end of a single-storey thatched cottage. It was made of breeze blocks and had a six by eight foot wooden door, held in place by a plank of wood and some corrugated iron. On either side of the door, there were two metal-framed, three-by-four foot windows divided in two halves. A hedge, which ran from the road back past the cottage, obstructed the view to the area in front of the building from the road. The hayshed, as the building became known, was central to Stalker's investigation in Northern Ireland. It was owned by Kitty Kearns who came from a strongly republican family. She died on 17 February 2010, just 40 minutes after reaching her 100th birthday – ironically, too late to know that the Queen of England and the Lord Lieutenant of Armagh had written letters congratulating her on 'such a special occasion'.

The Troubles, as the conflict was euphemistically called, were in their thirteenth year. When seen in comparative perspective, the conflict was by far the most internally politically violent of any liberal democracy during the period 1948 to 1977, both relatively per capita and absolutely in terms of numbers killed.[2] 1981 was a particularly turbulent year which saw a second protracted hunger strike by republican prisoners demanding changes in their prison treatment. Margaret Thatcher, the British Prime Minister, refused to give in to their demands. The protest was eventually called off after ten prisoners had starved themselves to death. The strike further polarised political opinion in Northern Ireland, with unionists enraged by the huge funerals of the hunger strikers and Sinn Féin becoming a mainstream political party.[3]

The hayshed shooting

On 24 November 1982, Martin McCauley picked up Michael Tighe on the back of his Montesa 250cc trail bike. They drove to the hayshed as Kitty Kearns had asked them to keep an eye on it while she was away. When Tighe and McCauley arrived, they saw that a window had been left open. They looked inside and saw something in the hay. Within a matter of minutes, Tighe lay dead and McCauley seriously injured, shot by the police or army – it remains unclear.

McCauley told his uncle, who visited him in hospital the next day, that after climbing in they found three pre-Second World War Mauser rifles in the hay. As they were looking at them, two men, whom he described as SAS, burst in, and opened fire on Tighe and then turned their guns on him. He made it behind a stone wall, but they shot him too. They were then both dragged out by their hair. A gun was put down McCauley's throat and he was threatened with the words: 'I will kill you, you fucking bastard'. Another said: 'Let him die like his mate'.[4] The shooting had all the hallmarks of a planned attack and an extra-judicial killing.

That evening the RUC issued a statement:

> Shortly after 4.30 p.m. yesterday afternoon a police mobile patrol had noticed suspicious activity at a shed close to the road at Ballynery Road North and decided to investigate. As the RUC men approached the shed ... they were confronted by two men carrying rifles. They opened fire, killing one of the men and seriously injuring another, who was taken to Craigavon hospital. Three rifles were recovered at the scene and the search of the area was continuing.[5]

Local people queried the police version of events. They said that the two youths were close friends who lived in adjoining houses and confirmed that they were keeping an eye on the farm where the shooting took place. Kitty Kearns was away staying with relatives because she was in poor health. They pointed out that the police statement could not be true because all the sheds attached to Kitty Kearns' farm were behind the cottage and well away from the road. The hayshed would not have been visible to a passing patrol. A person who lived nearby said that he had heard two bursts of automatic fire.[6] Seamus Mallon, the Social Democratic and Labour Party (SDLP) deputy leader, condemned the incident as an act of 'murderous brutality' and demanded a full and independent inquiry.[7]

Tullygally East Road shooting

Thirteen days earlier on 11 November 1982, there was another controversial killing. Sean Burns and Gervaise McKerr, together with Eugene Toman, were shot dead by the police at Tullygally East Road, in Lurgan. None of them was armed. The RUC press office issued a statement that evening. It claimed that the car, when signalled to stop at a checkpoint, slowed but then accelerated away, hitting an officer as he attempted to get out of the way. Other police officers in a patrol car parked nearby witnessed the incident and gave chase. While doing so, they thought that they were being fired at and they opened fire. The car careered off the road and down a bank. When the police arrived on the scene, all three occupants were dead.[8] A further statement was issued the following morning.

> A green Ford car owned and driven by Mr McKerr had stopped at a checkpoint manned by uniformed police at the junction of the Old Portadown Road and the Tullygally East Road, about two miles outside of Lurgan. The car then accelerated towards a policeman who had waved it down, it struck him and then had been driven off along the Tullygally East Road. Other police opened fire on the vehicle, which drove on in an attempt to escape. In doing so it careered off the road, down a bank. When the police arrived at the scene it was found that the three occupants were dead.[9]

This statement made no mention of the car chase. An eyewitness, who was not prepared to be named, claimed that the RUC had 'pumped volleys of bullets' into their victims after stopping the car.[10] One woman, who lived about 50 yards from the scene, said she heard four sustained bursts of automatic gunfire. Tom French, a Workers' Party councillor, who also lived nearby, said the fact that so many bullets had entered the driver's side indicated that the police were not firing from behind. Instead, it looked like the police fired into the car after it had come to a halt. He sought a proper inquiry, preferably by another police force.[11] This attack had all the hallmarks of another extra-judicial execution.

Mullacreevie Park shooting

The above two controversial shootings were followed by a third on 12 December. Seamus Grew and Roddy Carroll, members of the Irish National Liberation Army (INLA), died in similar circumstances to Burns, McKerr and Toman, when police fired a hail of bullets into the car in which they were travelling, at the entrance to Mullacreevie Park estate off the Killylea Road, outside of Armagh city. The two were unarmed. After the shooting the RUC issued this statement:

> At approximately twenty past eight a two vehicle uniformed police roadblock was in operation at Girvans Bridge on the Armagh Keady Road. A number of vehicles had passed through the roadblock when a car approached and was signalled to stop with a red light. It accelerated through the road check, knocking down and injuring a police officer. Police at the scene radioed another police vehicle in the area, which moved in to give assistance and gave chase to the escaping vehicle, which by then, had been identified as belonging to a known leading terrorist. The police vehicle, which was attempting to cut off the escaping car, followed it at speed for some distance.

When the escaping vehicle turned into Mullacreevie Park the police vehicle forced it to stop. The car then reversed at speed with its headlights full on, clearly identifying the police in uniform, who had dismounted from their vehicle and called the occupants to stop.

The driver jumped out of the vehicle and the police, believing they were about to be fired on, themselves opened fire. Both the occupants were shot. The police officer who was injured at the roadblock was taken to Craigavon hospital suffering from injuries to the head, legs and hands. An extensive search of the area from the road check to the scene of the shooting is being carried out.[12]

Once again, the circumstances were disputed. A local priest, Fr. Denis Faul, who together with Fr. Raymond Murray had done much to expose the abuses of the army and police,[13] said the shootings realised his worst fears provoked by the recent 'stake outs in Lurgan' – a reference to the two previous shooting incidents. He said that the RUC's new policy of apparently shooting to kill was a disastrous one since the law should be based on the sacredness of human life.[14] It was the third incident in just over a month that again had all the hallmarks of an extra-judicial killing. The key question in all three incidents was whether the six men could have been arrested without 'shooting to kill'.[15]

The six men had been killed by members of the RUC Headquarters Mobile Support Units (HMSUs), which were under the control of RUC Special Branch (RUC SB). The units had been established in the early 1980s and were trained by the SAS in Hereford, England, and their key objective was to 'neutralise' the enemy with 'firepower, speed and aggression'.[16] There were two units comprised of 24 men in total. Each one was, in effect, the equivalent of an 'anti-terrorist flying squad'.[17] Their forerunner was the Special Patrol Group which operated throughout Northern Ireland.[18] The intelligence for the units was supplied by E4A, which specialised in covert surveillance and formed one of the five branches within RUC SB.

Kinnego explosion

Before the three shooting incidents, there had been an IRA attack on a police patrol. On 27 October, Sergeant Sean Quinn and Constables Paul Hamilton and Alan McCloy were dispatched to investigate the theft of a battery in North Armagh. Sergeant Quinn, who headed the patrol, was a Catholic from Banbridge. Hamilton, who lived in Armagh, and McCloy, who lived in Lurgan, were both Protestants. The composition of the RUC at the time was 90 per cent Protestant and so this was an unusual 'mixed' patrol, policing a predominantly Catholic area around Lough Neagh.

As the police drove along Kinnego embankment on the south side of Lough Neagh, the IRA detonated a massive landmine from high ground, which propelled the patrol's armour-plated Ford Cortina into the air, leaving a crater 15 feet deep and 40 feet in diameter. The three officers were killed instantly. It brought the police death toll since the start of the Troubles to 169.[19] Chief Constable Hermon was at a prize giving event at Lurgan College and heard the explosion. When the ceremony was over, he made his way to the scene. He was observed talking angrily with a colleague.

It later emerged that there was a connection between the Kinnego explosion and the shootings in the hayshed and at Tullygally East Road. According to Peter Taylor, several weeks prior to the Kinnego landmine a highly-placed informer had provided the RUC with information that one thousand pounds of explosives had been smuggled across the border and was stored in the hayshed. The explosives were then removed undetected and used in the Kinnego explosion. The informer's handler wanted to know who was involved and two people were named – Sean Burns and Eugene Toman.[20] According to investigative journalist Ian Cobain, the mole also mentioned McCauley.[21] A few weeks later, Burns, McKerr and Toman were dead and McCauley, seriously wounded. As Bill Rolston, an academic sociologist, expressed it: 'It was difficult to avoid the conclusion that the RUC were out to even the score.'[22]

More information about each of the three shooting incidents slowly emerged during various criminal proceedings. Constable John Robinson was charged with the murder of Seamus Grew in the Mullacreevie Park shooting and appeared in court on 20 March 1984.[23] Sergeant William Montgomery and Constables David Brannigan and Frederick Robinson, who were charged with the murder of Eugene Toman in the Tullygally East Road shooting, appeared in Court on 29 May 1984.[24] Martin McCauley was tried on 15 January 1985 for possession of the old Mauser rifles which he and Tighe had found in the hayshed.

All three cases were heard in what are known as Diplock courts. These were introduced into Northern Ireland in 1972 following the recommendations of Lord Diplock, a judge who had been asked to examine ways to deal with political violence in Northern Ireland.[25] He recommended major reforms in policing and the criminal justice process. These included increased street powers for the police and the army, and the building of two special interrogation centres in which those detained would be 'more likely to confide in their questioner than remain silent'.[26] In addition, he argued for far-reaching changes in the criminal justice process for those charged with 'scheduled offences' – broadly, those offences arising from the political conflict. He recommended the replacement of trial by jury with a single judge responsible for hearing all the evidence and then directing him or herself on points of law, before bringing a guilty or not guilty verdict. Changes in the rules of evidence were also recommended.[27]

In 1971, Brigadier Frank Kitson published a book called *Low Intensity Operations* which was based on his experiences during the closing days of the British Empire.[28] One of his key messages was the need to adapt the rule of law to counter-insurgency ends. Diplock had achieved just that by transforming how trials would operate. The rule of law was to be further eroded with changes in the methods of policing and the development of widespread collusion between the security forces and loyalist paramilitaries.[29] Kitson subsequently became commander-in-chief of the UK Land Forces between 1982 and 1985.

Robinson trial, 20 March 1984

The official story of the Mullacreevie Park shooting turned out to be false. Constable John Robinson was not on a routine patrol when he received a radio message that Seamus Grew's car had passed through a check point. This was no chance encounter: it was part of a secret operation to capture Dominic McGlinchey, a prolific killer,[30] who had joined the INLA after being expelled from the IRA. Information had been received from an informer in the Republic that Grew was to pick up McGlinchey for an operation across the border. Grew was trailed by the RUC into the Republic, without any prior authority from the Irish government. McGlinchey was not picked up for some reason.

After returning north, Grew and Carroll came across a traffic accident at a joint police/army roadblock and drove through. The RUC SB Inspector who had been trailing them from the Irish Republic, stopped and picked up Constable Robinson, who was armed and part of the highly trained police squad. Together, they continued to pursue Grew and Carroll's car. They overtook and stopped the car at the entrance to the Mullacreevie Park housing estate. Robinson got out and fired nineteen shots into the car, killing Grew and Carroll instantly. The SB Inspector immediately left the scene. CID and the DPPNI were never informed of his presence or the possibility that he could give an eye-witness account.[31]

In court, charged with murder, Robinson admitted that he had shot both men using a high-powered handgun but said that he acted in self-defence, as he feared his life was in danger. He told the court that he was instructed by senior officers to tell a cover story to avoid mentioning the involvement of RUC SB and a British army surveillance unit, all to protect the life of an informer. The cover story was hatched when he and other members of his patrol were debriefed by a

Superintendent, a Chief Inspector and RUC SB officers. They were informed that the Official Secrets Act placed constraints on them. As part of the cover-up, instead of a road traffic accident at a check point, a story was invented about a vehicle not stopping. A fake radio message was constructed along with a manufactured story about an injury to the police officer who, in fact, was not injured when attempting to stop the car at the roadblock, but as a passenger in the car in the road traffic accident.[32]

Lord Justice MacDermott, the trial Judge sitting alone, pointed out that the Crown did not dispute these claims of a cover-up and, in any event, none of the others involved in the cover-up were charged. What he had to do as a Diplock Court Judge was to ascertain the facts in the case. While Robinson's version of events may have been 'distorted', this could be explained by the fact that events were happening faster than the time it took to describe them. In his summing up, MacDermott said that: 'while policemen are required to work within the law, they are not required to be supermen... I am satisfied that the accused honestly believed he had been fired at and that his life was in danger.'[33] Robinson was duly acquitted.

There was considerable nationalist anger at the verdict. Seamus Mallon described the decision as a 'deadly blow' to the hope that justice would ever be fairly administered in Northern Ireland. The courts had chosen to be protectors of the establishment and had failed to protect the citizen's basic right to life:

> Once again, the carefully planned and cynical execution of unarmed people by the security forces has been judicially exonerated. The process of law and justice has again been devalued in a manner that will have a devastating effect within the community.[34]

According to Fred Holroyd, Grew had been wanted by the police and army for several years. Holroyd was a British army Intelligence officer stationed in Northern Ireland in the early seventies and he later exposed the extent of collusion between the security forces and loyalist paramilitaries.[35] In 1974, the British army developed a plan to abduct Grew from the Republic and bring him across the border. But the plan was aborted because of police activity in the area following the murder of an Irish Senator, Billy Fox. Undeterred, 3 Infantry Brigade continued with their policy of attempting to kidnap republicans from the Republic. On 29 March 1974, another attempt was made to abduct Grew, along with Patrick McLoughlin. Three loyalists were recruited for the task and provided with maps and photographs of the area around Grew's house. Once again, the plan failed when two of the gang were seen acting suspiciously. A neighbour called An Garda Síochána and the men were arrested. They were jailed for five years each at Dublin Special Criminal Court.[36]

Montgomery, Brannigan and Robinson trial, 29 May 1984

The official version in the Tullygally East Road shooting was also false. Once again it was no chance encounter. Burns, McKerr and Toman had been under surveillance by a RUC SB/E4A surveillance team for days and the plan was to intercept them at a completely different place from the one where they were killed. No serious attempt was made to stop the car. It was ambushed by two members of the HMSU team on foot but sped away. It was then chased by other members of the squad waiting around the corner in an armour-plated Ford Cortina. A total of 109 bullets were fired from a Sterling sub-machine gun, Ruger rifles and a handgun[37] – one more shot than fired by the British army on Bloody Sunday.[38] The car struck no policeman. All three men died instantly. None was armed.[39]

Sergeant William Montgomery, Constables David Brannigan[40] and Frederick Robinson, appeared before Lord Justice Gibson charged with the murder of Toman. In a detailed and highly controversial analysis, Gibson claimed that there was no evidence, or alternatively no evidence on which 'a judge of fact', could properly reach a verdict of guilty.[41] Each of the officers, who were all members of a special support group and highly trained, had been told that the men were wanted on suspicion of having committed terrorist acts, including murder, and that they were on their way to commit another and were probably armed. The threat was deemed to be serious and hence they were issued with one sub-machine gun, two Ruger rifles, three semi-automatic pistols and 200 rounds of ammunition.

In reaching his verdict, Lord Justice Gibson arrived at two highly problematic conclusions from the evidence. The first was that he convinced himself that the bullets hitting the rear of the car would have emitted 'flashes, which could have readily been mistaken for muzzle flashes of guns fired from the back of the car',[42] and hence it was a reasonable conclusion that the officers were being fired at. The second concerned the noise of a passenger door opening. Gibson reasoned that as the car was driven at speed, 'it failed successfully to negotiate a turn to the right into a slip road' and ended up on the sloping left-hand verge of the slip road. All the accused, he emphatically stated, 'jumped out'. He then accepted the evidence of Mr Wallace from the Forensic Science Laboratory, who had carried out experiments on the opening of a passenger door. Wallace discovered that it produced two distinct metallic sounds: 'the first like the slide of a gun hitting the back plate and the second like the slide hitting the front plate'.[43] He claimed that 'these sounds were distinctly audible by him at a distance of 20 feet'.[44] The noise, the judge concluded, therefore established that one or more of the occupants were alive and were attempting to escape down the hill, or were taking up position behind the car with the intention of opening fire. In these circumstances, he argued, the officers' actions were 'the only means of self-defence and the only step consistent with their duty', apart from running away. In his view then, the use of force was 'reasonable' given the circumstances and the officers' understanding of the mortal danger they were in.

Lord Justice Gibson was highly critical of the prosecution's case. He criticised 'the entirely false and artificial division' between what happened when the car was moving and what happened when it was at a standstill.[45] The Crown had argued that when the car was stopped the situation was under control and further shooting was unnecessary. The Judge disagreed because there was no evidence, he claimed, of any appreciable interval between the two events and, in any event, the basic situation remained unchanged, other than there was now the possibility of escape. He further criticised the evidence that the Crown had presented at the preliminary inquiry. This had left the clear impression that the accused had simply driven through a vehicle checkpoint, that they had no weapons and that the police had chased the car discharging over 100 bullets, killing the three occupants.[46] The Crown had failed to acknowledge other evidence that the accused were part of a special unit and were working with another officer. They had been alerted that Toman and Burns had set off 'on their murderous enterprise' and as a direct result, the checkpoint had been established specifically to stop them.[47]

Justice Gibson reflected on the notion of intention in a murder case. He pointed out that it wasn't to be judged in some lawyer's study, a forensic science laboratory, in the full knowledge of hindsight or what one thinks should have been done in the situation. The question is:

> has the Crown proved beyond any reasonable doubt what was the actual state of mind, belief and understanding of the accused in the heat and anxiety of the moment, faced, as they understood it, with but a fleeting second to decide and to act, and is the state of mind so proved one which in law brings the case within the legal concept of murder?[48]

He concluded that at all stages the Crown's case fell far short of that, whatever hypotheses may have been advanced. He finished his judgment by saying that he considered the three accused to be 'absolutely blameless'.[49] He pointed out that normally acquittal can mean anything from probably guilty to absolutely guiltless, but he wished to make it clear that in this case they were blameless and this ought to be recorded, together with his commendation 'for their courage and determination in bringing the three deceased men to justice, in this case, *to the final court of justice*' (emphasis added).[50]

The verdict, like the verdict in the Grew and Carroll case, produced instant criticism from the nationalist community and from the Republic's Foreign Affairs Minister, Peter Barry. In a speech in Cork, he said:

> As regards the comments by Judge Gibson following his verdict, we have stated that these are absolutely unacceptable and give rise to widespread resentment and indeed fear. While Judge Gibson found that the defence found no case to answer, it should be recalled that the Director of Public Prosecutions brought the charges in the first place. Clearly the DPP felt that the evidence was sufficient to bring charges in both this and the previous case ... We believe that it is essential that the British authorities distance themselves from the implementation of these comments of Judge Gibson. It is deeply regrettable that these comments attributed to Judge Gibson could be read as in effect justifying a shoot-to-kill policy.[51]

The controversial Judge Lord Denning went on record and supported Gibson's interpretation of the law. It was most unlikely that Denning was familiar with the facts of the case, but this did not stop him saying that the three acquitted RUC men should never have been charged. 'They were doing their duty', he told BBC Radio. The legal basis for police action, Denning argued, was laid down by statute.

> A Constable can use such force as is reasonable in the circumstances, either to prevent a crime, or to assist in the lawful arrest of an offender. The law is perfectly clear. He can use whatever force is reasonable. Now, if there is a terrorist who is armed, it is quite clear that a policeman is entitled, in point of law, to do all that is reasonable to assist him to bring him to justice.[52]

Apart from showing his ignorance of the case – none of the three was armed – it was not the first time that Denning had made contentious comments. In 1976 six men, originally from Northern Ireland, were convicted of the Birmingham pub bombings and were sentenced to life imprisonment.[53] They always claimed they were innocent and that their confessions were beaten out of them. In 1976 they made their first appeal against their sentence. This was dismissed by Lord Widgery, who had cleared the army of any responsibility for the killings on Bloody Sunday.[54] In 1980, while still in prison, the Birmingham Six pursued a civil claim against the police, which Denning dismissed saying:

> Just consider the course of events if this action were to proceed to trial ... If the six men fail, it will mean that much time and money and worry would have been expended by many people to no good purpose. If the six men win, it would mean that the police were guilty of perjury; that they were guilty of violence and threats; that the confessions were involuntary and improperly admitted in evidence; and that the convictions were erroneous ... That would mean that the Home Secretary would have either to recommend that they be pardoned or he would have to remit the case to the Court of Appeal. This is such an appalling vista that every sensible person would say, 'It cannot be right that these actions should go any further'.[55]

Eventually in 1991, the convictions were overturned and the six men received compensation for having been wrongly convicted and spending over 17 years in prison.

Denning's remarks reflected two things. First, he considered that the integrity of the criminal justice system was more important than justice for the individual. Confidence in the system had to be preserved at all costs. A few miscarriages of justice were neither here nor there. Second, notwithstanding the long time he was on the bench, he could not conceive of the police committing perjury, being violent, producing false confessions or that the system could convict the innocent. Yet there was mounting evidence in the 1970s and the 1980s that these were not isolated phenomena.[56] The *appalling vista* could not be contemplated by one of the most senior judges in the land and he appealed for support for his view from every 'sensible person'. Ironically, these sensible people were likely to include those who were affected by the behaviour of the police in numerous miscarriages of justice cases, and who would have been hanged if capital punishment had still been in place.[57]

There was consternation in Whitehall over Justice Gibson's comments. Graham Angel from the Northern Ireland Office (NIO) in London wrote to Henry Steel, Legal Secretary to the Attorney General, seeking advice on whether there was anything they could or should do about the comments which were made in both the Mullacreevie and Tullygally cases. He considered the comments 'both unnecessary and silly', bringing discredit to the judiciary. He suggested that judicial independence 'should be complemented by a measure of restraint and judgement in comments made in court, which may have broad political and international implications'. He complained that they have created the opportunity 'for those who wish to distort RUC policy' and 'created unnecessary problems as regards our relations with the Republic'.[58]

The type of surveillance used by E4A to monitor Burns, McKerr and Toman did not emerge until six years later. In 1988, journalist Chris Moore revealed that their car had been bugged and E4A operatives were able to listen to conversations in the car.[59] They were convinced that the men were on their way to murder a UDA man, although when shot, they were all unarmed. Crucially, the bug recorded the last moments of the three men. None of this information was revealed to the court.[60]

McCauley's trial, 15 January 1985

McCauley went on trial at the beginning of 1985. Once again, a different version of events unfolded. He was charged with possession of the Mauser rifles which he and Tighe had found in the shed. He was represented by Pat Finucane of Madden and Finucane, a well-known and respected firm of solicitors in Belfast. Stalker, by this stage, had started his investigation and he sat in on the trial. In court, the officers changed their original statements that they had been on a routine patrol when they had seen a man with a gun move from behind a nearby cottage to the hayshed. No routine patrol was passing, as had originally been claimed. In fact, a two-vehicle patrol backed up by a third vehicle had been tasked to go to the hayshed by RUC SB. After the shooting they had been instructed to tell the 'routine patrol' story that had been invented for them by senior officers, and were told that the Official Secrets Act protected them in these circumstances. The defence counsel, Mr Harvey QC, pursued the issue of why the police had initially lied. He put the following questions to the officer:

HARVEY: What was the reason for giving the first account?

OFFICER: It was stressed to me, my Lord, that under no circumstances to disclose that we were working on Special Branch information, my Lord.

HARVEY: That was stressed to you?

OFFICER: That is correct, my Lord.

HARVEY: Why did you invent – I take it that you did invent it?

OFFICER: I did not, my Lord.

HARVEY: Did you not invent the account of seeing the gunman moving from the cottage to the outbuilding?

OFFICER: I did not invent it, my Lord.

HARVEY: You did not invent that?

OFFICER: I did not, my Lord.

HARVEY: That was invented for you?

OFFICER: That is correct, my Lord.

HARVEY: And that was invented for you by senior officers?

OFFICER: That is correct, my Lord.

HARVEY: Did they indicate to you or were you given any reason as to why it was necessary to invent an account as to the events leading up to this shooting?

OFFICER: Just as I have stated, my Lord, that it was on Special Branch information.

HARVEY: You didn't have to reveal that it was on Special Branch information, isn't that right?

OFFICER: It was to protect the source of that information, my Lord.

HARVEY: Were you not concerned about that?

OFFICER: I was reassured by two senior officers, my Lord.

HARVEY: Reassured about what?

OFFICER: That the statement was to be made in the way it was, my Lord.

HARVEY: Reassured that it was to be made the way it was, but reassured tends to mean that you had doubts, or tended to suggest that you had doubts, or were concerned about it?

OFFICER: I was naturally concerned, my Lord.

HARVEY: And how did they reassure you?

OFFICER: They said it would be covered by the Official Secrets Act, my Lord, and not to disclose the fact that we were working under Special Branch information, my Lord.

HARVEY: Of the two officers who were there, were they both of the same rank?

OFFICER: They were not, my Lord.

HARVEY: Can you say if it was the more senior or the less senior officer who invented the story about seeing the gunman moving from the cottage to the hayshed?

OFFICER: I can't recall which one it was, my Lord.[61]

The defence argued that the police evidence was so discredited and unreliable that no court could convict, and that the case should be dismissed in the light of strong evidence that there had been a conspiracy to pervert the course of justice.

During the trial one piece of remarkable evidence emerged, which to this day has never been satisfactorily explained. Dr Press, the assistant state pathologist, was cross-examined on the post-mortem examination which he had carried out on Tighe. He explained that there were four gunshot wounds. The shot, however, that killed Tighe entered slightly to the left of the breastbone and would have exited six inches lower if it had not shattered the spine. But if Tighe was standing on the bales of hay and the police were on the level outside, how was it possible that the entrance wound was higher than the exit wound?

Harvey pursued the issue of Tighe's position with Dr Press:

HARVEY: If the deceased was upright and facing directly front on to the position at 'Y', can you say what you would have expected if he were stuck by someone firing from the position marked 'Y', in relation to the entrance and exit wounds of the bullets?

PRESS: Well, if he were erect, one would have expected the entrance wounds to be lower than the exit wounds, considerably, I would have thought.

HARVEY: Were your findings consistent with the firing coming from this position?

PRESS: They would be consistent if the deceased was bending forward …

HARVEY: Well, from the exits and entrances that you found, were you able to conclude whether or not this person was bending forwards?

PRESS: I don't think I can say whether he was bending forward or not, from the actual wounds, he could have been shot from a height or, if he was shot from the position 'Y' then he would have had to be bending forwards.[62]

Tighe's position when he was shot was, therefore, critical. If he was standing up, he could have only been shot by someone higher up on the bales of hay and this could only have occurred if there was a soldier or a member of the HMSU hidden in the hayshed in a Static Observation Post (SOP). As RUC SB prevented the CID from entering the crime scene for an hour or more, there was ample opportunity for the crime scene to be tampered with.

There was also unexplained evidence in relation to the wounding of McCauley. He had been shot in the back of his left shoulder with the bullet exiting through his throat. Another bullet hit the top of his spine and came out under his right arm pit. A third hit his right thigh near the groin. It was put to one officer that if McCauley was in the position claimed, then the bullet tracks would have been from front to back instead of entering the left-hand side of his body. The officer could offer no explanation. Another officer was asked to demonstrate how McCauley held the rifle, saying he held it in his right hand with his thumb on the trigger. Defence counsel pointed out that McCauley was left-handed; nevertheless the officer continued to insist that the weapon had been in his right hand.

In his judgment, Lord Justice Kelly expressed concern about the credibility and accuracy of the police evidence. He was particularly sceptical of the position of the police officers when they fired the shots and whether they had ever seen Tighe and McCauley holding the rifles which were in the hayshed. Nevertheless, he disbelieved McCauley and found him guilty, giving him a suspended two-year prison sentence.[63] The trial turned out subsequently to have been a farce because crucial evidence was withheld from the judge, the prosecution, and the defence. No one was told that MI5 and the army had placed listening devices in the hayshed and the shooting had been recorded on tape by the police and an army technical unit. This only emerged much later, following the referral of McCauley's case by the Criminal Cases Review Commission (CCRC) to the High Court, which allowed the appeal against his conviction.[64]

Shoot-to-kill

Following the three shooting incidents, there were widespread allegations that the police were operating a shoot-to-kill policy.[65] There were demands for an inquiry from the nationalist population. A senior officer in the RUC expressed his concern to leaders of the Catholic Church, who in turn, reported his concern to the Irish government.[66] These concerns culminated in pressure being put on the British government by both the Irish and American governments to set up a public inquiry into the shootings. In the absence of any immediate response, an International Lawyers' Inquiry was established with the support of several human rights organisations. It was chaired by Kadar Asmal, a South African-born lawyer, then teaching law at Trinity College Dublin and subsequently a minister in the post-apartheid South African government. The inquiry concluded that undercover units of the British army and the RUC were trained to shoot-to-kill, 'even where killing is not legally justifiable and where alternative practices could and should be used'.[67]

The extent of lethal force used in the three incidents was considerable, amounting to over 150 shots in total. Fionnuala Ní Aoláin, an academic lawyer, studied all incidences of the use of lethal force between 1969 and 1994 and demonstrated that it was not an isolated aspect of state practice but an integral part of the overall counter-insurgency strategy along with the emergency legislation and the legal process.[68] Her key argument was that the use of lethal force could not be explained away by spur-of-the-moment decisions by members of the army or the police, but was structurally part of the overall legal apparatus, which involved a systematic failure of the state to protect the right to life. The study identified only 24 prosecutions against 34 members of the security forces and only eight of these were successful; the majority were charged with murder or manslaughter.[69] She argued that the police and soldiers were given preferential treatment compared with civilians as they had immediate access to counsel and their statements were simply handed over to the police.[70] Similarly, in the courts the differential treatment continued and sympathy for members of the security forces was a common feature in the judgments, giving the benefit of doubt to the law-enforcer.[71] More disturbingly, Ní Aoláin argued that many judgments were characterised by the misapplication of international legal standards and terminology.[72]

Cover stories

Hermon was appointed Chief Constable in January 1980. He was born in Larne and had joined the RUC in 1950 after studying accountancy. I first met him in the very early 1970s when he was deputy commandant of the RUC training college in Enniskillen. He came to the New University of Ulster to discuss the possibility of a course for senior officers covering psychology, sociology, criminology, and community relations. He was determined to have a professional, well-educated unarmed police service. When Tom Hadden, Kevin Boyle and myself later published a short book, *Ten Years on in Northern Ireland: the legal control of political violence*, a socio-legal study of the operation of the law, he asked us to meet him at RUC headquarters where he told us in no uncertain terms that such a critical analysis was unhelpful. After a decade of violence, his attitude towards the role of social sciences had changed. As we were ushered out, he showed us the roll of honour to all the police officers who, by the end of 1980, had been killed by the IRA.[73] He slowly turned over the pages saying that 'this was the reality'.[74]

In his autobiography, Hermon argued that cover stories were 'a routine police procedure ... to prevent arousing the suspicions of terrorist organisations that their internal security had been breached'.[75] Although they were included in public statements given to the media, he went on to say that, 'they were never to be included in police statements or given as evidence'.[76] This prohibition, however, contradicts the purpose of the cover story: to conceal the police sources of intelligence. The only way to be certain that police sources are protected was to continue with the lie in evidence presented to the court.

In May 1983, Hermon and the Head of RUC SB, ACC Trevor Forbes, met Sir Michael Havers, the Attorney General, and Sir Barry Shaw, the DPP for Northern Ireland, to discuss the three police reports which had now been prepared on the incidents by the RUC CID.[77] Hermon had appointed Forbes head of SB in September 1982 because of his 'recognised energy and enthusiasm' but exceptionally, he had no CID or Special Branch experience.[78] At the meeting, Hermon threatened to resign if any of the police officers were prosecuted for murder. In a television interview, he had argued that any prosecution would be disastrous as they would never be convicted, certainly not of murder. Moreover, a trial would damage the sources of intelligence.[79] He was informed that his resignation, however, would not affect the decision to prosecute. After the meeting he ordered that comprehensive intelligence briefs should be prepared by all the RUC SB officers concerned. After receiving them he wrote:

> I realised fully, for the first time, the extent to which the operational officers had been instructed to conceal from the CID the very sophisticated counter-terrorist activities which had preceded the shootings on 11 November and 12 December. The failure to disclose this information to investigating CID officers, even after caution, had negatived the statements of the policemen concerned. This in turn had seriously damaged the credibility of the CID investigations.[80]

The comment was disingenuous as the protection of informers and state agents was an essential element of the secret counter-insurgency strategy introduced in 1981.

The 'Stocker' inquiry

The RUC subsequently supplied more information to the DPPNI in relation to the three incidents but this was not considered sufficient. Hermon appointed DCC Michael McAtamney to liaise directly with the DPPNI's office. On 11 April 1984, the DPPNI made a formal request to Hermon for full information concerning the circumstances in which false or misleading evidence was provided by any member or members of the RUC. Hermon was also asked to investigate if there was evidence of several specific offences, including perverting, or attempting to pervert, the course of justice or any other offence in relation to the three shooting incidents.[81] Subsequently, the DPPNI raised further issues, at which point Hermon asked Sir Philip Myers, who had responsibility for the RUC within HMIC, to nominate a person to conduct an independent inquiry into the three incidents.[82]

On 23 May 1984, Graham Angel in the NIO wrote a memorandum to Jim Prior, the SoS for Northern Ireland, confirming that the Chief Constable had appointed 'Mr Stocker (sic), the Deputy Chief Constable of the Greater Manchester Police, to conduct an investigation into the alleged "cover-up" in the Robinson case'.[83] He went on to describe the terms of reference which were to investigate, 'a) whether there was any criminal conspiracy, b) the incursion into the Irish Republic; and c) the problems facing the RUC in the protection of information and sources during criminal investigations'.[84] He concluded by noting that 'Mr Stocker' has assembled his team and was making a start on his work in Northern Ireland right away. Hermon informed the Police Authority that a 'Mr Stocker' had been appointed to conduct the inquiry.[85] Even *The Times* misspelt the name.[86]

It is remarkable that a senior civil servant, the Chief Constable, and *The Times*, all failed to check how Stalker's name was spelt, particularly if the information was being relayed over the telephone. It would have been relatively easy to check with GMP. What is even more surprising is that civil servants continued to misspell Stalker's name for nearly a year.

* * *

There were so many unanswered questions about the killings in October and November 1982 that began to circulate. Why were three police officers allowed to investigate a minor burglary in an area considered to be unsafe for the RUC? Were the officers allowed to proceed to protect a highly placed and important informer? Crucially, were all six men shot dead in retaliation for the killing of the police officers? Was there an unwritten shoot-to-kill policy to kill suspected IRA or INLA members? What really happened in the hayshed? Specifically, how was it possible for Tighe's entrance wounds to be higher than his exit wounds if the police said they were outside the hayshed and firing into it? Were cover stories a key policy element in the security strategy?

There was certainly a conspiracy by senior officers to cover-up what had occurred at the scene of the three shooting incidents and to hide any connections between these incidents and the Kinnego explosion. The police reports were either false, embellished or misleading. There was a deliberate strategy to conceal the truth from the DPPNI and hence pervert the course of justice. No doubt the motivation stemmed, in part, from the need to protect informers and state agents, and to reveal nothing about the extensiveness of surveillance methods and operations. Maybe there was also a desire to cover up for intelligence errors made in allowing three police officers to enter an out-of-bounds area. Just as plausibly, however, there could have been a more sinister motive for the cover-up: to hide a deliberate decision to allow the police officers into the restricted area to protect a highly placed state agent.

The police officers prosecuted for their part in the killings must have felt a considerable sense of betrayal, anger, and bitterness. They had been briefed that they would be facing armed and dangerous individuals, told to tell lies, and threatened under the Official Secrets Act if they failed to do so. They had shown considerable loyalty and obeyed orders, only to face prosecution. In contrast, those who had developed the counter-insurgency strategy privileging the protection of informers and state agents over the rule of law, and those who conspired together to invent cover stories, for whatever reason, have never faced the full rigours of the law.

Chapter 3

Recruiting Spies, Transforming Policing

IN 1981 THE CONSERVATIVE GOVERNMENT secretly introduced radical changes to its counter-insurgency strategy in Northern Ireland, privileging intelligence gathering over the prosecution and detection of offences. The use of spies was further extended and strengthened. The strategy was the brainchild of Patrick Walker, a senior officer in MI5, and it formed the backdrop to the three incidents which Stalker investigated.

Walker was born in February 1932 in Kuala Lumpur, Malaysia, where his father was an official of the Federated Malay States. After three years in Malaysia, his parents moved to Kenya where his father became chief accountant for the Kenya and Uganda Railways and Harbours. At the tender age of six, he was sent off to a local boarding school and then to King's School Canterbury (England). He went to Trinity College Oxford and studied Modern History, obtaining a third-class degree.[1] In 1956, he joined the Colonial Administrative Service in Uganda. He was baptised a Presbyterian but in 1957 he converted to Catholicism. Walker returned to England after Uganda gained its independence in 1962 and was recruited to the Security Service, MI5.[2] Like General Sir Frank Kitson, who also had widespread experience in British colonies, Walker brought back ideas developed there. As the French philosopher, Michel Foucault argues, colonisation had a considerable 'boomerang effect' with a whole series of colonial practices being adopted within colonising countries themselves.[3]

Following the introduction of direct rule in Northern Ireland in 1972, MI5 and MI6 established the Irish Joint Section (IJS) with shared offices in Belfast and London. The role of IJS was to run agents to obtain 'strategic and political intelligence about the intentions and plans of paramilitary organisations'.[4] In the early 1980s, there were thought to be about 60 MI5 operatives in Northern Ireland with responsibility for running agents, bugging cars and premises, and supporting the Director and Co-ordinator of Intelligence (DCInt). The key role

29

of the DCInt was to provide ministers and officials in Northern Ireland and London with assessments of the security situation, based on accumulated intelligence.[5] Another 30 operatives concerned with Irish affairs worked in Great Britain.[6] The head of MI5, or Box 500, as it was popularly referred to within Whitehall, reported directly to the Joint Intelligence Committee (JIC) at the heart of government. This Committee was made up of the Chair, the Director of the Government Communications Headquarters (GCHQ), the Chief of the Secret Intelligence Service (SIS or MI6), the Chief of the Defence Intelligence Staff (DIS) and the Director of MI5. It met every Thursday on the second floor of the Cabinet Office in Whitehall. The Prime Minister and a few other people would receive personal briefings from the JIC and had access to the most highly classified one-off reports.[7]

A career in MI5

Little is known of Walker's career during his first seventeen years in MI5.[8] As MI5 remained a secret organisation until 1989, cover names were used in the Civil Service handbook to list the employment of MI5 personnel. The DCInt in the NIO had the cover name: 'Under-Secretary (Liaison Staff)' and was responsible for several 'Assistant Secretaries (Liaison staff)'. One of these was a P. Walker from 1979-1980.[9] The DCInt at the time was believed to have been David Ranson, who was recorded as having been present at a meeting in May 1981 with the Prime Minister, heads of the army and RUC, and the SoS for Northern Ireland, to discuss the political situation during the hunger strike of that year.[10] The first hunger striker, Bobby Sands, died on 5 May. In June 1981, Ranson prepared 'an intelligence-based analysis' entitled 'The Provisionals – Political Activity', which was forwarded to the Prime Minister's private secretary.[11] By the time of the 1984-85 Miners' Strike, Ranson was head of F Branch, dealing with counter-subversion.[12]

Walker's actual position in MI5 in 1980, when he penned the controversial security strategy, is unknown. *The Daily Telegraph's* obituary noted that he was 'assistant to David Ransen (sic),'[13] but provided no dates. *The Times* obituary was equally vague. It jumped from stating that Walker was involved in the expulsion of more than a 100 soviet intelligence officers in 1971, to the statement: 'There followed a spell in the Northern Ireland Office in Belfast, where Walker specialised in police issues and produced several significant reports on internal Royal Ulster Constabulary relationships.'[14] In April 1984, the Irish Joint Section was wound up and FX branch in MI5 reorganised, gaining undivided responsibility for counter-terrorism. Patrick Walker became its director.[15] In 1987, he was appointed Director General of the Security Service – the head of MI5.[16]

INLA and PIRA attacks

Three deadly incidents, one in England by the INLA and two in Ireland, led to the development of the new counter-insurgency strategy. On 30 March 1979, a bomb exploded under Airey Neave's car as he drove out of the House of Commons car park, killing him instantly.[17] Neave was the Conservative Party's spokesperson on Northern Ireland and the mastermind behind Margaret Thatcher's successful bid to become party leader and Prime Minister. Thatcher was devastated but defiant. She said:

> He was one of freedom's warriors. No one knew of the great man he was, except those nearest to him. He was staunch, brave, true, strong; but he was very gentle and kind and loyal. It's a rare combination of qualities. There's no one else who can quite fill them. I, and so many other people, owe so much to him and now we must carry on for the things he fought for and not let the people who got him triumph.[18]

A few months later, on 27 August, a small fishing boat left the beautiful little harbour of Mullaghmore in County Sligo. On board were Lord Louis Mountbatten, his daughter Lady Patricia Brabourne, her husband, Lord Brabourne, their twin sons Nicholas and Timothy, Dowager Lady Doreen Brabourne and Paul Maxwell, a fifteen-year-old from Enniskillen who looked after the boat during his school holidays. As they left the harbour, a fifty-pound bomb exploded on board. It had been triggered by remote control. Lord Mountbatten, Dowager Lady Brabourne, Nicholas Brabourne and Paul Maxwell were killed.[19]

Later that day, a convoy of soldiers from the 2nd Battalion of the Parachute Regiment were driving along a road by the side of Carlingford Lough when the IRA detonated a remote-controlled bomb in a hay lorry by the side of the road. Six soldiers were killed and many others injured. Soldiers from the Queen's Own Highlanders were quickly deployed to the scene. There was then a second massive explosion close to where the soldiers from the first blast had sought cover. Twelve more soldiers were killed. It was the Parachute Regiment's biggest loss since Arnhem and the British army's greatest loss of life in a single attack during the conflict in Northern Ireland.[20] A wall mural quickly appeared in West Belfast linking the events to 'Bloody Sunday'.[21] It read: 'Thirteen gone and not forgotten – we got eighteen and Mountbatten.'[22]

The three attacks caused consternation in Britain and Thatcher took decisive action. She sent Sir Maurice Oldfield to Northern Ireland to be the Security Coordinator (NISC) in the NIO with the aim of improving the quality of intelligence and co-operation between agencies. Oldfield served in the British army between 1940 and 1947 and then joined the Secret Intelligence Service (SIS). According to Dorril, when Oldfield was in Palestine in the late forties, he was involved in interrogating Zionist suspects and would talk 'cheerfully about beating them up and pushing people's heads under buckets of water'.[23] A similar waterboarding technique was used by the British army in Northern Ireland in 1972.[24] Oldfield took up his appointment on 2 October 1979, but resigned in June 1980.[25]

The MI5/Walker report[26]

In early 1980, Oldfield and Hermon asked Patrick Walker to prepare a report on the interchange of intelligence between SB and CID. This was not the first occasion that MI5 had been tasked with the job of examining the role of RUC SB, nor the last. In 1973, the then head of MI5, Sir Michael Hanley, suggested to Sir Graham Shillington, the RUC CC, that an MI5 officer conduct a review. Shillington turned to John Percival Morton CMG, OBE, a former colonial police chief in India, who was the senior MI5 officer in Northern Ireland at the time. Morton held strong colonialist views as expressed in a memoir:

> It dawned upon me, and became deeply ingrained, that the British were rulers of India and that the Indians were a sort of immature, backward and needy people whom it was the natural British function to govern and administer.[27]

It is not known if he considered the people of Northern Ireland in the same way as his report was never published.

Walker's report was prepared in 1980 and it was to transform policing in Northern Ireland. Yet it was never shown to, or discussed in Parliament, the supreme legal authority in the United Kingdom – reflecting the unaccountable power of the intelligence agencies within the British establishment at that time. It will be referred to as the MI5/Walker report, to emphasize its secret origin. Its existence only became public knowledge in 2001, thanks to a UTV Insight programme.[28]

In January 2016, the Committee on the Administration of Justice (CAJ) made a request to the PSNI for a copy of the MI5/Walker report. This was refused under section 23 of the Freedom of Information Act 2000, on the grounds that the report contained information supplied by, or relating to, bodies dealing with security matters. Following an internal review, which produced the same result, CAJ complained to the Information Commissioner who, in a skeleton argument, accepted that the appeal should be partly upheld and partly dismissed.[29] However, during the hearing the PSNI agreed to release all of the MI5/Walker report with a few sections redacted.[30]

The MI5/Walker report began by making a distinction between 'informants' (hereinafter informers) and 'agents'. The former were described as individuals recruited by the CID to provide information on criminal activities and are normally paid on results. Agents, however, are individuals recruited to provide information on a 'subversive organisation'. They are paid on a regular basis even when not producing results.[31] It recommended that all agents recruited by CID should be handed over to SB and, if this was not possible, they should be handled jointly.[32] The army had already agreed to share information on their agents.[33] Walker further recommended that all arrests must be first cleared by SB and that the charging of an agent should result from a 'conscious decision' by both SB and CID.[34]

The report emphasised that CID officers should be alert to the possibility of recruiting agents from individuals who are being interviewed. When the opportunity to recruit occurred, SB must be involved at an early stage.[35] CID officers should always be aware of the possibility of obtaining intelligence in addition to admissions. Where an interviewee was not going to make an admission, the CID officer should arrange for the interview to be taken over by SB, but even if the person has made an admission, SB must be allowed to question the individual on more general matters.[36]

It is significant that nowhere in these paragraphs is there any reference to a 'suspect'. The description is always an 'individual'. Under the Prevention of Terrorism (Temporary Provisions) Act 1976, which was in force at the time, police officers may arrest without a warrant where they have reasonable grounds for suspecting that the individual is either subject to an exclusion order or guilty of some offence under the Act, or is or has been concerned in the commission, preparation or instigation of acts of terrorism in connection with Northern Ireland affairs.[37] Yet the omission of the word 'suspect' from the report implies that people in Northern Ireland could be arrested and detained for the sole purpose of intelligence gathering rather than the prosecution of crime.

Walker was concerned about the absence of a coherent policy for reviewing and exploiting CID coverage of criminal activities. He recommended that a survey of CID informers be carried out as quickly as possible and consideration given to establishing a system of CID intelligence gathering.[38] This could then be exploited by SB, giving it even more control of CID. The centrality and power of SB was further enhanced by the recommendation that other units be brought under its control, including the Weapons and Explosives Intelligence Unit (WEIU) which was responsible for the analysis of firearms and ammunition recovered from paramilitary organisations. The justification for bringing the WEIU 'in-house' was that SB 'will always have serious reservations about supplying their most sensitive reports on a regular basis to a group operating outside SB'.[39] Walker also proposed that the Data Reference Centre (DRC) be brought in-house on the grounds that in the past it had been without access to 'a large proportion of the intelligence available to SB'.[40] These units joined the HMSUs, which were already under the control of RUC SB – illustrating the extended power of RUC SB in all aspects of policing.

The MI5/Walker report created a fundamental conflict between the role of the police and the role of MI5 in Northern Ireland, which centred around the concept of intelligence. Traditionally, MI5 was tasked with collecting and disseminating *strategic* intelligence, providing advice to Ministers about threats from paramilitary organisations and key political developments. The police, on the other hand, were tasked with collecting *tactical and operational* intelligence which could be used to detect crimes and prosecute offenders. Raymond White, a former head of SB in Belfast, pointed out that there was always a pressing requirement for strategic intelligence. He then described the dilemma:

> Each piece of intelligence had to be looked at both in its capacity to advance a criminal investigation and its potential future intelligence use. There was always a balance to be struck between preserving the life of people who are still alive on the one hand and solving crime on the other. It could not just be open disclosure.[41]

The classification of a piece of intelligence either as strategic or tactical was a central task of SB and it was inevitable, given political imperatives, that strategic intelligence would be considered more important than tactical or operational intelligence. Hence the detection and prosecution of crime became secondary to protecting agents, the non-disclosure of the security methods used and agent 'product'. SB regularly withheld information from CID concerning the methods used and the intelligence gained in relation to any incident.[42] The consequences were disastrous. The CID was effectively neutered and instead of the two branches of the RUC – SB and CID – working together in the most constructive and co-operative partnership, considerable antagonism developed between the two.[43]

Following the implementation of the MI5/Walker report, the role of RUC SB was greatly enhanced in controlling all intelligence and making decisions on who should or should not be arrested. The protection of agents became its 'prime consideration', although Walker admitted that 'the system will not work at full efficiency if SB are over-protective of intelligence, which should be exploited'.[44] It was inevitable, however, that SB would become over-protective and secretive. As Cobain eloquently put it:

> Quietly, with no public announcement, the RUC had been turned from a police force whose priority was detecting crime and putting criminals before the courts, into one whose principal aim was to spy on terrorists.[45]

The downplaying of the prosecution and detection of crime did not go unnoticed in the United States. In 1984, Walker's successor in F5, a section of MI5 responsible for countersubversion, wrote a memorandum on the reluctance of the FBI to exchange intelligence on Irish matters. He described it as a one-way process with the British supplying much information and the US very little. Some FBI officers were said to be 'very much "Police oriented" and take exception to our "intelligence" approach to investigations'.[46]

Role of state agents

The MI5/Walker report placed state agents and informers at the heart of the new counter-insurgency strategy. The implications were far-reaching. As the *raison d'être* of political violence is to create fear through murder and bombings, agents had to participate in these activities to become trusted members of paramilitary organisations. For the strategy to work, they had to commit heinous crimes in the full knowledge of their handlers. When their handlers were given accurate information about some planned attack, SB faced an ethical and moral dilemma. Did they inform the target and try to stop the attack and arrest those involved, or did they allow the attack to go ahead to avoid exposing their agent and the danger that they could be killed for being a 'tout'?[47] This dilemma occurs in the use of informers in normal policing, but the issues are far more serious in a society in deadly conflict.[48] Those who devised the strategy no doubt justified it, claiming that in a 'dirty war' an agent could not infiltrate the highest echelons of paramilitary organisations without committing serious crimes, including murder. Innocent people who lost their lives did so for the greater good, to save the lives of many others based on the intelligence gained and the prevention of even worse atrocities. It was a policy, to borrow Paul Brady's words from *The Island*, of 'trying to carve tomorrow from a tombstone'.

CID officers investigating murders and other offences were routinely denied information in order to protect agents and informers. Documents detailing sensitive intelligence, often relating to the identities of persons suspected of murder or other serious crime, were marked '"NDD" and/or Slow Waltz' – indicating that RUC SB must not disseminate the information downwards, or that a period of time should pass before CID was given the information.[49] Similarly, key files to the DPPNI were carefully sanitised to disguise the source of information. CID officers inquiring into specific incidents were also denied information about state agents and their handlers. Various deceits and subterfuges were used to prevent the truth from emerging. The MI5/Walker report, therefore, involved a fundamental tilt towards intelligence gathering.

Prior to the Regulation of Investigatory Powers Act 2000 (RIPA), the UK had no statutory or judicial controls over the deployment of agents or informers. In so far as there was *any* regulation, it was in the form of guidelines contained in a Home Office document published on 12 May 1969.[50] These made it clear that informers must never be used as *agents provocateurs* or to initiate crimes that would otherwise not take place. Notwithstanding this instruction, there was always the danger that the informer or state agent became a bounty hunter, dependent on large payments. The guidelines also emphasised that informers must not be allowed to commit crimes themselves in return for giving information. Crucially, the guidelines were drawn up to deal with 'ordinary' criminals rather than those involved in political violence. When Stalker began investigating the three shooting incidents there was, therefore, no statutory footing for the running of state agents. It was a situation that continued throughout the conflict.

Desmond de Silva, who in 2012 carried out a desktop review of the February 1989 murder of solicitor Pat Finucane (see Chapter 22), pointed out:

> In my view, the running of effective agents in Northern Ireland was such a fraught and difficult task that it manifestly required the support of a clear legal policy framework. I have established, though, that there was no adequate framework in Northern Ireland in the later 1980s. Accordingly, each of the three agencies running agents – the RUC SB, the Army's Force Research Unit (FRU) and the Security Service – operated under their separate regimes.[51]

The RUC on several occasions raised its concerns about the lack of a legal framework with successive governments. For example, a letter from the RUC to the NIO in 1987 stated: 'Given our special situation the restrictions placed upon us by virtue of the guidelines are unrealistic if we are to continue paramilitary penetration/source protection.'[52] Yet, the NIO and successive governments were singularly reluctant to develop a legal framework for the running of state agents. The issue was considered extensively at Cabinet level and with various government ministers who were all made aware of the lacunae in the law but: 'Ministers nonetheless continued to place a high priority on pursuing an intelligence-led approach to the terrorist threat.'[53]

As Mark McGovern emphasises, the absence of guidelines was not a failure of policy but its actual purpose, which was 'to open up a space of legal obscurity and plausible deniability that facilitated, rather than hampered, counter-insurgency practice'.[54] Raymond White, head of RUC SB asked Margaret Thatcher personally for legal clarity on the running of agents in paramilitary organisations and her response was: 'Well carry on doing what you're doing but don't get yourself caught.'[55] The rule of law had been abandoned with the agreement of the Prime Minister. Agents could commit freely the most serious of crimes, including murder, without fear of punishment.

In short, the MI5/Walker report heralded in an antinomian system and dangerously strengthened SB as a 'force within a force'. It transformed much of policing from the detection and prosecution of crime to a system of intelligence gathering based on hundreds of agents. In consolidating the use of state agents within armed groups, it laid the foundations for widespread collusion between the army, police and MI5, and loyalist paramilitaries. It permitted the security forces to outsource the war against the IRA while distancing themselves from the illegal activities of the state agents they directed.[56]

Caroline Elkins in her landmark study of the British Empire used the term 'legalised lawlessness' to describe 'the tautological process of law creation' – a process which involved 'incrementally legalizing, bureaucratising, and legitimating exceptional state-directed violence when ordinary laws proved insufficient for maintaining order and control'.[57] A similar process occurred in Northern Ireland. Temporary emergency legislation was followed by far-reaching changes in policing and the criminal justice system culminating in the introduction of M15/Walker strategy.

This new counter-insurgency strategy was well summarised in an article in *Just News*:

> All in all, the Walker Report is a blueprint for how to turn a police force into a conflict-fighting weapon where victory against the 'subversives' is the overriding priority and traditional functions such as preventing crime and upholding the rule of law are side-lined. You create a relatively small group of officers, distinct from the rest of the force, able to maintain their war-fighting ethos by vetting all recruits to their ranks, you concentrate intelligence gathering, analysis and dissemination in their hands, you give them direct access to overt and covert operational resources, you allow them a veto over arrests and charges and you give them the ability to place agents of influence in armed groups, some of which claim to be fighting on the same side in the 'war'. Of course, the RUC was already sectarian in composition and ethos, heavily armed and well used to repressive methods, but this report created an elite, counter-insurgency unit which chose who to allow in its magic circle and with access to and authority over all the resource of the wider force.[58]

On 23 February 1981, Walker's recommendations were circulated within the RUC to 'C' Department, all Chief Superintendents, Superintendents, Chief Inspectors, and Inspectors. Its focus was on making it clear that all decisions about arrest, the investigation of criminal activities and the responsibility for the circulation of intelligence rested with SB.[59] From this date onwards, SB took the lead in deciding who to arrest, if and when a criminal investigation should take place into any crime, and controlled all intelligence whatever the source.

At the same time as these fundamental changes were made to policing, changes were also made to the way the army collected intelligence and handled agents. Until 1977 each battalion ran its own agents. The function was then passed to brigades, and each established what was called a 'Research Office'. In 1980, Major General James Glover established the Field Research Unit in army headquarters in Northern Ireland, centralising the collection of intelligence. In 1982, the unit was renamed the Force Research Unit (FRU).[60] MI5 had an officer based in the FRU operation room in army HQ and had access to all the intelligence generated by it. FRU had its own budget and was represented on the Tasking Coordination Group (TCG) which was responsible for coordinating all intelligence from MI5, RUC SB and the SAS in Northern Ireland. FRU's existence remained secret for a long time before Mark Urban revealed its role in 1992.[61]

MI5 having devised the Walker strategy, which placed SB as a force within a force, was now in a dominant position. For all practical purposes it was running RUC SB and in control of all policing in Northern Ireland.[62] Any form of public accountability of policing in this context was a sham.

It is not known how many state agents and informers were recruited by the police, army, and MI5 under the MI5/Walker strategy. It was probably in the hundreds and they were drawn from both loyalist and republican communities, but those deemed most valuable were embedded in the IRA. They were recruited through a variety of methods based on the exploitation of some known personal vulnerability or using threats to family members, blackmail, and inducements. Over the years, the horrific nature of some of their crimes and the longevity of the period that they were allowed to operate with impunity, have slowly emerged (Chapter 21).

Covering-up

The production of the cover stories in the three incidents investigated by Stalker strongly suggested that the introduction of the MI5/Walker recommendations was accompanied by the development of a press and media strategy within the RUC, designed to hide the truth about surveillance methods and to protect the identities of state agents. Moreover, the carefully constructed cover stories for each of the incidents provided legal justifications for the officers to open fire. In all three, it was alleged that the officers were on routine patrols when something suspicious or untoward occurred that justified the shooting. In the Tullygally East Road incident the car failed to stop at a routine roadblock and sped away. In the Mullacreevie Park incident the same occurred – strong 'evidence' that the individuals were trying to avoid capture. In the hayshed incident, a routine patrol was confronted by two armed men with rifles – again, strong 'evidence' that their lives were in danger and a justification for their actions. Decisions on the content of the cover stories would therefore have been taken at the highest level among senior officers with legal expertise in the RUC and MI5, with the aim of preventing any possibility of a prosecution for murder.

The cover stories, however, went much further than false media reports. The CID officers tasked with investigating the three incidents were kept in the dark about key aspects of the shootings, and false or embellished documentation was given to the DPPNI, as revealed in the McCauley trial. The aim was clearly to influence the decision not to prosecute the officers involved in the shootings. All those involved in the cover-ups were guilty of perverting the course of justice. This dishonest and criminal behaviour arose directly from the MI5/Walker strategy which corrupted all aspects of policing.

* * *

The MI5/Walker strategy was to have a devastating impact. The rule of law was severely compromised along with the state's fundamental obligation to protect the lives of its citizens and not to murder them by proxy. Moreover, there was no independent oversight. Hundreds of agents were recruited by MI5, the army and RUC. The priority was to build up intelligence, not to arrest and prosecute those involved in political violence. State agents were allowed to continue their deadly activities for years and their role was often hidden from the CID, which was tasked with investigating the murders they had carried out. Maurice Punch, an academic specialising in the study of policing, eloquently described the situation as largely 'an intelligence war fought with the full gamut of dirty tricks, grubby hands, and unfortunate victims'.[63]

The allegations of shoot-to-kill, the cover-up by the RUC in the three incidents, and the rigorousness of Stalker's investigation were to lead to a profound change in the counter-insurgency strategy by the late 1980s. The RUC's deployment of its own anti-terrorist flying squads was reassessed and the British army once again assumed an enhanced role in the strategy to defeat the IRA. To avoid further allegations that the security forces were shooting to kill suspected members of the IRA and to avoid the intense legal and judicial scrutiny arising from a security force killing, the army increasingly outsourced the war against the IRA to loyalist paramilitaries. It recruited its own agents within the UDA, assisted them in purchasing arms and provided them with intelligence on suspects.[64] These developments, combined with the MI5/Walker strategy, were even more deadly. By the early 1990s loyalists were killing more people than the IRA (Chapter 22).

Chapter 4

Conspiracies in Life

KENT STREET IN BELFAST runs up from Royal Avenue to Carrick Hill and today the whole street has a run-down feel to it. There are some new buildings, but old, dilapidated structures and boarded-up vacant lots dominate. The only place, until recently, that had brought any life to the street was the famous Sunflower pub, known for its music scene, with its iron cage and gate surrounding the entrance – a reminder of the days of the Troubles. Now, one of the hoardings is also attracting visitors. It has a painting of a smiling Lyra McKee, the journalist shot dead by the New IRA in April 2019 – a reminder of the fragility of peace. Towards the top end of the street there once stood a building with a big sign: 'Cut Price Fancy Goods'. On 26 January 1981, it was destroyed in a contract bombing. It was to become a pivotal incident in the Taylor/Stalker affair.

Long Firm Fraud

Cut Price Fancy Goods was owned by Mark Klapish who lived in Manchester but had extensive business interests in Northern Ireland from the early 1960s. He would fly to Belfast on a Tuesday and return to Manchester on the Thursday. He stayed in the Dunadry Hotel, situated close to Belfast International Airport, often in the company of a friend. He would then travel around Northern Ireland in a silver Rolls Royce. He was well-known to many retailers in Belfast, who often wondered how he could sustain such a lifestyle, particularly when all his outlets were of the pound-shop variety. Some had formed the conclusion that most of his wealth was obtained through illegal activities – his premises appeared to suffer disproportionately from incendiary devices and bombs.

Klapish's persona as successful businessman hid a secret: he was an expert in the crime of long firm fraud or LFF, for short.[1] The origins of the term are obscure, but it is an intricate crime and involves several key players, all of whom have specialist names to denote their specific roles. The overall aim is simple: to purchase as many goods as possible on credit from the widest range of businesses, without any intention of paying for them; then, through a variety of techniques, to maximise the amount of money that the goods can raise. The key to a successful LFF is establishing confidence with businesses to obtain credit. In the 1970s and 1980s this did not appear to be a major problem, particularly if the managing director of the company appeared to be a successful businessman and there was a highly plausible individual doing the ordering.

Everyone involved in a LFF has a title. The person who brings together the team and arranges the initial finance is called the 'organiser'. Mark Klapish took on this role himself. The people who put up the money are called 'backers' and they normally put in place a 'minder' on the team to look after their financial interests. In this case it was alleged that the backers were Vincent Schiavo and Joseph Monaghan. They were involved in a wide range of businesses, including boxing promotions, and were alleged to be central figures in the QSG. Another key person in a long firm fraud is the 'frontman' or 'blowerman'. Their role is to order the goods, look after the office and 'take the rap'. In this case, the frontman was the police informer David Burton.

The initial creditworthiness is typically built up through several deceits including fraudulent references, the use of corrupt bank officials and *bona fide* businessmen who may be prepared, for a variety of reasons, to write a letter in support. Once the account has been established, it is consolidated by payment for the first orders with valid cheques. Sometimes, however, 'dud' cheques may be sent off, or sent with only one signature, when two are required, but new orders are placed in the expectation that they will be delivered before it is discovered that the cheque is invalid. Another ruse is to inform the creditor that there are problems paying at the present time because they have recently changed bank accounts. Most LFFs are begun in the summer months with small orders that are increased as Christmas approaches, mirroring normal business cycles. Just before Christmas huge orders are placed, then the goods are sold, and the firm closed.[2]

David Burton

David Burton had a long history of criminal deception, a string of convictions to match and had spent many years in jail. In 1963, aged 18, he was fined £50 for issuing dud cheques.[3] Five years later, he stole two cheques from his mother and bought £285 worth of jewellery which he then sold for £110. He was charged with theft and received a nine-month suspended prison sentence.[4] In 1972, he was sent for trial at Manchester Crown Court charged obtaining £1,156 by deception – over £12,700 at today's prices (March 2023).[5]

He was highly intelligent but a narcissist. From all accounts, he was a superb liar, a confidence trickster and very plausible. Several people regarded his ability for recollection as remarkable and he intuitively knew just how much information needed to be correct among a pack of lies. He appeared to have a need to ingratiate himself with the police as if, despite his own extensive criminality, he wished to be on the side of the law. While in his early twenties, the Krays tried to move into the club scene up north and they visited Manchester on one occasion. Burton served as their errand boy but made much of it for the next 20 years, telling everyone that he was once the Krays' chauffeur.[6]

Micky Martin, a ticket entrepreneur and showbusiness promoter, who knew Burton well, described several instances of his deceitfulness. He recalled one occasion when Burton came to his house and walked out with his wife's lighter and expensive pendant. On another, he stole £2,000 from his girlfriend, Elizabeth MacDonald, when helping with her hairdressing salon accounts. Martin claimed that: 'Burton knew what the police wanted to hear, and nine-tenths of the information were lies. He was rotten to the core, and I was ashamed to call him a friend.'[7]

Burton had known Klapish since childhood as they had grown up together in the Cheetham Hill area of Manchester. When Burton came out of jail in 1974, after serving his sentence for obtaining £1,156 by deception, Klapish employed him for a short while. In March 1976, he was sentenced to another six years in prison for deception. Judge Sir William Morris, before sentencing him, described him as 'one of the most plausible rogues ever to stand in that dock'.[8] Burton had admitted to 44 offences of obtaining property and money worth over £13,000 by deception and fraud. The Judge went on:

> These were gross deceptions born out of your overwhelming desire for wealth and you are a liar of incomparable skill and experience. I have little doubt that if you were released shortly, you would start again on your nefarious plans for taking money from innocent people.[9]

Sometime after completing this sentence, Burton ended up working for Klapish's company Cut Price Fancy Goods, which was specifically set up to run the LFF. It was based in Progress House in Salford. Burton was given the job as frontman, with responsibility for running the office and doing the purchasing. Progress House had, for many years, been seen by the police as a centre for fraud of one type or another and it had been under surveillance on several occasions. Why the two men came together at this time is unclear.

Klapish may have approached Burton because he was fully aware of his ability to deceive. Alternatively, and equally plausibly, Burton may have approached Klapish who had helped him out after the last time he was in jail. A further possibility is that Burton was encouraged by the RUC or even MI5, to find out more about Klapish and his activities in Northern Ireland. In 1982, a special team of RUC detectives was tasked to investigate how Manchester criminals were using the IRA to make bogus claims against the NIO.[10] An obvious source of intelligence would have been Burton. The team was headed by Bill Mooney who had visited GMP in 1976 and had been entertained by Stalker and Taylor on that occasion (Chapter 6).

Klapish used the address 'International Trade Showrooms, Progress House' to add to the company's credibility. Burton was very skilful. In a few months, he had purchased thousands of pounds worth of goods, some of which were sold in Manchester at cost, and some made their way across the Irish Sea to other firms owned by Klapish in Northern Ireland. But Klapish had a grander plan than simply defrauding creditors: he wanted to treble his money. First, he planned to sell off most of the goods he had purchased but for which he had no intention of paying. Then he would arrange to have the warehouse belonging to his company, Cut Price Fancy Goods, in Kent Street, destroyed. Finally, he would make a fraudulent claim to the NIO Criminal Compensation Fund (CCF), not only for the building but also for the full retail value of the goods which, he would falsely claim, were in the building at the time.[11]

Klapish's misfortune

Klapish was a most unfortunate businessman. Research shows that his premises in Belfast were fire-bombed or subjected to some other form of attack on numerous occasions. Klapish made 29 separate claims to the CCF amounting to nearly £2 million, for which he received over £300,000 in compensation payments.[12] In 1977, John Carson, MP for North Belfast, raised the issue of 'contract bombing' at Westminster and suggested that Klapish – who, at the time, had been cleared of a £450,000 fraud in Manchester – was suspected of arranging for two of his recently purchased Belfast premises to be fire-bombed.[13] The RUC SB and MI5, too, would have been aware that Klapish was involved in contract bombings from his long list of claims to the CCF, as well as his links to paramilitaries, well before he executed the grand plan for Kent Street.

In October 1980, Burton, who had for many years provided information to the police and was described as an 'historic informant',[14] learnt of Klapish's plans to blow up the warehouse in Kent Street. He tipped off DSgt Derek Burgess from

GMP's Commercial Fraud Squad hoping, no doubt, to avoid arrest for his part in the fraud.[15] This appears to have been one of Burton's few 'genuine tips'[16] and was 'spot on'.[17] Prior to Christmas 1980, he contacted the police again and told them that the Kent Street premises would be blown up within a couple of weeks 'by the IRA'. Before it was destroyed, a group of men went over to Belfast to remove stock from the warehouse. The RUC mounted a surveillance operation on their large orange and brown box van as it left Stranraer.[18]

The premises were eventually attacked on 26 January 1981. Shortly after opening time, several men entered the building and the staff were ordered to lie on the floor at gunpoint while two firebombs were planted. Mr Stewart, the manager, was in the main showroom when the gunmen walked in. He was a former Lord Mayor of Belfast. He described what happened: 'I had my back to the door and the first thing I heard was a voice saying, "Don't move, down on the floor".' After he lay down, a second gunman came in and planted a petrol can, with some sort of device attached to it. He could hear the bomb ticking. After a few minutes, he shouted: 'Are you gone?' When there was no answer, the staff escaped through the back door. The first firebomb exploded at 10.12 a.m. and the second twelve minutes later. Two firemen who arrived at the scene to fight the blaze were injured during the second explosion.[19]

The firebombs caused little damage. The loss assessors visited the building and estimated the stock to be worth about £52,000.[20] With a keen sense of irony, the contractors returned later that evening and completed the job, for which presumably they had been paid. It was too late. Klapish was prevented from making another highly inflated claim to the NIO to recoup the investment in the LFF. The backers lost thousands of pounds and were none too happy at the turn of events. A few months later it was rumoured that one of Klapish's backers took his Rolls Royce in lieu of payment.[21]

It is unclear which organisation was involved in the contract fire-bombing of Kent Street. Burton made no distinction between the PIRA and OIRA. He simply alleged that 'the IRA' were going to blow up the building. It is possible that Kent Street was one of the targets among the bombings claimed by PIRA that day: car bombs were planted in Portadown, Omagh, and Derry and a bomb was placed on the Belfast to Dublin rail line.[22] In addition, there were explosions in Lisnaskea and Newry. On the other hand, it is more likely that Klapish had arranged for either the Official IRA (OIRA) or loyalists to destroy the Kent Street premises. The OIRA – the armed wing of the Workers' Party – was involved in a wide range of criminality, including bank robberies and extortion. Other possible suspects for the contract bombing were members of the loyalist criminal community. Klapish, at one time, had premises on a loyalist section of the Crumlin Road, premises that were firebombed in the mid-1970s. It is known that he had contacts within the UVF and the UDA and was friendly with two brothers with substantial criminal records.[23]

Whoever was responsible, the Kent Street operation indicated that they were carrying out selected fire-bombings to raise funds for their campaign and had connections with criminals in Manchester. Any actions in England would be helped considerably by established and trusted relationships built up in Northern Ireland. GMP at the time suspected that people from Northern Ireland were committing armed robberies in jewellers in Manchester before disappearing back to Northern Ireland. On one occasion, they mounted surveillance on two suspects at Stranraer port but by the time they got to Gretna Green the suspects realised they were being followed and abandoned their car and made their way back to Stranraer by train. The Regional Crime Squad (RCS) contacted the RUC, who confirmed that the suspects were heading to Manchester to meet up with Manchester criminals.[24] Again, it is not known which organisation was responsible for these robberies. The crucial point, however, is that by the early 1980s, the RUC had considerable intelligence on the connections between paramilitaries in Northern Ireland and criminals in Manchester. The extent, if any, to which this shared intelligence was used to remove Stalker remains one of the many unexplained aspects of the Taylor/Stalker affair.

RUC and GMP meeting in Belfast

On 4 and 5 February 1981, a meeting between the RUC and GMP took place in Belfast to discuss the Kent Street operation. It was chaired by the RUC's Detective Superintendent Drew. Inspector Born from GMP was present as were other GMP officers including Burgess, who had been put in charge of the investigation into the LFF, and Detective Inspector David Patterson, from the No. 1 RCS, presumably because he had been, or was, Burton's handler. It is not known how many RUC officers were present or who they were. But as the case concerned apparent links between Manchester criminals and paramilitary organisations in Northern Ireland, RUC SB and MI5 may have attended or taken a very close interest in the details.

In a remarkable coincidence, Drew, who had been responsible for the CID investigation into the hayshed shootings, was subsequently interviewed by Stalker during his Northern Ireland investigation three years later.[25] Inspector Born later headed up the secret unit in GMP, which investigated Taylor and Stalker – another remarkable coincidence. Whether there was, of course, any connection between the presence of these two officers in the meeting and subsequent developments in the Taylor/Stalker affair is unknown.

The meeting was opened by DCI Waite, who stressed the seriousness with which the RUC considered the fire-bombing of Kent Street.[26] Over the two days a considerable amount of information was exchanged. GMP were told how members of staff, including the ex-Lord Mayor, were ordered to lie down on the floor while the bombs were planted. They would have been told about Burton, the blowerman and lifetime fraudster, and how he had told Burgess that the premises were to be blown up 'by the IRA'. He was described as 'a loyal and most reliable informant'.[27] Burgess told the meeting that Klapish had not got two brass farthings to rub together, and he had borrowed money to finance his business from the QSG. Patterson then elaborated on the personalities and modus operandi of the QSG. Schiavo and Monaghan's names were mentioned.[28]

It has been difficult to trace any follow-up actions of the police on either side of the Irish Sea after the Belfast meeting. One assumes, given the seriousness of the information, there would have been considerable activity to investigate Burton's claims that there were connections between 'the IRA' and the QSG. The Kent Street bombing appears to have alerted the RUC that Klapish was possibly a fraudster because almost two years later, on 15 December 1982, he appeared before Belfast Magistrates' Court. He was charged with defrauding the NIO and Legal and General Assurance Group of £81,000 between October 1975 and January 1976, suggesting that they had trawled through his old claims.[29] Together with Alfred Osbiston, also from Manchester, he was charged with conspiring to defraud the two organisations of £77,000. Other charges against Klapish included obtaining money by deception, false accounting and unlawfully inciting a Belfast based builder, Joseph Murray, to produce false documentation to substantiate a claim for repairs. Klapish and Osbiston were remanded on bail totalling £12,000. The outcome of the case is not known but it did not relate to the bombing of Kent Street or the LFF.

Burgess was left to carry out the investigation into the million-pound LFF single-handedly.[30] He did ask for a special team to cover all aspects of the inquiry, but his requests fell on deaf ears. He was told to concentrate on the fraud aspects, with all other aspects being referred to GMP's specialist units.[31] The lack of resources for Burgess to investigate a million-pound fraud would contrast sharply with the huge resources later allocated to investigate Stalker's friend – Kevin Taylor – also for fraud. Burgess, however, did have the help of Burton. Burgess, like Klapish, had grown up in the Cheetham Hill area of Manchester and was at school with Burton. This appeared to have led to a trust between the two when Burgess became Burton's police handler – trust that did not exist with any of Burton's other handlers, to whom he was more willing to lie.

Burton's allegations

Having reported the LFF to GMP, Burton was now in a vulnerable position. He went from one law enforcement organisation to another and passed on bits of information, gleaned in one department, as new information to another. It is now known that, as well as being an informer to GMP Fraud Squad, he was also an informer to No. 1 RCS, and American Express and, in all probability to Customs and Excise.[32] It is not known if he was also working for RUC SB and/or MI5.

One of the people Burton reported to the police in 1981 or 1982 was Kevin Taylor – a man he had never met.[33] He allegedly told his handler in No. 1 RCS, DI Patterson, the following information about Taylor:

1. Known supplier of monies for the importation of drugs and the purchase of properties;
2. Loans money to gamblers at large interest rates;
3. Firearms dealer in the past and a minder for firearms used on jobs by the QSG;
4. Known associate of IRA members.[34]

Patterson produced a report recording the above information and instructed some of his staff to research Taylor's background.[35] They found nothing, and Patterson took no further action as he appears to have concluded that Burton was inventing information to save his own skin. Burton later told a friend, Martin, that he had, indeed, made up the stories about Taylor.[36]

Operation City

There were two other significant pieces of information which Burton reported to the police at this time. The first was that there was an ACC 'on a pension'.[37] In 1981, GMP had six ACCs, including Stalker. The second piece of information was perhaps even more serious. Burton claimed that Klapish and members of the QSG were gun-running for the IRA.[38] No. 1 RCS took Burton's allegations seriously and sought permission to mount a surveillance operation on the Schiavo and Monaghan brothers – four alleged members of the QSG. It was called Operation City. Before any RCS carries out an operation of this type, they must first seek the permission of the Chief Constable of the force in whose area the surveillance operation will occur. If the operation involves phone tapping, the RCS must also make a specific request to the Home Secretary. Once granted, the Chief Constable must review the situation every month.[39]

DI Wilson made the case for Operation City in a memorandum dated 18 March 1982. He noted that the Schiavo and Monaghan brothers 'make up the inner circle of a crime [syndicate]', that 'they have many fingers in the criminal pie…' and are 'held in high esteem by Manchester criminals'.[40] He also noted that during a recent investigation, the British Transport Police learnt that 'GMP could not be trusted in the arrest of criminals', which Wilson considered an indictment against GMP.[41] The implication was that the brothers had police officers in their pockets; hence arrests and surveillance operations were 'blown out'. The report noted that they have 'runners' who watch out for the police, and therefore can avoid surveillance. The syndicate was suspected of handling foreign currency, theft of high-value mail, and handling and disposing of high-value loads.[42]

Crucially for later developments in the Taylor/Stalker affair, the memorandum made two references to 'the IRA'. First, it suggested that there was a connection between the four suspects and the IRA because of the IRA's suspected involvement in the fire-bombing of Cut Price Fancy Goods' premises in Kent Street.[43] Second, it noted that *'reliable information* (emphasis added) has been received that they in fact are gun-runners for the IRA'.[44] The so-called 'reliable information' had clearly come, once again, from Burton.

Operation City began on 21 April 1982 and ended on 19 October 1983.[45] It generated 203 pages of surveillance logs but not one of them was examined in Taylor's civil action as a claim for privilege was made on all the documents.[46] This was now a common practice when covert surveillance had taken place and was provided for in the Interception of Communications Act 1985. Although Operation City continued for more than eighteen months, 'no useful product' emerged.[47] While there may have been several minor charges for people who were associated with the four main targets, there was no evidence to link any of the four to the major crimes for which Operation City was established – drug smuggling, theft of high value mail, handling or disposing of high-value loads, and gun-running for the IRA. Yet Burton's information was to re-emerge in report after report prepared by the secret unit set up to investigate Taylor and Stalker four years later (Chapters 7 to 9).

Burton's further allegations

Having made up stories about the criminality of Taylor, the gun-running activities of the QSG, and that an ACC was 'on a pension', Burton became a total nuisance. He would ring DI Patterson in No. 1 RCS so often that he could not get on with his work. As a result, DCI McGourlay took some of the load off Patterson by having the calls diverted to him. McGourlay admitted he got to know Burton fairly well over the telephone, but he too kept away from him physically as much as possible.[48] He described Burton as a dangerous informant pointing out that he would push out information to various sources for the reward money. On one occasion four different departments, including the police and Customs and Excise, were all looking at the same incident causing all sorts of problems. His information, therefore, needed to be treated very carefully.[49] Stalker was told by colleagues that Burton was the 'most dangerous, unreliable informant that anybody could be involved with'.[50]

Later in 1982, Burton was on remand in Strangeways Prison charged with cheque fraud. DS Ankers, from the Discipline and Complaints Department, was informed that Burton could be of use in relation to an investigation of a police officer who was suspected of involvement in a robbery in a supermarket. Ankers and DI Richardson visited him in Strangeways. When Burton's bail application came up in early 1983 before Justice Prestt in Manchester Crown Court, Ankers spoke on his behalf and of his potential use to the police corruption inquiry, and presented the Judge with a sealed envelope with the details. At the end of the hearing Justice Prestt remarked, 'The police really want you out!' and out he went.[51] The importance of the hearing, however, was that Burton learnt that helping with investigations into police corruption was an excellent 'get out of jail card'.[52]

Burton was also providing or recycling information to American Express (AMEX) under the codename 'Barbara Codd'. In early 1983, Amex compiled a report based on information provided by Burton. It noted the names of people allegedly in the IRA with whom Klapish had arranged to blow up Kent Street. One was from Newry, who had since left Ireland for the USA to avoid arrest, and the other was from Dundalk.[53] This report reappeared in 1985, when the Taylor/Stalker relationship was being investigated.

Blown out

By May 1983, Burgess had obtained enough information to close in on those involved in the LFF. He had been helped by Burton whose primary motivation, no doubt, was to reduce any sentence for his role in the fraud. On one occasion, Burton recorded a conversation for the police via a wire in an expensive overcoat which Klapish had bought him only a few weeks earlier.[54] Burgess obtained several search warrants from Salford Stipendiary Magistrates. A meeting of senior officers was held to prepare for the execution of the warrants and to muster a large team of officers to carry out the searches throughout Greater Manchester. The officers reported early for duty without knowing anything about it. But the searches were a complete failure, and the whole operation was 'blown out':

someone had tipped off the suspects. They had time to dispose of any incriminating evidence. It could only have been a corrupt police officer.

One of those who had been tipped off was Vincent Schiavo. When DI Anthony Stephenson arrived at his house to arrest him, he discovered that Schiavo had left in the early hours of the morning after attending a boxing match at Belle Vue the night before. At the time, he was on bail after his friend, Jimmy Monaghan, provided the surety of £25,000. When Schiavo failed to appear in court, Monaghan forfeited his money. According to Jimmy Donnelly, Monaghan said: 'I'm shattered. I will have to sell my house'. He said that his house was worth only about £50,000 and he earned only £250 a week selling cars.[55] Although Schiavo had surrendered his passport, he later obtained a British Visitor's Passport and made his way to Spain.[56]

Schiavo's absconding led to a flurry of communications between GMP and Interpol. A telex from Interpol on 27 July 1983, noted that a boat called *Sherama*, owned by Schiavo, was moored at Pier 1 and a yacht called *Diogenes* was moored at Pier 2 in the harbour at Puerto Banus.[57] Taylor owned *Diogenes*. GMP therefore knew, in July 1983, that there was a possible connection between Taylor and Schiavo. But this was hardly a revelation, as Taylor had never made a secret of the fact that they had known each other since the 1960s when they both were trying to make a living in the Ancoats area of Manchester. It only became important when the telexes were later discovered by the special unit set up to investigate Stalker.

'I have found your rat'

The failure to arrest the principal suspects in the LFF, no doubt, added to existing suspicions that there was widespread corruption in GMP. It is not known what action the Discipline and Complaints Department took. Nothing emerged in the civil action as to the form the inquiry might have taken, nor the outcome. However, Taylor's papers included an unsigned, undated, and cryptic document which, if authentic, challenges GMP's chronology of events presented in the civil action.

It was an angry document reflecting a profound disappointment of those in authority.[58] Although mostly written in the third person, it was obviously composed by Burgess because he reverted to the first person in a sub-heading. Instead of writing 'Burgess was Burton's handler', he wrote, 'I was Burton's handler'. It was written after the collapse of Taylor's criminal trial in January 1990 and was obviously designed to challenge the official narrative. Most importantly, it contained a conversation which Burgess had with Burton shortly after all the arrests were blown out in May 1983. Burgess described it as a scene from Bruce Forsyth's 'Play your Cards Right'. It read as follows:

BURTON: I have found your rat.

BURGESS: Who?

BURTON: Have a guess.

BURGESS: (Names of two suspect police officers given).

BURTON: No.

BURGESS: We are having a guessing game, are we?

BURTON: Go on, it's obvious. I'll give you a clue – It's one of your CID bosses.

BURGESS: Geoff Bennett? (Fraud Squad Investigator).

BURTON: No, higher.

BURGESS: Collison? (Fraud Squad Inspector).

BURTON: Higher.

BURGESS: O.K. Bruce, Ted Hughes. (Fraud Squad Superintendent).

BURTON: Higher.

BURGESS: Geoff Rimmer? (Head of CID).

BURTON: Higher.

BURGESS: There is only one left – Charlie Horan? (ACC Crime).

BURTON: There's one higher.

BURGESS: Christ, there is only one higher. You're not suggesting Jim Anderton, are you?

BURTON: No, not that high. Do you know your own Chiefs?

BURGESS: You have lost me.

BURTON: Stalker, it's John Stalker.

BURGESS: I've not seen him for ages, he's with another force down South. (Two other
               Fraud Squad Officers were within earshot of this conversation and
               interjected thus.)

OFFICER 1: He's back here now

OFFICER 2: He's been back a while, he's an ACC. (The conversation with Burton
               continued as follows)

BURGESS: How do you know?

BURTON: He's 'on a pension' from the QSG.

BURGESS: Let's have something a little more concrete.

BURTON: I was at (associate's) house last night and I saw photographs of Stalker with
               the QSG. They were all dressed in dickie bows and penguin suits at an
               Anglo-American boxing night at the Piccadilly Hotel.

BURGESS: Who was in the photographs?

BURTON: All the QSG.

BURGESS: That doesn't prove that Stalker blew out my job.

BURTON: No, but it's obvious isn't it. Are you not pleased with this information? I've
               worked hard trying to find out who the rat is.

BURGESS: I could have done without it.

The document made it clear that Burgess did not think Stalker was the mole.
He was not close enough to the inquiry and Burgess considered Stalker's
dedication as a police officer ruled out the possibility. Given his 'social style and

sporting interests', it was not surprising that he associated with members of the QSG. He was 'a man's man', the report noted, and regardless of his position he was frequently seen at rank-and-file functions and was not averse to playing the drums. What Burgess did not know was that, throughout 1983, Stalker was attending a Royal College of Defence Studies course and therefore could not have tipped off Schiavo and his co-conspirators.

Following the conversation with Burton, Burgess prepared a report noting it *verbatim*. He submitted one copy to his Fraud Squad Superintendent and another to the Discipline and Complaints Department. If this conversation is true, there was a report in GMP suggesting that Stalker was corrupt a year before he was appointed to the Northern Ireland inquiry. It would be inconceivable that he was recommended for such an important inquiry in Northern Ireland if this information were believed.

Burton's LFF statement

The failure of the police raids exposed Burton. It would not have taken much for the various people whose homes were raided to guess that the police were very well informed. They would have immediately suspected Burton because it was widely known that he had been a police informer for years. Burton began to receive threats. His girlfriend, Elizabeth MacDonald, and his mother were also threatened. He moved out of the house he shared with his mother and moved to a safer address.

Burgess interviewed Burton over a five-week period and diligently produced a very long book of evidence on the LFF. This document potentially exposed Burton further as, in any trial, it would be revealed to the defence. In the event, Burton never signed the statement and the evidence was never used. But then, like so many documents in this saga, it went missing. It could not be found for Taylor's criminal trial, but a document purporting to be the original book of evidence eventually reappeared and was obtained on discovery in the civil action. This made no mention of Stalker, but it did allege that Taylor was a member of the QSG. His name, along with several others, however, appears to have been added to the document. There are dark lines above and below the names on the photocopy. When a ruler is placed along the line of type, Taylor's name is out of alignment, suggesting it was pasted in and then the document was photocopied again.[59]

During the preparation of the prosecution of the LFF, Burgess became ill and went on long-term sick leave. The stress of preparing a complex fraud case virtually single-handedly, with little support from senior management, and covering two jurisdictions and paramilitary connections, had taken its toll. He was never to return to work and his health never satisfactorily recovered. He was the first of several police officers in the Taylor/Stalker affair to take early retirement, resentful of their treatment. He left with a deep sense of injustice against the police force he had served for many years.[60] The case was taken over by DSgt Keith Ware and DC Alan Gregory.

LFF prosecutions

In September 1984 – nearly four years after the bombing of Kent Street – Klapish, Burton and Joseph Monaghan appeared before Judge Brown in Manchester charged with various offences relating to the LFF. Klapish was originally charged with conspiracy to defraud and 'making a deal with the IRA'.[61] As he pleaded guilty and there was no examination of any of the evidence, the details of a possible connection with the IRA never emerged in court. Klapish was sentenced to four years.[62] Burton also pleaded guilty. The court was then cleared and McGourlay revealed that Burton was a police informer and had received £2,000 for the information which he had given to the police.[63] Once again, Superintendent Ankers spoke on Burton's behalf and told the Judge about his help with allegations against corrupt police officers. Consequently, his sentence was reduced to two and half years.[64]

It is not known why Klapish, Burton and Monaghan were not brought to trial in Northern Ireland. In 1979, the DPPNI opened a file on Klapish concerning earlier fire bombings of his premises, but there was no file concerning his activities in January 1981.[65] There was certainly a strong *prima facie* case that Klapish had deliberately conspired to have his Kent Street premises burnt down to make a fraudulent claim to the Northern Ireland Criminal Compensation Fund. This was a much more serious offence than conspiracy to obtain goods by deception, for which Klapish was convicted in Manchester. In Northern Ireland, the case would have been held in front of a single judge without a jury in a Diplock Court.

Occasionally, offenders were prosecuted in Britain for offences committed in Northern Ireland, particularly if the authorities wished to avoid any adverse publicity. According to a Dublin Magazine, *The Phoenix,* one such case concerned Mark Philip Jackson, a former colleague of Constable John Robinson, the RUC officer acquitted of murder in relation to the Grew/Carroll shooting (Chapter 1). Jackson appeared before Taunton Magistrates where he was charged under the Official Secrets Act in October 1986. Like Constable Robinson, he had moved to Britain after leaving the RUC. He was charged with two offences under Section 2 of the Official Secrets Act.[66] This section relates to the passing of RUC documents and would have caused considerable embarrassment if the case had been heard in Belfast. It is not known to whom he passed the documentation.

According to one security expert interviewed for this book,[67] the person who carried out the fire-bombing of the premises for Klapish was a state agent who was being handled by MI5. He had been in the PIRA but later joined the OIRA because of a cloud of suspicion over his behaviour. This would possibly explain why Klapish, Burton and Monaghan were not being brought to trial in Northern Ireland on the more serious charge of conspiring to cause explosions: this would have exposed the identity of the state agent. The protection of state agents was the basis of the cover stories following the fatal shootings in Northern Ireland investigated by Stalker. If the security expert was correct – unsurprisingly it has not been possible to obtain any supporting evidence – history was repeating itself. Moreover, a trial in Northern Ireland could have exposed the close relationship between the OIRA and the RUC.

* * *

In retrospect, the LFF was a crucial event in the history of the Taylor/Stalker affair. Following the fire-bombings of the premises in Kent Street, alarm bells must have been ringing in both Belfast and Manchester concerning the implications that the IRA were involved with suspected major criminals in Manchester in a sophisticated LFF, and were also allegedly gun-running for them. It is inconceivable that this information was not carefully examined by RUC SB, the Anti-Terrorist Squad and MI5. As the MI5/Walker strategy encouraged the widespread recruitment of state agents, it is not beyond the bounds of possibility that Burton was a state agent at some point. The question then arises: was he used in a RUC/GMP plot to remove Stalker?

What is known for certain is that Burton played two central roles, first as the frontman in the LFF, and then as an informer to the police, American Express and, possibly, Customs and Excise. He did, occasionally, provide accurate information, as in his report that Kent Street would be firebombed, but so much of his information was inaccurate or untrue. Life was like a play for him. It did not really matter if he was frontman, blowerman or police informer, all the roles involved deception and deceit. Oddly, Burton's allegation that Stalker was corrupt, which Burgess reported in May 1983, was never mentioned in the civil action. Yet, according to the official story, Donnelly made an almost identical allegation concerning Stalker during a conversation with Burton in June 1984.

Chapter 5

Stalker in the Jungle

IT WAS LATE May 1984 when the Chief Constable of GMP, James Anderton, entered Stalker's office and asked him if he would head an inquiry into the shooting dead of the six men in Northern Ireland by the specialist anti-terrorist units of the RUC. It was only a few months after he had been appointed DCC of GMP. He did not hesitate for long before accepting the post.[1] Soon after, Stalker went to Summerseat, the home of his friend Kevin Taylor, and joined him in the jacuzzi. He told Taylor about his new but challenging task to conduct an inquiry in Northern Ireland. Taylor was under no illusions about the difficulty of such an investigation. He told him bluntly not to take it.[2] He pointed out the RUC was predominantly a Protestant police force and that he, Stalker, was a Catholic.

The Investigation

Stalker ignored his friend's advice and began assembling a team. He picked two detective sergeants, two inspectors and two DCIs, and one CS - a team of five men and two women.[3] He selected Chief Superintendent John Thorburn as his second-in-command – a gritty 50-year-old Scot whose CID experience and stature would have been difficult to surpass anywhere in England. He and Stalker had joined GMP at about the same time and had worked together in the detective branch. Stalker held him in very high regard.[4] He selected CI John Simons because he was a Special Branch officer[5] who had been positively vetted to the highest level and therefore had clearance for top secret documents. He would subsequently regret it (Chapter 15). According to *The Observer*, Simons was the brother-in-law and associate of Detective Chief Superintendent Peter Topping, who would later lead the investigation into Taylor and Stalker.[6]

The investigation into the three shooting incidents was never going to be easy. Few within the RUC wanted an outside inquiry. There was a vicious war going on. The police and the army, as they saw it, had to fight the war with their hands tied behind their backs, while republican and loyalist paramilitaries could do what they liked. CC Hermon was only too aware that the officers involved in the three incidents had been tasked to deal with some of the most wanted men in Northern Ireland based on information from state agents. He was opposed to any criminal proceedings being brought against the men.[7] Stalker had been warned by Myers, from HMIC, that Hermon would be most reluctant to assist, having been forced to have an inquiry.[8] Similarly, MI5, who had developed the policing strategy which made extensive use of spies and had placed the bug in the hayshed, would certainly not welcome an investigation.

Some of Stalker's problems in Northern Ireland stemmed from the lack of clarity about the constitutional status of his inquiry. He and his team were only too aware that a police officer from England did not have any power or legal authority in Northern Ireland because of its separate legal system. As Stalker remarked, 'for all practical purposes Northern Ireland was a foreign country'.[9] The problem lay in the lack of any sanctions against those officers who refused to co-operate with an inquiry.[10]

Stalker's terms of reference were to investigate:

1. the circumstances of the three shooting incidents in which six men were shot dead and one seriously injured, and in which certain members of the Royal Ulster Constabulary provided false or misleading evidence to members of the CID;

2. the conduct of members of the Royal Ulster Constabulary in connection with the investigation of all three incidents;

3. any evidence to suggest that any person was guilty of perverting or attempting to pervert the course of justice, or of any other offence in connection with the shooting incidents;

4. the circumstances in which members of the Royal Ulster Constabulary on duty entered the Republic of Ireland on 12 December 1982; and

5. the handling of informants by police officers and which information they cannot disclose to other policemen or the courts due to the need to protect sources.[11]

From the outset, Hermon and Stalker interpreted these terms of reference differently. Stalker wanted to reconstruct each of the three incidents to look for evidence of possible offences by the police and others, and then to submit the information to the DPPNI.[12] Hermon, however, wanted a 'review' of what happened in the three incidents: Stalker should 'read papers, speak to some key people about what had undoubtedly gone wrong, and submit a report containing a few operational recommendations for the future'.[13] Within a very short period there was little trust between the two men. Hermon was later to write that he deeply regretted his naivety in accepting Stalker's nomination without first asking questions about his qualifications. He considered that Stalker lacked 'experience at both operational and senior command level' and, rather disparagingly, pointed out that he had remained in CID for nineteen years before becoming an ACC.[14]

An unwelcome guest

On May 24, shortly after Stalker had arrived in Belfast, Hermon took him to a golf club for lunch. Stalker claimed that during the meal Hermon handed him a handwritten note, sketched on the back of a flattened-out cigarette packet. On it was his mother's family tree. She was Catholic and her parents were born in the Irish Republic. Stalker suggested that this would have involved a lot of research as it traced his relatives back to 1900 and included some he had never heard of.[15]

Hermon strongly denied that the cigarette packet incident ever took place and he later successfully sued *Private Eye* over 'the wholly fictitious conversation' which it had reported.[16] Hermon pointed out in his book that he had no knowledge of Stalker prior to his appointment and even got his name wrong noting it in his diary as 'Stocker' – the very same mistake that the officials in the NIO made. Hermon continued to make the same mistake in a note to the Northern Ireland Police Authority (NIPA) on 4 June.[17] But Hermon's mistake over Stalker's name does not in itself disprove the cigarette packet incident. A stronger point is that he was said to be a non-smoker.[18]

When I interviewed Chris Ryder, the writer and journalist, about Stalker's investigation in Northern Ireland about which he had written extensively, he told me that he too had had a cigarette packet incident with Hermon. One day he was summoned by Hermon to meet for lunch, after he had written a critical piece in the *Sunday Times* about the RUC. During the lunch, no mention was made of the article, but on the way back to RUC headquarters in the car, Hermon wrote his criticisms on the back of a cigarette packet and handed them to Ryder.[19] This suggests that Hermon sometimes did use a cigarette packet as a form of communication and adds credibility to the *Private Eye* story. Stalker later claimed that a police officer had sworn an affidavit to confirm that he had carried out the research into Stalker's family background.[20] If true, the intention was no doubt to indicate that Stalker potentially had a pro-Catholic bias. On leaving the restaurant, Hermon remarked: 'Remember, Mr Stalker, you are in a jungle now.'[21]

A few weeks later, Stalker received an anonymous phone call at his hotel from a 'sincere-sounding man with a Northern Ireland accent who said he was a Catholic RUC sergeant'.[22] He said that Stalker's suite of offices was bugged and the telephone was tapped. He then went on to tell Stalker the names of people to beware of in RUC SB. He then suddenly hung up.

Much later in his investigation, Stalker personally was to experience the hostility held by the ordinary rank and file towards his investigation. While attending Martin McCauley's trial in Crumlin Road Courthouse, he spoke to McCauley and his solicitor. He was then confronted by an RUC Sergeant who asked him if he knew to whom he had just been speaking. Stalker told him. The Sergeant then proceeded to inform him, with a vehemence that shocked Stalker:

> The solicitor is an IRA man – any man who represents IRA men is worse than an IRA man. His brother is an IRA man also and I have to say that I believe a senior policeman of your rank should not be seen speaking to the likes of either of them. My colleagues have asked me to tell you that you have embarrassed all of us in doing that. I will be reporting this conversation and what you have done to my superiors.[23]

The solicitor was Pat Finucane. Four years later, he was shot dead by loyalists in front of his family. Two of the assassins were state agents (see Chapter 22).

Controversy over Stalker's contribution

During their investigation, Stalker's team arranged for the reconstruction of the shootings, they read all the CID files and interviewed over 300 officers.[24] They took more than 600 written statements from policemen, forensic scientists, doctors, pathologists, members of the public and relatives of the dead men.[25] Stalker states that he himself interviewed officers of inspector rank and above, and saw 35 in all, including four ACCs.[26] Hermon, however, contradicted this. He claimed that Stalker was involved in only eight interviews and conducted only three himself, and 'only' 201 people made written statements. Moreover, Hermon claimed that Stalker 'travelled fewer than twelve times to Northern Ireland, while his team spent approximately 150 days there'.[27] Hermon recorded that he was reliably informed of these details 'by a member of his [Stalker's] team'.[28]

The information had come from Simons, the SB member of Stalker's team. He had been asked to prepare a report for Anderton in March 1988, who must have passed it onto Hermon. In the civil action, Thorburn was cross-examined extensively on the detail but was in no position to refute it as he had not prepared the report. He pointed out that Stalker would come across to Northern Ireland if and when he was needed and, of course, he had other duties back in Manchester. Thorburn claimed that there was nothing unusual in an ACC or higher rank leaving the groundwork to a lesser rank.[29]

The mysteries of the hayshed

By far the most important finding by Stalker's investigation team occurred in the early winter of 1984,[30] when they discovered that the hayshed had been bugged by MI5 and all sounds of the shooting of Tighe and McCauley were recorded on a series of tapes in a nearby listening post staffed by the RUC and army. Stalker demanded access to the tape of the actual shooting. This was to become,

> the rope in a bitter tug-of-war between those who believe that methods of intelligence gathering should be protected at all costs and those who regard the tape as possible evidence of murder committed by police, and therefore belonging in a wider arena.[31]

After more than 36 years, the unresolved question remains: was this 'tug-of-war' between Stalker on the one hand, and the RUC and MI5 on the other, the reason for his removal from the inquiry in Northern Ireland?

In his various reports and books, Peter Taylor has provided the fullest public account of the hayshed bugging. In the Panorama programme, *Stalker: Coincidence or Conspiracy* (broadcast 16 June 1986), he revealed that prior to the shooting of Tighe and McCauley a hay lorry was stopped at a routine checkpoint outside of Banbridge, having crossed the border from the Irish Republic. He continued:

> Under the bales of hay was concealed a ton and a half of explosives, one of the biggest hauls ever discovered in Northern Ireland. There was intelligence that part of that consignment was headed for the Ballynery hayshed. It was already in use as a secret IRA explosives store. The police now started watching it.[32]

In his books published in 1987 and 2001, Peter Taylor provided more detail. He reported that a highly placed state agent, or 'mole', who had first been recruited by the army, then taken over by SB and placed on MI5's payroll, had informed the police about the consignment of explosives. A few weeks later the mole reported that a further consignment would be coming across the border. On this occasion, there was no vehicle check point and no arrests. The plan, Peter Taylor suggested, 'seems to have been to catch an IRA active service unit with its hands on the explosives'.[33]

Electronic listening devices were then placed in the hayshed to be monitored 24 hours a day in a Portakabin some distance away. An MI5 technical officer planted a device in the rafters and an army technical officer planted one that would send a message if the explosives were removed. According to Peter Taylor, the authority to plant the devices was given by the Home Secretary. He queried whether the Joint Intelligence Committee (JIC), at the heart of government, knew about the operation. The devices then malfunctioned which meant that no message was sent when the IRA moved the explosives and used them with deadly effect on Kinnego embankment, killing three police officers.[34]

Subsequently, the malfunctioning devices were replaced by more sensitive devices, which transmitted all sounds to the listening post where they were recorded on tape. Officers in the listening post produced 42 tapes from the new devices in the hayshed. The last tape – tape 042 – was the crucial one. It had recorded the actual shooting of Tighe and McCauley and would prove or disprove whether any warning had been given prior to the shooting. It would also confirm or contradict McCauley's evidence that he was dragged out from the hayshed after being wounded, had a gun put down his throat and that there was a discussion about whether to 'finish him off'.

The failure of the first two devices at the same time, however, seems implausible. Was this another fabrication along with the cover stories to provide some sort of mitigation for the MI5, RUC and army's failure to prevent the removal of the explosives, and to allow the three police officers to investigate the theft of a battery, leading to their deaths? If the devices failed, there were obvious dangers to the public and the security forces if the IRA removed the explosives. Peter Taylor pointed out that a Static Observation Post (SOP) had been considered but was rejected because it would be too close to the road and the cottage, and there was the possibility that it 'would be sniffed out by republican-minded dogs'.[35] The most obvious place, however, for an SOP was inside the hayshed. It was known that no-one was living in the cottage in front of the hayshed and it would have been relatively easy to support one or two SAS trained soldiers hidden in the bales of straw.

So many key questions, therefore, remain unanswered. When was the hayshed first bugged? Stalker, unlike Peter Taylor, suggested that the hayshed was bugged before the arrival of the explosives. It seemed remarkable that the devices failed to capture either the placement or the removal of the explosives. Was Stalker able to see the authority for the use of the technical devices and the date on which it was issued? Was it before or after the Kinnego explosion? If it was before, it would lend some support to the faulty bug explanation. If it was after the explosives were removed, what was the purpose of the new device? Was it to monitor a further consignment of explosives or was it part of a trap to lure members of an IRA ASU into the hayshed? The 'convenient presence', as Stalker described them, of the old rifles, without any ammunition, raised the possibility that they were planted there 'by the informant or by someone else', perhaps an '*agent provocateur*'.[36] They could equally have been planted by MI5 or FRU.

Crucially, as well as the new monitoring devices, was there also an SOP manned by soldiers among the bales of hay? During McCauley's trial, two possible explanations were adduced for the fact that Tighe's entrance wounds were higher than the exit wounds: he was either standing or he was bending. If he was standing, he could only have been shot from a higher position inside the hayshed and not by any of the police outside the building. This would support the view that there was an SOP among the bales and would perhaps help explain why the CID were not allowed to the crime scene immediately.

Stalker wanted access to the intelligence on the movement of the explosives. He was particularly concerned over the use of informers and state agents, whom he thought might be used as *agents provocateurs* or bounty hunters. He wanted to know who they were and how much they were being paid. Peter Taylor claims that Stalker discovered that 'the mole' was paid £30,000 in a relatively short period of time.[37]

Stalker's requests went to the very heart of the counter-insurgency strategy which had been devised for the very purpose of protecting informers and state agents who were at the front line of the war against political violence in Northern Ireland. To concede to the requests would place the whole strategy at risk. Hermon's position was clear – he would not allow Stalker access to this information:

> I told Stalker that, whether or not it frustrated his investigation, I myself would not make a decision which could jeopardise police intelligence sources … Under no circumstances would I divulge anything to Stalker, or Thorburn, without the express approval of the Director of Public Prosecutions or, at his direction should he think it necessary, the Attorney General. I viewed the matter as one of national security, which ultimately rested with the Prime Minister.[38]

Stalker not only had problems obtaining the tape and details about informants and state agents, but he was also obstructed in several other ways. First, officers were not available for interviews; secondly, he was misinformed about the existence of files;[39] and thirdly, no action was taken when he recommended that SB Detective Superintendents, Thomas George Anderson and Samuel George Flanagan, should be suspended. They had played a central role in constructing the cover stories.[40] He also considered that a few key officers in RUC SB had taken a decision to obstruct the progress of his investigation.[41] Hermon, however, denies there was any obstruction. He had appointed David Chesney, a Senior ACC, to be Stalker's direct point of contact at chief officer level if he or his team required advice or help. But at no time during his entire investigation did Stalker or members of his team contact Chesney.[42]

According to Stalker, the CID investigation into the hayshed shooting, which he described as 'the act of a Central American assassination squad',[43] was seriously flawed. Shortly after the shooting, the DCS, who was head of the CID in the Southern region, was told by RUC SB officers, who were junior to him, that the crime scene was currently out of bounds. Consequently, he did not arrive at the scene until 90 minutes later. RUC SB were still there, yet the CID officer failed to question their presence or purpose. It was suggested that their presence was to ensure that MI5 removed the eavesdropping device,[44] but it could equally have been to reconstruct the scene, moving the position of Tighe's body and the rifles to avoid any chance of prosecution and perhaps to hide the fact that he had been shot by a member of a SOP inside the hayshed.

The actual investigation into the hayshed incident was carried out by Detective Superintendent Drew, whom in Stalker's words, 'figured deeply' in his inquiry.[45] He had responsibility for collecting all the forensic evidence, determining the number of shots fired, their direction and the distribution of the spent cartridge cases. It was his task to interview all the police officers involved in the shooting and resolve the conflict between their statements and the forensic evidence. Coincidently, he attended the meeting in Belfast in 1981 between the RUC and GMP following the bombing of Klapish's premises in Kent Street.[46]

Stalker made several criticisms of Drew and his team. The photographic evidence was useless and provided no evidence of angles or distances.[47] Drew failed to attend the post-mortem of Tighe, which would have provided him with immediate information about the trajectories of the fatal bullets. Stalker's overall conclusion was that the RUC CID detectives were either 'amateur and inefficient', or they had been 'deliberately inept'.[48] Drew's investigation, however, was severely compromised. None of the officers who fired the shots, nor their weapons, were immediately made available to the CID. All those involved were debriefed before they were interviewed by the CID officers and were instructed to make false statements.[49] In such circumstances, it was perhaps inevitable that Drew did not recommend any of those involved should be prosecuted.

Stalker made other discoveries about the hayshed incident. He learnt that McCauley's name had been mentioned by an informer in connection with the Kinnego explosion,[50] which would give some credence to the view that McCauley was lured into the hayshed in a planned revenge killing. Stalker also found that RUC SB had prepared an official record *after* Tighe's death, which posthumously associated him with IRA activity. Yet Tighe had no security record or criminal convictions. Stalker was 'uneasy' about the posthumous record.[51] Although he does not say why, presumably he thought that it had been produced to provide some justification for the killing of Tighe. While Tighe's friend McCauley was alleged to be in the IRA, Tighe's parents were adamant that Tighe was not a member. Traditionally, any member of the IRA was given an IRA funeral on their death. Tighe received a normal burial.

Stalker's other discoveries

There was also a catalogue of errors in the investigation of the killing of Burns, McKerr and Toman at Tullygally East Road: CID officers were denied access to the officers involved and to the forensic examination of the car; they were given incorrect information about where the shooting commenced; an independent witness was never interviewed; the state pathologist did not examine the bodies *in situ*; the photographic evidence was virtually useless; a fragment of the bullet which killed the driver was left unexamined, embedded in the car; numerous cartridge cases were missing; and no officers visited or contacted the dead men's families.[52] Most importantly, no one told Stalker's team that MI5/MI6 had bugged McKerr's car, allowing the security forces to listen into, and tape, any conversations within the car (Chapter 2). If Stalker, and subsequently Sampson, had known about this other tape, they would presumably have recommended that further officers should be prosecuted for perverting the course of justice.

The investigation into the Mullacreevie Park shootings of Grew and Carroll was just as shoddy: an independent witness to the shooting was not interviewed; it was suspected that the 'injured' officer had rolled in the dirt some distance from the scene to bolster the false claim of an injury; again, the photographs were useless; and the State Pathologist had not attended the scene. Stalker concluded: 'The shockingly low standard of basic techniques evident in the Tullygally East Road shootings had been repeated'.[53]

In all three cases, the files were poorly prepared and presented. According to Stalker, they were little more than a collection of statements and bore no resemblance to a murder prosecution file.[54] He commented upon the slack way in which certain terms were used, such as 'wanted' to refer to suspects, and the 'abuse of police evidence notebooks'.[55] Basic rules, known as 'preservation of evidence', were ignored. Crucially, a different detective officer had authored each report and no senior officer had seen fit to draw the reports together.[56]

Obstructing the CID in their investigations was a common practice within the RUC and stretched back over many years. For example, following the horrific bombing of the Step Inn, Keady, in August 1976, which caused the deaths of Betty McDonald and Robert McGleenan and injuries to 22 others, RUC SB built up a comprehensive picture of those involved and information about the planning and planting of the bomb. Yet all this detail was withheld from the CID investigating team. In the absence of any meaningful forensic evidence, there was little for the CID to investigate.[57]

What was new in the three cases investigated by Stalker, was that there was now systematic obstruction of CID as a direct consequence of the MI5/Walker strategy. All intelligence was now firmly controlled by RUC SB, and it decided who should have access to it. Since the protection of sources was paramount, the CID was effectively side-lined. Members of the CID could not challenge Force Orders. Against such a background, Stalker's criticisms of the CID were too stringent. In particular, the CS who was told not to attend the scenes of crime in the hayshed shooting and failed to question the presence of a SB officer had no option. RUC SB were firmly in command, under the control of MI5.

RUC Special Branch

Stalker rightly reserved his strongest criticisms for RUC SB. It had been investigated only two years earlier in 1982 following the leaking of secret information about informers to journalists. The investigation had been conducted by Joe Mounsey, an ACC from Lancashire, who led the team which played a key role in securing the conviction of Moors Murderers, Myra Hindley and Ian Brady – the killers of five children in the 1960s. His investigation in Northern Ireland is reported to have soured relations between RUC SB and Hermon. Members of the Branch considered 'the inquiry as a "witch hunt" and "counter-productive"'.[58]

Little appeared to have changed over the two years since the Mounsey inquiry. This was Stalker's damning indictment:

> The Special Branch targeted the suspected terrorist, they briefed the officers, and after the shootings they removed the men, cars and guns for a private debriefing before the CID officers were allowed any access to these crucial matters. They provided the cover stories, and they decided at what point the CID were to be allowed to commence the official investigation of what had occurred. The Special Branch interpreted the information and decided what was, or was not, evidence; they attached the labels – whether a man was 'wanted' for an offence, for instance, or whether he was an 'on-the-run terrorist'. I had never experienced, nor had any of my team, such an influence over an entire police force by one small section. We discovered an instance of a junior Special Branch officer's giving operational instructions to much more senior CID officers – and of his being meekly obeyed. Most CID officers we saw seemed resigned to the supremacy of the Special Branch. Some of them wearily said that there was no point in fighting it – that the power of Special Branch pervaded the RUC at all levels. One Chief Superintendent said to me, 'I did not ask what was going on. I knew I would not be told'.[59]

Stalker's extensive criticisms of the RUC reflected badly, not only on Hermon, but also on Myers who was responsible for carrying out periodic inspections into the RUC for HMIC and compiling reports on any shortcomings. Both men must have been distinctly unhappy with the thoroughness of Stalker's investigation and would have wished to see the back of him. Despite Stalker's apparent lack of 'experience at operational and senior command level', as claimed by Hermon, he produced a comprehensive, if incomplete, report that revealed the lack of professionalism in the RUC and the limitations of attempting to use the police as a counter-insurgency force in a deeply divided society.[60]

A year after Stalker's removal from the Northern Ireland inquiry, he remained a major topic of conversation within the RUC. David Donoghue, a Department of Foreign Affairs official, who later served as Irish Ambassador to Russia, Germany, and Austria, penned a note following the receipt of information from one of his contacts in Northern Ireland. He reported that at a dinner in April 1987 attended by Hermon, McAtamney and three ACCs, they 'engaged in a character assassination of John Stalker', claiming that he had not done detective work since the Moors Murders and was a 'shameless publicity-seeker', who had left all the hard work to Thorburn.[61]

They claimed that he had revealed the existence of MI5 bugging devices to the media, but Donoghue's contact rejected this allegation because he had been told by journalist Peter Taylor that James Prior – SoS for Northern Ireland from September 1981 to September 1984 – had accidently revealed its existence. During the dinner, someone asked whether the RUC's actions, presumably in relation to inventing cover stories, amounted to conspiracy to obstruct the course of justice. McAtamney is reported to have responded by saying: 'There's no law in the land against telling lies.' Hermon, who earlier had praised his deputy in whom he had the 'greatest confidence', supported McAtamney's comment.[62]

The merry-go-round

Early in 1985, Stalker began making demands on the police and MI5 in Northern Ireland to supply him with all the information he required to complete his investigation. In particular, he wanted access to the information concerning the murder in the hayshed, including tape 042. Stalker met Hermon in January 1985 and spelt out the absolute importance to his inquiries of the tape, the transcript of it and the evidence of the monitoring officer who might have been witness to murder. Hermon said that the tape was not his to give since the bug had been installed by MI5 and it was their property. Stalker later reflected: 'For the first time MI5 came into the picture.'[63] Hermon denies, however, that he met Stalker in January 1985. He claims that the first occasion he met him, after their lunch together in May 1984, was on 15 May 1985 – eleven months into the inquiry.[64]

On 28 January 1985, Stalker went to London and saw the Executive Head of Legal Services at MI5, who said that he could have access to everything he was seeking and that if MI5 was used as a delaying tactic by the police, he should contact him again immediately. The Head of Legal Services at the time was

Bernard Sheldon.[65] According to Stalker, Sheldon 'appeared to support and accept the absolute need for me to listen to the tape'.[66] On returning to Belfast, Stalker phoned Myers and told him that MI5 appeared to support and accept the absolute need for him to listen to the tape. Stalker, according to his own account, now considered that the main hurdle had been cleared. His primary concern at this stage in the investigation was the recruitment and use of informers, and whether any had been *agents provocateurs*. He suspected that Home Office guidelines on informers were regularly breached. 'My interest seemed to set off panic bells that reverberated throughout the Special Branch', he commented.[67]

Over the weekend of 16/17 February 1985, at a crucial stage in Stalker's investigation in Northern Ireland, Hermon and his wife were invited by Myers to his home in Colwyn Bay. It has been suggested that Myers and Hermon were close friends, and that Hermon often visited Colwyn Bay to stay with him. Hermon, however, refutes this as a 'travesty of truth'.[68] They were professional associates, each with their own independent role, and he had only once before, in August 1982, been a guest at Myers' Colwyn Bay home. The visit at this crucial time raises questions as to what was discussed. Myers had chosen Stalker to head up the Northern Ireland inquiry and would have been very familiar with the problems he was experiencing.

On 20 February, Stalker followed up on the meeting with the Legal Executive of MI5. He wrote a letter to ACC Trevor Forbes, head of RUC SB, listing his demands. He had waited until the end of the McCauley trial before pursuing the matter in case other information was revealed. He made a formal request for access to the tape and to the file on the informer who supplied information in both the Tullygally East Road and the hayshed shootings. Stalker had discovered that the same person had supplied intelligence for both events.[69] Once again, the RUC appeared to adopt delaying tactics.

On 4 March, Stalker sent a report to Myers, which 'spelt out in very graphic and detailed form' the position that his Northern Ireland inquiry had reached, what he was about to do and what he felt still needed to be done.[70] Stalker's cover letter and the report disappeared, and could not be found for the purposes of the civil action ten years later.[71] On 5 March, Stalker sent a formal request to the Chief Constable asking for access to the tape and any transcripts or logs, together with the identity of any person in the police, army or MI5, who had monitored the tape or listened in at the time of the shooting in the hayshed.[72] He received a telephone call saying that his request would be turned down unless the Chief Constable agreed. Clearly, his formal request had not been forwarded to the Chief Constable.

Stalker then wrote to the Chief Constable personally. He received a reply on 13 March refusing his request. He was informed that all the information requested was classified as Grade A intelligence by RUC SB and therefore he could not have it. As Stalker pointed out, the department which he was investigating, was now determining what he should or should not see.[73] Stalker at this point gave serious thought to resigning and had even drafted a press statement, but he decided against it.[74]

On 9 April, Stalker wrote another letter to Hermon requesting access to the tape.[75] He also asked to examine the papers on the 'highly paid' informer. At the same time, he wrote to DCC McAtamney to inform him that the evidence suggested that two RUC SB officers, Superintendents Thomas George Anderson and Samuel George Flanagan, together with a retired CS, were 'the principal initiators' in the cover-ups of the killings in November and December 1982. Stalker recommended that they be suspended immediately.[76] He received no response and, therefore, sought advice from Myers, who suggested that he write to Hermon about his recommendation that the two officers be suspended, or at least, removed from operational duties. According to Stalker, Myers, who had only recently entertained Hermon and his wife for a weekend at his home, added that Hermon was angry and offended at Stalker's persistent requests and 'would need careful handling'.[77] Stalker, by this stage in his quest for the tape, had long since abandoned any compromise. 'The naked hostility and opposition shown to me and my officers by Special Branch left no room for it', he later recorded.[78]

On 22 April, Stalker wrote yet again to Hermon, presenting him with a full outline of the evidence against the two officers. He pointed out that no fewer than sixteen junior officers had made full statements implicating the superintendents in the formulation of false cover stories and that one of the superintendents refused to accept fully the responsibility of Stalker's rank. The letter was delivered by hand and his request was rejected the same day. According to Stalker, Hermon argued that agreeing to the requests would create a most dangerous precedent. As Chief Constable, he could not expose those involved in undercover and surveillance work to external investigation. It was his duty to protect them.[79] In Hermon's account, he discussed Stalker's recommendation with Myers. At the time, Anderson was a fully operational RUC SB officer, while Flanagan was a highly regarded instructor at Bramshill Police College in England. It was decided that he should remain there, and Anderson was transferred from his operational post to an administrative role at RUC headquarters. It is unclear whether Stalker was informed of these decisions, but

Hermon was 'impatient and irritated' that Stalker's investigation was raising what Hermon termed 'procedural problems'.[80]

May and June 1985 turned out to be crucial months in Stalker's investigation. On 9 May Myers phoned Stalker and said that Hermon wished to see him the following Monday.[81] Stalker flew to Belfast and met Hermon for an hour. He asked Hermon to reconsider his decision not to allow him to have possession of the hayshed tape. Hermon replied that he would think about it. The meeting resumed on 15 May. Towards the end, a man 'who works in a certain department' – in other words MI5 – came into the meeting and Stalker was asked to leave for 20 minutes.[82] Hermon subsequently agreed to release the tape, if it existed, subject to the approval of MI5.[83] The next day Hermon phoned Stalker and told him that MI5 must vet the tape before he received it. Once again, those who were being investigated were determining what he could or not see.

On 14 June, six months after his first visit, Stalker was summoned to another meeting with MI5 in London. Other people present included the Senior Legal Executive from MI5, a representative of MI5 from Belfast and Hermon himself. This is Stalker's account of the occasion:

> The meeting was opened by the senior MI5 man. He made it absolutely clear, as he had six months earlier, that his department was not standing in the way of a murder investigation. He said that MI5 was prepared to release all information to me. Sir John was forcibly told that MI5 should not be used as a reason for my being denied access to any evidence or information. The MI5 officer turned to me and said that he would, however, be very reluctant to discuss the authority for the use and installation of the device. He asked me to accept his word that he had personally examined the papers relating to the installation of the bug in the hayshed at Ballynery Road North, and that everything was politically and legally in order. He said that my report could include his assurance that the necessary legal steps had been taken. My prime need was to listen to the tape – the correctness of its installation was of secondary importance. I agreed not to pursue this. He had behaved in a briskly honourable way throughout, and I had no reason to doubt his integrity on this relatively peripheral matter.[84]

Stalker then asked Hermon when he could have access to the tape. After a moment of silence, Hermon said, 'Never, I am afraid. The tape has been destroyed but a transcript exists'.[85] Stalker had indeed been given the run-around.

But Stalker's humiliation was not yet over. He could have the transcript provided he signed a secrecy form like the one that the RUC officers involved in the shootings had been required to sign. Stalker considered the forms to be 'dangerous and misleading' and refused to sign one.[86] 'I was bitterly disappointed by the Chief Constable's attitude', he remarked, 'and I regarded his decision as unashamedly obstructive'.[87] At least six months after he had first learnt about the existence of the tape of the hayshed shooting, Stalker had still not received any of the information requested.

His investigation was at an impasse. He could do no more. On 26 June, Stalker wrote to Hermon and placed on record the implications for his inquiry. He informed him that he would provide extra evidence,

> that would indicate that the five men shot dead in their cars were unlawfully killed by members of the Royal Ulster Constabulary. I believed I could safely say that the evidence available to put before the adjourned Coroner's Hearings was substantially more than that presented by the RUC at the criminal trials, and would attract much public interest when the inquests were eventually reopened.[88]

Little did he appreciate that successive governments would do everything in their power to prevent the adjourned Coroner's hearings ever being reconvened.

NIO's monitoring of developments

The NIO was kept regularly updated on the problems Stalker was experiencing but it continued to misspell his name as 'Stocker'. On 6 March, following Stalker's 4 March 1985 letter to Myers spelling out what was going to be in his report, Myers met the SoS for Northern Ireland. The Private Secretary penned a minute of the meeting which covered a range of policing issues including 'Incidents in Armagh'. This noted that 'Mr Myers reported on progress made by Mr Stocker' and that:

> It would be highly critical in such areas as doctoring of evidence, inadequate work by the pathologist, lack of coordination between the CID and Special Branch etc. It was likely that very senior officers would be shown to have behaved improperly.[89]

The political implications were obvious and must have caused widespread concern in Whitehall. The minute tried to lessen the impact by pointing out that the report itself would not become public, but it would be known that it would have been submitted to the DPPNI. Prophetically, it went on to say that, 'the affair would drag on for some time as the question of prosecutions was considered, as inquests took place and with pressure from Parliament'.[90] Stalker's findings also reflected badly on Myers himself who was responsible for annually assessing the operational efficiency of the RUC for the HMIC. His 1984 Inspection failed to highlight any of these short-comings, particularly the lack of coordination between CID and SB.[91]

On 25 April, a Mr Buxton wrote to the Permanent Secretary (PS) and Permanent Under Secretary (PUS) and copied to Mr Stephens, Deputy Under Secretary (DUS), concerning the demands that Stalker was making for access to the hayshed tape and the officer who listened into it. Buxton wrote that the DPPNI was very concerned about the outcome of Stalker's inquiry and was expecting more disturbing news as Stalker was still facing obstruction from the RUC, and was not getting to the bottom of the story. The letter finished by noting that, although the DPPNI was not specific, 'it was quite clear that Mr Stocker (sic) had encountered these blocks at a very high level'[92] – an obvious reference to the Chief Constable.

In a letter dated 16 May and headed 'The Stocker (sic) Inquiry', Buxton informed Stephens that Hermon had had lunch with the SoS on 13 May and had told him of 'the difficulties he was having with Mr Stocker'.[93] Buxton went on to say that he had spoken to the DPPNI, who informed him that matters had not moved on and that he feared that, 'the point would be reached when either Stalker would get the information he wanted, or he would withdraw from the case'.[94] The DPPNI pointed out that if Stalker did resign,

> apart from the ripples that that would cause, he (the DPP) would necessarily be involved to the extent that the information withheld had a bearing either on a past criminal prosecution or a possible future one.[95]

The DPPNI was indirectly referring to the case of McCauley and presumably cases which might emerge from the Stalker inquiry.

The next day, in another minute headed 'The Stocker Inquiry', Buxton noted that an 'intermediary' was able to reassure Hermon that there was 'no objection to Mr Stocker's (sic) being given access to certain equipment and to an individual RUC officer who could give evidence about it'.[96] In a follow-up minute, Mr Buxton confirmed that the intermediary was the Security Service, but now noted that, instead of releasing the information to Stalker, 'the Security Service should itself make the necessary investigations into the equipment which is at issue and interview the RUC officer involved'.[97] Buxton further noted that the Chief Constable was insistent that Stalker 'should not himself be permitted access to these sources of information' and that 'the terms of the arrangements have yet to be approved by the Deputy Director-General of the Security Service'.[98] Once again, MI5, a secret unaccountable body, was determining what a police officer carrying out an inquiry into six potential murders, could or could not see. The rule of law was being subverted.

On 1 July, Robert Andrew, PUS in NIO, wrote to Stephens and explained that Myers had telephoned him to report that the arrangements that had been put in place had broken down and that Mr Stocker (sic) would be unable, because he had been denied certain information, to carry out his investigation properly. Andrew commented that: 'This would be a very serious matter, implying as it did that the Chief Constable was seeking to cover up illegal actions by his force.'[99]

The next day Mr Buxton penned a minute under the heading 'Stalker Inquiry' – the first time in over twelve months that the NIO spelt his name correctly. He began by noting that the DPP had shown him a letter that Stalker had sent to the Chief Constable, adding that: 'He was not disposed to let me keep one, but that Sir P Myers and Mr Sheldon also had copies.'[100] He said that the main purport of the letter was to put the Chief Constable on notice and if further evidence is found, then it will cause the DPP to consider further prosecutions of police officers. Buxton surmised that, by giving the Chief Constable early notice, Stalker eased his 'conscience especially in view of the other's intransigence over the other pieces of evidence, but it will be of little comfort to Sir J Hermon'.[101] Buxton and the DPP then considered the range of prosecutions which might be forthcoming:

> They run from quite senior officers involved in the cover-up to the nasty thought that fresh evidence might give grounds for fresh prosecutions of officers involved in the actual incidents. In one of the three incidents no police officer has hitherto been prosecuted (only the surviving terrorist). In another, three policemen were prosecuted for the murder of only one of three terrorists killed, and evidence might be adduced indicating guilt in the death of the other two. In the third case, such a possibility scarcely seems to arise.[102]

Stalker scared

Stalker became very concerned about both the lack of co-operation and the hostility that his team was receiving from the RUC, and was concerned for the future of his inquiry. He was even worried about his own safety. In May, he took the unprecedented step of contacting the editor of the *Manchester Evening News*, Michael Unger, and began to let him have regular reports on the progress of his investigation.

In January 1988, these were serialised in *The Guardian* under the title of the Unger Diary. The first read as follows:

> 13 May 1985

> John Stalker rings me early this morning at the office about his inquiry into an alleged shoot-to-kill policy by the RUC. Stalker tells me that he is seeking some papers from Chief Constable Sir John Hermon that could show that RUC officers murdered members of the IRA. He is seeing Sir John tomorrow to get the papers, and if he doesn't get them, he will resign from the inquiry. He says that if the inquiry were conducted into a mainland police force then the problem wouldn't arise.

> I ask Stalker why he is telling me this, because I hardly know him and the information, if published, would be extremely damaging.

> Stalker says it helps him keep going – it forces him on – if he knows that someone outside the police force knows what is happening. If he begins to waver

about the sensitivity of highlighting the problems of another police force, then my knowledge will force him to carry on his investigations.

He also says that it is an insurance policy if anything happens to him.[103]

In the civil action it was put to Stalker that his contact with a local newspaper was extremely damaging to the Northern Ireland inquiry and to give details, which were highly confidential and sensitive, was ill advised. Stalker responded:

It was the most carefully considered and most difficult [decision] I've ever had to make in my professional life, and I think having raised it I'm entitled to explain why it happened. You have to look at the time, you have to look at the date and you have to look at what was happening not just to me but to the investigation. All the certainties in my life were being removed. The people who I thought supported me, the people who I thought were anxious for an honest investigation were suddenly disappearing. The support of the law, which I've always taken for granted as a police officer, through no fault of it, was impotent. The DPP was impotent to help, the Chief Constable no longer gave me any support whatsoever. Her Majesty's Inspector of Constabulary gave me no support whatsoever. On top of that a highly respected and probably the most experienced Special Branch man in Manchester – a man with very strong formal and informal contacts within the Derbyshire police and the R.U.C. – told me that I was being targeted by a terrorist group – the IRA. He gave me the name of the man who had been given the job of targeting me. He told me where he was from and, I have to be circumspect here my Lord, it wouldn't be right to name the man, sufficient to say that a file in GMP HQ which should have referred to this man, had been removed. As I understand, it has never been found. I had good reason [to believe] that the Manchester police in certain areas were not particularly to be trusted … I found myself isolated. I found myself in a position, which I never dreamed in my professional life, I would have ever to cope with. I needed a respected person, a man of integrity, a highly respected newspaper editor in this case … in order to know if anything happened to me what the truth was, because my clear understanding to myself was that the finding of my investigation might never see the light of day.[104]

There was a final reason why Stalker was scared, which he did not mention in the civil action. Rob McLoughlin, the producer of Granada's TV programme *Pawn in the game*,[105] had interviewed John Thorburn who told him that Stalker's team had started to investigate something very serious. He would not provide any details to McLoughlin because in Thorburn's words, 'it might lead to a bullet to your head'.[106] Thorburn added that Sampson did not follow up on this line of inquiry. In the absence of any judicial inquiry, it is only possible to speculate on what this line of investigation involved and why it was so threatening. But it is probable the Stalker team had discovered that state agents had been knowingly allowed to commit murders as part of the MI5/Walker counter-insurgency strategy.

Stalker's Interim Report

In the summer of 1985, Stalker and his team worked on producing an interim report in the absence of the information requested which had been promised nine months earlier. It had been agreed with MI5 that the report should be forwarded to the DPP but without the 'highly classified information' which Hermon had been reluctant to give to Stalker. It should, however, be drawn to the DPP's attention and if he thought that Stalker should have it, then Stalker should ask for it and the Attorney General would instruct the Chief Constable to make it available to Stalker.[107] This again reflected the power of MI5 to determine what should be disclosed in an investigation of the possible murder of six people by the RUC.

The interim report recommended the prosecution of eleven police officers – including the deputy head of RUC SB, three superintendents and a chief inspector.[108] Moreover, Stalker was concerned that perhaps several more senior officers might have committed offences. The report ran to sixteen volumes. Arrangements were made to deliver it personally to Hermon. On 18 September 1985, it was put on an early morning RAF flight accompanied by two GMP officers. Stalker and Thorburn took a scheduled flight and met the two officers with the report at RUC HQ. They were shown into the Deputy Chief Constable's office only to be told the Chief Constable had other business. In the absence of Hermon, McAtamney signed for the report, and they left.[109]

The description 'interim' was to become the subject of a diplomatic row following Stalker's removal. On 17 June 1986, at the Anglo-Irish Intergovernmental Conference at Stormont, Tom King, the SoS for Northern Ireland, informed Peter Barry, Ireland's Foreign Secretary, that Stalker's report was the final one. This, of course, precluded any suggestion that Stalker had been removed to prevent further enquiries and would negate any conspiracy theories. Following fierce protests from the Irish government that it was an interim report and was marked as such in gold letters,[110] Nicolas Scott, a junior Minister at the NIO, confirmed to the House of Commons the next day that it was indeed an interim report.[111]

On receipt of the report, Hermon took the unprecedented step of instructing two experienced Chief Superintendents to study it. According to Hermon, they expressed 'grave concern about its content'.[112] He then expanded the study team with a legally qualified ACC and the RUC's internal legal advisor. It took the team over four months to complete the analysis. On 13 February 1986, Hermon sent Stalker's interim report, together with the internal analysis, to the DPPNI.[113] He informed the DPPNI that he accepted the analysis by his study team and their overall recommendation that no further prosecutions were justified. He also informed the DPPNI that he was highly critical of Stalker's report and the failure to produce evidence to support its conclusions.[114]

Within a month of delivering the report, Hermon was authorised by the Attorney General to make available to Stalker certain classified material. In mid-March 1986, Hermon wrote to Stalker informing him of the decision. Stalker arranged to see Hermon to pick up the material on 30 April. On arrival at RUC HQ with Thorburn, they were told that the Chief Constable was at a passing-out parade at the Police Training Centre at Enniskillen. They met ACC Forbes instead and were given various documents, but they were not given tape 042.[115] It is now known that several of the key intelligence documents they received were unsigned and undated, and fabricated after the incidents.[116] Ironically, this was to be a common feature in the investigation of Stalker himself. Stalker, however, was to have no time to analyse the material before he was removed from his inquiry less than a fortnight later.

Destruction of the hayshed tape

Many years afterwards, it emerged that Stalker had indeed been given the run-around concerning the tape. In September 2014, McCauley appealed his conviction for possession of the rifles in the hayshed and his conviction was overturned by Declan Morgan, the Lord Chief Justice of Northern Ireland, and Lord Justices Girvan and Coghlin.[117] Crucially, the judgment spelt out the history of Tape 042. It was disclosed by more than one police and army personnel, who had listened to the tape, that no warning had been given by the RUC officers before they opened fire on the hayshed.[118] They had exceeded their orders and had given the occupants no time to surrender. Subsequently in November 1982, the Deputy Head of RUC SB destroyed what he believed was the only copy of the tape because 'he considered it potentially damaging to the RUC'.[119]

But the conspiracy deepened. An unauthorised copy of Tape 042 had been made by the army, perhaps as some trophy, and this copy came into the possession of MI5. It was held by them at the time of McCauley's trial but was destroyed in 'the summer of 1985'.[120] Thus, both MI5 and the RUC were aware of the tape, yet neither was prepared to release it in the interests of justice in the prosecution of McCauley. Moreover, the CID officer carrying out the investigation into the shooting was not informed of its existence. The rule of law had been abandoned.

When Stalker met MI5 on 28 January 1985 and was told that it would co-operate fully, and supported and accepted his need to listen to the tape, it was a total sham. The senior legal advisor to MI5 knew that it had a copy of the tape and failed to inform Stalker. Whether the Chief Constable knew that MI5 had a copy is not known. In any event, all of Stalker's requests to the Chief Constable from January to September 1985 to have access to the tape failed.

In his judgment in the McCauley appeal, the Lord Chief Justice does not note the precise date when the tape was destroyed. It is therefore not known whether it was destroyed before or after Stalker's second meeting with MI5 on 14 June. It does not matter greatly because this meeting, like the one in January, was yet another carefully constructed deceit on the part of MI5. It had no intention of releasing the tape to a police officer carrying out murder investigations. Unsurprisingly, the Lord Chief Justice considered that the behaviour of the police and MI5 'amounted cumulatively to grave misconduct'.[121]

* * *

It was 'an appalling vista', to use Lord Denning's phrase from his Birmingham Six judgment: MI5, RUC SB or the state agent had in all likelihood lured Tighe and McCauley into the hayshed; they were then shot without warning; the crime scene was cleared up or reconstructed before CID arrived; all those involved in the shootings were told to produce cover stories; an RUC SB intelligence report was produced to suggest that Tighe was a member of the IRA; and both tapes of the fatal shooting were destroyed, perverting the course of justice. In relation to the other two shootings, Stalker had found extra evidence that the five men shot dead in their cars were unlawfully killed and the cover stories were untrue. Against such a backdrop, several people in both the RUC and MI5 would have had a very strong motivation to try and remove Stalker from his Northern Ireland inquiry.

There were several linkages in the events in Northern Ireland and Manchester: the LFF; the Belfast meeting between GMP and RUC; the alleged connection between the QSG and IRA; the close collegiate relationship between Simons and Topping; and Burton, the principal police informer, providing information on alleged criminal activities in Belfast and Manchester. Any one of these linkages would have been invaluable in constructing a conspiracy. But if there was a conspiracy, GMP needed time to put it into action and to 'dig for dirt' on Stalker's friend, Taylor, to show proof of his alleged criminality. Would this then explain the obstructions and delays which the Stalker team experienced in Northern Ireland?

PART II
MANCHESTER

Chapter 6

Friendships and Policing Problems in Manchester

THE FRIENDSHIP between Kevin Taylor and John Stalker stemmed from a meeting of their two wives in the grounds of a convent school, Werneth Grange, Oldham, in 1973. On one wet morning as Beryl Taylor was crossing the school playground, a woman came up behind her and asked if she could share her umbrella. She introduced herself. It was Stella Stalker. Their daughters attended the same school. The two husbands were subsequently introduced. Taylor was immediately drawn to Stalker's wit, intelligence and good company, and Stalker to Taylor's gregariousness and generosity. They became good friends and they and their families would meet intermittently. Stalker was also close to his Chief Constable, James Anderton – a highly controversial chief police officer. They had known each other for nearly 40 years by the time of the civil action.[1] Their families were very close. Stalker's children referred to Anderton's wife as Aunty Joan.[2] By the summer of 1986, all these friendships were shattered.

John Stalker

John Stalker was born on 19 April 1939.[3] His first love was writing, and he would have liked to become a journalist, but the opportunity didn't arise. On leaving school he joined the Police Cadets and then on his nineteenth birthday he joined the Manchester City Police. He was interviewed for the job by Chief Superintendent Robert Mark, who later became Commissioner of the Metropolitan Police.[4] After pounding the streets of Manchester for three years, he was transferred to CID. He then made rapid progress up through the ranks. In 1961 he married Stella, and they had their first daughter, Colette, shortly after he was promoted to Detective Sergeant in the City Centre Division. As a Detective Sergeant he was involved in the investigation into the Moors Murders carried out by Myra Hindley and Ian Brady. In 1969, he became a

Detective Inspector in Salford and between March and September of that year he attended a full-time course for middle ranking officers at the Police Staff College at Bramshill. The average age of students was 36, but Stalker was only 30.[5] During that year, their second daughter, Francine, was born.

After Stalker completed the Bramshill course, he was asked by the head of CID to take over the operational side of the Drugs Squad. In 1972, he joined GMP SB and had general oversight of 'registration of aliens' and examined applications for nationalisation.[6] Two years later, with the amalgamation of Manchester and Salford police with several borough forces to form GMP, there were several promotions. Stalker was promoted to Detective Chief Inspector and headed the newly formed GMP SB. He was 'positively vetted' for the first time.[7] While in SB, he was responsible for investigating several IRA attacks on government buildings in Manchester, including the Stationary Office and the Department of Health and Social Security.[8]

Security vetting is a common practice before an appointment to a sensitive or high-powered post. It involves two stages. In the first stage, a routine check is made of the person's medical records and other public records, including criminal records, to ascertain if there are any problems. This is known as 'passive vetting'. The second stage concentrates on examining the background of the person and involves enquiries of their friends, relatives, family, and organisations and institutions to which they may belong. In Stalker's case it also involved an interview with his family doctor. The purpose is to assess the person's suitability for the post as well as checking that there is nothing untoward in their background. All vetting is carried out by a specialist team of investigators in the Ministry of Defence.

In 1976, Stalker was promoted to Detective Superintendent at the young age of 37 and he took over as head of CID in Manchester. By this time, he had considerable experience as a detective. He had investigated many murders, dealt with IRA bombings and shooting incidents, and had experience in the robbery and fraud squads.[9] At some point during the year, he met RUC Superintendent Mooney, who along with Chief Superintendent Hylands was trying to arrange a safe house for a 'supergrass' from Northern Ireland.[10] Mooney, a former head of RUC CID, was a senior detective in Castlereagh Interrogation Centre at a time when there were numerous allegations of beatings, sleep deprivation and other tortures.[11]

Stalker and Taylor were both interested in boxing and had an engagement at an Anglo-American boxing match in the Piccadilly Hotel in Manchester. Stalker invited Mooney and Hylands to join them. After the boxing tournament the party visited a local casino.[12] In 1982, Mooney headed up the special RUC squad which investigated the IRA's involvement in the LFF organised by Klapish (Chapter 4), establishing a clear link between the RUC and the GMP which was to figure prominently following Stalker's removal from the Northern Ireland inquiry.[13]

To become a chief officer in the police, it helps to have experience of working in different police forces. Stalker, therefore, made the move to Warwickshire in March 1978, where he became Chief Superintendent in charge of the CID. During his time in Warwickshire, he was again positively vetted, as he was required to oversee the work of the SB but also because positive vetting must be carried out every five years.[14] While in Warwickshire, the Chief Constable recommended that Stalker should apply for a senior command course. It was a six-month course and involved training officers for various senior posts in the police.[15]

During this period, he maintained his friendship with the Taylors. When Stalker was reporting back to Michael Unger, the editor of the *Manchester Evening News*, during his investigation in Northern Ireland, Unger asked him why he had not stopped his relationship with Taylor when he went to Warwickshire. Stalker explained that when he was a young detective, he had a 'major domestic problem', and the Taylors were the only friends to stick by them and he was forever grateful for this – an answer which Unger claimed was revealing because it highlighted 'Stalker's strange mixture of loyalty and naivety'.[16]

Stalker returned from Warwickshire in April 1980 and became one of the six ACCs in GMP. His roles covered the budget, the administration of the force and the development of a community relations strategy.[17] In 1983, Stalker was selected to attend a Royal College of Defence Studies course, which ran from early January to late December. Its aims were,

> to give selected senior military officers and officials of the United Kingdom the opportunity to study, with representatives of the Commonwealth and NATO and certain other nations, defence issues affecting the western democracies and other countries with similar interests, and the strategic, political, economic and social factors that bear on those.[18]

Each year two ACCs – who are regarded as civilians for the purposes of the course – are invited to participate along with Brigadiers and those of similar ranks in the Air Force and Navy. There is a practical element and attendees are required to complete a project. Stalker studied crime and social conditions in Colombia, Chile and Brazil.[19] After completing the course, Stalker returned to Manchester in January 1984 and was promoted to DCC in March. He had an office on the top floor of Chester House, next to the Chief Constable's but separated by their secretaries' office.[20] This provided an ideal layout for the maximum interaction between the two most senior officers in the force. Stalker's primary duty was to cover for the Chief Constable when he was absent, but there was also a statutory requirement for the Deputy Chief Constable to be the disciplinary authority for the force.

All the evidence suggests that Stalker was well regarded. There were, however, aspects of his career, which like Taylor's, would give rise to adverse comment. One aspect was his, and his Chief Constable's, attendance at numerous social events. Another was his use of a police driver for social occasions.[21] This was to figure in his disciplinary hearings in 1986. According to insiders, however, Stalker made little use of a police driver compared with his Chief Constable.

Stalker's glowing career was supported by his superiors. Given the hierarchy of the police, the Chief Constable of Warwickshire, Roger Birch, would have written a reference for him when he applied to be an ACC of GMP in 1980. He would also have needed a reference from his own Chief Constable for the Royal College of Defence Studies and, crucially, when he applied to be DCC in early 1984. The competition for the DCC of the largest force in the United Kingdom outside of London was no doubt very strong and hence Stalker would have required a glowing reference from Anderton himself, with whom he would have to work closely. For all these posts, he must have been considered to have the highest integrity, together with the necessary leadership skills and experience. Thus in early 1984, he continued to have the full support of his own Chief Constable when he was appointed to head up the Northern Ireland inquiry.

Stalker was an obvious candidate for the inquiry for several reasons. First, the context of the structure and responsibilities of HMIC meant that a choice would be made from within GMP rather than some other police force. At the time, Byford was the Chief Inspector and there were five inspectors, each responsible for a few police forces.[22] Myers was responsible for both GMP, and the RUC and it would, therefore, have been understandable for him to approach the one Chief Constable with whom he was in regular contact and seek a nomination. Second, Stalker had considerable detective experience and had completed the prestigious Royal College of Defence Studies course.

Little is known about the appointments of police officers to key police investigations. As with so much in the culture of the British state, the selection method used is not transparent, open, and subject to equality of opportunity principles. HMIC would have been formally responsible for making the recommendation to Hermon, and Sir Lawrence Byford, as Chief Inspector, would, almost certainly, have signed it off. But as it was such a sensitive inquiry, it would, in all likelihood, have been discussed with the Home Office and senior politicians. It may well have been an item for discussion at the heart of government at JIC, the intelligence steering group in the Cabinet Office, whose key role was to advise the Prime Minister and cabinet ministers on intelligence collection and analysis. At the time, there were more than 150 CCs, DCCs and ACCs in England and Wales from which an officer could have been selected.

Kevin Taylor

Kevin Taylor was born during the Great Depression in Salford on 2 January 1932, the eldest of three children.[23] His father left home when he and his two sisters were very young, and his mother was left to bring up the family. Taylor first started earning money at the age of 12 when he delivered three-piece suites using a most unlikely delivery van – a tricycle. It earned him £2 for a week's work. He left school without any qualifications at 14 and became, on his mother's insistence, an apprentice joiner at 4s.6d. per week. At sixteen, he switched jobs and became qualified as a fireman on the railways and with overtime earned £11 per week. He worked on the railways until he was called up for National Service. He then served with the Fifth Inniskilling Dragoon Guards in Germany, Korea, and the Middle East. As well as being trained by the army in various roles, he also learnt many of his entrepreneurial skills during four and a half years of service. He used to exploit the differential distribution of consumables and equipment between the British and American forces. He bought British beer and spirits and bartered it for American linen, toilet paper, coffee, and the occasional jeep. He then sold the goods behind the British lines.

After leaving the army, he had several jobs as a salesman, but in 1961 he became a full-time professional gambler. He moved to London and concentrated on playing Kaluki, a card game based on rummy, which could accommodate any number of players, but was normally played with four or five. It was at a time when the gaming laws had been radically changed and gambling had become an acceptable social activity. He would play all night and all day, sometimes for more than 24 hours, and would then go home and sleep before beginning another game.

On a visit to Manchester in 1964 he met Beryl Rooney and they were married in 1965. Initially they lived in London, but they soon moved back to Manchester. Kate, their first child, was born in 1967. Taylor set up a business called Vanland, specialising in the sale of commercial vehicles and he had a small showroom with a large open space situated in Ancoats, close to the city centre. This was a popular area for those without formal skills or education to seek a living in the business world, as the rents for premises were cheap. He worked a twelve- to fourteen-hour day developing various skills including spray-painting. Their second child Emma was born in 1969.

It was while working in Ancoats that Taylor first met two brothers who were to feature prominently in the Taylor/Stalker affair: Louis and Vinnie Schiavo. They rented the next-door pitch and sold second-hand cars. They all got on well together and used to help each other out. Around this time, Taylor also became acquainted with another set of brothers – James and Joseph Monaghan – and Jack Trickett, who was involved in boxing promotions. Another person whom he met during this period was Jimmy Donnelly. The Schiavos, the Monaghan brothers, Trickett and Donnelly, according to the police, were all said to be members of the QSG.

Taylor was to remain friends with Vinnie Schiavo and Jimmy Donnelly. These friendships were the first of many things in Taylor's life which were later to be interpreted in two opposing ways. For Taylor, loyalty was an important principle. Having been successful in business did not mean that you then turned your back on people whom you had known from the hard times. But to the police this loyalty to old friends was later to be seen in the most malevolent way.

Their logic went something like this. No successful businessman would maintain a friendship with people with criminal records; Taylor remained friends with a few of them; therefore, Taylor must be involved in crime. There are parallels here with the judgments made by the police in the Birmingham Six case, in which six men were arrested on their way to attend the funeral of James McDade, who had blown himself up while planting a bomb.[24] The police assumed that innocent people would not attend the funeral of a bomber, reflecting little cultural understanding of the strong Irish tradition of attending funerals, even of those with whom one is only slightly acquainted.

From selling vans, Taylor moved into property development. Gambling on the possibility that a very short-term lease would materialise into a long-term one, he acquired some semi-derelict land near Strangeways Prison on a three-year lease from Manchester City Corporation. The Corporation was not prepared to grant a longer lease because the land was on the route of a proposed road to Salford. But Taylor did his homework and discovered that Salford Corporation planned to build a housing estate in the path of the new road. He therefore started to build several units for rent with the help of his father-in-law, a master builder, on a site known as Moulton Street precinct. His gamble paid off and a longer lease was granted in 1977.

The first group of units consisted of about 35 small warehouse blocks of 500 square feet. They were built to a low-spec design. The units were leased as soon as they were put up and proved to be very popular with the Asian community. Taylor charged advance premiums of £1000, which he then ploughed back into building more units. Because of the demand, he could charge nearly four times the going rent.[25] This rather unusual method of financing the building of a set of warehouse units was another aspect of Taylor's life which was to be interpreted in two totally opposing ways. For Taylor, it was the only way to increase the commercial potential of the site when no bank would lend money on such a risky venture. For the police, it was to be seen in a very different light: a vehicle for laundering money.

In 1979, Taylor bought a derelict mill in Summerseat, just outside Bury, which he converted for the family home. Following the purchase, Taylor took advantage of the deep recession which accompanied Mrs Thatcher's first term in office and bought a marble tile company which had gone into liquidation. Taylor re-employed one of the redundant workers to do all the tile work for the house. He also bought a job lot of high-quality timber for the windows and floors from another company that had gone into liquidation. Through these and other means he built a luxurious and spacious home for half the normal cost.

In early 1981, Taylor made another purchase, which, like his friendships, was to play a significant role in the police investigation in the years to come. He went to the Miami Boat show with Edward Heginbotham and Arthur Bowen-Gotham, and bought a boat called *Diogenes* for £85,000. Mr Clucas, a Financial Management Consultant, recommended that Taylor acquire an offshore company called Gantry Ltd to hold the ownership of *Diogenes* to reduce any tax liabilities. Following the granting of access orders and search warrants in 1986, the police came across a letter that Clucas had written to Taylor after setting-up Gantry Ltd, in which he was critical of Taylor for not establishing the company prior to the purchase of the boat. He recommended that Taylor get rid of the letter after reading it because, in the wrong hands, it could destroy him.[26]

This was yet another aspect of Taylor's life which would be viewed in two different ways. For Taylor, and many others in business, an offshore company was a valid way of reducing the amount of tax they paid in the future on their wealth. It was an arrangement that was widely recommended by tax consultants throughout the United Kingdom and adopted by many.[27] For the police, it was impossible to think of any legitimate reason for 'hiding' the ownership of *Diogenes* behind an offshore company. It was clearly a wall against which any investigation would end abruptly, disguising some nefarious activity, such as drug smuggling.

In 1983, Taylor became Chair of the Manchester Conservative Association, of which he had been a member for a few years. By 1984 he was the owner of a very successful business venture. He had turned the five to six acres of land within the inner-city area of Manchester into a thriving wholesale trading area. It was a social as well as a commercial success. The rental income from the units was more than £350,000 per year. People came in buses from as far afield

as Ireland and France to buy goods on a Sunday. In May 1984, Taylor decided
to sell the property and reinvest the money in land that could be enhanced in
value through a change in the planning status. It was sold to the Viranis, a
wealthy Asian family, for £2.75 million. They bought it with a Liechtenstein
Company, Zelva Anstalt, and Taylor heard later that they subsequently sold it
on to a public company, in which they had a substantial interest, for £12
million.[28] A few days after Taylor made the decision to sell Moulton Street
precinct, Myers appointed Stalker to head up the Northern Ireland inquiry.
From then on, the two men's lives were inextricably linked.

Taylor now began to look for potential value-adding property. He judged
that a whole area between Trafford Wharf Road and Trafford Park Road had
considerable potential and he began to purchase several separate sites. The
first – a derelict 80,000 square foot warehouse – he bought from Robin Arnold
for £160,000. Before exchanging contracts, he approached Trafford Council
to ask if they would look favourably on an application for non-food retail
development and the planners indicated that they would be happy with the
proposed 40,000 square foot development. When asked if they would be
interested in a larger development, they again gave a positive response.[29] He
then decided to buy further sites, which although outside the Trafford
Enterprise Zone, and therefore not eligible for grant aid, had commercial
potential even without grants. He subsequently purchased two sites, one at
£150,000 and another at £240,000.

In July 1984, Taylor's company Rangelark, purchased a site outside of
Manchester, at Pool House Farm, Poynton, for £100,000. The site had come
to the notice of Vincent McCann, a surveyor and a friend of Taylor's, while
he was negotiating with Robin Arnold over the purchase of the land at Old
Trafford. It was an old brickworks with a large hole in the middle. It was
another risky venture, but Taylor hoped that with planning permission for
tipping, which he obtained a few months later, he would raise between
£300,000 to £1 million in tipping rights alone.[30] In addition, there was an
unknown quantity of poor-quality shale on the site, which could be sold,
releasing more land for tipping. When Rangelark later went into liquidation,
the Official Receiver sold the site for £180,000 – a sum which, Taylor
considered, was much below its true value. His commercial acumen was to
be proved right. In the early 1990s the site was offered for sale again at
between £560,000 and £580,000, with planning permission for a leisure
complex and motel. Later, planning permission was granted for over 100
houses on the site, which are currently valued at over £345,000 each.[31]

Taylor's final successful purchase, this time through another of his companies, Lacerta, took place in April 1985 when he bought a 5.75 acre site at Tottington at the cost of £65,000. A portion of it fell within the Green Belt, but he judged that he would obtain permission for housing development on part of it, which he did. He then asked Fyers Bell to sell it and the site was quickly sold to McAlpine Holt for £170,000. It is now another attractive housing development worth millions of pounds.

Taylor and Stalker socialised intermittently with one another. On 28 November 1980, Taylor was Stalker's guest at a Senior Officer's Mess dinner attended by Anderton, who signed Taylor's programme for the occasion: 'Best Wishes, Jim.'[32] In March 1982, Stalker invited Taylor and his wife to the annual police ball, held in the Tyldesley Suite at the Lancaster County Cricket Club. Anderton, gave the welcome speech. The GMP band played the music. A few years later, GMPA attempted to get rid of the band on the grounds of costs and objected to the band being used for police social occasions.[33]

In April 1982, Stalker and Taylor attended a St George's Night Officers' Mess dinner.[34] Later in the year, on 29 October, Taylor was invited to be Stalker's guest at GMP's Senior Officers' dinner held in the Haworth Room at the University of Manchester. It was a dinner jacketed, all-male affair and was attended by over 130 men drawn from the top echelons of Manchester civic and public life.[35] In April 1984, Stalker again invited Taylor to the George's Night dinner. As usual it was attended by many senior police officers, including Anderton, who again signed Taylor's programme, this time saying: 'Good luck, Jim.'[36] Taylor certainly needed it.

As chair of the MCA, Taylor organised several fundraising events in the Piccadilly Hotel in Manchester. Stalker attended one in November 1985, at which he and his wife were guests.[37] His attendance at this and other political fund-raising events subsequently formed one of the disciplinary allegations investigated by Sampson.[38] Gabrielle Cox, who was chair of GMPA in 1985, was later to remark, 'even mayors of the same party leave their chains behind and know where to draw the line'.[39] She further observed that Stalker did not realise 'the distaste which many people feel for the excessive socialising which seems to go with chief officer posts in Greater Manchester'.[40] While many of the events involved the attendees paying, nevertheless there were public subsidies such as the use of police vehicles to go to and from the events, the use of the police band and perhaps other hidden subsidies, of which the public was unaware. Moreover, attendance at an all-male event and at Conservative Party balls did not reflect well politically on either the Chief Constable or the Deputy Chief Constable of GMP.

James Anderton

James Anderton was born on 24 May 1932. His father was a Wigan miner. After National Service in the Military Police, he joined the old Manchester City Police on 30 March 1953. He made a meteoric rise through the ranks, and on 2 April 1976, he was appointed head of GMP, aged 44. GMP had been formed by the amalgamation of the Manchester City Police and various borough forces in 1975 to become the second largest police force in England and Wales. It covered an area of nearly 320,000 acres and had a population of over 2.5 million people. It was divided into fourteen divisions and had, at the beginning of the 1980s, approximately 6,500 police officers. The headquarters was in a purpose-built eleven-storey building, Chester House, in south Manchester. Anderton's office was on the top floor and overlooked Manchester United's Old Trafford football stadium. It was the scene of many dramatic press conferences.

Anderton was a highly controversial chief officer.[41] He was deeply religious and saw licentiousness as demons of the devil. Martin Walker, an author on a number of books on policing, described him as 'a Mancunian Ian Paisley'.[42] According to Michael Prince in his book, *God's Cop: the Biography of James Anderton*, Anderton claimed that the graph of his life was a straight line up to God without a dip or plateau.[43] He believed in reincarnation[44] and considered that in a previous existence he had been the puritan Oliver Cromwell.[45] Like Cromwell,[46] he believed that God was guiding him, as many of his ideas came as revelations in dreams.[47] In one Police Authority meeting during which he was being criticised, he waited for a moment and then said: 'Now I know how Christ felt when he was being crucified'.[48] He had a particularly strong belief in the notion of duty, which was underpinned by his religious beliefs and understanding of his role in the world. He was man full of confidence and claimed to one journalist: 'I never look over my shoulder.'[49]

Anderton's Christian beliefs guided many of his force's policing priorities. In a moral crusade, he orchestrated a crackdown on licentious behaviours from prostitution to drunkenness. In the year after taking up office, a specially selected squad raided nearly 300 newsagents and other premises and seized over 160,000 articles alleged to be obscene under the Obscene Publications Act, with a face value of just under half a million pounds.[50] Eight years later, GMP was still on a moral crusade against pornography, carrying out raids and together with other forces, a co-ordinated action was taken against 'sex shops'.[51] Pubs and clubs were also targeted for after-hours drinking and breaches of the licensing laws. On one occasion, his officers took over a youth worker's office on a Sunday without permission and spied on a gay pub using video equipment.[52]

Early in his career, Anderton argued that the 'race relations industry' should be abolished.[53] During the 1984 Miner's Strike, he condemned mass picketing as 'an act of terrorism, without the bullet and the bomb'.[54] He wanted homosexuality to be an offence[55] and argued that criminals should be flogged.[56] On 11 December 1986, he gave a talk at Sedgely Park Training School at which he told police officers that drug addicts, prostitutes and homosexuals were spreading aids 'by swirling around in a cesspit of their own making'.[57]

He held particularly strong opinions about police committees. He talked about the 'enemy within' and called for non-political boards to be set up to replace police committees: 'I sense and see in our midst an enemy more dangerous, insidious and ruthless than any faced since the Second World War'.[58] He felt that there was a long-term political strategy to destroy the proven structures of policing and turn them into an exclusive agency of a one-party state. It was powerful stuff and aimed directly at police committees, which he could no longer trust because of a growing risk that information passed to some members may be used to prejudice the operations of the police or fuel propaganda against them.

In June 1985, Anderton returned to this theme in a speech to the Association of Chief Police Officers Annual Conference, in Bristol. Coincidently, on the first day of the conference, Thorburn, Stalker's second in command on the Northern Ireland inquiry, had delivered Stalker's letter to Hermon demanding to know who gave the authority for the hayshed to be bugged (Chapter 5). The following day, Anderton spoke about the politicisation of the police and there were several indirect references to his own Police Committee which was attempting to develop some accountability over policing.[59] The police function, 'is now in need of protection. You cannot police by committee', he said, an undisguised comment on the difficulties he was experiencing with his own committee. Yet the practices within his own police force cried out for some sort of outside scrutiny and accountability to reflect the interests and demands of the community, at a time of record increases in the level of crime. He further bemoaned the 'singular lack of resources'. Yet, as will be shown, this was at the very same time GMP was prepared to allocate huge resources to investigate Taylor and Stalker (Chapters 14 and 15).

Insightfully, criminologist Eugene McLaughlin pointed out that Anderton likened the nature of the relationship between the police and community 'to that which operates in a well conducted family where there is complete trust, confidence and an absence of any kind of deception whatsoever'.[60] His was a

Victorian notion of the family, 'which is structured hierarchically with one party, the father, unquestionably in control'.[61] Like the Victorian father, he had total power and defended the autonomy of chief constables from political interference of any kind, and he saw anyone who demanded a strengthening of police accountability as subversive.[62]

Anderton was an excellent administrator and 'the most incorruptible police officer he [Stalker] had ever met'.[63] Every morning he would hold a conference with his chief officers and receive reports on problems arising.[64] He was meticulous in his paperwork and would sign or initial every document and copies of documents.[65] Perhaps crucially, he had little CID experience and, according to Stalker, had never actually 'questioned a suspect in any detective sense, certainly not for any serious crime'.[66] The pinnacle of Anderton's ambitions, in Stalker's view, was to become head of the Metropolitan Police or Chief Constable of the RUC.[67] He admired Hermon and his approach to policing. During a discussion of police anti-terrorist tactics, he told Stalker that, 'it is impossible to make an omelette without breaking eggs'– a comment which implied that the rule of law could be ignored in some circumstances.[68]

Policing problems faced by GMP

Anderton faced several policing problems prior to Stalker's suspension in 1986. During the first five years of the 1980s, overall crime in the GMP force area increased by a third. There were staggering increases in murder and rape. Burglary and car theft also saw large increases. Armed robberies jumped by over a third in 1982 alone. A criminal elite with sawn-off shot guns, stocking masks and getaway cars was causing havoc. It did not reflect well on the Chief Constable. By 1989, GMP had the second highest density of crime out of all the police forces in England and Wales.[69]

GMP also had a reputation for corruption. In 1979 it investigated a Detective Constable who was the son of a senior officer.[70] There were allegations that he was involved with a prostitute and had handled stolen goods.[71] An inquiry was set up under the control of Superintendent Peter Topping. He assembled a team of trusted officers – DI David Booth, DI Norman Collison, DI Christopher Baythorpe, and DSgt Rodney Murray. Subsequently, DI John Simons, DI Joyce and DSgt Ronald Gaffey were added to the team.[72] It was a highly secretive inquiry, using a 'force within a force' similar to that which investigated Stalker and Taylor. It took five years to complete and ended in two trials. In the first, DC Kirwin was sent to prison for four years[73] and Mrs Ethel Parkes, a 'female Fagin',[74] was sentenced to two years. Three police officers were acquitted.

During the trial, the judge, Mr Justice Caulfield, said he was shocked at the maladministration in the police documents which had come before the court. He expected police officers to have documents which would bear scrutiny by a criminal court: 'I am astonished at the errors that have appeared.'[75] Topping, Murray, Baythorpe and Simons all played significant roles in the investigation into Taylor and Stalker, and the maladministration of documents continued to be a major problem.

In the second trial, another police officer, DI Jack Butler, was found guilty of corruption and perverting the course of justice and was sentenced to four years in prison.[76] According to investigative journalist, Eamonn O'Neill, Butler and Baythorpe interviewed Robert Brown who confessed to the murder of Annie Walsh.[77] Brown always claimed he was innocent and that his confession had been beaten out of him. He was freed in November 2002, having served more than 25 years in jail, after the Court of Appeal accepted that he did not commit the crime.

While Topping was conducting his inquiry into police corruption, Baythorpe never told him that he had worked with Butler during the Robert Brown murder inquiry and was present either as a participant or a witness during Brown's 32-hour interrogation without a solicitor. Baythorpe had ample opportunity during Topping's three-year corruption inquiry to tell him that an innocent young man had been wrongfully convicted, but he did not.[78] At some point Topping produced a report on his inquiry, which, if it had been made available to Brown's legal team, may have shortened his time in prison. However, a PIIC had been issued preventing the report's disclosure. It was only made available shortly before Brown's conviction was squashed by the Court of Appeal.

Although Operation City run by No. 1 RCS had come to nothing (Chapter 4), the QSG continued to be a particular focus of police corruption. A number of them were suspected of having close ties with police officers of various ranks. One officer suspected of tipping-off members of the QSG had the nickname, Treacle Charlie.[79] On 16 May 1984, CS Topping and DS James Grant visited Leonard Pilot in Reading jail. Grant compiled a report of the visit and noted that the interview with Pilot was of considerable use and only heightened the suspicions they already had about police corruption.[80] Two weeks later, they both travelled to a prison to interview a man called Thomas Donovan, again about police corruption.

In October 1984, Jimmy Donnelly and Clifford Sirs were prosecuted for offences arising out of the theft of airline tickets. Donnelly pleaded guilty to conspiring to obtain services by deception and was given a twelve-month sentence suspended for two years. Prior to being prosecuted, he alleged that a

Coroner and two Chief Constables had used the stolen tickets and he threatened to gain as much publicity as possible to direct attention away from his own activities.[81] In the end, he did not make this information public during his trial. The original informant for the airline ticket job said she would not tell GMP because of alleged leaks and went to Cheshire police instead.[82] Further suggestions of police corruption emerged a month later. Burgess was told by David Middleweek, a local solicitor, that he could write a book on police corruption if he was ever cornered.[83]

Linked to the issue of corruption was a concern that Freemasonry had a poisonous influence on policing in GMP. While Freemasons have long denied that there was any conflict between membership of a masonic lodge and a job in the police, membership of a secret organisation can undermine public confidence in the institution. The problem was recently expressed succinctly by Duncan Campbell, a crime correspondent for *The Guardian*, who wrote: 'If the public thinks that a secret handshake can still swing a prosecution and officers themselves feel that the same handshake can affect a promotion, then it is as clear as ever that membership of both bodies is incompatible.'[84] During the Taylor/Stalker affair, there was a strong belief in GMP that being 'on the square' was important in promotion decisions.[85] The Brotherhood was strong in Manchester. There were 130 Masonic Lodges in the city alone, including Lodge 7441, named 'Manchester Ulster'. Cusick, in a long article in the *Manchester Evening News* at the time of Stalker's removal, suggested that this was one of several 'police' lodges where the predominant occupation of the brotherhood was Her Majesty's police.[86]

Anderton faced severe pressures on police resources. On 6 March 1984, the National Union of Mineworkers (NUM) called a strike in opposition to the Conservative government's policy of closing Britain's collieries. It was to last a year and was one of the most intense struggles in British labour history. Thousands of police were involved in preventing pickets arriving at the collieries and providing access for the small minority of miners who defied the strike action.[87] GMP committed its quota of officers. Hundreds of miners were arrested, most for breaches of the peace or obstructing roads. Contrary to government statements, few miners were charged with violent offences.[88] The most violent incident occurred on 18 June when 5,000 miners attempted to block the entrance to the Orgreave coking plant. Mounted police rode into the protesters and attacked them with truncheons. Many miners and policemen were injured. It became known as the Battle of Orgreave and further added to the miners' determination to win the dispute. They lost, however, and the strike ended on 3 March 1985.

The dispute affected policing at several levels. The perceived independence of the police was severely compromised as they sided with the Conservative government in defeating the miners, whose livelihoods were to be decimated as a direct result of the government's economic policies, which involved the closure of many mines. Thousands of police constables were introduced to physical force policing on the picket lines, for which they had little training. The dispute increased the closeness of Chief Constables to the centre of political power. It further strengthened their ability to resist any move to make the police more answerable to the communities they serve.[89]

The Miners' Strike also led to a major rethink about how to deal with public disorder and many police forces developed what were known as Tactical Support Units (TSUs), trained to deal with violence on the streets. GMP was no exception and, on 1 March 1985, deployed their TSUs against protesting students. The incident was to transform the lives of two Manchester students – Sarah Hollis, a third-year medical student, and Steven Shaw, a politics student. That evening, Leon Brittan, the Home Secretary, had been invited to attend a meeting at Manchester University Students' Union to give a talk on 'Law and Order' – ironically, given the events that were to transpire. About 400 students gathered on the steps of the building to protest against the visit and various government policies.[90]

At around 7.10 p.m., the students noticed columns of police marching in military formation towards them. It was assumed that they would form a cordon at the base of the steps. Instead, without warning, they started to assault the students and fought their way up. They punched and kicked students indiscriminately, and threw them down the steps. Some were dragged by their hair.[91] Steven Shaw was pulled out of the crowd by his leg and his girlfriend was punched. Sarah Hollis, after Leon Brittan had left, protested to a police officer about the student being dragged by her hair. Suddenly, she was grabbed by the back of her head and pushed. She fell to the ground. The next thing she remembered was being in the ambulance. The violent methods used to defeat the miners were now being used to disperse a peaceful student demonstration.

Over the following months the trained violence of the TSU paled into insignificance in the face of police deviance and lawlessness. Steven Shaw was repeatedly harassed and on two occasions assaulted by the police.[92] Sarah Hollis' treatment was similarly frightening. She received several phone calls in the middle of the night and when she answered, the caller hung up. She was stopped by the police and told her bike was unroadworthy. On another occasion, when stopped at traffic lights on her bike, two men got out of a car and said: 'Just remember we can pick you up any time we like, and we know the date of your exams'.[93] Her flat was burgled, and it subsequently emerged that a known burglar was encouraged by the police to raid her flat. A number of GMP police officers considered themselves to be above the law.

The friendship between Taylor and Stalker ended in late 1985. Their last social occasion together was when Taylor invited Stalker to the Conservative Party Ball, which took place on 23 November. Sometime after that, Taylor rang Stalker and asked about DI Stephenson who was a member of the Commercial Fraud Squad. Stalker asked him why he wanted to know. Taylor replied, 'he is investigating me'. Stalker then said, 'in that case our friendship must end' and put the phone down.[94] They were never to be in each other's company again – until the civil action ten years later. Stalker's friendship with Anderton lasted a little longer but ended in May 1986 when he was rung by Rees, clerk to GMPA, and told to take extended leave. Stalker phoned Anderton to try and find out what was happening. Eventually, Anderton phoned him back with the cruel words: 'Mr Stalker from now on you must look after yourself.'[95]

* * *

Prior to Stalker's suspension, GMP faced several major policing problems: widespread allegations of corruption; rising crime; severe demands on police resources; and officers who considered themselves to be above the law. It was a force led by a man with strong religious convictions and, surprisingly, with limited detective experience – a characteristic he shared, as will be seen, with the two senior officers in charge of CID, ACC Ralph Lees and CS Topping. These factors may have played a part in Stalker's downfall.

The main conclusion from this analysis, however, is that it was most odd that Stalker and Taylor's twelve-year friendship appears to have only become problematic in 1984 or 1985. It was a very public friendship. Over the years, the two men and their wives attended several social events, some of which were organised and attended by GMP. Stalker was positively vetted in 1973, 1979 and 1982. His first vetting occurred a year before the friendship with Taylor began. During his second vetting in 1979, it is unlikely, but not impossible, that the friendship was not unearthed. But it must have been discovered by his third vetting in 1982 unless the vetting process was very perfunctory. It can, therefore, be safely concluded that the third positive vetting found nothing damaging, otherwise Stalker would not have continued his rapid advancement up through the senior ranks, attended a prestigious course, and would not have been appointed to the Northern Ireland inquiry.

Chapter 7

Documents of Deceit

JUNE 1984 WAS a highly significant month in the Taylor/Stalker affair. If the official narrative is to be believed, this was the month that GMP received three pieces of intelligence which were central to removing Stalker from the Northern Ireland inquiry. The first concerned a report of a post-match golf conversation between a police officer and a businessmen who mentioned that Stalker attended parties at which criminals were present. The second involved a conversation between Jimmy Donnelly, a reputed QSG member, and police informer David Burton. Donnelly told Burton that Stalker was corrupt. The third related to a report that *Sherama*, a boat owned by Vincent Schiavo, another member of the QSG, had sailed from Puerto Banus to Gibraltar with some of the most wanted English criminals on board. All this evidence, if genuine, would support the view that there was no conspiracy to remove Stalker because he had only just started his inquiry, the implications of which were unknown. The remarkable feature of the three pieces of information was that they all occurred on the same day – 11 June 1984. The probability of this happening seems most unlikely.

The golf conversation

On 9 June 1984, Superintendent Bernard McGourlay, Gerald Wareing and Desmond Lawlor played in a three-ball Stapleford golf competition at Northenden golf club. After the game, the three retired to a nearby pub. During the conversation Wareing, who ran a painter and decorator's business and had recently returned from a holiday on Taylor's yacht, *Diogenes*, mentioned the names of several people whom GMP associated with the QSG, including Vincent Schiavo and James Monaghan. He also mentioned to McGourlay that Taylor threw parties after boxing matches which were attended by one of McGourlay's bosses. McGourlay later discretely established that the boss was none other than John Stalker.

According to McGourlay, he pondered on the information and his major concern was to make sure that someone tipped off Stalker that people were mentioning his name in the same conversation that they were also talking about the QSG. His wife suggested that he owed Stalker a duty to let him know what had been said. He could not, however, go to see the Deputy Chief Constable himself as he thought that Stalker 'may have taken umbridge' at being told he should change his friends because they were being talked about.[1] He was, after all, three ranks below Stalker and the hierarchical structure within the police did not encourage contact between such a range of ranks, particularly on such a delicate issue.[2]

McGourlay was in a difficult position. As acting Co-ordinator of No. 1 RCS, he had no immediate superior. Technically, he had a link back to his own force, GMP. Through this route, his direct superior was Head of Crime, ACC Charles Horan. McGourlay does not appear to have considered reporting the matter to him. Instead, he chose to approach CS Topping in GMP's Discipline and Complaints Department.

On Monday morning, 11 June, after he had cleared his desk, McGourlay is adamant that he rang Topping and told him that he wanted to speak to him confidentially. Topping asked him to visit him immediately. McGourlay places the time as 'the middle of Monday morning fairly early on'.[3] The timing is crucial. McGourlay related the golf conversation to Topping, who asked him to put it in writing and not to let anybody see it. McGourlay cannot now remember whether he committed it in writing in Topping's office or whether he went back to his own office. But according to Peter Taylor, McGourlay had made a detailed resumé of the golf conversation over the weekend.[4] It was, therefore, odd that he did not say this to Topping and hand over his notes. McGourlay did remember that during the meeting Topping left the room for a minute or two and spoke to somebody else, and then came back. He had no idea to whom Topping spoke.[5] At some point, McGourlay was introduced to John Richardson, a Detective Inspector who worked with Topping and had joined the department in 1982. McGourlay was told that he would be the person to contact if he came across any further information.[6]

In the civil action, McGourlay was cross-examined by Anderton's counsel, Mr Morrow, on when he reported the golf conversation to Topping. Morrow asked him if he had a contemporaneous note of the meeting with Topping. McGourlay admitted he had not. The meeting would have been noted in his desk diary, which had long gone. Morrow then suggested that his memory might be at fault as he was asked to recall the detail many months after the event.

McGourlay said that he was sure it was on Monday morning. Morrow then put it to him that it was not Monday 11 June but much latter and that McGourlay was mistaken when he said it was 11 June.[7] For some reason, the defence was making great efforts to suggest that the golf conversation was not reported on the Monday, but later. McGourlay was having none of it. He had told his wife about the conversation and went into his office with one thing on his mind on the Monday morning: to report the conversation to Topping.[8]

McGourlay's report of the golf conversation, 11 June 1984

McGourlay's written report to Topping of the golf conversation, like so many documents in the Taylor/Stalker affair, has been lost. Oddly, there is only a typed copy of it, which was minutely analysed during the civil action. It emerged that it contained several major errors or deliberate alterations. First, there were several narrative changes. In one place, the first person was changed to the third person. It noted that 'Lawlor must have told Wareing that *he* was a policeman'.[9] The original written by McGourlay would have said, 'Lawlor must have told Wareing that *I* was a policeman'.[10] It was suggested by the defence that as McGourlay had already admitted that he had difficulty reading his own handwriting, a typist might have misread or hit the wrong keystrokes – an implausible suggestion as the relevant keys are far apart.[11] It was then suggested that it 'doesn't make a ha'peth of difference', which was a most disingenuous response for such a crucial intelligence document.[12]

Second, the copy of the original document noted that McGourlay was 'anxious' when he was told about Stalker. McGourlay claimed, however, that he was not anxious but 'curious'. Again, the defence made little of this and suggested that it was another possible typographical error.[13] Third, the document noted that Wareing said to McGourlay: 'Do you know Kevin Taylor'? It then noted that McGourlay 'pretended' not to know him.[14] McGourlay insisted that at the time the name Taylor meant nothing to him and therefore he did not have to pretend that he did not know him. All these changes strongly suggest that there was some ulterior motive in making the alterations.

There were further problems with the document. Before giving evidence to the Sampson inquiry investigating the disciplinary charges against Stalker, McGourlay asked Topping if he could see his original report of the golf course conversation which was not missing or lost at this point. Topping allowed him to look at the report and to take notes under supervision. It emerged that there were a number of errors in the report: he never said that Wareing had been on Taylor's yacht *Diogenes*, nor that he himself had been present at the parties that

Stalker attended.[15] The report also wrongly stated that McGourlay knew that Trickett, Monaghan and Donnelly were involved in boxing promotions.[16] Morrow asked if McGourlay was saying that their involvement in boxing promotions was a false attribution. McGourlay simply repeated that he had no knowledge of their involvement.

Morrow finished his examination of the document by suggesting that the reference to the boxing promotions was not the most significant of paragraphs in the report. He suggested that if someone wanted to deliberately alter the meaning of the report they could have added or deleted something 'more sinister'.[17] It was a revealing comment and implied that Morrow had thought that there may have indeed been a deliberate attempt to change the meaning of the original report. In any case, such carelessness in reproducing a copy of the original report of the golf conversation either reflected sloppy work by officers in the Discipline and Complaints Department or it was an attempt to 'gild the lily' and increase the suspicions about Stalker.

At some point – McGourlay cannot be precise about the time, but he thought it was on the day he reported the conversation or a little later – Topping asked him if he could conduct low-key surveillance on Taylor to see if there was any information that could be picked up to corroborate what McGourlay had already reported.[18] Topping's request to McGourlay was most irregular. Normally any request to make use of the RCS would have to be made formally through the ACC responsible for crime. No officer, particularly not of Topping's rank, could make a request of this sort to the RCS without going through the hierarchy. Yet here was Topping asking a member of the RCS to do an investigation for him and not to put anything in writing. It was most unusual and ran counter to all procedures. McGourlay, however, went along with the request and selected his best surveillance officer, DSgt Henri Exton. He asked him and his partner to have a look at Taylor's house and to report back directly to him, but not to put anything on paper. McGourlay told Peter Taylor, the journalist, that 'wild horses wouldn't drag out of them what they were doing'.[19]

The Bridge Street conversation

A potentially more damning piece of intelligence on Stalker emerged from the second conversation. On 11 June at around 3.00 p.m., police informer Burton rang Richardson in the Discipline and Complaints Department and reported the following conversation between himself and Jimmy Donnelly, which had supposedly taken place on Bridge Street, Manchester, half an hour earlier.

Donnelly at the time was on bail for conspiring to steal airline tickets. The conversation apparently went like this:

DONNELLY: My case is listed for 7th July you know.

BURTON: Can't your man straighten it for you?
(B knowing there is a police connection inside the QSG).

DONNELLY: Who Stalker?

BURTON: Well, isn't he a Top Jolly now?

DONNELLY: He is Jimmy (Jimmy Swords) and Kevin's man.

BURTON: Haven't you got your own man?

DONNELLY: My man's a tosser (B mentions the name of 'the tosser'). Anyway, I shouldn't be talking to you Bertie. (B is giving evidence against the QSG re £600,000 of fraud including IRA activities) And don't come to the pub in case you are seen by one of the lads.[20]

The pub, the Brown Bull, was on the junction of Bridge Street and Chapel Street. It was run by Donnelly and was a meeting place for some members of the criminal fraternity in Manchester. There are two remarkable features of this conversation. First, it contained the same allegation that Burton made about Stalker to Burgess in May 1983, in the 'I have found your rat' conversation, which Burgess reported to both the Fraud and the Discipline and Complaints Departments – a report which never re-emerged among the 110,000 documents used by GMP in their defence of the civil action taken against them by Kevin Taylor (Chapter 24). Second, the very same people who were mentioned in the golf conversation – Donnelly, Monaghan, a.k.a. Jimmy Swords, Taylor and Stalker – were all mentioned in this conversation too.

Given the importance of this intelligence alleging that the DCC of GMP was corrupt, it might have been expected that Richardson would write a contemporaneous report on a standard form recording the call from Burton. But no such report was produced on discovery in the civil action. In addition, there was no reference to this Bridge Street conversation in Richardson's pocketbook. In the civil action, Taylor's counsel, Mr Roger Farley, asked Stalker to read out the entry in Richardson's pocketbook for Monday 11 June 1984:

7.40: Commenced duty, clerical in Y Department.

8.15: Gone with the Superintendent Elder.

9.35: Writing up a complaint file from the year before.

12.00: Refreshment.

13.00: Continuing with a Y department re complaint file.

14.00: To Albert Court, Miles Platting. Interviewed Thomas Freeman re MC [A miscellaneous complaint] in presence of Mr Manning.

18.30: Off duty.[21]

As can be seen, there was no mention of a call from Burton. On the contrary, Richardson appears to have been out of his office conducting an interview in Miles Platting, Manchester, at the time the Burton call was supposed to have come in. Farley continued:

FARLEY: If you received a complaint from a department that a Deputy Chief Constable was potentially corrupt do you think that something like a note would have been made of it?

STALKER: Absolutely, it would appear from that, that the Inspector, who is in the Y department at the time, that it's actually his own boss, his statutory boss, is being complained against. It's absolutely vital that you would put in there, if only it said: conversation with Chief Superintendent Topping … He needn't go into full detail, but he should make a reference to it.

FARLEY: If there's no reference to it what inferences can be drawn.

STALKER: *My inference is that it did not take place* (emphasis added). It couldn't have taken place. It is too important to be regarded as a routine entry in a diary… It did not take place.[22]

Stalker was then asked how he would rate the reports of the two conversations in terms of police work. He replied:

Disgraceful my Lord. It's disgraceful whether or not it had happened to me. The essence of good police work is to realise the powers the authority that you have in your hands and it's to be exercised responsibly and properly because of the enormous repercussions if it's handled badly, if it's handled maliciously well it's even worse. I can only say that if all the things that have happened, which you have rightly said happened as a result of this dross, it is a disgrace on the people involved. I don't blame the police force my Lord. I blame the people who misused such information to the detriment of so many other people.[23]

Later in the civil action, McGourlay appeared to accept that the Bridge Street conversation did take place, but thought it was 'an amazing coincidence' that, on the very same day he had reported the golf conversation, Burton should discuss with Richardson similar matters.[24] He remarked: 'Quite frankly my Lord, I just wondered what was going on'.[25]

There is further evidence that the Bridge Street meeting never occurred. Most importantly, Donnelly denied that it ever took place.[26] Moreover, as a reputed member of the QSG, he was most unlikely to have stopped and talked to Burton, who had recently supplied information to the police leading to the eventual prosecution for the LFF of two of Donnelly's associates. It is known that at the time Burton was extremely frightened for his own safety, the safety of his mother and of his girlfriend, Elizabeth McDonald.

The dialogue was highly questionable. In response to Burton asking if his 'man can straighten it', Donnelly replied: 'Who Stalker?' But later in the conversation Donnelly admits: 'My man's a tosser'. The obvious response to

Burton's initial question would therefore have been the name of the officer who Donnelly considered to be a tosser, rather than Stalker. Alternatively, instead of the name of a policemen, most people would have responded with the name of a lawyer. The other point to note is that Burton's response – 'Isn't he a top jolly now?' – suggested that he was familiar with Stalker's career. Yet, in February 1985 during a police interview, he stated that the Bridge Street conversation was the first time he had heard of Stalker's name.[27]

Peter Taylor, who produced a special Public Eye programme following the collapse of Kevin Taylor's trial in 1990, reported that the meeting was 'remarkable' and that the allegations were 'astonishing', and that the 'encounter seemed to be incredible beyond words'.[28] McGourlay, speaking to camera, said: 'I was amazed that such a coincidence happened.'[29] But nowhere in the programme does Peter Taylor suggest the possibility that the Bridge Street meeting was a complete fiction.

The lack of any contemporaneous report or pocketbook reference and the denial by Donnelly, strongly suggests that the meeting was a fabrication. It is claimed that Richardson noted all conversations with Burton in an A4 Blue book which went missing. This would explain why there is no report of the conversation on an official form, but it does not explain why there is no mention of the phone call from Burton in his pocketbook. All of this then raises many questions. Did Burton make up the Bridge Street encounter to enhance his reputation with the police or did officers in GMP fabricate the story in order to strengthen the suspicions about Stalker? In the absence of a contemporaneous dated report, there remains the question of when it was made up: was it June 1984 or much later?

Document 7, date unknown

The only existing documentary reference to a Bridge Street conversation was in a handwritten report by Richardson, on plain paper, entitled: 'Doc. File 7 – Kevin Taylor' (hereinafter Document 7). It carried the sub-heading: 'Informant – David Burton, known throughout report as 'B'.' Then, centred underneath, was simply the letter 'S' – a reference to Stalker. It then reproduced what purported to be a verbatim record of the Bridge Street conversation. This was followed by several other pieces of information allegedly provided by Burton. It noted that 'B' had learnt through different sources that Stalker was a close 'associate' of Taylor and in the past had visited his house for drinks and parties.[30] This again suggested that Burton knew a great deal about Stalker – something he would later deny. Under the pejorative heading 'Taylor's Pedigree',[31] the document listed the four items of information about Taylor which Burton had given Patterson, his handler, in 1982 - namely that Taylor was financing drug smugglers, lending money to gamblers, minding firearms for the QSG and was an associate of the IRA. It will be recalled that Patterson investigated the information at the time but found no evidence to support it (Chapter 4). Yet, here it was all being reproduced as fact.

Document 7 noted that at 11.50 a.m. on Friday 15 June 1984, Richardson spoke to McGourlay – another meeting which was not recorded in his pocketbook – who told him about the golf conversation.[32] This chronology, of course, was at variance with McGourlay's account. He claimed he reported the golf conversation to Topping on the Monday morning (11 June), who would presumably have reported it to Richardson. Why would Richardson now be noting that he heard about on it on the Friday? Document 7, therefore, reverses the order in which the two conversations took place with the Bridge Street conversation being reported before the golf conversation. This order of events supports Topping's claim in his book that the information on Stalker first came from Burton followed by more intelligence from the golf conversation.[33]

Document 7 further noted that McGourlay had contacted Burton and asked him what he knew about Taylor. Richardson then added the highly significant comment that 'McGourlay did not tell Burton about Stalker'.[34] Had McGourlay told Richardson that he had not mentioned Stalker's name, or did Richardson note the comment because he was only too aware of the possibility that Burton would use this information to the maximum of effect and go around to various agencies linking the names of the two men together? It would then mean that the whole investigation into Taylor and Stalker was based on recycled information from the police to an informer and back to the police.

In the civil action, McGourlay challenged some of the detail. He had not contacted Burton as he did not have Burton's telephone number.[35] On the contrary, Burton had managed, presumably using his considerable guile, to get into Salford police headquarters to see him.[36] He wanted to talk to McGourlay about his up-coming trial, as McGourlay had promised to speak to the Judge concerning the help he had given to the police in informing on his co-conspirators in the LFF.

Richardson's report noted several other random pieces of information all apparently supplied by Burton. It revealed the name of the policeman Burton believed was Donnelly's 'tosser'. In the civil action, Stalker instantly dismissed the suggestion. He pointed out that if GMP considered that there was any truth in what Burton was saying, they would not have subsequently promoted the named officer and moved him to serious crimes.[37] In one place in the document, Stalker's name was crossed out and replaced by 'Costi', but no explanation was given.[38]

The report contained another reference to 11 June 1984 – the fourth piece of evidence relevant to the Taylor/Stalker affair logged by GMP on that day. It recorded that a mere fifteen minutes after Burton had met Donnelly, he met a man known as Larry or Harry, who was a barrow boy in Manchester. He told Burton that 'Jimmy Swords', whose real name was James Monaghan, did not mind about being charged with fraud because they can't touch him. It then noted in brackets, incorrectly, that Swords had recently had his case concerning his involvement in the LFF in Belfast withdrawn at committal proceedings. Finally, it reported that 'Costi' had told Burton that several jobs had been 'blown out' by an Inspector who had since left the force. If only a small bit of all of this was true, it presented GMP with a serious problem.[39]

Document 7 had all the hallmarks of being carefully constructed. To begin with, in specifically noting that McGourlay did not tell Burton about Stalker, it excluded the possibility that Burton recycled the information from McGourlay among other agencies. Second, it suggested that Stalker's 'top jolly' status, as Burton allegedly called it, was generally known within the QSG, as seen in Donnelly's response. Thirdly, in noting that Richardson did not hear about the golf conversation until *after* the Bridge Street conversation, it strengthens, as will be seen, Topping's claim that the information on Stalker first came from Burton, followed by more intelligence from the golf conversation.

Crucially, Document 7 was not dated. If it was written shortly after Burton reported the Bridge Street conversation on 11 June, then it would support the official narrative that GMP had information relating to Stalker that needed to be investigated in June 1984. If, however, it was written much later, then it challenges the chronology of when the investigation into Stalker began. Incredibly, for such an important document in the Taylor/Stalker affair, the two men responsible for initiating the inquiry into Stalker – Topping, the head of the Discipline and Complaints Department, and Richardson, an Inspector in his department – disagreed on the date when it was written. Richardson claimed it was written on 28 June 1984. Topping claimed that it was written after the formation of DIU (February 1985). It could have, of course, been written even later – at the time of Stalker's removal.

McGourlay's lie, 11 June 1984

The difficulties of making sense of what was known, and when, is further compounded by a staggering admission by McGourlay in the civil action. He admitted that in his exchange with Burton in Salford police headquarters in June 1984, he *did*, in fact, mention Stalker's name.[40] He admitted that he had lied in his statement to the Rothwell inquiry – set up in 1990 to investigate the collapse of Taylor's criminal trial – by saying he had not mentioned Stalker's name to Burton.[41] He now claimed that, as he was showing the informer out of the building, Burton turned to him and asked if there was anything he could do for him. McGourlay responded:

> So, I said to him: 'Do you know a chap called Kevin Taylor'. There is a little pause, then he said: 'Oh he's a big financier'. I think he mentioned one or two other things ... So I said: 'Well he's supposed to be friendly with a police officer'. Burton said: 'Who is that'. I said: 'John Stalker'. And he immediately said: 'Who'? I repeated: 'John Stalker'. So, I got the impression that Burton at that stage didn't know John Stalker. Whether it was right or wrong I'll never know but he then said: 'I'll do what I can. I'll do my best and see what I can find out'. I'd got him downstairs and that was the last time I ever saw him.[42]

McGourlay explained that he felt extremely embarrassed and ashamed that he had asked somebody like Burton if he knew anything about Stalker as he knew 'what sort of person he was'.[43] His intention in reporting the golf conversation was only to warn Stalker that people were talking about his friendship and not for GMP to initiate an investigation into him. Mentioning Stalker's name to Burton increased the possibility that Burton would use this information to increase his status as an informer and feed it back to other law enforcement agencies. Mr Morrow, Anderton's defence counsel, foresaw this possibility.

MORROW: Isn't your concern now perhaps in retrospect that, particularly with your knowledge of Burton, if you feed something to Burton, he could feed it back to either another officer of the RCS or another agency within GMP or outside agency?

McGOURLAY: That was a great worry if he fed something back to the RCS or other agency. I wouldn't have been aware. That's why I felt ashamed that I had spoken to him.

MORROW: Knowing David Burton as you do, you could see the possibility of him feeding that information that you'd given him back to another source? That was your error.

McGOURLAY: Yes.[44]

McGourlay's admission forces a reassessment of the story about the Bridge Street meeting. It would increase the possibility that Burton had made up the conversation to curry favours. This would help explain the odd response to the question, 'can't your man straighten it for you'. The normal response would have been for Donnelly to name his 'tosser' or a lawyer, but allegedly he put Stalker's name in the frame, linking Jimmy Swords and Taylor – a formula he had used in 1983. None of this speculation holds up, however, because McGourlay did not speak with Burton until some days *after* 11 June – the date recorded by Richardson for the Bridge Street meeting. McGourlay's mention of Stalker's name to Burton would, therefore, have come too late to have any relevance to Burton's alleged utterances. The provenance of the Bridge Street meeting remains an enigma.

Sherama's trip to Gibraltar

The third piece of intelligence which GMP claimed further justified an investigation into Taylor and Stalker was the arrival of *Sherama* in Gibraltar on 11 June 1984 – the same day as the two conversations were reported to the police. The boat had sailed from Puerto Banus in Spain. On board were several notorious criminals including Freddie Foreman and Ronnie Knight, who were suspected of being involved in the robbery at the Security Express headquarters in Shoreditch, East London, on Easter Monday 1983 when £6.6 million in used bank notes was stolen.[45] Two more of the passengers – John Mason and Ronnie Everett – were also suspected of being involved in the robbery. Another member of the party was Maurice O'Connor, who had made a living from importing hashish from North Africa.[46] In addition, there was a group from Manchester – Vincent Schiavo, the boat's owner, Jack Trickett and Ashley von Meppen-Walter. Foreman was accompanied by his wife and Knight by his new girlfriend, Susan Haylock.

GMP was notified on 10 July 1984 of *Sherama's* arrival in Gibraltar a month earlier, and it was logged in Vincent Schiavo's intelligence report. Subsequently, GMP obtained a copy of what was claimed to be the crew/passenger list for *Sherama's* arrival in Gibraltar. In the civil action, Stalker was taken through each of the named individuals on the list and was asked if he knew any of them. He was also shown an article from *The Sunday Times* which noted that two of the people on board – Everett and Mason – financed a drugs operation in Spain.[47] Stalker's cross-examination on the crew/passenger list ended with Anderton's defence counsel suggesting that *Sherama* should have been 'flying the Jolly Roger' when it entered Gibraltar.[48] Stalker could only reply that he knew nothing of the people mentioned and had never met them. Oddly, none of the wanted criminals on board was arrested when they entered Gibraltar – a British Overseas Territory.

Among Taylor's papers, I found two sets of the crew/passenger lists dated 11 June 1984. Both listed the same names in identical handwriting over two pages. The top section of each set, however, was very different. One set noted that *Sherama* sailed from 'P. Banus to Gibraltar', while the second noted that *Sherama* sailed from 'P. Banus' but the destination section was left blank. On both pages, this set carried the official stamp: 'Yacht Reporting Station, 11 Jun (sic) 1984,

Customs Gibraltar' with a clear signature. The other set had no official stamp and no signature. The address of the registered owner of the *Sherama* also differed between the two sets. The two sets had all the hallmarks of being part of a scissors and paste job. Was this another fabricated document?

In 2012, Maurice O'Connor, one of the people on the list, published a book entitled: *The Dealer*. In it, he provided a description of *Sherama* visiting Gibraltar with a group of his criminal friends.[49] Unfortunately, he did not mention a date. However, he provided a lot of detail about the visit. Apparently, *Sherama's* original destination was Algeciras, a port about 80 miles down the coast. The plan was to watch Manchester United play against the local town. But at the last minute someone decided that it would be sensible to check that the match was actually on. They discovered that Manchester United was in fact playing Algeria in a friendly – not Algeciras. *Sherama*, which seldom left its home port, could not have made such a long trip and the passengers were not up for it. As provisions were already purchased, it was decided to go to Gibraltar for the day instead. O'Connor describes how the boat barely made it and had to be towed in by a police launch. The engines required repairs, forcing them to stay overnight. Two of them checked into a hotel, one of whom then stayed out late celebrating his birthday. When he returned to the hotel, he discovered that there were no covers on his bed as his friend had taken them to keep warm.

These details provided by O'Connor help to pinpoint the date of the trip (which was supposed to have taken place on 11 June 1984). The Manchester United curator confirmed that one of its teams had played a friendly against Algeria on 28 January 1984. The average night-time temperatures at that time of year were around 10 degrees centigrade, which would have made bed covers essential.[50] These two facts suggested that the visit was in fact in January and not June as written on the crew/passenger list. This only increased my suspicion about the document.

In 2018, I interviewed O'Connor in Barcelona. He expanded on the details of *Sherama's* trip to Gibraltar. He remembered the engine breaking down and the boat being towed into the harbour by a police launch. I showed him the crew/passenger list. His immediate response was that he did not remember some of those listed as being on board. He also remembered several others who were on board but not on the list. One was a marine engineer who spent the night fixing the engine. He was convinced that the trip had taken place in late January or early February. He was later able to confirm that his friend's birthday was on 28 January.

O'Connor put me in touch with one of the passengers on the crew/passenger list with whom he had kept in touch. In correspondence, the person, a student at the time, was certain that the trip happened in June and not January. We agreed to meet up. During our conversation she again emphasised that the trip took place in June. She remembered it well as she had obtained her first passport especially for the trip and had visited the monkeys on the Rock in the heat of the day. She told me that she had completed the crew/passenger list, with instructions from the captain. She distinctly remembered noting 'Co Director' alongside the name of the infamous criminals on board.

When I showed her the crew/passenger list, she immediately said that it was not her handwriting. I dictated several of the passenger names and the word, yacht, which was misspelt. Her spelling was impeccable, and her writing was very different from that on the document. It proved beyond any doubt that this was not the original which she had completed years previously. A few months after our meeting, she emailed me to say that she had found her passport and enclosed a photo of the stamp. It was dated 11 June 1984 – concrete proof that the date of the trip was correct but the crew/passenger list itself was some sort of a forgery. O'Connor's January trip was evidently a separate event.

Apart from showing that GMP were prepared to forge documents, it is not known why they should do so when the date and, as far as can be ascertained, the list of people on board were correct. In April 1999, I interviewed the immigration officer in Gibraltar who had stamped one of the sets of the crew/passenger list. He told me that in 'about October 1985' he was asked by the Deputy Commissioner of the Gibraltar Police, Mr Mario Payas, who was later convicted of embezzling money from the fund used to pay informers,[51] to prepare a statement describing *Sherama's* arrival in Gibraltar as it was needed for Vincent Schiavo's trial in Manchester in November 1985. Schiavo had been charged with several offences including deception, handling and making a false statement to obtain a passport.[52] The officer had been ready to fly to London and then to Manchester for the trial. A day had been set aside for him to give evidence and he was then to return. He thought that GMP must have been confident that it could all be done within the day. In the end he was not required.

The crew/passenger list may, therefore, have been forged to prove that Schiavo had travelled on an invalid or false passport when he jumped bail. To get to Spain, he needed to obtain a British visitor's passport shortly before or on the day of his departure. Alternatively, he already had another fraudulently obtained passport in case he had to surrender his authentic passport following an arrest. To guarantee a conviction, the police needed proof that he had obtained a passport fraudulently.

This could only be achieved if they had documentary proof. Perhaps, the original of the crew/passenger list was therefore changed to note the number of the fraudulent passport rather than the visitor passport.

Whatever the reason for the forgery, it was a very useful document for GMP. Along with the two conversations, it added further support to its narrative that there was 'strong' evidence to justify an investigation into Stalker and Taylor. It provided proof that the QSG were friendly with major wanted criminal fugitives from England and were perhaps involved in drug smuggling. It cast suspicions on Stalker's friend, Taylor, because the *Sherama's* home port, Puerto Banus, was the same harbour where Taylor's yacht *Diogenes* was moored. But in June 1984, GMP would not have known that Taylor owned a yacht, let alone that it was moored in the same harbour as the *Sherama*. This would have only been discovered *after* the DIU started to investigate him in 1985. The forged crew/passenger list would, therefore, have played no part in triggering an investigation into Taylor and Stalker in June 1984.

Topping's claims

To confuse matters further about what was known, and when, Topping's autobiography claims that he received the information about a possible corrupt relationship between Stalker and the QSG in May, not June 1984. The information was passed on to him by 'an inspector' who acknowledged that it had come from Burton.[53] Topping did not mention the name of the inspector or when in May he received the information, but he noted that it was while the Northern Ireland inquiry was still cloaked in secrecy and therefore Burton's allegations could not have been part of a conspiracy to get rid of Stalker. He concluded:

> John Stalker's suspension had nothing to do with his role in Northern Ireland. It was a decision based entirely on information and events that occurred in Manchester. I was the person who initiated the 'Stalker Affair' – and at no time did I have any detailed knowledge of what was going on in Northern Ireland.[54]

There are problems with Topping's claim that he received information about Stalker in May 1984. Although Topping did not name the inspector, it was obviously Inspector David Patterson, who was Burton's handler at the time. But Patterson, in evidence to the Sampson inquiry, could not 'recall Burton referring to an ACC' – Stalker's earlier rank. Burton only referred to 'senior officers' whom he did not name.[55] Patterson's evidence, therefore, undermines Topping's claim that he received information about Stalker in May 1984. But the claim becomes even more problematic in the light of Burgess' report to the Discipline and Complaints Department in May 1983, in which he noted that Burton alleged that Stalker was 'on a pension' with the QSG. Topping, who had been in that department in a senior rank for over six years, must have been aware of Burgess' earlier report.

Topping noted that following the initial information in May 1984, 'totally independently of anything Bertlestein' (Burton) had said, he received more information about John Stalker's connections.[56] Topping then described McGourlay informing him about the golf conversation. Thus, Topping supported the chronology outlined by Richardson in Document 7: Burton's information came first and was then backed up by a 'respectable Manchester businessman'.[57] The order of these two events is no academic point. The intelligence is much stronger if it first comes from an informer, who was prone to lie, and then backed up by someone respectable rather than the other way round. To confuse matters further, in the civil action no document was examined to support Topping's claim that he initiated the investigation into Stalker in May. On the contrary, the defence argued that the trigger for the investigation was the receipt of the reports of the golf and Bridge street conversations in the second week of June.

* * *

The overall conclusion from the analysis of the reports which allegedly began the investigation into Stalker, is that each one was possibly a document of deceit. The golf conversation obviously did take place, but McGourlay's original report was conveniently lost, and a copy was substituted which corroborated the suspicion in the Bridge Street conversation that Stalker was corrupt. The Bridge Street conversation was another possible fabrication by either Burton or someone else. It was almost identical to Burton's May 1983 allegation that Stalker was 'on a pension' from the QSG, which he made to Burgess who then reported it to the Discipline and Complaints and Fraud departments. It was obviously not taken seriously at the time otherwise Stalker would have been investigated and he would certainly not have been promoted to DCC or asked to investigate the killings in Northern Ireland.

The crew/passenger list for *Sherama*'s visit to Gibraltar on 11 June 1984 was a further document of deceit. There is no doubt that all the wanted criminals visited Gibraltar on that date. Why none of them was arrested remains a mystery. Similarly, why the crew/passenger list was not the original and was forged, can only be guessed at. It showed conclusively, however, that GMP were prepared to doctor documents for whatever reason, casting doubt on all other documents and reports produced on or after 11 June 1984.

Deceit in the preparation of documents, together with the absence of any contemporaneous reports and the lack of any reference to key events in police pocketbooks, severely undermines any claim that the investigation into Stalker, began in June 1984. It raises the obvious question: when did GMP start to investigate Stalker? If it was much later in 1984, when Stalker was making demands in Northern Ireland, this strengthens the possibility that there was a conspiracy to remove him.

Chapter 8

Criminal Intelligence

POLICE FORCES routinely collect information on sections of the population, which is maintained in their Crime Intelligence Units (CIUs). The reasons a person may arouse police suspicion leading to a CIU entry are varied. The individual on whom information is collected, collated and circulated has no right whatsoever in law to challenge the accuracy of the information. Nor is there any legal obligation on the part of the police to check its validity, evaluate and grade it. Yet information remains in the system indefinitely and can be accessed by the police at any time. By June 1984, when the official narrative claims the investigation into Taylor and Stalker began, GMP's CIU had eight items of information on Taylor – reproduced in the report by CC Colin Sampson following his investigation into Stalker in 1986.[1] The DIU had collated all the entries in 'Taylor Doc 1' which was examined in the civil action. The items provide a graphic illustration of the dangers of police intelligence gathering and the disastrous impact that it can have on a person's life.

Eight CI entries, 1973 to 1984

The first entry was dated 27 March 1973. It noted that Taylor was receiving metal stolen from the docks by two men with previous convictions, George Downing and Harvey Sefton. It further claimed that Sefton worked for Taylor and that Taylor had taken Sefton 'flying in a light aircraft'.[2] There is no evidence that the allegation was investigated further or who supplied the information to the police.

The second piece of information on Taylor was entered in GMP's CIU a couple of months later by a Cheshire police officer. It recorded that on 28 May 1973, Taylor had been to Spain on four occasions in the previous fortnight.[3] Once again, there is no record of where this information came from or whether it was evaluated. It would have been perfectly simple to check with Taylor the purpose of his visits. According to Taylor himself, his wife and two young daughters were on holiday for a fortnight on the Costa del Sol, and instead of joining them, because he detested lying on the beach in the hot sun doing nothing, he made visits during the fortnight to see them.[4]

The next two entries concerned Taylor's businesses.[5] The first, in July 1973, noted that his business was in financial difficulties. According to Taylor, this was incorrect, but even if it was correct, why would the police want to record it? A year and a half later, it was reported that Taylor had built a shopping precinct behind Broughton Lane, Salford. Again, the central question is why would the police wish to record this information? Was it part of GMP's policy at the time to collect intelligence on every new business in Manchester, or only those belonging to people who came from the poorest neighbourhoods?

There were then no entries for the next four years. But on 3 April 1979, PC Brew is recorded as having observed Taylor in a lengthy conversation with Vincent Schiavo and James Patrick Monaghan.[6] This was the beginning of several entries concerning his 'associations' with suspected or known criminals. In March 1981, Sergeant Moss reported that Trevor Goodwin, convicted in 1976 for handling stolen goods for which he had been fined £25, was living at Taylor's home.[7] Two years later, DSgt Reynolds recorded that Taylor was 'an associate' of James Anthony Donnelly, a.k.a. Jimmy the Weed.[8]

There was a further entry concerning Vincent Schiavo dated 15 June 1983. Reynolds recorded that Schiavo had obtained a 6.52-ton yacht named *Moriarty*. This had come from Taylor in payment of a gambling debt. Schiavo's vessel was said to be in Marbella, Spain.[9] Again, the source of this information is not recorded, and it was false. Taylor never owned a yacht called *Moriarty*. Interestingly, David Burton reported this same misinformation to the police in 1985 and was probably the source of the original falsehood in 1983.[10]

When the Sampson inquiry was established to consider the possibility of disciplinary charges against Stalker, it reproduced all of the CIU entries. In addition, it recorded that both Taylor's home and workplace telephone numbers were in Mark Klapish's telephone indexes. These indexes were seized when search warrants were executed in respect of the LFF investigation in May 1983.[11] These shared telephone numbers were unsurprising: Taylor had grown up with them and had remained friendly when he became a successful businessman.[12]

But police suspicion is constructed around people's associations. If you talk to, or appear to be 'friendly' with, someone who has a criminal record, you may come under suspicion yourself. Similarly, if your telephone number is in the possession of a suspected or known criminal, you may come under suspicion as an 'associate'. The possibilities of making connections based on associations to create 'guilt by association' are almost endless and, with the potential of computerised databases, awesome. By June 1984, all that GMP had in their CIU on Taylor were a few items of information that stretched back over an eleven-year period covering his holidays, his businesses and his association with known criminals, in one case via gambling.

The closest any of the entries got to suggesting that Taylor was involved in criminal activity was the 1973 entry that recorded he was receiving metal stolen from the docks. It was yet another piece of information in the Taylor/Stalker affair where there was a conflict over dates. Taylor Doc 1 recorded the date of the entry as 20 March.[13] The Sampson report, however, noted that it was dated 27 March – a week later.

Taylor Doc 1 was undated but was probably the first document that DIU prepared in 1985. At the time, the head of the Criminal Intelligence Unit was Detective Chief Inspector Baythorpe. Coincidentally, Baythorpe had submitted the 1973 entry when he was a detective constable. Given his current position, it would have been relatively easy to construct the entry to increase suspicion about Taylor, who has always denied that he received any stolen goods. Only four years after the date of the entry, Baythorpe witnessed or participated in obtaining the false confession from Robert Brown who then spent 25 years in jail for a murder he did not commit (Chapter 6).

RCS Report, 14 June 1984

Following the golf conversation, Topping asked McGourlay to submit a report on Taylor. In turn, McGourlay asked a member of his squad to pull together the information. An Intelligence Report headed 'Kevin Taylor' and dated 14 June 1984 was allegedly prepared by No. 1 RCS headquarters. It was examined in detail in the civil action, and it was implied that this was the report that Topping received. It was, however, another questionable document. There was a standard form in No. 1 RCS for an intelligence report which required the officer submitting it to note the target of the investigation, his or her name, and to whom the report was to be distributed. It was routine practice for the officer receiving the report to check each item of intelligence and initial them, stamp the report, and sign it, before copies were sent for distribution. The recipient then dated and stamped the report. Most of these standard completion requirements were missing on the document. When shown the document, Stalker said: 'I accept the headed note paper sir but there is absolutely no name on it that, if I were still in the police force, I could make reference to … There is no detective's name attached to it.'[14]

The report Topping claimed to have received consisted of the No. 1 RCS standard Intelligence Report form, but without any of the completion requirements, and two sheets of *plain* paper. The three pages recorded nineteen separate items of information, five on the required form and fourteen on the two plain pages. The report noted the following:

> This man believed to live in Summerseat is an associate of a number of known or suspected criminals.
>
> 1. Was in partnership with James Monaghan in Vanlands.
>
> 2. Now owner of Moulton Street precinct and has offices in Broughton Lane. (Suspected that recently sold the precinct for £2.25 million. Money maybe owing to the bank of Credit and Commerce in Peters Square and to the Nat Westminster).
>
> 3. He is a big gambler and will bet in thousands of pounds. Gambles in Sid Otty's.
>
> 4. Said to have financed a DT in drug deals.
>
> 5. Associate of Ali-Hag-Hussani owner of Brambles and the Lincoln service flat.
>
> 6. Reputed to have a boat in Miami.
>
> 7. Believed to be a partner of James Monaghan in villas in the Marbella area.
>
> 8. Associate at (5) believed to own house in Shelbourne Road where 'business' meetings take place.
>
> 9. Has a driver known as Fat Trevor.
>
> 10. Throws big parties at his home usually after boxing matches. Guests include gentlemen Trickett, James Monaghan (currently spending a lot of time in Spain), Joe Monaghan and other criminal associates.
>
> 11. Informant states police officers from time to time have been guests at these parties.
>
> 12. Informant states Taylor launders cash for James Monaghan.
>
> 13. Associate of some police constable etcetera.
>
> 14. Currently arrested in Spain – four names noted. Two of them are heavies, one of them is wanted here for fraud. Another one is wanted here for fraud. Three are associated with the Quality Street Gang and known to Taylor.
>
> 15. Michael Roy Brown is an associate of the Quality Street Gang and Taylor. Brown supposed to have visited Taylor's boat in Miami.
>
> 16. Brown is strongly suspected of buying or organising couriers. He has two girl couriers who are believed to carry currency travellers' cheques and goods.
>
> 17. Brown is believed to be an associate of ... who deals in currency and stolen travellers' cheques via the Lebanon and Morocco (drug sources).
>
> 18. Brown connects Taylor and Gleeson with Vincent Schiavo resident in Puerto Banus on the yacht Sherama. Schiavo wanted in Manchester.
>
> 19. Freddy Capper.[15]

The report was clearly attempting to suggest that, at best, Taylor was an immoral reprobate and, at worst, a key figure in the drugs and criminal underworld. Through the constant use of the word associate, it implied that he was involved in organised crime which stretched from Manchester to Spain. The report did not note that he was a man of respectability in the local community, having been a one-time Chair of the MCA and was seen, by many, as a successful property developer, who had regenerated an inner-city area of Manchester, providing much needed retail outlets. Perhaps, even more crucially, the report failed to record that he had no criminal record whatsoever.

Thousands of these types of documents are produced by the police on individuals every year and circulated internally. There is presumably some shared understanding within the police on how these documents should be read. If they were taken at face value, the police would be targeting most of the population. Nevertheless, the document provides a unique insight into the very sloppy and dangerous way GMP handled information in the 1980s. They appear to have been under no obligation whatsoever to note their sources, to verify their facts or record whether they had been verified. Looking at this report, it is simply not possible to know what information might be true and what may be rumour, gossip or plain lies.

Some items in the report were statements of supposed fact. For example, Item 1 noted, 'Was in partnership with James Monaghan in Vanlands (sic)'. It would have been very easy to check this information from the records at Companies House which would have shown that Taylor owned a company called Vanland, not Vanlands, and Monaghan was not a partner. Similarly, Taylor emphatically denies that he was ever a partner with Monaghan involving villas in Marbella.[16] Other items were prefaced by such phrases as 'said to have', 'reported to have', 'believed to be' and presumably this is police parlance that these items should be treated with some caution. The most absurd 'believed' was at the start of the report, 'This man believed to live in Summerseat'. This could have been checked out in seconds and his full address noted.

The report was peppered with subjective, pejorative and extremely vague descriptions. Taylor was described as a 'big' gambler who throws 'big' parties. He was 'said to have financed DT in drug deals' and 'launders cash for James Monaghan'. What these vague expressions mean in these contexts is nowhere explained but their overall impact is to create a highly prejudicial picture. Item 2 noted, in a revealing phrase, 'Suspected that recently sold the precinct for £2.25 million'. What does 'suspected' mean in this context? Anyone is legally entitled to dispose of his or her own property. To use the word suspected immediately made the link with some sort of illegality.

The vaguest description of all in the report was the word 'associate'. It was used no fewer than seven times linking Taylor to twelve people. Stalker considered associate to be a most dangerous word to which he always took exception. It was often used to mean somebody who knows someone but in intelligence terms it should, he argued, be used only for someone who was *criminally* associated with that person.[17] He provided the example of his brother looking at a car in a showroom. Suppose, he suggested, that it was under surveillance and his brother looked at a car and drove it away. Would his brother, he asked, be an associate of the people who sell the cars and an associate of people shown in a photograph with the car dealer?[18]

In the civil action, McGourlay was asked about the report. He said that the records at the No. 1 RCS were first examined to see if there was any information on Taylor but 'there was no reference to him'.[19] Then checks were made with the CIU at headquarters. He claimed that he received some information from there but cannot remember whether this was over the telephone or whether he was sent a typed document. No typed document, however, was presented in court from the CIU. But if CIU had indeed been contacted, as claimed, it was most odd that none of the Criminal Intelligence items held on Taylor and reproduced in the Sampson Report were included in the No. 1 RCS report. In particular, there was no mention of Taylor allegedly receiving stolen metal from the docks or the false information that Schiavo obtained a yacht called *Moriarty* from Taylor in payment of a gambling debt.

Similarly, there was no mention of any of the four items that Detective Inspector Patterson reported under the label 'Taylor's Pedigree', which were referenced in the undated report, Document 7, prepared by Richardson. At the time, Patterson was a member of McGourlay's No. 1 RCS, and one would assume that whoever prepared the intelligence report would have consulted with colleagues. This does not appear to have happened because the intelligence report did not note the most serious allegation of all, namely, the idea that Taylor was a minder for firearms used on jobs by the QSG or that he was a known associate of the IRA.

As there was no signature or official stamp on the report, there is, therefore, considerable doubt whether it was the original report or even a photocopy of an original prepared by the RCS and sent to Topping on 14 June 1984. McGourlay was unclear who had prepared the report. In the civil action, he pointed out that it could not have been him because he had written on it the comments 'known to me' and 'Number 4'.[20] Unsurprisingly, the report was referred to extensively by Anderton's defence counsel. At one point, Justice Owen became impatient with all the detail and asked: 'Would you like to tell me what the point is, then come back to it? It helps to keep awake.'[21] The point was no doubt to suggest that GMP had detailed information on Taylor's associates and alleged criminal activity in June 1984, which justified the subsequent investigation into Stalker.

A key question is where did all this information come from and when? It seemed unbelievable that only three days after Topping hearing about Taylor – a man with no criminal record – the RCS was able to collate a mass of information about him including the allegation that he was financing drug deals and laundering cash for members of the QSG. Item 15 – Brown's visit to Taylor's boat in Miami – may provide an explanation. Another visitor on the boat in 1981 was a man called Victor Roberts – a friend of Taylor's before they fell out. GMP, however, only interviewed Roberts in July 1985. This would suggest that the report was possibly another document which was produced after the setting-up of the DIU. McGourlay may have, indeed, prepared a report on Taylor as requested by Topping in June, but it was replaced by this more extensive version much later. This would explain why the report lacked the standard compilation procedures and why it was unsigned.

McGourlay's handwritten notes

McGourlay accepts that at some point he pulled together various items of information relating to Taylor. They were scribbled on top of an old No. 1 RCS intelligence report on Vincent Anthony Schiavo, dated 1 March 1984. In the civil action, Anderton's defence counsel suggested that the notes formed the basis of the 14 June RCS Intelligence report.[22] The document consisted of two typed pages relating to Schiavo with various handwritten notes on top of the typed report and a third page of handwritten notes on *plain* paper.[23] The notes on the typed report listed several items of information about Schiavo. It referred to Marbella and the boat *Sharama* (sic) having an American captain. It detailed how Schiavo had recently arranged, fraudulently, for the disposal of traveller cheques, how he was organising the movement of guns and drugs and was involved in the theft of Rolls Royce and Mercedes cars. The handwritten notes on the two typed pages referred to a number of people including the infamous Ronnie Knight, Micky Martin – a friend of Burton – and Semplicci.

There was, however, no mention at all of Taylor in the notes scribbled on either of the two typed pages. All references to Taylor were on the plain piece of paper. Here, the notes made specific reference to him and his business affairs: 'K Taylor, Vanlands (sic), J Swords'; 'Gambler, £5000, Sid Otty's';[24] and 'Moulton Street precinct Bank of Credit and Commerce'[25]. There was a reference to 'Treacle Charlie visits K. Taylor's premises and house'.[26] None of the items noted that Taylor was involved in any criminal activity except the very last, which stated 'KT believed to be storing guns'.[27]

There was nothing on the notes to indicate when they were compiled. In the civil action, Justice Owen suggested to McGourlay that if the notes formed the basis of the 14 June RCS report, they would have been produced sometime before or on 14 June. McGourlay, however, appeared confused and was not sure. He thought that not all the items listed in the notes were reproduced in the 14 June RCS report.[28] The most serious item, which was not reproduced, was: 'KT believed storing guns'.[29] If the notes had been used to compile the nineteen-item report, it is inexplicable why the most serious item of all is not included.

Stalker was taken through the notes in the civil action:

STALKER: Yes. Yes, I see it none of these are dated so I don't know when they have gone on. I suppose they could have gone on a considerable long time after 1984 but they don't seem to have. Certainly, most of those names have no significance to me. There is one mentioned at the bottom ... He had left the police force eleven years in eighty-four. Similarly, although it says at top of page 3 'K Taylor Vanlands', as I understand it, Taylor left Vanlands at least eight years probably ten years before that report was submitted. So, I am not sure of the value of those notes because I don't know who made them.

TABACHNIK: It looks as though they may have in fact formed the basis, on which other reports were prepared.

STALKER: I find it offends my sense of professionalism. It is probably the kindest thing I can say about it if there are no dates or signatures on it.

TABACHNIK: As I say it is scribbles on an intelligence document and that is clearly dated March 1984.

STALKER: Yes, but the scribbles could have gone on two or three [years later] we don't know.[30]

There was support for Stalker's insightful contention that the notes were perhaps written much later and therefore could not have formed the basis of the 14 June RCS intelligence report on Taylor. First, Burton reported the identical information that Taylor was 'storing guns' to GMP, but not until an interview in February 1985. He may have told the police about it earlier, in which case, given the seriousness of the information, it is inconceivable that there was no report. Yet none was produced in the civil action. Second, as noted above, Roberts did not tell GMP about Brown being on *Diogenes* in Miami, until 1985. There is, therefore, strong evidence to suggest that the notes – or perhaps only page three covering Taylor – were produced much later. Conveniently, in the absence of any dates, it could be suggested that the document was produced in June providing yet more support for GMP's official narrative.

Meeting with the Chief Constable

On 20 June, it is claimed, ACC Ralph Lees, the head of the CID, met James Anderton, the Chief Constable. It was suggested by Anderton's defence in the civil action that it was at this meeting that Anderton was informed of all the intelligence received on Taylor and Stalker in the preceding nine days.[31] For this to have happened, Topping must have related his information to his superior Lees sometime between 11 and 19 June. This would have given Richardson and Topping very little time to verify the information, much of it from Burton. Anderton's diary showed that he had been away in London prior to this date – it is not known for how long – but that on 20 June there was an entry stating that between 10.30 p.m. and 11.40 p.m. there was a meeting at his home re 'police inquiries', and the name Lees was circled.[32]

As a settlement was reached before Anderton was called to give evidence, neither the diary entry nor the nature of the discussion at the meeting were scrutinised in court. It could have been a meeting about some other police inquiry, as there appeared to be so many enquiries into corrupt police officers going on at the time. If the meeting did take place and Anderton was informed of the events, it is strange that he did not make a detailed record of what took place. It certainly contrasts with his behaviour from May 1985 onwards when he began to record detailed notes about his Deputy. Moreover, it was not until a month later that Topping wrote a letter to Lees which spelt out in detail the intelligence information on Taylor and Stalker, and suggested a course of action (Chapter 9). This would have been passed onto Anderton if proper procedures were followed. Why was this report necessary if Anderton had already been informed in a late-night meeting on 20 June and provided with the detail? The picture becomes even more confusing in light of a meeting two days later.

Heaton Park meeting, 22 June 1984

According to Peter Taylor, following the alleged Bridge Street conversation, Topping had 'grave' doubts about the conversation and arranged a meeting with Burton in Heaton Park.[33] Rightly, he needed to hear the allegations for himself and assess the credibility of Burton as an informer. Yet only two days earlier he had allegedly reported the information to Lees, who had then allegedly reported it to Anderton in their late-night meeting. The sequence of events, with Topping reporting the information upwards before checking it out, however, casts further doubt on the late-night meeting. Was it, as claimed, about Stalker or perhaps some other corrupt police officer? Another possibility is that the Heaton Park meeting did not take place, or involved a meeting about someone else.

Peter Taylor says that, during the Heaton Park meeting, Burton repeated the allegations about Stalker and said that Kevin Taylor was a member of the QSG as well as being chairman of the MCA. Topping confirms that he 'interviewed

Bertlestein on 22 June 1984'.[34] Peter Taylor then uses this point to refute any conspiracy theory. As it took place 'at a time when the Northern Ireland inquiry was still cloaked in great secrecy', he concludes that there was no possibility that Bertlestein, as he referred to Burton, 'could not have been prompted to lodge his allegations as part of a conspiracy to get Stalker out of Northern Ireland'.[35]

This suggestion would only hold true if Burton, and no one else, had alleged that Stalker was corrupt in the Bridge Street conversation. What makes it so difficult to assess the available information is that Richardson's diary entry makes no mention of Burton and there is no report of a Heaton Park meeting. Either Richardson and/or Topping failed to prepare a contemporaneous report or, if one was prepared, it has now suffered the same fate of so many of the key documents in this period and was lost or destroyed along with Topping's diaries.

Kwok Man document

Another suspicious document, dated 28 June 1984, recorded information from Burton who claimed he had spoken to the 'Head Chinaman' at the Kwok Man restaurant.[36] He was told that over the years the cost of providing free meals to the police had totalled between £20,000 and £30,000, and that Stalker had been going there for years with friends and colleagues, and had not paid. The information was recorded on a *plain* sheet of A4 paper and was undated, unstamped and not signed. Inspector Richardson was the officer who was most likely to have compiled the short report, yet again there was no record in his diary recording any call or meeting with Burton.

The document made similar allegations to those in an anonymous letter to GMPA in March 1984, claiming that both Stalker and Anderton had availed of freebies in the Kwok Man and that Stalker went regularly to casinos, including the Stanley Casino.[37] Anderton insisted that the accusation could not be ignored and that it should be properly investigated, overseen by HMIC. According to Stalker, Anderton was furious at the allegations. He always paid for himself and was deeply hurt by the comments. They were lies.[38] Stalker himself produced his credit card payments over the previous three or four years to show that he had always paid for his meals. He denied that he had ever been to the Stanley Casino.[39] That was the end of the matter as far as HMIC was concerned but it was raised again in Stalker's disciplinary inquiry in 1986.[40] In the civil action, Justice Owen asked why the accusations made about Stalker's friendship with Taylor could not have been treated in the same way as the allegation of free meals.[41] There has never been any satisfactory response.

* * *

These documents, like the documents examined in the previous chapter, are all problematic to some degree. They were unsigned, unstamped and most of the key information relating to Taylor was on plain paper. Remarkably, the RCS apparently managed to collate nineteen items on Taylor, a successful and well-known property developer, within three days of hearing his name after a round of golf which, apparently unknown to GMP and No. 1 RCS, suggested he was a major player in the crime scene in Manchester. It is impossible from the sloppy and scrappy way the reports and notes were prepared to ascertain when they were produced and by whom. Moreover, it is quite remarkable that the Chief Constable made no note of the meeting at which it is alleged his ACC informed him there was evidence that his DCC was corrupt. Once again there is evidence that the documents considered in this Chapter were also fabricated after the event to support the official GMP narrative that the investigation into Stalker started in May or June 1984. In this context, perhaps the word 'criminal' in 'criminal intelligence' is more appropriately read as an adjective rather than a noun.

.

Chapter 9

A Point of Disbelief

In July 1984, the Discipline and Complaints Department received a report from McGourlay linking Taylor to drugs. A car belonging to him was sighted outside a suspected drug-smuggler's house. If true, it supported, quite independently, informer Burton's claim that Taylor was involved in drugs. A few days later, Topping wrote a detailed letter to Assistant Chief Constable Lees outlining what he knew so far and making a recommendation on what should be done. The two documents further supported GMP's official narrative that there was sufficient evidence to begin an investigation into Taylor and Stalker in early summer. Once again, however, a detailed examination of the documents suggests that they may have been produced at a later date.

McGourlay's BMW report

McGourlay's report dated 12 July 1984 was short. It noted Taylor's home address incorrectly. It misnamed the name of the house as 'Woodrow Mill' instead of 'Wood Mill' and the name of the road was noted as 'Woodrow Lane' instead of 'Wood Road Lane'. Two careless errors. It recorded that two vehicles were seen in the grounds, a BMW registration number A180 LNC and a Fiat, registration number MRN 916T. It recorded that a check on the Police National Computer showed that they were owned by 'Listform' – another error. Following the check, a query was received from Detective Constable Robert Johnson, a member of the Drugs Squad, as one of the cars had been 'flagged' – a procedure which indicated that the same vehicle was already being watched and which informed the officer doing the check that another officer was already interested in it.[1] The Drugs Squad officer wanted to know the RCS's interest and was given an 'off-putting answer'.[2] The one-page report ended by noting that Taylor had a 'friend of rank' and 'the local lads do not like Taylor'.[3] As with so many other reports, it was not signed by the sender, nor initialled by the recipient – Topping. It was yet another document which aroused suspicions over authenticity.

The reason one of Taylor's cars was flagged was that it was seen outside the house of a suspected drug dealer and gambler – Mohammed Hanif, with an address at 30 Richmond Street, Ashton-under-Lyne. It was being watched by the Drugs Squad. There was, however, a simple explanation for the presence of Taylor's car – he had lost it in a gambling debt to Hanif. At the time, Taylor possessed three cars – the two recorded in McGourlay's report: the Fiat which was used by Taylor's caretaker, Trevor Goodwin, and the BMW, which was used by Beryl Taylor. A third car, also a BMW, registration FDK 821W, was used by Taylor himself. It was this car which he lost in the gambling debt and not the BMW noted in McGourlay's report.

Taylor instructed Derek Britton, his accountant, to complete a notification of sale or transfer to Hanif, which he did on 20 June 1984. All three cars had been registered to his company Mistform, not Listform. Once the notification of sale had been registered on the Driver and Vehicle Licensing Agency's (DVLA) computer, any police check on the PNC would show the current owner only – Mohammed Hanif – and not Mistform. It is understood that the name of the previous owner could only be obtained by writing to the DVLA. Thus, if this BMW was allegedly flagged after 20 June, the vehicle would have now been registered to its new owner and the police could not have known that it once belonged to Taylor. It was possible, of course, that Hanif was very slow in registering it and did not do so until after 12 July, when the report was prepared. This would explain the sighting, but it does not explain why the wrong BMW was noted in the report.

One possible explanation for the wrong BMW being noted in the report is that it was another document which was constructed much later. In May 1986, the police gained access to all of Taylor's personal files, following raids on his house and business premises. They included the transfer of sale document of the BMW used by Taylor to Hanif, the suspected drug dealer. This information would then have provided them with the opportunity to link Taylor to the drug scene. But in constructing a deceit, they made several mistakes: they noted an incorrect address; they misspelt the company's name, and most importantly, they noted the registration of the wrong car.

Meeting with Kerr

On the same day as McGourlay prepared the 12 July report, Richardson, from the Discipline and Complaints Department, supposedly visited 'A' Division and spoke with Detective Inspector William Kerr from the Drugs Squad, allegedly about the car which had been flagged on the PNC.[4] Unless McGourlay rang the Discipline and Complaints Department about the flagged car before submitting his report, Richardson would not have known about it when he visited the Drugs Squad, and the meeting was for a different purpose. But there was a further problem.

Kerr was asked about this meeting in the civil action, but he had no recollection of it. Mr Wells, Anderton's defence counsel, then tried to move quickly on, but was prevented from doing so. Justice Owen wanted to know the date. Richardson's diary entry was then produced for 12 July. But Kerr continued to be hesitant about the date of the alleged meeting. He pointed out that he always took his family on holiday during the first two weeks of July. Here is the exchange:

WELLS: My Lord the first contact that Mr Kerr had with Mr Richardson was when inquiries were made about a car registered to Mistform, one of Mr Taylor's companies. It was seen outside a street in Ashton-under-Lyne. Richmond Street was of interest to the drug [squad] because of who lived there.

J OWEN: Do you remember anything about that?

KERR: I can't remember that specifically sir. If Mr Richardson says that's the case, then there's no reason to doubt it. No.

WELLS: I'm grateful Mr Kerr if that's the case. Can I draw some things together?

J OWEN: Can we have a date for that because it might be …?

WELLS: Yes, my Lord 12 July 84.

FARLEY: My Lord, I don't want the witness to be misled. He did say to my learned friend that if that's in Mr Richardson's diary he would accept it and quite right to, but the diary entry was never put in…

J OWEN: Does it help, he's never seen the diary either.

FARLEY: But it does say why he went to see him.

J OWEN: Well if he can be given some details that might help.

FARLEY: If my learned friend put the diary entry, it may jog the witness's memory.

WELLS: By all means. I have no objection at all. It's item 273. It's dated 12 July 84.

J OWEN: Tell me where?

WELLS: 14.45, it says to A division.

J OWEN: At A division.

WELLS: To A division, spoke with the DI Kerr about re B. We'll hear in due course that's shorthand.

WELLS: And Mr Kerr, is it fair to say that so far as you can remember Mr Richardson never came to talk to you about anybody coded B?

KERR: I can't remember a code word B being mentioned to me.

WELLS: We can see 12 July 84. It's the same day as the document we've been looking at which mentioned Detective Constable Johnson's interest in the cars on the national computer. That's right, isn't it?

KERR: Yes.

J OWEN: We're back where we started from. You don't remember this but if he says that's what happened.

KERR: I'm just trying to contemplate what I was doing on 12 July 84 and…

J OWEN: Unless you tell me that it was your wedding day, I'm not likely to believe you can remember.

KERR: I can't remember. I am just concerned that I was actually there at the Drugs Squad because I always take the Wakes Week holidays at Bolton. It's the first 2 weeks in July ... I'm not for one minute suggesting John Richardson is telling anything other than the truth ... I really can't remember.[5]

Significantly, the diary entry recorded that it was a meeting about 'B' and not about the flagged car. Although Wells said that there would be reference to the shorthand in due course, this never occurred. But 'B' was shorthand for Burton throughout Richardson's pocketbook. If Richardson was seeing Kerr about the flagged car, as claimed, why was this not noted specifically in the entry? But did Richardson see Kerr or someone else on that day? There was not a discussion in court about the handwriting, but the name 'Kerr' could have been misread. Moreover, Kerr crucially was obviously doubtful that he ever met Richardson on the 12 July because he always took his family on holiday in the first two weeks of July.

Significantly, there was no mention in the Sampson Report on Stalker that Taylor's car had been flagged by the Drugs Squad. It would have increased the suspicion about Stalker's friend. Also, Peter Taylor made no mention of the BMW in either of the Panorama programmes broadcast in June and August 1986, although he did mention this detail in his book published in 1987.[6] The first traceable press report was in September 1986, when *The Observer* noted that 'the Drugs Squad confirmed that they were ... watching Taylor's BMW car'.[7] All of this adds support to the suggestion that the BMW report was created only *after* Stalker's removal in May 1986 and leaked to the press as part of a media operation, to show that its inquiry into Taylor was legitimate (Chapter 20).

Topping's letter

The next development in the official story apparently occurred a few days after the alleged sighting of Taylor's car. Topping sat down and wrote a long letter to ACC Ralph Lees. It was dated 17 July 1984. The letter began by asserting, in a confident manner, that Topping had over recent months been monitoring information from police officers and informants into claims that persons in organised crime in Manchester had been corruptly associating with police officers. He pointed out the obvious difficulties in obtaining evidence but did not wish to develop the point. He went on, beginning with a phrase popular with the top brass in GMP: 'Suffice it to say that I am now satisfied that there has been corruption on a large scale with that group of criminals known as the Quality Street Gang and members of the Regional crime squad including one of senior rank.'[8] He continued with a highly cryptic but crucial sentence: 'I would also not eliminate other detectives and police officers from a corrupt liaison with this criminal group.'[9]

Topping did not identify his informers which was most strange in a report destined for his CC. He pointed out that one of them was extremely close to the QSG and its criminal operations, and had once been Reginald Kray's chauffeur. It was obviously David Burton, who had on one occasion picked up Kray when he visited Manchester. But Burton and GMP subsequently turned this single lift into being 'Kray's chauffeur'. Topping's use of Burton's highly exaggerated description of himself as a chauffeur suggested that he wanted deliberately to boost Burton's credentials, or he was weak on assessing street talk. Topping then listed several criminals who were said to be part of the QSG, including Taylor, pointing out that, although 'many police officers do not normally associate Taylor with the QSG', his informer identified him 'as the financier of many of their large-scale operations', with a heavy involvement in drugs.[10]

One particularly 'disturbing aspect', according to Topping, was 'the increasing involvement of the QSG in drugs and a strong indication that the IRA was associating with them in this most criminal lucrative area'.[11] Top London criminals were also involved with the QSG because 'one of their boats *Sharama* (sic) has currently, on its passenger list, Ronald Knight'.[12] This information was only reported to GMP seven days earlier and logged in Vincent Schiavo's Intelligence Report (Chapter 7), but would it have been reported to the Complaints and Discipline Department?

Topping then noted that besides the QSG, 'the No. 1 man' in the drug scene in Northern England was Ali-Hag-Hussani, whom he described as 'extremely wealthy'.[13] His informer, presumably Burton, linked Hussani to Taylor. There was a further link, Topping argued, because 'a vehicle owned by Mistform' had been observed by members of the Drugs Squad in Aston-under-Lyne. But Taylor's BMW was seen outside of Mohammed Hanif's house and not at the address of Ali-Hag-Hussani. Topping, therefore, appears to have linked the wrong man to Taylor, or there was some connection between Hanif and Hussani – making the link to Taylor somewhat tenuous. There was a further problem with Topping's information. McGourlay had noted that the Police National Computer showed the car was owned by Listform not Mistform. How did Topping, only five days later, know that the correct name of the company was Mistform? Notwithstanding all these issues, the alleged 'flag' on one of Taylor's cars was proving to be a useful method of connecting him to drugs. Topping continued:

> That very roughly sets the frightening scene of one of the major aspects of serious crime in the Manchester area and brings me to what so far has been the most serious dimension coming from the information passed to me. Some weeks ago, my informant explained an association between a senior police officer who I will refer to as Mr Z and the Q.S.G. He was aware of a long-established corrupt police

involvement with a senior member of the Regional Crime Squad and Q.S.G. but was hearing from the street for the first time of a strong corrupt connection between Mr Z, James Patrick Monaghan and Kevin Taylor.[14]

Mr Z was Topping's pseudonym for his boss, John Stalker. Topping said he was surprised what he was hearing from the street, 'to the point of disbelief'.[15] Although he could not place much reliance on it, he could not forget it. But he went on to point out that *'following on the heels'* (emphasis added) of this information he learnt in confidence from McGourlay about the golf conversation.[16]

In the next and probably the most significant paragraph he said:

> I now have in my possession *documentary proof* (emphasis added) of Mr Z's association with Kevin Taylor. He has now in fact invited him to at least four social functions, which took place between March 1982 and April 1984 ... This openness it might be felt displayed a lack of knowledge on the part of Mr Z about Taylor's activities. Has he for instance met a seemingly respectable businessman not knowing of his background? I understand for instance that Taylor is a Tory party agent for this area ... I cannot accept that anybody who is so obviously astute as our Mr Z is not aware of Mr Taylor's background. There are of course intensive enquiries needed to test much of the information in my possession ... and his known criminal associates, but when account is taken of the link between Taylor, Q.S.G. ... it is extremely disturbing.[17]

The documentary proof in his possession were the mess dockets which Stalker had signed acknowledging his public attendance at the various GMP social functions with Taylor as his guest: the Spring Ball at Lancaster Cricket club, in March 1982; the St George's night dinner in April 1982; the Senior Officers' Mess dinner held at the University of Manchester in October 1982; and the St George's night dinner in GMP HQ in April 1984 (Chapter 6). But once again, would Topping have had this information in July 1984 or was this information only obtained much later?

Topping noted that the link between Taylor and the QSG, and the association between Mr Z and Taylor were 'extremely disturbing'. He concluded the report in prose which reflected the assertiveness and strategic thinking of a man who is full of confidence, arguing:

> What is clear is that this criminal ring must be smashed. It will, in my view, require a properly organised squad of officers, no more than ten, under the command of a senior officer.[18]

Topping had shown remarkable prescience. Just over six months later, GMP set up a special squad. He ended by apologising for the 'vagueness of the information which is reflected in the quality of this report' but claimed it was necessary to maintain confidence.[19]

In the civil action, Stalker appeared to accept that the report was genuine but was highly critical of Topping's proposal to form a squad of ten people. He said:

It was not the only approach, I would say on the information that is available there, [but] the effort that Mr Topping proposes to put into it. It would be wholly disproportionate certainly to strike off a superintendent in a team of ten for two years. It would be unheard of, unprecedented in police terms, unless there was very strong information. So, we go back to the information again: the informants of it, the value of it, and the officer handling him.[20]

Topping's letter painted the most serious and dangerous scene yet. It had all the ingredients of a Chief Constable's worst nightmare: widespread police corruption, involving his own Deputy Chief Constable; connections between several London criminals and the QSG; large scale drug and other serious criminal operations organised out of Manchester; and to crown it all, the involvement of the IRA. It relied on some of the information, but not all, provided in the previous alleged intelligence reports. Significantly, there were four new items of information. Burton was now described as having been Reginald Kray's chauffeur. Ronnie Knight – whose name was in McGourlay's scribbled notes only, and not in his submitted report – was recorded as being on the passenger list for *Sherama*. In addition, Topping had now obtained evidence of Mr Z's social engagements with Taylor. And, finally, the QSG were no longer simply associates of the IRA, they were actively involved with them in drugs.

Topping's comment – 'I understand for instance that Taylor is a Tory Party agent for this area' – raises serious doubts about how much he really knew about Taylor. While stating boldly that Taylor was very much involved behind a growing drugs scene in Manchester, he did not even know that he was Chairman of MCA and not an agent. According to Peter Taylor, Burton had informed Topping, during the alleged Heaton Park meeting in June, that Taylor was Chair of MCA, but now under a month later, Topping was wrongly noting that he was only a Tory Party agent.[21]

Crucially, the letter omitted information. There was no mention of Operation City, which was carried out by No. 1 RCS and involved the surveillance of the Monaghans and Schiavo brothers. Yet, despite the seriousness of the range of criminal acts – drug smuggling, theft of high-value mail, handling or disposing of high value loads and gun-running for the IRA – in which the targets were suspected of being involved, no concrete evidence was ever produced against the four (Chapter 4). Despite this, Topping in GMP was recommending another special squad to the smash the criminal gang in which Stalker and Taylor are now suspected of being involved.

Unquestionably, one of the more significant features of the letter was the order in which Topping claimed he received the two pieces of information suggesting that Stalker was corrupt. He claimed that his informant 'some weeks' ago was hearing of a corrupt connection between Stalker and Taylor. Presumably, this was the apocryphal information allegedly reported by Burton in the Bridge Street conversation and now repeated by Topping, in almost identical wording, from Donnelly's comment: 'He is Jimmy (Jimmy Swords) and Kevin's man.' Topping then stated, as if to create a public record of the fact, that 'following on the heels of this information' he learnt of the golf conversation from McGourlay. Yet, as shown, McGourlay was adamant that he reported the golf conversation to Topping on the morning of 11 June (Chapter 7). He was certain of the timing because he had spent the weekend worrying about the information he had received, and he wanted a senior officer to let Stalker know about the gossip on the street.

Stalker was examined on the order of the two events in the civil action by Taylor's counsel:

FARLEY: I am inviting you to consider what if Mr McGourlay's, if it had been the first information that had come to his [Topping] attention.

STALKER: Well, that seems to be the dates of the report... Mr McGourlay was 9th June, and the other informant supposedly street talk was on 11th June.

FARLEY: The order they reached Mr Topping's ears would be different.

STALKER: Well.

FARLEY: You don't know that of course.

STALKER: No.

FARLEY: But if they did come in that order, if it was golf club before top jolly... what do you make of that?

STALKER: I don't know what to make of it my Lord. I've not seen these documents. It is just very confusing and very confused. It seems to me that Mr Topping has set [off] a huge train of events that ruined so many lives on the basis of no information whatsoever. That's what it seems to me.[22]

The style of Topping's letter was notable. It suggested that a confident and assertive man, who had an excellent command of English, wrote it. In places, the style verged on the grandiloquent. For example: '*I have over recent months ... I will not develop this aspect further ... I have purposely included Taylor...*' There was also a marked use of modifiers between the subject and the verb: 'He has *these days* adopted something of an air of respectability'. 'He *clearly* is still active'. 'He has *in fact ...*' Moreover, the letter was littered with numerous clauses of concession: 'but *suffice to say* that I am now satisfied'; 'this openness *it might be felt* displayed a lack of knowledge'; 'There are *of course* intensive enquiries needed'. It also made much use of passive constructions: 'There are a number of criminals who *are said to be* part of the QSG'; '*it would be appreciated* that'. The final feature was the use of the adjective 'disturbing'. It was a word, or its derivative, which was subsequently used by Anderton in several documents in 1985 (Chapter 14). As Anderton had a confident and assertive writing style, could he have been involved in writing the document as part of the media operation following Stalker's removal? (Chapter 19).

There are two final points to make about Topping's letter. It was claimed that Lees, based on information from Topping, went to see Anderton about Stalker on 20 June (Chapter 8). If this occurred, why would Topping now be writing a detailed report to Lees? His letter did not begin with 'Further to our discussions' or some such phrase. It started with a clear statement that suggested he was informing Lees for the very first time of his worries and concerns about corrupt police officers, and Stalker in particular.

The second point is that there was no evidence that it was checked by a senior officer. Normal police procedures would demand that a document suggesting that the Deputy Chief Constable of their own force may be corrupt would be checked by one or more officers senior to Topping. At the very least, Anderton could have interviewed McGourlay but there is no evidence that he did so. This all adds to the suspicion that it was created at a later date. This would explain why it was on plain paper and there were no date stamps indicating when it was sent or when it was received.

Burton prison interviews, August 1984 to February 1985

It is very difficult to trace what happened from August 1984 until February 1985. It is as though the period has been air-brushed from the records of GMP. There was only one report noting some further intelligence on Taylor. Moreover, the loss of Richardson's blue books and the unavailability of Topping's desk diaries for the period mean that it is now impossible for anyone to verify any of the activities of two of the officers involved in investigating police corruption in GMP. The Discipline and Complaints Department, however, was not idle. By all accounts, they were extremely interested in David Burton. Notwithstanding the fact that several police officers considered him to be a pathological liar and a very dangerous informer because he recycled information, he was visited by different police officers on no fewer than eleven known occasions. The first interview took place on 4 September 1985 in a public house and then further interviews were conducted in Kirkham, Leeds and Lancaster prisons after he was sentenced for his part in the Cut Price Fraud scam (see Table 9.1).

There is an accepted procedure for visits to prison. Normally permission is required from a police officer of a higher rank than the one making the visit and approval must also be sought from the prison authorities. A form, noting the purpose of the visit, must be filled in and contemporaneous notes made of the interview, in accordance with Force Orders. Yet, in the case of the Burton interviews, GMP ignored all the rules. There was only one partially completed report of one of the interviews examined in the civil action. There was silence over the rest.

Table 9.1: *Interviews with David Burton between 9 August 1984 and 25 January 1985.*[23]

Date	Location	Officers
9/8/84	Belmont Public House	Not known
2/9/84	Belmont Public House	Sup Elder, Sols & Counsel
13/9/84	Kirkham Prison	Inspector Clarke
4/10/84	Kirkham Prison	Topping and Richardson
24/10/84	Leeds Prison	Topping and Richardson
29/10/84	Leeds Prison	Richardson and Russell
14/11/84	Lancaster Prison	Topping and Richardson
7/12/84	Lancaster Prison	Topping and Richardson
3/1/85	Lancaster Prison	Topping and Richardson
11/1/85	Lancaster Prison	Richardson
25/1/85	Lancaster Prison	Richardson

Topping first visited Burton on 4 October 1984. This is three-and-a-half months after it was claimed that he met Burton in Heaton Park about the allegation that Stalker was corrupt. It was an inordinate amount of time to wait before having a second interview with the informer making the allegation. The timing of this interview is significant as it coincides with events in Northern Ireland. Stalker and his team had discovered the existence of the hayshed tape 'in early winter 1984'.[24]

A month later, there were claims of phone tapping at GMP's HQ. It was reported that Anderton had made the disclosure privately to councillors following press reports that conversations were being recorded to trap 'a top-level mole'. Gabrielle Cox said: 'The Police Authority had discussed it and the Chief Constable has indicated investigations are taking place which could be of a disciplinary nature. It was decided to ask him to report to the committee when the investigation is over'.[25] There were no further reports. The fact that GMP were looking for a 'top-level mole' in relation to possible disciplinary charges raises the obvious question: was the mole believed to be Stalker?

What is extraordinary is that there is only one report of the eleven interviews with Burton in the public domain, despite the civil action. While there was no date on the lone report, it appeared to relate to the interview by Topping and Richardson with Burton in Lancaster prison on 14 November 1984. It noted that Burton informed Richardson that Ray Lamb, an ex-policeman in his late 40s or early 50s, had told him that 'he knows Kevin Taylor and does not agree with his activities in relation to drugs'.[26] An informer, therefore, provides hearsay evidence about Taylor from a corrupt police officer.

It was yet another document that is questionable and in all probability was constructed later. To begin with, why was it the only report, albeit partial, examined in the civil action from all the interviews with Burton between August 1984 and January 1985? Reports summarising the content of each interview would have strengthened GMP's case that its investigation into Taylor and Stalker was perfectly reasonable and not maliciously inspired and had started in the summer of 1984. Second, GMP had a standard form for reporting details of interviews. The top section required the officer to note the following details: Officer Reporting, Collar No., Warrant No., Section, Division, Sub-division, Date and who was the subject of the report. The report examined in the civil action, however, was compiled on a continuation sheet of a witness statement form. Consequently, none of the essential reporting information was noted and, in addition, the report was undated and unsigned. Stalker, in the civil action, was once again sceptical:

> He hasn't signed it. I don't, disagree, but I don't understand why it shouldn't be signed at the bottom. I obviously don't say it wasn't Richardson, but I just wonder why he didn't say it was Richardson. It is hand-written and it looks like that the pages are continuation sheets from Greater Manchester Police witness statement forms, but I would have thought it was easy enough to scribble an initial at the bottom. I accept it, but please I keep coming back to my sense of professionalism again.[27]

It is now known that in March 1985 Topping visited Burgess, who had retired from GMP in September 1984 as a direct result of stress involved in his single-handed investigation of the LFF.[28] He had suffered from acute anxiety and paralysis of his limbs. Topping wanted to know what Burton had told him in May 1983. Burgess repeated his account of the 'I have got your rat' conversation, which he had reported at the time to both the Fraud and the Discipline and Complaints departments.[29] Had someone discovered the 1983 report and informed Topping, making this, March 1985, the beginning of the investigation into Stalker and not June 1984? Was it significant that there was total silence about Burgess' report in the civil action and by Sampson in his report into possible disciplinary offences committed by Stalker? (Chapter 18).

No action

The period from July to December is not only remarkable for the silences, but also, given the intelligence suggesting that Stalker was corrupt, for the fact that no action was taken at any of three crucial points: when Anderton was allegedly first informed of the golf conversation on 20 June, on the receipt of Topping's letter of 17 July or after the many Burton interviews from August to January 1985. There were several options open to Anderton. He could have approached Stalker and said that he had worries about his friendship with Taylor and that he should distance himself immediately from him. But Stalker was clearly never approached. Another option was to ask one of his ACCs to discreetly investigate and carefully evaluate the information concerning Stalker. Third, he could have recommended that Stalker was immediately suspended and removed from the Northern Ireland inquiry and an outside force called in to investigate the allegations, but it was not until February 1985 that any serious action was taken. GMP then took the unprecedented step of establishing a secret unit to investigate its own DCC under the guise that it was collecting intelligence on the drugs scene. This was some seven months after the golf conversation. At no point was Stalker approached.

The procedures for the investigation of the behaviour of senior officers had been discussed and debated extensively within the police and in Parliament over the previous two years. The introduction of the Police and Criminal Evidence Act in 1984, made provision for a new system of complaints and disciplinary procedures against the police. It abolished the Police Complaints Board and established a Police Complaints Authority in April 1985[30] – at the very moment Stalker was being investigated by his own police force. The Act provided that, where it appears a senior officer may have committed a criminal offence or an offence against discipline and because of its 'gravity' or its 'exceptional circumstances', [31] the matter must be referred to the Police Complaints Authority. Under any interpretation of the wording of the Act, the circumstances in Stalker's case were either exceptional or grave. Once referred, the PCA must supervise the investigation.

Here was a senior police officer carrying out one of the most delicate and sensitive inquiries ever conducted into the activities of another police force, while at the same time, it was alleged that he was associating with criminals. In addition, it was alleged that these criminals had connections with the IRA. If any of this information was vaguely plausible, Anderton had a duty to set in train an investigation and inform the PCA. Yet he took no formal action until May 1986. This raises the distinct possibility that he was not told about the information until at least May 1985 when he started taking extensive notes on Stalker or, if he *was* told, he did not consider the information to be of any significance. It adds more weight to the probability that in fact there was no information in June and July 1984 apart from McGourlay's report of the golf conversation – and the rest was made up later.

* * *

There is little doubt that the six month period from June to December 1984 is the key to understanding the Taylor/Stalker affair. Yet many of the details are contradictory or problematic, and the silences and inaction profound. Anyone studying all the information would be surprised at its the poor quality, to 'the point of disbelief', to borrow Topping's phrase. While there is some documentation for the crucial two months in June and July, there is considerable doubt about its veracity. Topping's letter of 17 July is particularly problematic. It carried no stamp and contained information which was most unlikely to have been known at the time of writing.

In the near complete absence of any examination in the civil action of Topping and Richardson's interviews with Burton in the Autumn of 1984, it is impossible to know their true purpose. There are a several possibilities. The first is that Topping and Richardson were belatedly following up on Burton's allegation that Stalker was corrupt which he had allegedly made in June. The long period between the two events undermines this suggestion. The second possibility is that Burton was being reassured about his safety as it was known that he was being threatened. This suggestion is undermined by the fact that he is being reassured by the Discipline and Complaints Department rather than by the Fraud Squad who were handling the prosecution of the LFF and to whom he was providing considerable help.

The third possibility is that Burton was being encouraged to make false allegations against Stalker in order to remove him from the Northern Ireland inquiry. The timing would fit. Stalker's team had around this time discovered that the hayshed was bugged and that the shooting of Tighe and McCauley was captured on tape. Both the RUC and MI5 had the much to lose from his discovery. Was it perhaps the beginning of a conspiracy to remove Stalker?

Crucially, Richardson's blue books, in which he claims everything that Burton told him was recorded, are lost and Topping's diaries are no longer available. To lose one piece of documentation belonging to the principal investigators, as Lady Bracknell may have observed, is careless, but to lose two is a misfortune. Moreover, there is a total silence on Burgess' May 1983 'I have found your rat' report. It has been airbrushed from the narrative. And virtually nothing is known about the content of the interviews with Burton, in which Topping himself was heavily involved. All of this casts doubt on the integrity, honesty and professionalism of the officers concerned. But it also suggests that certain sections of GMP were part of a conspiracy to remove Stalker.

PART III
GET TAYLOR

Chapter 10

Secret Developments

IN THE AUTUMN of 1984, Stalker and his team in Northern Ireland pieced together various items of intelligence and reached the conclusion that the hayshed was bugged and that the killing of Tighe and the wounding of McCauley were recorded on tape. Stalker began to make demands for the tape, the names of any informers involved and their payments. Coincidently, back in Manchester there were several significant and far-reaching developments in GMP. The most important was the setting-up of a secret Drugs Intelligence Unit early in February 1985. This was preceded by several significant promotions stemming from retirements.

Retirements in GMP

At the end of September 1984, ACC Horan, who had overall control of 'V' Department – the main criminal investigation branch – retired. He had been a well-respected police officer with considerable investigative experience, who was a 'legend in his own time'.[1] Another person who retired around this time was CS Charles Abraham, who also had considerable investigative experience. ACC Ralph Lees, who had overall control of 'Y' Department – Discipline and Complaints – was given Horan's responsibilities and assumed overall control of 'V' Department. From several accounts, he was very close to Anderton, and this move increased Anderton's hold over this area of activity.[2]

Stalker was critical of Lees' move. While acknowledging that he was a good and effective uniformed police officer and administrator, Stalker pointed out that Lees had no CID experience and had not arrested anyone for a quarter of a century. He considered it not only inappropriate but also unfair for someone without even basic detective knowledge to head up a division of more than one thousand detectives and he expressed this view to Anderton.[3] Stalker's choice was Dan Crompton, who was subsequently appointed Assistant Chief Constable, but was put in charge of Administration and Technical Services. He resigned soon after and became Deputy Chief Constable of Nottinghamshire Constabulary. In 1995, he was appointed one of HM Inspectors of Constabulary.[4]

Topping's promotion

Each department was headed up by a Chief Superintendent and in January 1985 – a crucial period in the Taylor/Stalker story – Anderton made several significant changes. CS Topping, who was in the Discipline and Complaints Department, was appointed Deputy to Chief Superintendent Ken Foster, who was head of the CID, which was now under the overall control of ACC Lees. Anderton then decided to scrap the old structure of a head and a deputy head, and to create two equal positions with different responsibilities: one in charge of operations and the other, administration and policy. Topping was subsequently appointed to head up the former and Foster the latter.[5]

According to Stalker, Topping was another officer who lacked CID experience. He claimed that Topping had investigated less serious crimes while in his middle ranks and had little experience of investigating major crimes, such as murder or terrorism. As a result, he was 'markedly deficient in senior supervisory CID experience' and he could not have 'any confidence' in a man who had never investigated a murder in his life.[6] Foster felt he had not been consulted about these developments and the move devalued him 'as a man and as a detective'.[7] He retired from the force on 21 April 1985, shortly after Topping's appointment. Like DSgt Burgess, he retired early with a strong sense of injustice.[8]

To complete the picture, CS Thorburn was appointed to Foster's post in policy and administration. Thorburn was Stalker's second-in-command on the Northern Ireland inquiry and had carried out a large part of the investigation, including most of the interviews.[9] Thorburn would have been an ideal appointment to head up the operational side of the CID as he was one of the most experienced detectives in GMP and had shown, from the part he had played in the Northern Ireland inquiry, that he was a man of exceptional ability. Before going to Northern Ireland, he was seconded to the Home Office to develop the Holmes computer system for murder inquiries, which was then rolled out nationally.[10] Stalker could not understand why a man with extensive detective experience should be moved into an administrative post and replaced by a man who had little experience of investigations.[11] There must, therefore, have been a very strong reason to put him in charge of policy and administration rather than operations, particularly when, according to Stalker, the new head of 'V' department, Lees (like Topping), lacked investigative experience.

A trusted team

Other important staff changes involved the promotion of DS Grant to head up the Operational Support Group. This Group consisted of several different departments: the Stolen Vehicles Squad, the Commercial Fraud Squad, the Drugs Squad, SB, the Serious Crime Squad, the Cheque Squad, Force Criminal Intelligence, and Firearms and Explosives. Grant had been second-in-command to Topping in 'Y' Department and was once again directly responsible to him. The Commercial Fraud Squad, which had prosecuted Klapish and Burton, and subsequently played a key role in the investigation of Taylor, was headed up by Simons, Stalker's number three on the Northern Ireland inquiry, who had now been promoted to Superintendent. The Criminal Intelligence Unit was headed by Baythorpe.

These staff changes created a situation in which there was a distinct lack of investigative experience at the top of the CID and, indeed, at the very top of GMP – the Chief Constable also lacked detective experience (Chapter 6). How far this played a part in the subsequent developments in the Taylor/Stalker affair can only be surmised. Suspects are known to make up information on arrest to avoid being prosecuted or to reduce their time in prison. The interpretation of intelligence is a craft which is learned as police officers move up through the ranks. They learn to distinguish fact from fiction, to use key words in a consistent way and to judge how to interpret the meaning of expressions and phrases used by other officers. The lack of criminal investigative experience among the senior officers may therefore have led to a misreading of the 'dross' coming from the streets, particularly from one highly plausible informer.

The changes had several other results. They put in key positions several officers – Lees, Topping, Grant, Simons and Baythorpe – who had worked closely together either in the Discipline and Complaints Department or elsewhere. Topping and Simons were close. In their early policing career, they partnered each other and in 1969, when they were both feeling disenchanted with the long working hours, they gave in their notice and bought a lorry with the idea of going into the haulage business, but then decided against it. Topping's overall position was consolidated with trusted friends in positions of responsibility. Baythorpe possessed the dark secret of Robert Brown's wrongful conviction. Thorburn was side-lined although he was one of the best investigators in the force. If he had been the head of operations in the CID, he would, no doubt, have forensically examined all the information before jumping to a conclusion that Stalker was corrupt. Finally, the Chief Constable gained closer operational control than when Horan was in charge.

There were conflicting views about the extent to which Stalker, as deputy head of GMP, was consulted about these developments. The Chief Constable claimed that he talked to Stalker about the future role and structure of the CID, which needed substantial review. He then followed up the conversation with a memorandum dated 5 September 1984.[12] But Stalker had no recollection of the discussion or having seen the memorandum. When it was shown to him during the civil action there was considerable confusion over the document. Anderton's defence counsel initially claimed that it was Item 18,7e. Then it was suggested that it was in fact Item 18,7b. Mr Justice Owen said that he had Item 18,7a but not 7b. Whereupon the defence counsel handed up his copy to the judge, which was marked 18,7e. At this point Taylor's barrister complained that he had not got a copy of whatever document was being considered. Mr Justice Owen then asked for it to be photocopied. The confusion deepened when Mr Justice Owen emphasised that it was, in fact, Item 18,7b.[13]

What was clear from the interchange was that this highly important memorandum on the future role and structure of the CID was omitted from the bundle of documents held by both the Judge and the plaintiffs. The defence team had made sure that the plaintiff's solicitors and barristers would have had no time to consider the document within the context of all other documents or to consider its contents. Stalker was eventually presented with the memorandum.[14] He was asked if he now recalled the discussion that had taken place prior to it. He said that he could not recall it. Stalker was then asked if he was familiar with the document. He said that he had not seen it before. As perceptive as ever, Stalker pointed out that the Chief Constable had not signed it – a most unusual occurrence because Anderton always signed everything, even a photocopy of a document.[15]

Establishment of the DIU

The most important organisational change in GMP took place on 4 February 1985, with the setting-up of a special unit called the Drugs Intelligence Unit.[16] This occurred within months of Stalker discovering the existence of the hayshed tape and only a matter of days after Stalker's meeting on 28 January with MI5 in London, at which MI5 promised to co-operate fully with his investigation. This turned out to be manifestly a false promise as MI5 were later to destroy the only remaining copy of the hayshed tape. According to Anderton's defence in the civil action, the DIU was set up to investigate the activities of the QSG and their involvement in organised crime and drugs. In the words of his defence counsel, the primary purpose was: 'smashing the criminal ring'.[17] While Taylor was one of the targets, it has always been denied that it was established specifically to investigate the Taylor/Stalker relationship. There are, however, many factors which contradict this.

To begin with, 'DIU' was a misnomer. Typically, a drugs intelligence unit collates information and intelligence on all aspects of illegal drug use, but the DIU was focused on a specific group, the QSG. Stalker considered this focus to be 'fairly rare'.[18] The normal process is for a special squad to be established, which then sets its own targets. The introduction of the DIU was highly secretive and several senior officers were kept totally in the dark, including Stalker[19] and, initially, the Head of the Drugs Squad.[20] The Unit was located on the top floor of the Fiddes Building, just opposite police headquarters in Chester House. The most obvious place for it was, of course, within the force's Drugs Squad. It could then have been in close contact with those officers working in the same area. But, for reasons that have never been made clear, the DIU was to be kept, organisationally and physically, totally separate from the Drugs Squad.

Topping selected the DIU members with the help of Superintendent Grant. Initially four senior officers were recruited: DCI Norman Born, the head of the unit, DI Rodney Murray, DI John Richardson, and DI John Waterworth. Apart from Born, all of them had worked closely with Topping in 'Y' Department. Born had attended the two-day conference between the RUC and GMP in Belfast in January 1981 to discuss the LFF (Chapter 4). It is not known if other members of the unit had connections with the RUC. Murray was tasked with Waterworth to investigate drugs intelligence and Richardson with general inquiries.

It was an exceptionally top-heavy unit and would have drawn all the senior officers away from crucial work elsewhere at a time when overall recorded crime in GMP area had increased by 7.6 per cent over the previous year.[21] It was a close-knit team of officers whom Topping could trust. The absence of a body of foot soldiers to do the legwork, suggests that there was something unusual about its work. Typically, chief inspectors and inspectors have a supervisory role over sergeants but there was only one at the start – DSgt David Fiddler.[22] Stalker was highly critical of this level of staffing, describing it as 'wholly disproportionate' and he would not have permitted it.[23] The DIU was also made up of a similar composition of senior officers as the Butler inquiry, which Topping headed in 1979. This involved an investigation into corruption of detectives at Platt Road Police Station (Chapter 6). The similar top-heavy composition adds further weight to the suggestion that the DIU was principally about police corruption but under the disguise of collating drugs intelligence.

Initially, the Unit lacked any expertise in relation to the investigation of fraud. Richardson had no experience in the Commercial Fraud Squad and neither did the others. This gap was filled with the appointment of DSgt Keith Ware on 1 April. Ware came from the Commercial Fraud Squad and was a specialist in this area.[24] He had been involved in the prosecution of Klapish and Burton for the LFF. Ware was asked on one occasion whether he thought the DIU was 'over-ranked'. He quipped that he was the best-supervised sergeant in the force.[25]

Topping was in overall control and from the available evidence Lees' input as ACC crime appears to have been minimal for such an important development. Nothing has emerged indicating who precisely gave Topping the order to set up the DIU. There was no evidence in the civil action of a memorandum from any senior officer approving its establishment – an odd state of affairs. It was most improbable that Topping risked taking the decision himself to investigate his Deputy in case anything went wrong with the inquiry and he was left 'holding the baby', as one police officer expressed it.[26] A unit of this size required considerable resources, which needed to be taken from other departments. This naturally would have caused resentment.

The decision to set up the DIU presumably was approved by Anderton himself. Yet bizarrely, he continued writing positive references for Stalker during the summer of 1985. This raises the obvious question: did he know that one of its aims was to investigate his deputy and his relationship with Taylor, or had he been informed that its purpose was simply to investigate the QSG and drug smuggling?

DIU and the Drugs Squad

DI William Kerr, the head of the Drugs Squad, quickly became aware of the DIU. He had not been notified about either its establishment or its workings. He made enquiries of Grant, who was now in charge of the Operational Support Group. Grant informed Kerr that it was involved in work that would not interfere with the day-to-day work of the Drugs Squad. He accepted this and advised his own squad of the fact. Sometime later, he learned that cars which had been allocated to the Drugs Squad were now being used for surveillance work by the DIU. He submitted a report on the problems he was having trying to manage on the resources available to him. He was then summoned to see Topping.[27]

Kerr was informed in no uncertain terms that it was Topping's responsibility to decide on the distribution of vehicles and was dismissed from Topping's office. Later Kerr was ordered back to see Topping, who told him that he had decided to take him into his confidence about the work of the DIU, but whatever he said had to be treated in the utmost confidence. Topping then showed him a report and *two* dockets for officers' mess events with

Stalker's name on them. Kerr's overall impression from the document and the dockets was that Stalker was a 'crook'. He added: 'That was my over-riding impression and I found it surprising to say the least and extremely difficult to believe.'[28] Topping then remarked to Kerr: 'Those who have bitten the bag of corruption will pay the price.'[29]

In the civil action, Kerr was questioned about the two meetings with Topping and his concerns about the diversion of resources from the Drugs Squad to the DIU. He was first shown four officers' mess dockets and immediately said that he had been shown only two by Topping: one for the St George's night dinner and the other for the Spring Ball. He was then shown Topping's letter of 17 July 1984. It was implied by the defence counsel that this was the report that Topping had showed him. Kerr, however, said that he did not recognise it and anyway he distinctly remembered a document of two and not four pages.[30] Kerr's evidence therefore casts further doubt on Topping's letter and strengthens the argument that it was written at a much later date.

Stalker in the dark

Stalker himself had long been in support of a dedicated unit collating intelligence on the growing drug scene. The idea of specialised intelligence units was popular with some politicians. During the 1984/85 Miners' Strike, Margaret Thatcher instructed Chief Officers, via a senior Home Office official, to set up secret Public Order Intelligence Units to infiltrate and monitor groups and activities which threatened public order – an instruction which only some Chief Officers followed.[31] Whether this secret practice influenced the decision to set up the DIU will never be known. The crucial point, however, is that Stalker claimed that, as with the reorganisation of CID and the key appointments, he was kept in the dark.

This was challenged in the civil action. Tabachnik, Anderton's defence counsel, cross-examined Stalker on three documents allegedly stemming from the meetings of the Policy Review Committee (PRC). This met fortnightly and was made up of the most senior chief officers in the force, excluding the Chief Constable. Its role was to advise the CC on policy. The DCC normally chaired the PRC which dealt with resources and the financial implications of any new developments. Stalker considered it to be the single most important committee within the force.[32]

The first document was a minute from a meeting on 17 December 1984, which Stalker had chaired. It recorded the two objectives of GMP's drugs policy, but as Stalker pointed out, there was no reference to the establishment, function, or constitution of a DIU.[33] The second document was a minute from the PRC meeting on 6 February, two days after the setting-up of the DIU. It was numbered 24/85 and recorded that ACC Lees reported on the progress made in relation to drugs. It noted that the command structure of the Force Drugs Squad had been strengthened and that arrangements had been made for additional personnel to deal with the drug problem. Stalker said that he could not recall it, but again pointed out that 'there's no mention of a Drugs Intelligence Unit, separate from the Drugs Squad'.[34]

The third document was described as a 'Minute Sheet'. It was signed by Lees and addressed to the DCC. It was typed but had a handwritten number '24/85' in the left-hand corner. It noted: 'I have now formed an Intelligence Unit to cater for the targeting process of high-grade criminals involved in the trafficking of drugs ... May I discuss please?'[35] Stalker said that he could not recall the minute sheet or any discussion of its contents. Stalker was then asked to look at the handwritten number '24/85' on the minute sheet. It was claimed that it referred to the minute 24/85 of the meeting of the PRC of 6 February – refuting Stalker's claim that he was kept in the dark about the setting-up of the DIU. But as with so many documents in the Taylor/Stalker affair, there were problems.

To begin with, the minute sheet which was shown to Stalker was not dated 7 February, as claimed by Tabachnik, but 4 February. It was therefore unrelated to the PRC meeting minute 24/85.[36] Tabachnik backtracked and suggested that the number referred to the item to be discussed at the meeting. Stalker pointed out that if this were the case, the minute sheet would have been circulated to all members of the committee; it was only addressed to him. Finally, Stalker was asked what the policy was for putting a number on a memo, in this instance, a handwritten number. He replied: 'I have never seen it before, so I don't know whether that was policy, it was not my policy with documents, I did not do that.'[37]

Stalker's lack of knowledge of the DIU, the strange handwritten number and confusion over the date, all suggest that the minute sheet was constructed later to produce an official audit trail for the establishment of the Unit and to demonstrate that Stalker *did know* about developments, refuting criticism that the aim of the DIU was to investigate the Taylor/Stalker relationship. The handwritten number was added to the constructed minute sheet in an attempt to relate it the official 'Minute No 24/85' from the PRC meeting of 6 February, which made only a reference to the force objective relating to the misuse of drugs and failed to mention anything about a DIU.

After Thorburn had been appointed to head up policy and administration, he was asked to carry out a review of the use of resources. By this stage the existence of the DIU was known within the force. He asked the administration office to get him all the base documents in relation to the setting-up of the unit. None could be found.[38] Whereas Kerr was allegedly shown Topping's putative letter to Lees of 17 July 1984, the man tasked with reviewing resources allocated to the DIU was shown no accounts. Nor was he shown any of the PRC documents which supposedly recorded the decisions to set up the Unit.[39] His failure to obtain any records, coupled with the doubts over the PRC's documentation, suggests that, as well as Stalker, other members of the PRC – Dan Crompton, Bernard Divine, Robin Oake, David Phillips, and Paul Whitehouse[40] – were also kept in the dark over the establishment of the DIU and its true purpose. Everything pointed to the DIU being arranged in secret between Anderton, Topping and Lees.

* * *

All this evidence contradicts the idea that the DIU was established to investigate organised crime and the illicit drug trade. Rather, it points to the fact that the DIU's primary purpose was to target Taylor and Stalker. This would explain why Stalker, as Deputy Chief Constable, had no knowledge of this major policy development, which established the first ever dedicated intelligence unit in GMP. It would also explain why the head of the Drugs Squad was initially kept in the dark and why Thorburn, when tasked to look at resources, could not find any base documents on the formation of the Unit. Furthermore, it would explain why the DIU was top-heavy and its size and composition was almost identical to the unit which was set up to investigate police corruption in the early 1980s.

The only document that contradicts this explanation is the 4 February minute sheet, noting the formation of a unit to target drug trafficking. But in all probability, this was yet another document created after the event in order to produce an audit trail which supported the official narrative that the DIU was established to investigate the trafficking of drugs. Finally, the failure to make Thorburn, who was by far the most experienced investigative officer, head of CID, was an inspired decision, because it cleared the way for the investigation into Stalker without Thorburn being able to question it.

Topping's promotion to head up the operational side of the CID, while supervising the DIU investigation of Taylor and Stalker, placed him in a powerful position. His close friendship with Simons, who was number three on Stalker's investigatory team in Northern Ireland, established a direct personal connection between the two investigations. In such a situation, it would be surprising if Simons did not keep Topping informed of Stalker's investigation in Northern Ireland and the specific difficulties it was facing gaining access to the tapes and details of the informers. Similarly, it would be surprising if Topping did not tell his close friend of the investigation into their own Deputy Chief Constable.

.

Chapter 11

Death of the Informer

ONE OF THE FIRST tasks carried out by the newly formed DIU was to interview David Burton, the blowerman in the LFF in Belfast and police informer – or in popular parlance – a tout. The police carried out taped interviews with Burton on 7, 14, 21 and 26 of February and 7 March 1985.[1] All five interviews took place in prison while Burton was serving a two-and-a-half-year sentence following his conviction in September 1984 for his part in the LFF. Four interviews took place in Lancaster prison, where he had been moved following concerns about his safety in Kirkham.[2] The last interview took place in Preston prison. This brought the number of known interviews with Burton since August 1984 to sixteen. Exceptionally, the five new interviews were conducted by two senior officers – DI Richardson and DI Murray. The rank of the officers was unusual as junior officers normally carry out this sort of task. Unlike all the previous known interviews and prison visits with Burton in 1984 – for which there was no record of what was said – these interviews were recorded on tape.

Tape tampering

In the 1970s, there were several high-profile miscarriages of justice cases, in which there were allegations of incomplete, inaccurate, and fabricated defendant statements and false confessions due to coercive police pressure.[3] The government established the Royal Commission on Criminal Procedure to examine whether changes were needed in England and Wales. It reported in 1981 and led to considerable debate.[4] In 1984 the government enacted PACE, which made substantial changes to criminal procedure based on the Commission's recommendations. One significant change was the provision for the SoS to issue a code of practice in connection with the tape recording of suspects. But neither Burton's unreliability, nor the broader debate about taking accurate records of what is said during police interviews, had an impact on GMP and on the way in which the interviews with Burton were conducted.

An ordinary hand-held tape recorder was used for the Burton interviews and the tapes were not calibrated with time announcements. They were all subsequently transcribed, with many transcription errors. These were corrected by Anderton's defence team. The DIU had analysed the content of the tapes and indexed all the information onto cards. Overall, the 243 pages of transcript required over 370 cards to index and cross reference the information.[5] The transcription was not, however, a full record of the interviews.

One of the tapes was missing, perhaps lost or deliberately destroyed.[6] It is not known which of the five interviews it covered. Topping attended the second interview. Was this the tape that was missing? If so, what was the purpose of his visit? Was he hearing at first-hand what Burton was saying about Stalker or was he there to reassure Burton about his safety, as it was known he was being threatened at the time for informing on Klapish?[7] Neither of these reasons would have required the destruction of the tape. Did it show that Burton was being rehearsed or did it contain something that contradicted the GMP official narrative?

The tape recorder was turned on and off at various points during the interviews and, from the interruptions, it was obvious the interviewers were using an *aide-mémoire*. The interview on 7 February provided the first clue that the officers were using a list of names or incidents to guide the interviews. On one occasion, Richardson interrupted Burton and said: 'Right, just start it off with the names.'[8] Later, Burton referred to: 'Everybody on your list'.[9] In another interview, Richardson prompts Burton: 'We're talking about anything else to do with this man known as Febb' – the code name used by the DIU for Stalker.[10]

During the five interviews, Burton confirmed three pieces of information listed in previous documents and insisted at a number of points that the information would already be noted in various police officers' notebooks. The first related to the alleged Bridge Street meeting on 11 June. Burton started off by saying: 'Oh yes, I came out of Millers one day ...', and then he gave a description of meeting with Donnelly and the 'top jolly' conversation.[11] The 'Oh yes' suggested that he was responding to a prompt or question put to him by one of the two interviewers. He then emphasised that this was the first time that he had heard of Stalker's name, he didn't know him, and he had never seen him. Yet in 1983, he had informed Burgess that it was Stalker who had blown out the arrests in the LFF. His responses, however, corroborated the description of the Bridge Street conversation noted in the undated report by Richardson, Document 7, and the detail in Topping's 17 July letter, which obliquely referred to information he was hearing from the street – two documents that had the appearance of being fabricated.

The second significant piece of information was that Burton confirmed McGourlay had indeed asked him if he knew a high-ranking police officer named Stalker. McGourlay had denied this fact to the Rothwell inquiry (see Chapter 23) but admitted his lie in the civil action.[12] He may have also lied to Richardson because Document 7 noted specifically that McGourlay did *not* mention Stalker's name to Burton. In the interview, Burton initially claimed that having reported the Bridge Street conversation, McGourlay phoned him up that night and asked him about Stalker. But he then corrected himself and emphasised that it was the day after that McGourlay phoned him, adding 'luckily the day before McGourlay asked me this, I told you'.[13] It was a very odd comment. Why would a police informer consider it luck to have reported the Bridge Street conversation the day before McGourlay phoned him unless he was told to? He was most unlikely to have grasped the significance of this order of events, but to the police it was essential to place McGourlay's phone call after the reporting of the Bridge Street conversation otherwise it could simply be seen as recycled police information.

The third piece of significant information concerned firearms. It will be recalled that Burton told Patterson in 1982 that Taylor was minding guns for the QSG – information which Patterson checked out and dismissed, yet it was reproduced by Richardson in his undated report, Document 7 (Chapter 7). Burton now claimed on tape in February 1985 that he was shown a box by members of the QSG containing Israeli-designed and manufactured Uzi machine guns. Burton appears to have embellished his original story that Taylor was a minder of guns into a much more sensational one about the QSG hiding Israeli machine guns.

Perhaps most important of all, Burton claimed that he told Potts, Patterson and McGourlay in 1981 that the QSG had an ACC on a pension.[14] Sampson could find no support for this. Neither McGourlay nor Patterson could recall Burton referring to an ACC. Burton did, however, make allegations in relations to 'Senior Officers', but did not name them. Potts had no recollection of ever meeting him.[15] Burton, as we have seen, made the same allegation in the 'I have found your rat' conversation in 1983, but on that occasion named the ACC as Stalker.

Topping's letter 9 March

On 4 March 1985, shortly after interviewing a very senior RUC officer under caution,[16] Stalker sent Myers a brief that spelt out in detail the position that his Northern Ireland inquiry had reached and what more needed to be done. He also sent a copy to Anderton.[17] On 7 March, the police carried out the last taped interview with Burton. Two days later, on 9 March, Topping wrote a handwritten and very revealing note to Lees. It read:

> Sir, Brief notes to up-date you in relation to Taylor and Febb. Much of the information has yet to be tested, of course, and an in-depth study of Taylor's background is currently underway. A great deal is now known about the other key members of the QSG, but I have not yet decided our line of attack.[18]

Unlike so many other documents presented in court in the civil action, this one had all the hallmarks of being genuine. It was signed by Topping, now head of operations, and date-stamped by the sender and the recipient. Following reorganisation of the senior command structure, the head of operations and the head of policy and administration, were created as two equal positions. Yet, according to Stalker, the date-stamp indicated that Topping did not regard himself as on an equal footing with Detective Superintendent Thorburn, head of policy and administration, but in fact above him and second in command to Assistant Chief Constable Lees.[19]

The first sentence in the note made it unambiguous that one of the key objectives of the DIU was to investigate 'Taylor and Febb' – Febb was the secret codename for Stalker.[20] The note provides official confirmation that from February 1985, Stalker was being investigated internally. The new procedures, where a senior officer was suspected of a crime or disciplinary offence laid out in the Police and Criminal Evidence Act 1984, were being ignored. Junior officers were instructed to investigate their own Deputy Chief Constable under the disguise of investigating drugs.

The expression 'currently underway', to describe the in-depth study of Taylor, clearly implied that it had just started. Similarly, the phrase 'much of the information has yet to be tested, of course' left no doubt that it was a new investigation.[21] Topping's note, therefore, leaves little doubt that GMP only began to take a serious interest in Stalker and his relationship with Taylor in February 1985. The timing is critical. It came *after* intense demands by Stalker to be given key information about the informers involved in providing intelligence for the hayshed shootings – intelligence which Hermon refused to give, claiming that it was covered by national security, and it was also only a few weeks after Stalker had met MI5 in London.

In the civil action, Stalker was asked what inference he would draw from Topping's note as to the purpose of the DIU. He was unequivocal in his reply:

> Dated as it is so soon after the formation of the DIU and inferring as it does in the first line 'brief note to update you' my inference is that Taylor was the subject of investigation from day one of the DIU, within a very

short time, within a week of the DIU being set up. And the indications are to me, is that not too much consideration had been given to investigating anyone else.[22]

Topping's note also casts further doubt on the authenticity of his 17 July 1984 letter to Lees in which he alleged that there was a corrupt relationship between Stalker – codenamed Z on that occasion – and the QSG. In that letter he apologised for 'the vagueness of the information', yet nearly seven months later, notwithstanding the seriousness of what was being said, he admits that the information still needed to be tested.[23] Moreover, the letter argued forcefully that the criminal gang must be 'smashed' and recommended the establishment of dedicated team of officers for the task. Yet in this much later note Topping is undecided on his 'line of attack'.[24]

Topping's note was accompanied by a considerable amount of information on Taylor and Febb and hence his reference to them as 'brief notes' was very misleading. They covered three pages and contained no fewer than 35 items of information, which have been reproduced in Table 11.1 and Table 11.2, together with the probable source.[25]

Table 11.1: *Ten items relating to 'Kevin Taylor and Mr Febb'.*[26]

Item	Source
1. Informant B states that in 1981/1982 Taylor, Donnelly, Trickett, Schiavo, Monaghan and James Riley all went for a five-week holiday in Miami and whilst there stayed with Angelo Dundee, ex-manager of Muhammed Ali with believed Mafia connections, at his home. Also present was an associate of the QSG....	Burton interviews
2. On the 18 February 1985 Kevin Taylor and Angelo Dundee were guests of Mr Febb at the senior officers' mess in Chester House.	GMP
3. Donnelly has told informant B that Febb is Taylor and Swords man.	Burton interviews, Bridge St conversation
4. Mr Febb attends sporting venues with Taylor including ...	Burton interviews
5. Mr Febb speaks of dining with Taylor in the film exchange at the end of January 1985.	Burton interviews
6. Mr Febb may have been introduced in Peter Jessop's wine bar as John.	Burton interviews
7. Believed Mr Febb handling of nationality inquiries would not bear scrutiny.	Burton interviews
8. Taylor and Jack Trickett thought to have been in the company of a top jolly.	Burton interviews
9. Taylor and his wife were guests of Mr Febb at Spring ball on 19 March 1982	GMP
10. Mr Febb visited parties at Taylor's house and seen by Wareing there.	Golf conversation

Table 11.2: *Twenty-five items relating to 'Kevin Taylor'* [27]

Item	Source
1. 15 June 1983 is alleged to have owned a six-ton yacht Moriarty in Marbella Spain … debt.	Burton interviews
2. Owns large yacht moored in Miami.	Burton interviews
3. Was in partnership with Monaghan in Vanlands in early seventies.	Burton interviews
4. Believed to be a partner with Monaghan in villas in Marbella.	Not known
5. Suspected of laundering cash for James Monaghan and Vincent Schiavo …	RCS Report 14.6.84, Burton interviews
6. Michael Roy Brown suspected of being heavily involved in drug organisation in Lebanon and Morocco is associate of Taylor and is believed to have visited him at his boat in Miami.	RCS Report 14.6.84, Burton interviews
7. Known supplier along with James Monaghan of monies for drug importation.	Document 7, Burton interviews
8. Loans money to gamblers at large interest rates.	Document 7, Burton interviews
9. Minder of firearms used on robberies by QSG.	Document 7, Burton interviews
10. Known associate of IRA members through connections with Mark Klapish.	Document 7, Burton interviews
11. The golf conversation.	McGourlay, 11.6.84 Document 7
12. Holds parties at his home address after boxing promotions. Jimmy Donnelly visits there.	McGourlay, 11.6.84 Document 7
13. Vincent Schiavo laundered proceeds of several bank robberies through companies owned by Taylor.	Not known
14. Taylor and al Jaizani believed to have financed public house in Glasgow bought by Rob Carruthers.	Jessop Doc 2
15. Seen drinking with Peter Jessop in the wine bar.	Burton interviews
16. Taylor's alleged political ambitions.	Not Known
17. Sighting of Taylor's BMW outside of Hanif's house.	RCS Report 12.7.84
18. Extract from the Manchester Evening News.	MENS
19. Owns MBE properties now trading from two St. John St.	Not known
21. Reference to Godwin, who was Taylor's odd job man.	Burton interviews
22. Police at Ramsbottom say that Taylor does not associate with local police.	RCS Report 12.7.84
23. Maund thought to be an associate of Taylor.	Document 7 Burton interviews
24. Sold Moulton Street precinct for £2.75 million.	Not known
25. Referred to in telephone book from Joseph Monaghan's house.	Not known
26. Stayed at the home of Angelo Dundee with Donnelly Trickett Schiavo Monaghan and Riley in Miami.	Document 7 Burton interviews

The items, as can be seen, were a mixture of bold statements, suspicions, and guilt by association with suspected criminals. Once again, there was no attempt by the DIU to evaluate or grade the information. At that time, the Drugs Squad under CS Kerr had introduced a system of grading all information. The quality of the information would be graded from A to D and the reliability of the source from 1 to 4.[28] Yet, here was a team composed of a Chief Inspector, and three Detective Inspectors producing a document for Topping, who simply forwarded it to Lees, with a note saying that much of it needs to be tested. There appears to have been no attempt by Lees or Topping to ask for any supporting evidence to any of the items.

There were several certainties, but no evidence to back them up: 'Loans money', 'minder of firearms', 'known associate of IRA members', and 'laundered proceeds'. Stalker in the civil action took objection to the word 'known'. He pointed out that its use meant that the information had gone beyond the 'informant stage' and had moved into the realm of evidence. He added: 'It was not a very impressive document to be emanating from any sort of detective, never mind an experienced one.'[29]

Most of the information came from Burton (column 2). In Table 11.1, apart from the golf conversation and two GMP items, all the information linking Febb and Taylor came from the Burton interviews. Similarly, Burton was the source of most of the items on Taylor in Table 11.2. Of the 25 items, it is known that Burton provided the information for at least fourteen. Of the three most serious pieces of information relating to Taylor, all came from Burton. They had been reported to Patterson in 1982 and were found to have no substance: 'minder of firearms', 'known associate of IRA members' and 'known supplier ... of monies for importation of drugs' – all items which had been repeated in Richardson's Document 7.

Of the remaining eleven items, the source was unknown for six. McGourlay supplied the information for two items and the information for another came from a handwritten document by Richardson recording that Taylor was observed drinking in the wine bar owned by Peter Jessop. Only the first page now exists – all the other pages had apparently been lost. Stalker was once again highly critical of the single page. It was another example of poor detective work and it was on an official form normally used for a completely different purpose.[30]

When Stalker was presented with items of information relating to 'Kevin Taylor and Mr Febb' in the civil action, he was furious. 'These are absolute lies from beginning to end insofar as they relate to me.'[31] He drew attention to the fact that the Burton interviews had taken place when he had reached the most critical part of his investigation and was demanding access to the hayshed tape.

Tabachnik, Anderton's defence counsel, tried to insist that the information needed to be evaluated:

TABACHNIK: I understand … but what link do you say that there is between that and these interviews that were taking place with Burton over February and into March.

STALKER: The link is obviously for others to decide but as far as I can see they coincide at a particularly crucial time. I'd like to know, for example, why the decision to see Burton at this particular time, to take a statement of such great length from him and what the connection between what he said and the strength of what he said had in relation to the point I'd reached in my RUC investigation. I mean in February '85 it was well-known what I was finding and what I was about to say, and suddenly this man Burton appears, to have appeared from nowhere, and becomes very important. That's all I have said.

TABACHNIK: We've already seen that in the middle of '84 he was being interviewed and giving information in relation to you and Burton (sic).

STALKER: Well, he was being seen in relation to chit chat and little bits of information. This was extremely expensive in terms of resources … to sit down with a man in prison and take down reams and reams of transcript from him … I'm not in this witness box to say I can specifically say there was a connection. All I say is that it was a particularly crucial time of my investigation when Burton became important.

TABACHNIK: Are you or are you not saying that there's a connection.

STALKER: I say that on the balance of probabilities within my mind there is.

TABACHNIK: I see. What do you say the connection is?

STALKER: The connection is that a group, that a squad, that hadn't hitherto been formed was suddenly formed at exactly the same time as my Northern Ireland investigation involving very high levels. Until then it had been relatively low ranks. In early '85 I was dealing with the Chief Constable and Deputy Chief Constable amongst other people, who had been the subject of some very intense questioning by me. Here we had suddenly a squad formed for no apparent purpose other than to go and see Burton who had information or, so we are led to believe, about me.

TABACHNIK: Are you saying for example that the people who were conducting these interviews Murray and Richardson knew of the state of your inquiry in Northern Ireland.

STALKER: Probably yes but I can't say for sure.

TABACHNIK: How do you suggest that they would have come to know that.

STALKER: Well, there was no secret about it. I'd been making reports for some 12 months copying most of the letters that I sent to the RUC to the Chief Constable to Anderton and he may, I don't say that he did, but he may have passed that information on via Topping to the two detectives I have no idea.

TABACHNIK: As far as you know the two detectives would have had no direct access or knowledge to what was going on in Northern Ireland.

STALKER: They shouldn't have had there was no need for them to have. I can't say that they didn't.

TABACHNIK: What are you suggesting happened that in fact Anderton called them in and had a chat with them and said dig up the dirt on Stalker.

STALKER: No, it would be much more subtle than that my Lord. If it were to happen, there would be a half brief to those officers to go to the prison and see what they could find out with specific reference to Taylor and myself.

TABACHNIK: Are you suggesting that Burton himself was in on this and was involved in deliberately trying to supply the dirt.

STALKER: As I see it Burton was resurrected as it were from papers, that were in police possession from three to four years earlier, perhaps even 12 months earlier, when the information he'd given was regarded as worthless ... It suddenly became an opportunity to see him at great length over many days. Two experienced detectives with tape recorders to obtain information about me. I can put it no higher than that.[32]

Stalker was, therefore, of the strong opinion that the information given by Burton years earlier, but which was regarded then as useless, had been resurrected. There was much to support this view. Certainly, Burton's most damning allegations – Stalker's corruption, Taylor's drug smuggling, minder of firearms and financier for the QSG, and the connection between QSG and IRA – had been recorded by the police starting in 1982 and no action was taken. Although Burton was interviewed on several occasions in 1984, it was, therefore, not until February 1985 that there was a record of what he was telling the police when he was interviewed at length. But no assessment can be made of the content because he was obviously primed on occasions throughout the interviews, making it impossible to distinguish between information given freely by Burton and information given to him by the police.

The answer to Tabachnik's question to Stalker, 'Are you saying for example that the people who were conducting these interviews, Murray and Richardson, knew of the state of your inquiry in Northern Ireland', is crucial to assessing whether there was a conspiracy to remove Stalker. Stalker said that he could not be sure. But was he aware of a story in the *Manchester Evening News* in October 1984 that phones were being tapped in the GMP's HQ and tapes were being passed to the Discipline and Complaints Department (Chapter 9)? If the story was correct and Stalker's phone was included in the surveillance operation, Murray and Richardson would have been very much aware of the difficulties Stalker was experiencing in Northern Ireland.

Burton's death

Unfortunately, none of Burton's information could be tested in court because he died, aged 40 on 14 March 1985 in Preston Prison, a week after the conclusion of his fifth interview. Before his death various rumours had been circulating within the criminal fraternity in Manchester suggesting that perhaps someone was going to 'top him'.[33] At the time, he had already received one threatening letter while in prison, and both his mother and his girlfriend, Elizabeth MacDonald, had been intimidated. Burton, of course, had several enemies, particularly those whom he had told the police about, such as Mark Klapish, who was also in prison serving a four-year sentence.

Joseph Monaghan was another who was angry. Burton had implicated him in the LFF but then refused to sign a statement supporting his allegations. Although Monaghan was prosecuted for offences relating to the LFF, the jury could not agree on a verdict and he walked free. After the Taylor/Stalker affair became public knowledge in 1986, there was some speculation that Burton's death was contrived by one of his enemies or even MI5. The coroner nevertheless concluded that he had died from myocardial infarction, Coronary Thrombosis and Coronary Atheroma. In short, he died from 'natural causes'.[34] There had been a history of heart trouble in his family and his father had also died at a very young age.[35]

Burton's funeral was arranged quickly to observe the Jewish tradition of conducting the burial within 24 hours of death. He was buried the following day on the outskirts of Manchester at the Agecroft Jewish Cemetery on Langley Road in a grave prepared and tended by an Irishman from county Clare.[36] His inscription reads:

David Bertlestein
A beloved son who passed away March 14 1985
Aged 40 years
Deeply mourned by his devoted mother,
Uncle, aunts, relatives and friends.
Too sadly missed to be forgotten.

Anderton's letter to Myers

On the very same day Burton died, Anderton claimed he wrote a letter to Myers. This was a week after Topping sent his memo and the three pages of apparent 'intelligence' on Stalker and Taylor to Lees. No signed or stamped letter from Anderton was produced in court. Instead, Stalker was asked to examine what was claimed to be the draft of a letter prepared by Lees for Anderton to sign. This provided the first piece of evidence that Anderton was, at this stage, aware that his Deputy was under suspicion. Strangely, it was only a draft letter. Why was it not possible to produce the actual letter? As with so many other documents, the obvious question arose: was it authentic?

The draft letter, dated 14 March 1985, read as follows:

> You will know that one of the principal objectives of my force this year is to tackle the problem of the increasing misuse of controlled drugs and in order to make an effective effort in this regard ...

> The issue does however go deeper than that because I have become increasingly concerned about the activities of what perhaps could be described as a crime syndicate locally based who have enjoyed considerable financial reward from crime orientated matters in recent years. Initial intelligence indicates the syndicate are now channelling ... Spain. Evidence exists of an IRA connection, and it is also possible that members of this group have taken advantage of a close liaison with a senior police officer.

> Whilst I have mentioned the increase in the size of my force Drugs Squad ... people.

> You may wonder precisely why I am drawing these developments to your notice. [it is difficult] to present tangible evidence to support [what is clearly a matter] for cause for concern. People to whom I refer either have a considerable history of criminal activity ... Manchester area. It follows, therefore, that as the inquiry progresses, particular issues will emerge, which could be the source of considerable embarrassment in certain quarters ... nationally.

> While I know you will appreciate that it is not altogether necessary for me to give precise details of the persons to whom I refer ... I am mindful of my personal position in this matter ... in the inquiry.[37]

There were so many revealing but contradictory features in the letter. The most obvious was that this draft letter was very cryptic. The wording indicates that the draft was a formal acknowledgement of earlier conversations. It was obvious that Myers already knew that it was Stalker and Taylor who were under investigation. The wider implications of GMP's investigation into the two men were anticipated in the comment that, as the inquiry progresses, issues will emerge which could be the source of 'considerable embarrassment in certain quarters ... nationally'.[38]

The second significant feature was that Anderton had become 'increasingly concerned about the activities of what perhaps could be described as a crime syndicate locally based'.[39] But suspicions about the QSG had been a concern of GMP for many years. DI Wilson, in seeking permission to target the Monaghan and Schiavo brothers in 1982, used similar words and said that they 'make up the inner circle of a crime syndicate'.[40] Wilson also noted that he suspected that they were involved in drug smuggling and had connections with a police officer. In his putative 17 July 1984 letter, Topping also noted concerns about the QSG. Yet only ten months later Anderton was apparently writing to HMIC saying that he has become 'increasingly concerned' and that '*initial* (emphasis added) intelligence' indicates that the syndicate was operating from Spain. So, what has increased the concern over the period? The only new 'intelligence' had come from a series of taped interviews with informer Burton. No other intelligence of any significance had been received in the ten-month period.

The third feature, as pointed out by Tabachnik, Anderton's defence counsel, was that while Anderton was saying that there was 'a cause for concern', he was also saying that there isn't 'tangible evidence to support it'.[41] Stalker immediately pointed out the obvious contradiction. Here was Tabachnik presenting document after document to suggest that there was very strong evidence to support an investigation into Stalker in June 1984, yet here was Anderton allegedly writing to his superior in March 1985 saying that there was no tangible evidence.

The fourth feature was the grandiloquent style of the draft letter and the use of the personal pronoun: 'I have become increasingly concerned'; 'Whilst I have mentioned'; 'You may wonder why I am drawing these developments …'; 'People to whom I refer': 'While I know you will appreciate'; and 'I am mindful of my personal position in this matter'. It had all the hallmarks of being written by someone of authority with an excellent command of English and was very similar in style to Topping's putative letter of 17 July 1984. Did Anderton, in fact draft Topping's letter *and* this one?

A final significant feature of the draft letter was that it was not signed and carried no typist reference on it. It led to this exchange in the civil action:

STALKER: That is the second time I have to say in all my time working for Sir James Anderton I cannot recall any occasion when he didn't initial copies or sign copies. That is two letters I have been shown over the last two days, which have left the second page blank with no signature.

TABACHNIK: What do you say is the significance of that: he was going to deny authorship of the letter?

STALKER: I don't know it certainly gives no indication if there was a need to deny it. It could be denied. His typist reference isn't on it. I don't understand that. It always used to be unless he typed it himself.

TABACHNIK: It is clearly on the note paper of the Chief Constable, isn't it? He would have some difficulty in seeking to deny that it was his letter.

STALKER: I don't deny that it's the Chief Constable's letter. That's not the purpose of this answer. What I am saying is the only two occasions in my thirty years knowledge of Anderton from being a Constable to Chief Constable he hasn't signed a copy.

TABACHNIK: If it plainly is his letter what do you derive from that. The fact there is no signature, so what?

STALKER: It is a comment. The only two letters ever in my experience [which were unsigned] have both appeared in this trial.[42]

One possible explanation for these features is that no letter was ever sent to

Myers on this date and the draft was typed at some later point to suggest that HMIC had been informed much earlier than in fact it was. This would explain why Farley, Kevin Taylor's counsel, described it as a draft (presumably on information supplied by Anderton's defence team) and why no final letter, signed and stamped, was produced. It would also explain its assertive style and why there was no signature or typist reference on it. Moreover, it was claimed that, on receipt of the letter, Myers phoned Anderton and arranged a meeting. Anderton tape recorded the phone conversation, but the tape experienced the same demise as others in the Taylor/Stalker affair and was missing, casting further doubt on when HMIC was informed about Stalker.[43]

Further support for this line of reasoning comes from a written question in the House of Commons in October 1986. This was tabled by David Waddington, who at the time was the MP for Ribble Valley and also a junior Minister at the Home Office. He had met Stalker and Taylor at a Conservative Party event in 1982.[44] Waddington asked when HMIC became aware of the allegations against Stalker. His colleague in the Home Office, Douglas Hogg, Parliamentary Under-Secretary of State, gave the following written answer:

Her Majesty's Inspectorate of Constabulary was advised in October 1985 of the existence of information alleging that a relationship might exist between the Deputy Chief Constable and certain persons whose activities were under investigation in Greater Manchester. No evidence was available to justify any action in respect of this information until May 1986.[45]

This directly contradicts the claim by Anderton that HMIC was informed by him in March 1985. Following Hogg's statement to the House, Anderton wrote to Myers challenging the government statement that HMIC only became aware of the investigation into Stalker in October 1985. This was followed by an exchange of letters, with Anderton insisting it was March and Myers that it was October.[46]

If the government's account was correct then Anderton had failed to tell Myers that his DCC was under investigation and was now using a fake draft letter to claim otherwise. On the other hand, if Anderton was right and the draft had turned into an actual letter sent to Myers, then the government was misinforming parliament and distancing itself from any prior knowledge of a GMP investigation into Stalker.

There is, however, another aspect to the Lees' draft letter. In the civil action Stalker drew attention to its date. It was a mere ten days after Stalker himself had sent a letter to Anderton, Myers, and his second-in-command, Thorburn, which set out the impasse he had reached in his inquiry. Stalker described the information in his letter as 'politically extremely delicate and very volatile'.[47] This exchange then followed:

TABACHNIK: What do you say is the significance of this letter in the context of Northern Ireland.

STALKER: The significance of it is that suddenly here on the 14th March, when I have spelled out probably in more detail than I had ever spelled out before in the way of a consolidated briefing paper to Sir Philip Myers, here we have the first hints at people connected with me – namely Taylor and IRA connections … It may be of considerable embarrassment in certain quarters nationally. Does that mean politically nationally? I don't know. Coming from the Chief Constable it is difficult to think what else it could possibly mean. This is a letter which … I wished I had seen … before my Lord because what it [says] crystallises my thoughts in a way that I had already decided. It adds, in my view, [gives] strength to my opinion about what was happening in March 1985 in relation to my investigation. That's the first formal letter, of which sets out to discredit me and the investigation.

TABACHNIK: I see. So, this is you see a step really in securing your removal and dealing with the position in Northern Ireland?

STALKER: These were warning lights, these were flags going up if anything turns out we are not happy with we are formalising our conversations. Until then [nothing] had been recorded. They were on a man-to-man basis, HMI to Chief Constable basis …

TABACHNIK: Why should Sir James have wished to interfere in Northern Ireland matters simply because you were from his force and conducting the inquiry.

STALKER: This was far bigger than me my Lord. John Stalker was merely an investigating officer investigating six alleged murders involving police in Northern Ireland. We have here a situation, which has suddenly changed up a gear from … the 4th March when I sent that report to Sir Philip Myers. For the very first time both he and Sir James realised that this was threatening not just a few detective constables and sergeants and possibly inspectors in the RUC but the very high leadership of the RUC Sir John Hermon and Michael McAtamney, his deputy. This was for the first time spelled out. This was not some low-level investigation; it involved very senior people and I believe warning bells began to ring both with Sir James and Sir Philip and elsewhere in the Northern Ireland Office.

TABACHNIK: Let's just concentrate on Sir James are you saying that he got himself involved in your inquiry in Northern Ireland why because he was trying to protect Sir John Hermon?

STALKER: I believe that that may have been a factor but there were also other factors not the least of which his relationship with the HMI. It is very important to have a relationship with HMI … It can be a very bad enemy … It is very important the Chief Constable keeps his local HMI on his side.

TABACHNIK: Tell me this Mr Stalker if there was such anxiety about your report and such a desire to get rid of you at that time why not simply appoint an outside investigating officer in February or March that would have been the end of you wouldn't it?

STALKER: It wouldn't have been the end of me because I would have had nothing to fear it would have been the end of the Northern Ireland inquiry. I accept that.

TABACHNIK: Why not do that in February or March if Sir James was so anxious to get rid of you.

STALKER: Politically that would have been utter dynamite for that to have happened in the middle of an investigation, during which time it was known by honourable people in the security services I was seeking a tape and I appreciate my Lord that I can't say too much because much of this evidence is being given in open court but there in '85 my investigation had reached a most critical point and for me to be taken from it would have certainly raised more problems than it did when I was removed a year later. And may I say there was no reason to remove me from it.[48]

This exchange would suggest that Stalker did believe that the Lees draft letter was authentic and highly significant. It crystallised his thoughts about what had happened to him. There was a direct connection, he believed, between his investigation in Northern Ireland, where he was about to interview the top echelons of the RUC under caution, and developments in Manchester with the Chief Constable writing a damning letter leaving no doubt that Stalker had a corrupt relationship with the QSG. But it is equally plausible that HMIC were not informed until much later and the draft was an attempt to cover-up the fact.

The final point to make about the letter relates to what was meant by the phrase, 'I am mindful of my personal position'.[49] Was this simply making some oblique reference to his position as a Chief Officer, which placed him in a delicate situation of having to do his duty and authorise an investigation into his deputy, or did he feel that his personal position was compromised in some other way, and he was being asked by his superiors to do something with which he was distinctly unhappy? Whatever was meant, Anderton would have been fully aware of the implications and it was, therefore, even more strange, that once again, he did not make the decision to call in an outside force to investigate the existing information relating to his deputy.

It is also inexplicable that Myers, on receiving the letter, did not immediately insist that an outside force carry out an investigation, particularly as he was already fully briefed about Stalker's inquiry in Northern Ireland. Although the relevant section was not yet in force, the Police and Criminal Evidence Act was on the statute book, requiring that any serious suspicions against a senior officer should be immediately referred to the PCA and investigated by an outside force. There must, therefore, have been some reason why Anderton decided to keep the investigation in-house. Perhaps he was still in the dark about his own police force's investigation into Stalker and the letter was created later.

If Anderton did write a letter to Myers on 14 March, as is claimed, it would have caused considerable concern. It is inconceivable that HMIC did not immediately report the detail to the Home Office, and hence to the SoS, as it would, in Anderton's phrase, create 'considerable embarrassment in certain quarters … nationally'. There was no letter from Anderton among the Stalker/Sampson papers which were eventually deposited in the National Archives (Chapter 17), providing further evidence that no letter was sent at that time.

* * *

Once again, the evidence in the public domain for this period is partial and highly contradictory. But it adds further weight to the view that the investigation into Taylor and Stalker did not start until the beginning of January 1985. Stalker, having heard the evidence in the civil action, certainly believed that Burton's information only became important when his Northern Ireland inquiry became 'politically extremely delicate and very volatile' at the end of 1984 and beginning of 1985. This was the moment when he started rocking the boat in Northern Ireland, insisting on access to the hayshed tape and names of informers, interviewing senior officers under caution and potentially undermining the whole counter-insurgency strategy put in place by the Director of MI5, Patrick Walker. This may well have been the start of a conspiracy – with or without the knowledge of the Chief Constable – to remove Stalker based on Burton's babblings and a plan to construct a basis for prosecuting his friend Taylor through the work of the DIU.

It was claimed that the DIU was established to collect and collate intelligence on the growing drug scene and one of its first tasks was to record all the information which Burton had previously given to the police. Unsurprisingly, this was the same as most of what the police had on file.

This, however, is all too neat, particularly given the suspicion that much of the earlier documentation was created later. A much more plausible explanation is that Burton was being used to create a narrative of suspicion against Stalker at the very moment the implications of his inquiry in Northern Ireland were being realised in the top echelons of government.

Burton is certainly 'too sadly missed to be forgotten' as poignantly noted on his gravestone. He had perfected 'fake news' long before it had become a household concept. Lies were his commodity to be bought, sold, and recycled for a price. Sometimes they could be used for self-aggrandisement and, at other times, to bargain for more lenient treatment. They opened doors for judicial and other favours. He understood the importance of information to all the law enforcement agencies and the need for records. Like GMP, he appreciated the legality of forms, which played such a central part in the Taylor/Stalker affair, as well as forms of legality.

Chapter 12

Digging for Dirt

STALKER'S REPORT to Myers at the beginning of March 1985, telling him about his investigation in Northern Ireland, had enormous political implications, but he was determined to gain access to the hayshed tape. He sent a formal request to the Chief Constable asking for access and any transcripts or logs. He had no success. During March, Stalker interviewed a very senior RUC officer under caution as a criminal suspect. He wrote again at the beginning of April and then again towards the end of April requesting the tape. In May, he had a meeting with the Chief Constable and an MI5 officer, who was Director and Co-ordinator of Intelligence (DCInt), and was informed that MI5 were to act as honest brokers between him and the RUC. It would assess the tape before passing it on. MI5, of course, had every reason to want to control the information from the tape. They had failed to disclose its existence in the trial of McCauley and were therefore guilty of perverting the course of justice. A potential suspect in a crime was now controlling the intelligence. Stalker refused the deal.

Back in Manchester, the DIU, under the command of DCI Norman Born and staffed by DIs Murray, Waterworth, Richardson and DSgt Fiddler, continued its investigation into Taylor. They visited Taylor's banks and other organisations, and interviewed a range of people with whom he had been associated at some stage in his life and who could be expected or would be willing, for one reason or another, to supply the police with information. Some were people who never liked him, others were his political opponents in the MCA, and some had been friends but had fallen out. Several were his business associates. From a police perspective, chats with bank managers, inland revenue officials, businessmen, and former friends and enemies, is all good police work. From another perspective, it suggests that the police were 'digging for dirt' on Taylor who was seen in police jargon as 'a tasty' individual.[1] In short, they were on a fishing expedition.

The 'Drugs Intelligence Unit' was an inspired choice of title because of the moral opprobrium that goes with drug dealing. It was used to great effect to open doors and to gain the co-operation of reluctant individuals and, of course, to denigrate Taylor's character. In one documented example, two members of the DIU informed a senior development manager with a well-known building firm that Taylor was being investigated in relation to drugs and organised crime. It would have been extremely prejudicial to Taylor and would, no doubt, have made the likelihood of co-operation that much greater.[2]

Financial and commercial affairs

The inquiry focusing on Taylor's financial and commercial affairs began in earnest with the appointment of DSgt Ware to the DIU on 1 April 1985. At the time, he was working in the CID office in Bootle Street in the centre of Manchester.[3] He had considerable experience in the investigation of fraud. Significantly, he had spent some time helping DSgt Burgess prepare the LFF case against Klapish, Burton and others, and would have known all about the allegations that the QSG had connections with the IRA (Chapter 4). His appointment to the squad indicated that a decision had been made to investigate not only Taylor's alleged involvement in drugs but also his financial and commercial interests. It was to be a two-pronged strategy against a man who had no criminal record. Ware would have been very much a 'foot-soldier' carrying out the instructions of senior officers. During the first month, Ware familiarised himself with the files and carried out basic research, including enquiries at the Manchester Central Library, checking records.

This was an active and critical period for Taylor. He had sold the Moulton Street precinct and had already purchased several other properties. On 10 May 1985, Taylor requested a facility of £345,500 from the Co-operative Bank. Four days later, the bank confirmed the offer, which included £65,000 for Rangelark to buy land at Tottington, Bury.[4] This loan application was highly significant because it was used by the DIU to build a case against Taylor and others that they had conspired together to defraud the Co-operative Bank by deception.

On the same day that Taylor applied for the loan facility, Ware visited the Inland Revenue at Chorlton, a place he visited on numerous occasions over the coming months.[5] Public bodies, such as the police and the Inland Revenue are established by statute, and they cannot do anything which is not expressly or implicitly authorised by legislation. Where legislation permits the communication of information between public bodies, for specific purposes, details may be shared. In 1985, there was no legal provision for the Inland Revenue to provide the police with confidential information regarding Taylor's tax affairs, but according to Ware, it was entirely happy to co-operate throughout and to release information. There appears to have been no restriction on the time period and the Inland Revenue was happy to go back as far as the files existed.[6]

Hassling banks

The legal position relating to banks was also clear. The banker-customer relationship imposed on the bank a duty of confidentiality. It is not an absolute duty and banks must provide information if compelled to do so by the law or with the consent of the customer.[7] At the time, neither of these two conditions applied but this did not deter the police making numerous visits to Taylor's banks.[8] Ware first visited one of Taylor's banks on 28 June 1985 when he and DI Waterworth went to Lloyds Bank in King Street, Manchester and spoke with a Mr Cross.[9] The purpose of Ware's visit was subsequently contested during Taylor's criminal trial. Taylor's barrister, David Hood suggested to Ware that the reason stemmed from the fact that it was this bank that had issued Taylor with his American Express card which had been used by Taylor to purchase the tickets for him and Stalker to holiday in Miami in 1981 (Chapter 13). Ware denied this and argued that the purpose of the visit was to ascertain whether Taylor held an account there. Hood pressed the point:

HOOD: You went to Lloyd's Bank at 8.30 a.m. and returned at 10 a.m.?
WARE: Yes.
HOOD: It is not a tremendously long journey to that bank?
WARE: No, it is not, and it is early in the day – rush-hour time.
HOOD: You could have spent one and a half hours on that journey and that bank could tell you absolutely nothing?
WARE: Yes.
HOOD: When you go to a bank as a police officer, do you telephone in advance, making an appointment?
WARE: More often than not.
HOOD: Did you on this occasion?
WARE: Yes. That is why I went at 8.30 a.m. before the bank opened.
HOOD: You do not recall why that was the very first bank to which you went?
WARE: No.
HOOD: You dispute the suggestion because that is where the American Express card was held?
WARE: Yes.[10]

On 24 July, Ware visited Barclays Bank in Aston-in-Makerfield and spoke to Mr Parkinson, the Assistant Manager.[11] He left his office at 10.20 a.m. and returned at 3.10 p.m. Hood estimated that on this visit he probably spent well over an hour speaking with Parkinson. Was he perhaps chatting away about drug running and matters of that nature? Ware denied it and said that the purpose of the visit was again to ascertain whether Taylor had an account there and it took some time to be informed that he no longer banked with Barclays.

Three days later Ware's diary notes: 'On duty at Drugs Unit. Engaged re enquiries on current matters. 3.30 p.m. engaged with contact (bank) re above.'[12] Hood pressed for details about who the contact was and in what bank. Ware could not remember. Hood suggested that it might be a reference to a sort of 'deep-freeze' person – someone who was prepared to divulge confidential information – within a banking institution. No, it was not. Why then was the entry put in such a covert way? Ware denied that it was noted in any way covertly.

In late August, Ware travelled to Birmingham for an appointment with a Mr Cooper at the headquarters of the Trustee Savings Bank which had provided Taylor with a mortgage on his home. Hood pointed out that banks have a privileged position with their clients and must not divulge information unless required to do so by a court order. He then asked Ware whether he was carrying out his enquiries within the law or without it. Ware argued that it was his view that there is nothing improper in a police officer going to a bank to find out whether a person holds an account at that bank, whether he holds a mortgage with the bank and the state of the mortgage. He went on to point out that initially Cooper refused to release any information but was eventually persuaded to do so. Hood then forced Ware into an admission:

HOOD: You were after whatever information you could get?
WARE: Yes.
HOOD: You were finding out about Mr Taylor anything you could rather than pursuing a particular line of inquiry?
WARE: Yes.
HOOD: You say that it was part and parcel or instructions from Mr Topping that you have been out finding everything you can about Mr Taylor?
WARE: Yes.[13]

Hood suggested that by September 1985, Lloyds Bank, Barclays Bank and the TSB had already been visited. Ware had not yet visited the Co-operative Bank which was the most important bank in terms of Taylor's financial and commercial affairs at the time. Hood went on to point out that on 30 September, Ware had made enquiries at Tottington concerning the site Taylor had purchased in the area. This information could only have come from the Co-operative Bank. Hood suggested that Ware must, therefore, have had some covert contact with the Co-operative Bank by then for him to be able to make his enquires at Tottington. Ware denied it.[14]

Ware also made enquiries into Taylor's properties and land acquisitions. Several visits were made to the Land Registry at Lytham St Annes, which contained records of land transactions in the area, charges on land and other details. Police are required, before making enquiries at a Land Registry, to be in possession of an order signed by a police officer of at least superintendent rank, which gives a broad outline of the alleged offences that are being investigated and something to identify the property that is the subject of an inquiry.[15]

Hood enquired whether there was a copy of the form, but Ware said that he had handed it into the Registry. Hood further enquired what was on the form and whether it specifically mentioned drugs. Ware did not think so. When visiting the Registry, Ware would have had to detail and specify information about each of Taylor's sites before he could have obtained any information on the date of sale or purchases and any charges on the land. Taylor's ownership and sale of Moulton Street precinct was public knowledge in Manchester and Ware would have had no difficulty obtaining these records. Information about the sites at Tottington and Trafford Park, however, was not in the public domain at the time and the information could only have been supplied by one of Taylor's banks.

Interviewing enemies

Other lines of inquiry concerned interviewing people who had never liked Taylor or had fallen out with him at some time. In June 1985, the police interviewed Kim Berry. She had been employed by the MCA in 1983 but had left after six months. She took the car, with which she had been provided on employment, in lieu of wages that she claimed the Association owed her. Stephen Hayes, an ex-police officer, who ran a successful security business, was given instructions by the Chief Constituency Agent for the Association, Clive Webb, to re-possess it. Berry refused to hand over the car and sat in it, informing Hayes that her solicitor had instructed her to keep it. Berry alleges that Hayes then forcibly removed her from the car, during which time she dropped the keys. Hayes picked them up and drove the car away. Berry's mother had seen the argument and called the police, but there were no subsequent police proceedings against either party.[16] Her mother denied the implication made in a Sunday newspaper that it was her complaint that initiated the investigation into Stalker's conduct. She is reported as saying: 'I'm just an ordinary person. They shouldn't be concentrating on me. The incident is insignificant.'[17]

Richardson, in the company of Ware, conducted the first interview with Berry on 18 June and then again on 26 June, from which he compiled a seventeen-page report. She told him about the Hayes' incident and Taylor's lifestyle and habits. She described Taylor's house as 'a mansion' which she had visited on two occasions, once when interviewed for the job and again when she took back Taylor's BMW.[18] She reported hearsay information from Angela Britton, the daughter of Taylor's accountant, who allegedly told her that Taylor had many parties at the house and that it was common for drugs to be available and for 'couples to be naked or scantily clad when in the swimming pool or Jacuzzi'.[19] The report contained a subheading, 'Dubious or Villainous Associations',[20] and the first person mentioned was Stephen Hayes. The report was not a full contemporaneous record of the interviews with Berry, but a summary. It was another undated report prepared by Richardson, which presented Taylor in the worst possible light.

During the civil action, Stalker was highly critical of the report:

STALKER: I have to say that it is quite unprecedented in my experience that report after report after report. It almost appears as if people have been instructed not to date them. I say no more. I draw no conclusions from it. I've never seen it. It's totally against all police practice and training.

TABACHNIK: Mr Stalker there can't be a great mystery about the date of these reports once there is a dated card index being dated on every document?

STALKER: In that case I see no purpose in not dating them. I'm not here to say why they've not been dated. It is not consistent with any police practice anywhere in the country, anywhere in the world I would say.

TABACHNIK: Are you in fact suggesting that somebody has given specific instructions that reports are not to be dated?

STALKER: I can't say who it was. It appears to be so frequent that there must … It's either gross incompetence or else it's an instruction …

TABACHNIK: Mr Stalker it's right isn't it that not only is there a card index system operating but these people are keeping diaries, notebooks and so on in which they are recording on a day-by-day basis what they doing, who they are seeing and so on?

STALKER: I don't know my Lord, that's the truth.

TABACHNIK: There would be no point in deliberately not dating reports if these things are going to be recorded in officers' notebooks and diaries, is there?

STALKER: For me to stand here and say there's never been any malpractice in relation to diaries and notebooks, I'm not alleging it now. I've not seen them all. I'm saying that for an experienced detective time after time after time not to date a report strikes to me of something being very unusual, perhaps acting on instructions …

TABACHNIK: Are you actually suggesting … that it's somehow sinister?

STALKER: How can I possibly say that from the witness box … I've not had access to diaries nor to notebooks … It is wholly improper for the submission of a document without date. If I were the supervising officer, I would take these things seriously. I would say, when did you put that in? It's the first thing that we ask.[21]

Another person whom the DIU visited on a number of occasions in this period was Ann Carroll who became a key informant. She had been heavily involved in the MCA and was an ex-Vice Chair. In 1982, Taylor made a bid to become Chair of the party and she was strongly opposed to his nomination. On 15 July 1985, Waterworth and Richardson conducted an interview with her.[22] Once again no contemporaneous note of the interview was taken but an eight-page report was prepared subsequently. Carroll began by telling the police about Taylor's connections with the MCA. She then went on to describe Taylor's 'associates' and claimed that he 'moved between two circles of friends, businessmen and villains', but the only person she was sure had a criminal record was Michael Roy Brown,[23] contradicting her belief that Taylor moved in a circle of villains – plural. The use of the word 'villain' was not a word that would commonly trip off the tongue of a member of the Conservative Party and indicated again that the report was not a verbatim account.

During the interview, Carroll provided the police with a table plan for a MCA dinner in March 1982.[24] The police report, however, noted only the names of a few of the 700 people who attended the event. It recorded that Carroll had introduced David Waddington, then Parliamentary Under-SoS in the Department of Employment, to several guests, including Stalker. Waddington later became Home Secretary.[25] In addition, the police report described how attempts were made in August 1984 to eject Taylor from the Association. Someone put up a resolution, but it was defeated. At about this time, Carroll claims she received an anonymous phone call at her home.[26] In another interview Carroll is alleged to have told the police that when selling vans in the early 1970s, Taylor had re-wound the milometers to record lesser mileage. As she did not know Taylor in those days, she was simply repeating a widely held view that this was common practice among those trying to sell vehicles. She also told the police that there were irregularities with the finances of the MCA and suggested that he was using party funds for his own benefit.[27]

Another person interviewed on several occasions by the DIU around this time was Neil Westbrook, who had also been active in the MCA and was an ex-Chair. He was Managing Director of Trafford Park Estates Ltd which held a large portion of the land in Trafford Park. Following the sale of the Moulton Street precinct, Taylor had purchased a derelict warehouse in Trafford Park for £160,000 (Chapter 6). In January 1985, he obtained planning permission for it, which immediately doubled the property's value. He then bought several separate but adjacent plots of land in the area, building up a portfolio of more than eight acres.[28] In September 1985, a month or so after Westbrook had first been seen by the police, Taylor decided to sell the whole portfolio. Trafford Park Estates Ltd were potentially an interested party and any approach by the police to the Managing Director, irrespective of what may have been said, would have been potentially damaging to Taylor's financial and commercial interests.

According to the police, Westbrook was interviewed by Richardson on 28 June, 4 July and 10 September 1985. Westbrook was alleged to have told the police that on one occasion he met Taylor at the Stanley Casino and that Taylor had exchanged £1,000 into £50 Bank of England notes and lost the lot within a period of four minutes, playing £200 stakes per game.[29] In another interview, Westbrook told the police that Taylor had said he was friendly with the Deputy Chief Constable.[30] Richardson's reports of the meetings were again written after the interview and presented Taylor in a bad light through inferences and facts taken out of context.

Another informant whom the police interviewed extensively was Victor Roberts. Of all informants during this period, he was perhaps the most important, as far as the police were concerned. In the late 1970s, Roberts had been seriously injured in a motoring accident and Taylor had found him work. Over the next few years, he was the recipient of Taylor's widely known, but often abused, generosity. He visited America at Taylor's expense. When he announced that he was to be married, Taylor bought the engagement ring, financed the wedding, paid for the honeymoon and put down the deposit on the matrimonial home.[31] According to Taylor, the two men parted company in about 1982 or 1983 over a suspicious property deal involving Dulcie Street School. Roberts had a contact within the City Estates and Valuations Office of Manchester City Council and had arranged a tender. Taylor did not want to be involved with the project. The deal, however, went ahead with others.

Members of the DIU compiled several retrospective reports of the interviews with Roberts. One report states that he told the police about the Moulton Street precinct and was 'dismayed' to know how Taylor could have financed the development because he lived in a semi-detached house in Failsworth. The report also states that it was not uncommon for the odd unit to be used to store stolen goods and that the tax people would have a ball if they were to question Taylor.[32] In a report prepared by Richardson on 31 July 1985, it is noted that Roberts no longer associates with Taylor and 'is agreeable and will help all he can but makes it clear that the network within the organisation is so big that our task is almost [impossible]'.[33]

Roberts suggested the QSG had had their contacts within the police for years. He told Richardson that he was aware that Taylor and Stalker had known each other for a long time and that Taylor made no secret of their friendship. Roberts dined with Taylor and Stalker and their wives 'on many occasions' and 'on each occasion Taylor footed the bill, which was always at least £200, sometimes as much as £500 depending upon the food consumption and type of champagne bought at the time'.[34] He added that Stalker was very tight and seldom bought a drink. Richardson also noted that Roberts claimed Stalker knew of the association between Taylor and the QSG, 'but appears to turn a blind eye to their activities because of his position'.[35] Stalker was furious when presented with Richardson's report in the civil action:

> Well, that whole paragraph is quite wrong and false and mendacious my Lord. It says there [that I] appear to turn a blind eye to their activities; that is a clear allegation that I am in some way involved with the Quality Street Gang and, I completely deny that of course ... I have never walked away from Taylor because I have never seen him speaking to anybody who was suspicious. Most of the functions would be at police headquarters and that's unlikely to be an occasion where there would be suspicious characters.[36]

Crucially, Roberts told the police that Taylor and Stalker had been on holiday together on at least two occasions. On the first occasion, Stalker and his wife flew out to Los Angeles with Taylor and his wife for a two or three-week holiday. The second occasion was between 'November 1980 and June 1981' when the two men went alone. 'Roberts cannot prove it but knows that Taylor financed the holiday with Febb because as he puts it that's his style.'[37] Richardson added that, 'the disturbing feature so far as this enquiry is concerned is that Roberts is adamant that Taylor would not spend money without something in return'.[38] According to Richardson, Roberts also emphasised the importance of the masonic connections, pointing out that Stalker and Taylor were members of the same lodge.[39]

Stalker was again furious. He emphasised that he had never been on holiday with Taylor and his wife on any occasion, 'not even to Blackpool never mind Los Angeles'.[40] It was complete lies and, as far as he was concerned, threw the whole police report into disrepute. He pointed out that his eight-day holiday to Miami with Taylor took place in December 1981 rather than sometime during the eight-month period suggested by Roberts. As far as his membership of the masonic order was concerned Stalker had this to say:

> This is maliciousness to a point that has become ... well I find it very difficult to keep control my Lord. These are just words, there is not a shred of truth in any of them. I have never been a mason not that there is anything dishonourable in that itself but certainly I have not been one. I have never particularly wanted to be, and Taylor has never invested money in me. Anything I have had with Taylor has been reciprocal.[41]

Subsequently, Roberts claimed that much of what he said was untrue or had been taken out of context. He never said that: Taylor was a member of the QSG;

there was a network within the QSG which would be impossible for the police to do anything about; Taylor would only spend monies on Stalker to get something in return; the tax people would have a ball if they investigated Taylor's affairs; and Taylor had paid for the Miami trip. While he had commented on Taylor's financial affairs and had pointed out that his records were somewhat loosely arrived at, he was not suggesting that Taylor was guilty of tax evasion.[42]

Around this time, the DIU made a blunder in its search for information on Taylor. Ware was tasked with the job of interviewing a certain Mr Waterhouse to ascertain whether he would be a prospective informer. Mr Waterhouse was Taylor's brother-in-law, but Taylor and his sister had had a family row, which was soon patched up, but at that time they were not on speaking terms. Ware first called at the Waterhouse's home at the end of May, when Waterhouse and his wife were away on holiday. He then made another visit in July, when he spoke to Waterhouse about Taylor's business activities, including Vanland. In the criminal trial, Hood suggested that the DIU knew of the row between Taylor and his sister, and this was a further example of the DIU 'digging for dirt' on Taylor. Ware denied it and claimed that he did not know that Waterhouse was Taylor's brother-in-law.[43] This was odd given the enormous resources that had already been directed at investigating Taylor. Whether the DIU genuinely did not know of the relationship, or they were interviewing anyone who might provide them with information on Taylor, the visit was immediately reported to Taylor by his sister.

The Robson correspondence

Taylor's suspicions were at last confirmed: he now had concrete evidence that the police were investigating him. He took immediate action and obtained the services of Guy Robson, a partner with Kenneth Robson, Solicitors. On 9 August 1985, Robson wrote to the Chief Constable, James Anderton, expressing his concerns. It was to be the first of ten letters which Robson wrote to the police to seek clarification and to offer his client for interview. The letters subsequently became known as the Robson correspondence.[44]

The first letter began:

Dear Sir,

We have been consulted by Kevin Taylor of Wood Mill, Summerseat, Bury, in connection with a matter, which to say the least, is causing him some embarrassment.

Last week our client who is a well-respected member of the community received a telephone call from his sister, one Margaret Waterhouse, indicating that a police officer had been to interview her, not about herself but about her brother, our client. She was naturally curious to know why she should have been interviewed, hence the reason for contacting our client, and that in turn has caused the embarrassment we have referred to.[45]

The letter asked the Chief Constable to clarify the purpose of the visit and offered assistance on any matter GMP required. It ended by pointing out that, in view of the embarrassment and distress caused so far to their client, they asked for a speedy reply.

On 15 August 1985, CS Thomas Ryan from Bury Police Station replied, saying that: 'Without more information as to the nature of the inquiry by the police and the address of the sister, it is not possible to ascertain the purpose of those enquiries or which department is involved.'[46] It is possible that Ryan was totally honest in his reply. He could have been told nothing whatsoever about the inquiry when the letter was forwarded to him from the Chief Constable for a reply. On the other hand, the letter could have been forwarded to him with strict instructions as to what to say in reply. In either scenario deceit was involved.

A week later, Robson replied to Ryan with all the information requested, including a description of the officer who attended. He said that, 'he was attached to a small squad of five or six people'.[47] Robson also pointed out that an interview with his client was now inappropriate, as no one seemed to know who was investigating him or for what purpose. But on 6 September Ryan replied, saying that he had made further enquiries, 'but I have not been able to establish that any officer of the Bury Division has been making enquiries regarding your client. I have therefore passed the correspondence to the Chief Superintendent (CID Command) at Force headquarters, so that he may look into the matter further and he will no doubt communicate with you in due course.'[48] This suggests that Ryan genuinely did not know who had visited Mrs Waterhouse and he had made efforts to find out. Presumably, he would have contacted the various squads at headquarters, such as the Commercial Fraud Squad, the Drugs Squad, the Stolen Vehicle Squad, and the Cheque Squad, but not the DIU because it still remained a secret within the force.

On 11 September, Robson received a reply from Superintendent Philip Machent for the Chief Constable, noting that: 'Enquiries have been made but, from the information available, it is not possible to identify the officer involved.'[49] This was nonsense unless Machent had been kept in the dark. Anderton knew that Stalker and Taylor were being investigated by the DIU. After all, the draft letter composed by Lees, if genuine, had been sent to

HMIC in March informing it of that fact. It seemed that under no circumstances were the police going to admit to any enquiries into Stalker's friend, and the DIU's blunder of contacting Taylor's brother-in-law had to be covered up at all costs.

Dublin robbery

On 3 December 1985, five armed and masked men burst into the home of Brian and Linda Comerford in Tallaght, Dublin. They forced Mrs Comerford to go next door and fetch the neighbour, postmistress Ann Whelan. Then they took the Comerfords and the Whelans, apart from Mrs Whelan, to a disused house in Rathmines where they were kept overnight. Mrs Whelan was then forced to go to her post office, take out all the money and bring it to a predetermined point. She subsequently handed over seventy thousand in Irish pounds.

Back in Manchester, the police were hunting for the killers of Sergeant John Speed, who was shot after going to the aid of a colleague during what was a routine check on two men near Leeds parish church in October 1984.[50] They raided six houses in Manchester and arrested five men. Four were released but they detained Michael Roy Brown.[51] Following a search of his house, they found ten thousand pounds in Irish notes. At the time, Brown was suspected of drug trafficking and was connected with 'Cahill in Dublin'.[52] This presumably was the infamous Martin Cahill, who was killed, it is widely believed, by the IRA, in 1994.[53]

On 21 December, Brown was interviewed by Murray and Born from the DIU. They made a report of the interview which was examined in the civil action.[54] No explanation was given as to why members of the DIU interviewed Brown in what appeared to be a murder inquiry. During the interview, Brown claimed that Taylor had a 'top man' in GMP, was into drugs and was the best long firm frauds man. Tabachnik, Anderton's defence counsel, put it to Stalker that this was 'another source other than Burton suggesting a connection between Taylor and a top jolly'. Stalker disagreed and said that he had no reason to believe that Taylor had ever been a frauds man and pointed out: 'We've got a man [Brown] who did not know who his father was until recently who suddenly seems to know a great deal about him [Taylor]. It seems like a novel.'[55] Tabachnik pursued the issue and insisted that it was another source that needed to be tested. But Stalker was having none of it. He argued:

> The inference being that these people have suddenly appeared and given this information. They have been sought out. It seems to me the inference that I get is that one thing has led to another, and these people have been sought out. I'm

not criticising that, but it makes it appear these are unconnected bits of information that they are putting in and adding up to something. In fact, they are a chain of events which have been manipulated by the police.[56]

It then emerged that Brown had been interviewed the day before when he denied having any connection with a 'top copper'.[57] Then, during the interview with Born and Murray the following day, he said that he thought that he had been confused with Taylor who *did* have a top man. It was a highly significant allegation because it provided the only corroboration of Burton's Bridge Street conversation that Taylor had a top man in GMP. The interview occurred only a few weeks after the DIU had reached an impasse in its drugs' investigation into Taylor (Chapter 15) and here was Brown apparently confirming GMP's suspicions that Taylor was, indeed, into drugs. Following the impasse, the DIU had shifted its attention to Taylor's financial affairs and now Brown was confirming that Taylor was the best long firm frauds man.

It was all highly suspicious, and it was significant that no report on the first interview was examined in the civil action. Brown could easily have made up the allegations because he was in a very vulnerable position, having been arrested in relation to the murder of Speed. Alternatively, the DIU could have made up the story based on information it already knew about Brown, Taylor and Stalker, in order to justify its investigation.

At the time, the police had strong suspicions that John Speed had been killed by the IRA. Brown's Irish background, coupled with his known visits to Dublin, had led to his arrest along with the others. Subsequently, it transpired that the shooting had nothing whatsoever to do with the IRA. John Speed was killed by a career criminal called David Gricewith. About two years after the murder, the police rammed a getaway car driven by Gricewith after an armed robbery and the impact caused his shotgun to discharge, shooting him in the stomach. He died from the injuries. His girlfriend later confessed to the police that he had been responsible for other armed robberies and the murder of John Speed.[58]

* * *

All the evidence from the initial stages of the investigation by the DIU further confirms that its focus was principally on Taylor, a man with no criminal convictions and who was not suspected of committing any specific crime. There were only rumours from Burton, an inveterate liar. Yet huge resources were committed to 'digging for dirt' on Taylor. As Ware admitted in court, the police were not pursuing any particular line of inquiry; they were simply trying to find out anything they could about Taylor. Considerable time was spent visiting official bodies – Inland Revenue, banks, and Land Registry – and people with whom Taylor had fallen out. There were few contemporaneous notes taken with those interviewed. Retrospective reports were prepared on unofficial forms and without dates. For several interviews and meetings no reports at all were compiled. Subsequently, a number of those interviewed denied some of what they were alleged to have said. There was, in short, a total disregard for police procedures. Had specific orders had been given not to date reports and not to use official forms? All the available information suggests that Taylor was being 'fitted-up' to build a case against his friend, John Stalker.

Chapter 13

Diogenes, Drugs and Dead Ends

IN EARLY 1981, Taylor asked Lieutenant Commander Arthur Bowen-Gotham, a yacht master instructor, if he would accompany him to Miami to help purchase a boat.[1] He was happy to do so. While there, Taylor bought *Diogenes* for £85,000 at the Miami Boat Show. Later, Taylor reflected that: 'It was possibly the single worst mistake I ever made and was to have far-reaching repercussions in years to come.'[2] In March and June 1981, while *Diogenes* was in the United States, Taylor entertained a few of his old friends on board the boat, some of whom were alleged to be members of the QSG. Six months later, in December 1981, he invited Stalker to spend a few days on the boat. It was a disastrous trip. Stalker became very ill with seasickness. The engine broke down and Taylor scalded himself trying to fix it. The boat ran aground, and they were stranded on a remote island in the Bahamas.[3] They cut short the holiday and flew home. Then, when Taylor was trying to sell *Diogenes* at the beginning of 1985, it was suspected of being used to smuggle drugs. This mix of information, once discovered, proved to be very convenient for those who wanted Stalker removed.

Guns on board

Before cruising in the Bahamas, Taylor had been advised to purchase some guns for his own protection against pirates. Subsequently, he arranged for Colin Faulkner, a professional skipper, to bring *Diogenes* back to England from the United States. Before leaving Florida, Taylor showed him the guns and ammunition. During the voyage back to Manchester, Faulkner experienced bad weather and was forced to have storm damage repairs carried out in Bermuda. Faulkner met further bad weather approaching Ireland, and as he was low on fuel, he decided to dock in Cork to refuel. On approach, Faulkner alerted Customs by flying the yellow flag, and on arrival the Irish Customs thoroughly searched the boat. Off the North Wales coast, Faulkner radioed the coast guard and asked them to inform H.M. Customs of his arrival in Ellesmere Port and requested their assistance. On arrival, Faulkner declared the guns to Customs and Excise and insisted that they took possession of them. He recalls, however, that they were somewhat reluctant to do so.[4]

Taylor was interviewed about the guns at the time by Mr Liddle from Customs and Excise in Newcastle.[5] Taylor thought that this was the end of the matter, as the guns had been declared and he had given written instructions to Customs and Excise for their disposal. But the report made by Liddle was resurrected by the DIU four years later in 1985 and reinterpreted to suggest that Taylor was in fact 'gun-running for the IRA' because it had called into an Irish port and had guns on board when it arrived in Manchester. In the civil action, Justice Owen sarcastically remarked:

> There aren't very many gun runners for the IRA, I would imagine, who go into an English port without a licence for a gun, leaving it lying round in the boat to be found. I would have thought most of them would have got rid of the armaments a bit earlier.[6]

Customs and Excise clearly did not suspect that Taylor was gun-running, as Stalker pointed out, otherwise he would immediately have become a subject of interest to SB, and his friendship with Taylor would have been the subject of an investigation back in 1981.

Puerto Banus

In late July 1982, Taylor sailed *Diogenes* from Manchester to Puerto Banus in Spain with several friends: Stephen Hayes, Kevin Shaw, Howard Tebay and Matthew Butler. Although some repairs were made to the boat after crossing from the USA, it was, as one of the passengers described it, 'falling apart'.[7] The autopilot had not been repaired and consequently everyone had to do two-hour shifts. During the trip, they stopped at several ports, including Gibraltar, before arriving in Puerto Banus in Spain at the beginning of August. *Diogenes* was then moored at Pier 2. *Sherama*, owned by Vincent Schiavo, who was wanted for deception in Manchester, was moored at Pier 1. This information, when discovered by DIU, only added to their view that Taylor was indeed part of the QSG.

At the beginning of 1985, Taylor decided to sell *Diogenes* and put it up for sale in Puerto Banus. Alan Brooks expressed an interest and Taylor gave permission for him to take the boat on what is known in the yachting fraternity as a 'proving trip', but only in Spanish and Portuguese waters. This was normal practice when a boat was advertised for sale. The owner would entrust their boat, often to complete strangers, for days at a time. On 3 February, just one day before the DIU started work, *Diogenes* turned up in Dartmouth.[8] Customs and Excise strongly suspected the boat had been used to traffic drugs into England. Although no drugs were found on board, Customs and Excise considered that there were three suspicious aspects to the boat's arrival in Dartmouth: it had travelled from southern Spain close to north Africa; there were deodorant blocks in the cabins; the suspected smugglers – the skipper William Whittaker and Alan Brooks – spent the night on arrival in separate hotels.

Customs and Excise called Taylor after *Diogenes* had arrived in Dartmouth. He was shocked and shared their suspicions that it may have been used for the smuggling of drugs. He explained the circumstances to them and asked them to search the boat, but they informed him that they already had, but had found nothing. The boat needed extensive repairs and, while it was in the repair yard in Dartmouth, Taylor completed the sale of the boat to Brooks on 1 April 1985. It left Dartmouth for Portugal on 19 April, skippered by a professional yachtsman who had agreed to take it to Portugal. It arrived in Vilamoura on 25 April and was handed over to its new owner.[9]

Numerous documents were produced by the defence in the civil action to prove that the police had a reasonable belief that Taylor was involved in drug smuggling. As with so much in this story, it has been difficult to establish precisely how, when and from whom all the information concerning *Diogenes* came to the attention of the DIU, and whether it was tested or simply taken at face value. A crucial question in relation to the chronology of the Taylor/Stalker affair is, when did the DIU first receive the intelligence from Customs and Excise that *Diogenes* had arrived in Dartmouth?

CDIU intelligence

It appears that the DIU first began to contact various agencies involved in monitoring and collecting intelligence on drugs sometime in late April 1985. The agencies included Customs and Excise, the Central Drugs Intelligence Unit (CDIU) based at Scotland Yard, and American Express, which, as well as having an interest in fraud and money-laundering, also investigated drug trafficking and smuggling. In addition, the DIU contacted C11 at Scotland Yard. This was the Metropolitan Police's own CID, and was responsible for surveillance relating to No. 9 RCS, which covered the City of London and the Metropolitan Police.[10]

On 24 April 1985, Murray and Waterworth from the DIU visited both C11 and the CDIU at Scotland Yard. A report on the visit was not filed until 16 May – some three weeks later.[11] The aim of the visit was to establish a productive working relationship with the two units. From all accounts, the visit to C11 was not very fruitful and they received what was described as a 'polite brush-off'.[12] They were disappointed and upset about their reception. Stalker, however, pointed out that any detective superintendent surprised by that attitude obviously doesn't have a great deal of experience. C11, as he pointed out, was a department purely intended for use by the Metropolitan Police; it has no national role, unlike the CDIU which is required to co-operate and share intelligence with other police forces.[13] At the CDIU, they had a better reception and met DSgt Green. At some point, they were in contact with George Atkinson, from Customs and Excise, who was attached to the CDIU.[14] He was later to supply the DIU with a lot of information.

Once again, however, much of the documentation relating to these meetings and the information obtained was problematic. Some of it was on scraps of paper and not on official forms. Telephone conversations were not followed up with written reports. Several of the documents did not have a date when they were received and possessed only a date when they were filed by the DIU. One of the first intelligence reports provided by the CDIU was bizarre. It was a contemporaneous note of a telephone call at the beginning of May – the actual date is unknown – between Ware and DSgt Green of the CDIU. It recorded that four men had been arrested in 'Columbia'(sic) and linked them to one of the country's most respected television producers. Stalker, once again, was very critical of the documentation and the nature of the intelligence:

> I find it strange ... and unusual that a hand-written note about a telephone call from a Detective Sergeant at the CDIU is all that there is to see. I would have expected a report, if not a back-up report following on from the phone call from the CDIU. They are very keen and very particular to commit these things to paper ... I find that piece of paper is not something I would regard as professional ... The CDIU are pretty well obliged to submit these things to paper: it is in their interest to show the sort of work they are generating to show that they are contributing to the anti-drug effort in the country ... I find it most unprofessional ... I know the esteem he's [the television producer] held in internationally. I found it very wrong on the same sheet of paper to link people arrested for cocaine smuggling in 'Columbia' as opposed to 'Colombia'.[15]

On what appeared to be the same day – although once again there was considerable confusion over the date – Richardson produced a five-page report from telephone conversations with George Atkinson in the CDIU.[16] It listed the names of several people, including Taylor, Brooks and Whittaker, whom it boldly noted were 'involved in the large-scale importation of cannabis from North Africa', and were using different vessels including *Diogenes* and a boat called *Olympus Nova*.[17] When *Diogenes* arrived in Vilamoura on 25 April, Richardson noted that Taylor and Whittaker were waiting at the quayside with 'a number of heavies'[18] – a most unlikely event as Taylor had sold his boat to Brooks on 1 April. Taylor, in fact, was not waiting at the quay side. He was in England negotiating a loan with the British Linen Bank in Manchester – a detail which the police could have discovered from their investigation into his financial affairs.[19]

Richardson's damning report not only linked Taylor to the importation of drugs but also to firearms. He noted that Taylor 'first came to the notice of Atkinson' when *Diogenes* arrived in Manchester 'containing firearms' and was 'turned over' – a totally distorted account of what had actually happened.[20] Richardson further noted that Atkinson felt that there was very little doubt that Taylor was involved in firearms, adding that he had stored Uzi machine guns in the Moulton Street precinct[21] – a repeat of Burton's original allegation that Taylor was a 'minder of guns for the QSG' which he then morphed into storing Uzi machine guns (Chapter 11). Thus, a distorted account about *Diogenes* from a customs officer, together with an embellished allegation from an inveterate liar, was deployed to suggest that Taylor was involved in both smuggling and storing guns.

Following the telephone calls from Richardson, Customs and Excise forwarded the DIU a sixteen-page report and two pages of notes. Both were prepared by Christopher Martin, a Customs and Excise officer, and it was thought they were probably received by the DIU sometime in early May, as they were indexed on 9 May 1985.[22] It is not known whether any intelligence was passed to Customs and Excise by the DIU and subsequently incorporated into reports and notes. If this had occurred it would, of course, have created an absurd circle of intelligence that made it impossible to tell which piece of information corroborated another. Even if the information had come solely from Customs and Excise, the source was not declared.

The sixteen-page Customs and Excise report provided a detailed history of the activities of Brooks and Whittaker, whose nautical movements had been observed over 1984 and the early part of 1985. It recorded that:

> During July 1984, I.D. Manchester [Investigation Department of Customs and Excise in Manchester] received information to the effect that a group of criminals known as the 'Quality Street Gang' were organising a run of arms and drugs. A Provisional IRA connection was mentioned. A yacht named *Sherama* was to be used to smuggle the contraband.[23]

The most likely source of this information was Burton, who was now linking *Sherama* – a boat which could hardly have made a journey of more than 20 nautical miles let alone a trip to North Africa and back – with the QSG, IRA, drugs, and arms. It was very similar to the information which he had been peddling since the LFF in 1981. It suggested that as well as being an informant for GMP, he was also providing the same information to Customs and Excise, which was now being fed back to the DIU. The report also noted that *Sherama* had been in Gibraltar on 11 June 1984 with several criminals on board, including Ronnie Knight.[24]

In early May 1985, Customs and Excise passed on other information to the DIU. This included the passenger list of people from *Diogenes* on 2 August 1982, when it docked in Puerto Banus. Customs and Excise – or the DIU – must have obtained the list from the port authorities. All the people who had been on board appeared to have been checked out against SB files, presumably at the request of the DIU. SB discovered that one of the passengers, Matthew Butler, had purchased a raffle ticket in 1973 for a Prisoners' Dependant Fund from a Mr O'Reilly, who was suspected of 'having Republican sympathies'.[25] Absurdly, this was considered by the DIU to lend further support to its view that Taylor had connections with the IRA.

Raffles for Prisoners' Dependant Funds, however, were regularly held both in Ireland and Britain, and many people of Irish origins would contribute to them for welfare or philanthropic rather than political reasons. A contribution, even to a vendor who had republican sympathies, did not make the purchaser a supporter, let alone an active member of the Provisional IRA. The search revealed not only the extent and depth of intelligence that SB hold on the Irish community in Britain, but also how innocent actions can be interpreted in the worst possible light.

Stalker was again very critical of this intelligence:

> This is the worst form of intelligence keeping … If it's to mean anything to people who pick it up 12 years later, it should say what the strength of it is. A police officer making a report has an enormous important duty to let people know what he thought when he wrote it. And to put that he was a republican sympathiser in contact with the PIRA without saying how or why … is wrong in my view.[26]

On 10 May 1985, DCI Baythorpe interviewed an informer who told him that he did not think that enough was being done to arrest the top drug dealers in the city. He mentioned that a Pakistani man was involved in drug dealing and that Taylor, Chairman of the MCA, was one of the major financiers.[27] The informer also told Baythorpe that Taylor's income was not sufficient to cover his lifestyle and he used drug deals to maintain it, which, of course, contradicts the allegation that Taylor was a 'major' financier.

Baythorpe told the informer that he 'found it very hard to believe' and then noted in his report that, 'the name meant nothing to me'.[28] This was most surprising. Taylor was a well-known businessman in Manchester and apparently a major player in the criminal life of the city. According to GMP, McGourlay had submitted a nineteen-item report on Taylor to Topping in June 1984 and the DIU had been investigating Taylor for four months. Yet the head of CIU noted that he knew nothing about him in May 1985. It was bizarre. The informer's name was never revealed in the civil action, but it could have been the ubiquitous Burton.

Manchester City Football Club luncheon

Baythorpe's informer was not the only one who considered that GMP was not doing enough to arrest the drug smugglers in Manchester. Taylor was of the same opinion. On 16 May, a few days after DIU had received all this information suggesting that Taylor was not only involved in drug trafficking but also possibly the importation of arms for the IRA, Taylor attended a lunch at Manchester City Football Club. These were held monthly and were designed to bring together people to promote the interests of the club. Attendees paid an annual fee and then extra for the meal and any guest whom they invited. On this occasion, Taylor invited John Stalker.

The guest of honour was James Anderton, the Chief Constable. With so much 'serious intelligence' in its possession, it is highly surprising that no-one in GMP tipped off Stalker or considered that Taylor might pose a security risk to the Chief Constable. Yet after the meal was over, Taylor wandered over and joined Anderton at his table. Among other matters he discussed with the Chief Constable was the growing drug problem in Manchester. Taylor told Anderton that he didn't think the police were doing enough to deal with the heroin and cocaine problem, and he thought that 'the Pakistanis' were mainly responsible for the importation of the drugs.[29]

Taylor also told Anderton about his concerns with his yacht. He related how he had been trying to sell it in Puerto Banus but there were many other people trying to do the same. A common practice, he said, was to leave the boat in the hands of an agent and allow potential purchasers to try the yacht out. He had left his with a man called Whittaker, who had found a potential purchaser called Alan Brooks, and he had given permission for it to be tried out in Spanish and Portuguese waters, but then it had ended up in Dartmouth. Taylor told Anderton that the boat had probably been used for a drug run. He then went on to say that it seemed the drug runners were involved in a sophisticated ruse whereby they would pretend to be potential purchasers and then use a yacht for drug smuggling, thereby implicating the real owners in the importation of drugs. He informed Anderton that he and Stalker were working on the problem and would soon produce a file for Interpol. Taylor never did produce a report because he shortly afterwards discovered that he was himself subject to a police investigation.

In retrospect, this conversation had an element of farce about it. Anderton would have known about all the intelligence which Customs and Excise and

CDIU had supplied to the DIU. In particular, he would have been familiar with the details of *Diogenes* entering Dartmouth after being suspected of dropping off a haul of drugs. Now he was being informed of the same event by the ex-owner of the boat. It must have been very difficult not to convey to Taylor that he already knew the details.

After the lunch, Anderton returned to his office and dictated a long memorandum to himself regarding the background to the social event, Taylor's approach, and the details of their conversation.[30] It noted that Taylor 'is currently suspected of being involved in major crime and somehow involved in the illegal importation of dangerous drugs including cocaine and heroin ... There could also be an IRA dimension'[31] – identical information to that supplied by Burton.

Anderton's memorandum also noted that Taylor was under investigation and police surveillance. He went on: 'I was mindful, above all, of the position of my own Deputy ... whose relationship with Taylor is causing me acute concern.'[32] As a result, he had referred the matter to 'an independent higher authority'.[33] The higher authority was presumably HMIC. Anderton finished by noting that enquiries 'will either confirm or remove' his suspicions. These enquiries, incredibly, never did include an interview with Taylor about the use of his boat, suggesting that GMP was more concerned with investigating Stalker than dealing with the drug problem.[34]

Anderton's memorandum contained a highly significant comment: 'I also knew that connection between Taylor and Stalker and members of the QSG has recently been firmly established.'[35] This was simply untrue. The connections between the QSG and Stalker were never firmly established and raised the question as to what information Anderton was receiving from the DIU. Was it, by late May 1985, feeding false or exaggerated information to Anderton to secure Stalker's removal? For Anderton to record that there could well be 'an IRA dimension' beggars belief. Was he told that the 'dimension', as he put it, originated four years earlier from a dangerous informer, Burton, who alleged that Klapish and the QSG had contracted the IRA to blow up Kent Street in Belfast?

The reference to the independent higher authority – HMIC – was also significant. This memorandum – dated May 1985 – is the only actual documentary proof from Anderton himself that he had informed HMIC about his concerns over his deputy, raising considerable doubt about the earlier claims. As mentioned above, GMP claimed that in March 1985, a letter had been drafted by Lees for Anderton to send to Myers in HMIC, stating his suspicions about Stalker. But no original was produced in court and the authenticity of the draft was questionable.

If Taylor, at the time, had known that he was under suspicion, it is remotely conceivable that his conversation with Anderton was a highly sophisticated attempt to put the police off the trail and place the blame elsewhere. But he did not know he was being investigated until the end of July 1985 and therefore this conversation was that of an innocent man expressing his concerns to the police. In any event, Taylor had sold the Moulton Street precinct for £2.75 million in May 1984 and was now buying several other development plots. It did not make sense to put this considerable profit at risk by drug smuggling. Moreover, if he was a drug smuggler why sell the boat?

At around this time, the DIU also received at least four documents from Alan Chapman, who worked for American Express and was described as a 'Special Agent'.[36] One of American Express's informers was none other than 'Barbara Codd' – alias David Burton (Chapter 4). In February 1982, Burton provided Chapman with various information about members of the QSG and the names of two IRA men suspected of blowing up Kent Street.[37] Anderton's defence counsel made much of the fact that the DIU was getting information from at least two different agencies – American Express and Customs and Excise – implying that this was good detective work.[38] It was only good detective work, however, if the source of the information was different and not recycled information from the same informer.

Recruiting another informer

On 16 May 1985, *Diogenes*, which was now owned by John Allan Brooks,[39] arrived in Guernsey with Whittaker and a crew member called Eric Worswick who was wanted for various offences.[40] Worswick was arrested and brought back to Lancashire.[41] Over the following weeks, he was interviewed extensively by members of the DIU and admitted that he had been involved in the importation of drugs in the time between leaving Britain and his arrest.[42] On 25 June, he appeared before Preston Crown Court, but charged only with handling stolen goods. He pleaded guilty and was sentenced to 150 hours of community service.[43] He had obviously done a deal with the DIU to become an informer in exchange for more serious offences being kept off the charge sheet.[44]

Before formally recruiting Worswick as an informer, Topping and Born went to London on 23 July 1985 to seek advice, or perhaps approval, from the Acting Deputy of Public Prosecutions, Mr Wood.[45] It is not known why Topping considered it necessary to seek approval because he had the authority under Force Orders to recruit Worswick.[46] Presumably, it was to cover his own back in recruiting someone who was believed to be heavily involved in the importation of illegal drugs. Topping would no doubt have given details of his belief that GMP was facing a major problem of organised crime involving the QSG, IRA, a prominent Manchester businessman and a corrupt police officer. He would also have provided details of *Diogenes* and his belief that it was being used for drug smuggling. Although some of the information had been around for at least two years and had a nasty habit of re-emerging from different agencies at regular intervals, it is most unlikely that the DPP was informed of this fact, or the fact that Taylor had sold his boat or had raised his own suspicions directly with the Chief Constable.

The visit by Topping to the DPP, together with his prison interviews with Burton, reflected the extent of his continuing involvement in the investigation. He was now head of CID Operations and oversaw hundreds of detectives within the various Specialist Units: Criminal Intelligence, Criminal Records, Fingerprint Department, Serious Crime Squad, Cheque Fraud Squad, Commercial Branch, and the SB. Normally CID heads would not become involved in specific investigations as it would conflict with the officer in charge. It would also take them away from their primary responsibilities. Topping's continuing involvement, therefore, suggests that it was much more than a drugs inquiry and lends support to the view that, from the outset, the purpose of the DIU was to investigate the Deputy Chief Constable.

Worswick, once recruited, was armed with a tape-recorder, and sent back to Spain to record any conversations with drug smugglers.[47] During the next few weeks Worswick supplied the DIU with details about the drug scene in Spain and numerous tapes of conversations with people suspected of being involved. In total his information came to a staggering 1,800 pages.[48] On 2 July, he told Murray in the DIU that a Michael Green had contacted him and had asked if he would take *Diogenes* back to Spain, and also if he would go to see Brooks, who was now in prison, having been arrested leaving the country.[49] Green, originally from London but now based in Marbella in Spain, was building up a vast empire running drugs into Europe from North Africa.[50]

On 15 July, Worswick supplied more information. He provided a description of how *Diogenes* was used to smuggle drugs into a little beach called Blackpool Sands, a privately managed Blue Flag beach close to Dartmouth in south Devon.[51] The trip began with *Diogenes* sailing from Puerto Banus to just off the coast of North Africa, where it met a Moroccan boat, and containers of cannabis were transferred on board. It then sailed over to England and, when just outside the three-mile territorial limit, the drugs were transferred to a large inflatable dinghy and towed by a smaller inflatable with an outboard motor in order to reach the beach. The engine was then turned off and the large inflatable quietly paddled ashore. Following the unloading of the drugs, the inflatables were destroyed.[52]

At the end of July, GMP made another visit to London. A high-powered delegation of GMP police officers, which included ACC Lees, DCS Topping and DCI Born, met first with the Metropolitan Police and then with Customs and Excise. At the first meeting with Commander Corbett of the Metropolitan Police, Born took the minutes. The purpose was to update Corbett on the problems they were having and seek further help. They then moved onto a meeting with Customs and Excise, with whom they tried to arrange a joint strategy, presumably using Worswick, to get at the root of the organisation suspected of drug smuggling. Customs and Excise were not prepared, however, to co-operate.[53]

On 7 August, Anderton met the deputy head of Customs and Excise, no doubt as a result of the rebuff which Lees, Topping and Born had received to their suggestion of co-operation.[54] The meeting, as Stalker pointed out, was again unprecedented and it was extraordinary that a Chief Constable himself would get involved in a run-of-the-mill drugs investigation unless, of course, it was no ordinary investigation but, instead, a determined effort to find evidence on which to prosecute Taylor in order to remove Stalker from the Northern Ireland inquiry.

Towards the end of August, the DIU became weary of Worswick. They called a meeting with Customs and Excise on 22 August. The DIU asked them to confirm or corroborate at least some of the things that Worswick had been telling them about the drug scene.[55] They were reassured. However, only a week later, DI Murray was expressing the opinion that he considered Worswick had divided loyalties and could not be trusted.[56] A criminal, who appeared to promise so much, was now turning out to be like Burton – very unreliable. He was potentially giving the DIU the run-around.

The 'History of M/V *Diogenes*'

In September 1985, a summary of all the information on *Diogenes* was produced in a report entitled 'History of M/V *Diogenes*'. It is not known who prepared this report, but it might have been Baythorpe as head of CIU. It began by noting that *Diogenes* was searched in Liverpool docks in 1982. It then noted that in July 1982: 'Vessel again checked, this time in Gibraltar'.[57] The source of this latter information was unknown. The report was highly illustrative of the way intelligence can be given a totally different meaning as it is reproduced from one document to another. The wording suggested that the yacht was under some sort of constant surveillance. It was not. As already noted, the boat was not searched in Liverpool. Colin

Faulkner, the skipper, contacted Customs and Excise himself and handed in the guns and ammunition.

In late September 1985, the DIU received confirmation that Taylor was not involved in the illegal importation of drugs. Customs and Excise reported that one of their informers, whose identity was not given, told them that Taylor had no connection with any form of drug dealing. He described Taylor as a successful businessman, who was involved in property and land deals, an assessment based on first-hand information from political sources at the Town Hall.[58] However, it was not until 27 February 1987, that GMP eventually admitted that Taylor was not involved in drugs. In an action heard in front of Lord Justices May and Nolan, Mr Andrew Collins Q.C., who was briefed on behalf of GMP, said that there was no suggestion that Taylor had ever been involved in drugs in any way and that he wished to make that clear in open court.[59] By then, Taylor's businesses had been ruined and he had lost everything. The DIU was eventually disbanded in 1989. It was admitted in court that the DIU had arrested no-one for drug offences in its entire four year history.[60]

* * *

The arrival of Taylor's yacht, *Diogenes*, in Dartmouth after a suspected drug run was a seminal moment in the Taylor/Stalker affair. It is not known precisely when the DIU received the intelligence from Customs and Excise, but it was at least a month or two after the DIU started work and it would not have influenced the decision to set up the unit. This strengthens the argument that the DIU was clearly a disguise to investigate the Taylor/Stalker relationship based on informer Burton's babblings. *Diogenes'* drug run, however, may have convinced those working in the DIU that Burton's information had substance. Their conviction would have been strengthened by Burton recycling the information through different agencies. Against such a background of suspicion, the information was carelessly embellished as it was transferred from one agency to another and back to the DIU. The curious spectacle of Taylor approaching Anderton in May 1985 and telling him of his suspicions about the use of his boat – hardly the behaviour of a drug smuggler – did not deter the investigation. Minds were made up. The DIU was less interested in drugs *per se* and more interested in discrediting Taylor because of his friendship with Stalker.

PART IV
BANKING ON A CONVICTION

Chapter 14

Operation Kaluki

STALKER DELIVERED an interim report to the RUC on 18 September 1985. At the same time, despite many months of work by the team of senior officers and one sergeant, the secret DIU still had no tangible evidence to link Taylor to organised crime, drugs, or the IRA. At this point, it might have been expected, particularly in the context of rising levels of all types of crime in Manchester and its surrounds, that GMP would have taken the decision to disband the Unit and terminate the investigation. Instead, a decision was taken to intensify investigations into Taylor under the codename Operation Kaluki, named after Taylor's favourite card game. The operation involved one of the most intensive surveillance operations ever targeted on a British citizen. A dedicated surveillance unit observed Taylor's offices from 25 September 1985 to 21 March 1986, with an extra two days on 8 and 9 May – a total of 114 days. It is hard to avoid the conclusion that GMP were desperate to find evidence on which to convict Stalker's friend – and at any cost.[1]

The Miami tickets

In July 1985, Roberts, the former friend of Taylor, had told the DIU about the holiday Taylor and Stalker took together in Miami in 1981. The DIU went to considerable lengths to obtain evidence of the vacation and who paid for it. It obtained the details of all transactions which Taylor had made on his Gold Card from American Express, stretching back over many years. No Access Order was obtained for these documents. It was another breach of the law and the principle of confidentiality.

After two months of checking every transaction, the DIU discovered one recording the purchase of two plane tickets from London to Miami. Stalker's name was noted on the copy. On the very same day that Operation Kaluki began work, Ware went to Travelmaster Ltd in Prestwick and saw Alan Derbyshire who found the receipts and documents relating to the flights, and handed them over to Ware. Stalker's fate was slowly being sealed. After DI Stephenson joined the DIU in November, he prepared a schedule of all Taylor's American Express payments but only from 1981, although the transactions went back much further. In the whole of the schedule, there was only one that carried an asterisk: the flight of 'KT and Febb'.[2]

When Anderton received the information from Lees that Stalker had visited Miami, he made two notes to himself on consecutive days. On 25 September 1985, he recorded that Lees had passed on the information to him and added the comment 'very disturbing'.[3] The following day he wrote another note, which described how he had spent over an hour in secret session with RL discussing the Miami visit and how it would be 'damaging to Stalker'.[4] The existence of these notes contrasted with his action following the claimed meeting with Lees in June 1984. On that occasion, it was claimed that Lees had reported to him the suspicions about Stalker, yet he made no note.

In the absence of any evidence of personal corruption or crime, the only way in which the information could have been considered by Anderton to have been 'very disturbing' or 'damaging to Stalker' was because he had accepted a gift from a member of the public whom some of his officers considered to be a major criminal. The possibility that Stalker had paid Taylor his share did not seem to have occurred to Anderton or Lees, perhaps because Anderton had noted down the detail incorrectly. He seemed to be under the impression that only Stalker was going to Miami, rather than the two men together.[5] Moreover, Anderton did not appear to entertain the possibility that Taylor was innocent of any crime.

Kaluki Report

On 26 September 1985, members of the DIU were instructed to prepare a detailed report for Anderton on Taylor and Stalker. Why he wanted a report urgently at this moment is open to conjecture. It could have been precipitated by the findings of the American Express transaction or, more likely, the submission of Stalker's interim report on the RUC a week earlier. During the criminal trial in 1990, Taylor's defence counsel, David Hood, was determined to find out more about the preparation of the report and who gave the order for it to be produced. He examined Ware on his pocketbook entry for 26 September 1985.

HOOD: Let us move through September to the 26 September – 'On duty at 7.45 a.m.'?

WARE   Yes.

HOOD: What does that refer to – 'on duty @ Drugs Unit. Engaged in urgent request – CC's report.' What is 'CC'?

WARE: I think 'CC' means Chief Constable. It will be exactly what the report says.

HOOD:	You have been assigned to the DIU since the 1 April and you told us that it is a dedicated Unit, a Unit dedicated to performing certain tasks and that it is a small team?
WARE:	Yes.
HOOD:	Here we are only five months later doing an urgent report for the Chief Constable?
WARE:	I did say initially the Chief Constable, yes.
HOOD:	It could not have anything to do with your duties with the DIU, would it?
WARE:	I very much doubt it.
HOOD:	Can you recall what it was?
WARE:	It was informing the Chief Constable about the work I had carried out so far.
HOOD:	Mr Topping was in charge?
WARE:	Yes.
HOOD:	Who asked you to do an urgent report for the Chief Constable in September 1985?
WARE:	I cannot say that I have been asked by any specific person to compile an urgent report, but that is what it says, and I have no doubt at all that the request probably came from the Chief Constable through Chief Inspector Born, who was head of the Unit, but I cannot say categorically because I do not know.
HOOD:	You do not send off reports to the Chief Constable every day, do you?
WARE:	No.
HOOD:	Let me ask you again: Who asked you to do it? What were you specifically asked to do?
WARE:	I cannot recall who asked me to do it. Chief Inspector Born was head of the Unit and I am almost certain – as certain as I can be – that the request came from him. I am almost as certain that the information in that report was information regarding work I had done so far, and although it says 'Urgent – Chief Constable's report', you must be aware that reports do not go direct through to the Chief Constable: they have to go through the chain of command, which included, on this occasion, Chief Inspector Born.
HOOD:	It is an urgent report for the Chief Constable?
WARE:	Yes.
HOOD:	You told us, going back to July 1985, that you can remember all the way back through four years that first interview with Mr Roberts and that no notes were taken. You remember that?
WARE:	I can remember that no notes were taken.
HOOD:	Let us go to the Chief Constable's report matter. Is your answer still going to be that you do not know what it was, and it was probably a resumé of what had happened, and you cannot remember who asked you to do it?
WARE:	Yes, exactly. That would be my answer.
HOOD:	In what circumstances in the course of police business do you fill out urgent reports for the Chief Constable?
WARE:	Very rare.
HOOD:	Are there any circumstances in which you can recall doing it on any other occasions?

WARE: Me personally?

HOOD: Yes?

WARE: No.

HOOD: This is the only time in your entire life as a police officer that you have performed this function, and your memory, I suggest is so utterly vague about it?

WARE: Yes.

HOOD: How long have you been a police officer?

WARE: Since 1967.

HOOD: 20 years – getting on for 23 years?

WARE: Yes.

JUDGE: Why was it urgent?

WARE: Because I seem to remember that the head of the Unit, the Chief Inspector, had requested that a report be filed and submitted on an urgent basis; exactly why he considered it to be urgent I just don't know.

After a lunch adjournment, Hood was in a kinder mood and now suggested that Ware was a small part of a much wider conspiracy.

HOOD: Mr Ware, finally, the report of the 26 September 1985, I would like to be a little more specific as to the criticisms I am making. Let me make it plain: Mr Taylor's case is that you are guilty of the worst behaviour and it goes higher up the ladder than yourself and other officers that we heard from in this case. We have heard of Mr Topping before lunch; we heard of a report going to the Chief Constable. I wish to make it plain that Mr Taylor's case is that it was at the higher levels that the real wrong-doing took place in all this, and I am suggesting that you have been guilty of wrong-doing: you were, as it were, one of the 'foot-soldiers' rather than one of the 'generals'. Do you understand?

WARE: I understand. If you do accuse me of anything at all I will deny it if it was right and proper at that time.[6]

The Kaluki report was in two parts and provided an insight into the information that the police had on Taylor after fifteen months of investigation, if taken from the date when Topping claimed the investigation began, or eight months since the establishment of the DIU. The first part contained an Anacapa Chart. These were first developed by Anacapa Sciences Inc. and apply network analysis to law enforcement problems. They provide a visual representation of complex data. A good summary is provided by Sparrow:

> Anacapa charts generally depict individuals by small circles, and relationships by lines (solid or dotted according to whether the relationship is confirmed or unconfirmed). The charts may also show rectangles enclosing one or more individuals as a method of representing membership of corporations or institutions. They clearly show who is central, who is peripheral, and visually reveal chains of links connecting one individual to another. To a network analyst they look like typical network diagrams.[7]

Anacapa Chart

It has been possible from the information presented in the civil action to reproduce what the chart might have looked like.[8] Along the top of the chart there were links between Taylor and his accountant, Derek Britton, who shared the same office at 2 St John Street Manchester. Then, to the right of Taylor there was a square enclosing Stanley Casino, presumably making a link between him and the fact that he sometimes gambled there. To the left of it, there was a circle enclosing the word Febb and linking Stalker to Taylor via the Stanley Casino.[9] Down the righthand side of the chart there was a series of squares enclosing circles representing individuals. Alongside the squares was a list of companies associated with each individual. In the centre of the chart, there were four squares representing the land purchases that Taylor had made, with links to the TSB and Co-operative banks. The left-hand side was headed M/V *Diogenes*, with the reference: 'Firearms and Drugs'.[10] Beneath it was a list of names of alleged members of the QSG, various other suspects as well as the names of two retired police officers. One circle contained the name of a man from Manchester. Stalker pointed out that he was a registered firearms dealer who used to supply guns to the RUC, amongst others, and was subject to licensing by the Home Office.[11] Why he was on the list never emerged.

Anacapa charts are intended to inform and clarify the relationship between different elements in a complex set of data. This amateur attempt at the use of this method of visual presentation achieved neither. It appeared mainly to present the viewer with details of the perfectly legitimate business and financial activities of Taylor while suggesting that there was a connection between him and a list of suspected criminals via his yacht *Diogenes*. Most of the information had been in the police domain for months, sometimes years, and no attempt had been made to produce any evidence to suggest that Taylor was involved in any of the criminal activities of those named in the circles. Once again, alleged membership of the QSG was used to imply criminality.

The second part of the Kaluki documentation consisted of an eight-page report. It recorded a whole series of statements, which were intended to be read in conjunction with the chart. Some of these statements were simply factual. For example, Taylor was purchasing the Film Exchange 'for a large sum of money' – as reported in the Manchester Evening News.[12] Other statements were highly prejudicial and presumably were intended to be read in this light.

Incredibly, the report noted that *Diogenes*, 'is alleged to have been used for the transportation of firearms and drugs on 8 June 1982 and the vessel was searched at Eastham Dock by customs officers who found two guns on board'.[13]

Drugs have now been added to the allegation that firearms were smuggled into England on board *Diogenes*. There was, of course, not a shred of evidence that *Diogenes* was transporting drugs in 1982. Moreover, while it did have firearms on board, the skipper of the boat, it will be recalled, had declared the firearms, and asked for them to be impounded (Chapter 13). The vessel was not searched. The report illustrated yet again how easy it was to reproduce items of information from earlier reports and then to combine them to suggest criminality. It seemed to be a crude and sloppy attempt to validate Burton's allegations of 1982 linking Taylor to drugs and guns.

Much was made of Taylor's gambling and there was a reference to members of the DIU observing him the day before the report was prepared, 'gambling in his city office during working hours'.[14] The report further noted that an informer 'states that he has seen Taylor and Febb' at Stanley Casino and the Playboy Club.[15] Stalker once again challenged the facts. He pointed out that he had been to the Playboy Club on only one occasion, after he had been the judge at the Lord Mayor's Show. A table had been booked by the Manchester Chamber of Commerce at the Playboy Club and he had had no part in choosing or booking the venue. Taylor certainly was not there.[16]

Apart from the fascinating insights which the report revealed about the way facts can be embellished and distorted, there was no evidence in the report which connected Taylor to any criminal activity. What the report did show, however, was the large amount of help that several of Taylor's banks had given to the DIU. It recorded for example, two mortgages and the amount which Taylor had been granted from two separate banks for his house – referred to pejoratively as 'palatial'.[17] It also noted the details of several loans which his companies had with various banks and recorded that all these pieces of information had come from a 'bank source'.[18]

All the visits to the banks had been initiated by the police: none of the banks or other financial institutions had approached the police or cast doubt on their client's integrity. Nor had any access orders been sought by the police at this stage to obtain legal access to any of Taylor's documents. The title of the Unit – the Drugs Intelligence Unit – had obviously opened doors and the many hours spent at various banks had not been in vain in obtaining detailed information on Taylor's financial and commercial activities. Yet during Taylor's criminal trial, members of the DIU continually denied that they had received any information about Taylor's accounts from any of the banks until after access orders had been obtained in 1986. The Operation Kaluki report provided irrefutable evidence that they had.

Surveillance marathon

With the Chief Constable's report out of the way, GMP began to intensify their investigation into every aspect of Taylor's life. Prior to 1985, GMP did not have a dedicated surveillance team. In about April 1985, shortly after the setting-up of the DIU, a decision was taken to establish one. DSgt Fiddler was put in charge of it and tasked with its development.[19] DS Simons, according to one newspaper, was in overall command.[20] After undergoing several months of training, the team then started watching Taylor. Once again there was no documentation in the public domain explaining the rationale for the unit.

Police surveillance teams follow a standard procedure. The priority is to find a good static observation post from which to observe the target, a location that must not give rise to any suspicions. In residential areas, it may be an unoccupied flat or house, or a room in a private house that the owner has been persuaded may be used for the common good. In commercial areas, it is often an empty office which is rented for a period, or some other site which does not give rise to suspicions. In targeting Taylor, two buildings were used, as well as observation points on the street.[21]

Teams are trained in techniques of observation and in providing accurate descriptions of people observed. This is a skilled task, as the description must be good enough to be able to help other officers identify the person. Typically, each person observed will be given a codename which reflects some aspect of their appearance, demeanour, or dress. Nicknames are sometimes sexist, such as 'legs', or pejorative as a 'slouch'.[22] A typical team will have up to fifteen members, who can be drawn upon to carry out observations or follow-up tasks. Normally, there will be two officers carrying out the static observation using powerful binoculars and cameras with telephoto lenses.

All observational details are noted on a standard operation log sheet, which notes the time of the observation, the intelligence and the officer who recorded it. These then give rise to what are known as action sheets. Again, these are standard forms. The top half of the form notes the nature of the action. For example, to trace and identify a white male, six-foot tall with a scar over the left eye, wearing a smart blue suit and carrying a black leather briefcase. Other instructions may task an officer to find out the owner of a specific vehicle or check out premises which a target has visited. The middle section of the sheet notes the officer allocated the task, the date, time and by whom. The bottom half of the sheet is used to record the 'result of action'.[23]

Property development involves long periods of time waiting for decisions to be taken. Taylor never tried to disguise the fact that he often filled his time in his office playing cards or backgammon by himself or gambling with others. A wide cross-section of Manchester society visited his office during working hours and gambled with him. The surveillance team must, therefore, have spent a considerable proportion of its time observing the great and the good, and the not so good, playing cards, and then attempting to identify each and every one of them.

Over the six months of observations, the surveillance team produced 415 pages of logs and generated 287 action sheets, which led to 1,395 pages of reports. It is not known whether any wanted criminals were observed and subsequently arrested as part of the operation. No evidence emerged from this costly surveillance to link Taylor to a specific crime, let alone the crime of which he was ultimately accused. The whole operation cost many thousands of pounds. Moreover, it was outrageous that the only dedicated surveillance unit in GMP had been deployed to watch people playing cards instead of supporting the detection and prosecution of individuals suspected of murder, rape and other serious offences.

Since about August 1985, Taylor suspected that both his house and office phones were being tapped and conversations recorded. He made enquiries but in vain. Then in June 1986, there was a faulty line in his office and the British Telecom engineer who came to test the phone said that there was unusual resistance on the line. Taylor asked if this could result from a phone tap and the engineer replied that this would explain the interference and the unusual resistance.[24] During the criminal trial, the police would admit only that a less sophisticated form of phone tapping had been used, whatever that might mean.[25]

Following Stalker's removal from the Northern Ireland inquiry in May 1986, he was informed by a colleague that his phone was tapped. His solicitors also believed their phones were tapped and their offices were also under secret surveillance. Anderton denied this in a carefully worded statement, in which he said: 'Neither Mr Stalker's nor Mr Lakin's telephones have been tapped under any authority granted or obtained by me.'[26] This left open the possibility that they were being tapped illegally.

The Anglo-Irish Agreement

As the surveillance team was observing Taylor playing cards, secret discussions were taking place between the British and Irish Foreign Offices and pressure was being exerted by President Reagan on the two governments to find a solution to the intractable problem of Northern Ireland. These talks eventually led to the Anglo-Irish Agreement, which was signed by the Prime Ministers of Britain and Ireland, Margaret Thatcher and Garret FitzGerald, on 15 November 1985. It was, according to two eminent political commentators, 'the most far-reaching political development since 1920 and the creation of Northern Ireland'.[27] The UK and Irish governments committed themselves to working much closer together on Northern Ireland and the most radical element of the agreement was the setting-up of a joint ministerial conference of British and Irish Ministers, supported by a permanent secretariat in Belfast. While supported by much of the nationalist community, most unionists were adamantly opposed to the Republic having any say in the North and organised mass demonstrations. The Agreement had major implications for the RUC as it was required to police the widespread anti-Agreement protests. As Chris Ryder, a Northern Ireland journalist and one-time member of the NIPA, put it:

> It sucked the force into the eye of the Northern Ireland political storm as never before and provoked a crisis of confidence among the members and their families on a scale that the IRA could only hope for. Unionist politicians actually attempted public subversion of the force and faced it with the most serious test ever of its professionalism, integrity and impartiality.[28]

* * *

September 1985 was a key month in the Taylor/Stalker affair. In Northern Ireland, Stalker delivered his interim report, minus his final assessment of the hayshed shooting. He was still waiting to obtain access to the tape and details about the informers involved, and wished to interview senior officers in the RUC and MI5 under caution. Widespread protests against the Anglo-Irish Agreement by unionists and loyalists were expected, requiring the police to deal with the impending violence. In Manchester, GMP intensified their investigation into Taylor by deploying a newly-created surveillance team for 114 days to watch his offices. Even a suspected serial killer was unlikely to be under surveillance for this length of time, yet here was a man with no criminal record being watched for nearly four months. Once again, it is difficult not to conclude that Taylor was being intensely investigated as part of a plan to remove Stalker from the Northern Ireland inquiry.

Chapter 15

Banks, Banquets and Boats

ON 11 NOVEMBER 1985, there was another highly significant development in the Taylor/Stalker affair. DI Stephenson replaced DI Richardson in the DIU.[1] Stephenson was a specialist in fraud and had worked for some time in the Commercial Fraud Squad. He had been involved with the LFF investigation in Belfast and Manchester, and was one of the officers who went to arrest Vincent Schiavo only to find that he had hot-footed it to Spain the night before (Chapter 4). The change in personnel indicated that a decision had now been taken to focus the investigation on Taylor's commercial activities, as the drug investigation had reached a dead end. Following Stalker's submission of his interim report in September, GMP seemed more determined than ever to find an offence for which to prosecute Taylor.

Investigation impasse

In the criminal trial, Hood cross-examined Stephenson on his appointment to the DIU. He made the remarkable admission that the DIU investigation into Taylor was at an impasse when he moved to the secret unit.

HOOD: While I am interrupting, you said earlier that you were under a lot of pressure at this time, that was about November 1985?

OFFICER: Yes.

HOOD: Where from?

OFFICER: From senior officers, to resolve the matter one way or the other.

HOOD: By senior officers?

OFFICER: Particularly from Mr. Topping. When I joined the unit, the enquiry was at an impasse as regards Mr. Taylor.

HOOD: He was wanting a result, Topping?

OFFICER: Yes, one way or the other.

HOOD: One way or the other?

OFFICER: Yes.[2]

It was now over six months since Burton had been interviewed on five separate occasions repeating on tape several very serious allegations against Taylor – that he was a member of the QSG, had stored guns for them, and was involved in drugs, organised crime, and had a police officer on a pension. Yet a team of senior officers had been unable to provide a shred of evidence to support any of them.

Police visits to the Co-operative Bank

The shift in the investigation towards Taylor's commercial and financial affairs appears to have begun a month or so before Stephenson's appointment. On 8 October, Ware and Richardson visited the Co-operative Bank, Taylor's principal bank. They met with Mr Hylie Sheppard, the assistant general manager and the bank's chief inspector of its fraud department. According to the police, the purpose of the visit was to try and persuade the bank that it was being defrauded by Taylor. The bank, however, had not reported any fraud but was then visited on no fewer than nine times between this date and 19 February 1986.

During the criminal trial, Hood was particularly interested to ascertain from Ware what information led to the first visit to the bank. More specifically, he asked Ware: 'What acts were perpetrated by Mr Taylor that you could legitimately confront the bank about and put to Mr Sheppard?'[3] Ware replied that Mr Sheppard was told to look more closely at the facilities that had been afforded to Taylor. The cross-examination then continued:

HOOD: Will you answer the question?

J SACHS: What factual basis had you which enabled you to make that assertion to Mr Sheppard?

WARE: The source of information was one man – Mr Roberts.

HOOD: What was it that Mr Roberts told you?

WARE: That we, as the police, should look carefully at the relationship between Mr Taylor and the people with whom he banked.

HOOD: In the light of that answer about Mr Roberts, let me suggest that Mr Roberts didn't have a clue about Mr Taylor's bank, that they had not spoken to each other for several years. There was no way that Mr Roberts could have said anything at all about the bank.

WARE: Mr Roberts suggested that we should investigate, if possible, about the relationship between Mr Taylor and Mr Taylor's bankers.

HOOD: Answer the questions, please. You are saying that you recall Mr Roberts going on saying something quite specific – that you should go and have a look at the Co-operative Bank and also to investigate Mr Taylor's relationship with the bank over cash? That is what you are saying on oath to the Court?

WARE: Yes.

HOOD: In the light of your happy recollection of that fact, it was the case, was it
           not, that by 1985 Mr Roberts and Mr Taylor had not been speaking for
           some considerable period of time? Mr Roberts was not privy to Mr
           Taylor's private or commercial activities? Mr Roberts could not possibly
           have known of his relationship with the Co-operative Bank?

WARE: I don't know. Only Mr Roberts can tell you that.[4]

Hood pressed Ware on whether any check had been carried out on the
reliability of the information from Roberts before visiting Taylor's bank and
prejudicing him there. Had he made any efforts to ascertain whether Roberts
might have malicious motives? Ware said that he had made no such efforts, only
that Richardson had seen Roberts on several occasions.[5]

On 26 November, Ware went again to the Co-operative Bank. The purpose
of this visit, according to Ware, was to introduce Stephenson to Sheppard. Hood
considered this incredulous: 'You do not seriously suggest that you and Mr
Stephenson went all the way to the Co-operative Bank merely to tell Mr
Sheppard that Mr Stephenson had replaced Mr Richardson? Yes, of course I
did.'[6] Hood asked him if Sheppard had given him any details of Taylor's account.
Ware denied it. Hood asked again and Ware responded with the definitive
statement: 'Mr. Shepherd did not give me information regarding Mr. Taylor's
accounts before access orders were in fact applied for and granted.'[7]

Hood then interrogated Ware on how long he spent with Sheppard, as his
pocketbook noted that they began the task at 10.13 a.m. and returned to their
office at 12.45 p.m. Hood suggested that they were probably at the bank for some
time. The cross-examination continued:

HOOD: Yes. Let us fix an approximate figure. An hour?

WARE: Quite possibly.

HOOD: You were there quite possibly for a whole hour. Let us follow this through,
           Mr Ware. It is not going to take much more than, let us say five minutes,
           let us say ten minutes, fifteen minutes, for you to tell Mr Sheppard that Mr
           Stephenson is now heading the inquiry instead of Mr Richardson?

WARE: Yes.

HOOD: What happened during the other 45 minutes?

WARE: Nothing whatsoever. The reason for the visit was to do nothing more than
           introduce Mr Stephenson.

HOOD: We have what you say the reason for the visit was; we have at the moment
           an unexplained period of 45 minutes when you were there?

WARE: Yes.

HOOD: What went on during those 45 minutes if you say Mr Sheppard told you nothing?

WARE: You are trying to imply that Mr Sheppard in fact imparted something to me
           during that period.

J SACHS: I think it is suggested that you did not sit in silence for 45 minutes. What
           did you discuss for the balance of the notional hour?

WARE:	Other than an introduction of Mr Stephenson – and going back that long, I can't remember exactly what was discussed. I don't know and I am certainly not going to guess.
HOOD:	Mr Ware, it will not do, will it? You understand the suggestion I am putting to you – you are disputing that?
WARE:	Exactly.
HOOD:	Let us go for (what I think you called yesterday) an educated guess. What on earth could you possibly have discussed for 45 minutes – two police officers, part of a unit dedicated to make certain investigations? What could you have discussed for 45 minutes?
WARE:	I don't want to make an educated guess, Mr Hood.
HOOD:	What could you possibly have discussed with the details of Mr Taylor's account at that bank?
WARE:	You are really asking me a hypothetical question – I don't know.
J SACHS:	I do not think he is, sergeant; I think he is asking you a question.
HOOD:	It is not a hypothetical question, is it, Mr Ware, because that is not an imaginary situation. We have here a real situation – your own evidence that you were at that bank quite possibly for as long as an hour.
WARE:	My apologies.
HOOD:	With the most generous time calculation possible, your introduction of Mr Stephenson could not have taken longer than 15 minutes, so we have a straightforward factual position – 45 minutes, which I am asking you for an explanation.
WARE:	And because I can't remember, I will not guess.
HOOD:	Let me suggest to you, that of all the banks you went to you found gold at the Co-operative Bank in Mr Hylie Sheppard, a man ready (let me suggest) to help you in any way he could from the very outset in complete breach of his duties of confidentiality to Mr Taylor.
WARE:	No, he was willing to accept the inquiry from the police that he should, in fact – either he or his staff should look closely at Mr Taylor's banking facilities with the Co-operative Bank.
HOOD:	And then he started to give you information, did he not – documents, papers and the like?
WARE:	Not at that stage, no.
HOOD:	With his Honour's kind indulgence, I will ask you once more and then move on. What happened during the unexplained 45 minutes?
WARE:	I can't remember, and I will not guess.[8]

A few weeks later, on 16 December, Ware and Stephenson made yet another visit to the Co-operative Bank to talk to Sheppard. Ware, while he made no notes, again claimed he was told nothing other than that Sheppard had started an inquiry within the Corporate Business department of the bank, an inquiry that was ongoing. Once again, Hood worked out how long they must have been at the bank and suggested it might have taken fifteen minutes to find out how the bank's inquiry was going, leaving another 45 minute gap. Ware insisted that the purpose of this visit was to ascertain whether his enquiries had given the bank enough suspicion to be able to say to the police that: 'We, as the Co-operative Bank, wish you, the police, to become fully involved in this enquiry.'[9]

The following day Ware and Stephenson returned to the bank with CS Topping, now head of CID in GMP. Even Justice Sachs showed surprise and asked what time he had left on the previous day. Hood then asked with an air of sarcasm: 'What on earth could have altered in the meanwhile, unless Mr Sheppard had got an absolute storm of energy on him in the meanwhile?'[10] The explanation, however, was the same as on Stephenson's first visit: it was another introduction, and he could not remember what was said. Hood pushed hard:

HOOD: Mr Ware, a detective Chief Superintendent – your boss – head of the whole division, accompanying you to the bank?

WARE: Yes.

HOOD: No doubt an event you will remember to your dying day. Tell us, please, what was said? Two hours, Mr Ware, including travel. What was said?

WARE: I am sorry, I cannot recall exactly what was said.

HOOD: Generally?

WARE: It would have been much easier, much better, to have made notes of some description of every time I visited any premises whatsoever, made any enquiries or spoke to any persons whatsoever. On this occasion I went there with Mr Stephenson and Mr Topping; I can't really recall, and I will not guess at what was said, but Mr Topping was quite adamant that he wished to be introduced as the head of this unit to the Co-operative Bank.

HOOD: What was said?

WARE: I can't recall.

HOOD: What did Mr Topping do?

WARE: He stayed in my company and spoke to Mr Sheppard.

HOOD: Did he take notes of what was being said?

WARE: I don't recall notes being taken.

HOOD: You do not recall anybody making any notes at all?

WARE: At that time?

HOOD: Yes.

WARE: I don't recall any notes being taken. I certainly didn't take any; I don't recall Mr Topping taking any, and I am also just as certain that Mr Stephenson didn't take any.

HOOD: If we look through over three years of your pocketbooks, we will not find a single other occasion, will we, when Detective Chief Superintendent Topping accompanied you on an inquiry outside of Fiddes Building?

WARE: I don't think you will.

HOOD: Do you recall any occasion in your 20 years in the police when a detective superintendent, the head of the whole of the C.I.D., has accompanied you on a field inquiry?

WARE: No.

HOOD: So, just like the report to the Chief Constable, it is the only time in your whole career that such a thing has happened and just like with that urgent report, your memory is completely lacking?

WARE: It is also the only time in my career that I have been involved in an investigation, which has involved, one way or another, a man so senior as the Deputy Chief Constable of a police force.[11]

Topping, despite being head of the CID with many other responsibilities, was keeping a very close eye on this investigation by insisting that Stephenson take him to the Co-operative Bank and introduce him to Sheppard. This was no run-of-the-mill fraud investigation. GMP, and Topping in particular, were making every effort and using considerable resources to investigate all aspects of Taylor's life. Either he firmly believed that Stalker was in a corrupt relationship with Taylor and was trying desperately to find concrete evidence to bring disciplinary or criminal charges against him, or the true purpose of the intense investigation was to construct an offence on which to convict Taylor to support a disciplinary charge against Stalker.

Stephenson made yet another visit to the bank just two days before Christmas. This was the fifth visit made by members of the DIU. Hood, once again, wanted to know the purpose of the visit.

HOOD: You have gone there four times with that in mind, you have told us you wanted them to consider their position and complain, and they would not?

OFFICER: In due course.

HOOD: You wanted them to complain?

OFFICER: Once they satisfied themselves that they were the victim of a fraud.

HOOD: The sooner the better as far as you were concerned?

OFFICER: Yes, indeed.

HOOD: So, we have it. You wanted them to complain and to complain as soon as possible.

OFFICER: Yes.

HOOD: Even on your evidence, with a year to talk about it, the best you come with, you went back again for a fourth visit, fifth visit in all, to give the bank more information to update them?

OFFICER: Yes.[12]

On 22 January 1986, Stephenson went back to the Co-operative Bank. He was there for nearly four hours. Hood points out sarcastically that it was rather a long time to be updating him with information. 'What on earth – you have been updating him for nearly four hours on what is your sixth visit to the bank – seventh in all accepting that on one occasion no-one was available – what on earth could you have been telling him?'[13] Stephenson lamely suggested that perhaps he had been exploring how the bank operated internally, only to be told that he had already done that during another visit.

Five days later both he and Ware were back again. By now, Hood was losing patience.

HOOD: Mr Stephenson, let us see if we can do a little calculation just to put your answers in perspective. We have you, including travelling time, at the bank by 27 January on seven different occasions and we have you with Mr Sheppard for seventeen hours and ten minutes. I suppose we should take three and half hours from that total [for travel]. That still got you there in the region of thirteen to fourteen hours.

OFFICER: Yes.

HOOD: During which time you told us on oath you were not given any information at all by Mr Sheppard.

OFFICER: That's right.

HOOD: Mr Stephenson, let me put it to you again this simply is not the truth, is it?

OFFICER: It's very much the truth.[14]

It was far from the truth. Both Stephenson and Ware knew that they had persuaded Sheppard to provide them with detailed information about Taylor's loans and commercial affairs. The key meeting took place on 29 November 1985. Following the visits, Stephenson wrote an extensive report on the information which Sheppard had provided. He also noted a list of actions for Sheppard and GMP.[15] In the absence of any legal obligation, there was a clear breach of confidentiality to Taylor. Further information was obviously supplied during following meetings. The late November meeting explains Topping's unprecedented visit to Sheppard in December, to hear for himself what the bank official was saying. It also explains why in the criminal trial, Ware and Stephenson strenuously denied that Sheppard had supplied them with information, otherwise the trial would have collapsed.

Police pressure on bank to report a fraud

During the bank visits, the Co-operative was put under considerable pressure by the police to report Taylor for fraud. To this end, they gave the bank three pieces of false information. They told Mr Chadwick, Head of Advances Department, that there was a legal time limit on registering legal charges. This was untrue. Second, they told him that the amount of shale on the Poynton site was only 20,000 to 30,000 tons. This was incorrect. Third, they informed him that there was no planning permission on the Poynton site, which was also untrue.[16]

Within the bank there was concern at the behaviour of the police. Mr Collier, a senior official in the bank, later told Chadwick that he hoped he was right in what he had told the police. He pointed out that if Bowley – who headed up the Corporate Business department in the bank and who was charged along with Taylor – wins in court, he will be taking action against the bank and 'you might get your arse kicked'.[17] He made it clear that he didn't trust the police and that Chadwick shouldn't either.

The taped meeting

Towards the end of November 1985, Stephenson contacted First Interstate Capital Markets, an American bank which made a loan in 1982 to Propwise, one of Taylor's companies. The bank liaised with their London solicitors, Travers Smith Braithwaite, who wrote to Propwise on 3 December. The letter recorded that the bank had been approached by the police and was prepared to assist with their enquiries, provided Propwise gave its full and unlimited authority to divulge such information.[18] Stephenson had told the bank that he was from the Commercial Fraud Squad rather than the DIU.

Taylor's solicitor, Guy Robson, had already tried in August 1985 to ascertain who was investigating Taylor in GMP, and had written several letters without success (Chapter 12). Following the letter from the First Interstate's lawyers informing him that Stephenson was making inquiries of his account, Taylor asked Robson to follow this up with the police. Robson contacted the Commercial Fraud Squad and was told Stephenson was not with them.

On 6 December 1985, Robson spoke with DS Simons, who was now head of the Commercial Fraud Squad. Although not a member of the DIU, Simons must have been familiar with its secret work, as Stephenson, a member of his department, had been seconded to the unit only a month earlier. Simons was still Stalker's number three on the Northern Ireland inquiry at this time. Robson was informed by Simons in a telephone call that the inquiries had 'gone past Mr Taylor and no longer involved him'.[19]

Robson followed up this conversation with a letter to the Chief Constable on 13 January, noting the sequence of events to date and the fact that Simons had declined the offer to interview Taylor. He finished by drawing attention to the impact it was having on Taylor.[20] Anderton was away from his office when the letter arrived. Stalker, as his Deputy, opened it. The letter confirmed that his friend Taylor was under investigation. When Anderton returned, Stalker gave him the opened letter. Following their meeting, Anderton wrote a note about the incident, recording that he felt in a 'delicate situation'.[21]

The key question is why did Anderton feel that he was in a delicate situation? As Farley, Taylor's counsel, pointed out in his opening address for the civil action, Anderton only had to advise his deputy to distance himself from Taylor. But Anderton was obviously concerned that to give this advice would confirm that the enquiry was serious. However, not to give the advice would be irresponsible. Stalker's knowledge of the investigation was, of course, immaterial: Anderton had a duty to advise Stalker to distance himself from Taylor. His failure to do his duty, Farley suggested, was not an attractive attitude in a chief constable.

A meeting was subsequently arranged between Robson, Simons, and Taylor. It took place on 16 January 1986.[22] After a short introduction to the meeting, Simons requested that Taylor leave the room. He did so, leaving behind his briefcase with a tape-recorder running.[23] Robson began by emphasising the impact that the inquiry was having on his client. He recalled that Simons had said in their telephone conversation before Christmas that the inquiry had 'gone past Taylor'.[24] Robson wanted to know whether there would be any further letters written to banks. After all, to his knowledge, some investigation into Taylor had been going on for at least five months. Simons gave no answer.

Robson pointed out that in civil law, 'there is consequential foreseeable loss'.[25] He went on to say that he would make a note of the fact that he had offered Simons the opportunity to interview his client at a time of mounting losses. He was leaving Simons in no doubt about the possibilities of a civil action. The interview finished with Robson trying to establish whether there were any other departments, or in Robson's quaint phrase, 'special little ones' involved.[26] Simons avoided the question by pointing out that he and his colleagues worked in the Commercial Fraud Squad.[27] He was not going to admit that a special unit had been investigating Taylor for the best part of a year, or that Stephenson had been seconded to it.

Robson received no reply to his letter to Anderton. On 3 February, he wrote to him again by recorded delivery, drawing attention to his letter of 13 January. He received a reply a day later, in which Anderton said that it was the practice of the police to neither confirm nor deny that enquiries are being undertaken. Robson wrote further letters in March and April following the discovery that access orders had been issued under PACE in respect to Taylor's personal and business bank accounts.[28] On 28 April Robson received a long, dismissive but highly revealing letter from Anderton:

Dear Sir,

Re: Kevin Taylor

With reference to your letter of 25th April I have to inform you that it is not my policy in particular circumstances of cases of this sort, to disclose at this stage any information you seek respecting points at issue. If and when it is necessary for your client to be interviewed by investigating officers of the Greater

Manchester Police Force you and your client will, of course, be advised and relevant information communicated to you.

This latest letter of yours which has been sent to me personally at my office now prompts me to raise an important matter. Whilst I fully appreciate that it is the rightful prerogative of any legal representative to write to me personally as Chief Constable in the interests of or in connection with a client, your persistence in doing so in the case of Mr Kevin Taylor is, to say the least, unusual and, in my experience as Chief Constable of Greater Manchester during the past ten years, also quite unprecedented.

I am sure you will appreciate that officers in the various investigation branches in my Force conduct many enquiries of different kinds involving numerous people, and subject to my being satisfied as to the propriety and necessity of these investigations, and there is orderly and correct supervision of them, I must allow them to continue towards a proper conclusion.

Yours faithfully

J. Anderton

Chief Constable.[29]

The letter showed that Anderton was now well aware of the case, but was obviously not concerned about the impact which the investigation was having on Taylor's businesses. The implicit message was that he was only doing his duty.

In the middle of the exchange of letters, on 8 February, Stephenson and Ware travelled to London to liaise with Angela Simpson at Amex and to collect all the documents for both the green and gold accounts of Taylor.[30] They visited her again on 17 March when her diary entry read: '10.30 DI Stephenson, Manchester, re drugs Kevin Taylor'.[31] The DIU was determined to use the drug card to open doors and obtain co-operation notwithstanding it was now over four months since Customs and Excise informed them that Taylor was not involved in drugs (Chapter 13).

Investigating Taylor's social life

Apart from investigating Taylor's commercial activities, the DIU was also interested in Taylor's social life, or rather a few social events at which Stalker was in his company – events that had nothing whatsoever to do with the alleged crime of perpetrating a fraud against his bank. The first was a dinner at the Belfry Hotel, Wilmslow in Cheshire held on 27 September 1985. It was organised by the Alexian Brothers – a Catholic charity established to provide for 'the sick, the aged, destitute and the insane'. The Stalkers were there as guests of Taylor. Anderton also attended the event and was the guest of Luis Anton, the Portuguese Consul in Britain.

According to Taylor, during the evening Anderton wandered over to their table and exchanged pleasantries with their party. Later, Taylor paid a visit to Anderton's table and spoke with him. He remembered that he talked about the Police Committee and made some remark to the effect that Anderton must be pleased that a Tory councillor had been elected chair. The previous Chair, Gabrielle Cox, was a Labour councillor with whom Anderton had had numerous battles. Taylor also remembered chatting briefly with Luis Anton, whom he had met on several occasions.[32] After the event, Anderton once again made a note to himself of the discussions between them and he recorded that Stalker was 'uncomfortable' – a remark which Stalker strongly challenged in the civil action.[33] On 4 October, the DIU dispatched Sergeant Ware to the hotel to obtain full details on who organised the event and who attended.[34]

The second event took place on 12 October 1985. According to Taylor, a group of his friends went to the Belle Vue greyhound track for an event in aid of Swinton Rugby League Club. There were about 50 people in the party including Stalker and his wife. After the races they went to a Greek restaurant in Princess Street in Manchester. Many months later in April 1986, Ware was dispatched to the greyhound track to try and obtain more details about who was present, and presumably to confirm that Stalker was in the party.[35] He prepared a report, which was then summarised in a document presented in the civil action. It noted that Stephen Hayes, the ex-policeman who now ran a security business, was in the party and implied that either Taylor or Hayes had paid the bill. Stalker denied this and said that it was a charity affair for a local sporting club and the bill was divided up with everyone paying their share.[36]

The third event was the Annual Ball of the MCA, which took place in the Piccadilly Hotel, Manchester, on 23 November 1985. Taylor organised a party for the ball. Although he now suspected that he was being investigated, he decided nevertheless to invite Anderton to join the top table. Unsurprisingly, Anderton turned down the invitation. Taylor also invited John and Stella Stalker. A couple of weeks before the event, Stalker had asked Anderton if it was alright to attend the ball, given that it was organised by a political party. At no time did Anderton indicate to Stalker that he disapproved. On the contrary, according to Stalker, he expressed his support.[37]

After the discussion, Anderton once again wrote a personal note to himself. His version of events was very different. He noted he told Stalker that it would be 'quite improper' politically for himself to attend, but it was different for Stalker.[38] As Stalker pointed out, this was contradictory. What was 'quite improper' for the Chief Constable, would also be 'quite improper' for his Deputy

– a contradiction upon which Mr Justice Owen also commented.[39] In any event, Anderton had told Stalker that the reason he turned down the invitation was because he had a previous engagement and not because it was a Conservative Party event.[40]

A few days after the event, Ware was again tasked with the responsibility of finding out more. He saw a Mr Groves in the Piccadilly Hotel. In the criminal trial, Hood asked Ware what he was doing at the hotel as part of an investigation into the commercial aspects of Taylor's life. Ware replied that he was there to find out what functions had been attended or organised by Taylor. Hood continued his cross-examination:

HOOD: Did Mr Groves make a statement?

WARE: A written statement?

HOOD: Did he make any statement to you at all, an oral statement or a written statement?

WARE: Certainly not a written statement. I believe he made an oral statement, or more to the effect that Mr Taylor had in the past organised or attended certain functions at the Piccadilly Hotel, which was involved in the boxing or football fraternity (if you will forgive me for calling it that).

HOOD: Did he make a statement? You say he made merely an oral statement, do you?

WARE: Yes.

HOOD: Did you note down the details of that conversation?

WARE: No.

HOOD: Here you are, being sent by senior officers to make enquiries to collect any information you can. You go to the Piccadilly Hotel, you speak to Mr Groves, and you say you do not write down any of that information at all?

WARE: Yes.

HOOD: So, you carry it in your head, do you?

WARE: Yes.

HOOD: And you take it back, and what do you do then – report it orally or write it down back at Fiddes Building?

WARE: Report it orally.

HOOD: So, your evidence is that at no stage do you write down this sort of information?

WARE: On this occasion, I didn't, no.

HOOD: Mr Ware, what happens if you forget? Is the unit not then deprived of a possibly vital piece of information?

WARE: But I didn't forget.[41]

Diogenes and commercial developments

As well as banks and banquets, Operation Kaluki was concerned with boats. The DIU had possession of the airline tickets for Taylor and Stalker's holiday on *Diogenes* in Miami in 1981. They now sought more information about the yacht and who might have sailed on it. On 3 December 1985, Ware and Stephenson travelled from Manchester to Poole in Dorset, to interview Lieutenant Commander Bowen-Gotham, who had flown to Miami in 1981 to help Taylor buy *Diogenes*.[42] In the criminal trial, Ware denied that the visit to Bowen-Gotham was specifically to find out about Stalker's trip to Miami but admitted that his name may have come up during conversation. Ware was unable to explain how the visit was remotely relevant to a fraud investigation. They took no statement from Bowen-Gotham, but Ware thought that Stephenson did take notes.[43]

The final area of interest to the DIU concerned Taylor's commercial development activities. In the absence of any access orders, the information leading to these enquiries could only have originated from the Co-operative Bank. At the beginning of October 1985, Ware and Richardson visited the Land Registry at Lytham.[44] Two days later, they travelled to London to interview Mr Virani, who had bought the Moulton Street precinct from Taylor for £2.75 million in May 1984.[45] He was interviewed again a fortnight later.[46] In November, Ware visited one of Taylor's purchases – the Tottington site – to see if the demolition which had been organised on the site had taken place.[47] In December a visit was made to Bury Town Hall to liaise with the Planning Officer.[48]

The mystery of Simons' role

There is a mystery surrounding the role that Simons played in the whole Taylor/Stalker affair. He was part of Stalker's team in Northern Ireland and had been selected principally because he had been positively vetted.[49] At the time, he was head of the Commercial Fraud Squad, from which Stephenson had been seconded to the DIU to pursue the investigation into Taylor's commercial activities. As noted above, Simons told Robson on 6 December that the inquiry had gone past Taylor. Hood pursued the issue with Stephenson in the criminal trial:

HOOD: Are you aware of Chief Superintendent Simons?
OFFICER: Yes.
HOOD: The officer at the material time, who was a GMP Officer?
OFFICER: Yes.
HOOD: The officer was also, at the time, Mr Stalker's number three in his Northern Ireland inquiry?
OFFICER: That's correct.
HOOD: And you say that he played no role in the DIU activities?
OFFICER: No, he didn't.

HOOD: None whatsoever?

OFFICER: Not as far as I'm aware. He replied to some correspondence.

HOOD: Do you remember me asking you about the early days at the old-style Committal last year?

OFFICER: Yes.

HOOD: Saying that [he] had nothing whatsoever to do with the inquiry, and when I showed you some correspondence suggesting that he might have been assigned to the operational side of the group at some time or other?

OFFICER: Yes.

HOOD: And you had become aware that from as early as August 1985 Mr Taylor was writing letters to the Greater Manchester Police, indicating he knew there were enquiries against him and that they were crippling his business?

OFFICER: I understood so, yes.

HOOD: Offering himself up for interview, offering access to his bank accounts and the like?

OFFICER: Yes.

HOOD: Do you recall such correspondence?

OFFICER: Yes, I do.

HOOD: Asking, with increasing urgency as the months progress, this inquiry to be made and he would be told what it was the DIU were after, and he is co-operating in any way he can?

OFFICER: Yes.

HOOD: Did you become aware, as the correspondence progressed, Mr Taylor's then solicitors spoke to Superintendent Simons of the Greater Manchester Police force on the 12th of December 1985?

OFFICER: I'll accept that, yes.

HOOD: Mr Simons told him that the inquiry had gone past Mr Taylor and no longer involved him?

OFFICER: Yes.

HOOD: Something that was untrue?

OFFICER: No, it wasn't, because Simons was misinformed. There was an on-going inquiry at the Moulton Street precinct being conducted by the Commercial Fraud Squad at the time in relation to other matters.

HOOD: And the answer to my question, on your evidence, is true but, as you say, Mr Simons did not realise it?

OFFICER: Basically.

HOOD: It is true at the time DIU inquiries had gone past Mr Taylor, they were going into top gear.

OFFICER: Mr Simons didn't have any knowledge of the DIU inquiry.

HOOD: Will you answer my question. I'm asking you about Mr Simons and the answer is it was untrue?

OFFICER: It was, in fact, yes.

HOOD: Tell me, Mr Stephenson, if Mr Simons was never involved directly or indirectly with the DIU inquiries, what was he doing on the 6th of January 1986 at a meeting with Mr Robson, Mr Taylor's solicitor? You are aware of that meeting are you not?

OFFICER: Yes, I am.

HOOD: And indeed, we went at length through the notes and indeed the tape recording that was made of it.

OFFICER: Yes.

HOOD: Mr Simons purported to give answers to questions without knowledge of what was going on, did he not?

OFFICER: Yes.

HOOD: Mr Stephenson, what was he doing that for if he was no part at all of the DIU inquiries, directly or indirectly?

OFFICER: I can only assume that he was asked to go and attend to the correspondence.[50]

Hood returned to this issue three days later and reminded Stephenson that at the Committal he said: 'I accept that on 6th January 1986 Mr Simons knew there was an inquiry into Mr Taylor by the DIU.'[51] Stephenson claimed that he could not recall having said it. But it was too late as it contradicted what he said in his cross-examination. The police, however, were determined to stick to the official line that Simons knew nothing about the DIU's investigation into Stalker, despite seconding one of his officers from the Commercial Fraud squad to the DIU.

On 12 December 1985, just a few weeks before the meeting in January between Robson and Simons, Stalker asked Simons if there was an inquiry into Taylor. Simons told him that there was no investigation into Taylor, but there was one into a tenant of his.[52] It was a lie. In the civil action, Stalker was asked if he would exempt Simons from his praise for his handpicked Northern Ireland team. His response was bitter: 'I didn't know then what I now know. Mr Simons had told me lies. If I'd known he was an officer who would tell lies, I wouldn't have taken him to Northern Ireland.'[53]

Later in his evidence, Stalker again implied that Simons was not truthful. He was shown a report which Simons had prepared for Anderton in March 1988, noting how often Stalker visited Northern Ireland during his investigation (Chapter 5). In one place it commented that Stalker did not see the relatives of the deceased and had to be persuaded to interview McCauley, the survivor of the hayshed shootings. Stalker responded:

> … it gives me no pleasure to accuse a fellow police officer of lies but it always seems to be Simons and that is not true. McCauley was very important: he was the only survivor of seven people who'd been shot by the police and to say I had to be persuaded to see him is a travesty of the truth, that just wasn't the case.[54]

Simons made a long entry in his notebook about the 12 December conversation between himself and Stalker. It contrasted sharply with the lack of detailed entries by members of the DIU investigating Taylor. The general gist of the entry was that Stalker had told him 'that a long-standing friend of some twenty years' had been in contact and was worried that the police enquiry would have an impact on 'his business and his credit worthiness'.[55] Simons specifically noted that Stalker did not mention the name of the friend. He also noted that Stalker had been assured by the friend that 'everything was above board and legitimate'.[56]

Tabachnik, Anderton's defence counsel, questioned Stalker about the claim that Simons had told him emphatically that Taylor was not the subject of an investigation. Stalker replied:

> My recollection was, that is what Simons said to me. In all the time I was a senior officer, this is the only time I ever did this. So, I can remember what happened, but I can't argue. I didn't write it down. I didn't see the purpose, but what I can say is that Simons said to me, your friend is not under investigation but one of his tenants is. It doesn't affect your friend. I left it at that because it had helped clear my mind that the head of the Commercial Fraud Squad didn't know there was an investigation into Taylor. I don't believe that he didn't know.[57]

Tabachnik went on to suggest that Simons' account was much more likely to be accurate than Stalker's because Simons had written it down and knew very little about the matter as it was not happening in the Commercial Fraud Squad but in the DIU. Justice Owen was not convinced by this argument. He was baffled by the fact that Simons had specially noted that Stalker had not mentioned the name of his friend. He pointed out that, 'It would be difficult to make an inquiry if he did not know the name' and it was a 'rather odd detail to put in'.[58] As Simons and Topping had a longstanding and close relationship, it is most improbable that Simons was in the dark about the depth of the investigation into Taylor and his own Deputy Chief Constable (Chapter 10).

On his return to work in August 1986, Stalker confronted Anderton about what Simons had told him. In his book published in 1988, Stalker described how he was told by a 'flustered and red-faced' Chief Constable that no inquiries had properly started into Taylor until October 1985 and no police officer was under investigation in April 1985. Stalker was now convinced that his removal was connected to his investigation in Northern Ireland and concluded:

> Those few blurted words confirmed for me, however, all that I suspected: that investigations into Kevin Taylor did not truly begin until after I had delivered my report into the RUC to Belfast on 18 September 1985, and that enquiries into me did not begin until after I had been given clearance in March 1986 to have access to the tape and to see Sir John Hermon and his Deputy.[59]

But Stalker was wrong. The evidence indicated that the investigation into Taylor and Stalker began at least in February 1985 with the establishment of the

DIU, if not before. This was confirmed in Topping's authentic 9 March letter beginning with the sentence: 'Brief notes to up-date you in relation to Taylor and Febb.' (Chapter11)

* * *

Following the delivery of Stalker's interim report on 18 September 1985, all the evidence indicates that the investigation into Taylor further intensified with the appointment of Stephenson to the DIU, strongly suggesting that there was a determination to prosecute Stalker's friend for fraud when no evidence of his involvement in drugs materialised. The numerous visits to the Co-operative Bank –Taylor's main bank – totalling over thirteen hours, were remarkable. The explanation that the police were performing 'introductions' was absurd. The bank was being pressured to supply information. At the end of November, the bank, illegally, finally gave the police all the confidential information about Taylor's loans. The police could now construct an offence on which Taylor could be prosecuted. Once again, Topping was heavily involved. The police enquiries into Taylor's boat and the social events which Stalker attended as Taylor's guest, show that Taylor and Stalker were, beyond doubt, the primary focus of the DIU's investigation. While Simons' precise role in the investigation into Taylor and Stalker remained a mystery, he was the only GMP officer who knew everything about Stalker's investigation in Northern Ireland and shared a very close relationship with Topping.

Chapter 16

Accessing the Inaccessible

BY THE BEGINNING of February 1986, Stalker's interim report, which he had delivered to the RUC five months earlier, had still not been passed on to the DPP in Northern Ireland; and Stalker and his team were still no nearer to obtaining access to the contents of the hayshed tape. According to Stalker, routine calls from his officers to the RUC were met with the standard response that the Chief Constable was still studying the report.[1] In fact, it was being minutely examined by a team of two DCSs, a legally qualified ACC and the RUC's internal legal advisor.[2] According to Stalker, in England and Wales an investigating officer's report would have been delivered simultaneously to the commissioning Chief Constable and the DPP.[3] The RUC finally delivered Stalker's report to the DPPNI on 13 February 1986. Was the long delay connected with the investigation of Stalker in Manchester?

Taylor's downfall

Back in Manchester Taylor's business was steadily deteriorating. The police investigation into his affairs was having a disastrous impact on all his commercial activities. Taylor's excellent relationships with the banks and planning authorities had deteriorated greatly. His word was no longer trusted and everyone was now treating him with suspicion.[4] He believed that the police had deliberately damaged his business reputation so that banks would curtail or stop funding, planners would be suspicious of him, and potential buyers would back off. The very name – Drugs Intelligence Unit – was sufficient to cast suspicion. References to drug trafficking and suggestions that he was involved in organised crime, discredited him among all those on whom his business depended. In a matter of months, he had become an outcast in his own circles and was slowly bankrupted.

The DIU too was struggling. The drugs investigation into Taylor had come to nothing and none of the banks was prepared to report their client to the police for an offence which the police, and not the banks, had come up with. However, by the end of November 1985, the DIU had managed to persuade the Co-operative Bank to hand over confidential information on Taylor's loans. Unlike Stalker, who was pursuing an official murder inquiry and was still experiencing considerable difficulties obtaining the information which he required, the DIU appeared to have experienced few problems in gaining access to Taylor's confidential files. This information could now be used to construct an offence for which Taylor could be prosecuted. But first the DIU needed to access all of Taylor's bank accounts legally.

Access Orders

The legal means of access to a person's bank account are provided for in the Police and Criminal Evidence Act 1984 under special procedures, which came into force on 1 January 1986.[5] Access can be granted if several conditions are fulfilled. The first and most important is that there are reasonable grounds for believing that a serious arrestable offence has been committed. This is defined, in the case of fraud, as any offence where there is 'substantial financial gain or loss to any person'.[6] Second, the material sought is likely to be of 'substantial value to the investigation' and is likely to be 'relevant evidence'.[7] The third condition is that other methods of obtaining the material have been tried without success or have not been tried because it appeared that they were bound to fail. The final condition is that access is in the public interest.[8]

Stephenson prepared the access order application. It will be recalled that he joined the DIU on 11 November 1985. In his evidence in Taylor's criminal trial, Stephenson agreed that he was brought in when the drugs inquiry had reached an impasse[9] and admitted that without access orders the inquiry would have ended.[10] His role was to examine Taylor's commercial activities 'to resolve the matter'.[11] In other words, to construct a case against him. During the Committal Proceedings (held to determine whether the case should to go to trial) Stephenson admitted that he had been authorised to prepare the application by the Chief Constable. When asked why he thought the Chief Constable was consulted, he said it was because it was the first occasion in Manchester that the procedure had been used and because the subject of the application was Kevin Taylor.[12]

Stephenson applied for access orders to eight of Taylor's bank accounts and the accounts of the Virani Group, to whom Taylor had sold Moulton Street precinct for £2.75 million in May 1984. The application was heard in private before the Recorder of Manchester, Mr Justice Prestt, on 27 February 1986 [13] – a fortnight after Hermon had passed on Stalker's interim report to the DPPNI. Taylor knew nothing of the hearing.

Before making the application, Stephenson obtained legal advice from Mr Hooley in the CPS,[14] who would have been fully aware that for the offence to be a serious arrestable one, there had to be serious financial loss or gain to someone. In February 1986, however, there was no suggestion that the Co-operative Bank had suffered any financial loss. On the contrary, it had made substantial sums from the interest on Taylor's loans. Nor was there any evidence that Taylor had made a serious financial gain out of the alleged offence. He was now desperately trying to sell some of the sites but without any success. Nonetheless, Stephenson was prepared to confirm in the application that there were reasonable grounds for believing that there was a conspiracy[15] to obtain pecuniary advantage by deception against the banks.[16]

The third important condition which must be satisfied before access is granted is the need for other methods of access to be exhausted. Stephenson knew of the Robson correspondence in which Taylor had been offered for interview on several occasions. Not only did Stephenson not inform the Recorder that Taylor had offered to help the inquiry, but he stated that: 'there is no likelihood of Taylor authorising the financial institutions to make disclosure concerning his business dealings with the police'.[17] When GMP did eventually ask Taylor to sign one of its standard forms to grant access to his bank accounts in September 1987, he signed it, further undermining Stephenson's claims that Taylor would be uncooperative.[18]

Denigrating Taylor

The application, like so many of the reports prepared by the DIU, placed Taylor in the worst possible light. The application was full of smears, innuendo, and downright lies, despite all the evidence being presented under oath. It was written in such a way that it gave the clear impression that the investigation was principally about drugs, notwithstanding that after more than a year, the DIU still had no evidence linking Taylor to drugs. The document was headed 'Drugs Intelligence Unit, Greater Manchester Police' – a title, which once again was intended to open doors.

Stephenson began the application with the words:

> I am currently concerned with an enquiry into the financing of unlawful drug trafficking in the County of Greater Manchester.[19]

These words made the circumstances look as dire as possible and raised the worst possible spectre. The implication was obvious: Taylor was suspected of lending money to drug traffickers to purchase drugs – the very same information which informer Burton told the police in 1983, information that was then repeated through numerous police reports. At the criminal trial Hood put it to Stephenson, 'that is not very candid stuff' and went on:

HOOD: Your evidence is that you were brought into the DIU whose drugs inquiry had reached an impasse?

OFFICER: Yes.

HOOD: You were specifically assigned to enquire into the commercial activities of Mr Taylor?

OFFICER: Yes, I was.

HOOD: Without knowing very much about them, but having a synopsis of information and, by February 1986, having had no access to any bank accounts?

OFFICER: Yes.

HOOD: It was plainly put in that way Mr Stephenson, was it not, to make it look as dire as possible?

OFFICER: No, it was not.

HOOD: 'The financing and unlawful drug trafficking'. Could you raise a more serious spectre before a judge at the Crown Court?

OFFICER: The position was at that time …

HOOD: Mr Stephenson, do you agree with me it is as serious an allegation as you could make?

OFFICER: It is certainly a serious allegation, yes.[20]

A cursory glance at other details in the application, however, would have immediately contradicted Taylor's alleged involvement in financing drugs. Stephenson reported that Taylor's 'total indebtedness' to the various financial institutions for which he was seeking access came to £1.3 million.[21] On this evidence, Taylor was borrowing money and, in his own words, 'geared up' to maximise the profits on the sale of the various plots of land which he had assembled. The statement then went on to record that 'the main inquiry centres upon the commercial activities of one Kevin Taylor'.[22] The overwhelming impression, however, had been created that it was principally a drugs investigation rather than an investigation into fraud.

Stephenson noted that Taylor 'is currently purporting to be a respectable businessman and a figure of some repute in local politics'.[23] This was a baseless and unsupported smear on Taylor's reputation. A second smear followed: 'Taylor's main activity during business hours is that of card playing.'[24] It was claimed that this was based on 'observations over a substantial period of time'.[25]

This was about the only piece of intelligence which the DIU was able to substantiate in the whole application, because it arose from the 114 days of observations of his office by the dedicated surveillance unit from two buildings opposite his office.[26]

In an inelegant and tautologous sentence, Stephenson continued:

It is also known that he associates with major criminals known to be active in the Manchester area, and persons dealing unlawfully in drugs, and he is currently so doing.[27]

The implication from this statement was that Taylor was a criminal in all but name. It suggested that he was part of a major criminal fraternity dealing in drugs. There was no attempt to unpack what was meant by the vague phrases 'associates with' or 'major criminals' nor 'persons unlawfully dealing in drugs'. It later emerged that one of the 'known criminals' was a man whose criminal record consisted of one conviction in 1944 for handling two pounds of potatoes, as a ten-year old, during a wartime blackout.[28]

Diogenes, drugs and firearms

The application referred to Taylor's yacht *Diogenes*. It noted that it had been bought in Miami, but 'the source of the payment is not known', implying that there was something illegal about the payment.[29] It then went on:

It is known that a number of persons including Taylor's family, a solicitor and his wife, a senior police officer and a number of Manchester criminals departed from the United Kingdom on different occasions and spent time aboard *Diogenes*. Certainly, the flights and hotel bills for some of the persons concerned were paid for by Taylor.[30]

It gave no dates or the names of those involved. The comment about flights and hotel bills being paid by Taylor was an obvious indirect reference to the fact that GMP had discovered that Taylor had bought the flights for himself and Stalker to go to Miami. The possibility that Stalker might have reimbursed Taylor was not mentioned.

Much was made once again of the presence of firearms on *Diogenes*. It will be recalled that Taylor had been advised to purchase some firearms for his own safety when cruising in the waters off Florida (Chapter 13). The application claimed that firearms were 'found on board' after *Diogenes* arrived in Manchester and noted that 'no proceedings have resulted from that incident'.[31] In fact, the firearms were declared to Customs and Excise by Colin Faulkner, the professional skipper who brought *Diogenes* back to England. He had insisted that Customs and Excise take possession of them. They were not 'found'. Finally, the comment that 'there were no proceedings' suggested that there should have been when no crime whatsoever was committed. At the time, Customs and Excise were not remotely concerned, and they conducted no further inquiry.[32]

The application also mentioned that *Diogenes* was used to import 'hard drugs' into England. Again, this was a misrepresentation of the known facts. *Diogenes* made only one trip from Spain to England while in Taylor's ownership. He had granted permission for it to be used for a 'proving trip' as he was trying to sell it and he was surprised when it arrived in Dartmouth. Customs and Excise were suspicious, although there was no concrete evidence, that it had been used to import drugs, certainly not hard drugs. Taylor even informed Anderton about his suspicions. All the other trips from Spain to England occurred after Taylor had sold the boat. None of this detailed information was provided to the Recorder and showed how, through various techniques, the police were able to construct a story to convince the Recorder to grant access to all of Taylor's accounts.

Taylor's loans

The rest of the application focused on Taylor's businesses and commercial activities. Again, the language was prejudicial. It noted that Taylor had sold the Moulton Street precinct, which it described as 'a partially developed site'.[33] This was far from the case; there were only a few units still being built. It was the first inner-city rejuvenation scheme carried out in Manchester and was a thriving business community. This was very different from the description 'the partially developed site'.[34] The application also noted that it was not known what happened to the proceeds. The money, as the police knew, was used to purchase several other plots for development purposes.

Stephenson presented considerable detail in the application about Taylor's loans. He informed the court that after selling Moulton Street precinct, Taylor's company, Rangelark Ltd, sought loan facilities from the Co-operative Bank and offered the bank security, in the form of a charge on three parcels of land at Tottington, Poynton and Trafford Park.[35] This loan was not taken up at the time. But in September 1984, Rangelark secured a loan of £345,000 from the Co-operative Bank based on the same security.[36] Stephenson pointed out the land at Tottington, in fact, could not be considered as part of the security to the bank, because it was purchased by another of Taylor's companies, Lacerta Investments Ltd.

In several places in the application Stephenson hinted at a conspiracy – the offence, for which Taylor was subsequently charged. He pointed out that Taylor's solicitor must have known that the Tottington land could not be used as security.

He then continued:

> It must also have been apparent to certain persons in the employ of the Co-operative
> Bank, p.l.c. at a comparatively early stage of the transactions, that the security
> offered by Rangelark Limited could not in fact be secured to protect the Bank's
> interest, and yet nevertheless, funds continued to be authorised for payment to
> the account of Rangelark Limited, whose indebtedness to the Bank now stands
> at about £820,000.[37]

This implied that Taylor, his solicitor, and 'persons' in the employ of the
Co-operative Bank were all involved in a conspiracy. Stephenson argued
that it was self-evident that there was an agreement between the parties. The
description was nonsense. Just because three people were involved in carrying
out a set of professional tasks does not constitute a conspiracy. There must be
evidence that they were part of an agreement to deceive. Stephenson provided
no information to support such a contention.

During the criminal trial, Hood cross-examined Stephenson on where he had
obtained all the commercial information. He gave a range of answers. On
occasions, he said that it was from 'general knowledge' within the DIU; on
other occasions he suggested that the information came from Dun and
Bradstreet, the credit inquiry agency, or from the Company Market Register,
and on several occasions he said he just 'could not recall'. While some of these
bodies may have provided some of the information, they could not have
supplied it all. Stephenson admitted that the information had been written down
in note form, but the notes were subsequently destroyed. Justice Sachs asked:
'Do you not find that absolutely staggering, Inspector'. 'I do indeed' came the
plaintive reply.[38] Hood suggested that the source must have been the Co-
operative Bank itself. Stephenson denied this and said that the bank had
provided no information.[39]

Another possibility is that the information was obtained illegally. In his book,
Taylor noted that in early March his accountant Derek Britton entered the
Rangelark offices and found signs of a disturbance. The filing cabinet had been
opened and the files tampered with, but nothing was missing.[40] The application
for access orders was first presented to the court on 27 February and therefore
if there had been a burglary in March it would not have helped in the preparation
of the application. However, there does appear to be some doubt about the date
of the burglary. Later in his book, Taylor stated that it occurred in February.[41]

Inferences and omissions

The application contained several deductions or inferences. For example, when
Rangelark applied for an increase in the £345,000 loan, Stephenson noted that

'in support of that application for an increase, three valuations, all dated 7 March 1985, were submitted'.[42] Other examples included:

> It must also have been apparent to certain persons in the employ of the Co-operative Bank … that the security offered by Rangelark Limited could not in fact be secured to protect the Bank's interest.[43.]

> Had the Co-operative Bank plc been made aware of the true situation at the time Rangelark made their application for loan facilities to them, the applications would have been rejected.[44]

> They [the valuations] had the effect of assuring the bank that the loan facilities requested were well covered by the security offered.[45]

There was one crucial omission from the application. Under cross-examination at the criminal trial, Stephenson admitted that Sheppard, after checking all his files in the Co-operative Bank, said to him: 'As far as I am concerned, I could see no fraud that has taken place and I will not make a complaint.'[46] This crucial piece of information was not noted in the application. When asked if he had told the Recorder of Manchester this fact, Stephenson said he thought that he gave the information verbally, in response to a question from the judge.[47] During the Committal Proceedings, however, Stephenson said: 'I accept that I omitted to inform the Recorder of Manchester in February 1986; the Co-operative Bank have made no complaint.'[48] When Hood put it to him that the two bits of evidence were plainly directly contradictory, he admitted that 'they are indeed'.[49]

At the end of the access orders' hearing, Justice Prestt took the unprecedented step of placing the application in a sealed envelope with the instructions that it should not be opened, except with his permission. He had been led to believe that it was a very sensitive inquiry.[50] Prior to Taylor's criminal trial his solicitors tried to obtain a copy of the application which was now being held by the CPS. Initially, GMP said that they could have a copy but later claimed that it was covered by a PIIC.[51] It was hardly surprising that GMP was determined to use every tactic to keep the contents secret.

This was not, however, the first time in relation to the Taylor/Stalker affair that Justice Prestt handled a sealed envelope because of the sensitivity of the investigation. It will be recalled that in the early part of 1983, Chief Superintendent Ankers gave him a sealed envelope containing details of the contribution that Burton had made in relation to his investigation into police corruption. It led to Burton being released on bail (Chapter 4).

Outcome of the application

The Recorder adjourned the hearing on 27 February 1986, because he was concerned about the way the banks had been notified. PACE requires that a notice of access is served on an institution in writing. In this case, Stephenson had prepared and served notices on the branches concerned. The Recorder considered that the notice should have been served on the registered office of the banks. Stephenson then prepared fresh notices and served them on the registered offices of all the eight banking institutions, again stressing that no contact should be made with the account holder regarding the pending applications. At a re-hearing on 12 March 1986, all access orders were granted.[52]

All the relevant information on Taylor's loans had been obtained illegally, either from the Co-operative Bank providing confidential information, and/or from a break-in at the Rangelark offices. The details on the loans, which were subsequently noted in the indictment and in the prosecution's evidence against Taylor in the criminal trial, were almost identical to those noted in the application. Similarly, American Express broke the rule of confidentiality before access orders were granted. It provided the DIU with all of Taylor's transactions, including the one used to purchase the tickets for himself and Stalker to fly to Miami in 1981 – a discovery which led to the stepping-up of the investigation into himself and Taylor. Access orders were, therefore, essential to regularise the dishonesty and the breach of the law in obtaining confidential information about Taylor's finances.

Taylor attempted to challenge the abuse of law in the application for access orders but without success.[53] When he was bankrupted by the police investigation and the banks were foreclosing on his debts, he counterclaimed on the basis that banks were in breach of confidentiality in failing to challenge the access orders. On 18 July 1986, the Trustee Savings Bank commenced mortgage possession proceedings against him and agreed a series of payments. When Taylor failed to meet these, it issued a warrant for possession. On 3 June 1987, Taylor issued a counterclaim in relation to the bank's failure to uphold their obligation of confidentiality. He used the same tactic in relation to Barclays Bank plc when it brought a legal action against him claiming £3,586 in respect of a debt arising on his account. These counterclaims were, however, dismissed by the courts, principally because the full responsibility for determining whether the conditions relating to the making of the orders rests with the judge who made them.[54]

Search warrants

On 7 May 1986, Stephenson applied to the Manchester City Magistrates' Court for search warrants under section 8 of PACE to search various premises.[55] He appeared before the Stipendiary Magistrate, Mr Fairclough. Search warrants, like access orders, must satisfy several conditions before they can be granted. The police must have reasonable grounds for suspecting that a serious arrestable offence has been committed, the material must be of substantial value to the investigation and constitute relevant evidence. In addition, the material must not consist of documents covered by legal privilege or what is known as 'excluded or special procedure material'.[56] This covers anything that a person has acquired or created in the course of their trade, business or profession and holds in confidence. This would, for example, cover any documentation created by a lawyer liaising with a bank on behalf of their client, any material held by Taylor's accountant, Derek Britton, or any of the correspondence between Taylor and the banks, professional advisors and local authority planning departments.[57] In order to obtain special procedure material, an application has to be made before a circuit court judge.

Two other pertinent conditions apply to search warrants. The officer must have reasonable grounds for believing that entry to the premises will not be granted unless a warrant is produced or that the purpose of the search may be frustrated unless a constable arriving at the premises can secure immediate entry to them.[58] In the absence of either condition, the search warrant is illegal and redress can be sought for trespass to property and goods, wrongful detention of goods and abuse of power.

When a search warrant is executed, another set of conditions apply. The search must be conducted within one month and at a reasonable hour unless the search may be frustrated. The officer in charge must identify him or herself and produce the search warrant. Once the search is under way, it may only be carried out 'to the extent required for the purpose for which the warrant was issued', although the police may seize other articles if they have reasonable grounds for believing that it is 'evidence in relation to an offence' and 'that it is necessary to seize it to prevent it being concealed, lost, altered or destroyed'.[59] After the search is over, the officer must make an endorsement on the warrant, stating whether the articles or persons sought were found and whether any articles were seized, other than articles, which were sought.[60]

Stephenson applied for at least seven search warrants under PACE. Like so many documents in this story, the originals are now missing.[61] They covered the home and offices of Taylor, and two of his firms, Rangelark and Compallex Ltd. They also covered Taylor's accountant, Derek Britton, his solicitor A. J. Adler of Oldham, and the home of their solicitor's clerk, Edward Higginbotham. In addition, Stephenson applied for several other search warrants to search for stolen goods. These included the home of Colin Peter Brown, who was Taylor's chauffeur, and a couple of other people whom Taylor knew. The last three warrants were a blatant and not very subtle attempt to imply that Taylor was not only part of a professional conspiracy to defraud, but was also part of a 'criminal fraternity'. The warrants for the searches of Taylor's home, Rangelark and Britton's offices were identical except for the address. Stephenson stated on oath:

> that he has reasonable cause to believe, that a serious arrestable offence has been committed namely, a) conspiracy to obtain dishonestly from the Co-operative Bank plc £240,000 by deception, and that there is material, ledger accounts, accounting documents, correspondence, minutes and business records on premises ... which is likely to be of substantial value to the investigation of the said offence, and that the material is likely to be relevant evidence and that if it does not consist of, or include items subject to legal privilege or excluded material, or special procedure material, and that the conditions specified below apply.[62]

In each of the warrants, the two conditions specified were that: 'entry to the premises will not be granted unless a warrant is produced', and 'that the purpose of a search may be frustrated or seriously prejudiced unless a constable arriving at the premises can secure immediate entry to them'.[63] The warrants authorised the search and seizure of any of the material listed. As with the access orders, no record of the proceedings was taken, and it is not known what was said to the Stipendiary Magistrate. In the Committal Proceedings, Hood cross-examined Stephenson on what he might have said to the Magistrate:

HOOD: Very well. Moving to the search warrants, on the 7th May you applied for search warrants?

OFFICER: I did.

HOOD: Did you swear any information to obtain those search warrants?

OFFICER: Yes.

HOOD: Did you say that drugs were still of interest?

OFFICER: I am sure I would have done, yes.

HOOD: Did you tell the Metropolitan Stipendiary Magistrate that on that date there were no complaints from any banking institution against Mr Taylor?

OFFICER: Yes, I think I did.

HOOD: On that occasion you asserted to a court that a serious arrestable offence had occurred?

OFFICER: I did.

HOOD: Although no loss had been occasioned to anyone there was at best a
           potential loss?

OFFICER: The loss had not been discovered by the bank at that time.[64]

The reference to drugs was once again being used to open doors and to
build-up the seriousness of the alleged offence being investigated. Stephenson
would no doubt have informed the Stipendiary Magistrate that he was from
the special unit, the DIU, making the application look more serious. These
ruses may well have distracted attention from the obvious fact that much of
the material in Taylor's office and his solicitor's office was 'special procedure
material', as defined by PACE and therefore could not be obtained through a
search warrant.

Search of Wood Mill

All the search warrants were executed on 9 May 1986 and involved teams of
officers visiting all the addresses. No record is available of what may have
been said in the briefing prior to the search. The most important search was at
Wood Mill, Taylor's home. Six police officers arrived at 8.00 a.m. Trevor
Goodwin, who looked after the house and lived in the next-door cottage, called
Taylor from the phone in the hall to inform him of the police's arrival. Taylor
finished dressing and went down to the hall. The search team was led by
Murray and included Ware from the DIU, DC Brian Webb from the
Commercial Fraud Squad and two other Detective Constables.[65] According to
Beryl Taylor, she asked to see the warrant for the search, but none was
produced.[66] This was in violation of PACE, which provides that the officer in
charge must identify himself (sic), show the warrant and supply the
householder with a copy of it.[67] Taylor watched as they searched downstairs
and Mrs Taylor went upstairs with a police officer. It later emerged that the
officer was Eileen Scarrett (née Hurt), who had been part of Stalker's team in
Northern Ireland for two years and whose husband had submitted a report on
the QSG in 1983.[68]

Normally, a drugs search would take at least a day, and sometimes two.
Sniffer dogs are often used to help in the search and, typically, floorboards and
bath panels will be taken up or removed, and all tanks and cisterns are
systematically searched. Although the briefing team were, in all probability,
told that Taylor was suspected of the importation of dangerous drugs, the
search of his house took less than an hour and a half. Only fifteen items were
removed including two plastic bags of documents, a starting pistol and
cartridges, phone indexes, business cards, and two photograph albums.[69]

Within fifteen minutes of starting the search, Webb, who was not attached to the DIU, discovered two photograph albums among 20 albums under the stairs. In the criminal trial it was denied that the briefing for the search recommended searching for photo albums. Ware's explanation of the discovery was that 'police officers are rather nosey'.[70] The two albums consisted of a series of photographs of social events, including photographs of Stalker taken at Taylor's 50th birthday party. Webb showed them to Ware, who made the decision that they should be seized because he was 'disturbed' by the content.[71] He made, however, no note in his pocketbook about the seizure. Hood repeatedly asked why he was disturbed. What was disturbing about a senior police officer attending a social event of a friend? Ware eventually admitted that it was because a person with a criminal record was in one of the photographs. Hood pointed out that Taylor came from a humble background and had kept up a friendship with some of the people who came from the same humble background and would from time to time socialise with them. Hood suggested that the very purpose of the DIU was to use the social link to try and draw him into some sort of criminality with which he could be charged. Ware denied it.

Hood also pursued the question of how photo albums could possibly be considered to provide evidence in relation to the offence of fraud or, for that matter any other offence, as required under PACE. Ware could provide no satisfactory answer. During this cross-examination, Ware also confirmed the majority of his time was spent investigating Taylor. When Hood suggested that, in fact, it constituted about 90 per cent of his time – a figure, which also applied to other members of the DIU – Ware agreed.[72]

Once items are seized under a warrant, there is the requirement that all the items are labelled, recorded, and placed in safe storage. Ware accepts that the photographs were not registered in a book recording the recovery of property.[73] Nor were they signed out and then signed back in when used, ignoring the basic procedures.[74] The photograph albums were handed over to the head of the DIU, Chief Inspector Born. Subsequently, some of the photos were removed from the album and passed to the Sampson inquiry, which investigated the disciplinary proceedings against Stalker. None of the other items seized from Taylor's home were used in the prosecution against him.[75] As it was, not all the photographs remained in the possession of the DIU or the Sampson inquiry. One appeared in the Manchester Evening News in June, showing John Stalker in the background with Stephen Hayes, – the ex-police officer who now ran a security business – in the foreground with Beryl

Taylor.[76] Hood put it to Ware that the photograph was leaked to the press. Ware said that was absurd.

Other searches

Stephenson was responsible for searching the premises of A. J. Adler, Taylor's solicitor. He was accompanied by two other officers. They took away ten files from Edward Heginbotham's office, including a file which was not mentioned on the warrant, dealing with all the correspondence between Taylor and the Co-operative Bank. On 21 May, Heginbotham wrote to Stephenson personally and asked him to return the file. It was crucial in relation to Taylor's ongoing property deals. A week later Heginbotham received a reply which was headed, 'Drugs Intelligence Unit, our reference D.I. Stephenson, for the attention of Mr E.N. Heginbotham'.[77] The letter was signed by Superintendent Simons, providing further evidence of his involvement in the investigation of Taylor. In Taylor's committal proceedings, Hood asked Stephenson to explain Simons' involvement. He replied:

> I think at that time Mr. Simons had been transferred to Operational Support Group at Chester House and in that capacity Mr. Born may have passed the communications through to him for reply. That is all I can say about it at this time. I will check and determine when, in fact, Mr. Simons was in that position.[78]

From all accounts, these searches caused concern among lawyers, accountants and other professionals in Manchester. The Royal Commission on Criminal Procedure[79] had recommended that any expansion in police powers should only occur if they were balanced by sets of procedures which provided some external check on the powers.[80] In the case of police access to the most sensitive and confidential information, it recommended that this should be decided by a circuit court judge and all search warrants by a justice of the peace. Yet, notwithstanding these safeguards, within weeks of the legislation coming into force, several offices of professional people in Manchester were subject to searches and important commercial and professional documentation was seized.[81]

DIU's fourth report

Shortly after the execution of all the search warrants, the DIU was instructed to prepare yet another report on Taylor and his associates. This was the fourth such report and was dated 11 May 1986, just days before Stalker's removal from the Northern Ireland inquiry. It was claimed that the first report was prepared by Topping in July 1984 just after Stalker had started his inquiry in Northern Ireland. The second, also by Topping, was produced in March 1985, shortly after Stalker was making threats to interview under caution very senior officers in the RUC. The third, entitled Operation Kaluki, was prepared in September 1985, just days after Stalker submitted his interim report to the RUC.

This fourth report was prepared by three of the DIU staff – Born, Murray and Waterworth. It must have been required very urgently because the three of them worked on the report on the Sunday following the discovery of the photographs two days earlier. It was handed to Topping, who then passed it onto Lees, who then passed it onto the Chief Constable. It was subsequently given to GMPA.[82] Whether the report that was forwarded by Topping was precisely that which he received from the DIU is a matter of conjecture. When Inspectors Murray and Waterworth were interviewed for the Smethurst inquiry (Chapter 24) – the 1990 inquiry into DIU missing documents – Murray said:

> The report that we prepared was not totally to the satisfaction of Peter Topping who wanted the report more strongly worded than we thought was merited. We suspected that Topping may alter the report to reflect his wishes so someone may have kept a copy of our original report as evidence of what we have submitted.[83]

Later when shown a copy of the report, Murray said: 'To the best of my recollection that is similar if not identical to the report we prepared.'[84] When questioned by the Smethurst team, Waterworth said: 'There was a suggestion that we would keep a copy of our report because of a suspicion that Topping either would or did alter it in order to make the report stronger against Stalker.'[85] Whether or not the report was altered, Murray and Waterworth's evidence to the Smethurst inquiry strongly suggests that members of the DIU no longer fully trusted their boss and were concerned that Topping would paint the worst picture possible of both Taylor and Stalker.

The report considered in the civil action consisted of 16 pages. Although only very small sections of it were read into the court transcript, it was clear that it repeated much of what was in previous reports. The major items of 'intelligence' with which Topping was so concerned in his apocryphal report of July 1984 were all reproduced. Under the heading 'Investigation into Kevin Taylor', the report noted that 'documents recently seized from Taylor's home and business addresses show personal connections with major criminals based in Manchester' and that he 'consorts with them'.[86]

It then listed thirteen alleged members of the QSG, the first eight being considered the 'inner sanctum' – an interesting description given the concept's importance in the rituals of the masonic order. In 1983 when Operation City was mounted, there were only four members of the 'inner sanctum', the Monaghan and Schiavo brothers (Chapter 6). Now the inner core had doubled and the overall membership of the QSG had been expanded to thirteen members. The eight core members were suspected of armed robberies, the importation of dangerous drugs and of having connections stretching to Europe and the United States. *Sherama* was mentioned, together with the list of passengers on board when it visited Gibraltar in June 1984.[87] The only item recorded in Stalker's favour was that 'the informant' – no doubt David Burton – did not suggest that Stalker was involved in criminal activity.[88] The notion of a gang was once again being used as a convenient peg to link people together and to imply Taylor was a major criminal with whom Stalker was associating.

Most controversially, the report again attempted to link Stalker to the IRA via Taylor's 'association' with Michael Roy Brown and Klapish. Further, it noted that through Stalker's 'association' with Taylor, he had been in the company of 'known criminals', and from photographic evidence, was 'at complete ease in this situation'.[89] Specifically, photographic evidence allegedly showed his association with one of the leading members of the QSG.

Stalker was clearly shocked and angry when he read the report. He considered it to be malicious, incompetent, and unprofessional. He criticised it for repeating information from one document to another.

STALKER: This is another example of the contents of one document being transferred to another, being transferred to another one and then it being put forward almost as three or four separate pieces of information. It is a repeat of the same information.

TABACHNIK: Well.

STALKER: The wording is exactly the same.

TABACHNIK: Mr Stalker this is an update on information which is to hand.

STALKER: I accept that sir, but the information is being put to me from a different document when it's quite clear it's come from an earlier document as if it was some something separate and it's not something separate.

TABACHNIK: If we could not find the earlier document, you'd criticise the information as being imagined, one shows an earlier source you criticise it for being repeated. The author of the document loses each way.

STALKER: No, if a number of documents are put before me as being separate and independent and the wording is very similar and I can see that they have consecutive dates from a month after the inference, it is obvious that they are repeats of one document. A lie repeated is still a lie.

TABACHNIK: Nobody is suggesting they are separate or independent. This is an update of sources of information requested.

STALKER: It's not updating, it's repeating it.[90]

Stalker complained that the report represented him in the worst possible light. There was no mention of the fact that he had been a police officer for 27 years 'completely blameless in any sense, not a disciplinary mark, not a suspicion against me'.[91] He was furious at several inferences made about him. He challenged the comment that 'he was at ease in the company of criminals', which was supported by 'photographic evidence' – a photograph of him at Taylor's birthday party in 1982.[92] He said that he was not at ease with criminals apart from when they are in the dock and pointed out that after the party photograph was taken, he was positively vetted, promoted to Deputy Chief Constable, and encouraged to apply for two Chief Constable posts. To say he was at ease with criminals was just not true.

Stalker argued that the 'photographic evidence' was most misleading. It assumed that his photograph was taken at the same time as the photographs of several people with criminal records. He pointed out that the people who were alleged to have been in the QSG could have arrived after he had left.[93] He also challenged the comment that he did not pay his own way in relation to the party at the Belle Vue racetrack and the claim that Stephen Hayes was on his table at the Conservative Ball in November 1985. Stalker continued:

> Hayes nodded at me, as an ex-police officer there was no way that I was going to go within 50 yards of him even within a crowd of 500 people. Although Hayes may have fallen by the wayside, he understood the position that I and the Chief Constable would have been in. If you recall, sir, the Chief Constable was due to go to this dinner as well but decided he had something else to go to, but he knew I was going and did not say it was wrong to go. So [not] to put it in context is misleading. It is that that annoys and angers me about this report because it's not a balanced report; it's a report, which was intended to achieve a purpose, which was to get me from the Northern Ireland inquiry, of course, that's what it did.[94]

Tabachnik then moved on to the next item in the report, concerning Sergeant John Speed, who had been shot dead in Leeds in October 1984 (Chapter 12). It noted that Brown was an associate of an IRA member who was suspected of involvement in the shooting. Stalker was again outraged and argued that it was the third or fourth example of the IRA being associated with people who were associated with Taylor, and by inference associated with him. It was 'quite outrageous that these things should be regarded as high prominence or currency at all'.[95] He pointed out that nobody could have taken the associations seriously when they were first recorded, otherwise he would have been immediately removed from the Northern Ireland inquiry. They only became important, Stalker suggested, between March and May 1986 when his inquiries were at the point they were. They could not have been important before that, otherwise he would not have been allowed to stay.[96] As it transpired, the IRA had nothing whatsoever to do with Speed's murder.

Stalker was most angry with the final paragraph of the report, which suggested that:

> In the light of his association as shown in this paper it cannot be said that he is totally impartial and, whilst it is unlikely to be the case, it could well be said by some that he has reasons to be sympathetic to the IRA. It follows therefore that urgent consideration should be given to allowing Mr Stalker to continue to head this most sensitive inquiry.[97]

He said he could not imagine a more damning sentence, endorsed by his CC. It was a smear campaign at its absolute worst. He said he was almost speechless and the more he thought about it the angrier he got.[98] The paragraph was most unlikely to have been the comments of a middle-ranking officer in the DIU about his DCC, but was added, in all probability, by his own CC.

The fourth report also depicted Taylor in the worst possible light. His successful sale of Moulton Street precinct for £2.75 million was currently 'subject to police scrutiny as it was thought that Taylor and associates may have misappropriated some of the proceeds from this sale and placed them into offshore companies'.[99] The use of the words 'associates' and 'misappropriated' were clearly intended to suggest criminality. Yet Taylor and his wife were the sole owners. There were no other 'associates'. Similarly, 'misappropriation' suggested fraud but there was nothing illegal in putting your own money in an off-shore account. It has been a common practice, albeit a controversial one, for years, as revealed in 2021 in the Panama papers.[100]

Taylor's 'pinnacle of his aspirations politically so far' extended to him becoming Chairman of the Manchester Conversative Association and entertaining eminent personages including at least one Cabinet Minister.[101] The report continued: 'Despite the social and financial strides made by Taylor ... he has never forgotten his early criminal associates.'[102] Once again, the word 'associate' was being used to make connections – in this case with people he had grown up with. He was described as having 'a thirst for gambling' and was 'a compulsive gambler' – a description which Stalker challenged in the civil action.[103]

There were a number of references to Taylor's boat, *Diogenes*. It mentioned that while Taylor still owned it, the boat had been used to deposit a load of Moroccan cannabis in Dartmouth. Apart from the fact that it was only *suspected* that the boat had deposited drugs – there was no actual evidence – the report made no mention that Taylor was trying to sell the boat at the time, or that the smugglers had used it while it on a 'proving trip'. Also, the report made no mention of the fact that Taylor had reported his suspicions to Anderton. Furthermore, the report claimed that it was used on at least two further occasions whilst owned by Taylor. There was no evidence presented during the civil action to support such a claim.

A month after the fourth report was produced, four more police officers were seconded to the DIU tasked with collecting statements in the prosecution of Taylor: DS Kenneth Caldwell, DS Alan Corfield, DC Peter Hogg and DC David Knowles. Resources appeared to be limitless in GMP's determination to prosecute him, a clear contrast with the officer who single-handedly prosecuted Klapish, Burton and Monaghan for the LFF. All the new DIU officers had a reputation for producing results. Hogg had the nickname of 'Hotty Hogg' and was known for intimidating witnesses. Caldwell, following his promotion to Detective Inspector, was blamed by a judge for the collapse of a multi-million-pound gangland murder trial in 2003. He had removed vital documents which pointed to suspects other than those in the dock.[104] He was moved from detective work but despite two inquiries was not suspended. Caldwell retired soon after and it was announced that he would deliver two public lectures on policing at the University of Manchester at £24 a head.[105]

* * *

The principal conclusion from all the evidence in the first few months of 1986 is that GMP abused and manipulated the law to access key information on Taylor's financial affairs and to obtain photographic evidence that Stalker 'associated' with criminals. The application for access orders was full of untruths, smears and downright lies. The ease of access which the orders allowed to Taylor's private documents contrasted sharply with the difficulties experienced by Stalker in obtaining information in his investigation in Northern Ireland into the suspected murder of six young men by the police.

The 1986 report which formed the basis for Stalker's removal from the Northern Ireland inquiry shared similar characteristics to the access order application. It was full of distortions, unsubstantiated comments and presented both Taylor and Stalker in the worst possible light. The accusation, that it could be said by some unnamed people that Stalker had reasons, unstated, to be sympathetic to the IRA, was a damning indictment of a professional police force and its Chief Constable. In the absence of any supporting evidence, it could only be based on a flawed syllogism: the QSG had connections with the IRA; Taylor knew some members of the QSG; Stalker was friendly with Taylor; therefore, Stalker had connections with the IRA. The allegation was a deliberate falsehood designed to strengthen the case against Stalker to guarantee that he would be removed from the Northern Ireland inquiry.

Chapter 17

Scarborough Fair

SIR PHILIP MYERS, on retiring from the post of Chief Constable of the North Wales Police at the young age of 51, was appointed to HMIC as Inspector of Constabulary for the north-west region. Instead of working from one of the regional offices in Manchester, Preston or Lancashire, he insisted on opening an office around the corner from his home in Colwyn Bay, a seaside resort in North Wales overlooking the Irish Sea.[1] On Monday 12 May 1986, Anderton travelled to North Wales, a journey of seventy-five miles, to meet Myers and present him with a copy of the report which the DIU had compiled over the weekend containing the damning allegation that Stalker might have 'reasons to be sympathetic to the IRA'. There is no record available as to what was discussed, but Anderton must have persuaded Myers, on the basis of the highly tendentious 11 May report, that Stalker should be suspended.

On 14 May, Myers telephoned Stalker who explained his intention to return to Belfast the following week. Myers told him to cancel the flights and any hotels. A decision had obviously been taken to remove Stalker from the Northern Ireland inquiry. But who made it? Stalker asked why he should not go to Northern Ireland, but Myers said that he could not explain on the telephone. Stalker phoned Hermon and said that he and his team would not be coming. Hermon claimed that he insisted he still wanted to see Stalker so they arranged to meet on 21 May.[2] According to Stalker, he arranged to return to Belfast on 26 May, not 21 May as suggested by Hermon.[3]

This disagreement over the dates of the meeting was immaterial in the context of what happened next. According to Hermon, on Sunday 18 May, Myers phoned and told him that Sir Lawrence Byford, Chief Inspector of Constabulary, had received a complaint from Stalker about a row that he and Hermon had had on the telephone. Myers explained that he was meeting Byford at a conference in Scarborough the next day and would be in touch thereafter.[4] If true, it was most irregular that Myers would break confidences and inform Hermon of a complaint which had been made about him. Hermon made a brief note in his official diary of the conversation: 'Mentioned a CC seeing BS, RA, TK and that DH was *au fait* with developments.'[5] This cryptic note was to become the subject of considerable controversy

File note of Scarborough meeting, 19 May 1986

On 19 May 1986, Byford, Myers, Anderton, Sampson and staff officer Steve Vessey, all met in the Royal Hotel in Scarborough during the Police Federation Conference.[6] The report which the DIU team had prepared over the weekend of 11 May formed the basis of the discussion. Byford subsequently made a detailed file note of the meeting based on Vessey's notes.

Prior to the civil action brought by Taylor, Anderton's defence team sought files from the Home Office which might be pertinent to their case. In December 1993, the Deputy Under Secretary of State in the Home Office wrote to Chilcot in the NIO informing him that he had conducted an examination of the Stalker papers and had concluded that the only document which was relevant to the issue was the file note which had been prepared by Byford. He went on to say: 'It seems to us appropriate to make this document available to Sir James Anderton; it was prepared with this sort of contingency in mind, and its disclosure does not seem to me to be harmful.'[7] It suggests that the Home Office anticipated the need for an audit trail of the decision to remove Stalker. The question then arises, when did Byford prepare the file note?

The meeting opened with a discussion on the procedure that should be followed to initiate an enquiry into Stalker's relationship with Taylor.[8] It recorded that Stalker was 'closely associated with Taylor' who was 'an associate' of the QSG – a situation rendered more difficult because of links between the QSG and IRA.[9] Byford informed the meeting that DPPNI had recently sent papers to Stalker concerning misconduct by Hermon, which he had asked Stalker to investigate.[10] According to journalist Peter Taylor, Sampson knew nothing about the possible inquiry into Stalker, or that he was to lead it, until he arrived at Scarborough.[11] So at the meeting, Sampson was apparently being informed on the one hand that Stalker was investigating the CC of the RUC and on the other that Sampson himself was now being asked to investigate Stalker. This was an uncomfortable position for Sampson and the political implications were obvious. At this point in the file note, Byford added that it was essential for the DPPNI, Hermon, and Sir Robert Andrew, the

Permanent Secretary in the NIO, to be told that Stalker would be investigated by Sampson.[12]

Anderton made several contributions during the meeting. He said Stalker was one of those 'hard professional policemen' and one of the 'Manchester school of detectives who cut corners to get results'.[13] There were suspicions that Manchester detectives were involved in corruption, adding that, when he first arrived in Manchester 'he cleared out the Manchester CID'. [14] He had no doubts about Mr Stalker's integrity 'until about two years ago'.[15] When he was appointed to DCC, his appointment was subject to comment because of 'his interest in clubs'.[16] He mentioned that Stalker had a 'tight relationship' with Taylor.[17]

Anderton drew attention to the threat posed by organised crime in Manchester. He said that 'most of the serious crime in the city was linked with the QSG' which he described as a loose association of criminals. It had connections with the IRA and the Mafia in America.[18] Not a thread of concrete evidence appears to have been presented at the meeting supporting any of these claims. Anderton further informed the meeting that 'about two years ago' he asked Lees to set up a team of carefully selected officers to target the QSG. Then Kevin Taylor's name 'came into the frame'.[19] Anderton was clearly referring to the DIU, but this was not set up until February 1985 – well under a year and half earlier, not 'about two years ago'.

Anderton also described some of the disagreements he had had with Stalker. He mentioned that Stalker had objected to the decision to appoint Lees as the Assistant Chief Constable overseeing the CID and that Stalker had tried to replace Topping.[20] He did not elaborate on the nature of Stalker's objections – that Lees and Topping lacked CID experience. Anderton also reported on the infamous letter-opening incident in January 1986 when Stalker, in Anderton's absence, opened a letter from Taylor's solicitors seeking information about the police investigation into Taylor. Anderton informed the meeting that he thought Stalker was anxious about his position in the face of Taylor's eventual prosecution.[21] The wording is significant. He does not use the word 'possible' prosecution but 'eventual' prosecution. He was confident that Taylor would be prosecuted.

Anderton then explained some of the actions taken so far. He pointed out that warrants had been executed to search Taylor's premises. Back in September 1985 – the month Stalker had delivered his interim report – Anderton had considered appointing an investigating officer to examine the information against Stalker but had decided against it because such an inquiry might have prejudiced the criminal inquiry into Taylor.[22] Inexplicably, he considered that a single criminal inquiry, among thousands, was more important than investigating allegations against his second in command. As Stalker argued in the civil action, if he had sufficient evidence to justify an investigating officer at that time against a man who was deputy of a large police force and carrying out a sensitive inquiry in Northern Ireland, he should have appointed one. He had no constitutional choice.[23]

Much of the information which Anderton reported to the meeting was contentious or inaccurate. According to Stalker, it was not correct that Anderton had 'cleared out' the Manchester CID – eight of the current nine DCSs were members of either the Manchester City police or the Manchester Salford police.[24] Stalker also challenged Anderton's view that 'most of the serious crime' was linked to the QSG. Anderton's comment, claiming that he started to have doubts about Stalker's integrity as early as 1984, was contradicted by the fact that he continued to support Stalker's applications for further promotion during the summer of 1985.[25] Anderton also wrongly told the meeting that Stalker was appointed to the Northern Ireland inquiry while he was an ACC. In fact, he was appointed when he was a DCC.[26]

Stalker further challenged Anderton's description that he had a 'tight' relationship with Taylor. It implied that he was surveillance-conscious and very cautious about his relationship. He pointed out that the only times he saw Taylor he was totally open about it and it was, on occasions, at police functions. Anderton also claimed that surveillance had indicated Stalker had associated with criminals. But there was no such evidence. Apart from one casual snapshot of his wife, two places removed from a man who had a criminal conviction, there was nothing.[27]

Byford, Myers, and Sampson were all familiar with the DIU's 11 May report. At one point, Byford pointed out that the boat that Taylor owned had been used for drug smuggling, whereupon Sampson interjected and said that the boat had been used after Taylor had sold it, which was not correct. It had made one trip while Taylor was trying to sell it.[28] Mention was then made of the 1981 trip by Taylor and Stalker to Miami. Once again, the details were incorrect as it was said that Mrs Stalker was on the trip. She was not.[29]

Lees indicated that his file was a file of intelligence; it was not a file of evidence. In short, it still needed statements to be obtained. He emphasised that the information relating to Stalker came from the inquiry into Taylor – the airline tickets and presumably the photographs.[30] It was suggested that Lees should 'firm up' on the airline ticket information within the week.[31] What this meant was unclear. The DIU had already obtained Taylor's card transaction for the purchase of tickets for himself and Stalker from Amex. Apart from asking Stalker if he had paid his share, nothing more could be done to firm up the evidence.

There was much discussion on the procedures that needed to be followed. Anderton expressed the wish to get the Greater Manchester end clear first before involving Northern Ireland [32] and referred to the need 'to lay the foundation' of an investigation into Stalker's relationship with Taylor before Taylor goes to trial.[33] In other words, the focus was on his deputy and the need to collect information on the friendship with Taylor before anything else occurred. Anderton appeared determined to get rid of Stalker. Just two days after the meeting, Stephenson visited the Fraud Investigation Group (FIG) presumably to obtain their opinion on the strength of the evidence in relation Taylor.[34]

Byford said that Stalker would need to be seen to ascertain whether he made any admissions that would support proceedings. He appeared to be suggesting a two-part procedure. In the first part, Stalker would be interviewed on a formal basis about some of the information and then, if it was concluded that there was a case to answer, the disciplinary proceedings would kick in.[35] This course of action was rejected. There was a suggestion from Byford that Lees should report the intelligence to someone independent – thereby taking Anderton out of the inquiry. It is not recorded who rejected both of these proposals from Byford which would have introduced a step before moving to a disciplinary investigation. It could have been either Anderton or Sampson or both. Whoever it was, there was a determination to see Stalker removed.

Sampson referred to the need for the Police Authority to appoint him as the investigating officer into the allegations against Stalker. He added that no decisions about the Northern Ireland inquiry should be made until after this inquiry. This recommendation, however, was rejected and it was agreed that Stalker should be removed from the Northern Ireland inquiry immediately.[36] This decision was taken without a single question being put to Stalker and without any of the criminal intelligence accumulated under the command of senior officers, who lacked investigative experience, being independently tested. Basic principles of natural justice were ignored.

Sampson agreed with Byford's earlier suggestion that he should go to see the DPPNI and tell him that Stalker was 'involved with criminals and possibly with the IRA'.[37] The accusation that Stalker had 'reasons to be sympathetic to the IRA' had now morphed into possible involvement with the IRA – an accusation which Stalker found 'quite outrageous'.[38] Moreover, he added that

Sampson was an 'ultra-cautious man' who would never have passed on such an unsubstantiated comment to the DPPNI.[39] Subsequently, during the disciplinary investigation, Sampson never asked Stalker about any connection with the IRA. The totally unsubstantiated allegation, however, had been sufficient to remove him from the Northern Ireland inquiry and initiate disciplinary proceedings.

Sampson's proposed visit to the DPPNI suggested that he would be taking over Stalker's investigation and he 'was anxious to know the terms of reference'.[40] Yet, a little later the report noted that Sampson 'needed to know whether his appointment implied any responsibility for that enquiry', suggesting that no decision had yet been taken. It was all very vague. In the civil action, Stalker pointed out that constitutionally, this decision could only be taken by the Chief Constable of Northern Ireland after consultation with the SoS for Northern Ireland.

Myers and Anderton were only too familiar with the problems which Stalker had encountered throughout the two years he was struggling to seek the truth of what occurred in the three shooting incidents he was investigating in Northern Ireland. They were aware of the intense resistance that Stalker had experienced in his demands for key information. Myers knew too that Stalker had been about to return to Northern Ireland to interview under caution the CC, DCC, and an ACC on the very day the meeting was taking place in Scarborough. He knew because he had told Stalker to cancel his visit.[41] Yet neither man is recorded as saying anything about the wider implications of Stalker's removal. It is inconceivable that they were politically naïve.

The meeting remains an enigma. What was meant by the comment recorded in Vessey's notes – but not recorded in Byford's report – that the purpose of the meeting was 'to demonstrate action without malice and duty to report' (Chapter 1)? Had there already been discussions in the higher echelons of government, including MI5, that Stalker must be removed, and the meeting was a disguise to hide any political interference in the decision? As Sampson constitutionally could only be appointed by Hermon, the Chief Constable, when did he give his consent? One possibility is that he did so on the day of the Scarborough meeting.

Charles Buckley, who assisted Taylor's defence team, was convinced that Hermon was also at the meeting after seeing him interviewed on the Panorama programme – *Conspiracy or Coincidence?* He talked to Mr Carr, Secretary of the Police Federation at the time, who confirmed that Hermon had paid a flying visit. Buckley then leaked the story to *Private Eye* to see if Hermon would sue.[42] Hermon had already sued *Private Eye* once before and Buckley considered that if he did not sue, then it would confirm his presence at Scarborough. No writ was issued.[43] Hermon, in his autobiography, does not refute the allegation and makes no mention of what he did on that day.[44]

There is a strange sequel to the Scarborough meeting. A few years after the decision to remove Stalker, a postgraduate student at the University of Bristol, who was a warden at one of the halls of residence, told me about a conversation he had had with a young undergraduate. The student told him that he was related to a top policeman who had been involved in a controversial investigation and had now deposited his papers in a trunk with a family member. It was no normal trunk: when opened by someone not authorised to do so some chemical would automatically destroy all the papers. The student's story has not been verified but there was the possibility from other information that the 'top policeman' was Byford, raising the crucial question as to why a senior member of the Inspectorate should go to such lengths.

The answer can only be speculation. But one possible explanation is that Byford was so worried about what had occurred that he felt he needed a secure set of papers to cover his back. The investigation of powerful individuals or organisations would appear to be a fearful business.

Myers and Sampson visit Hermon

On 20 May, according to Hermon, Myers and Sampson visited him at police headquarters in Belfast and revealed that Stalker had been under investigation by GMP for several months. Hermon found it 'utterly shocking'.[45] They handed him a two-page document noting a series of matters of an extremely serious nature. Hermon said he did not wish to have a copy and handed it back. It was an extremely short meeting as they arrived at 2.25 p.m. and had to catch a plane from the City Airport at 3.15 p.m.[46] Hermon does not reveal what time they left. But they would have needed to leave at least twenty minutes for the journey to the airport and to check in. The meeting must therefore have lasted a matter of minutes. This was an incredibly short meeting in the circumstances and there is no evidence that he gave his consent during the meeting to Stalker's removal – something which he alone constitutionally could do.

Hermon would have immediately understood the implications of Stalker's removal and the widespread publicity it would receive, and would no doubt have wanted more information unless, of course, he already knew the details. The higher echelons of the police meet regularly and it is possible that Anderton had already tipped off Hermon about the investigation, knowing that it would have enormous political implications for the RUC. During my research of the *Manchester Evening News*, I came across a small item in Mr Manchester's Diary – a humorous column about local celebrities, dated 23 March 1986.[47] It was headed 'Chief blue comedian'. It noted that Anderton took the stage 'before 280 police officers from all over the United Kingdom headed by Ulster's Chief Constable, Sir John Hermon'. The occasion was the Silver Jubilee dinner of the Federation of British Police Motor Clubs held in the Cresta Court Hotel in Altrincham. The report noted that Anderton had the audience in laughter as he riddled his own Police Committee and its Chair Gabrielle Cox. This occasion, if not others, would have provided Anderton with the opportunity to inform Hermon that Stalker was being investigated by GMP.

Formal procedures

On 28 May, Anderton met the Chair of GMPA, Norman Briggs, and Roger Rees, the clerk to the Authority. Briggs agreed with Anderton and Rees that Stalker should be instructed to take extended leave and that Sampson should investigate the alleged disciplinary charge against him – decisions which he took, controversially, on behalf of the authority. He then set in motion the formal procedures for the investigation of his Deputy Chief Constable under the Police (Discipline) (Senior Officers) Regulations 1985 and Part IX of PACE. Later in the day, Rees rang Stalker informing him that he was to take extended leave because of allegations made against him. Rees also asked him to be in his office at 10.00 a.m. the following day. Stalker rang Anderton to try to find out what was happening. He was told: 'From now on you must look after yourself.'[48] These were cruel words from a Chief Constable who in the past had been so supportive.

On 30 May, GMPA met and confirmed the decision that Briggs had taken on 28 May. There was no opportunity for any discussion. Rees issued the cryptic press statement on behalf of the Authority which began with the comment that information on the conduct of a senior police officer suggests 'the possibility of a disciplinary offence' and ended six lines further on with the comment that 'the Deputy Chief Constable is on temporary leave while the matter was being investigated' (Chapter 1). On the same day, Hermon made another controversial entry in his diary: 'Expressed concern regarding structure of inquiry. Clearly collusion between PM/RA/CS and DPP. I must hold the line'.[49]

The cryptic statement from GMPA did not require too much intelligence to realise that 'a senior police officer' was none other than Stalker. *The Times* reported the statement in detail. It provided an extensive account of Stalker's eighteen-month investigation in Northern Ireland and some of the content of his report, which it described as being 'critical of the lack of supervision of the special anti-terrorist groups and recommended that at least three senior RUC officers in charge of the units should be charged with conspiracy to murder'.[50] It finished by noting that Stalker's report had caused resentment with some senior ranks of the RUC who believed that he 'had not understood fully the conditions and pressures under which the RUC operates'.[51]

During these developments, Michael Partridge, a senior civil servant in the Home Office, contacted Anderton pointing out that he was 'aware of the matter affecting his deputy'.[52] Partridge expressed concern over the impact it could have on the Northern Ireland inquiry. He then added, presciently, that he hoped Anderton had 'proper evidence' that Stalker was 'associating with criminals'.[53]

Hermon's diary entries

Early in 1990, Hermon's diary entries for the period 16 May to 2 June 1986 became public. They had been passed onto Rodger Pannone, Stalker's solicitor, after they were obtained on discovery in one of the libel actions brought by Hermon against *Private Eye*. Stalker claimed that the diary entry for 18 May (a Sunday), which 'mentioned a CC [later confirmed to be Sampson] seeing BS, RA, TK and that DH was *au fait* with developments', showed that he was removed from the Northern Ireland investigation 'by senior cabinet and Home Office officials'.[54]

On 25 January 1990, Stalker presented a document to the Home Office making the claim. It was quickly rebutted. A spokesperson said:

> The document fails completely to demonstrate that anyone other than appropriate authorities took part in the decision that Stalker should be removed from duty and consequently could not continue to head the investigation.[55]

The Home Office spokesperson said that the entry did not say 'had seen', as suggested by Stalker, but 'seeing' and referred to a meeting that a Chief Constable (Mr Colin Sampson) was attending the following day when the decision to remove Mr Stalker was taken. It confirmed that the initials referred to Sir Barry Shaw, the former DPP in Northern Ireland, Sir Robert Andrew, PUS in the NIO, Tom King, SoS for Northern Ireland, and Douglas Hurd, the then Home Secretary.[56] Hermon, in his autobiography, confirms that he was referring to these people and that the meeting was in the future.[57]

There was, however, a contradiction in the spokesperson's statement as reported. They claimed that the tense was 'all-important' because it specifically 'related to a meeting the following day'. This was no doubt a reference to the Scarborough meeting. But only Sampson and Hurd were in Scarborough on that day. Shaw, Andrew and King were certainly not there, adding some weight to Stalker's interpretation that 'seeing' referred to the past.

At the beginning of April 1990, Sir John Wheeler, a Conservative MP and Chair of the Home Affairs Select Committee, asked Mr Waddington, the Home Secretary, for a comment on the document which Stalker had handed in. On 4 April, Waddington made a statement to Parliament.[58] Waddington confirmed that the initials referred to the people listed by Hermon and then said:

> Mr Sampson has confirmed that he knew nothing about the possibility that Mr Stalker might be the subject of an investigation before he attended a meeting at Scarborough on 19 May chaired by the then Chief Inspector of Constabulary, Sir Lawrence Byford. The other persons present at that meeting were Sir Philip Myers, Mr James Anderton, Chief Constable of Greater Manchester Police, Mr Ralph Lees, Assistant Chief Constable of Greater Manchester Police and a staff officer. That was the meeting at which Mr Anderton decided to refer certain information relating to Mr Stalker to his Police Authority.[59]

Byford's file note contradicts Waddington's statement that Sampson knew nothing about the possibility that Stalker might be the subject of an investigation prior to his attendance at the meeting. Sampson's reported comments during the meeting showed that he was very familiar with the allegations against Stalker. Moreover, he would not have informed the meeting that he would take over the Northern Ireland inquiry unless it had been cleared with Hermon – the only person who could legitimately make the decision.

Waddington proceeded to regret that Stalker had 'misquoted' Hermon's diary entry emphasising that Hermon had written 'seeing' and not 'has seen'. The correct wording, he claimed, gave the clear implication that the entry referred to events in the future and that Sampson had at that time seen none of the persons to whom Hermon was referring. But the wording was ambiguous.

In the given context, the literal meaning of the words did imply that the CC had already seen BS RA TK, as the rest of the entry referred to the past. Moreover, if these three people were to be seen in the future, most people would have written 'will see' and provided a time reference – for example, on Thursday – rather than the word 'seeing'. Furthermore, if indeed Anderton had already informed Hermon, perhaps at the Altrincham meeting, he would certainly have been referring to the past.

Waddington's response to the *au fait* reference was also problematic. He began by pointing out that, 'it would have been perfectly natural for Her Majesty's Chief Inspector of Constabulary to have informed the Home Secretary that problems were arising in relation to Mr Stalker's position'.[60] But Waddington then contradicted this 'perfectly natural' action, by noting that 'there is *now* (emphasis added) no other record to show whether he did so before 19 May'. Waddington, however, then informed Parliament that Hurd's recollection is that 'he was first informed after 19 May'.[61] In other words, he was only informed *after* the Scarborough meeting. Consequently, Hermon's note of 18 May that DH was *au fait* with events was either wrong, or Hurd had been informed, and Waddington's statement to Parliament was incorrect.

On 8 June 1990, Sir Lawrence Byford joined the debate and wrote a letter to *The Times*. He argued that Stalker's removal was not part of an 'establishment cover-up' but action taken 'to protect the investigation'. He refuted the ongoing speculation that Ministers and/or senior civil servants were involved. He insisted that: 'The first they knew of the decision to refer the matters to the appropriate authorities in Manchester and Belfast was when I briefed them at a later stage'.[62] While not providing a date, presumably he meant after the Scarborough meeting on 19 May or after 30 May when the GMPA made the formal decision to initiate disciplinary proceedings against Stalker.

Stalker replied to Byford's letter drawing attention to Hermon's diary entry of 18 May. He pointed out:

> This entry directly contradicts Sir Lawrence Byford's claim that 'Ministers and/or senior civil servants' knew nothing of the decision to refer the matter of my removal to the Greater Manchester Police Authority until a later stage … The inescapable fact is that my removal … was under discussion at national political levels both here and in the Province before the official decision to do so was made and well in advance of the first notification to the Greater Manchester Police Authority.[63]

Only a year later, Byford contradicted his earlier position. In the TV programme *Stalker: The Final Chapter*, presented by Peter Taylor, he claimed that he had informed the Home Secretary about Stalker at the Police Federation Conference in Scarborough on May 19, not after it. Peter Taylor then asked:

P TAYLOR: Was this the first time that the Home Secretary had heard about the allegation?
BYFORD: Yes.
P TAYLOR: Are you sure about that?

BYFORD: I'm absolutely positive about that. I mean, again my experience of being a
                policeman, I think I am able to detect whether somebody is expressing a
                false surprise or not. He was greatly surprised when I told him and the
                developments which are taking place.

P TAYLOR: He hadn't heard a whisper before, no suspicion?

BYFORD: I'm sure about that; he had not.

P TAYLOR: What was his reaction?

BYFORD: His reaction I suppose was a mixture of surprise and concern.[64]

Incredibly, therefore, there are now three dates in the public domain when
Home Secretary Douglas Hurd was possibly informed about Stalker's removal:
18 May or before according to Hermon, 19 May according to Byford and
sometime after 19 May according to Waddington in his statement to
Parliament. Hermon's written record, which was made shortly after the
telephone conversation on 18 May suggesting that Hurd had already been
informed, is the most credible. It is another crucial element in the
Taylor/Stalker affair where there was conflict in the versions given by those
in authority.

This was not the end of the controversy over this diary entry. *Private Eye*
suggested that 'BS' referred to Bernard Sheldon, who at that time was Head of
Legal Services in MI5, and 'RA' was in fact Sir Robert Armstrong, the cabinet
secretary to Margaret Thatcher.[65] To support the suggestion, it referred to the
Attorney General's response on 28 June 1986 to a question from Alf Morris.
This was his reply:

> I take the question to refer to the decision by the Greater Manchester Police
> Authority to request the deputy chief constable to take leave of absence. *This
> was a decision for the authority alone and not for the Director. Neither the
> Director of Public Prosecutions for England and Wales nor the Director of
> Public Prosecutions for Northern Ireland had any involvement in events leading
> up to that decision* (emphasis added). For completeness, I should add that
> subsequently the Director of Public Prosecutions (England and Wales) has
> received a preliminary report concerning Kevin Taylor (whose name has been
> associated with the Deputy Chief Constable) with a view to him advising as to
> appropriate lines of inquiry. However, that is a separate matter.[66]

The crucial passage is italicised. If Barry Shaw, the DPP for Northern Ireland,
'had no involvement in the events leading up to that decision', Hermon's
initials, BS, could not have referred to him. It therefore increased the
possibility that it referred to MI5's Bernard Sheldon and the initials RA
referred to Robert Armstrong.

Some support for this interpretation comes from Hermon's diary entry for 30
May: 'Expressed concern regarding structure of enquiry. Clearly collusion
between PM/RA/CS and DPP. I must hold the line.' Here Hermon refers to the

DPP, as 'DPP' and not by the initials BS. This adds more weight to the suggestion that the initials BS in the 18 May entry referred to Bernard Sheldon and not Barry Shaw. If they did refer to Sheldon, it increases the likelihood that PM and RA refer to Prime Minister and Sir Robert Armstrong and that there was collusion between the three of them.

Some sixteen months after Hermon made his controversial diary entries, Sheldon and Armstrong were in Australia together for Margaret Thatcher's government's ill-fated attempt to ban the publication of Peter Wright's book *Spycatcher.* Wright had been a member of MI5 in the 1970s and his book claimed that MI5 had tried to undermine Harold Wilson's Labour government.[67] In March 1974, the card referring to the file on Wilson was removed from MI5's central index and its existence was known only to a few people.[68] One of those with full access was Sheldon.

It is known that Thatcher took a close interest in developments in Northern Ireland and must have approved the secret MI5/Walker counter-insurgency strategy in 1981. When a SB officer raised his concerned about the lack of legal framework for running agents, she famously said: 'Well carry on doing what you're doing but don't get yourself caught' (Chapter 3). She would have been very aware that Stalker's investigation was exposing elements of the secret strategy and could lead to criminal or disciplinary charges against the Chief Constable, and his Deputy. Moreover, any criticism of the RUC would have been most unwelcome after Thatcher had successfully negotiated the Anglo-Irish Agreement with the Irish government which required the RUC to police unionist/loyalist protests against it.

Sheldon, for his part, was closely involved in the negotiations with Hermon over the hayshed tape and intelligence relating to informers and state agents which Stalker was demanding. Moreover, he would have been aware that a number of MI5 personnel could be prosecuted for perverting the course of justice following the destruction of the tape of the actual shooting. Robert Armstrong, as Cabinet secretary, would have been party to a decision of this magnitude.

The government robustly rejected any suggestion that the highest echelons of government had anything to do with Stalker's removal. In his statement to Parliament, Waddington explained that Hermon had felt annoyed at not being adequately consulted over Stalker's replacement and the arrangements for the continuance of the inquiry. He pointed out that Hermon had already publicly stated that nothing 'sinister' should be read into the reference to 'collusion'. Waddington ended by saying:

> I am entirely satisfied that, contrary to the assertion made by Mr. Stalker in his statement of 25 January, Sir John Hermon's diary entry for 30 May 1986 had nothing whatever to do with Mr. Stalker's removal from the inquiry in Northern Ireland.[69]

Hermon, in his autobiography written some ten years after the events, unsurprisingly, supported a similar explanation. He said that his cryptic note reflected his 'anger and sense of frustration, even bitterness, that the RUC was going once again to become embroiled in controversy' and he felt that he 'had not been consulted at any early stage about Sampson's appointment'.[70] He added, somewhat lamely, that: 'in retrospect, I know that there was no such "collusion"'.[71]

Government papers

It is a legal requirement under the Public Records Act 1958 that government departments must normally deposit documents in the National Archives after 20 years. Files, however, may be retained after this time if they are 'required for administrative purposes or ought to be retained for any other special reason'.[72] This power has been used extensively over the years to delay, or retain indefinitely, files which could shed more light on controversial allegations, events and issues.[73]

In December 2023, following a successful appeal to the Information Commissioner, the NIO transferred thirteen files with the title: 'RUC: Stalker/Sampson inquiry, inquiry by John Stalker and Colin Sampson into police shootings in Northern Ireland' [hereinafter NIO Stalker/Sampson papers] to the National Archive. This was 17 years after the files were due to be deposited and 37 years after they were compiled. It was hoped that they would shed light on the controversy over Hermon's diary entry and, in particular, whether the decision to remove Stalker from the Northern Ireland inquiry was taken, as claimed by Stalker, 'by senior cabinet and Home Office officials'. But there is a dearth of documentation covering the crucial period in which the decision to remove Stalker was taken.

On the 15 May 1986, just four days before the decision was taken, there is a minute recording that some supplementary enquiries would be necessary as Stalker had not been given 'highly classified' intelligence information.[74] The minute also recorded that the Attorney General had asked to see Tom King to inform him that it was his view that he considered it necessary for the DPPNI to see Stalker 'at first hand – without the chief constable present'.[75] For Stalker to see the DPPNI in the absence of the CC indicated the seriousness of the situation and that the discussion was about the possible culpability of the CC. The minute suggests that the NIO was being kept well-informed about the progress, or rather the lack of it, of Stalker's investigation in Northern Ireland.

Then there is nothing about Stalker in the deposited files until 22 May when Myers wrote a letter to Andrew confirming a conversation the day before in which he informed Andrew of GMP's investigation into Stalker.[76] According to the files, the very first occasion that government officials in the NIO were informed about GMP's investigation was therefore 21 May.

Myers' letter began: 'I forward a note concerning our conversation of yesterday'. It continued:

> It is a distilled version of a much longer report prepared by an Assistant Chief Constable who has been conducting the investigations into a group of criminals referred to. The team has steered clear of Mr. Stalker up to now and most of what they know about him at this stage is 'intelligence' rather than 'evidence'.[77]

The letter noted that Byford had told Sir Brian Cubbon, Permanent Under Secretary of State in the Home Office, that 'something is afoot which may have serious repercussions'. The letter recorded three things that had been agreed:

> a) That I tell you [Andrew] as soon as possible.
>
> b) That Colin Sampson and I see the Northern Ireland Director of Public Prosecutions. He has the same 'distilled' version as you.
>
> c) That Colin Sampson and I see Jack Hermon. He has not the 'distilled' version but is broadly aware of the contents.[78]

This last point, of course, contradicts Hermon's account of events. Myers and Sampson had already seen him on 20 May – two days before this letter was written.

The letter further recorded that Stalker's team was due to 'start afresh' on Tuesday 27 May. This was when Stalker had planned to return to Northern Ireland to interview Hermon under caution, having been instructed by Myers to cancel an earlier planned visit. Myers noted that, 'I will somehow put this off'. According to Stalker, Myers phoned him on 23 May and asked him to cancel this rearranged visit.[79] Under no circumstances was Stalker going to be allowed by HMIC to return to Northern Ireland to complete his investigation.

HMIC distilled report

The distilled report, which Myers mentioned in his letter, was obviously a précis of the much longer DIU's report prepared over the weekend of 11 May. The distilled report was even more tendentious than the original. It began by stating that the GMP was carrying out an inquiry into the activities of a group of criminals who were 'strongly suspected of financing armed robberies, long term fraud and the importation of drugs'. This was obviously a reference to the loosely connected group of criminals referred to as the QSG. Although, there was little evidence that they acted together to commit crime, it was a convenient label to link a varying number of people together and to blame them for unsolved crimes (Chapter 1).

It then stated that 'Kevin Taylor, a businessman, is involved with this group of criminals' and 'is believed to finance certain ventures of the group and also to dispose of illegal monies via his business connections'. It added that Taylor had 'connections with a police officer and used the association to his own ends'. The allegation that Taylor disposes of illegal monies had been provided by the Walter Mitty police informer David Burton during the taped interviews with him in February and March 1985 (Chapter 11).

The distilled report continued:

> Information was also received to indicate that the criminal group was connected with members of the IRA. They are said to assist the IRA in the importation of drugs, arms and laundering money. Whilst further enquiries are now needed to investigate this claimed association, there is currently a member of the criminal group charged with handling Irish currency directly identified as being the proceeds of an armed robbery in the Irish Republic in 1985. This Manchester criminal is linked in intelligence reports to a man [heavily redacted section] who is currently in custody, being one of the persons arrested in 'The Dublin Guinness Kidnapping case'.[80]

There was, however, no definitive evidence that 'the criminal group' was connected to the IRA. The LFF which Klapish and other alleged members of the QSG organised from Manchester culminating in the contract bombing of Klapish's premises in Kent Street, Belfast, could have been carried out by either the IRA or loyalist paramilitaries. It was Burton who had alleged it was the IRA (Chapter 4). The next two incidents mentioned – the robbery and kidnapping – both occurred in Ireland where during the Troubles it was widely assumed by outsiders that the IRA were involved in all serious crimes. Yet there was nothing to suggest that the IRA had anything to do with either of these two offences.

The armed robbery took place on 3 December 1985 when a postmistress was forced to hand over 70,000 Irish pounds (Chapter 12). If it had been carried out by the IRA, it is most improbable that Brown would have been only charged with handling and released on bail. The kidnapping case, to which Brown was tenuously linked, occurred on 8 April 1986, when Jennifer Guinness was abducted from her home. Eight days later she was released, and the kidnappers captured. They were subsequently convicted and sentenced to prison. At no time was it alleged that the IRA was involved. But in linking a mythical IRA kidnapper to Brown and Brown to the QSG, it added to the suspicion that the QSG was heavily involved with the IRA.

There was no mention of the Guinness kidnapping case in the civil action during the examination of the DIU's 11 May report. This suggests that the kidnapping had been added by the HMIC in their distilled report to embellish the supposed connections between the QSG and the IRA, hoping that it would provide stronger support for Anderton's remarkable statement in the 11 May report that Stalker might have 'reasons to be sympathetic to the IRA'.

At this point, the distilled report noted: 'The police officer associated with Kevin Taylor is John Stalker, the Deputy Chief Constable of the Greater Manchester Police'. It went on to note that Taylor was currently being investigated for conspiracy to defraud a sum in excess of £1 million. There was no mention that this related to loans from the Co-operative Bank nor that the police and not the bank had 'discovered' the alleged fraud. It further mentioned that the police had observed members of the criminal group visiting Taylor's premises. It will be recalled that his offices had been under surveillance for an unprecedented one hundred and fourteen days (Chapter 14). The paragraph finished by noting that Stalker had attended 'lavish parties given by Taylor' at which members of the group had been present and a photograph album had recently been recovered which indicated that Stalker and his wife were there at the same time as 'at least one prominent member of this group'.

The distilled report finished by alleging that Stalker had accompanied 'Taylor on *holidays* (emphasis added) to the United States of America and Spain' and that recovered documents show that Taylor had purchased air tickets for himself and Stalker to fly to Miami in 1981. In fact, Stalker had been on only one holiday – the Miami trip – for which he had reimbursed Taylor for the airline tickets. He was never on holiday with Taylor in Spain. All this information could have been easily checked by asking Stalker. The mystery remains as to why Anderton never asked Stalker about these matters before initiating the disciplinary procedures.

On 30 May, Andrew wrote a minute which confirmed that Stalker was to appear before the Police Authority and would be suspended. He went on to note that 'I was first alerted to this unfortunate development by Sir Philip Myers a few days ago' and informed SoS for NI.[81] In the same minute, Andrew noted that he had attached 'a letter from Sir Philip with a summary of a report prepared by the Greater Manchester Police'. This was obviously a reference to the distilled report. He continued: 'Until allegations against Stalker have been investigated, I suggest that the papers should not be given wider circulation.'[82] They were not and at some point, both the letter and the distilled report were removed from file CJ4/6285 before it was lodged in the National Archive. Fortunately for this research, they had not been removed from file CJ4/7464.

Retained or missing documents

There were a number of significant gaps in the deposited NIO Stalker/Sampson papers. Partridge's letter to Anderton, in which he expressed hope that he had 'proper evidence' against Stalker, could not be found. There was no record of Sampson 'seeing' Andrew or King in any meeting in this period as forecast in Hermon's 18 May diary entry and confirmed by Waddington to Parliament. Nor was there any reference to a meeting on 20 May when Hermon recorded that Byford and Sampson saw King, or Andrew – it is not clear which – before they visited him at RUC police headquarters in Belfast. Moreover, there remained contradictory evidence as to when precisely Hurd became *au fait* with the issues. The only reference is in Myers' letter to Andrew in which he notes that Byford 'has told' Cubbon, who would have informed Hurd.

There was also nothing in the files noting that Hermon had phoned Andrew in the evening of 31 May to convey his 'deep anxiety at the possibility of Colin Sampson assuming control of the RUC investigation'.[83] Hermon considered that Sampson carrying out both investigations would be disastrous for the RUC and 'to retain Stalker's own team under Thorburn would be even more unfortunate'.[84] Furthermore, he felt his position had been compromised by the premature disclosure to the media of Sampson's probable appointment to the Northern Ireland inquiry.

It was not until the beginning of June that Hermon appears to have granted his consent to Sampson's appointment. On 3 June, Myers met the Attorney General and the outcome of the meeting was reported to the NIO by David Haggan. He explained that 'it had been agreed that Sir John Hermon, who was content to do so, would appoint Mr Sampson to complete Mr Stalker's RUC inquiry'.[85] It was agreed that Hermon should issue a press statement. On 6 June, the RUC duly did so. Hermon is quoted as saying:

> In view of the leave of absence of Deputy Chief Constable Stalker the same inquiry team, consisting of the same officers, is now, after consultation with Her Majesty's Inspector of Constabulary, and on his recommendation to be headed by the Chief Constable of West Yorkshire Mr Colin Sampson, whom I have asked to do so and who will report to me. I am anxious that this extended investigation be completed quickly and professionally so that I may receive the directions of the DPP. [86]

Haggan further reported that the AG had expressed doubts about the same officer undertaking both inquiries. It was a view also held by the NIO who favoured a separate officer for each. But Myers had 'strongly argued' against. No reason was given, but having the same person to conduct both investigations would have provided the HMIC with greater control of events.

* * *

The period from 18 May to 31 May, when the decisions were taken to remove Stalker and appoint Sampson to carry out both inquiries, remains shrouded in secrecy, controversy and contradictions. The release of government papers has provided some clarity. But it has been impossible to ascertain precisely who knew what and when, or to substantiate much of what was known from other sources.

The information in the deposited files does, however, resolve the controversy over the interpretation of the initials in Hermon's diary entry of 18 May. As there is documentary evidence that the NIO, Home Office and DPPNI were all informed by Myers shortly after the Scarborough meeting, it confirms Hermon and the government's claim that the diary initials referred to Barry Shaw and Robert Andrew and that they were going to be informed sometime in the future. The initials did not refer to Bernard Sheldon and Robert Armstrong. But this does not, of course, exclude the possibility that Sheldon and Armstrong were involved in the decision to remove Stalker.

They could have exerted pressure on Anderton and the HMIC, perhaps with the agreement of Thatcher, to help remove Stalker from the Northern Ireland shoot-to-kill inquiry without informing the Home Secretary or the Secretary of State for Northern Ireland. It would explain why HMIC – a body tasked with upholding standards in policing – was prepared to produce such a tendentious distilled report. It used absurd logic linking different events and people together and distorted, embellished and provided inaccurate information. There is no doubt that Stalker at the time posed a real threat to policing in Northern Ireland: he was recommending the prosecution of a number of officers; he was highly critical of the power of the RUC SB; and he was still demanding access to the destroyed tapes. Moreover, the culpability of the CC was uncertain.

The Scarborough meeting was in all probability an obvious disguise to hide decisions which had already been taken, certainly by HMIC and possibly at a higher level in government. The Home Office official admitted as such in his comment that, 'it was prepared with this sort of contingency in mind'. The meeting was a shambles, jumping back and forth from one topic to another. There was no systematic presentation of the evidence against Stalker, nor any analysis of it. Several incorrect statements were made either to the meeting or recorded in the minutes. Byford's proposals that either Stalker should be asked about some of incriminating information or someone independent of Anderton should look at the evidence, before moving to a formal disciplinary investigation, were both rejected. One or more key participants were determined to see Stalker suspended immediately.

The outstanding feature of the meeting, however, was Anderton's preparedness to undermine his Deputy with negative comments and falsehoods, and to support an investigation into him based on unsubstantiated and untested information. Only two years previously he had appointed him his Deputy and had recommended him to conduct the Northern Ireland inquiry. A year later, he was writing references for him for senior posts. Then he changed his mind. This adds further weight to the possibility that he too had been asked by the security establishment to get rid of Stalker, leaving Byford with no option, but, in his eloquent words: 'to demonstrate action without malice and duty to report'.

PART V:
COVERING UP

Chapter 18

Sampson's Inquiry in Manchester

ON 29 MAY 1986, Sampson began his investigation into the disciplinary charges against Stalker with a team of fourteen officers and two support staff. It will be recalled that Sampson had been appointed, according to the official narrative, at a meeting ten days earlier in Scarborough. He was tasked not only with investigating the disciplinary charges but also with completing Stalker's investigation in Northern Ireland. The latter decision was politically contentious because it suggested that there was indeed a connection between events in Northern Ireland and Manchester. Sampson completed his inquiry into Stalker quickly, in just over two months at a cost of £250,000.[1] His report was submitted to the PCA and GMPA on 6 August.[2] It was considered at a meeting of GMPA on 22 August. Sampson's Northern Ireland inquiry took longer and was completed sometime in the first three months of 1987. It has never been published.

Prior to the meeting of GMPA, Sampson's report on Stalker was leaked to the press, providing a rare opportunity for critical assessment by the press and others.[3] It did not inspire confidence. GMPA expressed concern that the report had been given to the press – a criminal offence – and asked Anderton to investigate. He appointed Mr Tony Mullet, of the West Mercia Police, to carry out an inquiry.

Investigating Stalker

The terms of reference for Sampson's investigation into Stalker's conduct were broad:

> 1. To supervise in accordance with Section 89(2) of the Police and Criminal Evidence Act 1984 an investigation, to be conducted by the Chief Constable of the West Riding Police Authority, Colin Sampson, Esq., Q.P.M., at the request of the Greater Manchester Police Authority, into the information received by the Police Authority and all related matters appertaining to the conduct of the Deputy Chief Constable of Greater Manchester Police, John Stalker, Esq.

2. In accordance with Part IX of the Police and Criminal Evidence Act 1984 to make such recommendations and statements to the Greater Manchester Police Authority and to take all such action as may be necessary and desirable to carry out their statutory powers and duties and to ensure that the complaint is fully and fairly investigated.[4]

The inquiry was supervised by the Rt. Hon. Roland Moyle in the PCA. He had been a Minister of State for Northern Ireland from 1974 to 1976, under the Wilson government. Moyle became deputy chair of the PCA in 1985.[5] He supervised several controversial inquiries. In 1989, he was responsible for overseeing the West Yorkshire police investigation into the West Midland Serious Crime Squad, which had been responsible for the wrongful conviction of the Birmingham Six and many other miscarriages of justice.[6] In the early 1990s, he supervised the police investigation into the Assistant Chief Constable of Merseyside Police, Alison Halford, who had brought a sex discrimination claim against the Merseyside Police, having failed repeatedly to win promotion.

On 29 May 1986, Sampson and his Assistant Chief Constable, Donald Shaw, met Stalker in his office at Chester House. Sampson informed Stalker that he had been tasked by GMPA to investigate certain matters concerning his conduct. Stalker asked what the matters were, but Sampson said that it was not possible to say at this point as they amounted to rumour, innuendo and gossip, and enquiries would have to be made. Stalker asked how long the inquiry would take as he had planned to return to Northern Ireland for a protracted stay. He was then informed that he had been taken off the Northern Ireland inquiry, 'forever'.[7]

On 3 June, Topping wrote to Sampson, enclosing several documents. What these were exactly is not known. His covering letter, however, noted that some of the information about Stalker had not yet been verified or tested. Stalker was highly critical of this and found Topping's comment very strange. It implied that new information had come to light, whereas it was evident to Stalker from documents he had been shown previously that the information referred to had been around for some time. Also, there had been plenty of time to make proper inquiries into the truth or otherwise of whatever was being said in the documents.[8]

At a meeting on 9 June in Sedley Park and armed with all the documents from Topping, Sampson told Stalker why he had been suspended. He said:

Information has been received which indicates that during the past six years you have associated with persons in circumstances that are considered undesirable, and by such association you may have placed yourself under an obligation as a police officer to those persons.[9]

But it was not until 23 June that Stalker was at last provided with the charge against him. It had taken Sampson over three weeks to formulate it:

> Between 31 March 1980 and 31 December 1985, John Stalker, an officer of the Greater Manchester Police associated with Kevin Taylor and known criminals in a manner likely to bring discredit upon the Greater Manchester Police.[10]

The wording of the charge was sloppy, misleading, and highly damaging to the reputation of Taylor. Taken literally, it could be read as meaning that associating with Taylor alone was likely to bring discredit upon GMP. But this was absurd because Taylor had no criminal record whatsoever. It was obviously intended to mean that associating with Taylor, when both men are in the company of known criminals, brings discredit. But there are further ambiguities. What is the meaning of 'known' in this context? Does it mean 'known' to the police in general, in which case it is superfluous, because if someone has a criminal record, he or she will be 'known' to the police in any case. Perhaps it means 'known' to Stalker, but this is far from clear.

Finally, there is the problem of the meaning of 'in a manner likely' to bring discredit. What sort of manner is envisaged here? The possibilities are endless. Does being in the same room, together with a few hundred other people, form the disciplinary offence, or is it necessary to talk to the criminal for the offence to occur? In between and beyond there are numerous other possibilities. For example, if Stalker's wife is photographed in a group in which there is a 'known criminal', does this constitute 'a manner likely to bring discredit'?

An investigation based on such a vague and imprecise charge is further compounded by research at the time, which suggested that in any cross-section of the population a large proportion will have a criminal record. Using data from a longitudinal survey, David Farrington, a Cambridge criminologist, found that one third of the population of men could be expected to have some sort of criminal record by the age of 30.[11] Police officers attending any social function, or any public meeting are likely to be in the company of people who have criminal records and hence 'likely to bring discredit' to the police, on this measure. From the outset, it was obvious from criminological research that such an investigation was bound to find Stalker or any other senior officer guilty of 'associating with known criminals'.

The association charge, however, was not the only one put to Stalker. Contrary to all principles of natural justice, further possible breaches of police discipline were discovered during the investigation itself, including 'acting in a manner likely to give rise to the impression amongst members of the public that he may not be impartial in the discharge of his duties', as well as eight counts of misusing police vehicles.[12] Stalker considered that his use of official vehicles had been far less than that of his predecessor and also less than his colleagues in Chief Officer ranks. He therefore requested an official scrutiny of the use of official transport for similar functions by others. Sampson, however, rejected this as he claimed it was outside his terms of reference and would delay the inquiry. In general, Sampson did not appear to consider the vehicle charge as particularly serious as he notes that Stalker had misused police vehicles 'only five times' in the last two years.[13]

It was inevitable, given the nature of the first charge against Stalker, that the focus of the inquiry would be on the social occasions that both Taylor and Stalker were believed to have attended together. There were five main ones listed in the Sampson report: the holiday on board Taylor's yacht *Diogenes* in Miami in 1981; Taylor's 50th birthday party on 2 January 1982; the Taylors' wedding anniversary at the Masons Arms Hotel near Bury, on 7 August 1985; a fundraising evening at Belle Vue Greyhound Stadium on 12 October 1985 followed by an impromptu meal at a Greek Restaurant in Manchester; and a Conservative Party Ball in Manchester on 23 November, 1985.[14] The first four events related to the charge of association with criminals. The last concerned an allegation that Stalker had displayed bias by attending a Conservative Party Ball. Two of these events took place prior to Stalker's inquiry in Northern Ireland. The other three events took place after he had carried out most of his investigation and had submitted his interim report in September 1985. There was a further occasion when the two men were together: a dinner at Belfry Hotel, Wilmslow, on 27 September 1985, in aid of the Alexian Brothers – a Catholic charity. There was, however, no mention of this occasion perhaps because it was also attended by Anderton (Chapter 15).

Sampson was particularly interested in interviewing members of the QSG who might have been present at any of the first four social functions. This ageing criminal fraternity, many of whom, from the evidence of several different sources, had now retired from an active life of crime to a relatively affluent life of legitimate activities, were no doubt amazed at the amount of attention to which they were now subject.

The investigation team was divided into two sections. One section – comprising a DCS, four DIs and two Sergeants – was engaged on 'directed inquiries'. The other section was made up of one DI, three constables and two typists, who provided the support and administration. One of their principal tasks was to list all the documents, index all the material and input it all into a computer database. The team carried out 335 actions, obtained 169 statements, and collated 146 documents and 50 exhibits.[15] Several people, who were not prepared to make a statement, were tape recorded and transcripts made. It is not known whether the recordings were made in secret or with the interviewees knowledge.

About 500 people were of some interest to the investigation. They came from all walks of life in the Greater Manchester area, reflecting the nature and extent of Taylor's very wide circle of friends, acquaintances, and fellow gamblers. All of them had their personal details, such as their names, addresses and any other information that the police had collected on them during the inquiry, entered into the computer database. None of them, presumably, was aware of this invasion of their privacy.

The investigation was far from independent or fair. Sampson's position was compromised because he was present at the Scarborough meeting. At no stage had Anderton given Stalker any opportunity to challenge the evidence or offer an explanation. The investigation was also heavily reliant on the information supplied by the DIU. It even recommended people to interview and on at least two occasions, it assisted in the investigation. On 16 June 1986, Stephenson recorded in his notebook: 'With D.S. Ware, Britannia Building Society, Cross Street, and saw Mr Allen. Inquiry for West Yorkshire.'[16] Stalker had a bank account at the branch and a few days earlier had given Sampson's team permission to look at this account, but it was members of the DIU who visited the bank. This was unprecedented as there was always the possibility that Stalker would be reinstated to his post and here were junior officers from his own force investigating his private finances.[17] On 15 July, DC Hogg, from the DIU, travelled to London and obtained a statement from Angela Simpson, an employee of American Express. It was then taken to the supposedly independent police officers investigating Stalker at Bishopsgate Police Station, Wakefield.[18]

Sampson's report

Sampson's report was headed: ALLEGATIONS OF MISCONDUCT AGAINST DEPUTY CHIEF CONSTABLE JOHN STALKER. But at no stage had there ever been allegations of misconduct against Stalker. Sampson had made this clear to Stalker when interviewing him.[19] The report itself was disjointed, repetitive, and contained numerous errors. There was no attempt to define what was meant by 'associating with known criminals in a manner likely to bring discredit upon the Greater Manchester Police', or to explain why particular people were selected for interview. Overall, the structure was very poor. It did not follow a chronological or a thematic presentation of the events and issues.

Under a section headed, Police Inquiries, the report listed six lines of inquiry that the investigation pursued. They were:

1. To establish the existence of a friendship between Deputy Chief Constable Mr Stalker and Kevin Taylor and to determine the length and nature of that relationship.

2. To verify the believed association between Kevin Taylor and known criminals.

3. To establish Deputy Chief Constable Mr Stalker's knowledge of Taylor's association with known criminals.

4. To investigate the association of Deputy Chief Constable Mr Stalker with known criminals.

5. To establish if Deputy Chief Constable Mr Stalker had received hospitality, holidays and/or financial reward from Kevin Taylor during their period of friendship.

6. To investigate alleged disciplinary offences discovered during the investigation.[20]

There was no explanation why these lines of enquiry and not others were chosen, and there was no systematic analysis of the evidence under each of the six areas, or any conclusion.[21] The six lines of inquiry appear to have been quickly forgotten and were not referred to again in the report.

Credibility of the evidence

The bulk of the evidence which was considered and described in the report came from just two sources: informer David Burton, who died more than a year before Sampson's investigation of Stalker began, and friends of Taylor who had fallen out with him over the years – one of whom made anonymous telephone calls to the West Yorkshire police and made numerous allegations against both Taylor and Stalker.[22] All these people, therefore, had some ulterior motive for discrediting both men. Burton was vulnerable and wanted to curry favour with the police. Taylor's former friends and colleagues were provided with an opportunity to return to battles which had been lost elsewhere. From the outset, therefore, Sampson had the challenge of distinguishing fact from fiction and presenting the truth in an unbiased manner.

Naturally, Burton and his evidence were subject to much attention. The report provided a short biography of the man, noting that he was born in 1944 and died in prison in 1985 'from natural causes'. It then went onto say:

> Burton's criminal career involved him in various capacities with the Kray twins, to whom he was a chauffeur, and various members of the Quality Street Gang. As a result, he built up a remarkable knowledge of criminals and their activity on both a local and national scale. Burton did not keep all his knowledge to himself and provided useful information to the police on a number of occasions.[23]

The first sentence was presumably attempting to suggest that he was a major criminal because of his association with both the Krays and the QSG, but no evidence was provided to indicate what these 'various capacities' were, apart from being a chauffeur.[24] Similarly no evidence was produced to support the claim that he had 'a remarkable knowledge of criminals'. The paragraph was, therefore, no more than a series of vague and unsubstantiated assertions that does little credit to a serious police investigation.

The report noted that Burton was interviewed on four occasions between February and March 1985. In fact, he was interviewed on five occasions as noted in the civil action.[25] How could such a basic error be made? Richardson and Murray who carried out the interviews presumably made statements to the Sampson inquiry in which they would have noted the number of interviews they had conducted. Did they simply both forget that they had conducted five interviews, or did they deliberately misinform Sampson for some reason? Sampson noted: 'Those conversations [with Burton] were tape recorded and extracts relevant to this enquiry have been transcribed for inclusion in the statement/exhibits bundle.'[26] This makes it even more mysterious that one interview from the key informant in the Taylor/Stalker affair should have been overlooked. To compound matters, there was no reference to the missing tape of one of the interviews.

The report then continued:

> It can be seen that Burton refers in general terms to Kevin Taylor's connection with the Quality Street Gang but also alleges his complicity in drugs trafficking. Much of what Burton has alleged is still the subject of discreet inquiry. This aspect of this report is extremely sensitive, and confidentiality is absolutely essential to current operational matters in this field.[27]

Sampson accepted without any apparent scrutiny the DIU's assertion that Taylor's alleged involvement in drug trafficking was still subject to 'discreet inquiry'. Yet it was over a year and a half since Burton was taped making this allegation and DIU had found no evidence to support it. Moreover, it will be recalled that Stephenson admitted in the criminal trial that when he was appointed to the DIU in November 1985, the drugs element of the inquiry was at an impasse.

Sampson and his team did attempt to assess the credibility of Burton's evidence. It examined eight pieces of information provided by him.[28] The first, and most important, was Burton's allegation that the QSG had an ACC 'on a pension' in 1981. The report simply noted that McGourlay and Patterson regarded him as a good but dangerous informer who needed careful handling as he was prone to embellish information. Neither officer could remember Burton making the specific allegation but confirmed that he did make allegations in relation to senior officers whom he did not name (Chapter 4). As with the other lines of inquiry, the report made no attempt to reach a conclusion. Yet all the evidence suggested that Burton was using police concerns about the QSG and police corruption, intelligently, to link them together with a generalised allegation to add to his credibility within GMP at a time when he was extremely vulnerable following his involvement in the LFF.

Another of Burton's allegations was that various senior police officers had obtained free meals at the Kwok Man Chinese Restaurant – the same allegation made in 1984 in an anonymous letter to GMP. This had been reported to the Police Authority, investigated by Anderton and dismissed (Chapter 8). Nevertheless, Sampson made his own investigation into the allegation. He recorded that DSgt Burgess could recall an occasion when he visited the restaurant with his family and Stalker and his family were just completing their meal when they arrived. Sampson continued:

> Mr Burgess is not able to say whether or not Mr Stalker paid for his meal and no precise date can be placed on this incident. A statement was not obtained from Mr Burgess who was formerly involved in the prosecution and conviction of several Quality Street Gang members against whom David Burton gave evidence.[29]

The investigation into Stalker was bordering on the absurd. It was not surprising that Burgess was unable to say whether Stalker paid for his meal. Most people when they go out to a restaurant do not watch other customers paying their bills. The owner of the restaurant, however, did make a statement, that Stalker always paid for his meals[30] – a fact which would have been confirmed by Sampson's examination of the bank accounts of Stalker and his wife.

Unsurprisingly, Sampson concluded the obvious, namely that overall: 'There is remarkably little corroboration of what Burton has alleged.'[31] However, Sampson was determined to give the informant some credibility and qualified this statement by adding: 'Yet there is evidence from other sources, including Mr Taylor himself, connecting him with members of the Quality Street Gang and with Mr Stalker.'[32] As David Murphy pointed out, it is hard to grasp the logical status of the 'yet' in this context.[33] It implies that there was, after all, some truth in what Burton said.

The evidence presented in Sampson's report was thoroughly investigated by several journalists based on a critical reading of the report and backed up by numerous interviews.[34] At least three people challenged the evidence presented in the report. Wareing denied the official version of the golf conversation. He was reported as saying that Stalker had been at parties at Taylor's house when 'known criminals had been present'. Wareing, who had played the round of golf with McGourlay, said that he did not know any criminals and had only seen Stalker once at Taylor's house.[35] Cecil Franks, Conservative MP for Barrow and Furness, also claimed that the police had completely distorted a statement that he had given. He was quoted in the report as being 'rather surprised to see a senior officer in Mr

Taylor's company'.[36] Franks, however, could not see how his comment could be used to support the view that Stalker was bringing discredit to the police force.[37]

The other person who challenged Sampson's evidence was Chief Superintendent Arthur Roberts. He was a friend of Ian Burton, Taylor's solicitor. They occasionally played squash together. According to Topping, Ian Burton told Roberts after a game of squash that Taylor had said that he would 'blow out Stalker and his associates', if the police did not stop investigating him.[38] This implied that Taylor had some information on Stalker and other police officers that he could use to discredit them. Roberts, however, denied he told Topping any such thing and made it known within the police that he was incensed that Topping even reported a conversation without informing him.[39]

Inaccuracies, errors and unsubstantiated comments

The report was riddled with inaccuracies and errors. It recorded that Stalker was appointed to investigate 'the deaths of three men shot by members of the Royal Ulster Constabulary'.[40] Stalker investigated six deaths. It noted correctly that Burton had alleged that the QSG had an 'Assistant Chief Constable on a pension'.[41] Yet only a few paragraphs later the report noted: 'Having regard to the allegation of Burton that Mr Stalker was "on a pension" from Mr Taylor or the Quality Street Gang …'.[42] Burton, however, never alleged that Stalker was 'on a pension', only an ACC. In one place in the report, it noted that Taylor's early business was called Vanlands,[43] but later the business is noted correctly as Vanland.[44]

Numerous dates were wrong. During his investigation, Stalker received a threat from the IRA. Sampson recorded that Stalker brought the threat to Anderton's attention in February 1986. But according to Stalker, the true date was February 1985.[45] The report noted that Stalker attended 'the Over the Bridge Restaurant, Millfold, Ripponden regularly (sic) on three occasions in 1983 and once in 1985'.[46] Three paragraphs further on it records that the four visits were in 1983 and 1984.[47] It noted that Born and Murray interviewed Michael Roy Brown on 20 December 1985.[48] In the civil action it was noted that he was in fact interviewed by these two police officers on 21 December.[49]

Sampson strongly denied that DS Simons, who was part of Stalker's investigation team in Northern Ireland, was involved in 'the instigation and supervision of the investigation into Taylor'[50] – an allegation made in *The Guardian*.[51] Moreover, Sampson specifically claimed that the suggestion that there was a relationship between Simons and Topping was 'wholly inaccurate' – an untrue disavowal reflecting the sensitivity of the friendship for GMP. While Simons may have played no part in 'the instigation and supervision', he nevertheless played a role, as has been shown (Chapter 15). He spoke with Taylor's solicitor about the police enquiries into his client and subsequently met with him. At the time, he was head of the Operational Support Group and had responsibility for GMP's only surveillance squad which had observed Taylor's offices for 114 days. For a squad to be deployed for this phenomenal length of time, Simons must have been part of an inner circle of trusted officers behind the secret investigation into Taylor and Stalker.

The report noted that the QSG was 'a group of Manchester criminals who are regarded by a number of senior police officers as being the organisers of incidents of major crime in the city'.[52] It does not mention who these officers were and produced no evidence to support the assertion. It could, no doubt, have found a similar number of officers to contradict this assertion. It continued:

> As a group the QSG acquired a considerable reputation with fellow criminals, the public and the police for although individually they were dealt with by the courts for relatively minor offences it seemed by reputation at least, they were making a good living from crime and not getting caught.[53]

Again, no evidence was produced to support any of these assertions. It simply perpetuated the myth that the QSG was a gang and a convenient vehicle to blame whenever there was some major unsolved crime, or to link people together as 'associates'.[54] As Murphy concluded, the Sampson report 'speaks with its own voice. It constitutes its own authority without either referring to sources of factual verification or support for opinions'.[55]

Denigrating Taylor and Stalker

There was considerable evidence in the report that its aim was to discredit both Taylor and Stalker. Many of the actions of Taylor were interpreted by Sampson in the worst possible light. For example, during the search of his home Taylor made the comment: 'This has been going on for two years and I'm going to find out who keeps pushing this. When I find out I'll have someone out of Chester House for this.'[56] Sampson considered that this would lead the police to gain the impression that: 'Mr Taylor was indicating he was in a position to exercise some influence within Greater Manchester Police headquarters.'[57] But it was equally plausible to interpret this statement as a comment from a man with a deep sense of injustice.

The report was replete with pejorative adjectives, adverbs and verbs to denigrate both men. For example, the verb 'admit' was used 36 times in the report, principally in relation to Taylor, Stalker, and men with criminal records.

It was employed only once to describe the evidence of others. It was certainly never used to describe the evidence of any police officer apart from Stalker. Stalker 'admits' to attending numerous events from boxing tournaments to the Conservative Association Ball, knowing certain criminals and opening the letter addressed to Anderton. Taylor 'admits' that he is a gambler, knows some criminals and has talked to Stalker about public order and drugs.

The denigration of the two men was a continuation of the strategy begun with the DIU and reached its pinnacle with the granting of access orders and search warrants, whose purpose, according to Charles Buckley, one of Taylor's solicitors, was clearly revealed in the report. He was quoted as saying:

> I have always thought the first fourteen pages of the Sampson Report one of the most dramatic documents on the Taylor case. The rhythm and momentum of those first twenty-three paragraphs show beyond any peradventure or shadow of doubt that the real purpose of the access orders and the search warrants on Taylor was to get material to dish the dirt on Stalker.[58]

There were several references in the report to the photographs which had been seized during the search of Taylor's house in highly questionable circumstances, as it was difficult to see how they could possibly be considered evidence in relation to the offence of fraud or, for that matter any other offence, as required under PACE (Chapter 16). The chain of custody was therefore broken, providing further support for the view that the whole purpose of the intense investigation of Taylor was to obtain evidence on Stalker.

The official narrative

The Sampson report presented the official narrative based on information supplied to it by GMP, challenging the widespread press and media speculation that there was a conspiracy against Stalker. It claimed that, shortly after Stalker was appointed to the Northern Ireland inquiry, information came to the notice of the police that he had a corrupt relationship with criminals, which needed to be investigated. 'During the first half of 1984 Superintendent Topping' was monitoring and collating information on alleged police corruption. There was nothing startling about this, as he was in charge of the Discipline and Complaints Department whose role was to do just that. The report continued:

> *By July 1984* (emphasis added) he had received information from a number of sources indicating that Kevin Taylor was involved with the Quality Street Gang. In particular, one informant said that he was involved in the financing of drugs trafficking. The same informant whilst making reference to another alleged corrupt police officer, who has since retired, said that there was a strong corrupt connection between Mr John Stalker, James Patrick Monaghan and Kevin Taylor.[59]

The report provided no precise dates indicating when Topping received each and every piece of evidence from 'a number of sources', nor when he received the two items from the same informant. The vagueness of the phrase 'by July' suggests that the Sampson team could not establish precisely either the source or the date when this information entered the police domain. The report was only slightly less imprecise in its reference to the famous golf conversation between McGourlay and Wareing, noting only that it took place in June. Based on this information, the report claimed that Topping prepared 'a four page' report on 17 July and submitted it to Assistant Chief Constable Lees, who referred it to the Chief Constable.

Why Sampson thought it necessary to mention that Topping's report was four pages in length is significant when it was so imprecise on so much else. The most likely explanation is that he was aware that there was some dispute over the length of the original report – one officer, who had seen the original, thought that it was only two pages long[60] – and wanted to confirm that Topping's putative report, which had all the hallmarks of being constructed at a later date, was four pages in length.

David Murphy pointed out that if this is an accurate account of the order of events, then it was Taylor's association with Stalker that led to Taylor being investigated. Stalker, in this version of events, whatever the press argued at the time, was not investigated because he associated with Taylor. Stalker was already in the frame and his friendship with Taylor was the key to the long investigation into him and his consequent downfall.[61] Yet, the report concludes emphatically that: 'They [members of the DIU] were not tasked to investigate Mr Stalker or his friendship with Taylor.'[62]

Another crucial aspect of the official narrative concerned when precisely Anderton informed Myers in HMIC. Sampson recorded:

> Since March 1985 Mr Anderton had kept Sir Philip Myers OBE QPM DL, Her Majesty's Inspector of Constabulary, informed of the allegation in respect of Mr Stalker and the progress of the investigation.[63]

Again, the report was vague on when precisely in March he was informed. This is not immaterial, however. It will be recalled that Waddington, the Home Secretary, was specifically asked in a Parliamentary Question in October 1986 when HMIC first heard about the investigation into Stalker. The reply was 'October 1985' (Chapter 11). Incredibly, there are now two different dates, over six months apart, when it is claimed that the Chief Constable of GMP informed HMIC that his Deputy was subject to an investigation.

It was very strange that there was no analysis by the Sampson team of the documentation produced by the DIU. Earlier Chapters in this book have provided numerous examples of reports whose authenticity was questionable, based on an analysis of only those parts of documents presented in the civil action. The absence of any forensic analysis of the documents allowed the Sampson team to simply reproduce the highly questionable chronology of the official narrative, in which it was claimed that the investigation of Stalker started in July 1984.

Plausible deniability

The most unsatisfactory aspect of the whole Sampson report concerns the RUC and MI5. In a sub-section headed 'Media Coverage', in which it described the coverage as 'speculative, scurrilous or inaccurate', it stated boldly:

> It is necessary that I should make it clear to any reader of this report that no evidence has been found that officers of the RUC or members of the Security Services have in any way been responsible for the instigation of allegations against Mr Stalker.[64]

This is unsurprising. If the army, RUC or MI5 had spread rumours about Stalker to get rid of him, it is most unlikely that there would be an audit trail. In the inquiry into the murder of Billy Wright in the Maze Prison in 1997, a former ACC in the RUC, Sam Kinkaid, was tasked to explore the apparent lack of documentation supplied to the inquiry. He used the expression 'plausible deniability' to account for its absence and explained:

> It was a culture or practice that existed in an organisation where the members did not keep records, so there was no audit trail. Nothing could be traced back, so that if they were challenged, they denied it, and that denial, being based on no documentation, would become 'plausible deniability'.

The system in SB was such, he said, 'that it didn't give proper audit trails and proper dissemination, and at times it would appear that it allowed people at a later date to have amnesia, in the sense that they couldn't remember because there was no data on the system'.[65]

Although it is unlikely that there would be any documentation, there was nothing in the Sampson report to suggest that he even sought permission to examine RUC SB or MI5 files. There was no discussion of the possibility that Burton was an informer for MI5 or RUC SB, nor any reference to the visit of a RUC officer to GMP HQ in March 1986 when Ware, a member of the DIU, was instructed to take the officer to Manchester airport for his or her return flight. At the very least, Sampson needed to explain the purpose of the visit to dispel the suggestion that there was indeed close co-operation between the two police forces shortly before the decision to suspend Stalker.

Omissions

There were many glaring omissions in the report. The most obvious was the failure to make any reference whatsoever to Burton's allegation that Stalker was corrupt in the 'I have found your rat' conversation with Burgess in May 1983, which Burgess reported both to the Fraud and the Discipline and Complaints Departments. [66] There must have been a record of Topping visiting Burgess in January 1985 and asking him about his report. Yet there was no mention of it. Could this be explained by Sampson's desire not to undermine the official narrative that the investigation into Stalker started in June, rather than perhaps late 1984?

Another glaring omission in the report was the failure to discuss the known connections between Manchester and Northern Ireland. There was a mention of 'a fraud investigation in May 1983',[67] but no further details of the fraud were provided. The comment clearly related to the LFF and the contract bombing of Klapish's premises in Belfast which led to the two-day meeting in 1981 between the RUC and GMP (Chapter 4). Burgess, who so meticulously put together the mountain of information which led to the conviction of Klapish and Burton for conspiracy to defraud, was effectively written out of the official story. The only reference to him was in relation to the Kwok Man restaurant.

Very oddly, the alleged Bridge Street conversation between Burton and Donnelly was also omitted. During the conversation, it will be recalled, Donnelly implied that Stalker was a 'top jolly' for Taylor and Jimmy Monaghan. The detail of the meeting was confirmed by Burton in one of the five interviews with him in February 1985. Its inclusion would have corroborated other information and added more weight to Burton's credibility. Similarly, there was no reference to the numerous interviews with Burton, conducted by Topping, Richardson and other police officers, in late 1984. Two explanations are possible for these lacunae. Either the DIU withheld the information from Sampson, or the inquiry team believed that the conversation was a fabrication and the subsequent interviews with Burton had nothing to do with Stalker but other corrupt police officers. To have included the conversation and the interviews would have further undermined the credibility of Burton and cast further doubt on the evidence which led to the investigation into Stalker.

A further glaring omission was any reference to one of Taylor's BMWs being seen outside a drug dealer's house. The alleged sighting was noted in McGourlay's 12 July 1984 report, which had all the hallmarks of being fabricated at a later date. The information would have strengthened the suspicions against Stalker's friend. Either the Sampson team were suspicious and therefore did not mention it, or it was only produced after Sampson had carried out his investigation in August 1986 to deal with the adverse publicity. It was certainly in the public domain by late September when *The Observer* reported the information.[68] Peter Taylor also mentioned it in his book published the following year.[69]

There was one other significant omission. Sampson's report made no mention of the US authorities watching *Diogenes* – a most obvious line of inquiry for the Sampson team to explore. This detail had been provided to a meeting of GMPA by its chair, Norman Briggs. At a subsequent meeting, Labour members had pressed Anderton on the source of the information. Anderton said he could not recall providing the information. Whereupon, Rees, the clerk to GMPA, turned to him and said 'Your memory must be at fault. You did indeed tell the Chairman about *Diogenes.*'[70] The information, no doubt, helped secure Stalker's suspension, but it was untrue. The US Drug Enforcement Agency had never shown any interest in the *Diogenes* or Taylor, which may explain the omission.[71]

Re-instatement and retirement

The report concluded, 'despite some misgivings', there was no evidence that Stalker had accepted a gift or undue hospitality from Taylor or that the relationship was corrupt or criminal.[72] Unsurprisingly, given the poor quality of the report, it failed to spell out what the 'misgivings' were, but the comment was sufficient to cast doubt on the conclusion that there was no evidence. It concluded:

> There was 'no allegation made of any criminal offence being committed' by Stalker, there were, however, a series of disciplinary offences 'demonstrating a less than excellent standard of professional performance'(underlining in the original). It continued: This standard of excellence is that which is set by the Service itself and expected of it by the public. In consequence, therefore, I have given the most careful consideration to the whole of the circumstances of this case and having regard to the considerable amount of public speculation and interest it has generated, I am of the opinion that the evidence supports, indeed *demands* (italics in the original), that it be ventilated before an independent Tribunal.[73]

GMPA considered the report on 22 August 1986. It rejected the recommendation that ten charges should be considered by an independent Tribunal. Instead, it recommended that Stalker should return to work, but with the proviso that he should be more circumspect in his friends and contacts as Deputy Chief Constable. Shortly after, Stalker returned to work. Ten days later, on 1 September, Anderton issued a press statement defending his role in the Stalker case. He claimed that the inquiry was 'justified, necessary and properly conducted', adding that 'he did no more or less than his duty'.[74]

Stalker's return was never going to be easy, as the investigation into him by Anderton, Lees and Topping had severely undermined any future relationship with them. He was now once again Topping and Lees' superior and had to deal with issues as they arose. For example, on one occasion, he received reports from some of his officers, who alleged that good, efficient, and capable officers were being moved out of key departments and replaced by Topping's nominees who were masons. Stalker confronted Topping over the allegation. Topping denied it. He said that the first consideration was ability but added that, other things being equal, he would favour a mason.[75]

Within a few months, Stalker decided to leave and handed in his notice. The trigger was Topping and his decision to mount a huge police operation to search for the bodies of two victims in the notorious Moors Murders case of Myra Hindley and Ian Brady. Neither Anderton nor Topping informed him of the pending search. Anderton himself was absent from the office for the first two days of the search, leaving Stalker in charge of the force and to face the press and media, in total ignorance of developments.[76] Stalker remarked it was 'the cruellest and most obvious insult it was possible to deliver to a Deputy Chief Constable'.[77] He had exhausted any respect for the Chief Constable and decided it was time to go.[78]

* * *

The leaking of Sampson's disciplinary report to the press provided a unique insight into a police investigation which would normally be kept secret from public scrutiny. It was a report whose true purpose remains obscure and was compromised as Sampson was party to the discussion at the Scarborough meeting. Moreover, it relied heavily on information provided by the DIU and there was no attempt to examine critically the unsigned and undated reports, several of which appear to have been produced retrospectively. It appeared blinded in its belief that Stalker was corrupt.

The report itself was poorly structured, full of inaccuracies, errors, and numerous unsubstantiated comments. It could find little to support Burton's information. When there was little or no evidence to substantiate the vague charge of associating with known criminals, Sampson resorted to new charges against Stalker of attending party political functions and the misuse of police cars. His report, however, provided the government with some comfort, because it supported the official narrative that there was no conspiracy to remove Stalker from the Northern Ireland inquiry.

Chapter 19

Sampson's Inquiry in Northern Ireland

IN JUNE 1986, Sampson took over Stalker's inquiry in Northern Ireland. Thorburn was replaced as second-in-command by West Yorkshire Police Assistant Chief Constable, Donald Shaw. Thorburn and the rest of Stalker's team remained on the inquiry. There were a number of serious outstanding issues that required further investigation: the destruction of the hayshed tapes by both the RUC and MI5; the production of routine cover stories in each of the three shooting incidents; the construction of false, distorted or embellished information submitted to the DPPNI; the withholding of key intelligence from the CID; and the lack of any legal framework for running of state agents.

Unlike Sampson's investigation report on Stalker, which was leaked in full to the press (Chapter 18), Sampson's reports on his inquiry in Northern Ireland have never been published. This followed the usual practice in police investigations in order to protect confidentiality and allow their authors to be frank. It has been possible, however, to build up a fairly detailed picture of Sampson's investigation and recommendations, based on leaks to the press, the criminal trials which followed the three incidents, and the release in December 2023 of the 1986 NIO Stalker/Sampson papers to the National Archive.

Structure and content

During his investigation, Sampson provided government officials with a synopsis of the structure and content of his reports. On 17 October 1986, he met Sir Robert Andrew in the NIO in Belfast and informed him that he would submit three reports. The first would cover the investigation into the hayshed incident, which would be ready on 22 October. It would deal only with criminal charges against the officers involved in the incident and not the allegations of a cover-up. The second report would deal with Stalker's recommendations on the other two incidents, together with Sampson's own recommendations on the hayshed incident. This report would also address the cover-up allegations in all three incidents, including the possibility of charges of conspiracy to pervert the course of justice. A third report would deal with what Sampson labelled as 'public interest' aspects of his inquiry. This would include the management of SB, the use of informers, and cross-border incursions.[1]

The Home Office was not happy with having three reports. Sir Brian Cubbon, Permanent Under Secretary of State in the Home Office, in a letter to Andrew, considered it 'somewhat complicated and messy' and was concerned that the structure did not reflect on the integrity of the exercise as a whole. He thought that if Sampson was seen as 'shilly-shallying', or the DPP had to ask him to do something again, it would reflect badly on Sampson's Manchester report.[2] By the beginning of February 1987, Sampson had still not finished the second report. It had been delayed because the DPPNI had directed that Sampson carry out a further 21 interviews which the Attorney General was satisfied were necessary.[3] Presumably, they included interviews with all those in the army and MI5 who conspired to destroy the tapes.

The second report was eventually delivered to Hermon and DPPNI around 23 March 1987. It dealt only with the general question of cover-up in the three incidents. Contrary to the expectations of the NIO, it did not include a confidential annex dealing with the role of the Chief Constable and his most senior officers. This now was to be included in the third report divided into three sections. The first would deal with Sampson's criticism of the CC, DCC and ACC in charge of SB, 'which will be serious but will fall short of recommendations for prosecutions'.[4] The second would include Stalker's extensive papers on the management and organisation of the RUC which Sampson considered should be included, 'to avoid the accusation that he has suppressed anything'.[5] The final section would deal with Sampson's observations on the management and organisation of the RUC with an emphasis on the role of SB. The minute finished by noting that Sampson was still considering the position of members of MI5 involved in the hayshed incident and whether to make a separate submission to the DPP.[6]

The Secretaries of State in the Home Office and NIO must have been appalled by what they were hearing. Sampson was not only seriously considering charging the most senior officers in the RUC, the CC, DCC and an ACC, but also three senior officers of Superintendent and Chief Superintendent rank. In addition, he was considering prosecutions of members of the army and MI5. The implications were devastating. Trust in the forces of law and order would be damaged irrevocably, particularly within the nationalist community.

Principal recommendations

In the end, Sampson did not go as far as recommending that the top three officers in the RUC should be prosecuted. CC Hermon, DCC McAtamney and ACC Forbes were all interviewed under caution. Hermon was interviewed on 8 October 1986 after written questions had been given to him – a procedure not normally applied to ordinary suspects.[7] Sampson concluded that Hermon 'seemed not to have been involved in the details of what happened'[8] and therefore there was insufficient evidence to charge him. Hermon was highly dismissive of the interview. In his autobiography, he noted that his replies to questions were 'robust and somewhat disparaging', and he heard no more.[9] Although Sampson believed that 'it was possible that McAtamney, the Deputy Chief Constable, had knowingly suppressed evidence in his investigation into shootings',[10] he did not recommend prosecution of him either. Finally, Sampson considered charging Forbes, head of SB, and a Detective Chief Inspector, with conspiracy to pervert the course of justice, but did not do so.[11]

In light of his conclusion on the possible culpability of these three top officers, Sampson was concerned about submitting his report to the Chief Constable. During a meeting with Andrew, Myers and Saunders from the Attorney General's Office, Sampson strongly recommended that the report should not be sent to Hermon. He feared the 'integrity of the investigation would be compromised since the Chief Constable would show the report to the senior officers concerned' and they would be given an advance opportunity to prepare a defence.[12] Sampson also expressed his concern that Hermon would again delay passing the report onto the DPPNI. He pointed out that it took Hermon over four months before he forwarded Stalker's interim report to the DPPNI, and despite knowing that his deputy had yet to be interviewed, he allowed him full access to the report. Andrew, however, pointed out that the report had been commissioned by the Chief Constable and if it was not submitted to him, the media would suggest that charges had been recommended against him.

A few weeks later, Sampson was still insisting that this key part of his report should not be shown to the Chief Constable since it 'discussed the culpability of himself and other senior officers'.[13] Andrew pointed out that as there was not going to be a recommendation that Hermon should be prosecuted, it would be difficult to deny access to the report which he had commissioned. Again, Andrew pointed out that if it became known that Hermon had not seen the report, the construction would be that he was personally incriminated.

While not recommending prosecution of any of the three top officers, Sampson did recommend several significant prosecutions. Building on the work of Stalker's team and armed with new information from those that had listened to the tape of the hayshed shooting – the destroyed tape 042 – that no warning had been given, Sampson considered that there was a *prima facie* case against three of the police involved in the shooting. He therefore recommended that they be prosecuted for murder and attempted murder.[14]

Sampson also supported Stalker's recommendation that DS Anderson and DS Flanagan (Chapter 5) should be prosecuted for conspiracy to pervert the course of justice for overseeing the fabrication of cover stories in the form of doctoring and embellishing evidence. In relation to the hayshed, the deception included: claims that it was a routine patrol; false information about an armed person being seen walking towards the hayshed; altering log registers, making up posthumous intelligence on Tighe, and ending the transcription of the listening tapes at tape 041 with the comment: 'No further interest'.[15] In relation to the Mullacreevie Park incident, the deception included among other matters: a fabricated story about the vehicle checkpoint in which a police officer was injured, falsifying the colour of cars at the scene and destruction of physical evidence.

Finally, Sampson recommended that several MI5 officers should be prosecuted for perverting the course of justice relating to the destruction of the hayshed tape.[16] He considered that 'the fact that the Security Service was in possession of and retained the copy tape until the early summer of 1985 and did not bring it to the attention of Mr. Stalker is wholly reprehensible'.[17] It was more than reprehensible. It showed that MI5 was prepared to break the law and to pervert the course of justice to defend their reputation and that of the RUC.

From all accounts, Sampson followed in Stalker's footsteps and carried out a thorough investigation. He could be criticised, however, for not recommending the prosecution of SB officers for failing to pass on information to the CID investigating the three shootings. Stalker made this criticism and Sampson recognised that at the time of the three incidents: 'RUC Special Branch was taking a much too dominant part in operational matters to the detriment of the established CID.'[18] The failure to pass on information stemmed directly from the illegal MI5/Walker counter-insurgency strategy. Yet no SB officers are known to have been prosecuted for deliberately obstructing CID – a common practice in the investigation of many murders. If either Stalker or Sampson had recommended prosecutions, it would perhaps have curtailed the illegal MI5/Walker counter-insurgency strategy and strengthened the role of CID.

Peter Taylor argued that, as Sampson was prepared to recommend the prosecutions of both RUC and MI5 officers for perverting the course of justice, there was no cover-up and Sampson clearly wanted matters to be exposed in open court. Taylor continued:

> If there had been a 'Brit' conspiracy to get rid of Stalker (which I do not believe), then appointing Colin Sampson as his successor, in the expectation that he would collude in a cover-up, was a major mistake. This is one of the main reasons why the conspiracy theory does not hold water.[19]

This, of course, does not necessarily follow. It was still possible for a variety of reasons that a conspiracy was hatched to remove Stalker.

Operation Lexical

Late on in his investigation, Sampson discovered that the cover stories were not randomly produced in response to the shooting incidents, but part of a clearly defined policy designed to hide operational details. The policy was revealed by Hermon during an interview late on in Sampson's investigation when he produced a copy of a force order which had been in place since late 1981.[20] Neither Stalker nor Sampson up to this moment had known of the existence of such a policy. It provided for a specially constituted group in RUC Headquarters to meet after a fatal shooting in order to prepare a press release. The fact that the force order was introduced in 1981 suggests that it was all part of MI5/Walker counter-insurgency strategy designed not only to hide operational details but also to protect the lives of informers and state agents. Deception was at the heart of the strategy. Crucial information was therefore withheld from both the CID, DPP and the public.

Shoot-to-kill

Stalker, it will be recalled, was appointed because there was a widespread view among the nationalist community that the RUC had adopted a shoot-to-kill policy. In an interview in *The Times* nearly two years after his suspension, Stalker explained that:

> I never did find evidence of a shoot-to-kill policy, as such, There was no written instruction, nothing pinned up on a noticeboard. But there was a clear understanding on the part of the men whose job it was to pull the trigger that that was what was expected of them.[21]

Sampson too could find 'no evidence' of any instructions that there was a shoot-to-kill policy. In contrast to Stalker, he considered that the RUC used only 'legitimate methods to bring offenders to justice'.[22] But he did admit that, 'the three incidents which took place over a short period of time in November and

December 1982 are inextricably linked by the involvement of the same officers and specialist units as to give this impression'.[23]

Cubbon was sceptical about Sampson's conclusion. He wanted to know what 'objectively' was meant by the statement that 'there was no shoot-to-kill policy'. He went on:

> Sampson may be satisfied that there was no policy or instruction from the Government or the top of the RUC. But critics will immediately ask whether there are doubts about the vigour and effectiveness and even commitment of senior levels to ensure that junior officers did not in practice pursue such a policy. They will also ask about the attitude of senior officers to reports that junior officers had taken the law into their own hands in an individual incident. It seems to me that [if] the whole of [the] Sampson investigation is available for public consumption, in criminal proceedings or otherwise, it will be mistakenly incomplete to say simply that he is satisfied that there was no shoot to kill policy.[24]

Notwithstanding Cubbon's scepticism, in a meeting on 23 October 1986 between Hermon and Andrew, it was agreed that it would be very helpful if use was made of Sampson's conclusion that there was no shoot-to-kill policy. But only two weeks later Andrew wrote to Hermon informing him that the Law Officers had considered this possibility and advised strongly against, not because of the strength of evidence against such as conclusion, but in case it prejudiced any criminal proceedings. In addition, Andrew claimed that there was a danger that publicising one finding would make it hard to resist disclosure of all the findings.[25] Hermon was unhappy. He saw a clear distinction between the policy finding on shoot-to-kill and the possible prosecution against individual officers. He pointed out that the RUC had taken 'a great deal of unjustified and distorted criticisms from many sources' and had been unable to reply.[26]

Handling the Irish

Throughout Sampson's investigation there was concern within the NIO about how it should discharge its commitment to inform the Irish government about the outcome of the Stalker/Sampson inquiry – a task which it labelled patronisingly as 'Handling the Irish', as if dealing with some troublesome youth. In a minute of 7 November, Mr Bell noted that 'for all practical purposes we <u>are</u> (underlined) committed to telling them'.[27] This commitment was made following Stalker's appointment in 1984.[28] Bell continued:

> The Irish claim to view the whole affair as a serious impediment to relations between the RUC and the minority community and they do have a legitimate interest in the alleged border incursions. If we stand on our dignity and do

not at least give the appearance of being frank Stalker/Sampson will be quoted against us every time we step up pressure on cross border security co-operation.[29]

The minute claimed that the government was hamstrung because 'the Secretary of State will only (apparently) see as of right the promised section of the report dealing with "general management issues"'. The word 'apparently' is interesting and suggests that the SoS may well see the whole of Sampson's report. It then added 'our aim should be to persuade the Irish that they are only interested in the general management issues. In other words, they should have no interest in the allegation that there was a shoot-to-kill policy or that several police officers should be prosecuted for murder.

In a more expansive minute a month later, Bell developed the problems they were facing in providing information to the Irish government: Sampson had not yet finished his enquiry; even when it was finished the NIO could not make any comment until the DPP made decisions over prosecutions; and the NIO was unable to say that Sampson had concluded that there was no shoot-to-kill policy in case it prejudiced prosecutions. In the meantime, there were extensive leaks in the press and media. In these circumstances, Bell concluded, a policy of 'constructive stonewalling' was probably the best course of action and suggested that, 'we must abandon all hope of being able to satisfy the Irish'.[30]

Leaks to the press

During the Stalker/Sampson inquiry in Northern Ireland, there were numerous leaks of information to the press. On 20 June, Hermon wrote to Andrew complaining about the 'steady pattern of leakages' from early on in Stalker's investigation. He pointed out that Chris Ryder of the *Sunday Times* was particularly well informed. Then from the spring of 1985, 'it was evident that someone close to the investigation was feeding the Press'.[31] Hermon claimed the situation came to a head when Stalker was taken off the inquiry. He complained that 'Peter Taylor for Panorama, and associates in *The Irish Times* and *The Guardian*' had either seen Stalker's interim report or had been supplied with detailed information from it. He concluded: 'I need hardly say that this business causes me and the Force great concern. Methods of surveillance have been publicized to the benefit of the PIRA. Surveillance operaters (sic) feel unprotected.'[32]

Three days later Hermon rang the NIO on no fewer than three occasions concerned about articles in the papers, all of which he claimed were unfavourable to the RUC and there was no mention of Stalker's conclusion that there was no shoot-to-kill policy. The clear implication, he argued, was that Stalker or a member of his team was responsible for the leaks.[33] He demanded that something should be done. He wrote again on 17 July complaining about what he called 'a series of serious distorted disclosures' and insisted on an investigation.[34] Officials, however, were reluctant to take any action as they considered an investigation under the Official Secrets Act could be counter-productive and could fuel the allegations of government contrivance in a cover-up. Over the next few months, he continued to campaign about the leaks.

On 20 August, Hermon wrote to Andrew again about the leaks. He had met Myers and Sampson at the Home Office at the end of July to express his concerns and to seek reassurances from Sampson that he was satisfied that none of his present team were responsible for the disclosures. Sampson had given him reassurance to the limits of 'his professional and human judgment'.[35] But Hermon was not satisfied. *The Observer* had carried an article on 10 August in which it made reference to 'informers' code numbers'.[36] Hermon pointed out that the information could have only come from someone on Stalker's team or two RUC officers. He wanted his request for an investigation to remain on the table.

All of this was putting a great strain on Hermon. On 6 April 1987, Andrew had a long conversation with him which Andrew described as 'somewhat rambling'. He considered Hermon to be in 'rather a depressed state'. Hermon complained that 'the integrity of the RUC was not properly recognised by the NIO' and that the RUC was facing additional pressures as a result of the Anglo-Irish Agreement. He needed more resources. The most important part of the conversation concerned the Sampson report. Hermon informed Andrew that he was halfway through his examination of Part 2 and, as in the case of Part 1, he considered that:

> Sampson's attitude was naive: he had not understood the problems, had not asked the right questions, and had discovered sinister connotations where none existed. If prosecutions were mounted on this basis he [Hermon] did not think they would succeed; but if the cases came to court great damage would be done to the RUC; he [Hermon] was particularly concerned that the defence would press for the discovery of classified papers.[37]

Andrew was left with the impression that Hermon was under 'great pressure'. Apart from operational problems, Andrew considered that Hermon 'was anxious about his own position and that of the force in light of Stalker/Sampson; he is working long hours; and he is suspicious of almost everyone (the NIO, the HMI, the Police Authority, the GOC, the Security Service etc)'.[38]

The Northern Ireland Manchester connection.

Throughout the period of Sampson's investigations, there was considerable concern in the Home Office about the rumours and speculation that the allegations against Stalker had been instigated with the aim of discrediting him and thus frustrating his investigation in Northern Ireland. Pressure was mounting for a judicial inquiry. Salford City Council had called for an inquiry into the origins of the allegations against Stalker – a matter raised by Neil Kinnock in a letter to Douglas Hurd, the Home Secretary. In response, Hurd pointed out that Sampson, who had responsibility for both inquiries, had 'found no evidence that officers of the RUC had been responsible for the instigation of allegations against Mr Stalker'.[39] This, of course, left open the possibility that MI5 had been responsible. Hurd ended his letter by emphasising that Sampson's report was nearly finished and the Attorney General was of the view that a further inquiry at this stage might be prejudicial to any criminal proceedings that might follow – a disingenuous position in light of the Attorney General's decision, less than two years later, to cancel all the criminal proceedings recommended by Stalker and subsequently Sampson (Chapter 20).

* * *

All the available evidence suggests that Sampson's investigation in Northern Ireland was far more thorough than his investigation into the disciplinary charges against Stalker in Manchester. Stalker and then Sampson revealed considerable levels of deception, deviance, obstruction and criminality, all of which stemmed from the illegal counter-insurgency strategy put in place by MI5 in 1981. It had corrupted the rule of law to gain intelligence, neutered CID murder investigations by requiring the withholding of key information and deceived the public and DPP by releasing false information. The thoroughness of both investigations, together with the number of recommended prosecutions against the backdrop of continuing allegations that there had been a conspiracy to remove Stalker, placed the Thatcher government in a difficult dilemma: to fail to act on the recommendations would add weight to the idea of conspiracy, but to have key MI5 and other personnel cross-examined in court was unthinkable.

Despite both Stalker and Sampson's investigations, there remained many unanswered questions – about the hayshed shootings, in particular. Was Tighe shot by someone inside the hayshed? Who put the Mauser rifles among the bales? The official narrative was that they were hidden there along with the explosives by the IRA. But there is the possibility that they were planted by MI5, the army or RUC when the faulty bug was replaced, as part of a plan to trap members of the IRA in a shoot-to-kill operation in revenge for the murder of the police officers on Kinnego embankment. As well as serving as a trap, the presence of the rifles would have provided a strong claim of self-defence in any killing. Moreover, the existence of a shoot-to-kill plan would explain why there was no attempt to surround the hayshed and arrest Tighe and McCauley in a controlled and safe operation. Finally, there remains a mystery about what Thorburn meant when he revealed to a journalist that they were pursuing a very serious line of inquiry before Stalker was removed, which was not followed up by Sampson. What was it?

Chapter 20

Perverting the Course of Justice

STALKER'S REMOVAL at the end of May 1986 led to intense press and media speculation. He was widely perceived as the quintessential honest police officer with an unblemished police career. He was just about to complete a very sensitive inquiry in Northern Ireland concerning the death of six young men at the hands of the police. All he needed was access to the tape of the hayshed shooting, the intelligence behind the operation and information on any state agents involved. Against such a background, it was inevitable that there would be widespread allegations of a conspiracy to remove him. Anderton, in particular, came in for considerable criticism. The prosecution of Kevin Taylor became an imperative, to prove to the world that Stalker's removal was justified because of his association with 'known criminals'.

Meetings with DPP

On 19 June 1986, Topping, Born and Stephenson tried unsuccessfully to persuade the DPP to prosecute Taylor. The DPP's representatives, according to Farley in his opening address in the civil action, 'would not sanction such a course – not only had they not seen a word of evidence but at that time they expressed reservations about the merits of the case as it was then presented to them'.[1]

The Times duly reported that there was a file on Taylor with the DPP.[2] While only a report and not a file of evidence, GMP had now provided a justification for Stalker's suspension. The article finished by noting that friends and colleagues of Stalker remained convinced that he was a victim of a deliberate smear campaign to force his removal from the Northern Ireland inquiry.

A second meeting with the DPP occurred just under a month later on 16 July, at which Topping was recorded as 'being anxious' that Taylor was charged quickly. It was pointed out by the representatives of the DPP that the inquiry into Taylor would take months and no approval of the charges would be taken in advance.[3] The failure of these officers to get the DPP to change his mind, served only to increase Anderton's determination to have Taylor immediately prosecuted. He now persuaded Myers from the HMIC to join him in a visit to the DPP.

On 27 July, Anderton, Myers and Topping travelled to London. It was only eleven days after the DIU's second meeting with the DPP. Nothing, of course, could have changed in the meantime. Anderton was dressed in full uniform. According to Stalker, it was unprecedented that Myers, a Home Office official, should attend such a meeting with the DPP to participate in a decision over a prosecution. In the civil action, Anderton's defence counsel tried to suggest that there was nothing untoward in Myers' attendance:

TABACHNIK: Can you see any reason why as regional inspector Sir Philip shouldn't take an interest in something completely dominating the media?

STALKER: An interest yes but this is not an interest. This is a role.

TABACHNIK: Do you dispute that there was enormous media coverage of the matter at the time?

STALKER: Of course not.

TABACHNIK: Do you dispute that there were a lot of allegations and a lot of speculation flying about?

STALKER: Yes, still is.

TABACHNIK: Do you dispute that much of the media coverage was hostile and could affect the reputation and good name of the force?

STALKER: I accept that there was some hostility but much of it was self-administered by the police by appointing Mr Sampson to both enquiries.

TABACHNIK: Do you dispute in fact that there was public concern about the matter?

STALKER: There was public concern yes.

TABACHNIK: Do you dispute that the reputation of a number of people including senior police officers was being sullied and bandied about in unfavourable and critical ways in the media?

STALKER: Yes, but that is not unusual and the point I make, and I make it again my Lord, is that I have never ever known, and I defy another chief constable to tell me when an HMI went to the DPP [and told the] office: 'pull your finger out, get a move on, this is causing embarrassment.' That is no basis on [which] to make a decision on whether or not to prosecute.[4]

Stalker rightly emphasised that adverse publicity should have nothing to do with the prosecution of an individual. Yet it emerged that this was the principal reason for the presence of Myers and Anderton at the meeting. Anderton had made an *aide mémoire*. One item on it related to the prosecution of Taylor. This stated that he was 'a central figure in the criminal life of Manchester and had connections with organised crime'.[5] It was a damning comment on a man with no criminal record and must have caused bewilderment in the meeting, as GMP had only demanded that Taylor be prosecuted for allegedly stealing from his own companies and defrauding a bank – hardly the activity of a 'central figure' in the criminal life of Manchester.

Most of the other items on the *aide mémoire* concerned the adverse publicity which GMP was experiencing following Stalker's removal. One noted 'the disruptive and damaging speculation inside and outside the force'.[6] This was certainly true. Links were being made in the press and media between the Northern Ireland inquiry and the investigation into Stalker. Taylor, too, was receiving considerable publicity protesting his innocence and informing the public that he still did not know the nature of the police inquiry into his affairs. The leaking of the Sampson report and its extensive criticism would have only added to Anderton's concern.

GMP's secret press and media operation

During the meeting, Anderton revealed that he had mounted an 'operation' to deal with the adverse publicity. Topping explained some details of the operation 'in the strictest confidence',[7] but there is no record in the public domain of what he told the DPP. It was an extraordinary admission. Any comment or story would prejudice Taylor's trial. The operation was therefore a deliberate and planned contempt of court. Anderton then informed the meeting that the BBC Panorama team was making a programme about Taylor – no doubt with the considerable help of GMP – which would make 'possible connections with international drugs trafficking'.[8] This must have confused the DPP still further as GMP was attempting to prosecute Taylor for fraud.

The media operation appears to have started shortly after Stalker's removal. On 5 June, the *Daily Mail* – a paper which was often ahead of other papers in reporting on the Taylor/Stalker affair – stated that Stalker had 'been accused of accepting hospitality from a known criminal', and the headline implied that it was related to a holiday.[9] This information could only have come from the police. No one outside the force would have known that the investigation involved looking into Stalker's 1981 holiday with Taylor.

On 15 June, *The Observer* carried the headline: 'Stalker "smear" hinges on old photograph'.[10] It reported that a four-year-old photograph of Stalker attending a birthday party for 100 guests given by Taylor was the sole evidence against Stalker. The article described how newspapers 'were fed stories of "lavish hospitality from known criminals"' and Dublin officials were told that there were 'serious disciplinary charges against Stalker – so serious that his whole inquiry into the RUC might be invalidated'.[11] Peter Murtagh, *The Guardian* journalist, confirmed that the extensive leaking of information went beyond GMP. In a review of Stalker's book, he reported that the Home Office and Northern Ireland sources at the time were contacting newspaper editors and leader writers to offer 'guidance' and 'some fairly senior political figures' were offering to brief reporters strictly off-the-record.[12] They were informing journalists that Stalker was 'up to his neck in it'. The 'it' was unspecified but ranged from drugs, women, young men, to backhanders, and he had to be got rid of to 'protect the integrity of the RUC inquiry'.[13]

On 16 June, the BBC broadcast the first of three television programmes produced and narrated by Peter Taylor. The first was entitled *Stalker: Coincidence or Conspiracy*. It began:

> Two weeks ago, John Stalker was removed from his inquiry into the Royal Ulster Constabulary. After months of delay, he was finally given access to top secret intelligence records concerning one of the shootings he was investigating. Was it coincidence or conspiracy? [14]

The programme put key questions to several people: Kevin Taylor; James Prior, SoS for Northern Ireland; Lord Rawlinson, Attorney General; Sir Cecil Clothier, Chair of PCA; John Stalker; and John Hermon. Kevin Taylor was asked several questions: 'Do you know which branch the police officers were from?'; 'Have you defrauded anybody?'; 'Might they have been from the drugs squad?'; and 'You've been involved in drugs?'[15] His reply to all the questions was in the negative and he was particularly emphatic about drugs: 'I have two young daughters. Is it likely that I would be involved in drugs? I detest the stuff'.[16] The questions suggested that Peter Taylor knew that GMP was pursuing two lines of investigation into Taylor – one focusing on drugs and the other on fraud.

The second Panorama programme was broadcast on 19 August, just three weeks after Anderton had informed the DPP that he had established a special press and media operation, and that the Panorama Team would make connections between Taylor and international drug trafficking. The programme began:

> Tonight, Panorama reports on the real reason why Stalker was taken off the Northern Ireland inquiry. We investigate his association with Kevin Taylor and the connection between Taylor's yacht and an international drug smuggling ring.[17]

The wording in the second sentence was almost identical to the words used by Anderton to the DPP. The only difference was that Anderton did not mention a yacht. The programme dealt with Taylor's ambitious property development in Old Trafford, his friendship with some members of the QSG, and his 50th birthday party, at which some people with criminal records were present. The programme then focused on *Diogenes*. Peter Taylor asked Kevin Taylor about Stalker's holiday on the yacht and who paid, and if Stalker knew that some people with criminal records had been on it previously. The rest of the programme focused on drug smuggling and the use of *Diogenes* for a drug run by Whittaker and Brooks. The programme failed to explain that Taylor was trying to sell the boat and had allowed it to be used on a proving trip.

Although the programme did report that a file on Taylor relating to *fraud* had been sent to the DPP, the viewer was left with the distinct impression that Taylor was involved in drug smuggling. Unlike the previous programme, which lent towards a conspiracy, this programme came down firmly in support of a coincidence of events. It stated boldly, in relation to the Northern Ireland investigation, that action was taken 'to preserve the inquiry not to destroy it'[18] – the very same line that Murtagh reported was being spun by the Home Office and Northern Ireland sources. It emphasised that there was no evidence that Stalker's problems had anything to do with Northern Ireland; they arose entirely from his friendship with Taylor and his associates.

The only source of much of the information in the programme, once again, could only have been GMP and influencing the programme was part of the operation mounted by Anderton to counter the adverse publicity.

Only the programme makers can answer what information they were fed or had access to. For instance, were they shown some of the documents which previous chapters have suggested were likely forgeries? In particular, was the team shown McGourlay's 12 July BMW report which alleged that Taylor's car was flagged by the Drugs Squad because it was seen outside an alleged drug smuggler's house? As was argued, this report had all the hallmarks of being a much later creation rather than a report contemporaneous to 1984 (Chapter 9). Nothing about the press and media operation was disclosed on discovery in the civil action, suggesting that either no detail was noted, apart from Anderton's *aide mémoire*, or the documents relating to it were subsequently destroyed.

At the end of September 1986, *The Observer* published another piece under the banner 'the Irish Connection', detailing the role of David Burton in the LFF in Belfast and how he made money acting as a police informer in Manchester. The story was not going away and there continued to be adverse publicity about the force. The following month, Topping reopened the investigation into the notorious Moors Murders case of Myra Hindley and Ian Brady, amidst allegations that the primary purpose was to distract press and media attention away from the Taylor/Stalker affair. On 26 November, Born and Ware from the DIU went to the moor to see Topping, who was obviously still centrally involved in the Taylor/Stalker investigation, and informed him that Stalker was seen watching a warehouse which Taylor was purchasing from the G.E.C.[19] It was either a case of mistaken identity or a piece of fiction, but nevertheless considered important enough that Topping should be told immediately.

Three weeks later, on 16 December 1986, Topping arranged for Saddleworth Moor to be sealed off by hundreds of police officers and Hindley was flown in by helicopter to help the police locate the bodies of Pauline Reade and Keith Bennett. It was inevitable that the event would receive maximum publicity. Resources for the search, as with the investigation into Taylor, seemed limitless. Bernard Levin wrote a highly critical piece in *The Times*.[20] He asked: 'Why is the macabre farce on Saddleworth Moor allowed to continue?' And added: 'Who, if anybody, is in charge and what does he think he is doing?'[21] The article was accompanied by a picture of police officers digging in the middle of a snowstorm. It was an absurd and ghoulish exercise. Taylor's legal team, along with many others, were now even more convinced that it was an expensive publicity stunt to distract attention away from the adverse publicity which GMP continued to receive.

GMP made several other visits to the DPP demanding that Taylor should be prosecuted. But they received the same answer. The DPP insisted on seeing the evidence before he could prosecute. On 30 September, Sir Brian Cubbon, Permanent Under Secretary in the Home Office, wrote a long letter to Douglas Hurd, Secretary of State in the Home Office, in which he made an incredible admission:

> It now seems that Taylor will not be prosecuted for fraud. No final decision has been taken. Informal indications are that the Director and counsel whom he has consulted do not consider the police evidence sufficient. That news underlines the need for a waterproof position on the allegations that Stalker was framed. No prosecution of Taylor will be seen by some to confirm that the whole Manchester episode was a smokescreen for getting Stalker off the backs of the RUC.[22]

As a consequence, Cubbon considered holding a judicial inquiry into whether there was any connection between allegations against Stalker and Stalker's own investigation in Northern Ireland.[23] The Home Secretary's first instinct was for an independent enquiry although he recognised that it could prejudice any criminal proceedings.[24]

Eventually in early summer 1987, however, nearly a year after the high-powered police delegation, a file of statements and various exhibits were sent to the DPP. On 9 August, *The Mail on Sunday* was once again ahead of the pack. It ran a story that Taylor might face criminal charges and announced that the DPP would decide that week whether to prosecute.[25] But it was not until late September 1987 that the DPP formally agreed that Taylor and the others should be prosecuted for conspiring to obtain pecuniary advantage from the bank. This was some sixteen months since Anderton had informed the meeting in Scarborough that Taylor would go for trial.

No prosecutions: Attorney General's statement

On 18 January 1988, the Attorney General, Sir Patrick Mayhew, made a historic statement to the House of Commons which fundamentally undermined any belief that the rule of law was respected in Northern Ireland. He announced that no officers in either the RUC or MI5 would be prosecuted, contrary to the recommendations of both Stalker and Sampson. He said:

> The Director [of Public Prosecutions in Northern Ireland] has, however, concluded that there is evidence of the commission of offences of perverting or attempting or conspiring to pervert the course of justice, or of obstructing a constable in the execution of his duty, and that this evidence is sufficient to require consideration of whether prosecutions are required in the public interest, and he has consulted me accordingly. I have therefore taken steps to acquaint myself with all relevant circumstances, including matters concerning the public interest and, in particular, considerations of national security that might properly affect the decision whether or not to institute proceedings. I have informed the Director fully with regard to my consultations as to the public interest, and in the light of all the facts and information brought to his notice, the Director has concluded, with my full agreement, that it would not be proper to institute any criminal proceedings. He has given directions accordingly.[26]

The Irish government was furious that they had not been informed, in breach of the Anglo-Irish Agreement. In an informal ministerial meeting between Tom King, SoS for Northern Ireland and Mr Collins, Minister of Justice in the Irish Republic, King said that Stalker's suspension had been highly embarrassing and that the speculation that there has been some form of Cabinet plot to remove him was 'absolute rubbish'.[27] He produced a copy of Peter Taylor's book presumably to support his argument that there was no conspiracy. Collins responded angrily that the Attorney General in reaching his decision had 'done nothing serious to consider Irish interests'.[28] He said that many people in Ireland believed that the responsibility for the cover-up went all the way up to the British cabinet. He argued that King's appeal to Stalker's view that there was no actual shoot-to-kill *policy*, was irrelevant and added that: 'Stalker did not understand Ireland and did not understand the terrorist scene.'[29]

The Attorney General made his statement in the same week that the Court of Appeal, presided over by Lord Chief Justice Lord Lane, ruled that the convictions of the Birmingham Six were 'safe and satisfactory', despite substantial new evidence that their confessions had been beaten out of them and then fabricated. The six men would spend another four years in jail – sixteen years in total – before they were released. The Birmingham Six case was one of the worst miscarriages of justice in British legal history.

Sir Robert Andrew later described the reasoning behind Mayhew's statement in an interview with Peter Taylor. On the one hand, prosecutions would have demonstrated that the government was not covering up illegal activities. On the other hand, if the police and MI5 officers were prosecuted, and had to answer questions under oath, then the effectiveness of intelligence-gathering operations would be jeopardised, as the methods would be revealed. Mayhew therefore decided on balance that prosecutions were undesirable.[30]

Chris Ryder, however, argued that there was a very specific reason related to the intelligence-gathering operations. One of the officers whom Stalker recommended for prosecution was Superintendent Anderson, a key figure in RUC SB. The British government feared what he might say in court, in particular that he would disclose details of unauthorised security operations in the Irish Republic, threatening Anglo-Irish relations and future co-operation.[31] Politics, therefore, trumped all other considerations. Those who allowed or even encouraged state agents to commit murder, who perverted or conspired to pervert the course of justice, or who obstructed a constable in the execution of his/her duty were beyond the law in Northern Ireland. As one commentator put it: 'rule of law yields to the rule of war'.[32] The decision poisoned the whole of the policing and justice system in Northern Ireland, and an entire generation of young lawyers became disillusioned and angry.[33]

The Attorney General made the historic announcement abandoning the rule of law on the grounds of public interest just three days after HMIC held its annual luncheon for the top echelons of those responsible for law and order. It was a smaller event than in 1987. The principal guest was again Douglas Hurd, the Home Secretary, and he was accompanied by Douglas Hogg, Parliamentary Under-SoS at the Home Office – who a few months later would make the dangerous and defamatory comments alleging that some Northern Ireland solicitors were in the pockets of terrorists. Top civil servants, Sir Robert Armstrong and Sir Robert Andrew, once again attended, along with John Chilcot, from the NIO. HMIC was represented by Sir Lawrence Byford, Sir Philip Myers, and Mr Charles McLachlan. Most of those in attendance had played some role in the decisions about policing and security in Northern Ireland and perhaps had hoped that this was a moment of closure on the Stalker/Sampson investigations. However, the matter was far from closed. There would be further police investigations and inquests into the 1982 incidents (Chapter 26).

SB 'reforms' in Northern Ireland

The following month, on 17 February, Tom King, now SoS for Northern Ireland, made a statement in parliament on the police reforms in Northern Ireland following the Stalker and Sampson reports. He informed the House that he had received a special HMIC inspection report by McLachlan, who had reviewed the procedures and practices of the RUC, focusing on the idea that RUC SB was a 'force within a force' and on CID investigations. King said that McLachlan's report made it clear that while Stalker and Sampson had focused on the situation in 1982, 'matters were substantially improved shortly afterwards'.[34] This was simply untrue.

King also revealed the existence of yet another secret review by MI5 into policing in Northern Ireland. This was carried out only a few months after the Mounsey review of RUC SB in 1982 (Chapter 5). He told the House:

> In 1983, at the request of the Chief Constable, a former very senior officer of the Security Service carried out a special review into certain aspects of Special Branch management and its relationship with the CID. His recommendations were implemented in full. The new rank of senior assistant chief constable was introduced for the RUC in 1984. Since then, both the Special Branch and CID have answered to the same senior assistant chief constable, so that their work has been fully co-ordinated.[35]

The identity of the 'very senior' MI5 officer is unknown. It could have been Patrick Walker reviewing his own 1981 strategy. Whoever it was, MI5 rather than Parliament was once again developing policing policy in Northern Ireland, reflecting the enormous political power of an organisation which was still formally secret – it was placed on a legal footing for the first time in 1989.

The whole thrust of King's statement was that RUC practices and procedures had been substantially improved since the Stalker and Sampson reports. He admitted that work still needed to be done so that the policies and practices of the RUC should 'in future reflect the paramountcy of CID'. He intended to discuss with the Chief Constable and Deputy Chief Constable safeguards to ensure that facts and information given to the DPP were 'full and accurate'.[36] He failed to tell Parliament that the MI5/Walker strategy was still without a legal framework and the non-prosecution of most state agents involved in criminality, including murder, continued.

The NIO was only too aware of the lack of a legal framework which had been the subject of continual discussion. On 3 March 1988, a senior official wrote to the Home Office and copied to the AG's Office. The letter pointed out that Stalker/Sampson had raised the question of guidelines for the running of informers and that the McLachlan report had noted that existing ones were not appropriate to the RUC in their 'counter-terrorist operations'.[37] The official pointed out that the guidelines were 'essentially aimed at ordinary decent crime and in any case do not bind the RUC'.[38] Towards the end of the month, the Attorney General was concerned that his officials should not be involved in drawing up guidelines which condone the commission of criminal offences. By September, still nothing had been resolved, and there was continuing frustration within both the RUC and MI5 that the NIO had failed to deal with the problems and provide a statutory framework for running state agents.[39]

No disciplinary charges against RUC officers

Following the Attorney General's announcement that no-one should face criminal charges in relation to the three shooting incidents, there was still the possibility of bringing disciplinary charges against all those involved. On 29 June 1988, the Northern Ireland Policing Board met to decide whether charges should be brought against the three senior officers with ultimate responsibility for the cover stories: for the withholding or embellishment of intelligence given to the DPP; the doctoring of records; and the destruction of the tapes. In a narrow vote of four to three it was decided that no disciplinary action should be taken against Hermon, McAtamney and Forbes. The vote represented less than half of the sixteen-person board. It is not known if the full board were present when the vote was taken.[40] It paralleled GMPA's decision to suspend Stalker: it lacked transparency and appeared procedurally to have been carefully arranged to achieve the desired outcome.

In contrast, the following month it was announced that disciplinary proceedings should be heard against 20 constables and sergeants, two superintendents and an inspector, based on the recommendations of Charles Kelly, Chief Constable of Staffordshire Police, who investigated the matter. It brought a unified response from Seamus Mallon, SDLP, and Ian Paisley, DUP, on the fact that the lower ranks were to be subject to proceedings while higher ranks and politicians, who were also involved, were not. The scales of justice were not evenly balanced. Paisley was reported as saying: 'Sir John will go down in history as the buck passer' and that Mrs Thatcher as head of the security forces should bear the responsibility for any alleged 'shoot-to-kill policy'.[41]

In August 1988, it was announced that Superintendents Anderson and Flanagan, who had been suspended on full pay, had retired on health grounds.[42] In March 1989, the first of several of the expected disciplinary hearings took place before a tribunal headed by Sir Kenneth Oxford, the Chief Constable of

Merseyside Police. He was the fourth English Chief Constable, but not the last, to carry out a role in Northern Ireland connected to the three shooting incidents. The hearings were expected to last several months and to involve a detailed examination of the charges against each of the men. Instead, it was announced that the hearings had been completed and eighteen officers implicated in the three incidents had been reprimanded. Another officer was cautioned, and charges against the twentieth member of the force were dismissed.[43]

Seamus Mallon, Deputy leader of the SDLP, described the decision as 'outrageous', and went on to say that 'the effect of the killings and their aftermath has eaten deeply into the psyche of the nationalist community and had made the whole problem of respect for the law and the police more difficult'.[44] Apart from the four police officers who were prosecuted and acquitted of murder in two of the three incidents, no-one has faced criminal or disciplinary charges over the cover stories, the conspiracy to deceive the DPPNI, destruction of tapes, the doctoring of records, or in relation to the hayshed rifles. Nor have any ministers or civil servants who devised the lethal and illegal MI5/Walker strategy faced any criminal or disciplinary action.

Abandoning inquests

On 14 November 1988, the inquest into the deaths of McKerr, Burns and Toman reconvened in front of coroner, Mr James Elliot. It had been opened originally on 4 June 1984 but was adjourned after a request from the lawyers to study the transcript of the trial of the three RUC officers acquitted for murdering Toman.[45] The inquest into the deaths of Grew and Carroll was due to begin in September 1984 in front of Mr Gerry Curran. However, Curran resigned, claiming that he had found grave irregularities in the case files. He was replaced by Mr Rodgers, Curran's deputy, who then was unable to take on the case because of a busy workload. Rodgers issued a statement:

> It is apparent from an examination of the material documented and recorded on those (police) files that statements originally made during the initial police investigation into the deaths do not accord with the evidence given during the trial of a police constable at Belfast Crown Court in March and April of this year charged with the murder of Peter James Grew. [46]

Subsequently, a third coroner, Mr Rainey Hanna, was asked to take over the inquest, but he said that it would be premature to hold one before a police investigation had ended. An RUC spokesman was reported in *The Irish Times* as not knowing when the police investigation would end. He added that it was headed by Deputy Chief Constable 'John Stocker of the Greater Manchester Police'.[47]

At the resumed 1988 inquest into the deaths of McKerr, Burns and Toman, Belfast solicitor Pat Finucane represented Eleanor McKerr, the widow of Gervaise McKerr. Controversially, coroner James Elliot admitted unsworn statements of three police officers involved in the killings. Finucane asked for an adjournment while he sought judicial review of the decision. It was refused. Seamus Mallon interrupted the inquest, demanding that the proceedings be adjourned because it did not command the confidence of a sizeable section of the community. He said: 'On their behalf I ask you to adjourn this inquest until such time as those people who have material evidence to give can give it in this inquest and be subject to the type of cross-examination that is required.'[48] The failure to adjourn the inquest led to a walk-out by two of the three families.

The next day, Finucane submitted an application for judicial review seeking suspension of the inquest proceedings pending the review. He also sought the quashing of the coroner's acceptance of Public Interest Immunity Certificates (PIICs) which Tom King, the SoS for Northern Ireland, had issued a few days before the start of the inquest. These prevented the disclosure of the identity of key personnel and, crucially, 'the organisation, chain of command, methods of operation and capabilities of the units', effectively preventing the truth about the shootings becoming known.[49] Mr Justice Carswell, however, ruled that the Coroner had been right to admit unsworn statements and it was not contrary to the coroner's rules or a breach of natural justice. But it was wrong not to adjourn the inquests.[50]

Finucane appealed to the Appeal Court in Belfast. In a decision which Seamus Mallon described as a victory for judicial independence, the judges ruled that the RUC men could be compelled to give evidence but not to answer questions which might be incriminating. This overturned rules for the practice and procedures of coroners' courts introduced by the old Ministry of Home Affairs in 1963. The judges considered that the old rules constituted a major departure from the general law relating to compellability of witnesses in coroners' courts.[51] They argued that compellability was a matter of substantive law and not mere practice and procedures. It was a landmark decision which contrasted sharply with the decision of the Attorney General to stop all prosecutions in relation to the six killings.

Sir Patrick Mayhew, the Attorney General, appealed to the House of Lords (at the time the highest UK court) which reversed the decision of Appeal Court.[52] Seamus Mallon was highly critical and argued that the coroners' decisions were now going to be a sham. The Committee on the Administration of Justice considered that the ruling would affect 21 other inquests,[53] including those pertaining to the six other killings which Stalker investigated. The decision of the Lords initiated by Mayhew, together with his decision to stop prosecutions in the 'public interest', effectively prevented the truth from emerging about the circumstances of the six killings, despite the legal efforts of Finucane who, by now, was seen as a thorn in the flesh of the authorities.

On 5 May 1992, some twelve years after the shooting, the inquest opened into the killings under a third coroner – John Leckey. During this inquest, one of the police witnesses admitted he had had access to his statement made after the shooting. Counsel for McKerr asked to see the statement, but was refused. This set in train further legal actions which followed the same pattern as before, with the lower courts rejecting the appeal and the Court of Appeal granting the right to see the document. In early 1994, Leckey dismissed the original jury. On 8 March, he issued *subpoenas* for the release of the reports prepared by Stalker and Sampson. On 22 March, new inquests opened into the six killings investigated by Stalker/Sampson. Subsequently, the government prepared another PIIC to prevent the release of the reports. After a judge set the *subpoenas* aside and upheld the PIIC, the Coroner abandoned the inquests in early September 1994.[54] The inquests have still not been held. They were scheduled for 2024 – 42 years after the killings, but then fell foul of the Legacy Act (see Chapter 26).

* * *

The period from mid-summer 1986 to the end of 1988 was characterised by the extensive abuse of the law, both in Manchester and Northern Ireland. GMP put enormous pressure on the DPP to prosecute Taylor for a crime which the police effectively constructed, accompanied by a special operation to leak information to the press and media, in contempt of court. The pressure to prosecute Taylor, a man with no criminal record, was in sharp contrast to the Attorney General's decision not to prosecute or discipline anyone in relation to the six suspected murders and numerous other crimes investigated by Stalker and Sampson, on the grounds that it was not in the public interest. Compared with prosecuting Taylor for a relatively minor potential fraud, the catalogue of possible RUC and MI5 criminality ranged from: murder; encouraging state agents to commit crimes; doctoring information; withholding, concealment, and destruction of surveillance evidence; inventing cover stories; obstructing police enquiries; and perverting the course of justice. The Attorney General's decision, coupled with the failure to hold inquests into the six killings, meant that the rule of law was effectively being abandoned in Northern Ireland.

Moreover, the rule of law in Northern Ireland was further undermined by the continuing failure of the United Kingdom government to provide a statutory framework for the running of agents, allowing them to commit crimes without any control over their deadly activities. The issues were considered extensively by the NIO and at Cabinet level. Ministers were fully aware of the lacunae in the law. However, there was a conspiracy by ministers and top civil servants to delay developing a statutory framework because this would interfere with intelligence gathering in Northern Ireland. The failure to introduce any legal controls on the deployment of state agents was to continue to have a deadly impact.

Chapter 21

Arrests and Committal Proceedings

IT HAD BEEN ARRANGED through their lawyers that Taylor and Derek Britton (Taylor's accountant) would walk over to Bootle Street police station to be charged at 10.30 a.m. on 30 September 1987. It was not to be. Instead, a posse of police officers arrived at their offices at 10.00 a.m., arrested the two men and then humiliatingly marched them across Deansgate, the main street in Manchester, to Bootle Street police station. They were fingerprinted and photographed. Around noon, they appeared in court and were committed to appear at some future date. No bail was set and there were no travel restrictions – an odd decision for the man who was suspected in report after report of being at the heart of organised crime in Manchester.

Taylor's other two alleged co-conspirators were arrested on different dates. On 15 September, two weeks before Taylor's arrest, Bowley, the head of the Corporate Business Department in the Co-operative Bank, had been arrested. He had been told that he was wanted for further interviewing but mentioned that he was going on holiday. On his return the police arrested him at his home in Newcastle at 6.30 a.m. His house was searched and it appeared that the only things the police were interested in were photograph albums. They showed no interest in documents, which might have been relevant in a fraud inquiry. They then took him to Manchester where they interviewed him over the next two days. During his time in police custody, it was put to him that if he helped with the investigation into Taylor, the police might take no action against him.[1] Vincent McCann, a quantity surveyor and associate of Taylor, was arrested on 5 October. It was to be another year before they appeared in court.

The 'Big Bang'

The changing nature of banking is crucial to an understanding of the context in which the police decided to prosecute Taylor and his three co-accused. In 1983, the Thatcher government made the decision to deregulate the financial and banking sectors. The main change came into force in October 1986 when radical changes were made to the stock market – the 'Big Bang' as it was called – leading to a radical deregulation of financial markets. In the same year, legislation was introduced which removed restrictions on the range of services offered by building societies, enabling them to compete with banks on a level basis.[2] As a consequence, banks too became much more competitive. They cast aside the old three-six-three adage – paying three per cent interest on deposits, charging six per cent on loans and being out on the golf course at 3.00 p.m. – and became risk-takers.

The Co-operative Bank had anticipated the need to become more competitive and in 1979 had recruited Bowley to generate corporate business, at a time when it had very little. When he moved to Newcastle six years later, the amount of business going through the department stood at over £65 million. It represented about a third of the bank's lending throughout the country and bad debt was non-existent at the time.[3] Bowley was very successful at his job and was skilful at identifying entrepreneurial individuals. He had sought out Taylor and saw him as a good bet.

As head of the Corporate Business Department in 1984, Bowley had discretion to lend up to £25,000 on an unsecured basis and £100,000 on a secured basis. Any sum above this amount had to be approved by the Advances Department, whose main function was to assess loan applications from the Corporate Business Department and other branches within the bank. There were several controllers in the Advances Department, and they could lend £75,000 unsecured and £150,000 secured, at their discretion. The senior advance controller, Mr John Cowburn, could lend £150,000 unsecured and £250,000 secured. Above Cowburn, stood Mr Roger Gorvin, the general manager of domestic banking. His lending discretion was £500,000 unsecured and a similar amount secured.[4] Loans above this sum had to go to the bank's Advances Committee. This had a discretion up to a limit of one million pounds secured and unsecured. This committee was made up of the advance controllers, including Cowburn, Gorvin and the chief general manager, Mr Ruck.[5]

There was considerable tension between the Advances Department and the Corporate Business Department, principally because the former was thought to be too slow and too rule-based, with little understanding of the realities on the ground and the need to move fast to secure a deal. However, everybody in the Advances Department including Gorvin, the general manager, knew that rules were being broken.[6] The police were able to exploit this tension to the full.

Overseeing the whole of the bank's activities was the Inspection Department, which was the bank's internal police force, headed by Hylie Sheppard. He had the power to request any file and inspect it.

Committal proceedings

On 18 September 1988, the committal proceedings against Taylor, Britton, Bowley, and McCann, began in Manchester. They were heard in front of Mr David Loy, a stipendiary magistrate. Their purpose was to decide whether there was enough evidence to warrant committing the defendants to trial at the Crown Court.[7] Taylor was represented by David Hood – a junior barrister at the time – Britton by Martin Steiger, Bowley by Peter Larkin, and McCann by Guy Robson. The prosecution was composed of two QCs, a most unusual occurrence for a minor fraud. It was led by Michael Corkery, who was brought up from London and was considered one of the best prosecuting counsels in England, and his junior, Michael Shorrock, a QC from the Manchester circuit.[8] Although Corkery's presence was perceived as an insult to the quality of the Manchester Bar, the authorities were taking no risks in this prosecution.

The principal offence against the four defendants was a charge of conspiracy to obtain pecuniary advantage by deception. The charge of conspiracy has been a feature of English criminal law for a long time and has been used extensively in Ireland over the centuries.[9] It substantially increases the possibility of a conviction.[10] Lord Widgery, the Judge who exonerated the soldiers of any wrongdoing on Bloody Sunday, noted:

> The use of the conspiracy charge has been criticised so often and for so many years that it would no doubt have been abolished long ago unless there was some real merit left in it.[11]

The real merit rests with the procedural advantages for the state and prosecuting authorities. The charge implies that the alleged crime is more serious as it involves several people conspiring together, and it allows the net to be spread more widely, bringing lesser fry to court. It means that evidence, which otherwise would be inadmissible on the substantive charge, becomes admissible. It places co-defendants in a more difficult position than if they were making their own case on its merits and in a long and complicated fraud trial, jurors find it hard to remember which evidence applies to which defendant. To sustain the conspiracy charge, it was imperative to charge Bowley, the Co-operative Bank's business manager, along with the others.

The committal proceedings lasted seven weeks. The prosecution's case rested on the various applications Taylor had made for funding to the Co-operative

Bank and claims that: he had failed to inform the bank of crucial facts; provided misleading information; overvalued his assets; told several lies; and cross-fired cheques to make it appear that there were sufficient funds in one of his accounts. The police claimed that if the bank had known the extent of the deceptions, they would not have granted the loans. The strangest feature of the case was that no complaint or concerns had come from the Co-operative Bank itself. Indeed, following pressure from the police for it to complain, the Bank carried out an internal audit of Taylor's accounts and found no irregularities. It was left to GMP to construct the alleged crimes.

There were advantages and disadvantages of old-style committal proceedings. On the one hand, the prosecution's case is revealed and hence it is possible to plan a defence. On the other hand, in trying to prevent a case going to trial, too much of the defence's case may be revealed, which can then be countered in the trial itself. But one strong advantage is that there is an opportunity to compare what a witness says in these proceedings with what they say in the trial itself. DI Stephenson, who oversaw the case and had prepared the application for access orders, was considered a key witness. The defence, therefore, arranged for a court reporter to produce a transcript of his cross-examination on 18 and 20 October. This proved to be critical in the trial itself, as Stephenson produced contradictory evidence under oath at the trial.

Examination of Stephenson

Early on in his cross-examination of Stephenson, Hood focused on the application for access orders, which Stephenson made on 27 February 1986, and on the fact that the application had been put in a sealed envelope by the Judge. Hood revealed the various efforts that had been made by those representing Taylor to obtain access to the application (Chapter 16). Several legal actions were refused on various grounds.[12] Direct requests to the prosecution were also denied, first on the ground that the Judge had given an order for the envelope to remain sealed, which was untrue, and then that it was covered by a PIIC. Finally, Taylor's solicitors wrote to the DPP requesting disclosure under the Attorney General's Guidelines. The document was finally disclosed.[13] The court was left with the clear impression that there was something to hide. As Taylor said in his book:

> It is probably the most crucial document in the whole case and the one which reveals most clearly the determined effort of the police to get what they wanted, without any regard for truth and justice.[14]

Hood also examined Stephenson on the file of evidence which he sent to the DPP. During his meticulous analysis of all the documents, Hood had discovered that a crucial file – the Bernard Thorpe and Partners' valuations – had been omitted from the exhibits in the case. Crucially, these showed that the Trafford Park site which Taylor had purchased was valued at £864,000 in February 1986. With development potential it was considered the site would be worth around £1.5 million, and with planning consent, £4 million. Hood asked Stephenson if the omission was 'deliberate or accidental'.[15] He replied: 'I consciously omitted it'.[16] It was a damning omission because it showed, beyond any doubt, that the Bank's lending was adequately covered.

During cross-examination of Stephenson, Hood asked if a member of his team could look at Stephenson's pocketbook. There were no objections. Mr Fox, a retired Manchester police inspector, who was now a clerk with Adlers, the instructing solicitors, began to copy as much of the relevant detail as possible. After a while, Corkery made a sarcastic and somewhat disingenuous intervention:

CORKERY: May I mention one thing, if it is not inconvenient to my friend. This witness has referred from time to time to his notebook and in answer to my friend's desire to look at the notebooks they were duly handed over. I do not know how much confidential material there may be in those books in relation to other matters and other enquiries, but I do notice (I have had it brought to my attention) that the representative of the solicitor in the back of the court has been making copious notes from those notebooks. I appreciate there will be no harm done whatsoever, but if those books do cover sensitive areas relating to other matters, then it is most unfortunate that this conduct should be continuing. There may be nothing in it at all. I only raise it at this moment so that Mr Hood can take instructions and in effect satisfy himself that all is well. I only mention that so that there is no misunderstanding and no danger.

FOX: I will produce the notes made, sir. Every entry relates to visits to the Co-op.[17]

The diary entries revealed the numerous visits which had been made to the bank prior to the granting of access orders and proved invaluable in destroying the prosecution's case against the four defendants.

Dubious police practices

Several other points emerged which were to help the defence's case. To begin with, for several of the witnesses called by the police, there were inconsistencies and contradictions between their statements and the evidence they gave in court. This was a strong indictment of methods used to construct the case. Moreover, witnesses were required to sign statements prepared by the police, without being shown crucial documents. In addition, the prosecution failed to call one important witness – Sheppard, the head of the fraud department in the Co-operative Bank. The defence suspected he had given the police details of Taylor's accounts prior to them obtaining access orders. His absence confirmed the suspicions of the defence lawyers.

Throughout the proceedings, doubt was raised about the origins, quality, and interpretation of the evidence. Yet the magistrate considered that there was a case to answer in relation to all four defendants. He hesitated over sending Bowley for trial as Corkery had made it clear that Bowley had not gained financially from his alleged recruitment by Taylor. Realising the importance, no doubt, of having him as part of the conspiracy, Corkery, was able to convince the magistrate that financial gain was not necessary for the offence.[18] It only added to Bowley's predicament. While driving to the committal proceedings one day, he knocked down and killed a woman and was charged with dangerous driving, and a summons was sworn for dangerous driving. The police waited until the day the fraud trial started in October 1989 and then served the summons.[19]

Press and media campaign continues

A few months before the trial, there was further evidence of the continuation of the special press and media operation which Anderton told the DPP in June 1986 he had established. On 27 July 1989, the *Manchester Evening News* published a long interview with Anderton. He talked about the 'Stalker Affair' and said that 'he took decisions based on the best advice available'. He added: 'It may be some time yet before we truly understand, on careful reflection, the right action was taken and whether indeed all the parties involved collectively reached proper conclusions. Who is to say?'[20]

The phrase 'some time yet' was significant. Anderton clearly expected the successful prosecution of Taylor. This would then show conclusively that Stalker did have criminal friends and that Anderton had made the right decisions. Another significant phrase was 'all the parties involved collectively'.[21] Was this a reference to more than the police and DPP, including the higher echelons of government? There is little doubt that the interview would have adduced public sympathy for Anderton and his predicament. 'It was hell', he said, and caused him considerable stress both personally and professionally.[22] His comments could be seen as an attempt to influence potential jurors in the upcoming trial of the four defendants.

On the same day as the *Manchester Evening News* interview with Anderton, the *Daily Mail* published another positive GMP story. It reported that the early-evening train from London to Manchester sped through the countryside with the soup in the first-class dining car slopping everywhere. A Chief Constable came to the rescue of the distraught diners and exerted his authority. He demanded of a steward that the train slow down. This was easier said than done as there was no way for the guard to communicate with the driver other than by pulling the communication cord, which he did.[23] The Chief Constable was none other than James Anderton. Taylor's solicitors, Betesh Fox & Co, wrote a strongly worded letter to the Chief Constable arguing that the articles were an attempt to influence jurors and to show GMP in a favourable light. Read together, they were clearly part of a public relations exercise.

This was not the only action with the potential to influence the jurors in Taylor's criminal trial. In early autumn 1989, Topping, now retired on medical grounds, exploited his decision to reopen the Moors Murder investigation in 1986 and published his autobiography under the grand title: *Topping: The Autobiography of the Police Chief in the Moors Murder Case.*[24] It was co-authored with Jean Richie, who wrote a book on Myra Hindley published in 1988.[25] While a large section of the book focused on his role in the Moors Murder case and the confession of Myra Hindley, the final Chapter was entitled 'The Stalker Affair'. Although he pointed out that Taylor had no previous convictions, on the very next page Topping stated: 'But professional criminals often have no, or very few convictions; the man with the long criminal record is the habitually unsuccessful criminal, as detectives like Mr Stalker know.'[26] In an attempt no doubt to emphasis the point, he continued: 'It is naïve to think that all criminals have criminal records.'[27] It was a clever piece of writing but highly prejudicial.

In the final Chapter, Topping took the opportunity to re-state the official line that Stalker's suspension had nothing to do with Northern Ireland: it was based entirely on information and events that occurred in Manchester. He strenuously denied that he reopened the Moors Murder case to divert attention from the Stalker case. He refuted Stalker's criticism that he lacked detective experience and pointed out that he had a proven record in dealing with all levels of police corruption. He proudly concluded that: 'I doubt if there were many senior policemen in the whole of Britain with greater relevant experience than I had.'[28]

Inevitably, the publication led to a number of civil actions. Myra Hindley applied to the High Court to seize the profits from the book, as Topping had revealed private conversations in a breach of confidence. She sought a ruling that it was improper for a police officer to make a profit from confidential information obtained in an interview with a suspect. She dropped another injunction, because of costs, which sought to ban the book.[29] The GMPA also issued a writ against Topping alleging breach of confidence.[30] This was an unprecedented move for a police authority to bring an action against a former police officer.[31] Finally, Taylor himself brought an action against Topping. He argued that the book created a substantial risk that his fraud trial would be prejudiced.

* * *

By the autumn of 1988, GMP had achieved their objective of bringing Taylor to court. They had at last managed to construct a crime for which to prosecute him. The committal proceedings, however, revealed that to achieve their objective GMP had to resort, ironically, to the charge of conspiracy and to various dubious practices in making the case against Taylor and his co-accused. They employed one of the best prosecuting lawyers in the country and tried to influence potential jurors in the forthcoming trial by planting positive stories about the Chief Constable who approved the sacking of his own Deputy. Taylor's conviction was imperative, to show in the Chief Constable's own words, that 'the right action was taken and whether indeed all the parties involved collectively reached proper conclusions'.

Chapter 22

Murder of a Solicitor

ON 12 FEBRUARY 1989, loyalist gunmen burst into the home of Belfast solicitor, Pat Finucane, and shot him fourteen times, killing him instantly and wounding Geraldine, his wife, while they were eating Sunday lunch. DS Alan Simpson, the Senior Investigating Officer (SIO) for the murder, later admitted that he had never attended a murder scene of such ferocity and he had attended the scenes of over 200 murders, suicides and sudden deaths.[1] The gunmen had fired several rounds into Pat Finucane's face at close range. Two paid agents of the state were involved in his murder. A third was recruited as a state agent after his involvement in the murder became known.

It was a significant event in the Taylor/Stalker affair for several reasons. First, Finucane had been involved in legal proceedings arising from the three shooting incidents investigated by Stalker and Sampson, and was seen as a problem for the authorities. Second, his murder stemmed directly from the deadly outworkings of the MI5/Walker policing strategy which formed the backdrop to Stalker's investigation. Third, the various police and judicial inquiries into Finucane's murder provide strong evidence that the Stalker/Sampson investigations resulted in a shift in the use of lethal force. This was necessary because the investigations failed to counter the belief that HMSUs were following a shoot-to-kill *policy* (a belief partially supported by Stalker but denied by Sampson (Chapter 19); they had raised the threat of criminal prosecutions for members of HMSUs and handlers of state agents, as well as the possible trial of senior police officers for perverting the course of justice.

While the main elements of the MI5/Walker strategy remained in place, there was a curtailment in the deployment of HMSUs. Instead, the fight against the IRA was increasingly outsourced to loyalist paramilitaries. 'Institutionalized collusion' with both loyalist and republican paramilitary groups[2] became the norm, as detailed in a forensic analysis by McGovern.[3]

A 'thorn in the side of the authorities'

Finucane was a partner in the law firm, Madden and Finucane which conducted a range of civil and criminal work. He represented people from both communities and was highly successful in using the law to challenge the authorities during the conflict in the 1980s. He became well-known for representing people arrested under the Prevention of Terrorism Act and he was involved in several high-profile cases. He represented Bobby Sands – the first of the 1981 hunger strikers to die. He used civil actions to make claims for assault and false imprisonment against the police. He brought the first successful *habeas corpus* petition in relation to an individual detained under the emergency legislation. As described in Chapter 20, he represented Eleanor McKerr, the widow of Gervaise McKerr, in a judicial review of the Coroner's decision in the inquest into the shooting of the three men to admit the unsworn statements of the police. Of particular note, less than two weeks before his murder, he filed two applications with the ECHR challenging the UK's derogation from the Convention.[4] He was, in words of a group of New York lawyers, 'a thorn in the side of the authorities'.[5]

Finucane's murder sent a chill through the legal profession in Northern Ireland and illustrated starkly how verbal attacks on lawyers by politicians can not only undermine the rule of law but can have lethal consequences. On 24 November 1988, Douglas Hogg, a junior Home Office Minister, visited Belfast and attended a briefing by the Chief Constable and other senior officers of the RUC. Hogg was informed that some solicitors in Northern Ireland were 'effectively in the pockets of terrorists'.[6] This was just two weeks after the inquest had opened into the deaths of Burns, McKerr and Toman. On 13 January 1989, the RUC provided Hogg with 'profiles' of Pat Finucane and Oliver Kelly, another Belfast-based solicitor.[7]

During a debate in the House of Commons on 17 January, Hogg stated that were a number of solicitors in Northern Ireland who were 'unduly sympathetic to the cause of the IRA'.[8] This was 26 days prior to the murder of Finucane. The words were very similar to those used in the DIU report which sealed Stalker's fate at the Scarborough meeting on 19 May 1986. Seamus Mallon was outraged with Hogg's use of parliamentary privilege and, prophetically, commented that lawyers would become 'targets for assassins' bullets'.[9] Journalist, Nicholas Davies, argued that Hogg's speech had been carefully planned. He claimed that it had been drafted by senior MI5 officers and Hogg had been specifically asked to make the statement. Davies continued with the bold, but otherwise unsubstantiated statement, that 'senior MI5 officers in London' were ultimately responsible for organising Finucane's murder.[10]

Demand for a public inquiry

Following the murder, the family called for a public inquiry. There was no response from the British government. On 1 November 1998, Geraldine Finucane applied to the European Court of Human Rights (ECtHR) on the grounds that no proper investigation had been carried out into her husband's death. In May 1999, the Chief Constable of Cambridgeshire, John Stevens, was asked by RUC Chief Constable Ronnie Flanagan to re-investigate Finucane's murder and allegations of collusion. In addition, he was asked to consider various issues around the handling of agents.[11] This was Stevens' third inquiry into various aspects of policing in Northern Ireland. His first investigation in September 1989 was into the theft of montages from the charge room and administrative offices at Dunmurry police station,[12] the disappearance of confidential material from Ballykinlar Army Camp on or about 1st September 1989, and video tapes stolen from UDR barracks. His second inquiry concerned the murder of Terence McDaid by loyalists in 1988, again following allegations of collusion.[13] None of the reports from the three inquiries has been published. There is only a short summary report of 20 pages available.[14]

The Finucane family continued to demand a full public inquiry into his murder. In 2001, at a meeting in Weston Park between the British and Irish governments, the British government agreed that if a judge of international standing recommended a public inquiry, 'the relevant Government *will* (emphasis added) implement that recommendation'.[15] In 2004, Justice Peter Cory, a Canadian Supreme Court Justice, after reviewing the available material, recommended a public inquiry on the grounds that there was *prima facie* evidence of collusion between 'state security forces' and loyalist paramilitaries.[16]

On 1 July 2003, the ECtHR reached a judgment on Geraldine Finucane's application. It considered that the British government had failed to carry out an Article 2 compliant investigation[17] on the grounds that the original police investigation was not independent, the original inquest failed to consider allegations of state collusion, the necessary public scrutiny element was missing, the DPP had failed to give his decisions in relation to the prosecutions, and there was undue delay.[18]

Seven years after Judge Cory's report, the Finucane family flew to London on 11 October 2011 and met Prime Minister David Cameron in the expectation that after 20 years, the British government would honour its international commitment to hold a public inquiry. Their expectation was shattered: they were informed that there would be no public inquiry, only a desktop review by an eminent QC.[19] Cameron added, as if by way of an apology: 'There are people around here who would never let it happen'.[20] It was an oblique reference to MI5 and MI6. There was obviously much to hide. The day after the meeting, on 12 October, the Rt Hon Sir Desmond de Silva QC, was appointed by the SoS for Northern Ireland to conduct an independent review into 'the question of state involvement' in Finucane's murder.

State agent Brian Nelson [21]

The three inquiries into Finucane's murder – Stevens, Cory and de Silva – despite falling far-short of a public inquiry, at which people can be cross-examined, painted a shocking picture of state collusion in the murder of Catholics and republicans, and revealed more detail on the operation of the MI5/Walker strategy.[22] Stevens was the first to discover that two state agents were involved in Finucane's murder: Brian Nelson, an agent for the British army, and William Stobie, an agent for RUC SB and a quartermaster for the UDA. Stobie was subsequently arrested and charged with murder, but the trial collapsed after a witness failed to testify. Two weeks later Stobie was shot dead by a loyalist group called the 'Red Hand Defenders'.[23]

The information on Nelson which emerged from the various inquiries made disturbing reading. In 1973, he and others kidnapped Gerald Higgins, a partially-sighted Catholic, and took him to a club on the Shankill Road where he was tortured: he was beaten, set on fire and electrocuted. Nelson was jailed for seven years for his part in the kidnapping and torture. In May 1984, Nelson offered his services to the British army. He was recruited as a state agent with full knowledge of his violent background.[24] He joined several others who were all run by a specialist army unit called the Force Research Unit (FRU) – a secret wing of army intelligence set up in 1979. From 1986, Major James Gordon Kerr became its commanding officer.[25]

After two years as a state agent, Nelson moved to Germany with his family. Army personnel from FRU went over to the continent to persuade him to return to Belfast and encouraged him to become the intelligence officer for the UDA/UVF. He was promised a house and £200 a week for his services as a state agent. He took up the offer, joined the UDA and very soon was appointed its intelligence officer.[26] He was to become one of the deadliest assassins, targeting

Catholics and republicans to be murdered, with the help of the army who supplied him with the intelligence.

Stevens summed up Nelson's role as follows:

> [...] he had been tasked by both the British Army and the Protestant paramilitaries with the job of pulling all the intelligence together, to make the UDA a far more effective killing group. He was privy to information that should have been confidential to the Army, including index numbers, people's backgrounds and movements. Feeding this information into a computer, he had produced dossiers that he called 'intelligence packages', which he gave to the killers so that they could go out and shoot people who *they* (italics in original) thought were members of Sinn Féin or the IRA.[27]

Paul Larkin, who was one of the first to document the extent of collusion between loyalist paramilitaries and the British security forces, described the strategy as 'a macabre scenario where you have British soldiers leaking information on Catholics and nationalists to paid state agents who can then arrange for the murders to take place'.[28] According to Ingram and Harkin, Stevens concluded that Nelson had a role in fifteen murders, fourteen attempted murders and 62 other murder conspiracies, including the attempted murder of Alex Maskey.[29]

At some point, MI5 tried to poach Nelson from the army. It wanted him to join three of their own agents who were already in place at the top of the UDA.[30] There was a strong belief among MI5 and the RUC SB that intelligence was nullifying the threat from the UDA.[31]

The opposite was the case. The number of murders by the UDA increased after Nelson became its intelligence officer. As Stevens commented: 'He was at the very centre of all intelligence which came out of the Protestant paramilitary terrorists and the targeting of people who were subsequently killed.'[32]

Stevens' inquiries showed that the various criticisms which Stalker made of the MI5/Walker strategy remained unaddressed. Moreover, like Stalker, Stevens experienced extensive problems during his inquiries. The army lied to him and informed him 'that they never ran agents'.[33] At some point, it secretly seized Nelson's intelligence dump, no doubt fearing the consequences if their illegal activities in supplying intelligence to loyalists were discovered. Stevens was told that documents did not exist, but they were then subsequently discovered, necessitating the re-interviewing of individuals. In addition, hundreds of documents held by the Ministry of Defence, which opened up new lines of inquiry, were disclosed late. Stevens described the obstruction he experienced as being 'cultural in its nature and widespread' and recorded that he was concerned at what level the decisions had been taken to obstruct his inquiry. He noted no further details.[34]

Shortly after his arrival in Northern Ireland, Stevens met ACC Wilfie Monahan, head of crime, who had informed Simpson – the investigating officer in Finucane's murder – not to get too deeply involved. Monahan told Stevens:

> I want to make sure that you succeed, because our force cannot afford another fiasco like Stalker. I give you my word that we'll do whatever is necessary to help you get to the truth.[35]

They discussed where Stevens' team should be based, and one suggestion was Holywood Barracks.[36] Monahan responded: 'If you go there, they'll burn you down.'[37] They chose Seapark, a highly secure complex near Carrickfergus. Monahan's flippant comment about a fire turned out to be prophetic.

Nelson's arrest and trial

On 11 January 1990, Stevens' team planned to arrest Nelson in a dawn raid. The night before the arrest, they returned to their base to find a fire raging in their offices. Fire alarms, telephones and heat-sensitive intruder alarms had all failed. Many files were destroyed. It was suspected that a Covert Methods of Entry Team (CMET) from the Intelligence Corp in Ashford Kent was responsible. Detective Superintendent Simpson was tasked to investigate the fire. He concluded, however, that the fire was accidental and had been caused by a careless disposal of a lit cigarette in a wastepaper basket – the seat of the fire.[38] There was no foul play. Stevens, however, thought otherwise and saw it as a further attempt to obstruct his inquiry.[39]

In January 1992, Nelson eventually came to trial. Beforehand, there were extensive discussions at the highest level – as there were over Stalker's recommendations – as to whether the prosecution of Nelson was in the public interest.[40] The Ministry of Defence submitted advice to Tom King against a decision to prosecute. In an open acknowledgment of the 'dirty war' and the abandonment of the rule of law in Northern Ireland, it argued that a prosecution would:

> [...] challenge the integrity of the system ... by revealing that ... [Nelson] ... was not merely a paid informant but a long-term agent who was allowed to continue as an active member of a terrorist organisation which committed many murders while he was acting as its intelligence officer. It would feed the speculations of those who believe that the security forces are involved in a 'dirty tricks campaign' and are in collusion with loyalist paramilitary groups.[41]

It would, of course, have done much more than feed speculation. It would have provided concrete evidence that the security forces were indeed involved in a 'dirty tricks campaign' and were in collusion with loyalist paramilitary groups.

Sir Patrick Walker, now Director General of MI5 and the architect of the deadly MI5/Walker strategy, joined the debate and wrote to the Home Office outlining his concerns. His advice was copied to the AG's Office. He later met the AG and emphasised that a prosecution would damage the morale of state agents, a view shared by the cabinet secretary Sir Robin Butler. Walker even went as far as to suggest that those MI5 officials who gave evidence might be at risk of kidnap.[42] Writing to the prime minister, Sir Robin Butler noted that Nelson, according to the AG's evidence, had only saved two lives. He stated that the real argument against prosecution was that it would harm intelligence operations in Northern Ireland compared with 'the good that could possibly be done by prosecution'.[43] No one in the security establishment wished to see Nelson behind bars.

Nelson pleaded guilty to only 20 offences, including five counts of conspiracy to murder. Conveniently, his guilty plea precluded any details of his role directing murder as a state agent being revealed. At Nelson's trial, Colonel Kerr spoke on his behalf.[44] He claimed that Nelson's information allowed him to hand over to the RUC 730 reports of possible assassination attempts against 217 individuals.[45] On 3 February 1992, Nelson was sentenced to ten years imprisonment. Kerr's unsubstantiated claim that Nelson saved hundreds of lives contrasted with accumulating evidence that paramilitaries were encouraged to commit murder and that people targeted were not warned, in order to protect the identities of state agents.

In response to the broader issues which arose from the case, Sir Patrick Mayhew, who was now SoS for Northern Ireland, asked Sir John Blelloch, a former Permanent Secretary in the NIO, to conduct a review of agent handling. In July 1992, Blelloch circulated his paper to John Chilcot, Permanent Secretary in the NIO.[46] Chilcot must have felt uncomfortable on reading it because according to 'Robert', the MI5 officer who played a fundamental role in bringing about the IRA ceasefire, 'he was not sympathetic to the world of espionage and agents and basically disapproved'.[47]

In June 2003, Kevin McNamara asked the SoS for the Home Office if he would place Blelloch's report in the House of Commons library. He was informed that it dealt with matters of 'national security and its sensitivity precludes publication'.[48] It was another report on some aspect of the deadly MI5/Walker strategy in Northern Ireland which was kept from parliamentary scrutiny, reflecting yet again, the power and unaccountability of the security establishment. Subsequently, the Blelloch report led to the setting up of an Interdepartmental Working Group chaired by Chilcot. The Working Group pointed out that the existing law left agents, their handlers and ministers exposed, yet the government continued to postpone putting in place adequate guidance and regulation for the running of agents.[49]

The Retired Police Officers Association issued an open letter in response to Stevens' investigation and allegations of collusion which was, in effect, a defence of the MI5/Walker strategy. It argued that there was a fundamental difference between the operational imperatives of intelligence agencies and their criminal intelligence counterparts. Actions arising in the intelligence world when viewed from a criminal investigation perspective 'can be regarded as irregular or suspicious behaviour' but were 'eminently sensible and acceptable' from an intelligence perspective. There always had to be a balancing act between the disclosure of intelligence and what it might provide, and the duty of care owed to covert intelligence sources. The letter went on:

> In such instances, the occasion invariably arose whereby some information had to be held back or not fully exploited in order to preserve the life of a source, i.e., the withholding of intelligence, or it is the necessary and prudent action required to protect the life of a valuable agent. How you interpret such matters is strongly influenced by the breadth of the perspective adopted. As the intelligence world never viewed its existence as being solely a vehicle by which to serve the needs of crime investigation, it therefore, on specific occasions, quite justifiably adopted, in its opinion, the position that the priority to preserve life and secondly property, came at the expense of solving crime.[50]

Barrett's confession to Finucane's murder

On 3 October 1991, there was a significant development in the murder investigation of Pat Finucane. Detective Sergeant Jonty Brown, who was part of the CID team investigating Finucane's murder, had received a call from a man called Ken Barrett – a prolific killer suspected of being involved in Finucane's murder.[51] He wanted to meet with Brown to arrange a deal on all he knew about UFF operations, past and present. The UFF, in fact, never existed as such, but was a flag of convenience for the criminality of the UDA. Brown and his partner, Trevor McIlwrath, met Barrett at his home during the morning. As required by the MI5/Walker strategy, Brown reported the meeting to RUC SB. It was then agreed that Brown, McIlwrath and an SB officer should pick up Barrett at Nutt's Corner, outside of Belfast, and use a concealed tape recorder in the car to record the conversation. Later that night, Barrett joined them in their car, as arranged.

At some point during the conversation, Brown asked Barrett directly: 'Who murdered Pat Finucane?' He replied: 'Hypothetically me.'[52] Barrett then proceeded to describe the shooting in detail. Subsequently, Brown wanted a copy of the tape, but SB refused to give it to him. On 10 October, they met Barrett again in the same place, but on this occasion, the SB officer instructed Brown not to ask anything about the murder of Finucane. Brown and McIlwrath met Barrett a few more times but were then instructed by RUC SB that there would be no more meetings. In the meantime, no effort was made to arrest Barrett despite his taped confession. Brown, in his own words, was left 'in the dark'.[53] RUC SB were determined, for whatever reason, to pervert the course of justice and prevent a possible suspect from being arrested for the murder.

Some eight years later, on 27 April 1999, Brown was summoned to Seapark RUC complex at Carrickfergus and interviewed by a team of detectives from Stevens' third inquiry team. He told them how on 3 October 1991, he had interviewed Barrett who had admitted to the murder of Finucane, and how an RUC SB constable had recorded it all on tape. The following day after further interviews, he signed his six-page witness statement. Brown was then informed that the tape had been tested at the Metropolitan Police laboratory and it had not been changed in any way. He was then informed that there was no murder confession on the tape in relation to the Finucane killing.

Brown was stunned and asked to listen to the tape. It was true. Incredibly, there was no confession on the tape. However, Barrett did mention two other murders. Brown rang the regional intelligence officer to find out the date of one of the murders. He was told it was 10 October 1991. This proved that this was not the tape of his interview with Barrett of 3 October on which there was a confession regarding the murder of Finucane, but the tape of the interview on 10 October. RUC SB had deliberately switched the tapes.[54]

RUC SB had been involved in an extensive deceit, perverting the course of justice.[55] They had deliberately set up the second meeting a week after the first to record Barrett and they made sure he did not repeat the confession. They failed to take the simple precaution of checking the details on the second tape to make sure that there was nothing on it which would allow the date of the interview to be ascertained. But why did SB not wish to arrest Barrett? After all he had confessed to this murder and was known to have been involved in many others. The despicable reason emerged many years later. RUC SB had decided after Finucane's murder to recruit Barrett as an agent.[56] The murder investigation against him was dropped and from that moment onwards he became a paid agent of the state.

Justice Cory's findings

In 2004, Justice Cory published his findings into Finucane's murder. As with Stalker and Stevens, he reported that his inquiry had been obstructed. The worst incident involved MI5 raiding his team's offices in London and wiping clean all the hard drives of their computers on the grounds of national security. It must have been known that the drives would have been backed up. The destruction must, therefore, have been a deliberate an attempt to intimate the investigators. It failed because Cory recommended a public inquiry into Finucane's murder.[57] He concluded that the police and army were guilty of collusion and connivance in serious crimes.

Cory considered that the documents which he analysed raised 'serious and perplexing questions' concerning the extent to which FRU had advance knowledge of the targeting of Finucane by Nelson. He concluded that an inference could be made that they did, but this was a matter for a public inquiry.[58] He discovered that MI5 knew that Finucane was being targeted but did not warn him – in 1981, again in June 1985 and December 1988. He commented: 'This is an indication that both the Security Service and RUC SB saw agent security as taking precedence over the need to warn a targeted individual that his life was at risk.'[59] He also criticised RUC SB for treating threats made by republican groups as more dangerous and deserving of attention than those made by loyalist groups.[60]

As with the Stalker investigation, RUC SB failed to pass on key intelligence to CID. Simpson, the senior investigating officer, was not informed that Nelson was a state agent for FRU or that Stobie was a state agent for RUC SB. It frustrated the murder investigation and, according to Cory, in such a manner that this could be judged as a collusive act.[61] Cory also drew attention to the lack of co-operation between FRU and RUC SB, and between RUC SB and CID.[62] Again, this had been a major concern of Stalker four years earlier.

Arming loyalists

One of the most significant of Cory's findings was that the British army was helping to arm loyalist paramilitaries. He discovered that in July 1985, FRU arranged for Nelson to go to South Africa to purchase arms for the UDA, paying for his flight and hotel expenses.[63] In his investigation into Finucane's murder, de

Silva found documentary evidence from both the army and MI5 that the plan was to intercept the arms *en route* to Northern Ireland.[64] But this made no sense. Why go to such efforts only to intercept the arms, arrest those involved and at the same time risk the UDA unmasking Nelson as an agent?[65] In any event, the detection and prosecution of crime was certainly not a high priority in the MI5/Walker strategy. All this strongly suggests that the documentary evidence was part of a cover-up to disguise the conspiracy to import arms for loyalists.

In South Africa, Nelson met an arms dealer from Armscor, the arms procurement agency of the South African Department of Defence, but he denied that any deal materialised. However, it is thought that some weapons came back following his visit.[66] Whatever the truth, in 1987 the UDA was able to exploit the relationship which Nelson had established with Armscor and learnt, via one of their European agents, that there was a cache of arms held by the Lebanese militia in Beirut which had come on the market.

Following a £325,000 bank robbery in Portadown, the UDA was subsequently able to purchase these arms. The huge cache was landed at Belfast docks in December 1987, hidden in a consignment of ceramic tiles to be divided up between the three loyalist paramilitary groups who had sponsored the enterprise: UDA, UVF and Ulster Resistance.[67] While the UDA weapons were sized, those for Ulster Resistance and UFF were not. Ulster Resistance then rearmed the UDA. With so many state agents, it is remarkable that the authorities allowed the weapons to be landed in Northern Ireland, unless it was part of a deliberate strategy to allow them in. According to interviews conducted by the investigative journalist, Ian Cobain, Nelson was kept informed throughout the operation.[68]

The outcome of the shipment was immediate. From 1985 the number of people killed by loyalists began to rise and by 1992 had exceeded the number of people killed by republicans, who, up to that point, had been responsible for more deaths than loyalists in every year apart from 1976.[69] A subsequent Police Ombudsman for Northern Ireland (PONI) investigation concluded that the imported arms were used in the murder or attempted murder of seventy people in Northern Ireland.[70] It was also discovered that the police had destroyed all documents relating to the 1987 weapons' shipment.[71]

Castlereagh break-in

On Sunday 17 March 2002, St Patrick's Day, highly sensitive material was stolen from the reformed and renamed Police Service of Northern Ireland (PSNI) SB offices in Castlereagh police station. It was reported that codes used by SB handlers and their informers, and personal information about handlers –

including some home addresses and mobile phone numbers – were part of the haul. The break-in had all the hallmarks of a highly professional job: the Castlereagh complex had tight security, the raiders knew the layout of the facility and they had up-to-date information as this particular office had only been in use for five days.

According to Rosie Cowan in *The Guardian*, three men in smart suits had driven up to the base, waved their IDs at the officer on duty and driven in.[72] They then walked into the building and again waved their IDs at the officer on duty and went up to the office to which SB had just moved. They knocked out the only officer in the room, put a bag over his head and tied him up. They checked his pulse regularly. They left after about 20 minutes.[73] Comparisons were made with the mysterious fire in 1990 in the offices of the Stevens team in Seapark – the highly secure complex near Carrickfergus.

The break-in was a huge embarrassment for the newly formed PSNI. Throughout the Troubles, the police had a policy in which the protection of state agents and informers took precedent over the detection and prosecution of offenders. This, of course, was the reason that the RUC refused to give Stalker any information about its intelligence sources in the six murders he investigated. Yet nearly 20 years on, security in the building housing the command centre for all informers and state agents was so lacking that three smart-suited men were able to walk in unchallenged and steal the documentation. Even the office door did not appear to have a lock or, ironically, a 'spyhole' to check those who wished to have entry. Moreover, there were no reports of CCTV cameras in any of the passages leading to the office.

There was speculation that the break-in was related to the Stevens' inquiry into the murder of Pat Finucane. The principal suspect within the press and media was FRU whose officers had been Nelson's handler. It had been renamed and was now called the Joint Support Group.[74] In the absence of any legal framework for the running of informers and state agents, there would have been concern among the army, and indeed, police and MI5 handlers, that they could be prosecuted for a range of offences and, therefore, it was essential to destroy any incriminating intelligence. On the other hand, as much of the information would have been also stored elsewhere, its value was questionable. Like the fire in Seapark, the raid may have been an attempt to intimidate or hinder the police investigations. Others speculated that it was intended to derail the peace process at the very moment the IRA was preparing for a second round of decommissioning.[75] Two weeks after the raid, this speculation increased when six people were arrested in republican areas of Belfast and Derry.

Chief Constable Sir Ronnie Flanagan immediately set up a police inquiry into the Castlereagh break-in. Separate from the police inquiry, John Reid, the SoS for Northern Ireland, appointed Sir John Chilcot to head a government investigation to consider the wider implications for national security. Chilcot had been PUS in NIO from 1990 to 1997 and had played a key role behind the scenes in the peace process. But it was an odd appointment as possible suspects included MI5, and Chilcot was currently a staff counsellor for both MI5 and MI6 (the Secret Intelligence Service). On 16 July 2003, the SoS for Northern Ireland, now Paul Murphy, issued a written statement on Chilcot's inquiry. He informed parliament that Chilcot 'did not uncover any evidence whatsoever that members of government agencies were involved'.[76] All of this frenetic activity to ascertain who was responsible for stealing documents from Castlereagh, contrasted sharply with the continuing failure to set up a public inquiry into the murder of a solicitor.

De Silva's report

In 2012, Desmond de Silva published his desktop review into Finucane's murder. While subject to several criticisms,[77] it nevertheless provided more evidence on the deadly counter-insurgency strategy put in place by MI5 in 1981 and the failure to implement Stalker's recommendations. De Silva stated bluntly that, 'a series of positive actions by employees of the State actively furthered and facilitated his [Finucane's] murder and that, in the aftermath of the murder, there was a relentless attempt to defeat the ends of justice'.[78]

De Silva documented the history of the numerous failed endeavours to develop a legal basis for the deployment of state agents in Northern Ireland and stated:

> My overall conclusion is that there was a wilful and abject failure by successive Governments to provide the clear policy and legal framework necessary for agent-handling operations to take place effectively and within the law.[79]

This 'abject failure', as McGovern has argued, served a deliberate purpose. It opened up 'a space of legal obscurity and plausible deniability that facilitated, rather than hampered, counter-insurgency practice'.[80] Senior civil servants were complicit in deliberately delaying the development of a legal framework. De Silva recorded that on 13 March 1987, senior NIO officials and senior RUC officers met to discuss guidelines for agent handling, and it was agreed that the RUC would draw up a draft paper for discussion. But a month later, the PUS in

NIO wrote an internal minute noting that 'it would not be wise to take any steps at this juncture to halt it [the development of guidelines], we should simply desist hastening it'.[81] The RUC SB 'slow waltz' in the dissemination of information to CID was now being adopted by senior civil servants in putting the brakes on developing legislation to control agent handing.

De Silva produced shocking evidence on the extent to which both the RUC and UDR leaked intelligence to loyalist paramilitaries. He noted that in 1985, MI5 was so concerned about the extent of leaks that it carried out a detailed assessment and found that 85 per cent of the UDA's intelligence came mainly from the RUC and UDR, and that the proportion had increased since the signing of the Anglo-Irish Agreement.[82] A further MI5 report in 1986 noted that the UDA Inner Council now considered that it was 'able to mount an effective campaign' because of the level of intelligence it had on republicans – a situation which could not have occurred without the considerable assistance of the security forces. In the late 1980s, De Silva reported that senior police and army officers 'may have been providing assistance to loyalist paramilitaries'.[83] A few months after Finucane's murder, there were continuing concerns over the leaking of intelligence from the security forces to loyalist paramilitaries.

Colonel Kerr submitted a statement to the De Silva inquiry. In it he produced a chilling justification for Nelson's recruitment:

> We carefully developed Nelson's case in conjunction with SB with the aim of making him the Chief Intelligence officer for the UDA. By getting him into that position FRU and SB reasoned that we could persuade the UDA to centralise their targeting through Nelson and to concentrate their targeting on known PIRA activists, who by the very nature of their own terrorist position were far harder targets.[84]

When interviewed by de Silva, he claimed that 'by involving the UDA in targeting PIRA activists, we were engaging them in work that was really rather nugatory because the targets by their positions and locations were too difficult'.[85]

Prime Minister David Cameron made a statement to parliament following the publication of de Silva's report. It was the most damning statement on collusion to date and an indictment of the counter-insurgency strategy in Northern Ireland. He began by noting that it was 'an extremely dark and violent time in Northern Ireland's history'. Cameron went on to say:

> The report sets out the extent of collusion in areas such as identifying, targeting and murdering Mr Finucane; supplying a weapon and facilitating its later disappearance; and deliberately obstructing subsequent investigations. ... but

while [de Silva] rejects any state conspiracy, he does find frankly shocking levels of state collusion. ... He finds that "a series of positive actions by employees of the State actively furthered and facilitated his murder". ... "there were extensive 'leaks' of security force information to the UDA and other loyalist paramilitary groups."... "an extraordinary state of affairs ... in which both the Army and the RUC Special Branch had prior notice of a series of planned UDA assassinations, yet nothing was done by the RUC to seek to prevent these attacks." ... it is really shocking that this happened in our country. ... state agents played "key roles" in the murder. ... "two agents who were at the time in the pay of agencies of the State were involved". ... the RUC Special Branch "were responsible for seriously obstructing the investigation." ... Most shockingly of all, Sir Desmond says that "on the balance of probabilities ... an RUC officer or officers did propose Patrick Finucane ... as a UDA target when speaking to a loyalist paramilitary."[86]

Deadly assassins

Nelson, Stobie, and subsequently Barrett, were just three state agents who were recruited as part of the MI5/Walker strategy. There were hundreds of others. In evidence to a parliamentary committee considering an extension of further exceptional policing powers in 2011, Stevens said:

> When you talk about intelligence, of the 210 people we arrested, only three were not agents. Some of them were agents for all four of those particular organisations, fighting against each other, doing things and making a large sum of money, which was all against the public interest and creating mayhem in Northern Ireland.[87]

Over the years, the names of several other state agents have entered the public domain, together with the extent of their criminality, following police inquiries and PONI investigations. They include Gary Haggarty, Mark Haddock and Freddie Scappaticci. Their murderous behaviour illustrates the way the rule of law was set aside in favour of intelligence.

Haggarty went on trial in 2008 when his sixteen-year criminal career in the UVF eventually came to an end. He pleaded guilty to 201 crimes, which included five murders, five attempted murders, 23 conspiracies to murder, four kidnappings, five hijackings and numerous other crimes. He asked for another 304 offences to be taken into consideration. He was, in Ian Cobain's words, 'a serial killer, kidnapper, drug dealer, racketeer, a one-man tsunami'.[88] He had been a state agent for eleven years.

Following his arrest, Haggarty became an 'assisting offender' or in common parlance, a 'supergrass'. He provided the police with a mass of information, which they claimed saved lives and prevented numerous crimes. Because of his co-operation, Haggarty was entitled to a discount on his sentence and a further discount for pleading guilty. His 20-year sentence was therefore reduced to four years and six months. As he could apply under the Good Friday Agreement for release after two years and he had already spent four years on remand, he was freed and immediately joined a witness protection scheme. There was no justice for his victims, the hundreds affected by his reign of terror and criminality as a paid state agent.

In 1997, Raymond McCord's son was killed by the UVF and his battered body found dumped in Ballyduff quarry, Newtownabbey. McCord began a personal crusade to find out who killed his son. In 2007, he made a formal complaint to PONI about the failure of the police to investigate his son's murder properly. The Ombudsman opened an investigation. She discovered from intelligence reports and other police documents that Haddock, an RUC SB informer, was linked to the murder of Raymond McCord junior and ten other murders. There was some intelligence linking him to five additional murders over a twelve-year period. There was also evidence that Haddock was involved in seventy-two different crimes including: armed robbery, grievous bodily harm, criminal damage, drug dealing, extortion, hijacking and threats to kill, in the period 1991-2003.[89] He was paid over £79,000 as an informer.

The year before the Ombudsman carried out her investigation, Haddock was prosecuted for an attack on Trevor Gowdy, a pub doorman, who had been hit with an iron bar and a hatchet. McCord, who sat through the trial, was shocked at the length of Haddock's criminal record and later commented: 'I cannot understand how any law enforcement agency in the world would employ a murderer, a drug dealer and an extortionist with so many criminal convictions and claim it is for the greater good.'[90] When the UVF discovered that Haddock was a police informer, Haggarty was dispatched to murder him.[91]

The Ombudman's report laid bare the corrosive impact of the MI5/Walker strategy on policing in the period 1991-2003. She listed sixteen actions which gave rise to 'grave concerns'. Some of the more important criticisms included: failure to arrest informers or treat them as suspects following confessions of crimes or following finds of ammunition in their houses; concealment of intelligence indicating that informers had been involved in murders and other serious crimes; withholding intelligence from CID; destroying or losing forensic exhibits; doctoring documents; and failure to inform DPPNI that an informer was a suspect in a crime. The Ombudsman concluded that the only explanation for these failures was that there 'was collusion by certain police officers with identified UVF informants'.[92]

Director of Relatives for Justice, Mark Thompson, commented on the report and argued that Haddock was 'the dime a dozen killer at the bottom of the chain'.[93] He stated bluntly that the evidence pointed to 'a highly sophisticated British government political and military policy of infiltration of loyalism for the purposes of murdering Irish nationals. The irony was that Haddock also killed numerous unionists and loyalists.'[94] In total, loyalist paramilitaries – Nelson, Haggarty and Haddock – are believed to have been involved in over 130 murders, attempted murders, and conspiracies to murder while acting as state agents or informers.[95]

Scappaticci – Agent 3702

As well as running agents in the loyalist community, the army had penetrated the republican community with state agents. The most significant known to date was Scappaticci – also known as Stakeknife.[96] He was recruited by the FRU sometime in 1978 and was paid £80,000 a year.[97] Scappaticci had been interned in 1971 and, following release in 1976, he became a trusted member of the IRA. By the early 1980s, he was deputy head of its internal security unit (ISU) – known locally as the 'nutting squad' – which interrogated, tortured, and killed those suspected of informing.[98] It is believed that John Joe Magee, as well as some other members of the ISU, were also state agents.[99] To protect Scappaticci, Stevens considered that FRU allowed the deaths of allegedly 'some thirty agents by feeding them to the PIRA'.[100] Harkin and Ingram list 36 killings while Scappaticci worked in the ISU.[101] These deaths alone resulted in over 50 children losing a father.[102]

There was speculation that when the UDA targeted Scappaticci, FRU steered them to another target, an innocent victim in Ballymurphy, Francis Notarantonio, who was shot dead to save their agent in the IRA.[103] On the other hand, Willie Carlin, who was an agent for MI5, describes how Scappaticci saved his life by tipping off the security services that the IRA were about to interrogate him.[104] The former Commander of UK Land Forces described Stakeknife as the military's 'most important secret'. 'It was the golden egg. It was the one thing that was terribly, terribly important to the army ... So, we were terribly cagey about Fred.'[105]

Scappaticci is believed to have been involved in the murder of one of the informers involved in supplying information which led to the first incident investigated by Stalker – the killing of Sean Burns, Eugene Toman and

Gervaise McKerr.[106] The tip-off came from Gregory Burns – the brother of Sean Burns. It is a complicated story.[107] In the early 1980s, Gregory Burns applied to join the UDR to earn some extra money – an odd decision for someone from a strong republican family. He was informed that because of his background he would not be accepted; instead he could provide information to the authorities for which he would be paid. As a state agent for MI5, it transpired that he supplied the vital piece of information that led to the death of his brother, following which he became a loose cannon, and the FRU relocated him to Amsterdam, where he provided low-level intelligence on republicans in the city. After a period in other parts of Europe, Burns returned to Northern Ireland and re-joined the IRA at the invitation of Aidan Starrs. He continued supplying information to FRU. A third member of the unit, John Dignam, joined on release from prison.

Burns, Starrs and Dignam then became a three-person gang carrying out robberies and other offences in the name of the IRA, but in contravention of orders, they helped themselves to the proceeds. In 1990, Dignam and Starrs robbed a local snooker club. All three were then questioned by the IRA and suspended. They realised that they were in danger and made a request to the FRU to be relocated, but their request was turned down. Prior to the robbery, Burns was in a relationship with Margaret Perry, which soon ended. Margaret knew about their roles as informers and their involvement in the robbery. She posed a real threat to them so they hatched a plot to kill her. In June 1991, Starrs, under the pretext of taking her to see her old boyfriend in hospital, stopped the car not far from Mullaghmore, County Sligo, brutally killed her and buried her in a shallow grave.

According to Ingram and Harkin, the IRA ordered Scappaticci and John Joe Magee to carry out an investigation into Burns, Dignam and Starrs.[108] They were tortured and confessed to being state agents. Their confessions were taped and then they were shot. Only two months earlier, on 5 May 1992, Gregory Burns had interrupted the inquest of his brother Sean. He said that his family had no confidence in the inquest system and that the three had been deliberately murdered by the RUC. 'Justice could never be done because of the narrow remit of the inquest system'[109] – an abhorrent comment from someone who participated in the murder of an innocent woman.

In 2007, Police Ombudsman Nuala O'Loan produced a damning report on Perry's murder in which she stated: 'I am satisfied that police knew of the threat to Margaret in 1990. There was no assessment of that risk or of the general risk to Margaret. That should have been a priority, given the nature of the information received.'[110] The RUC SB, she claimed, had made a serious 'error of judgement' and 'the protection of the source became the primary concern for the police'. RUC SB also failed to assist the investigation into her murder by withholding intelligence which would have indicated who was responsible.[111] These were the very same criticisms which Stalker made eight years earlier.

Operation Kenova

In June 2016, Operation Kenova was established to investigate alleged murders, assaults, kidnappings and torture committed by Stakeknife, and to determine whether any of his crimes were preventable. This was part of a costly inquiry,[112] headed by Jon Boutcher, former Chief Constable of Bedfordshire.[113] Boutcher subsequently oversaw three other Troubles-related investigations: Operation Turma, an investigation into the murder of the three police officers at Kinnego Embankment 1982; Operation Mizzenmast, an investigation into the death of Jean Smyth-Campbell in 1972; and the Barnard Review, a review of the Glenanne Gang series of murders committed during the 1970s, which was commissioned as Operation Denton and is estimated to encompass over 100 incidents involving around 120 cases of murder.[114]

All of Boutcher's work was overseen by a Governance Board, whose purpose was to provide families and interested parties with reassurance that the investigation was Article 2 ECHR compliant. The Board has no influence on ongoing investigations, which was the responsibility of the Independent Steering Group (ISG). However, the appointment of Sir John Chilcot, who was PUS in the NIO from 1990 to the end of 1997 and was heavily involved in discussions about the lack of a framework for the running of agents, undermined the reassurance of compliance, as Article 2 requires that investigations are compliant in relation to the principle that they should be independent.

The origins of Operation Kenova can be traced back to years earlier. On 3 January 1990, Sandy Lynch, a police informer, was interrogated by Scappaticci in a house in Belfast.[115] Lynch was subsequently rescued by the police but only after Scappaticci had left the house, leaving several others to guard him. It appeared to have been a carefully planned police sting operation to arrest members of the IRA. They were prosecuted and convicted for Lynch's abduction and detention, but it subsequently emerged that the RUC had withheld crucial information from the DPPNI.[116] Following the quashing of the convictions of those involved in the kidnapping, Sir Alasdair Fraser QC, DPPNI, made a request to the Chief Constable under the Justice (Northern Ireland) Act 2002 for information about the case. Subsequently, Mr Barra

McGrory, QC made another three requests for further information to the Chief
Constable between 2013 and 2015, relating specifically to Stakeknife.

Nothing had, therefore, changed since the Stalker/Sampson investigation. The
RUC was still prepared to withhold files from the prosecution to protect state
agents and informers. In this instance, it also raised the terrible vista that many
deaths, in which it was suspected that Scappaticci was involved, were
preventable if there had been state intervention.

Kenova's terms of reference were wide-ranging:

> Whether there is evidence of the commission of criminal offences by the alleged
> agent known as Stakeknife, including but not limited to, murders, attempted
> murders or unlawful imprisonments.

> Whether there is evidence of criminal offences having been committed by
> members of the British Army, the Security Services or other Government
> agencies, in respect of the cases connected to the alleged agent known as
> Stakeknife. Regard in this context will be given to the Article 2 (ECHR) rights
> of victims and the associated responsibilities of the British Army, the Security
> Services, or other Government agencies.

> Whether there is evidence of criminal offences having been committed by any
> other individual, in respect of the cases connected to the alleged agent.

> Whether there is evidence of the commission of criminal offences by any persons
> in respect of allegations of perjury connected to the alleged agent.[117]

In 2020, the Kenova team submitted the first batch of files from its
investigation into Scappaticci to the DPPNI. It recommended he face
perjury charges based on the allegation that he had lied under oath. The
DPPNI concluded, however, that there was insufficient evidence to put
Scappaticci on trial. He also ruled out any prosecutions regarding the
misconduct in public office of two former members of MI5 and a former
member of the Public Prosecution Service. The DPPNI, Stephen Herron,
explained his reasoning:

> After a thorough analysis of all available evidence and with the benefit of
> independent advice from highly experienced senior counsel, I have concluded that
> in each case there is insufficient evidence to provide a reasonable prospect of
> conviction for any offence. In these circumstances the evidential test for
> prosecution was not met. The second limb of the test for prosecution, which relates
> to the public interest in bringing proceedings, did not therefore fall to be applied.[118]

Brian Rowan, a retired BBC journalist, acknowledged that Boutcher will try
to get at the truth, but many others will be equally determined to 'block his path,
to hide the very worst of this place, and the very worst of that war'.[119]

Scappaticci died in April 2023 – a death that appears to have been kept secret
by the authorities for some days.[120] He will now never face prosecution for any

of the murders he committed while working as a state agent. In December 2018, he was, however, prosecuted for possessing extreme pornography, including images of animals. It is not known if this perversion was used to recruit him as an agent. He received a three-mouth suspended sentence. The chief magistrate Emma Arbuthnot seemed to take pity on him and remarked on his serious health issues and lonely life, telling him: 'You have not been before the court for 50 years – and that's good character in my book.'[121] A quick internet search would have disabused her of her ignorance. More than 30 families of his victims are currently suing his estate.[122]

In December 2023, the DPPNI issued another statement concerning its decisions in relation to Operation Kenova.[123] He reported that, in total, Operation Kenova had submitted files on 28 suspects. Fourteen were members of the IRA and had roles within the IRA's ISU. Twelve suspects were retired soldiers attached to FRU, the unit responsible for recruiting and handling of agents, and two were retired RUC officers who were allegedly involved in 'an incident of false imprisonment'. The alleged offences ranged from murder, conspiracy to murder, false imprisonment, conspiring to pervert the course of justice and misconduct in public office. Three suspects have since died leaving decisions on 25 suspects. The DPPNI's statement considered decisions in respect of sixteen of the suspects and again he considered that there was insufficient evidence to provide a reasonable prospect of a conviction, principally because there were insurmountable difficulties in relation to using intelligence material as evidence.

On 6 February 2024, the DPPNI issued another statement concerning his decision not to prosecute a further four individuals reported by Kenova – two former soldiers who worked as handlers with FRU and two alleged members of the IRA.[124] Once again, the DPPNI considered that there was insufficient evidence to provide a reasonable prospect of a conviction because of the difficulties associated with the use of intelligence material.

At the end of February 2024, the DPPNI issued a final statement on the remaining Kenova files.[125] It dealt with decisions relating to a further seven members of the IRA, three agent handlers in FRU and two retired soldiers – an operations officer and a commanding officer. Although not mentioned by name, the latter was Colonel Kerr, who headed up the FRU from 1986 to 1990. The DPPNI, together with his earlier statement, provided information on the relevant factual and legal context focusing on the FRU, supplementing information which was already in the public domain from the de Silva inquiry.

In 1986, the army had issued 'an updated set of directives and instructions' for FRU.[126] It is not known if Stalker's interim report caused this revision. They stated that source coverage was the responsibility of the Director and Co-ordinator of Intelligence (DCI), who exercises this responsibility through the various Intelligence Committees. The DCI was represented in army HQ by the Assistant Secretary Political (ASP), who must be kept informed on a regular basis of the current status of the sources. Moreover, on behalf of MI5, he or she is responsible for the maintenance and safekeeping of all FRU source files.

In July 1988, Kerr issued a new directive 'which dealt with the re-organisation of the FRU and its establishment as a fully independent and operational unit within the army intelligence structure'.[127] He called it 'Perestroika'.[128] It stated that important intelligence or operational headlines, as well as daily reports on operations, were to be passed to him personally or, in his absence, to the operations officer. Previously, the operations officer had received all intelligence headlines after every meeting with a source. Kerr now took on this powerful role himself, leaving the operations officer to handle one source – Scappaticci. In addition, Kerr instructed that 'all agent case files were to be transferred from the offices of MI5's ASP to HQ FRU'.[129] This suggests that Kerr was now taking over MI5's role in the handling of agents, further increasing his power in the intelligence war.

Operation Kenova recommended that the army handlers of Scappaticci, the operations officer and Kerr should all be prosecuted for misconduct in public office. The offence occurs when a person wilfully neglects to perform his or her duty and/or wilfully misconducts themselves to such a degree to amount to an abuse of the public's trust in the office holder. In this case, the misconduct related to the general running of Scappaticci as an informer and their failure to share with the police certain intelligence information.

The DPPNI concluded, however, that there was no reasonable prospect of conviction of any of the suspects because, once again, of the difficulties over the admissibility of intelligence. This issue will be considered further (Chapter 26). He revealed that Kerr had been investigated before for alleged misconduct resulting from the oversight of a different source, probably Nelson, but was not prosecuted. The DPPNI considered whether Kerr's possible prosecution could be strengthened by the deployment of evidence in relation to the previous case, but rejected the idea as the misconduct was of a different nature. These final prosecutorial decisions mean that not one member of the army or MI5 has been prosecuted for any crime following the many murders carried out by state agent Scappaticci, despite a police investigation finally costing £40 million.

It is now safe to conclude that the many hundreds of murders committed by state agents as a key part of the MI5/Walker counter-insurgency strategy will never be prosecuted. Families who lost loved ones, and particularly, children who lost a parent, will continue to demand to know whether a state agent was involved in their murder. They will continue to seek the truth and justice.

The Kenova team promised to publish a report which 'will address high level themes and issues' into Scappaticci's activities, which may provide some solace to families. In October 2022, Boutcher announced that an 'interim report' would be published in the New Year (2023).[130] In August 2023, he announced that its publication had moved one step closer and had passed national security checking with 'no changes or redactions' – a surprising outcome given MI5's history and suggests that their role in the conflict has been heavily censored. On 8 March 2024, the interim report was eventually published.

Kenova Interim report

It was a damning indictment of the state and its legal and moral obligation to protect the lives of its citizens. Although it was widely known that Scappaticci was Stakeknife, bizarrely he was not mentioned by name as the government has yet to give Boutcher authority to do so. The report confirmed much that was already suspected. In order to protect the lives of informers and state agents, the RUC, police and MI5 failed to prevent murders and withheld, did not share or failed to act upon, key intelligence. Stakeknife was allowed to remain in place and continue his murderous activities for years. Overall, Kenova investigated 101 murders and abductions with Stakeknife being linked to at least 14 of the former and 15 of the latter.

Boutcher ridiculed the argument that Scappaticci saved 'countless' or 'hundreds' of lives – an assessment derived from the FRU's 'unreliable and speculative internal metrics which were also used to produce similar and equally exaggerated claims about Brian Nelson'.[131] He argued that no serious security and intelligence professional on hearing that Scappaticci was 'the goose that laid the golden egg' should have been alerted to the falsehood as 'the comparison is rooted in fables and fairy tales'. The comments were clearly directed at Sir John Wilsey, the general officer commanding the British Amry in Northern Ireland between 1983 and 1990 who made the 'golden egg' comment and also at Colonel Kerr who made the claim in Nelson's trial that he had helped save hundreds of lives.

Boutcher considered that Scappaticci's information probably saved 'between high single figures and low double figures and nowhere near hundreds sometimes claimed'.[132] His estimate did not take account of the lives lost as a consequence of Scappaticci being allowed to remain as an agent where he often ignored his handlers. Boutcher concluded: 'I think it probable that this resulted in more lives being lost than saved'.[133]

The Kenova team had a 'fractious' relationship with MI5.[134] Access to information was withheld or delayed and documents were reclassified as 'Top Secret'. Boutcher discovered that solicitors representing former security force personnel 'had been given greater and unorthodox access to MI5 materials'.[135] On one occasion, MI5 accused a member of the Kenova team of disclosing secret information. This was untrue. Following an independent review of the relationship between MI5 and Kenova, matters improved. But on the day Kenova was due to serve files on the PPS, MI5 informed Kenova that the building's accreditation to receive secret files had expired and that various building upgrades and staff training were required. It meant that there was a delay of over three months before the files could be submitted. Whether this was a deliberate attempt to delay PPS decisions on possible prosecution of MI5 personnel and agent handlers, or simply an oversight, remains unclear and may never be known.

Kenova investigated the incident reported in a BBCNI Spotlight programme that MI5 had entered the offices of Judge Cory in London and wiped clean the investigation's hard drives. According to MI5, the story was incorrect:

> It was, in fact, NIO officials – advised on occasion by MI5 concerning protective security measures – who were responsible for the physical and information security for Judge Cory's investigation and who, with the consent of Judge Cory's secretariat, removed the hard drive [sic], after their contents had been transferred from non-secure systems on which they had been stored onto encrypted laptops ... MI5 did not remove anything from Judge Cory's offices, nor did MI5 direct others to do so ..." [136]

Kenova interviewed Judge Cory and Judge Pomerance, a senior counsel to his inquiry. Both claimed that the individuals who entered the offices identified themselves to the secretary and the office manager as representatives of MI5. Boutcher was in no doubt who was telling the truth and concluded: 'It is a tribute to the legacy of Judge Cory to hold fast to the truth of his account in the face of efforts to mislead.'[137]

Unsurprisingly, the report confirms what has been known since Stalker's interim report in 1985, that there was no legal framework for the management and use of agents in Northern Ireland – a fact which was confirmed by possibly ten subsequent inquiries. The Home Office guidelines issued in 1969 were totally inadequate. Yet successive governments did nothing to rectify the situation until shortly before the GFA. It is abundantly clear that FRU, with Kerr in charge, exploited the situation and ran an unknown number of agents who were permitted to commit murder and other serious offences.

Although the ASP in army HQ kept the DCI informed about developments relating to the army's collection and exploitation of intelligence, MI5 appears to have supported the activities of FRU and believed the fairy tales of the success of the unit. Boutcher, however, concludes that MI5 'could not sensibly be criticised for the conduct or operation of the FRU or any of its agents'.[138] Why not? After all it had introduced the antinomian counter-security strategy and would have had first-hand information of what was happening. It should have raised concerns.

Denial of a public inquiry into Finucane's murder

Against such a background, it is little surprise that the government is using every tactic possible to prevent a public inquiry into Finucane's murder. The family is not giving up, however. Following the announcement that the government would not establish a public inquiry, only a desktop review, it began a judicial review of the decision. This was eventually heard by the UK Supreme Court and in a judgment issued on 27 February 2019, the Court held that there had not been an Article 2 compliant inquiry into Finucane's death but did not go as far as to recommend a public inquiry, leaving it up to the British government to decide on what action to take.[139] Of considerable significance as far as the analysis in this book is concerned, the Supreme Court noted that: 'The "strands of involvement by elements of the state" needed to be recognised and explained. These were necessary ingredients of an Article 2 compliant inquiry.'[140] In effect, although it does not mention the MI5/Walker strategy by name, all the strategy's various elements need to be analysed and explained in this and any other death for it to be Article 2 compliant.[141]

On 30 November 2020, the government eventually responded to the Supreme Court with a statement to parliament. The SoS for Northern Ireland said that the levels of collusion in the Finucane case were 'totally unacceptable' and he repeated the apology made by David Cameron. He told the House of Commons that the government would establish a public inquiry 'to look at any potential failings by government or State bodies'.[142] However, he announced that he had decided 'not to establish a public inquiry [into the Finucane murder] at this time', but to await a 'process of review'. It was yet another attempt to delay making any decision.

Geraldine Finucane then challenged the SoS decision not to establish a public inquiry and instead await the outcome of the process of review. Her case rested on the failure of the government: to identify the precise role of state agents and their identities; the precise assistance given to the murders by the state; and the means by which these matters might have been established. Moreover, she argued that the SoS decision 'gave rise to further excessive and egregious delay'.[143]

On 21 December 2022, Justice Scoffield issued a damning judgment in her favour. He announced:

> I have no hesitation in concluding that the United Kingdom Government (represented in these proceedings by the respondent, the Secretary of State) remains in breach of article 2 on the basis of the ongoing delay in completing an investigation which satisfies the requirements of that provision.[144]

He quashed the decision of the SoS not to hold a public inquiry and directed that a decision must be taken on how to deal with the investigative deficiencies within a specified timeframe. He also considered that the SoS had unlawfully failed to reconsider the position following the conclusion of the process of review. He recognised the 'sorry situation' in which Geraldine Finucane found herself noting that it was now over 33 years since her husband was murdered, nineteen years since the ECtHR judgment and three and a half years since the Supreme Court judgment.[145] He ordered the SoS to pay Mrs Finucane £7,500 in damages.[146]

At the beginning of January 2023, she began legal proceedings in the High Court to seek damages against the British government for continuing to remain in breach of its legal obligation to carry out an investigation into her husband's murder. Counsel for the SoS for Northern Ireland, in response, said that a decision had not been reached on the timetable for a decision, adding 'part of any decision of this nature which may involve a public inquiry involved consultation with the Prime Minister and across government'.[147] This was an obvious reference to MI5. In March 2023, the SoS was ordered to pay a further £5,000 to Mrs Finucane in damages.[148]

The SoS appealed the decision of the High Court findings and the award of damages. The Court of Appeal heard the case over two days on 19 and 20 September 2023. Paul McLaughlin, KC, representing the SoS, argued that the judge had gone too far, had failed to make a distinction between delay and culpable delay and had blurred the differences between public authorities, namely the SoS, Police Ombudsman and PSNI – arguments which appeared to have little or no merit. Fiona Doherty KC, for Geraldine Finucane, argued that the government's response had exacerbated the hold-up, pointing out that it was now 34 years on from the murder. She emphasised that the SoS had options but chose procedures that would take years to complete. She argued that a long line of SoSs have taken the decision 'to kick the can down the road and run down the clock'.[149] It was obviously another attempt to further delay the SoS making a decision as to whether or not to hold a public inquiry into Finucane's murder by state agents and at considerable cost to the tax-payer. Judgment was reserved in the appeal.

* * *

Finucane's murder and subsequent judicial and police inquiries provided more information on the MI5/Walker strategy and its continuation without any legal framework. Notwithstanding the recommendations of the Stalker and Sampson investigations, RUC SB remained a force within a force. State agents were permitted to continue their deadly activities and agent protection, rather than the detection and prosecution of crime, continued to be paramount. Their activities were often hidden from CID officers who were tasked with investigating murders. Deceit, deviance, and criminality within sections of both the army and the police continued.

The murder of Finucane arose from a change in the counter-insurgency strategy brought about by the Stalker and Sampson police investigations and their recommendations that several police and MI5 officers should be prosecuted for perverting the course of justice. Instead of a reliance on police special units trained in firepower, speed and aggression, the army now began to arm loyalist paramilitaries and to provide them with intelligence to 'take the war to the IRA' – leading to collusion between the security forces and the UDA and UVF. Finucane's murder was just one of many such killings arising from this change in strategy. The rule of law continued to be set aside, along with the state's fundamental obligation to protect the lives of its citizens.

It is an indictment on the part of successive British governments that they still remain, at the time of writing, in breach of their legal obligation to carry out a human rights compliant investigation into the murder of Pat Finucane. They have managed to introduce delay after delay, making it more difficult to establish the truth about the precise role of state agents in his murder arising directly from the deadly MI5/Walker strategy and, more importantly, the decision by the army to out-source the war to loyalist paramilitaries. An inquiry would expose those responsible for developing the original MI5/Walker strategy and, subsequently, the outsourcing of the conflict. Powerful interests within the British establishment are most unlikely to permit it ever to happen. Against such a background, in which the rule of law was subverted in the interests of counter-insurgency without any parliamentary scrutiny, the probability that MI5 or sections of the security forces in Northern Ireland conspired to remove Stalker does not appear to be so remote.

Chapter 23

Taylor's Trial

EIGHT MONTHS after the murder of Pat Finucane, the criminal trial against Kevin Taylor, Derek Britton, Terence Bowley and Vincent McCann started – on 2 October 1989. It was a crucial case for the police. If they won, it would help refute the conspiracy theory that the Deputy Chief Constable was removed because he was getting too close to the truth in his inquiry in Northern Ireland. It would show that Stalker's friend Taylor was indeed a criminal and that the investigation by GMP into the two men was justified. If Taylor was acquitted, however, it would provide further support for the view that Taylor had been pursued with the purpose of placing Stalker under suspicion. The police were taking no risks and continued to keep an eye on Taylor and his friends who noticed that they were being followed by police cars when visiting him.[1] During the trial, it emerged that the police had used every trick in their armoury, including deceit, to guarantee a conviction.

A valued client

From early in the trial, there was an astonishing admission which undermined the whole basis of the case against Taylor. Ferguson cross-examined David Davenport, who was an associate in the Corporate Business Department at the Co-operative Bank. He asked him if Taylor would have been able to repay all his bank loans if he had been able to sell his sites in Trafford Park. Davenport said that he would. Moreover, it emerged that the bank would have made a profit of £360,000 on the loans. It further emerged that the bank considered Taylor to be a good customer as loans to him were producing excellent returns. Ferguson then asked him if, at any time during his conversations with Taylor, he had ever, to his knowledge, wilfully misled him. Davenport said that he had not.[2]

Mr Cowburn, who had become head of the Corporate Business Department when Bowley moved to Newcastle at the end of November 1985, was also asked if he considered Taylor a good client, someone whom the bank was anxious to support and someone who would bring in other business to the bank. Hood continued:

HOOD: He was somebody who had shown his credentials as a property developer with the Moulton Street project?

COWBURN: Yes.

HOOD: He was somebody who had been lent money by another financial house and who had repaid them? I am thinking of the Continental Illinois Bank, yes?

COWBURN: I don't know that situation. I'm sure that's right.

HOOD: But he was somebody who was in the business of finding and developing property on quite a large scale?

COWBURN: Yes.

HOOD: Somebody who the bank would regard, looking at it at that time, as being a good risk?

COWBURN: Yes.

HOOD: Somebody who had shown preparedness to move from one financial institution to another?

COWBURN: Yes.

HOOD: And somebody who the bank would want, if it could, to keep?

COWBURN: Yes.

HOOD: And so far as the transaction hitherto, the bank regarded the monies advanced within the facility as wholly secure?

COWBURN: Yes.

HOOD: There was no security which he could give that he had not given so far as the bank knew, personal guarantee?

COWBURN: Yes.

HOOD: Of himself and his wife?

COWBURN: Yes.

HOOD: Charge on the house?

COWBURN: Yes.[3]

These were surprising pieces of evidence in a case based on allegations of overvaluing property, deceit, dishonesty and misrepresentation.

Harassment of witnesses

It emerged early on in the trial that some witnesses had been subject to harassment. Several of the bank employees were interrogated over long periods and were treated as if they were themselves suspects but were not accorded their rights as set out under PACE. Davenport was first seen by the police in July 1986 and was then interviewed on over twelve occasions by between eight and ten different officers. He was at home on the first occasion and had taken the day off work because his wife had just come out of hospital. The police were unconcerned and took him to the bank where he was interviewed until six o'clock that evening. The following day, a Saturday, he was picked up by the police in the morning and taken to the local police station. He was interviewed again until six o'clock in the evening.[4] The police claimed that they were interviewing him about his former colleague, Bowley, but it seemed clear that at this stage they were treating him as a possible suspect.[5] At the trial, further pressure was put on him when he was forced to wait for three days before being called to give evidence.[6]

Stephen Wood, a security clerk in the bank, received similar treatment and was subject to several interviews in police stations. On 30 September 1986, Caldwell and Knowles went to the Co-operative Bank and invited him to accompany them to Collyhurst Police Station. He was then interviewed by Stephenson for over three hours but at no stage was he informed that he might be considered a suspect and cautioned.[7] Hood cross-examined Caldwell on Wood's treatment:

HOOD: As far as you are aware, he was not under arrest?

OFFICER: No. He was perfectly happy to come and see us.

HOOD: And he was never cautioned?

OFFICER: Not by myself.

HOOD: Did I hear you say that he was perfectly happy to come and see us?

OFFICER: As far as I was concerned, and he came to see us on a number of other occasions at Bolton Police Station. That was as much a matter of convenience for him as anything else.

HOOD: A matter of convenience?

OFFICER: For him, yes.

HOOD: Would it surprise you to know that he told the court on oath that he was far from happy about being taken to various police stations?

OFFICER: I think he was far from happy being involved in the whole inquiry, but nevertheless he had to be spoken to.

HOOD: It is most interesting to know just why he said that. He told us he was far from happy because he felt he was being coerced by the police into signing statements that he did not agree with.

OFFICER: As I say, I did not conduct any formal interviews with him, and did not take any statements from him. Perhaps that is something that other officers can assist with.[8]

Hood pursued the same line of questioning with Knowles. He wanted to know, if they were not being treated as suspects, why the police demanded that they look at the bank accounts of both Davenport and Wood. They were then required to explain every transaction over a two-year period. Knowles said: 'It was simply finally to satisfy ourselves that as witnesses it was the correct thing to do.'[9] Wood claimed that he and Davenport were constantly told by the police that if they co-operated, they would put a good word in for them at the bank and implied that if they didn't, they would do the opposite. On one occasion they indicated to Wood that if he did not volunteer to go to the police station with them, they would charge him with a criminal offence.[10]

The treatment of Bowley was similarly heavy-handed. On 15 July 1986, Stephenson, Corfield and Ware went to the Co-operative Bank and asked him to accompany them to Bootle Street Police Station. He agreed and was then interviewed from 11.00 a.m. to 8.10 p.m.[11] In September, he went away on holiday to Menorca and stayed in Castell Playa Fiesta Hotel, but the police were not going to leave him alone. During the trial, Ware was asked by Bowley's defence counsel, Mr Birkett, what he thought of the chances of a member of his investigation team being in the same hotel at precisely the same time as Mr and Mrs. Bowley in September of 1987.[12] He thought the chances were remote, to say the least. It was then put to him that Bowley had seen Topping at the hotel. Ware was flabbergasted and added: 'You will forgive me, sir, if I faint – I did not know that.'[13] On returning from holiday, he was arrested, driven to the Newcastle-upon-Tyne branch of the Co-operative Bank, where his office was searched. He was then taken to Manchester and interviewed.[14]

Several other witnesses complained about the way they were treated by the police. For example, Brian Harris, who provided advice to Taylor on the Poynton site, was interviewed at Bootle Street Police Station. He was asked to sign a statement by Hogg – another officer with a reputation for producing results who had joined the DIU in June 1986. Hogg said: 'I don't see any great problems for you'.[15] Harris considered this a threat and that if he didn't sign the statement, he could become a potential defendant. He complained to Hogg about his treatment. Hood cross-examined him on this point:

HOOD: Does he not make a few complaints to you about the way in which he is dealt with by yourself?

HOGG: He certainly does, sir, yes.

HOOD: He suggests that he knows about you from other police officers he knows in another force?

HOGG: Correct – a force I used to be in.

HOOD: He suggested you have got rather a reputation within that force for intimidating witnesses?

HOGG: That's what he said.

HOOD: He goes so far as to suggest to you that your nickname in that force was 'Hotty Hogg'?

HOGG: Correct, that's what he said.

HOOD: He asks if he can take away a copy of his statement and consult a solicitor about it?

HOGG: Yes, sir.
HOOD: And he was refused that right?
HOGG: Correct.
HOOD: You would not allow him to consult a solicitor before signing it?
HOGG.   That's correct.[16]

Failure to show witnesses relevant documents

Several witnesses claim that they were not shown all the relevant documents before they signed their statements. In some interviews, the police failed to follow the standard procedure and attach exhibit labels to the document; it was therefore impossible to know what documents had been shown to the witness. Mr Colin Wicks, a Chartered Surveyor employed by Inland Revenue, who was asked to value the four plots of land that Taylor had purchased in Trafford Park, was shown only selected valuations in his interview with the police.[17] He was told that he could see the other valuations only after he had signed the statement. Hood put it to him that it would be rather difficult to un-sign his statement if there was anything in another valuation which caused him to change his mind. Wicks' understanding was that he could add a rider once he had seen the additional valuation.[18]

Mr Richard Weatherhead, another Chartered Surveyor, admitted to Hood that his statement gave a misleading impression concerning the amount of interest in the site at Trafford Park. Steiger, Britton's defence counsel, suggested that this was due to a misleading selection of documentation by the police and Weatherhead agreed.[19] A similar situation occurred with Mr David Appleton, who was not a Chartered Surveyor, but an associate of the Landscape Institute. He was not shown all the documents assessing the amount of shale on the old brickworks at Poynton before signing his statement. He noted that he was confident that there was no more than 30,000 cubic metres of shale.[20] Yet the ex-manager of the brickworks put the amount of shale considerably higher.

Several of the banking officials also made similar claims that they were not shown relevant documents. Chadwick told the court that the police showed him only documents which they wanted him to see.[21] Davenport, too, did not see all the documents before he signed his statement which was prepared by the police from notes taken in the interviews. When Wood was interviewed, he was shown only three or four documents at a time and invited to comment, instead of having a chance to look through all the bank files together.

Mr Derek Slade, a Chartered Accountant, and a partner with Arthur Young,[22] was asked to carry out an accounting exercise based on the records of Taylor's companies. However, he was not given key information in preparing his report. He was not informed that Trafford Park was made up of several individual sites, rather than just one site – substantially under-estimating Taylor's portfolio. Moreover, he was not given some key information about the Poynton site, such as the fact that it had been given planning permission in January 1985, the amount of shale on the site or the proposal that it was initially to be used as a tip.[23]

More importantly, Slade, as an expert witness, was given very narrow instructions in relation to one of Taylor's companies, Rangelark. He was simply asked to review its assets and determine if it was solvent. He concluded from the figures that it was trading insolvently. Hood put to him the example of a person who formed a company to buy a Ferrari car with a loan of £7,000. He then left the car in a garage for many years and eventually sold it for £8 million. If the only asset of that company was the Ferrari sports car, Hood suggested, it would mean that if one valued the company's assets purely on the cost of that motor car, that company would be technically insolvent for every year. Slade agreed. It perfectly illustrated the difference between the notion of technical insolvency and the reality within the property development world.[24] The police, however, wished only that the jury considered that Taylor was trading fraudulently.

Regina v Kevin Taylor and Others

The prosecution team was comprised of two QCs, Mr Corkery, and Mr Shorrock, and a junior – Mr Pearce. The trial Judge was Michael Sachs. He was the first solicitor to be appointed to the High Court bench, breaking one element of the Bar's monopoly of criminal trial proceedings.[25] There were several changes to the defence team following the committal proceedings. Mr Richard Ferguson QC and Mr Hood represented Taylor; Mr Birkett QC and Mr Morris represented Bowley from the Co-operative Bank; Mr Rhys-Davis QC and Mr Steiger represented Britton, Taylor's accountant; and Mr Jack Price QC and Mr Gee represented Mr McCann, the quantity surveyor.

Taylor's barrister, Richard Ferguson, was originally from Northern Ireland and he stood as an Ulster Unionist MP for South Antrim in 1968 at the start of the Troubles but gave up politics after his house was fire-bombed, and resigned from the Orange Order. He concentrated on his legal career defending republicans, loyalists and members of the police and army. In 1984, during a supergrass trial, he became ill and four of the accused were granted a separate trial.[26] Shortly afterwards, he moved his practice to England and became one of the Bar's most successful barristers.[27] Taylor thought that as he had represented families of the IRA, this might give him an interesting edge in the case.[28]

However, three weeks into the trial Taylor and his team were unhappy with Ferguson's failure to challenge Corkery's tactics and he agreed to step down.[29] Hood, who was not yet a QC, took over the case.

The defendants, in different combinations, faced a barrage of charges, including several counts of obtaining pecuniary advantage by deception, procuring the execution of a valuable security, furnishing false information, false accounting and fraudulent trading. All four were originally charged with conspiracy but at the last minute it was agreed to drop the conspiracy charge, leaving only the substantive charges. The conspiracy charge had served its purpose in guaranteeing that the case went to trial. The remaining charges related to several different statutes: Theft Act 1968, Criminal Law Act 1971, Criminal Attempts Act, 1981, Companies Act 1948, and 1985. The complexities of the case make it extremely difficult to summarise briefly the details, but the principal charge against all four defendants was related to the loans Taylor had obtained between January 1984 and November 1985, allegedly on the basis of false representation as to the value of the properties offered as securities and the true purpose of the borrowings. The charges against Bowley related principally to his role in providing the loans and overdraft facilities to Taylor, to causing loss to the Co-operative Bank and in gaining pecuniary advantage for Taylor by deception.

The trial started with a blaze of publicity. Corkery began the prosecution case by arguing that Taylor had run out of cash for his property developments and had turned to the Co-operative Bank, where he recruited Bowley for his dishonest schemes. Corkery emphasised that there was no evidence that Bowley had benefited financially, but that he was behaving in a dishonest manner. He approved a loan for Taylor of £240,000 without the approval of the Advances Department and he had then tried to cover it up by making an application to the Advances Department after it had been granted. Corkery also claimed that Taylor was involved in cross-firing of cheques from his different accounts so that one of the accounts was in the black when seeking the loan.

Valuations

Assets and their valuations were central. The police claimed that Taylor had deceived the bank by overvaluing his home and other property to obtain loans from the Co-operative Bank. He told the bank, when applying for a £2 million loan, which in the end he didn't take up, that he thought his luxury home was worth £500,000. But valuations are just that: they are estimates of the market value of land and property. Like most homeowners, he over-estimated the value, and it stretched the imagination to describe such behaviour as fraudulent. Bowley later testified that 'people do tend to, how shall I say, enhance figures sometimes but at the end of the day we would rely on our valuation'.[30] He went on to say that even when you have a formal valuation you have to make a judgement, adding that 'valuation tends to be a difficult scene. It can vary quite substantially'.[31] Gorvin, a director of the bank, admitted that you can 'run through until you find one you like'.[32] Davenport, too, when asked about one of the loan applications, made it clear that the bank relied on independent valuations and not on anything, which Taylor had told them.[33]

As well as over-valuing his house, the police also claimed that Taylor had deceived the bank in relation to the amount of shale on the Poynton site and hence over-valued the asset. McCann, who had been included in the conspiracy charge, had introduced Taylor to the vendor of the site. The police claimed that McCann had deliberately over-estimated the amount of shale which had then formed the basis of a valuation of the site for the bank by O'Hare Associates and he had deliberately withheld the Appleton report from them. But Appleton was not qualified to judge the amount of shale[34] and, in any event, the bank always relied upon its own independent expert valuations.

Stalker's invisibility

Throughout the criminal trial, the prosecution was silent on the connection between Taylor's prosecution and Stalker. The defence, however, took every opportunity to make the link. Early in the trial, Ferguson asked Davenport: 'Did you ever get the impression that Mr Taylor was being investigated as a means of getting at Stalker?' He replied, 'Yes, to discredit him.'[35] Later in the trial, Hood asked Ware:

HOOD: Is it your evidence that you were never part of the team dedicated to investigating Mr John Stalker, the then Deputy Chief Constable of the Greater Manchester Police Force?

WARE: That is so.

HOOD: You were never at any time in the course of your secondment to the Intelligence Unit so involved in inquiries dedicated to investigating Mr Stalker?

WARE: Dedicated to investigating Mr Stalker? No.

HOOD: Part of the inquiry team investigating Mr Stalker: would you say you were?

WARE: Again, No. Mr Stalker's name cropped up, as you are well aware.

HOOD: Was it ever any part of your duties to investigate Mr Stalker?

WARE: No.[36]

The following day, Justice Sachs became interested in exploring the Taylor/Stalker connection. After Ware claimed he could remember nothing about what was said during Topping's visit with him to the Co-operative Bank, Sachs asked Ware: 'Was Mr Stalker's name mentioned on that occasion?' Ware said he did not think it was.[37]

Hood was not going to let the issue drop. He asked Ware about a detailed entry in his pocketbook made on the day of the search of Taylor's house.

HOOD: Is it right to say that you have seen fit to note, for instance, at 9.35 a.m.: 'Conversation in hallway adjacent to big lounge and front door in the presence of Mr Murray. Mr Taylor: "We've had lots of parties here. On one occasion at least when John Stalker and Stella were here when they stayed until at least half-past three. I didn't get to bed until quarter-to-four. Search continued." Is that an accurate reading of your note?

WARE: Yes, it is.[38]

Hood asked him what possible relevance it had to his inquiries into the commercial activities of Taylor. Ware said it had none, but he thought the remarks were relevant.

HOOD: You see, Mr Ware, let me press you a little further. It was not just obvious in a roundabout sort of way that Mr Stalker was of interest to the DIU, it was plainly a part of their enquiries throughout, was it not?

WARE: From fairly early on since I joined the unit in April 1985 then the answer is yes, but what I don't want you to do is think perhaps that on my very first arrival at the DIU. someone said to me 'Forget the DIU, you are here to investigate Mr Stalker', because that simply wasn't the case.

HOOD: I did not suggest that Mr Ware.

WARE: I'm sorry.

HOOD: Regardless of that, using your common sense and putting two and two together, as a police officer it was obvious to you from a fairly early stage that it was?

WARE: It became obvious, yes.[39]

All the evidence suggests that the police witnesses were under strict instructions to keep the Stalker dimension firmly under wraps during the trial. Certainly, none of their notebooks referred to him. Ware made no mention of Stalker, for example, when he was dispatched to find out details of three social events (Chapter15) at which Stalker was in the company of Taylor: on 27 September 1985, Belfry Hotel, Wilmslow;[40] on 27 November 1985, Piccadilly Hotel, Manchester;[41] and on 28 April 1986, Belle Vue Greyhound Stadium.[42] When Bowley was taken to Bootle Street police station and interviewed for nine hours, he asked if 'it was something to do with John Stalker?'[43] Again, there is no mention of this comment in the interview notes. Even when a specific enquiry was solely related to Stalker, there was still no mention of his name. For example, when Stephenson and Ware from the DIU were tasked by the West Yorkshire Police – unprecedently for a supposedly independent inquiry into Stalker – to find out details of Stalker's account at the Britannia Building Society, Ware noted only: 'To Britannia Building Society, Cross Street, re current inquiry.'[44]

Later in the trial, Justice Sachs was obviously concerned that the DIU was, in fact, investigating Stalker and asked Ware:

J SACHS: Did you ever feel uncomfortable at all when you were taking part in this inquiry, Sergeant Ware?

WARE: Many times, sir.

J SACHS: Uncomfortable about what?

WARE: About the fact that the Deputy Chief Constable's name was involved, and then came the speculation in the newspapers about MI5, etcetera. That certainly made me uncomfortable.

J SACHS: Did you think you were being used in any way?

WARE: I think it is very fair to say, sir, at that time, no. Maybe now my view has changed somewhat.[45]

RUC officer's mysterious visit to GMP

On 26 March 1986, Ware's pocketbook noted: 'To Manchester Airport with senior officer from the RUC'.[46] Hood and Justice Sachs wanted to know more about the visit:

J SACHS: You do not come across that every day of the week, Mr. Ware. What was his name?

WARE: I didn't know his name, Sir, otherwise I would have recorded it. I think I said very early on I have no knowledge and I have had no involvement with matters involving the RUC. I think on this occasion this was a RUC officer who was visiting Chester House – to see whom, I do not know – and I was doing no more than returning that man to the Airport in order for him to return to Ireland.

HOOD: Mr. Ware, you are a detective sergeant. At that time, you were in fact attached to a small team dedicated to a particular task; you were engaged at that time in the most frenetic activity. You would not have been asked to act as a chauffeur unless that was CID business. I cannot put it to you that you would have known precisely what he was doing there, but you would not have been asked to do that unless he was there in relation to the DIU, would you?

WARE: I was asked on this occasion, I believe, because – when you brought it up today and this moment, I had no idea that that entry was in the book. It doesn't mean anything at all to me, and I believe and will state to you categorically that on this occasion that is exactly what was being asked of me – to be nothing more than a chauffeur and to return this man to the Airport. Who he was and whom he came to see, I don't know, and I can't answer you.

HOOD: These may be difficult matters to deal with. You do not ever get asked to act as a chauffeur, do you, on other occasions, for an officer who has got nothing to do with this enquiry?

WARE: Not that I remember, Sir, no.

HOOD: Let me put it to you again. This officer was plainly in Manchester for matters that concerned the DIU, and as an officer in the DIU you were asked to return him to the Airport, were you not?

WARE:	I'm sorry, I will state it again. I do not know who the officer was. I do not believe he was visiting the DIU – he was somewhere at headquarters.
HOOD:	Do you recollect this or not? Is this a memory lapse; something you say you remember in particular?
WARE:	I don't recollect it at all.
HOOD:	At all?
WARE:	At all.
HOOD:	So, you cannot state anything categorically, if that is right, can you?
WARE:	In that sense, no, but believe you me
HOOD:	Mr. Ware, why are you now wheeling out the big explanation, if your evidence is you cannot remember it at all?
WARE:	If I could remember this specifically and if I could remember the name of this officer – who he had been to visit – and if I was ever a party to what he came to visit for, then believe you me, standing here in the context of this trial, I would tell you, but I do not know.
HOOD:	I have not asked for a long speech. I have asked for an answer to my question. Do you want me to ask it again?
WARE:	Yes.
HOOD:	If your evidence is that you do not remember at all and you have refused on so many occasions to make a guess – 'I won't make a guess', you have told us – why have you given us this elaborate explanation about this particular incident?
WARE:	Because I consider it to be so insignificant inasmuch as I don't remember it at all, and yet at the same time I know full well that you again are trying to get back to the matter of the RUC and its involvement with Mr. Stalker etcetera. I am saying to you that I took no part in that and I want you to be absolutely 100 per cent certain about that, together with every other person in this Court, including yourself, Sir.[47]
J SACHS:	It does not matter what I think, Mr. Ware.

After a short adjournment, Hood returned to the issue. He asked Ware who gave him the instruction to go to the airport. He could not remember. Hood asked him how he knew that he was a senior officer as for security reasons he wouldn't be wearing a uniform. Ware thought that he had been told by either Topping or Born.[48] In the end, the court was no clearer about who the officer was, whom he met in GMP, or from where he was picked up, but Hood's cross-examination had firmly established yet again a link between Stalker's investigation in Northern Ireland and the investigation into Stalker and Taylor in Manchester.

Ruining Taylor

During the cross-examination of the police officers based on their police pocketbooks, evidence emerged which strongly suggested that the police were determined to frustrate the sale of Taylor's assets and prevent him releasing the sums that he had been loaned. The most egregious example occurred on 11

September 1986 when Caldwell and Knowles visited Mr George from Wimpey Homes Holding Ltd. – one of the largest house building firms in the Northeast and a potential purchaser of Poynton or Tottington. After providing a statement, George made a note of the meeting. It stated:

> They [Caldwell and Knowles] and other officers are preparing a case for the Director of Public Prosecutions to determine whether Taylor should be brought to trial. They regard this part of the enquiry as commercial fraud and are investigating Mr. Taylor on a question of drugs and also organised crime.[49]

George also noted that the two officers said that they were from Special Branch. Hood asked Caldwell how George could have known this. Caldwell admitted that Knowles may have said that he was from SB or seconded from SB. As SB deals with threats to national security, the police were clearly attempting to suggest that the investigation into Taylor was extremely serious. It further emerged that George was told that Taylor had committed a criminal offence in using the name of Wimpey Homes in trying to raise finance from the bank. They also mentioned that he had used the names of Manchester United Football Club and WH Smiths to suggest that they had also expressed an interest in the site. Hood put it Caldwell that this was calculated to destroy Taylor's reputation. Caldwell denied it.[50]

Officers from the DIU also made numerous visits to Taylor's property sites which he was attempting to sell. They were particularly interested in Pool House Farm at Poynton and went there on a least seven occasions to make enquiries, to observe the proposed tip and the movement of vehicles, and to see if there was any sign of recent workings. Similar visits, though less in number, were made to Taylor's property sites at Tottington and Trafford Wharf which included taking photographs.

There were similar visits to Taylor's family home – Wood Mill – first to ascertain if it was being sold, and then to find out if the Taylors had vacated the property. The police even made enquiries at Rains Estate Agents at Altrincham who were handling the sale and left with a brochure of the property.[51] On one occasion, Caldwell and Knowles obtained binoculars from Criminal Intelligence and observed 'Mrs Taylor leaving the house with a pile of folded towels and driving off'.[52] It is hard to imagine what this surveillance had to do with a fraud. It did, however, reflect a determination by the police to monitor Taylor's demise.

At the beginning of December 1986, members of the DIU visited Elliot Partnership – the landlords for Taylor's offices at 2 St Johns Street in Manchester – and then visited it twelve more times throughout 1987. In the criminal trial, Hood tried to ascertain the purpose of all the visits from both Caldwell and Knowles. Caldwell argued that the purpose was to find out what the current state of play was, and whether or not Taylor was going to leave the premises and if so where he was to be relocated.[53] Hood suggested to Knowles that the real purpose of the visits was to financially ruin Taylor and the police 'were digging up any dirt anywhere which might possibly be found'.[54] Knowles denied it.

It emerged that distress warrants had been issued on the premises for non-payment of rent which entitled the bailiffs to seize articles. Hood suggested that the police hoped to get hold of Taylor's computer and computer discs from the bailiffs. They could then have gained access illegally to the personal and private information stored on the computer. This was denied but there was evidence that Knowles had developed a close relationship with one of the bailiffs who had phoned him at his office and wished to provide information on Taylor. Hood suggested that he was acting as a police informer.[55]

It is hard to find a more wasteful use of police time than one in which police officers were observing possible development sites and making enquiries about whether or not a site has been sold, against the backdrop of increasing crime. None of this activity could have been relevant to the prosecution of a fraud but it would certainly have put off potential purchasers. Taylor's ruin was essential to achieve a successful prosecution. If he manged to sell all his property, as he anticipated, and repay his loans in full to the bank, it would be very difficult to persuade a jury that he had acted fraudulently.

Hood's car

On 5 January, after cross-examining Knowles, Hood drove home and parked, leaving the notes which he had prepared for questioning Knowles in the car. Within an hour of arriving home, his car was stolen and discovered the following morning burnt to a cinder some miles away.[56] Coincidently, it was just five days later that the Stevens' offices in Carrickfergus (Northern Ireland) suffered the same fate as Hood's car (Chapter 22). Taylor's defence team strongly believed that this was an attempt to sabotage Taylor's defence and to intimidate Hood at the very moment that the case against Taylor and the co-defendants was starting to fall apart.

The possibility that the destruction of Hood's car was arranged by the police cannot be ruled out. There had been previous examples of GMP acting beyond the law. In 1984, there was strong evidence that GMP arranged the burglaries of Steven Shaw's and Sarah Hollis' flats following their complaints about police tactics during the visit of Leon Brittan, the Home Secretary (Chapter 6). In February 1986, just before the granting of access orders, the offices of Rangelark, one of Taylor's firm, was burgled.[57] Hood suggested to Stephenson that it was to obtain material to substantiate the application for the access orders.[58] He denied it. Taylor, and subsequently Stalker's solicitors, believed that their phones were subject to some form of illegal electronic surveillance (Chapter 16).[59] The stakes were high and police deviance cannot be ruled out.

Contempt of court and other woes

When Stephenson took the stand on 15 January 1990, Hood wanted to know where the valuations concerning land at Poynton, Tottington and Trafford Park had been obtained. The details had been included in the application for access orders. There were two possibilities: the burglary of Taylor's offices in February 1985 or the Co-operative Bank. Hood suggested that they must have come from the latter. Stephenson denied it and gave a series of contradictory answers. First, he said that they came from an informer whom he was not prepared to name. Then he suggested four other possibilities: the DIU, Thomas Holt of Peter O'Hare Associates, the Land Registry, or Ware. The Judge intervened with the sarcastic remark that they might have been put in a dustbin or somewhere.[60]

The following day began with Stephenson admitting that he had spoken with Ware overnight, breaking the cardinal rule that a witness should not discuss their evidence with anyone. Stephenson was obviously desperate to find an answer to where the three valuations had come from. The court adjourned for an hour to discuss what should happen next. Ware was recalled and the Judge informed him that his conduct was 'purely unacceptable'. Ware responded weakly: 'I can only apologise, Sir'.[61] It was a contempt of court.

The jury returned and Hood continued his cross-examination of Stephenson. In one of his statements to the West Yorkshire police, Ware had referred to 'information sheets' which were compiled by members of the DIU after making a specific enquiry. They were placed in four or five-drawer metal filing cabinets in the DIU. Hood wanted to know from Stephenson what had happened to them following the disbandment of the DIU. Stephenson replied, 'They've gone'. He admitted that they 'had been destroyed'.[62] He tried to rescue things and suggested that only the interview notes with witnesses were destroyed on completion of the statements. This had been necessary because they had a problem with storage and security. Justice Sachs was surprised and asked if it was normal practice. Stephenson admitted that it was 'abnormal practice'.[63]

Hood then focused on the detail in Stephenson's application for access orders to Taylor's bank accounts. He began by asking where the figure for the loan facilities of £345,000 had come from.[64] Stephenson denied that it had come from the Co-operative Bank and said that he could not now recall but since the committal proceedings he had, along with all the other officers in the DIU, been trying to recall the source of the figure. The Judge asked him if he did not 'find that absolutely staggering'.[65] Hood pointed out that the information about the loan was only partially true. Stephenson admitted that he now knew that, but he had only found out after he had obtained the access orders.

Hood asked about the source of the information concerning the solicitors who dealt with the loan. Stephenson suggested that it came from Sheppard. Hood pointed out that earlier he had denied that he had received any information from the bank and added sarcastically, that it was a further advance. When asked why he had not offered this information earlier, Stephenson claimed that he had forgotten.[66] Hood then asked him for the source of the information concerning the increase in the loan facilities from £345,000 to £771,500, suggesting again that it could only have come from the bank. Initially, Stephenson said he didn't recall, but then suggested it was the Land Registry and finally he said that it was general knowledge in the DIU.[67]

Hood further questioned Stephenson on his claim that if the Co-operative Bank had been made aware of the situation at the time Rangelark made their application for loan facilities, the loan facilities would have been rejected. Hood said that it was a presumption and not a fact and it left a misleading impression. Stephenson disagreed.[68] At one point, Stephenson said that the DIU thought Taylor may have been laundering money.

Hood pounced. 'Was there not a fundamental contradiction between laundering money and borrowing money?'[69] 'Could there be any fact further away from laundering money but being indebted at over £1 million?', Hood asked.[70] Stephenson admitted that was true, but he didn't know the level of indebtedness at the start of the investigation.

Collapse of the trial

The following day, 17 January, things went from bad to worse for the prosecution. The day began with Hood confirming Stephenson's evidence that the inquiry was at a dead end when he was appointed to the inquiry. It could not proceed unless it was able to enquire into the financial dealings of Taylor and his companies. Stephenson admitted that was correct. Justice Sachs then asked:

J SACHS: You agree, there is no doubt that without those access orders this inquiry could not have proceeded and would have died a death.
OFFICER: It would not have got off the ground, your Honour.[71]

A little later in the proceedings Stephenson announced that he had brought along his records in relation to the land at Poynton and Tottington, but before he could add Trafford Park, Hood interjected. He demanded, 'Where are they?'

Stephenson responded: 'Here'. The Judge asked what was going to happen if 'this had not emerged rather accidently?'[72] Stephenson replied that he was going to produce them in view of the Judge's direction of yesterday. On further questioning, he confirmed that there were certain 'files' in the DIU. Hood pointed out that over the last two days of questioning he had not mentioned 'files' but referred to general knowledge. Were the files still in existence? Stephenson said that they should be. The Judge intervened again:

J SACHS: Just so that I understand this, Mr Stephenson, these files that you say should still be in existence, do they contain the information sheets and the general knowledge of which we have heard reference so often?

OFFICER: They should do, your Honour, yes.

HOOD: Why on earth did you not tell us that they may well still be in existence?

OFFICER: Because I can't find them. I have asked this. This has been a problem for some considerable time. I have been trying to determine the source of the information to his committal.

HOOD: You have just said that they may be with the drugs people, did you not?

OFFICER: Yes, but we have looked round everywhere for this original information. I have asked every member of staff and they are not available.

HOOD: You are a very experienced officer, Mr Stephenson. Documents in connection with a case are certainly maintained by the police until at least the case is concluded. Is that right?

OFFICER: The papers that I have obtained, yes.

HOOD: Have you never in your experience encountered a situation like this?

OFFICER: No, it was a unique situation.

J SACHS: I find it quite extraordinary. It does not matter what I think but that is what I say. Mr Corkery, it does occur to me that some officer should be called from this unit at some stage, either by you or possibly by me, if you can identify him, so he can try and assist us on this matter.

CORKERY: Certainly, your Honour, I agree entirely.

J SACHS: I am very concerned, Mr Hood.[73]

After an adjournment, Corkery arranged for Born, Murray, Waterworth and Richardson to be interviewed by Mr Worthington from the DPP's office. It was a humiliation and an embarrassment for officers who had worked in the DIU. Born was first up and denied knowing where the relevant files were now, as he was no longer in charge. He passed the buck to Stephenson and said that he thought that any relevant material would have been taken by Stephenson as he oversaw the fraud investigation. He denied knowing anything about the papers having been burnt, which one witness had suggested, or having been asked by Stephenson about the whereabouts of the key documents.[74] The maladministration of police documentation, which Justice Caulfield, had heavily criticised in the prosecution of Kirwin, under the supervision of Topping, was happening once again (Chapter 6).

The next day, 18 January, the proceedings began with legal arguments over Hood's request to see Born's notebooks. The police, however, were not going to throw in the towel too easily. They objected to the notebooks being made public on the grounds that they covered current serious crime investigations and that they related to informers. It was subsequently agreed that these parts should be stapled together so that the content could not be read. Born was then recalled and questioned further about the missing files. He was followed by Richardson, Murray and Waterworth. They all denied knowing anything about the present whereabouts of the files or if any of them had been destroyed. None of Stephenson's colleagues in the DIU were prepared to help him in his predicament. Hood suggested to him that he was 'left holding the baby'. He agreed.[75]

Stephenson knew the source of the information that he used to obtain access orders. He had prepared and signed, but not dated, a report of one of his visits to the Co-operative Bank before obtaining the access orders, which noted details of both the Rangelark and Propwise accounts, and Taylor's loan facilities.[76] Access orders were needed to regularise the situation. All the denials by the police – that the bank had not supplied them with information – were attempts to cover up the fact that the bank had indeed provided the police with confidential information. The use of the description 'information sheets' for what were substantive reports was a smokescreen. If it was admitted that the bank had in fact provided the information prior to the access orders, the trial would have been terminated as the evidence was obtained illegally. As it was, the trial collapsed anyway.

Throughout the rest of the morning, Hood questioned Stephenson on the access orders. He took him through the details concerning the sealed envelope and asked him about his statement to the Recorder. He then moved onto to the various letters written by Robson, Taylor's solicitor, offering Taylor for interview. Hood asked about the role of Simons and suggested that he was part of the investigation. Stephenson claimed that Simons was never an active part of the DIU.[77] It was put to Stephenson that the statement: 'In these circumstances there is no likelihood of Taylor authorising the financial institutions to make disclosures concerning his business dealings to the police', was untrue.[78] Stephenson denied it. Hood then made a dramatic intervention:

> In the light of that answer and numerous other officers' replies about this particular document and this particular application, I would seek to raise a matter of law with the court, I hope it would not be wholly inconvenient to do it now.[79]

At this point, the Judge gave the jury an early lunch and Hood made a key submission to the court.

In my submission – I hope properly I can put very straightforwardly – that, in the light of the evidence of Mr Stephenson and others, plus the explanation for access orders and sworn information, that materially misled his Lordship, Judge Prestt. It was done at a time when the inquiry had reached a dead end and, your Honour, at a period without any further evidence. In the light of that, in my submission, if the Recorder had been given truthful information – in accordance with that sworn information – he would never have granted the order. He has been misled. In my submission, that renders all the evidence, subsequently obtained, inadmissible. In my submission, any court having now heard the facts would never have allowed the material improperly obtained to go before a jury if they had known of them. I put it shortly and I know my learned friends follow me.[80]

The Judge then adjourned the proceedings. Corkery took the opportunity to consult and seek advice from the DPP over the difficulties which the prosecution was facing. The court returned two hours and 20 minutes later. Corkery began by saying that it was the duty of counsel always to 'grasp the metal and take a firm view' and if there is a view to be taken, to take it. He went on to say that he was concerned about a fair trial for all defendants and from the point of view of the public. He then announced:

I have taken the view that, in the circumstances of this case, it would not be proper that the prosecution should seek an adverse verdict, at the hands of the jury, against these four defendants.[81]

The jury returned and Corkery repeated his view that it would not be appropriate to ask it to bring a verdict adverse to any of the defendants in this case. The clerk of the Court read out each of the charges in turn and the Foreman announced 'not guilty'.

The collapse of the criminal trial was a disaster and an embarrassment for both the prosecution and GMP. The police had used every tactic to construct a case against Taylor and to secure a conviction: they harassed witnesses; they withheld key documents in the production of witness statements; they failed to follow the correct procedures in the use of exhibit labels; they gave expert witnesses restrictive terms of reference; they misrepresented the information in the key valuation reports; documents were lost or destroyed; and they told lies. Someone, Taylor's defence team believed, was instructed to torch Hood's car at the very moment the prosecution case was beginning to unravel.

Stephenson's misrepresentations and omissions in the access orders application, his failure to reveal the source of key information, and his contempt of court in speaking to a colleague while still giving evidence, all ran counter to his reputation for professionalism and integrity. On joining the DIU as a fraud officer, Stephenson would no doubt have been briefed that it was strongly suspected that Taylor engaged in drug smuggling and was laundering money for the QSG. As a Commercial Fraud Squad officer, he would not have interrogated the information about drugs or the QSG but would have accepted the dominant view of the DIU team that Taylor was a major criminal. Yet, when the bank informed him, after an internal review, that it still did not believe that Taylor had committed fraud against it and that their loans to him were secure, Stephenson, inexplicably, remained convinced of Taylor's criminality.

The collapse of the trial raised again the spectre that there had been a conspiracy to remove Stalker, but both the Cabinet Office and Home Office denied it. The Home Office insisted that the decision to suspend Stalker was an operational decision of the Chief Constable of Greater Manchester following consultations with the Inspector of Constabulary. It was acknowledged that the senior police officers involved in the decision discussed the issue with civil servants because of the implications of Stalker's suspension. But as Richard Norton-Taylor commented: 'Almost certainly, civil servants in this case were involved in a damage limitation exercise. But the precise role of these officials in the Taylor/Stalker affair is still far from clear.'[82]

In April 1990, *Pawn in the Game*, produced by Rob McLoughlin, was broadcast. It began by asserting that the Taylor/Stalker affair was 'the biggest scandal in post-war Britain'.[83] It sympathetically charted Taylor's path from poverty to riches and then back to poverty as a direct result of the police investigation. It revealed that seven months before Stalker was removed from his Northern Ireland inquiry, the police knew that there was no evidence to link Taylor to any criminal activity. The fraud case against him was a connivance and Taylor was a pawn in a far bigger game.

Six weeks later, the BBC broadcast Peter Taylor's Public Eye programme (Chapter 1). This took a very different position. The programme argued that Kevin Taylor's acquittal 'does not prove that he was a victim of the conspiracy'.[84] On the contrary, there was ample evidence that needed to be investigated. Towards the end of the programme, Peter Taylor interviewed Sir Thomas Hetherington, who was Director of Public Prosecutions at the time. He explained that the reason why it took so long to charge Taylor had nothing to do with the police desperately trying to dig up any evidence they could, but because they were having difficulty in finding the evidence which would satisfy the DPP. Hetherington confirmed that in the end they did find evidence that satisfied the officers who were dealing with the case in his department. They would not have gone ahead with it if there was not a realistic prospect of a conviction. In other words, notwithstanding that the drugs investigation had reached a dead end and the bank had made no complaint, there was nothing untoward in prosecuting Taylor for fraud.

The Rothwell inquiry

A month after Peter Taylor's Public Eye programme – on 19 July – the PCA announced the setting-up of an independent police inquiry, under Chief Superintendent Geoff Rothwell of Merseyside Police, to investigate the evidence given by both Stephenson and Ware, and the other officers at the criminal trial.[85] As revealed during the civil action, there had been a complete disregard in the investigation of Taylor and Stalker of the rules relating to the collection and storing of information and intelligence. Numerous reports were unsigned or undated and key documents were missing. The tape recording of the five Burton interviews, in which he was clearly being prompted, broke all procedures for the taping of interviews and one tape had disappeared. The single most obvious example of malpractice was the report of the golf conversation which contained errors proving beyond doubt that it was not an accurate copy of the original, and had been beefed up to make the information look more serious.

Yet there is nothing in the public domain which suggests that this caused Rothwell to recommend that any of the police officers face disciplinary charges. Several had retired and could not now be disciplined, but others were still in service. Moreover, given that there was a very strong probability that some of the documents were fabricated retrospectively, were any of the senior officers interviewed under caution? There is again nothing in the public domain which suggests that Rothwell recommended that any of the officers should face *criminal* charges. All this contrasts sharply with the disciplining of their Deputy Chief Constable four years earlier, based on nothing more than rumour and innuendo. As with the published Sampson report on Stalker, this was clearly another perfunctory police investigation which was not prepared to add to the opprobrium of GMP.

* * *

Any objective reader of the thousands of pages of transcript of the Taylor trial would be shocked at the incredible lengths to which the police went to find incriminating evidence against Taylor. The trial lasted seventy-three days and a mass of documentation was presented throughout the proceedings. In total, over 20 police officers were dedicated to investigating him. They pursued numerous lines of inquiry: his alleged membership of the QSG and drug smuggling; his commercial and financial affairs; his gambling activities and his social life. They visited banks, building societies, inland revenue, land registries, casinos and social venues, and they tracked down and interviewed people whom he had fallen out with over the years. The cost of the investigation appeared to have no bounds. And it all came to nothing.

The official narrative of the Taylor/Stalker affair was now in tatters. Both the Sampson report and the Panorama programme of August 1986 had suggested that Stalker was removed because of his associations with known criminals stemming from his friendship with Taylor. But all the evidence shows beyond a shadow of doubt that Taylor was investigated intensely as a means of getting at Stalker and the investigation began in all probability, not in June 1984, but either in winter 1984 or shortly after Stalker had submitted his interim report. Despite their enormous efforts and deviant behaviour, GMP could not construct a successful criminal case against Taylor. The evidence mounts that there was, indeed, a conspiracy to remove Stalker.

Chapter 24

Civil Action

AFTER THE CRIMINAL TRIAL collapsed, Kevin Taylor decided to start civil proceedings against GMP for malicious prosecution, offences of misfeasance, unlawful acts, and a claim for damages. On 16 May 1995, Taylor's counsel, Roger Farley QC, began his opening address. Taylor, once a wealthy businessman, but now bankrupt and dependent on legal aid, was challenging the second largest police force in the country, which was covered by insurance and rumoured to have over 20 lawyers working on defending the action. Unusually, the civil action was heavily reliant on documents disclosed by the defendants, GMP. Moreover, in the background was another far more powerful state body – the Treasury Solicitor Department.[1] This is a non-ministerial government department supplying legal services and, in this case, was responsible for representing Sir Patrick Mayhew in determining what could or could not enter the public domain on grounds of national security. Mayhew was now SoS for Northern Ireland.

Discovery

A civil action begins with the plaintiff pleading their case in writing, to which the defendant responds. When a set of pleaded facts are considered inaccurate or vague, requests can be made for further and better particulars. As a defendant, the technique is to make it as difficult as possible for the opposition to know what you have. Thus, lists are initially drawn up under vague headings, such as 'various police documents', perhaps hiding a vital document which could be of considerable benefit to the plaintiff. The other side will then come back and ask for further and better particulars. The rules in existence in 1995 – they were later radically changed following the recommendations of Lord Woolf – provided ample opportunity for lawyers to find ways to conceal and manipulate information.[2]

    In this case, it was far from a level playing field, as most of the important documents Taylor needed in order to prove his case were held by GMP. The latter took full advantage of their position to control the information needed by the plaintiff. They objected to the production of a wide range of documents covering nearly 20 different categories. They also flooded the plaintiff's lawyers with a tsunami of more than 110,000 documents,[3] a proportion of which were produced at the very last moment, no doubt with the aim of preventing the plaintiff from having sufficient time to go through and make sense of them. Most of the documentation was a product of everyday police activity covering many years. Its relevance to the case was often impossible to fathom, but it tied down Taylor's lawyers. The photocopying costs alone of producing several sets of all the documents must have been considerable.

Taylor was at another disadvantage. Anderton had access to a large team of lawyers to prepare his defence. All the statements would have been carefully constructed to support GMP's narrative of what had occurred and any inconsistency or contradiction changed. They would not, therefore, have been the officers' own statements written in their own words, but corporate statements on behalf of GMP containing identical descriptions for incidents in which two or more officers were involved.

An unprecedented example of the development of an official police narrative occurred a few years earlier following the Hillsborough disaster on 15 April 1989, in which 96 men, women and children were killed. Police officers on duty that day were instructed to note their recollections of the events on plain A4 sheets. As discovered by Professor Phil Scraton, these were then systematically edited and turned into statements by a team of solicitors acting for the South Yorkshire police. There was nothing illegal about this process and subsequent investigators and the DPP were aware of what had occurred.[4] In Taylor's civil action, a similar process occurred. All statements were prepared by Anderton's defence team and were, no doubt, checked for inconsistencies and contradictions – a very different process from a statements produced by criminal suspects.

An embarrassing liaison

During the preparation of their defence against Taylor's civil action, Anderton's lawyers discovered that Norman Born, head of the DIU which secretly investigated Taylor and Stalker, was in a relationship with Elizabeth McDonald – the girlfriend of police informer David Burton at the time of his death in prison. He had been GMP's key informant in the Taylor/Stalker affair and had provided extensive information to the DIU about the QSG, including saying that Stalker was corrupt. It was clearly embarrassing for GMP to discover that the officer who headed up the unit investigating Taylor and Stalker was in a relationship with someone who had previously been associated with Burton, a life-long criminal. Even more so, as the charge against Stalker was that his friend, Taylor, was alleged to be associated with criminals in the QSG. Crucially, the relationship could have influenced Born's objectivity and impartiality in assessing the intelligence provided by Burton on Taylor and Stalker. These issues, however, did not prevent Topping from subsequently appointing Born head of GMP SB.

The information emerged during a five-hour meeting in September 1993 held at GMP's headquarters. This was attended by Anderton's lawyers and eight key officers involved in the investigation of Taylor and Stalker. A barrister asked: 'Is there anyone in this room who has a liaison with a woman with links to a criminal?'[5] Born admitted that he had a relationship, but claimed it was a private matter. He added that the relationship had started after Burton's death. The meeting also discussed the loss of thousands of documents which the police had planned to use in the civil action. It erupted in anger when a barrister asked about the lost files. A senior CID officer accused the lawyer of treating the officers worse than 'criminals'.[6]

Following the meeting, the new Chief Constable of GMP, David Wilmott (who replaced Anderton in 1991) issued a statement.

> During the preparation of the defence of the civil action brought against GMP by Mr Kevin Taylor and others, matters came to light which require further investigation. Because of the history and degree of public interest in this case, the chief constable has invited Chief Supt Chris Smethurst to conduct the investigation for him.[7]

This was the fourth police inquiry set in train by allegations originating from Burton, the Walter Mitty police informer, twelve years earlier.[8]

An application or a jury trial

Early in the civil action, Taylor made an application for the case to be heard before a jury.[9] In making his ruling on this, Justice Owen said that it was inevitable that the case would necessarily involve the examination of documents and accounts of a substantial nature. But in refusing a jury trial, he relied principally on four factors raised in a previous case by Lord Justice Stewart-Smith:[10] the physical problem of a jury handling large bundles of documents, the prolongation of the trial, the added expense, and the risk that a jury might not sufficiently understand the issues. He was particularly concerned about the cost arising from the prolongation of the trial and the need to make copies of the documents for the jurors. He pointed out that both parties were, to a certain extent, being paid out of the public purse. Although there was insurance pertaining to the defendants, the Legal Aid fund was hard pressed enough.[11] He therefore refused to grant a trial by jury.

National Security

It was almost inevitable, given the secrecy of the modern British state,[12] that Public Interest Immunity Certificates (PIICs) would be deployed. These allow a litigant in a civil action to refuse to disclose evidence to the other side on the grounds that it would be damaging to the public interest. On 9 May 1995, just before the trial got under way, Mr Burnett, acting on behalf of the SoS for Northern Ireland, warned that Stalker's evidence could jeopardise the peace process and applied to the Judge to issue a PIIC on part of his evidence. He said:

> It remains very much in the public interest that all terrorist violence be permanently ended and that nothing should be done which would prejudice or impede the efforts of Her Majesty's Government to that end or which would be of assistance to terrorists now or in the future.[13]

As Lashmar pointed out, it was a 'stunning assertion', given that Stalker was suspended nine years previously and had had no contact with MI5 since then. He went on to suggest that: 'The immunity is clearly in the government's rather than the public interest.'[14] The Judge adjourned the proceedings so that he could read the 27-page application. Taylor remarked that he had been waiting four years for the case to come to court with so many setbacks, 'and now we have another one'.[15] Farley, Taylor's barrister, told the court that it was their case that Taylor was a victim of a high-level conspiracy to destroy him. He went on:

> This late intervention by the government can only serve to confirm in his mind that those forces that were then arrayed against him are closing ranks once more to prevent the light of truth shining through.[16]

Two days later, Justice Owen returned to court and gave his ruling. He accepted that part of Stalker's evidence should be suppressed on the grounds of national security but was unhappy with the secrecy. He was also highly critical of the PIIC certificate being presented at the very last minute, as a further delay to the trial was expensive and wasteful. It was also 'unfair to the court and to the cause of justice'.[17] He suggested that if he had had more time to investigate matters, his decision could have been different, and he was very unhappy about the way his hands were tied by earlier judgments in a way that allowed critics to point to 'an attitude which may seem supine and not providing that check on executive power which the courts should provide'.[18] He went on to say that he found it difficult to understand how Stalker's evidence, much of which was already published in his book, could damage national security.[19] But he had no power to reject the contents of the PIIC. His remarks were widely reported.[20]

Later in the trial, Justice Owen remarked that: 'Secrecy is a kind of British disease. It very rarely does any good but we all in our various jobs have to deal with it.'[21] On another occasion, he emphasised that he was not in favour of the secrecy demanded of the law currently. He regarded it as being of 'no functional value to anybody' but he had to accept it.[22] He conceded, however, that on occasions secrecy was necessary, but as an impartial tribunal in performing the required balancing act, he had come down in favour of Taylor when there was an issue on the extent of the PIIC.[23]

Taylor's team were extremely unhappy with the PIIC. Farley pointed out that it was no easy task to do as the Judge ordered in his judgment on the PIIC and there were broader implications. For example, any re-written general matter would then have an impact on the plaintiff's witness statements. At this point, the Treasury Solicitor, Burnett, intervened and made several points in relation to the Judge's ruling, basically emphasising that his hands too were tied. Farley took his comments to mean that there was nothing up for negotiation. The Judge concurred. To give the plaintiff time to go over his ruling and to recast Stalker's statement, the Judge agreed that the proceedings should be delayed for a few days.[24] He made it clear that if a witness was to give his evidence in chief by way of a statement, then the statement must be available to the public.[25]

Further issues

Before the trial got under way, Tabachnik, Anderton's counsel, complained about the order in which witnesses were to be called by the plaintiff. Back in April, he had expected Taylor to be the first witness, but had recently discovered that it would be Stalker.[26] He raised a series of arguments. First, as Stalker would cover extensive matters, they would require more time to pull out the relevant documents which would form the basis of their cross-examination. Justice Owen was having none of it. He pointed out that Tabachnik had behind him two lawyers who had done nothing else for two years and must know where everything was. That was the point of having specialist advocates. Tabachnik then argued that there were over 110,000 documents, to which Owen retorted, that was a problem of the modern world. Tabachnik suggested that there were wider implications as they must explore, with other witnesses, financial matters that needed to be explored first with Taylor. If they didn't, the costs of the trial would increase. Finally, he argued that Taylor would see the evidence that other witnesses were giving and would be primed and at an advantage. Owen was totally unsympathetic to this argument too, and pointed out that there would be very little overlap between the evidence of other witnesses and Stalker's evidence, which would focus upon 'the conspiracy', before correcting himself and saying 'the alleged conspiracy'.[27]

On Tuesday 16 May, the proceedings opened with further discussion of the impact of the PIIC. Farley admitted that some concessions had been made but argued that they were not enough. While the public purse was a consideration, they had a duty to their client to present his case in the best possible light. The Treasury Solicitor then complained that they had received Stalker's recast statement and it had virtually ignored Justice Owen's ruling and was unsuitable. He politely suggested that 'a misunderstanding may have crept into the thinking of my learned friends', and they had failed to understand that there was no negotiation.[28] Justice Owen expressed his exasperation and said he was not going to have any more of 'this nonsense' and told them that he would sit late to decide about the statement, but to 'get on with the case'.[29]

In a case of malicious prosecution, the plaintiff must prove that the defendant intentionally and maliciously instituted or pursued an investigation without any probable cause. To rebut the charge, GMP argued that it had sufficient information to believe that there was a corrupt relationship between criminals and the police which required investigation. In particular, the defence argued that the police were acting honestly and genuinely in believing that Taylor was involved in drug smuggling.

Farley's opening

Farley then began outlining the plaintiff's case which was delivered over two days and composed of more than 50,000 words. It was a powerful case which argued that Stalker's investigation in Northern Ireland was the root cause of Taylor's troubles. Stalker was making findings which were highly critical of the RUC and a way had to be found to remove him. The method adopted was his friendship with Taylor. It was alleged that Taylor had criminal connections and was suspected of being involved in crime.[30] Farley pointed out that Hermon, the Chief Constable of the RUC, was opposed to the inquiry from the start and numerous difficulties were placed in its way.[31] The discovery of the hayshed tape was central and 'the order of events was crucial'.[32] Farley argued that the establishment of the DIU was manipulated by Topping.

While lower ranks may have thought the DIU was investigating the QSG, Topping and his superiors knew that the central focus was on the Taylor/Stalker relationship. The codename Febb, to refer to Stalker, and Topping's letter dated 9 March 1985, which reported on the relationship between Taylor and Stalker, left no room for doubt. Farley argued that Anderton was obsessed with the position of his Deputy. The note he wrote to himself following the luncheon at Manchester City Football club on 16 May 1985 was proof. Farley drew attention to the important phrase: 'There could well be an IRA dimension'. Farley asked: 'Could that ever have been a serious suggestion?'[33] Farley submitted that it ultimately was used to engineer Stalker's removal from the Northern Ireland inquiry.

Farley described the discovery of the Amex transaction for the purchase of two airline tickets for Taylor and Stalker's holiday in Miami 1981, on 25 September 1985 – coincidently, the same day the sixteen-week surveillance operation on Taylor, under the codename operation Kaluki, began. The discovery caused Anderton to write two notes to himself. In the first he described the information as 'disturbing' and in the second as 'damaging to Febb' (Chapter 14). Farley pointed out that Anderton failed to consider the possibility that Stalker had paid his share. He also emphasised that the discovery could not have been the reason for the operation Kaluki as this would have been prepared weeks in advance. The trigger for the operation, Farley submitted, was the delivery of Stalker's Northern Ireland interim report.

On the same day as the discovery of the transaction for the airline tickets and the start of operation Kaluki, the DIU was asked to prepare a report for the Chief Constable. Farley submitted that the report showed how the enquiries had been conducted. He argued that:

> Any connection proven or otherwise to any offence proven or otherwise by any of his associates, or associates of associates, or in case an associate of an associate of an associate is not regarded as being too trivial to include in a report that is intended, we say to do very serious harm to a man on which there is no or no substantial evidence of any wrongdoing whatsoever. No evidence at all.[34]

He further argued that the intensification of the inquiry was from then on connected with the submission of Stalker's Northern Ireland interim report.

The political nature of the investigation became even clearer in the summer of 1986. Farley described the huge pressure that was brought to bear on the DPP. The message, he argued, was clear: Get Taylor. 'I don't care how you do it but get him.'[35] He pointed out that the message must have been intolerable for the investigating officers and would explain why Stephenson suppressed evidence and committed perjury at the trial. Moreover, it would explain the quite phenomenal lengths to which the police went to obtain evidence. In desperation, following the huge criticism of Stalker's removal, GMP leaked pieces of information to the press to try to stem the adverse publicity and in so doing, Farley submitted, was in contempt of court. He ended with a summary of the broad propositions of their case.

Following an opening address, Farley introduced a chronology of events which he hoped would be a useful management tool. It was divided into three columns: one for the date, another for 'Taylor' and a third for 'Stalker'. He pointed out that it was not always easy to see how one event relating to Taylor impacted on Stalker and *vice versa*, but he hoped this would help to keep things in chronological order. A similar chronology from this research has been constructed and is presented in the Appendix.

After Farley's opening statement, there was a brief adjournment during which his team considered a supplemental list of over 2,000 documents which had been served on his instructing solicitors after the close of business the night before by Anderton's solicitors. Among other things, the list included a response by the RUC to Stalker's book. In the absence of any explanation, Farley suspected that the disclosure of the documents was a tactic designed to prevent him calling Stalker first, because the contents of the documents would have to be considered by the Treasury Solicitor's Office. He asked for another short adjournment.[36]

In the afternoon, this proved to be the case and national security and secrecy once again became an issue. Another representative of the Treasury Solicitor's office, Mr Morton, pointed out that none of the new disclosures had been considered by the SoS with a view to determining if there were any national security considerations or whether any PIICs were applicable.[37] The two counsels agreed not to refer to the documents until they had been checked by the Treasury Solicitor in order that the proceedings could begin.

Stalker's evidence

On 17 May 1995, eleven years after Stalker had been asked to investigate police conduct over the killings in Northern Ireland, he took the stand in the civil action. He was examined for thirteen days. Farley took him through his career, his problems in Northern Ireland, hostility from senior ranks in the RUC and several other topics. He was then cross-examined by Tabachnik. At times, it was difficult to see the relevance of the information examined and Justice Owen was of the same opinion and, on several occasions, asked for clarification.[38]

Stalker was an excellent witness. His sharp intellect and his knowledge and experience of policing often left the defence barristers' assumptions and arguments in tatters. He drew attention to the numerous documents which were unsigned or undated, contrary to basic policing procedure. He constantly made a distinction between information and intelligence, and the need for intelligence to be supported by accompanying evidence, which in this investigation was sorely lacking. He pointed out that so much of the information appeared to come from the same source – David Burton – while it is accredited as coming from many different sources. He would have liked to have had the opportunity as a police officer to evaluate it all because it did not seem to be very valuable.

Anderton's defence counsel, Mr Tabachnik, tried unsuccessfully to illicit from Stalker several different dates as to when Stalker considered the conspiracy against him began. He started by getting Stalker to agree with the official line that there was an interest in him in June 1984 when there was nothing in his inquiry in Northern Ireland which would have attracted any concern before February 1985. The cross-examination continued:

TABACHNIK: Mr. Stalker would you accept that from the middle of '84 onward there was in fact a continuing interest in you.

STALKER: Would I accept that that's the case?

TABACHNIK: Yes.

STALKER: I would be very surprised if it wasn't given the type of investigation I was conducting in Northern Ireland.

TABACHNIK: There's nothing in Northern Ireland that could conceivably attracted any interest or concern before February '85 is there?

STALKER: Yes, of course there was. It was a constant escalation of the stakes as it were from the beginning of the investigation to the end. I briefed and kept informed, by copy memorandum and copy letters to the Chief Constable, the state that my enquiry had reached. H.M.I. Sir Philip Myers was also aware. What I'm saying is Burton became important at a very significant time of my investigation.

TABACHNIK: When do you say that this conspiracy against you had actually began?

STALKER: I said before, I do not say that there was a group of men in a smoke filled room. It was a developing picture over a period of months for a number of people including, particularly, the Inspector of Constabulary Sir Philip Myers. He realised his position was in very, very serious jeopardy. I can't say what the part Mr. Anderton played but he must have played some.

TABACHNIK: Mr. Stalker we're talking about February '85, months before your report delivered in September '85.

STALKER: In September '85, I'd completed 90 percent of that investigation and all parties at very senior levels both in government and police levels knew of what I was doing and where I got to. All that was needed for the next few months was to try to get hold of the tape. It was about 10 percent or less of the investigation. Even without the tape, it was extremely damning of RUC and the Inspectorate.

TABACHNIK: Mr. Stalker are you then saying that in fact the events of February are the first or an opening chapter in the moves to get rid of you?

STALKER: Yes. It seems to me that given papers that I have before me. There was a bit of information, which apparently was regarded as not very important in July '84, then suddenly in February '85 Burton was put under the microscope for a very long time. It was unprecedented that two experienced Detective Inspectors should spend so long with a tape recorder. We've seen the transcript today – they fill half a Court Room. It seems to me that they were far, far more than just interviews with a possible informant – a discredited one in many ways so I understand.[39]

Earlier in his evidence Stalker had claimed that the political decision to remove him was not taken until early in 1986. Tabachnik wanted to know how this fitted in with his previous insistence that the conspiracy started in February 1985.

TABACHNIK: Mr. Stalker, what you have told us is the decision to remove you was essentially a political decision made at highest level, you told us in March/April '86.

STALKER: Yes.

TABACHNIK: How do the events in '85 begin to fit into that pattern of a political decision made at the highest level, something like a year before you gave as the date when the decision was made?

STALKER: You will recall sir that I said that no politician can remove a police officer from an investigation: that has to be done by another police officer. What I'm saying is that February '85 was the beginning of the process. It was not by any means the complete process but at that time, for the very first time, really senior people including Mr. Anderton, the Chief Constable, and Inspector of Constabulary, Sir Philip Myers, knew what was going to be in that final report, which was extremely damning and extremely damaging to a number of people both in and out of the police force. I believe that that was the beginning of a process which reached its pinnacle, its finale, 12 months later.[40]

The clear implication from Stalker's response is that, as he could only be removed by another police officer, he considered Anderton and Myers to be part of the conspiracy conducted at the highest level of government. Tabachnik tried to suggest that Stalker was 'seeing demons' and that the Burton interviews were simply a continuation of a process of interviews begun in the summer of 1984. Stalker disagreed: on the contrary, the interviews were part a greater process, which eventually led to his removal from the investigation.

Later in his evidence, Stalker suggested that Anderton's desire for a knighthood may explain why he was prepared to go along with a government conspiracy to remove him from the Northern Ireland inquiry.

TABACHNIK: I want to be quite clear about what you are saying Mr. Stalker. Are you suggesting that at least one of the reasons why Sir James might have got involved in Northern Ireland was in pursuit of honours, a knighthood?

STALKER: One of the reasons and it is one of those rare areas of his professional life where he could be led by the nose by government.

TABACHNIK: Again, is this surmise or do you have some evidence to support this?

STALKER: Of course, I don't have evidence, who could possibly get evidence like that? All I can do is draw conclusions. I knew Mr. Anderton better than anyone else, apart from his wife. I had known him since 1956. I worked with him for most of that time. The last seven years of my service I worked alongside him and those are my beliefs …

TABACHNIK: Without a scrap of hard evidence you are prepared to make that sort of reflection on Sir James?

STALKER: You asked me what I thought, not what I could prove, and I answered what I thought.[41]

Thorburn's evidence

On 31 May 1995, Thorburn, Stalker's second-in-command on the Northern Ireland inquiry, took the stand. Much of the questioning centred around the setting up of the DIU. Thorburn pointed out the deceit involved in not informing him of this important development. The defence tried to suggest that Thorburn's views were based on resentment, as he failed to be appointed head of the CID and was forced to share the post with Topping. On the contrary, Thorburn emphasised that it was the deceit. Everyone was asking questions about the DIU, yet he was in the dark. He accepted in hindsight that the deception was run at the behest of Anderton, but it was wrong and undermined the efficiency of the senior ranks of the CID.

Referring to Topping, he said: 'No-one trusted him and because no-one trusted him, that's how it affected the efficiency.'[42] It was put to him that there was a need for a high level of security. Thorburn was indignant: 'You are not trying to tell me are you that the information could not be shared with me?'[43]

It was further suggested to Thorburn that there was 'no breakneck speed in setting-up the DIU'. Again, Thorburn was indignant. He pointed out that the QSG had been in existence for a number of years and by June 1984 there were allegations that the Deputy Chief Constable was involved with them and drug running. 'Do you think there was no urgency there?', he commented. 'That's not the view that I would take, I can tell you.'[44]

Thorburn was also asked about several of the key documents and was highly critical. He emphasised that he would have gone through their content with 'a fine-tooth comb to establish what truth was in the document'.[45] It was nonsense, he implied, to produce a document and ask him about it, as he didn't know if it was rubbish or truthful without further documentation. When asked specifically about Topping's letter of 17 July 1984, which alleged that Stalker was involved with the QSG – which in turn was involved in drugs and gun-running – he emphasised that he would have wanted every scrap of information to support such an allegation.[46]

Thorburn was specifically asked about his criticism of the Sampson inquiry in Northern Ireland – he had previously claimed that it had sacrificed truth and professionalism for speed and expediency. Thorburn responded by saying that it was an 'unfinished job'; other interviews needed to be conducted and further aspects followed up.[47] As a result, it was not done as thoroughly as it could have been. He pointed out that Stalker had a good grasp in the interviews of where you could go and how to lead the questions. But Sampson, Thorburn acknowledged, was in a terrible position, 'as he did not know where he could jump, and he had to accept a lot that possibly I would certainly have not accepted'.[48] When asked about what was 'unfinished', Thorburn refused to go into detail. When pushed for an overall description of the broad general areas which had not been investigated, Thorburn replied that they were 'too sensitive'.[49] It will be recalled that when Thorburn was asked by Rob McLoughlin , the producer of Granada's TV programme *Pawn in the Game*, if he could investigate these sensitive areas, Thorburn told him that he would get a bullet to the head if he attempted to do so (Chapter 5).

Justice Owen

From the outset, Mr Justice Owen emphasised that he was concerned about the delays in getting the proceedings started and then with the slowness of the trial itself. He pointed out to the two sides that it was costing £13,000 per day. He often showed his impatience: on one occasion, he commented, 'We spent one thousand pounds worth on these last two documents';[50] on another, 'You have taken a very, very long time to get nowhere';[51] and on a third, 'How can I possibly use that in any judgment ... what possible relevance has it?'[52] He was critical of much of the documentation and emphasised that if a document did not record who made it and when it was made, it would have no great significance for him.[53] And it was essential that every document was dated.[54]

On several occasions during the trial, Justice Owen appeared somewhat bewildered by what he was hearing about policing. For example, Stalker was cross-examined on a report of an interview which suggested that there was police corruption. Justice Owen intervened and said he thought that it seemed an 'extraordinary state of affairs' that no-one had gone to interview people who were thought to be involved in criminal activities.[55] He thought that it went to the very root of policing.

The settlement

Only three other witnesses took the stand before a settlement was reached – Superintendents McGourlay and Kerr, and Bowley from the Co-operative Bank. Key players in the investigation of Taylor and Stalker were never cross-examined. Throughout the action, enormous pressure was put on Taylor to settle as the costs of the case spiralled into millions. The Municipal Mutual Insurance (MMI), GMP's insurance company, was increasingly concerned at the costs. There were rumours that it was in financial trouble and was not taking on any new clients.[56] In early January 1995, Taylor was offered £625,000 in settlement of the case but refused. Six months later, on 18 June, Taylor was made a greatly increased offer which, after much deliberation, he reluctantly accepted because he was informed that if he did not do so, his legal aid might be withdrawn.[57] He wanted to continue with the action as he felt his case was becoming stronger by the day because of what was emerging in the proceedings. After the settlement, GMP issued a statement:

> Municipal Mutual Insurance Company plc are the insurers of the Greater Manchester Police Authority in respect of the defence of the proceedings and under the contract of insurance they have the conduct of the proceedings. It was the wish of those insurers to bring the proceedings to a speedy conclusion having regard to the enormous costs involved. The insurers have agreed to make a payment to Mr Taylor. That payment is to be made on the basis that Sir James Anderton's denial of liability is maintained, repeated and continued, and is to be made on commercial grounds only, having regard to the costs of the proceedings and the fact that Mr Taylor has the benefit of a legal aid certificate to pursue the proceedings. The parties have agreed that the sum to be paid to Mr Taylor shall remain confidential.[58]

Taylor was asked why he thought he had been made a new offer. He said that, while the defendant might claim it was a commercial decision, 'I believe they didn't want anything further coming out'.[59] It was claimed, however, that MMI's overall liability was approaching the maximum for which they were liable under the insurance policy. If GMP wished to continue with the case, GMPA would have had to find the £13,000 a day running costs. A confidentiality clause was included at the initiative of GMP.[60]

Taylor's three co-defendants also brought actions against GMP for malicious prosecution. Derek Britton, Taylor's accountant accepted an offer of £180,000 in early January 1995.[61] There is no publicly available information on when McCann and Bowley settled, and for how much. It is now known that the total sum for damages and costs of all the parties involved in the four cases was a staggering £10,593,574.[62] Taylor's settlement was over £2 million, making it one of the largest ever – if not *the* largest – settlements of a civil action against the police.[63]

The whole investigation into Stalker, Taylor and his co-defendants cost the British taxpayer and police insurers many millions of pounds. At today's prices, the cost of the DIU alone would have amounted to around £1 million and the surveillance unit possibility another £500,000. The criminal trial cost possibility another £1 million and the civil action £10.5 million. In addition, the four police inquiries by outside police forces probably amounted to another £2 million. A very rough estimate, therefore, suggests that the whole Taylor/Stalker episode cost about £15 million, excluding the private costs of the collapse of Taylor's property empire.

* * *

The civil action did not bring closure to the Taylor/Stalker affair. As a settlement was reached before all the evidence was heard and key witnesses, such as Anderton, Topping and Richardson, were not called, Justice Owen did not have to reach a judgment, on the balance of probabilities, that GMP intentionally and maliciously instituted or pursued an investigation without any probable cause. Although key information was not allowed to enter the public domain on the often-specious grounds of national security, the civil action opened the window on extensive police misbehaviour. There was, without doubt, a general failure of those working in the DIU to follow normal police procedures, raising the question as to whether this was deliberate. In the absence of a judgment, Farley's rigorous opening statement and all the details revealed in the civil action add further support to the view that Taylor was indeed maliciously prosecuted to get rid of Stalker from the Northern Ireland inquiry.

PART VII:
CONCLUSIONS

Chapter 25

Coincidences, Conspiracies and Consequences

IN EARLY 1980, the British state's response to the continuing conflict in Northern Ireland was to introduce the MI5/Walker counter-insurgency strategy, in effect privileging intelligence over the prosecution and detection of crime. State agents were permitted to continue their deadly activities with impunity. Drug barons, extortionists, domestic abusers, and petty criminals forged ahead with their numerous nefarious activities without fear of arrest, provided they supplied intelligence. At least two state agents were involved in the murder of Belfast solicitor, Pat Finucane. The protection of the lives of state agents became the top priority in the counter-insurgency strategy and RUC SB became a force within a force after being tasked with the control of all intelligence. During their investigation, Stalker and his team discovered many of the key elements of this secret and illegal strategy.

The key question remains: was there a conspiracy to remove Stalker from the leadership of the Northern Ireland inquiry in May 1986? Taylor's civil action against the GMP for malicious prosecution was based on the contention that Stalker's investigation in Northern Ireland was the root cause of Taylor's troubles (Chapter 24): GMP had constructed a case against him to discredit Stalker in order to remove him from the Northern Ireland inquiry. This was challenged in court. Instead it was claimed that there was sufficient evidence to justify an investigation of Taylor and Stalker in June 1984. From this it was argued that, as Stalker had only just begun his investigation and the outcome was unknown, there was, therefore, no basis for a conspiracy. There was simply a coincidence of events in Northern Ireland and Manchester, and Stalker's removal from the inquiry into the RUC was a *consequence* of what happened in Manchester. After extensive research at the time of Stalker's removal, BBC journalist Peter Taylor concurred with the official narrative that there was no conspiracy.

Dates and sequencing are obviously critical in making a determination. If the investigation into Stalker began before the implications of his investigation were becoming known, it reduces the possibility of a conspiracy. On the other hand, if the investigation into Stalker only began *after* his findings were becoming apparent to the security establishment, it makes a conspiracy more plausible. The implications of his investigation would have become obvious in November 1984, following the discovery that the hayshed had been bugged and an informer or state agent had supplied the intelligence which led to the shootings. From that moment onwards, Stalker pressed to find out what was on the tape and what was known about the informer's role. As a consequence, the evidence needs to be considered in two distinct periods. The first, from June 1984 until the establishment of the DIU in February 1985. The second, from February 1985 until May 1986 when Stalker was suspended from duty.

The standard of proof in a civil action is based on a 'balance of probability' – that, on the evidence, the occurrence of an event is more likely than not. This is a lower standard than in a criminal trial in which the burden of proof is 'beyond reasonable doubt'. Taylor's civil action was settled before a final judgment, and it is impossible to know what the Judge may have concluded after hearing all the evidence. In what follows, the 'balance of probabilities' is used to assess whether or not there was a conspiracy to remove Stalker. We begin with a précis of the official narrative.

The official narrative: denial of a conspiracy

GMP claimed that the start of the investigation into Stalker and Taylor was based on three pieces of key information: a post-match golf conversation in which a businessman told McGourlay, Deputy Co-ordinator of No. 1 RCS, that Stalker attended parties at which criminals were present (the golf conversation); a conversation on Bridge Street in Manchester, in which Burton, a regular police informer, alleged that Stalker was corrupt (the Bridge Street conversation); and a crew/passenger list from the *Sherama*, a boat owned by Vincent Schiavo, a member of the QSG, which entered Gibraltar with several wanted criminals on board. As Taylor was allegedly 'associated' with the QSG, the visit increased suspicions about Stalker. All three events, apparently and somewhat remarkably, occurred on the same day – 11 June 1984 (Chapter 7) – and several months before Stalker's hayshed/informer discoveries in Northern Ireland.

McGourlay says he reported the golf conversation to Topping, head of the Discipline and Complaints Department in GMP, late on in the morning of 11

June. In response, Topping asked McGourlay to find out whatever he could about Taylor. Coincidentally, according to the report compiled by Richardson, an inspector in Topping's department, Burton telephoned him on the very same day. He told Richardson that he had just met Jimmy Donnelly at 2.30 p.m. in a chance meeting on Bridge Street, Manchester. During the conversation, Donnelly was alleged to have said that Stalker was 'Jimmy (Jimmy Swords) and Kevin's man', in other words, he was corrupt.

On 14 June, apparently in response to Topping's request to McGourlay, No. 1 RCS compiled a nineteen-item report on Taylor which implied that he was a major player in the Manchester crime scene (Chapter 8). McGourlay sent it to Topping, who reported the detail to his boss, ACC Lees. On 20 June, Lees saw CC Anderton and informed him of their suspicions about Stalker. On 22 June, Topping met Burton in Heaton Park to hear at first-hand what he was saying about Stalker, Taylor and the QSG.

The following month, on 12 July – again according to the official narrative – McGourlay sent a report to Topping noting that a check on the PNC of two of Taylor's vehicles seen at his house, produced a query from the Drugs Squad, as one of the cars was seen outside the house of a suspected drug dealer (Chapter 9). On 17 July, Topping wrote a long letter to Lees documenting the 'frightening scene' of serious crime in Manchester, 'a long-established police involvement with a senior member in the RCS and the QSG', and an 'association' between Stalker and the QSG. He recommended that a properly organised squad should be formed to 'smash' the criminal ring.

Following Burton's conviction and imprisonment for his part in the LFF on 4 September 1984 (Chapter 4), Topping conducted extensive interviews with the imprisoned Burton between October 1984 and January 1985 (Chapter 9). On 4 February 1985, the specialist squad that Topping allegedly had recommended six months earlier to investigate the QSG and its involvement in drug trafficking and other criminal activities, was formed and began work (Chapter 10). One of its first tasks was to interview Burton and to capture on tape the allegations that he had made against Stalker and everything he knew about the QSG (Chapter 11).

In short, according to the official narrative, the instigation of an investigation into Stalker was based solely on information which came to the notice of the GMP, coupled with its suspicions of corruption among senior police officers. There was no connection whatsoever between Stalker's inquiry in Northern Ireland and events in Manchester. On the contrary, GMP knew little or nothing about the progress of Stalker's investigation in Northern Ireland and the difficulties he was facing.

Suspect evidence

On paper at least and regardless of the apparent linkage to Stalker's investigation in Northern Ireland, the official narrative appeared to justify an investigation into the Taylor/Stalker relationship on its own merits, particularly as the criminal intelligence against Taylor was said to be extensive. However, as shown in previous chapters, a forensic analysis of all the documentation raises serious questions about the authenticity of that official narrative (Chapters 7, 8, and 9). There were conflicts over dates and times, factual errors, and contradictions in the material. Moreover, there was widespread disregard of the rules relating to the reporting and recording of information. Basic procedures, such as noting information on the relevant standard form or observing the rules of contemporaneous reporting, were ignored. Plain paper was used instead of official continuation pages. Date stamps, indicating who sent the documents or who received them and when, were absent. In normal circumstances, such practices would be considered breaches of the police disciplinary code.

Crucially, several documents which were claimed to have been prepared in June 1984, appear to have been compiled at a later date. There is little doubt that the golf conversation took place, but McGourlay's original report of this was apparently lost and the typed copy of it contained errors and distortions which had the effect of increasing the suspicions about Stalker and his relationship with Taylor. There was considerable doubt over the Bridge Street conversation. As it was such an important piece of information and possibly fabricated, its provenance is carefully analysed at length below.

The *Sherama* certainly entered Gibraltar on 11 June 1984 with Ronnie Knight on board. Knight, along with several other wanted criminals, was suspected of involvement in the 1983 £6 million Security Express robbery in London. But the crew/passenger list which was examined as part of Taylor's civil action was a forgery, as confirmed many years later by the student who compiled the original list. She confirmed that it was not her handwriting or bad spelling. It is not known why it had been copied or how much it may have been altered in the process, but it was a clear act of deceit.

The 14 June No. 1 RCS document was also highly suspect, as it appeared to suggest that the police were totally unaware that Taylor was apparently a major player in organised crime in the city until after his friend, John Stalker, started the Northern Ireland inquiry in June 1984. Yet just days after the golf conversation, RCS officers were able to list nineteen separate items about Taylor, including a number alleging his association with major criminals. Fourteen of the items were on plain paper – again amplifying the risk that these could easily have been added later. Oddly, the list did not contain any of the eight entries on Taylor from GMP's own CIU, not even the only entry among the eight which alleged criminality. But even *that* entry was suspicious because of different dates reported in the public domain. According to the Sampson report, it was dated 27 March 1973, but in the civil action the same entry was claimed to have been compiled a week earlier and was dated 20 March 1973. It had been submitted by Baythorpe when a young constable. Much later, he was in charge of the Criminal Intelligence Department during the Taylor/Stalker investigation.

There was no contemporaneous documentation for the alleged Heaton Park meeting on 20 June at which it was claimed that Topping, along with Richardson, saw Burton in order to vouch for himself what Burton was saying about Stalker. Similarly, there is no record or report of the meeting on 22 June at which Lees allegedly reported Topping's and his own suspicions about Stalker to Anderton. The 28 June single page unsigned report, noting that Burton had provided information that Stalker had for a long time been party to free meals at the Kwok Man restaurant, was identical to the anonymous letter sent to the Police Authority making a similar allegation about Stalker and Anderton. Was the report manufactured and credited to Burton, based on this letter?

To further increase suspicions over the documentation, Topping's desk diaries for the period suffered the same fate as McGourlay's original report of the golf conversation and were no longer available. Also missing were Richardson's A4 blue books in which, it was claimed, he noted all information from Burton. Was this simple carelessness or were the documents deliberately lost or destroyed because they would have contradicted the official narrative?

The information in July was equally suspect. The 12 July error-filled report that one of Taylor's cars was seen outside a drug dealer's house, which then alerted the Drugs Squad, noted the number of the BMW used by his wife – a car which would *not* have triggered an alert. However, Taylor's BMW could have, because he had lost it in a gambling debt to someone suspected of drug dealing. Noting the registration number of the wrong BMW was a mistake which could easily have been made if the document was fabricated at a later date, based on information obtained in the searches of Taylor's offices in May 1986. Further, it was alleged that Richardson subsequently met Kerr, head of the Drugs Squad, to discuss the alert. Kerr, however, had no recollection of the meeting and it was most unlikely the meeting took place, as Kerr always took his summer holiday during the first two weeks of July – the period during which the meeting was supposed to have taken place.

Topping's 17 July letter summarising the information was only initialled and contained no stamps that it had been sent or received. It noted that *Sharama* (sic) currently had Knight on its passenger list, but it is unlikely that Topping, in the Discipline and Complaints Department, would have known about it entering Gibraltar, just over a month previously, when writing his letter. He wrongly claimed that Taylor was a Tory party agent rather than chair of the MCA. All of this documentation, therefore, like so much of the June documentation, had all the hallmarks of being constructed at a later date, to support the official narrative.

Provenance of the Bridge Street meeting

The suspect documentation, the contradictions in the information, the lost and missing reports all suggest at best a total disregard of recording and reporting procedures, and at worst some sort of nefarious activity or a conspiracy. The Bridge Street meeting is the key to any understanding as to what actually happened between June 1984 and the end of the year. It is claimed that the conversation occurred at 2.30 p.m. on 11 June (Chapter 7). If true, and Donnelly did imply that Stalker was corrupt, then along with the golf conversation, GMP had no option but to investigate the information further.

As police forces are trained in the collection and recording of information, it should be comparatively simple to establish when the information was received and assess its quality, particularly when it related to the DCC of the force in question. However, in reviewing all of the available information made public as a result of Taylor's criminal trial and civil action, as well as the interviews I conducted, the failures of police process are manifest.

Donnelly claimed emphatically to me that the meeting never occurred. If it had, he suggested, it would have led to a confrontation. Burton was a *persona non grata* at the time because he had 'ratted' on those involved in the LFF and, as a result, they had lost thousands of pounds in the botched fire-bombing in Belfast. Donnelly, however, was known to lie and his evidence therefore needs to be treated with caution. But there were other factors which suggest the meeting never took place. There was no contemporaneous dated and signed report on a regulation form of the meeting alleging that the DCC was corrupt. There was only an undated handwritten report – Document 7 – compiled by Richardson on some disputed date. Similarly, there was no entry in Richardson's pocketbook that he had received a call from Burton reporting the meeting. On the contrary, there was an entry which noted that he was out of his office at the time the call was supposedly made. Finally, both McGourlay and Peter Taylor, the journalist, considered the meeting 'remarkable' – it was improbable that the meeting took place.

The alleged Heaton Park meeting on 22 June casts further doubt on the Bridge Street meeting. Although Richardson did record in his pocketbook that he and Topping had a meeting in Heaton Park on that day, he did not record with whom the two officers met. It could have been with anyone. But even if it was with Burton, it may have had nothing to do with allegations about Stalker but with Burton's own safety and that of his mother and his girlfriend, Elizabeth McDonald, in light of the threats they were receiving (Chapter 4). The lack of any contemporaneous report of this meeting undermines the claim that it was about Stalker.

According to Peter Taylor, the purpose of the Heaton Park meeting was to assess the credibility of Burton's allegations about Stalker. But this is undermined by the fact that only two days earlier it was alleged that Topping had reported Burton's information to Lees who had in turn then reported it to Anderton in a late-night meeting. This was contrary to all police procedures because the information should have been assessed, particularly from a dangerous informer, who had a reputation of a lifetime of deceit, before reporting it upwards. In any event, Anderton took no action. This contrasted with his action over the far less serious matter of an anonymous letter accusing him and Stalker of availing of free meals at the Kwok Man restaurant – a matter which he immediately referred to the GMPA, carried out a detailed investigation and produced a comprehensive report rebutting the allegation.

All this evidence strongly suggests that the Bridge Street meeting never occurred and was a fabrication. But when was it made up, by whom and when did it come to the notice of Topping? Burton was certainly a credible suspect and could have made it up on his own volition. He had a vivid imagination and knew from past experience that allegations of police corruption opened doors. In 1981, he had alleged that an ACC was on a pension and Taylor was drug smuggling and storing firearms for the QSG. In 1983, he claimed that the ACC was in fact Stalker after he had 'blown out' the arrests of members of the QSG involved in the LFF.

In May and June 1984, Burton was helping Burgess in the prosecution of those involved in the LFF. He had completed a statement and was deciding whether to act as a 'supergrass' in their trial. No doubt he was hoping for a lighter sentence for his part. In the end, he did not sign his statement or act as a supergrass, presumably because he was being threatened. Instead, McGourlay spoke on his behalf at the trial. He continued to allege that he was being threatened after being sentenced and demanded to be moved from Kirkham prison where he had initially been sent along with Klapish.[1] Just over a month later he was moved to Leeds prison and then within a fortnight he was moved to Lancaster prison. Throughout these months, he was in a very vulnerable position and could have made up the Bridge Street conversation to curry favours.

There are, however, several factors which suggest that Burton did not make up the conversation on his own volition, but rather that the story was attributed to him. As he was being threatened by the QSG and knew that he would probably be beaten up if he met Donnelly, he was most unlikely to invent an improbable story about a friendly chat. Moreover, the wording attributed to him in the conversation seemed false and stilted. In response to the mention of Stalker's name, Burton was alleged to have said: 'Isn't he a top jolly now?' This was an unlikely phrase for a lifelong fraudster and police informer. It appeared to be a police expression and was used by them to describe corrupt senior police officers in two other documents examined in the civil action.[2] In any case, according to his handler, Burton always used the phrase 'being in his pocket' to describe a corrupt police officer.[3]

There were also glaring contradictions in the evidence which were unlikely to have occurred if the meeting took place and the conversation was authentic. The first related to the use of the 'now' in the 'top jolly' comment. It suggested that Burton was familiar with Stalker's career. Yet in his taped interviews in February/March 1985 after he described the Bridge Street meeting, following an obvious prompt, he said that this was the first time he had heard of Stalker's name. Then, after describing how McGourlay had rung him up and asked him if he had heard of Stalker – an impossibility according to McGourlay because he did not have Burton's telephone number[4] – he again said that he *had* heard of him. So, had Burton heard of Stalker or not?

The other, perhaps more significant, contradiction concerned the reporting of the Bridge Street and golf conversations. Document 7 noted that the Bridge Street meeting occurred at 2.30 p.m. on 11 June and that Burton rang Richardson and told him about it soon after. In the same document,

Richardson claimed that he spoke to McGourlay at 11.50 a.m. on Friday 15 June and was told about the golf conversation – another call which was not recorded in his pocketbook. This order of events would place the reporting of the golf conversation four days *after* the Bridge Street conversation. This was the order confirmed by Burton, following another prompt, in his February/March interviews.

Topping, in his 17 July letter, also claimed that this was the sequence of events. He could not have been more emphatic. 'Some weeks ago', his informer told him of a corrupt relationship between 'Mr Z, James Patrick Monaghan, and Kevin Taylor'. This was obviously a direct reference to the Bridge Street conversation in which Donnelly says that Stalker is Monaghan and Taylor's man. Then, 'following on the heels' of this information, he is informed of the golf conversation. He confirmed this order of events in his subsequent book.

Yet, McGourlay was insistent that he reported the golf conversation to Topping on the morning of 11 June and, therefore, *before* the alleged telephone call from Burton reporting the Bridge Street conversation. In the civil action, Anderton's defence counsel attempted to reverse engineer McGourlay's order of events and insist that he reported the golf conversation later in the week. McGourlay, however, remained adamant that he reported it on the Monday morning. These contradictions are perhaps more likely to occur when there has been a deceitful manipulation of the evidence, with no-one checking the information carefully.

All these factors taken together suggest that the Bridge Street conversation was most probably made up by someone other than Burton but attributed to him. He could, however, have been encouraged to confirm it in the interviews after the establishment of the DIU. In any case, it was similar to what he said to Burgess about Stalker in 1983, and *that* conversation may have been the inspiration for the Bridge Street conversation. His continued need to ingratiate himself to the police may have helped him agree to their demands. If this speculation is correct, the next question is: when was the Bridge Street conversation made up and Burton credited as the source?

Start date of a conspiracy

One possibility is that Burton was encouraged to recycle the information around the time of Stalker's appointment. This was the view of a retired intelligence officer who had worked in Northern Ireland. He claimed that as a matter of routine, MI5 always developed fail-safe plans to counter any action which might undermine national security. Hence, it is conceivable that there would have been a back-up put in place at the start of Stalker's investigation into the six killings which could be triggered if the need arose.[5] Stephen Dorril, an academic, author and journalist, who has written extensively on the intelligence services, also argued that the conspiracy to remove Stalker started on 'the day he arrived in Northern Ireland'.[6] This would have been the time Burton was most vulnerable while he was helping the police with their inquiry into the LFF.

There was a less clandestine possibility for a conspiracy to have developed around this time. In his book published in 1988, Stalker was convinced that there was a decision to obstruct his inquiry and he believed that most of his difficulties 'flowed from the belief of influential Special Branch officers that all I should be doing was to conduct a review of matters past, and not commencing a new investigation'.[7] Moreover, Stalker was perceived as unsympathetic to the difficulties the RUC was facing and was already seen to have taken sides. He had made the decision to regard the relatives of the dead men as potentially legitimate witnesses. But, according to Stalker, this was seen as naïve and harmful to RUC Special Branch.[8] In the civil action, Stalker was pushed on when he thought a conspiracy may have started. He certainly did not dismiss the possibility that it started shortly after he had begun his investigation pointing out that there was a 'constant escalation of the stakes as it were from the beginning of the investigation'.[9] As it progressed, he had kept both Anderton and Myers informed.

A stronger possibility, based on the available evidence, is that the conspiracy started after Stalker had discovered that the hayshed was bugged in late autumn 1984, and cover-stories had been constructed to disguise the intelligence sources which led to the three incidents. This was the moment when a number of those involved would have realised that they could be prosecuted for perverting the course of justice and possibly other offences such as malfeasance in public office. There are several factors which support this speculation.

To begin with, it would explain the extraordinary length of time between the golf and supposed Bridge Street conversations in June 1984, and the establishment of the DIU in February 1985. With information from two separate sources suggesting the DCC was corrupt, it is inconceivable that GMP would take over half a year before establishing a special unit to investigate the information, particularly when, at the time, there was strong evidence of police corruption at a high level in Manchester. It is also inconceivable that Topping, head of the Discipline and Complaints Department and instigator of the investigation into Stalker, did not bother to interview Burton again for over three months. He first allegedly interviewed him on 22 June in Heaton Park, but not again until 4 October.

Second, Topping's letter of 9 March 1985 contained the statement, 'much has to be tested', referring to the information on Taylor and Stalker collected to date. This was nine months after it was claimed that GMP had information that their Deputy was friendly with a suspected member of the QSG and according to Burton was himself in 'in the pocket' of the QSG. It would have been a serious derogation of duty not to have tested the information immediately, especially given that Stalker had just started a highly sensitive inquiry in Northern Ireland. Even the anonymous letter received a speedier response.

Third, the existing documentation on when Burton reported the Bridge Street conversation was tendentious. The only evidence confirming the reporting date was the handwritten Document 7 prepared by Richardson. It was claimed that the information was précised from his A4 blue books in which he had been told to note all the information from Burton. As noted above, these have been lost. There was no date on Document 7 and there was a dispute over when it was in fact written. Richardson claimed it was in June 1984 and Topping after the DIU was set up in 1985. The reference to Donnelly's upcoming trial in July, as well as a reference to Klapish's impending trial,[10] which occurred in September, suggest that the information was recorded by Richardson in his blue books sometime before these events. But it is equally plausible, if the document was compiled in 1985, for these dates to be included in the document to make it appear that Burton reported the information in June rather than much later in the year.

Fourth, no contemporaneous reports were examined in the civil action concerning actions taken between mid-July 1984 and the beginning of February 1985. There was no detail provided on the numerous prison visits to Burton in the latter half of 1984 apart from one partially completed report on a piece of scrap paper. This was an interview with Burton in Lancaster prison on 14 November 1984 in which he supposedly provided hearsay evidence from a fellow inmate – an ex-police officer – about Taylor. Standard police procedures required that reports of all prison visits were documented. Yet, there were no records.

On the balance of probabilities, all the available evidence suggests that the conspiracy to remove Stalker began in late autumn 1984, rather than in June with the fabrication of the Bridge Street conversation which Burton was encouraged to report. It does not immediately follow, however, that there was a conspiracy to remove Stalker related to his investigation in Northern Ireland. The fabrication of the Bridge Street conversation could have been part of an internal GMB plot to remove him. There are two possible variants of such an internal conspiracy.

A GMP internal conspiracy

One possibility was that there was a strong view within the Discipline and Complaints Department that Stalker was indeed corrupt, but there was insufficient evidence. To strengthen the suspicion, the Bridge Street conversation was fabricated, McGourlay's original report of the golf conversation was 'lost', and a typed copy was constructed with subtle changes to increase the suspicions about Stalker. It was simply an example of 'noble cause corruption' where unethical means were used to obtain a result for the greater good.

As noted, there was widespread speculation at the time that police corruption was rampant in the GMP. There were eighteen inspectors overseen by six superintendents investigating complaints and other matters in the Discipline and Complaints Department, headed by Topping, a man of strong moral principles. Operation City run by No. 1 RCS between 1982 and 1983 had been a failure. In addition, several GMP arrest operations had been 'blown out', including the one aimed at arresting those suspected of being involved in the LFF. The pressure on the Discipline and Complaints Department to act and produce results must have been immense. Doctoring some of the existing evidence was needed to convince officers higher up of the need for a special squad to investigate. It had nothing to do with Northern Ireland.

As Anderton took no action at this point, he may not have been informed about the suspicions that some of his officers had about his deputy. He was only told after the DIU had been established when Topping, in March 1985, wrote a clearly authentic, stamped and signed letter to Lees headed, 'Brief notes to up-date you in relation to Taylor and Febb'. Lees would have passed this letter and notes to Anderton. Even then, Anderton does not appear to have been particularly concerned as he continued supporting Stalker's applications for senior posts throughout the summer of 1985, although he did start dictating extensive reports on key events involving Stalker from May 1985 – perhaps to ensure that he personally was protected if details emerged confirming suspicions about Stalker's corruption.

A second possibility, again unrelated to Northern Ireland, was that there was an internal conspiracy based on the personal ambitions of two senior police officers in the GMP. This theory was put forward by Charles Buckley, who assisted Taylor's defence team in the criminal trial and civil action. He argued that it was a Shakespearean tragedy in which Anderton, the Moor, and Topping, his Iago, conspired together. Anderton, he conjectured, wished to become Commissioner of the Metropolitan Police or Chief Constable of the RUC, but he was concerned about possible competitors. One obvious rival was Stalker, who had been in his shadow for the last 30 years. Crucially, Stalker had extensive detective experience – a skill missing from Anderton's own CV. Removing Stalker would leave a clear run in for Anderton and a void in GMP to be filled by Topping.

From my perspective, neither of these two internal conspiracy possibilities to remove Stalker carry much credence. While there have been many examples of 'noble cause corruption' in attempting to put criminals behind bars – for example, the scandalous miscarriages of justice of the Guildford Four and the Birmingham Six – it is unlikely that police officers would risk manufacturing evidence against their own Deputy Chief Constable for fear that, if it transpires that there is no actual evidence, their jobs would be on the line. The possibility that the personal ambitions of two police officers was the source is also, in my view, quite weak. If Anderton did see Stalker as a competitor, it was foolhardy to recommend him, only months earlier, to carry out the Northern Ireland investigation. This would only have strengthened his career prospects. Moreover, he could simply have not supported Stalker in his applications for senior posts.

Possible conspirators

Once an internal conspiracy is eliminated, the possibility of a conspiracy linked to Stalker's investigation in Northern Ireland becomes more credible. Who initiated it and how precisely it was done is inevitably speculative – but it is possible to navigate through the publicly available evidence in a measured and analytical fashion. Several MI5 officers would obviously have had a strong motive to get rid of Stalker. These included MI5 officers who faced charges of perverting the course of justice following the destruction of the remaining tape of the hayshed shooting. In 1981, as extensively documented, MI5 developed the secret Walker counter-insurgency strategy based on the widespread use of spies but without a legal framework for running state agents and informers, thereby exposing handlers to prosecution (Chapter 3).

Over the years, MI5 has shown little respect for the rule of law and democratic values.[11] In Northern Ireland, there have been glimpses into its dark activities as described in previous chapters. The introduction of the secret

MI5/Walker counter-insurgency strategy in 1981 was one of MI5's most egregious acts. It ignored parliamentary sovereignty, prolonged the conflict and has made peace more difficult. But there are other examples. In the early 1980s, it possessed information that Pat Finucane, the Belfast solicitor, was being targeted for assassination by loyalists but did not warn him. Similarly in June 1985 and December 1988 it had further information that he was being targeted but again failed to warn him.[12] During Judge Cory's investigation into Finucane's murder, in an act of intimidation, MI5 entered his London offices and destroyed the investigation team's computer hard disks on the grounds of national security.[13]

During the 1970 and 1980s, there were allegations that a paedophile ring was operating out of Kincora Boys' Home and that the security services, including MI5 and MI6, connived in, or ignored, the sexual abuse in order to gather intelligence on loyalist paramilitaries.[14] The Historical Abuse Inquiry (HAI), set up in 2015, concluded that there was no credible evidence to show that MI5 was 'complicit in any form of exploitation of sexual abuse in Kincora for any purpose'.[15] However, a recent film, Lost Boys, makes a compelling case that there were links between the network of paedophiles, which MI5 apparently was fully aware of, but ignored, their crimes because some were state agents. The film suggested that five Belfast children who went missing in the early years of the Troubles, had been murdered.[16] During the making of the film, the Director claimed that the production team had been burgled and their phones hacked, implying that MI5 may have been involved.[17]

During the HAI inquiry, a telex was discovered written by MI5 Assistant Director and Co-ordinator of Intelligence who suggested creating 'false files' to withhold information from a police investigation into Kincora Boys' Home. MI5 apparently had failed to tell the RUC that a certain person was an MI5 agent and the suggestion was that 'false files' should be used to cover-up the fact.[18] While admitting that it was 'at best unwise and at worst demonstrated a willingness to deceive the police', the HAI concluded that the suggestion was not pursued. However, Lost Boys included an interview with Mike Taylor who claimed that his 1982 statement, which the HAI used to reject his evidence, had been fabricated.

In 2006, during a debate in Parliament, Mark Durkan, leader of the SDLP in Northern Ireland, summed up his views of MI5:

> MI5 have in the past comported themselves as para-terrorists in their handling of and engagement, involvement, collusion and complicity in all sorts of crimes committed by terrorists. They did not share intelligence that could have been

used to apprehend people, to alert people, or to save lives. Such was the nature of its operations that MI5 literally ... conspired to allow people to get away with murder. When the Government seem content to cover up those aspects of the past, I find it hard to accept their assurances about the future.[19]

Some members of the RUC are also obvious strong candidates for a possible conspiracy. Several of its officers faced prosecution: the HMSU officers who shot dead the six men; the senior RUC SB officers who constructed cover stories to protect the identity of state agents and informers, and instructed the HMSU officers to tell lies; the senior RUC SB officer who gave instructions for the hayshed tape to be destroyed because it was felt to be particularly damaging to the RUC; those who perverted the course of justice by not revealing evidence to the DPPNI; and RUC SB handlers who were running the state agents and allowing them to commit crimes, including murder, without a legal framework. All of them would have had a strong motive to remove Stalker who was threatening to expose what was going on.

The two-day meeting in Belfast between the RUC and GMP in relation to the LFF would have established relationships which could have been exploited in helping to remove Stalker (Chapter 4). Masonic connections may also have been relevant. In Northern Ireland, a serving RUC officer claimed that the Brotherhood influence was omnipotent and he claimed that Freemasonry wielded enormous power in promotion and selection, particularly for the RUC SB.[20] Trevor Forbes, the head of it, was known to be a mason and membership within the force appeared to be expanding. Three months before Stalker was appointed, 22 officers set up a new Masonic Lodge in Ballymena called 'Harp and Shamrock' – the symbols in the RUC coat of arms – suggesting that membership of the Brotherhood was popular within the RUC.[21] The report of the Independent Commission on Policing found that, in a survey of over six thousand officers, 8 per cent said that they were masons and some former members of the police told the Commission that masons have in the past been present in relatively large numbers in the Special Branch.[22] In Manchester, Cusick argued that a number of the officers investigating the Taylor/Stalker relationship were known to be masons.[23] Martin Short, in an extensive analysis of the Stalker affair argues, however, that 'a mason conspiracy demands more evidence'.[24]

The British Army, and FRU in particular, was another possible conspirator. Stalker was concerned with the recruitment and use of informers, and whether any had been *agents provocateurs*. He would have been aware that most agents were run by FRU and, given the lack of any legal framework for running of agents, would have been concerned about the role of FRU in the intelligence war. FRU in turn would have been worried that Stalker's investigation could lead to army handlers of agents, as well as the senior officers in overall charge, being subject to criminal prosecution. It will be recalled that Thorburn had told Rob McLoughlin, the producer of Granada's TV programme *Pawn in the game*, that Stalker had started to investigate something 'very serious' (Chapter 5). He refused to tell McLoughlin what it was as 'it might lead to a bullet to your head'. In all probability, it was an investigation into the maverick activities of the FRU.

Finally, there would have been major concerns within the higher echelons of government. Stalker's investigation would not only damage the secret counter-insurgency strategy but would fatally undermine the overall credibility of the RUC. At the time, there were negotiations between the British and Irish governments which would lead in November 1985, to the signing of the Anglo-Irish Agreement when the RUC would be required to police loyalist opposition to it (Chapter 14). Further, several senior civil servants in the NIO and politicians who had been directly responsible for not developing, or delaying, the introduction of a legal framework for agent handling, faced being charged with the common law offence of misconduct in public office, as they were in breach of their duties. The motive for getting rid of Stalker was widespread. Any one or more of these organisations could have conspired to remove Stalker by having Burton spread allegations about him and Taylor.

Modus operandi of an external conspiracy

Burton was in a very vulnerable position fearing for his life in the autumn of 1984, having provided information on Klapish and others in the LFF. He wished to be moved to a safer prison. In such circumstances, it is not difficult to imagine him being willing to spread an allegation about Stalker being 'Jimmy (Jimmy Swords) and Kevin's man'. Once the information was reported to Topping in the Discipline and Complaints Department, coupled with the much earlier report in June from the golf conversation and two mess dockets showing that Stalker had entertained Taylor at a police function, Topping would have been convinced and made the decision to investigate. It would have been relatively easy to persuade ACC Lees, perhaps sometime in November 1984, to set up a secret task force to investigate the Taylor/Stalker relationship under the guise of a Drugs Intelligence Unit.

The DIU's first task was to interview Burton. Richardson and Murray were tasked with conducting the interviews. Richardson was from Discipline and Complaints Department and Murray, according to Dorril, was GMP's liaison officer with MI5.[25] They clearly used an *aide mémoire* because Burton made several references to a list (Chapter 11). However, no *aide mémoire* or list was made available in the civil action. The detail must have been from existing reports, which again were not examined in the civil action, most likely, from reports of Burton's numerous prison interviews. He was clearly prompted to mention both the Bridge Street conversation with Richardson and that McGourlay had phoned him that same night and asked him what he knew about Stalker. As the alleged phone call from McGourlay was after Burton had reported the Bridge Street conversation, it guaranteed that the question about Stalker could not have been recycled information.

In carrying out their work, the members of the DIU may have been unaware of the unit's true purpose and believed that it was investigating Taylor and the QSG in relation to drugs. Anderton too may have been initially kept in the dark and believed that the unit was collecting intelligence on the drug scene in Manchester. It was only after he received Topping's 9 March 1985 letter that he had some documentary proof in relation to 'Taylor and Febb'. Even then, as previously noted, Anderton did not appear to take the matter seriously and continued supporting Stalker's applications for more senior posts throughout the summer of 1985.

All of this is inevitably speculative. However, I would argue that on the balance of probabilities there was a conspiracy involving the army, RUC SB and MI5 to remove Stalker in late 1984. It was initiated by MI5 who saw the possible dangers Stalker posed to the counter-insurgency strategy and the army's key role within it. It is the most plausible explanation for the events in the period June 1984 to February 1985. The Bridge Street conversation was central to its success and was fabricated only after Stalker had discovered that the hayshed had been bugged and was beginning to look into the murky waters of the running and management of informers. Such a conspiracy would explain most of the mass of conflicting and contradictory information; the failure to follow standard reporting procedures, and the 'loss' of Richardson's blue books and Topping's diaries as their existence would have undermined the official narrative that there was no conspiracy. Burton's death at the young age of 41, shortly after his fifth interview with officers from the DIU, meant that none of this speculation could be tested. His secrets and those of GMP died with him.

A convenient investigation

What happened in the period following the establishment of the DIU and Stalker's removal, however, is much less speculative. There is convincing evidence to suggest that the police investigation into Taylor and Stalker intensified. The ebb and flow of the investigation can only be explained by a determination to prosecute Taylor in order to justify the removal of Stalker. No police force would have committed so much expenditure and tied up so many senior officers in an investigation for a relatively minor fraud, unless there was some very good reason, such as pressure for a result from either MI5 or the highest echelons of government. The main factor in support of such a position is the remarkable closeness of developments in Northern Ireland and Manchester.

Towards the end of 1984, Stalker was putting increasing pressure on the RUC to provide him with the tape of the hayshed shooting and details of all the state agents involved in the three incidents. In January 1985, Stalker had his first meeting with MI5 in London. They agreed to co-operate fully and informed him that he could have access to everything he wanted, but failed to tell him that they themselves had a copy of the tape of the hayshed shooting. A few weeks later, the DIU began to investigate all aspects of Taylor's life.

Six months later, Stalker again met MI5 in London, together with CC Hermon. Bernard Sheldon, the Senior Legal Executive in MI5 said that his organisation would not stand in the way of a murder investigation. However, the meeting did nothing to reduce DIU's effort to find something on Taylor. On 17 July 1985, the DIU recruited a long-standing drug smuggler to act as an informer. At around the same time, they interviewed Victor Roberts, a onetime friend and colleague who had fallen out with Taylor several years previously. They interviewed him on a further six occasions. The DIU produced more unsigned and undated reports. But still there was no evidence to support Burton's 1981 allegation that Taylor was involved in smuggling drugs. Sometime in late summer, two top-level MI5 officers destroyed the only remaining tape of the hayshed shootings.

On 18 September 1985, Stalker delivered his interim report to the RUC. Two days later, Murray received a report from Customs and Excise that Taylor was not involved in drug smuggling. The information did not change minds. A week later, the DIU launched Operation Kaluki, named after Taylor's favourite card game, and deployed its newly established and only surveillance team to watch Taylor's offices for the next 114 days – a quite remarkable usage of a scarce resource. On the same day, Lees informed Anderton that Taylor had purchased Stalker's airline ticket for their holiday together in Miami – not an unusual occurrence among friends – but he wrote a note saying: 'very disturbing'. The following day he spent over an hour in secret session with Lees. Later he demanded that the DIU prepare another report on Taylor and Stalker.

On 11 November, the DIU was strengthened with the appointment of Stephenson, a fraud expert. He admitted in the criminal trial that, on his appointment, the drugs investigation was at an impasse. Four days later, the Anglo-Irish Agreement was signed by the British and Irish governments. It was feared that it would lead to widespread protests by loyalists. On 26 November, Ware accompanied Stephenson to the Co-operative Bank, Taylor's principal bank. This was GMP's third visit in as many months. Yet, the Bank had made no complaint to the police about their client. The police pressure, however, paid off. During this visit, the bank supplied the police with detailed information on all of Taylor's loans, in breach of its duty of client confidentiality. The GMP was now in a position to construct a crime against Taylor. In December, Topping, now head of the CID, took the unprecedented step of meeting Sheppard, the head of the fraud department in the Co-operative Bank.

By the end of 1985, Taylor, a man with no criminal record, had been under investigation, according to GMP, for a year and a half, including ten months by a top-heavy team of four senior officers and a sergeant, and two months by GMP's only surveillance unit. Again, huge resources were dedicated to the task, which contrasted with the known fraud and contract fire-bombing organised by Klapish in Belfast for which only one GMP fraud officer was tasked with investigating and prosecuting all those involved.

On 13 February 1986, after a five-month delay, Hermon eventually sent Stalker's interim report to the DPPNI. Two weeks later, an application for access orders, based on deceits, half-truths and silences, was made for all of Taylor's bank accounts (Chapter 16). Access was granted. This provided legal cover for the information which had already been obtained illegally. At the beginning of March 1986, the DPPNI instructed Hermon to release the tape and the other documents which Stalker had requested. At the end of the month, a member of the DIU drove an RUC officer from GMP headquarters to the airport. It has never been revealed who he was, the purpose of his visit and why a member of the DIU was tasked to be the chauffeur.

At the end of April 1986, Stalker flew to Belfast to see Hermon for a prearranged meeting accompanied by Thorburn, his second in command. Hermon was not there but they did receive from RUC SB the documents which they had been demanding for over a year. Despite promises, there was, of course, no tape of the hayshed shooting – they were told all copies had now been destroyed either by the RUC or MI5. Back in Manchester, search warrants had been obtained for Taylor's house and offices and various other people's premises linked to him, and were executed on 9 May 1986. In his home, during a very perfunctory search, the DIU discovered the family photograph albums and took them away. Their relevance to a fraud investigation involving a bank has never been explained.

On 11 May, the DIU was instructed to prepare the fourth detailed report on Taylor for the Chief Constable. Despite the ostensible focus of the DIU's investigation being on the QSG, the report which was prepared over the weekend contained the phrase that Stalker had reason 'to be sympathetic to the IRA'. This totally unsubstantiated comment would guarantee his removal from the Northern Ireland inquiry. The next day, Anderton, armed with the report, visited Myers at his home in Colwyn Bay. A week later the Scarborough meeting took place 'to demonstrate action without malice and to report', in all likelihood, as a cover for decisions which had already taken.

On 30 May 1986, GMPA was blindsided into accepting the decision that Stalker should take extended leave. Meanwhile, the investigation into Taylor continued with numerous police visits to his various properties. Taylor suspected that this was a deliberate attempt to undermine their sale and make it impossible for him to repay the loans and strengthen the case against him. Continual pressure was put on the DPP to prosecute, without success. Over a year later, the DPP finally approved his prosecution.

The synchronicity of events in the two jurisdictions is remarkable, with delays to Stalker's investigation in Northern Ireland appearing to trigger more frenetic activity into Taylor in Manchester. This, of course, is only speculation and not proof. But the investigation of Taylor was no run-of-the mill affair. It first focused on drugs and then switched to constructing a fraud in the absence of any report from Taylor's bank that it had been defrauded. His banking details, however, were essential in constructing a crime for which to prosecute him and to justify a disciplinary charge against Stalker, guaranteeing his removal from the Northern Ireland inquiry.

Political interference

As this was no normal criminal investigation, the obvious question arises: was Anderton approached by MI5, or perhaps Mrs Thatcher herself, to engineer the removal of Stalker? If this did happen, the most obvious time was in September 1985. This was the month when Stalker submitted his damning interim report which, if acted upon, would have had far-reaching national and international fallout. Moreover, Stalker had not finished his investigation and was still demanding information about the hayshed's intelligence and monitoring. Then, shortly after submitting his report, the DIU with information that Taylor was not after all involved in drugs, switched to his financial affairs and intensified its investigation.

There are a number of factors which support this possibility of political interference. At around this time, Anderton's attitude and behaviour towards his Deputy changed. On receiving the news that Taylor had bought Stalker's airline ticket to holiday in Miami, he did not take the obvious course of action and ask Stalker if he had subsequently paid Taylor for his share of the flight. Similarly, on receiving yet more information on Stalker and Taylor from the DIU, he did not instruct a senior officer to assess critically and grade all the information or call in an outside police force to investigate the allegations against his Deputy as constitutionally required. It was all out of keeping with a man who was widely respected for critical faculties, his sense of fairness and belief in due process.

Six months later, Anderton was clearly determined to have Stalker removed. He approved the damning phrase in the DIU's fourth report that Stalker had reason 'to be sympathetic to the IRA', which was then given to Myers. At the Scarborough meeting he portrayed Stalker in the worst possible light and provided false information (Chapter 17). It strongly suggested that Anderton had agreed to engineer Stalker's demise through the prosecution of Taylor to show that Stalker had criminal friends.

It is known that Anderton was very sympathetic to Hermon's approach in dealing with the IRA and wanted to be Chief Constable of the RUC. He had once said to Stalker when discussing anti-terrorist tactics that you cannot make an omelette without cracking eggs (Chapter 6). He would have considered it his duty if he was approached by MI5 or Thatcher to help remove Stalker. Anderton and Thatcher had met on a few occasions. When she visited Manchester, Anderton afterwards wrote in his diary 'Maggie Thatcher to me: I believe the Commissioner is going soon' [26] – a hint that he was in the running.

In December 1986, Anderton gave his highly controversial speech suggesting that homosexuals, who had HIV/AIDS, were 'swirling in a human cesspit of their own making' (Chapter 6). At the time, he was President of the Association of Chief Police Officers and Byford considered it brought ridicule on the Association – a view held by many Chief Constables. He was also heavily criticised by his own Police Authority. Yet Mrs Thatcher defended him. In addition, Thatcher subsequently turned down a demand for a public inquiry into the Stalker/Sampson affair.

Another factor suggesting political pressure in Stalker's removal was the extraordinary behaviour of the HMIC – a Home Office body tasked with upholding standards in the police (Chapter 17). The Scarborough meeting, comprising some of the most senior police officers in the land, accepted uncritically the alleged evidence against Stalker in the DIU's report, concurred with Anderton's view of his Deputy, and ignored the fact that no one had asked Stalker or investigated further any of the information in the DIU's report. The summary of the meeting prepared by Byford seemed to be solely focused on a 'duty to report'. Then Myers, or someone else in the HMIC, prepared a précis of the DIU's main report which Myers circulated to the Secretary of State for Northern Ireland and DPPNI. The distilled report used absurd logic linking different events and people together, and distorted, embellished and reported inaccurate information.

Finally, support for the theory that there was political interference in Stalker's removal came from Sir Michael Havers, the Attorney General in Thatcher's government from 1979 to 1987. According to Richard Ryan, who reported back to Dublin in February 1988, Havers was critical of his successor, Sir Patrick Mayhew, for not prosecuting those involved in the alleged shoot-to-kill incidents. He told an Irish diplomat in Dublin that he suspected that the matter was specifically covered up by 'MI5 and people within cabinet'.[27] The comment was contained in a public record in the Irish National Archives. A parallel report was not found in the UK National Archive.

Covering-up

Following Stalker's removal, it was widely believed that there was a conspiracy. To counter this, GMP set up a special press and media operation as revealed by Anderton during the extraordinary meeting at the offices of the DPP in London in July 1986 (Chapter 19). He attended the meeting in full uniform, and, unprecedentedly, was accompanied by Myers from the HMIC, a Home Office body with no responsibility whatsoever for prosecutions of suspected criminals. Anderton had made extensive notes for the meeting, focusing on the adverse publicity rather than the evidence against Taylor. The operation was a clear contempt of court, reflecting the extent to which GMP – like the RUC in 1982 when it produced 'cover-stories' in the three incidents investigated by Stalker – was prepared to pervert the course of justice (Chapter 19).

No details of the press and media operation emerged in the civil action, but to challenge effectively the widespread view that there was a conspiracy, it became essential to assert that the investigation into Stalker started in June 1984, pre-dating by several months any of Stalker's alarming discoveries in Northern Ireland – at this stage, Stalker had only just been appointed and the implications of his inquiry were unknown. If this is correct, it would explain why a number of the reports and papers had all the hallmarks of being altered or fabricated to create a narrative which started in June 1984.

Apart from the Bridge Street meeting, other reports, on the balance of probability, were altered or fabricated as part of the press and media operation. The latter may have included Burton's unsigned witness statement prepared for the LFF trial. This listed Taylor as a member of the QSG, but his name appeared to have been added to the document.

It would certainly have included altering McGourlay's report of the golf conversation to increase the suspicion that Stalker fraternised with criminals; the production of the extensive RCS 14 June report on Taylor, based on information collected by the DIU during 1985 and 1986; adding pages to Schiavo's intelligence report to implicate Taylor; and the construction of the 12 July BMW report. The doctoring of the crew/passenger list for the *Sherama* entering Gibraltar may also have been part of the operation. A number of these documents could have been shown to journalists in May 1986, as 'proof' that the investigation began in June 1984 and hence there was no conspiracy.

Sampson's report on his investigation into the disciplinary action against Stalker was a key element in the cover-up. It reproduced the GMP's narrative, uncritically, that the start of the investigation was in June 1984 and that there was no connection between events in Belfast and Manchester. Crucially, it failed to make any mention of Burton's 'I have found your rat' conversation with Burgess in May 1983 which Burgess reported both to the Discipline and Complaints Department and to his Superintendent in the Fraud Department. This was, of course, the very same allegation contained in the fabricated Bridge Street conversation. Similarly, Sampson omits to mention that Topping visited Burgess in January 1985, shortly before the establishment of the DIU and asked him about Burton's allegation.

To have revealed these facts would have undermined the GMP's narrative that Burton only made the allegation about Stalker shortly after the golf course conversation in 1984 rather than in 1983 when no action was taken by either the Fraud Department or the Discipline and Complaints Department in which Topping was then deployed. Burton's information became important only after Stalker was appointed to head up the Northern Ireland inquiry and was in all likelihood the basis for the fabricated Bridge Street conversation. The Sampson report therefore served several purposes: to cover up the truth of what occurred, to protect the reputation of the GMP and to ensure that Stalker would be removed from the Northern Ireland inquiry.

Destruction and retention of public records

A final element of the cover-up in the Stalker/Taylor affair relates to the public records. There is evidence that a number of key files have been withheld. There is a sparsity of documents for the key period in the last two weeks of May 1986 and no clarity on who knew what and when. In particular, there is no clarity on when Hurd was first informed despite three different dates being given by different officials (Chapter 17). As argued, Stalker's removal from the Northern Ireland investigation would have had widespread policing, political and national security consequences, and it is most odd that neither of the two departments most affected were only informed a matter of days before the GMPA took the decision to ask him to take extended leave before suspending him.

Successive governments have often delayed depositing controversial papers in the UK National Archive. The NIO Stalker/Sampson papers discussed above were only deposited seventeen years after the required date and then only after a four-year fight under the Freedom of Information Act, 2000 (FOIA). The struggle illustrates how various sections of the FOIA can be used to avoid any form of public accountability for years, often until those involved have retired or passed away. The ill-defined concepts of 'national security' and 'security matters' provide justifications to retain any embarrassing or illegal activity of the police, army or MI5. If these powers are deemed insufficient, then there is always Section 3(4) of the Public Records Act 1958 which allows files to be closed indefinitely for 'administrative purposes' or 'any other special reason'.

On 18 July 2019, I made a request to the NIO under the Freedom of Information Act, 2000 (FOIA), seeking access to eight of the files. I was refused under section 22 of FOIA on the grounds that they were needed for 'future publication', in this case, forthcoming inquests and police inquiries. The NIO pointed out that the information which I requested 'will be transferred to the National Archive in due course'.[28]

I requested an 'internal review' of the decision. On 8 January 2020, the review partially upheld my claim but only on the grounds that insufficient information was provided as to why, in all the circumstances, it was reasonable to withhold the information. However, it concluded that the balance of public interest lies in maintaining the exemption and in withholding the information on the grounds that the NIO 'is able to manage the transfer of files to the National Archive in an efficient and cost-effective manner that ensures compliance with its obligation to protect sensitive information'.[29] In other words, a bureaucratic reason trumped the public interest. No transfer of the files to the National Archive occurred.

On 31 March 2021, I made a further request for the same files, together with an additional five files. I emphasised that my request was limited to 'the advice and correspondence relating to Stalker's removal and Sampson's appointments'. I was again turned down by the NIO on the same grounds. It claimed that it was retaining the files 'in-house because there was a clear possibility of their being required by the Coroner in relation to the inquest, and by Police Scotland'.[30] Ironically, this decision meant that as long as the inquests into the six killings could be delayed through the use of PIICs, then it was possible to delay depositing the files in the National Archive. Any form of public accountability of state servants could conveniently be paralysed by this combination of the laws.

The NIO also noted that some of the information requested could be exempt from disclosure under section 23(1). This provides that information is 'exempt information' if it is supplied by or relates to bodies dealing with security matters. The exemption is absolute and is not subject to the public interest test. The NIO then added the Kafkaesque comment, 'it is also possible that the information relates to none of the bodies dealing with security matters'.

In other words, section 23 provides a convenient power to exclude from public scrutiny information which has nothing whatsoever to do with information supplied by bodies dealing with security matters. The response went further and also claimed exemption under section 24. This covers anything which is not captured under section 23 on the grounds of 'national security'. Compounding the Kafkaesque situation, the NIO pointed out that, 'we cannot say which of the two exemptions is actually engaged' as to do so would be to undermine 'national security'!

Section 24 is a qualified exemption and the NIO considered whether the balance of the public interest favours releasing or withholding the information. While recognising that openness in government may increase public trust and engagement in government, the NIO nevertheless concluded that there was 'a very strong public interest safeguarding national security'. [31] The information and advice to ministers was now nearly four decades old and it beggars belief how it could be a threat to 'national security' after this length of time. As if these powers were insufficient, the NIO also withheld the information on the grounds of section 40(2) – which exempts information if it relates to someone other than the applicant and disclosure would be against the Data Protection Act. The NIO was determined that no information concerning the Stalker/Sampson inquiries would be open to public scrutiny.

On 7 May 2021, I asked for another internal review of the decision not to release the requested files. I pointed out that in my original request for a limited number of files, there was no mention of the files being retained under sections 23, 24 and 40. I also noted that it was now publicly known that two state agencies – the RUC and the Security Service – had destroyed their copies of the surveillance tape of the hayshed shooting, which was one of the 'perverting the course of justice' incidents investigated by Stalker. The Lord Chief Justice described this behaviour as 'amounting accumulatively to grave misconduct'. I also noted that Stalker was deceived in a meeting with MI5 in June 1985 when told he could have access to the tape when in fact the remaining tape had been destroyed by the Security Service either shortly before or after this meeting. As the section 23 power covers two of the bodies which the Lord Chief Justice accused of 'grave misconduct', the decision to invoke this power prevented any public scrutiny of the correspondence and advice to ministers concerning those actions described as 'grave misconduct'.

I further pointed out that it was not clear from the NIO response the extent to which section 23 or alternatively section 24 were engaged, but that it was inconceivable that all of material in the files requested related to MI5. Therefore, regardless of other considerations, the files could have been released in a redacted form. Regardless of the general absolute nature of the exemption, it should not apply to historic records like these in accordance with s64(2) of FOIA. Finally, there are also rights to records of public interest that may expose wrongdoing under ECHR Article 10.

On 7 June 2021 I received a response. The internal reviewer concluded that retention under exemption 22 was 'both reasonable and appropriate'.[32] Moreover, following assurances, the reviewer concluded that I had received 'a reasonable and clear reply' in relation to exempted material under section 23 and 24, and agreed with the decision to withhold information under section 40. The NIO was not going to release any of the papers.

On 23 June 2021, I made a complaint against the decision to the Information Commissioner, who accepted my complaint for adjudication.[33] In July 2022, the NIO proposed an 'informal resolution request' which I turned down. On 13 September 2023, I received the ICO's decision. It began by noting that during the Commissioner's investigation, the NIO dropped the section 22 exemption, but added two further exemptions – under sections 31 and 38. Section 31 exempts anything which might prejudice law enforcement including the prevention of crime, apprehension and prosecution of offenders, and the administration of justice. This would exempt from public scrutiny any discussion of the possibility that members of the police and security services could be prosecuted for offences, including perverting the course of justice by destroying the hayshed tapes. Section 38 relates to health and safety. This covers any disclosure that would be likely to endanger the safety of any individual. Following the ceasefires and the Good Friday Agreement in 1998, it is hard to understand how releasing information on named individuals concerning events over 40 years ago would endanger the lives of anyone.

The decision notice accepted that the NIO was entitled to reply on exemptions 23, 38, and 40(2) in relation to all the information that was not withheld solely on the basis of section 22. But crucially, the NIO must now provide access to the requested information that does not fall within the scope of exempted sections – within 35 calendar days. Failure to do so may result in the Commissioner making written certification to the High Court. Failure to do so could constitute yet another contempt of court in the Stalker affair.

On 11 October 2023, I was informed that the files would be deposited in the National Archive by mid-December, but I could view the files in the NIO's London Office ahead of their transfer to the National Archives – an invitation which I accepted. As shown, they provided little clarification on who knew what and when (Chapter 17). It seemed that papers had been retained although there was no way of knowing. There was no marker, unlike redacted parts in a document which noted the FOI section used to support the redaction. The delay in depositing the files and the paucity of information in them increases the suspicion that numerous files had been retained under the Kafkaesque clauses of section 23 and 24 and that there had been some sort of cover-up of the conspiracy to remove Stalker.

The Stalker/Sampson files are not the only controversial files to be retained or hidden. Sam McBride, a Belfast journalist, reported that files dealing with agent handling, collusion and myriad other controversial areas have not only been withheld but have been excluded from a list of closed files given to journalists in Belfast.[34]

As well as the retention of files and delay in depositing them, it is known that a number of files have been destroyed. *The Detail* reported that several were destroyed just weeks before the inquests into the six deaths investigated by Stalker were due to begin. The Coroner was advised by the senior legal advisor, Sir Nicolas McPherson, the Treasury's Permanent Secretary, that his Department had undertaken a review to transfer records it held to the National

Archive. As part of that review a number of file series were destroyed whilst others were preserved.[35]

There is nothing new in this behaviour. The United Kingdom has a history of the destruction, retention or concealment of controversial state documents from the public. In 2013, documents relating to Britain's withdrawal from the colonies were finally handed over to the National Archives after 50 years. One document revealed that instructions were given that post-independence governments should not be given any material that 'might embarrass Her Majesty's government', that could 'embarrass members of the police, military forces, public servants or others e.g. police informers', that might betray intelligence sources, or that might 'be used unethically by ministers in the successor government'. Ironically, the protocol was codenamed 'Operation Legacy'.[36]

* * *

On the balance of probabilities, the most plausible explanation of all the available and very contradictory evidence is that there was a conspiracy by senior personnel in the army, RUC SB and MI5 to remove Stalker. MI5 used Burton to spread allegations about Stalker. But once Stalker was a suspect and the DIU had been set to work, MI5 and the highest echelons of government put pressure on Anderton and the HMIC to guarantee Stalker's removal. MI5 probably began the process in late autumn 1984 when it would have been only too aware of the danger posed by Stalker's insistence on gaining access to key intelligence, state agents and the hayshed tape. Then in autumn 1985, approaches were made to Anderton seeking his help in getting rid of Stalker. No police force would have committed so much expenditure and tied up so many senior officers in an investigation for a relatively minor fraud, unless there was some very good reason to do so. It was necessary to construct a crime for which to prosecute Taylor to prove that Stalker had 'criminal' friends.

Following Stalker's removal, an official narrative was constructed to suggest that there was sufficient evidence in June 1984 to mount an investigation into him and his friendship with Taylor. As Stalker had only just begun the Northern Ireland investigation, there was no reason to conspire to remove him immediately, thus avoiding any taint of conspiracy. The official narrative, however, is undermined if, as strongly suspected, documents were fabricated or embellished to make it appear that the start date was in June 1984 rather than in November 1984 when the implications of Stalker's investigation were clear to all in the security establishment. The official narrative was yet another 'cover story', paralleling the conspiracy to construct cover-stories in the three incidents investigated by Stalker.

The careers of two men in Manchester were subsequently ruined. The Rev Canon Michael Burgess, in his opening remarks at Stalker's funeral in 2019, talked about his integrity, single-mindedness, strength of character and courage.[37] A colleague described him as a 'copper's copper' and a man who attained high office 'but never forgot his roots'. Sampson investigated every aspect of his life. Stalker had to account for money lodged in his bank account and explain a holiday from years previously. Although reinstated, he was left with a legal bill of over £20,000. The events surrounding his suspension, removal and reinstatement also had a profound impact on his very close-knit family.[38]

A similar fate befell his friend Kevin Taylor. Every aspect of his life was minutely examined. His property empire was destroyed. He was made bankrupt and his family was forced to rely on the largesse of friends and on social security benefits. The stress of the intense police investigation into his life and business activities affected his health, and he had several heart operations. He died in 2001. The impact on his family, too, was considerable. The £2.4 million which he was awarded following his claim for malicious prosecution, failed to compensate for the £22 million he estimated he had lost. Both men, as well as sharing a friendship, also shared the characteristic of never forgetting their roots. Unfortunately for Taylor, it was his past friendships with the people with whom he had grown up which provided the authorities with information that enabled them to construct a crime against him and engineer Stalker's removal from the Northern Ireland inquiry.

During the conflict in Northern Ireland, the British state often sought to portray itself as the neutral referee adjudicating between two warring tribes.[39] Of course the reality is that the state was involved as an active participant in the conflict. It participated both in direct violence and in the killing by proxy of its own citizens by both republican and loyalist paramilitaries. No-one has been held accountable for the introduction and continuation of the secret MI5/Walker strategy. It prolonged the conflict and has left a legacy in which hundreds of families in both communities in Northern Ireland wish to know whether a state agent was involved in the murder of their loved one. Controversially, accountability is focused on prosecuting 'low-hanging fruit' – the soldiers and police involved in the killings. Those higher up, who devised and implemented the counter-insurgency strategy, withheld and destroyed evidence, arranged for cover stories, lied to police inquiries, perverted the course of justice and, in all probability, conspired to remove Stalker, are never likely to be prosecuted. The rule of law, accountability and transparency were all abandoned in the fight against political violence in Northern Ireland.

Chapter 26

Justice Removed is Justice Denied

THE SIX KILLINGS investigated by Stalker arose from the outworking of the illegal and secret MI5/Walker strategy which formed the bedrock of the intelligence war against the paramilitaries, supplemented by technical surveillance. There has been much discussion by academics, journalists, police officers and security experts on the success or otherwise of the intelligence war. For example, journalist Ed Moloney argues that intelligence was key in forcing the IRA to opt for peace.[1] Former police officers and other commentators have made similar claims.[2] On the other hand, Leahy, who carried out a detailed analysis of the role of informers and agents in different regions in Northern Ireland, concludes that the intelligence war did not influence to any great extent the IRA's decision to call ceasefires in 1994 and 1997. He argues that a number of other factors contributed to the decision, a crucial one being a decline in support for the IRA's campaign from nationalists across Ireland.[3]

Critique of MI5/Walker strategy

Missing from these debates is an assessment and critique of the MI5/Walker strategy itself. As we have seen, the strategy transformed policing in Northern Ireland. The principal aim was to take every opportunity to recruit people to supply intelligence. Hundreds of state agents and informers were recruited, some in high positions within the paramilitary organisations. They were, in many instances, allowed to commit offences with impunity. The detection of crime, protection of life and justice became subordinate to collecting intelligence. The strategy had a profound and long-lasting impact on the rule of law and perceptions of truth and justice in Northern Ireland. Moreover, it has made peacebuilding more difficult because those that lost loved ones in both communities want to know whether a state agent or informer was involved.

It is widely claimed that intelligence gained from informers and state agents saved thousands of lives during the conflict and prevented numerous bombings, hijackings, robberies, and other offences. According to Matchett, a retired RUC SB officer, state agents in republican organisations alone saved at least sixteen thousand lives over a 30-year period – a figure based on an absurd logic.[4] The true figure can never be known, but the 'lives saved' argument has been used constantly to justify the counter-insurgency strategy based on intelligence gathered through the widespread use of informers and state agents. The apparent success, however, is never discussed alongside the number of lives lost as a direct consequence of the strategy and in violation of the state's responsibility to protect the lives of its citizens.

Many lives were lost because people suspected of being agents or informers were subsequently murdered by the paramilitary group that they had infiltrated or were part of. The precise number of people killed is unknown. Sarma notes a figure of 71 in his detailed analysis of informers during the 30 years of conflict.[5] Matchett records the death of over 80 people, 46 of whom were killed after the introduction of the MI5/Walker Strategy in 1981.[6] It was noted (Chapter 22) that just four state agents and informers – Nelson, Haggarty, Haddock and Scappaticci – were suspected of involvement in over 160 murders post 1981. If the deaths of the 46 informers identified by Matchett are added to these killings, at the very minimum, nearly 200 people lost their lives through the outworkings of the MI5/Walker strategy. Moreover, in an unknown number of cases, lives could have been saved, but a decision was taken by RUC SB, or MI5, not to warn the individual but to protect the state agents, as in the case of Pat Finucane. The greater the importance of the state agent, the less likely the person whose life was threatened would be informed.

While prosecuting this deadly counter-insurgency strategy based on the widespread use of spies, MI5 was, at the same time, working to secure peace. This side of their work has been documented in a highly readable book by Peter Taylor.[7] Drawing on extensive interviews, interspersed with descriptions of violent incidents which had not been prevented by intelligence, he details how peace was eventually negotiated principally through the courage of an MI5 officer called 'Robert' and the Derry businessman Brendan Duddy who acted as a secret communication channel between the IRA and MI5. This will now become the dominant narrative of MI5's role in Northern Ireland during the conflict and its other role – running state agents who were allowed to commit murder with impunity – will be kept in the shade.

Lack of a statutory framework for state agents

The fundamental principle of British democracy is that parliament is sovereign, and all policies and strategies must be based on the rule of law. All of the early emergency legislation which transformed the justice system in Northern Ireland, was subject to debate and discussion in parliament before being enacted into law. Even the Prevention of Terrorism (Temporary Provisions) Act, which was rushed through Parliament in 24 hours following the Birmingham pub bombings in 1974, was nevertheless subject to some scrutiny, however perfunctory, before being enacted.[8] In contrast, the MI5/Walker strategy, which fundamentally changed the long-established model of policing and criminal justice in Northern Ireland, was developed in secret by MI5 and then implemented by the RUC, without parliamentary debate or approval.

The strategy was rationalised, no doubt, because of the threat posed by IRA insurgency following the murder of Lord Mountbatten and his boat party, and the death of eighteen soldiers at Warrenpoint in 1979. Apart from the failure to legislate for the broader transformation of policing, there was no specific statutory framework for the running of state agents and informers at the core of the strategy. In May 1987, the RUC wanted more 'realistic' guidelines for handling agents. However, senior civil servants were not enthusiastic about the RUC's initiative and were instructed by PUS in NIO to delay the development of new guidelines (Chapter 22).[9] Their failure to develop a policy to control the criminality of state agents had disastrous consequences for Pat Finucane and many others.

Over the years, there were numerous deliberations within government on the lack of a legal framework for agent handling. De Silva described how the NIO set up a working group, made up of representatives from the Home Office, MI5 and RUC, which developed a set of draft guidelines. It was followed by the Blelloch review and the establishment of an Interdepartmental Working Group under Chilcot's chairpersonship in 1992 (Chapter 22). De Silva provided some information of the content of the working group's draft guidelines and noted that there must be authorisation by an ACC if the informant was engaged in criminal activity.[10] He claimed that MI5 adopted these guidelines in January 1992 and the RUC and JSG likewise in March of the same year.[11] According to de Silva, the guidelines 'did not, in fact, represent the tightly defined framework (coupled with rigorous regulation to prevent abuses) that was required to deal with the complexities of agent-handling in Northern Ireland'.[12] Ironically, throughout the deliberations the principal argument against introducing a statutory framework appeared to be the view that it would not be approved by Parliament.

Authorising criminality of state agents

In 2000, the government introduced the Regulation of Investigatory Powers Act (RIPA) which provided a partial legal basis for the use of 'covert human intelligence sources', CHISs, – informants and state agents – using a system of 'authorisations'. These could be granted on a variety of grounds, including national security and public safety. But RIPA fell short of placing any legal control on the criminality of informers and state agents, and provided no legal protection for their handlers in the event of knowing that their agents are committing crimes. In de Silva's judgement, 'it [RIPA] provides little guidance as to the limits of the activities of covert human intelligence sources'.[13]

Government ministers arguably misled parliament that everything was now lawful. In a debate on the Stevens inquiries in 2003, Jane Kennedy, Minister of State in the NIO, in a carefully written response, said that the government has 'always required public authorities to act within established guidelines' in their use of agents. She continued:

> The Regulation of Investigatory Powers Act 2000 ensured that the guidelines set out by Parliament were compatible with the European Convention on Human Rights. That Act has improved the structures for the management of informants and has ensured far greater accountability than there may have been in the past.[14]

It was a highly ambiguous and disingenuous statement. Parliament had not set out any guidelines to make RIPA compatible with the European Convention on Human Rights. It was much later that MI5 devised a set of guidelines which were never seen or approved by parliament. As with the MI5/Walker report, this once again reflected the unaccountable power of the Security Service to devise policy within the higher echelons of government. The guidelines were dated March 2011 and were, in all probability, developed to deal with the expected criticism in the de Silva report that there was no legal framework for the running of state agents. This suggests that prior to this date state agents were permitted to participate in criminality without even an authorisation.

The existence of the guidelines only emerged in 2017 when Privacy International brought a case before the Investigatory Powers Tribunal (IPT), concerning Bulk Communications Data/Bulk Personal Datasets.[15] During the hearing, the bodies involved in defending the claim – the SoS for Foreign and Commonwealth Affairs, the SoS for the Home Department, GCHQ, MI5, SIS –

inadvertently revealed, because of a sloppy redaction, that the prime minister had issued three directions to the Intelligence Services Commissioner (ISC) – a post set up under RIPA which was meant to provide independent judicial oversight of the conduct of MI6, MI5, GCHQ and the MOD.[16] Two directions were already in the public domain, but the existence of the third direction had been kept secret.

Privacy International and Reprieve then issued proceedings challenging the secrecy and legality of the third direction. On 1 March 2018, Prime Minister Theresa May issued a written statement to the House of Commons, presumably because the existence of the third direction was now public knowledge, and stated disingenuously that: 'Issuing these Directions forms part of our rigorous intelligence oversight system'.[17] She revealed that the third direction instructed 'the Commissioner to keep under review the application of the Security Service guidelines on the use of agents who participate in criminality and the authorisations issued in accordance with them'.[18] In other words, it was revealed in parliament for the first time that authorisations allowed MI5 agents to conduct a range of activities which constituted criminal offences in domestic law.

Privacy International and Reprieve were then joined by the CAJ and PFC to make an amended claim.[19] On 8 June 2018, a heavily redacted copy of the 'Guidelines on the use of Agents who participate in Criminality (Official Guidance)' – hereinafter, the Guidelines – was made available to the claimants.[20] The Guidelines began by acknowledging the regime for authorising the conduct and use of CHISs under RIPA, and emphasising that neither the Act nor its Code of Practice allow CHISs to be authorised to participate in criminality.[21] It then points out that individuals and organisations often pose a threat to national security through the commission of serious offences. 'In these circumstances it may sometimes be necessary and proportionate for agents to participate in criminality' to obtain intelligence.[22] Hence: 'An officer empowered to issue a CHIS authorisation under RIPA may in appropriate cases authorise the use of an agent participating in crime'.[23]

Then, following two heavily redacted paragraphs, the Guidelines describe the 'effect of an authorisation'. It states:

> An authorisation of the use of a participating agent has no legal effect and does not confer on either the agent or those involved in the authorisation process any immunity from prosecution. Rather, the authorisation will be the Service's explanation and justification of its decision should the criminal activity of the agent come under scrutiny by an external body, e.g. the police or prosecuting authorities. In particular, the authorisation process and associated records may form the basis of representations by the Service to the prosecuting authorities

that prosecution is not in the public interest. Accordingly, any such authorisation should, on its face, clearly establish that the criteria for authorisation are met, in terms which will be readily understood by a prosecutor.[24]

It is Kafkaesque in intent and undermines the very purpose of granting permission to an agent to commit crimes as the authorisation has no legal basis. Cleverly, while the Guidelines have no legal basis, they confer some protection for MI5 personnel who run state agents, through an 'explanation and justification' to the prosecuting authorities, presumably from the Attorney General, on the grounds that it would not be in the public interest to prosecute. This is, of course, precisely the procedure adopted in relation to the recommendations of Stalker, and subsequently Sampson. They had recommended that various people should be prosecuted for perverting the course of justice. The Attorney General determined that it was not in the public interest (Chapter 20). As a result, the criminality of state servants never came before the courts. A similar procedure has, therefore, been adopted under the Guidelines permitting state agent handlers, who authorised criminality, to avoid justice. In contrast, the Guidelines provide no protection for the individuals who risked their lives providing information.

There are further problems with the Guidelines: they are contrary to the common law and incompatible with the European Convention on Human Rights; they provide no protection for citizens against whom the criminal acts are committed; there are no limits to the type of crimes that may be committed; and they run counter to the essential element of the rule of law that a citizen should know the law before committing themselves to any action.[25] Finally, the Security Service Act 1989, which placed MI5 on a statutory basis for the first time, contains no reference to authorisations. It is impossible to see how the function of MI5 to protect national security or to support police forces and other agencies in the prosecution and detection of crime, provides any basis for state agents to commit crimes with or without authorisations.[26]

The oversight of the authorisation policy was neutered from the outset. The Intelligence Services Commissioner (ISC) and their replacement, the Investigatory Powers Commissioner (IPC), were side-lined. On 27 November 2012, just days before the publication of the de Silva report, Prime Minister David Cameron wrote to Sir Mark Waller, the IPC, informing him of the secret policy that MI5 handlers can permit informants to participate in crime. But he went on to emphasise that the Commissioner was not to comment on the legality of the secret policy. Cameron continued: 'You would not be asked to provide a view on whether any particular case should be referred to the prosecuting authorities; and your oversight would not relate to any future consideration given by prosecuting authorities to authorisations'. He added that he had considered whether his letter should be published for transparency purposes, but 'concluded that it should not on the basis that doing so would be detrimental to national security and contrary to the public interest'.[27]

Cameron's letter further confirms that the MI5 Guidelines were an attempt to pre-empt de Silva's criticism that there was no law governing the running of state agents by suggesting that there was, in fact, a framework, albeit secret, based on authorisations. As the authorisations had no legal basis, there was a need to instruct the Commissioner not to investigate the legality of the practices. The government had pulled the rug from under the very body which was legally intended to provide oversight and transparency on the work of MI5. The letter made a mockery of the subsequent report from the Cabinet Secretary on 'the lessons learnt' by government departments from the de Silva Report.[28]

In the amended claim brought by Privacy International, CAJ, PFC and Reprieve, seven grounds were advanced to challenge MI5's ability to authorise the commission of criminal offences. The four major grounds were:

1. There was no lawful basis for the policy, either in statute or common law;
2. The policy amounts to an unlawful de facto power to dispense with the criminal law;
3. The secret nature of the policy, both in the past and now, means that it is unlawful under domestic principles of public law;
4. For the purposes of the ECHR, the policy was not and is not 'in accordance with the law'.[29]

On 20 December 2019, the IPT issued its judgment. It rejected all the grounds of the challenge by a majority judgment of three to two. The majority claimed that the Security Service Act 1989 has 'an implied power' for MI5 'to engage in the activities which are under challenge'.[30] But the ruling emphasised that this does not mean that MI5 has any power to confer immunity from liability either in criminal or civil law on either its own officers or on agents handled by them. While MI5 may not have the power, the Attorney General certainly does.

In arguing that the Security Service Act intended to 'continue' the existence of MI5 and the operations conducted by it, it retrospectively provided a legal basis for all the activities of state agents and their handlers, in stark contradiction to de Silva's view that there must be a 'rigorous framework' for the running of informers.[31] Moreover, the system of oversight by the IPT falls far short of a system 'structured as to ensure adequate oversight and accountability', as recommended by de Silva.[32] The judgment, therefore, raises profound and fundamental issues in relation to the rule of law in the United Kingdom. The appellants lodged an appeal against the judgment.

On 9 March 2021, the Court of Appeal dismissed the appeal.[33] It was heard in front of Lord Justices Davis, Haddon-Cave and Dingemans. Although the appeal was based on the lawfulness or otherwise of the Guidelines, the judges considered that the central point was whether there was any legal power on the part of the MI5 to 'authorise' agents' participation in criminality. The judges concluded that the provisions of the Security Service Act 1989, and the Royal Prerogative before it, provided the necessary power. They argued that although the 1989 Act is silent about any actual power relating to the running of agents who commit criminality, MI5 could not carry out its functions without them. Therefore, by implication, the 1989 Act confirms the continuance of the power which MI5 previously assumed under the Royal Prerogative. In short, conduct which is contrary to the criminal and civil law is deemed to be legal on the basis of some undefined, but implied power. As Professor Zellick argued in his minority judgment in the IPT in December 2019, 'to attribute an intention to Parliament in these circumstances is fanciful'.[34]

The Appeal Court judgment contains some remarkable statements which suggest that the eminent justices have little or no understanding of the 30-year long 'dirty war' in Northern Ireland, and implicitly accept that more innocent lives were saved than were lost through the criminality of state agents. They point out that the appellants drew on concrete examples to support their objections to the Guidelines, such as the Finucane case and that of Stakeknife. They refer to the Finucane case, insultingly, as 'a worked (albeit extreme) example, even if not proven' and concerning Stakeknife and Operation Kenova, 'nothing has yet been proved'.[35] They conclude that these are 'cogent points but essentially forensic'.[36] It is not clear what the judges meant by 'extreme example' when murder by state agents was commonplace, or 'nothing has yet been proved', when there is ample evidence that state agents were involved in Finucane's murder. In any event, the meaning is immaterial because the points are dismissed as irrelevant as they cast no light on the meaning of the 1989 Act.

The mindset that the running of state agents obviously saves more innocent lives than are lost is reflected in the statement:

> … in the circumstances of the present case it doubtless would be very surprising to many people that what is styled the 'rule of law' should require the Security Service to desist altogether from running agents who participate in criminal activities, notwithstanding that that is in fact designed to expose and prevent extreme criminal conduct intended entirely, on any view, to subvert the rule of law and (very often) to take innocent human lives in the process.[37]

It did not seem to occur to the eminent justices that the very opposite may be the case: that instead of preventing the loss of innocent lives the murderous activities of state agents subverted what is styled as the rule of law and led to the killing of many innocent people as witnessed in Northern Ireland during the conflict.

The implication of the judgment is far-reaching: it fails to respect parliamentary sovereignty; it allows MI5 to authorise crime without the knowledge of either the police or the DPPNI, usurping the independence of the DPPNI; it permits MI5 to decide whether a prosecution is in the public interest; and it runs counter to the Criminal Law (Northern Ireland) Act 1967, section 5, which requires disclosure of information about serious crimes to a constable.

Finally, and most importantly, it retrospectively confirms that notwithstanding de Silva's conclusion that there was no legal framework for the running of agents in Northern Ireland, the criminal conduct of state agents in Northern Ireland during the conflict was nevertheless lawful under the 1989 Act and previously under the Royal Prerogative, but at the same time such conduct could be liable to prosecution under provisions in the criminal law. Needless to say, these two positions are manifestly incompatible. The rule of law requires that the legal provisions which impact on civilians in their daily lives are spelt out in clear and unambiguous language, and not implied based on some obscure intellectual legal argument of necessity.

In September 2020, prior to outcome of the appeal against the decision of the IPT, the government introduced The Covert Human Intelligence Sources (Criminal Conduct) Bill which became law in 2021.[38] For the very first time, this provides a legal basis to permit state agents and informers to engage in criminal conduct following authorisation. It consolidates but widens the judgment of IPT and provides MI5, MI6, the police, the National Crime Agency, the Serious Fraud Office, and the armed forces, and nine other government departments and authorities, with the power to authorise criminality.[39] One critic described it as 'a license to kill', as there are no limits on the types of crimes permitted.[40] The widespread criminality of state agents, which characterised the conflict in Northern Ireland, will soon be a feature of a wide range of other government bodies. The British state, far from detecting and prosecuting crime, will become an even greater source of it.

The rule of law has been further undermined by the refusal of successive UK governments to uphold an international agreement and establish a judicial inquiry into Finucane's murder as agreed at one stage between the British and Irish governments. Successive Conservative governments have cynically used the law to delay honouring the international agreement made in 2001. In the meantime, evidence has been lost and key witnesses have died.

The reason for delaying any decision is obvious. An inquiry would reveal much about the intelligence-led model of policing and the extent to which state agents employed by MI5, the army and the RUC, were involved in murder. The failure to hold such a public inquiry has protected the higher echelons of government who devised, introduced and operated the illegal MI5/Walker strategy, from prosecutions which would inevitably have been demanded following a judge-led public inquiry. The central problem, as journalist Tom McGurk has pointed out, is that 'the British establishment has to protect those in their intelligence services and police forces who ran this operation and the politicians who approved it'. He went on to say that none of them will ever appear in court because it 'would open up an appalling vista of state-sponsored mass-murder and criminality'.[41]

The failure stands in sharp contrast to the decision of Theresa May, when she was SoS in the Home Office. In 2015, she announced the terms of reference for a judge-led public inquiry into undercover policing in England and Wales.[42] This followed an independent review by Mark Ellison, QC[43] which discovered that undercover police officers had infiltrated hundreds of political and other activist groups. It included spying on the families of Blair Peach who died after being hit on the head during an Anti-Nazi League demonstration against the National Front in London in 1979, and it found appalling practices, including the failure to disclose material to be used in criminal proceedings and deception of the courts.

The form of undercover policing was very different in Northern Ireland, with civilians, rather than police officers, being recruited as state agents in order to infiltrate paramilitary organisations. Moreover in Northern Ireland, the appalling practices related to murder carried out by state agents, as well as failures to disclose material in murder proceedings and deception of the courts and prosecuting authorities. In many respects, therefore, the demand for a public inquiry into undercover policing in Northern Ireland is much stronger than the case in England and Wales.

Historical police investigations

The decision of the Attorney General in 1988 that no-one should be prosecuted for the offences identified by Stalker and Sampson (Chapter 20) was a bitter disappointment to those who believed in the rule of law, particularly, as the Lord Chief Justice, Declan Morgan, considered that the destruction of the surveillance tape recording of the hayshed shooting and the misleading of the DPPNI by both the RUC and MI5 constituted 'grave misconduct' (Chapter 5). But this was not to be the end of the matter. On 14 January 2015, the DPPNI, Barra McGrory QC, requested that the Chief Constable and the Police Ombudsman carry out full investigations into the actions of former RUC and MI5 personnel in withholding, concealment and destruction of surveillance evidence in relation to the hayshed shootings.

Police Scotland were asked to carry out the investigation, which it called Operation Klina. It was staffed by eleven full-time and four part-time police officers and staff. A major part of the work involved collating, scanning and indexing approximately 14,500 documents, and interviewing over 200 potential witnesses. At the beginning of December 2020, Police Scotland submitted its report to the Chief Constable and the DPPNI. The cost of Operation Klina was over £5 million. At the time of writing, it is not known if anyone will be charged and prosecuted with perverting the course of justice or malfeasance in public office.

Operation Klina identified several potential areas for further investigation which lay outside its terms of reference. These principally related to the killing of the three RUC officers by the IRA landmine on Kinnego embankment and included, 'a failure to disclose information within the RUC which may have assisted the investigation; the conduct of senior officers in their assistance to the Stalker/Sampson investigations; and the potential criminal conduct of another person connected with these incidents'.[44] As a consequence, Operation Turma was set up in September 2019 to fully investigate the murder of the three police officers and whether there was evidence of the commission of criminal offences by any of the person(s) connected with the events. It has yet to make recommendations to the DPPNI.

Operation Kenova into the activities of Scappaticci and the DPPNI's decision that none of the 32 suspects should be prosecuted (Chapter 22) raises profound questions about the rule of law and the MI5/Walker counter-insurgency strategy. The DPPNI recommended that there should be no prosecutions on the grounds that the cases failed to meet the evidential test. The principal reason given for the failure was the inadmissibility of 'intelligence' because: a) it had been given on the grounds that it would not be revealed, b) it is generally not intended to be deployed in criminal trials; and c) it is mostly hearsay. To compound matters, the original intelligence record of what the source said was no longer available. Sixteen of the suspects included twelve military personnel attached to the FRU, with responsibility for the handling and management of agents, and two RUC officers. Operation Kenova had recommended that they should be 'prosecuted for perverting the course of justice in relation to the investigation and potential prosecution of a suspect against whom there was an allegation of false imprisonment'.[45] The officers had reached an agreement to ensure that the suspect did not stand trial. One of the military personnel was a lawyer who allegedly provided legal advice on the conspiracy. In short, they conspired to keep Scappaticci – the army's 'most important secret' – out of court.

The implication of the decision not to prosecute anyone is far-reaching. It means that, not only those who are suspected of perverting the course of justice by keeping state agents and informers out of court, but also those who knowingly allowed agents to commit crimes including murder as part of the MI5/Walker counter-insurgency strategy, cannot be successfully prosecuted because intelligence is inadmissible. Ní Aoláin showed that the law is 'structurally incapable' of responding to systematic violations of lethal force.[46] These decisions of the DPPNI show that the law is similarly incapable of dealing with widespread state criminality. In fact, it was probably designed to do just that.

Following the DPPNI's decision in 2020 not to prosecute Scappaticci for perjury,[47] Boutcher pointed out that there are many challenges in bringing prosecutions in legacy cases, and that legacy should not be judged simply through the prism of prosecutions, but also in terms of bringing truth to the families.[48] This is certainly correct. But Boutcher's family focus shifts attention away from the state and the deadly counter-insurgency strategy it pursued. As the veteran BBC reporter John Ware has noted, Boutcher's investigations raise new and searching questions and crucially,

> risk an official rewriting of history about the ultimate benefit of the intelligence-led policing model that dominated the UK's counter insurgency strategy from 1980. It was this approach that prioritised intelligence picture building through a prolific informer network over exploiting intelligence more fully for the benefit of the criminal justice system. Sometimes preserving that informer network also cost lives.[49]

The day after the DPPNI's December 2023 statement in relation to Operation Kenova, Boutcher insisted that prosecutions are peripheral. He pointed out that they formed only a tiny element for the 238 families affected by his investigations. He went on to say that families had spoken highly about the information which they had already been given and the way they had been treated. He ended by saying: 'This is the way to do legacy.'[50] But while helping some families, it shifts attention away from the activities of the state in running hundreds of agents who were permitted to commit murder with impunity.

The devastating conclusion is that the Northern Ireland criminal justice system has been politically neutered and has been totally ineffective in bringing criminal charges against state operatives, undermining the rule of law. They were responsible for: developing the illegal MI5/Walker strategy; running murderous state agents, such as Scappaticci and Nelson; destroying vital evidence, knowing that it was required in murder trials; and producing cover stories to deceive the DPPNI and the courts.

Legacy Plans

Over the years, there have been numerous discussions, consultations, and commitments from governments since the Good Friday Agreement on how to deal with the past, but there has been delay after delay, and no resolution.[51] In 2014, the British and Irish governments published the Stormont House Agreement (SHA).[52] It proposed four institutions to deal with legacy issues: a Historical Investigation Unit; an Independent Commission on Information Retrieval; an Oral History Archive; and an Implementation and Reconciliation Group. The proposals were supported by the main political parties. Under the SHA, the British government agreed to introduce legislation to honour these commitments. No legislation was introduced, however. In January 2020, agreement was reached in the New Decade, New Approach (NDNA) to restore the collapsed Northern Ireland Executive. As part of the agreement, the British government once again agreed to implement the SHA and to introduce draft legislation within 100 days.[53] It failed to meet this commitment too and the Secretary of State (Julian Smyth MP) who made the commitment was sacked in February 2020.

In March 2020, before 100 days had passed, the new SoS for Northern Ireland, Brandon Lewis, made a ministerial statement to the Westminster parliament on the government's 'new approach' to dealing with the past.[54] It overrode most of what had already been agreed in the SHA between the political parties in Northern Ireland, and between the British and Irish governments. In the context where a presumptive amnesty had been proposed after five years for veterans who served in Iraq and Afghanistan in the Overseas Operations (Service Personnel and Veterans) Bill 2020, the ministerial statement promised 'equal treatment of Northern Ireland veterans and those who served overseas'.[55] The Joint Committee on Human Rights was subsequently forthright in its criticism of the Bill. It argued against having two different classes of defendants or different classes of victims and was most opposed to the introduction into domestic law of a special category of defendant, namely members of the armed forces.[56]

The March statement emphasised that information recovery would be at the centre of the new legacy system, noting, cynically, that: 'The Government is committed to the rule of law but given the considerable time that has elapsed since many of these incidents took place it is vital that we swiftly implement an effective information recovery mechanism before this information is lost forever'.[57] In addition to hinting at the amnesty proposals to come, the statement proposed that the police would only investigate those cases in which there was compelling new evidence and a prospect of prosecution.

The Committee of Ministers, in reviewing the judgments of the ECtHR in relation to several cases arising out of the Northern Ireland conflict, was highly critical of the British government's new proposals. It expressed 'profound concern' that the British government had not provided any details in response to the Committee's request for information on the approach to legacy investigations set out in the March statement.[58] It had requested to know how the current proposal would meet its obligation under Article 2 of the Convention.[59] It called upon the British government to legislate for the SHA. All these failures reflected a broad disregard for the ECtHR.

The Queen's speech on 19 December 2020 announced that the government would bring forward proposals to seek better ways of dealing with legacy issues that provide better outcomes for victims and survivors.[60] On 14 July 2021, the government published a command paper with its proposals, formally abandoning the Agreement reached with the Irish government and local political parties in 2014.[61] It proposed a statute of limitations on all Troubles-related cases, bringing an immediate end to criminal investigations and barring PONI from carrying out investigations. It also proposed to end all 'judicial activity' covering current and future civil cases and inquests.

The government made a commitment 'to full disclosure in order to provide information to families'. It claimed that there would be a 'legal duty' on state bodies and agencies to provide full disclosure. This would extend to the armed forces, the police and the security services. The government insisted that it was committed to openness and transparency. Judging by past behaviour, it is a most disingenuous commitment. Throughout the Troubles, judicial and police inquiries reported that crucial documents and other evidence were withheld from them by the army, police and security services. Extensive use was made of PIICs to prevent disclosure of information in inquests and judicial actions, based upon the vague and ill-defined notion of 'national security'. As the PFC/JFF commented: 'it would be extremely naïve to expect that agents of the British state, who were involved in collusive acts, or indeed the British state itself, would participate openly and truthfully in such a scenario'.[62]

The legacy proposals were denounced by victim groups, Stormont's five main political parties, and the Dublin government. Barra McGrory, a former DPP for Northern Ireland, said he was shocked by the proposals and claimed that the government was seeking 'to abolish completely all meaningful and judicial accountable processes'.[63] The head of the Northern Ireland Human Rights Commission said that the proposals raised, 'profound issues about the veracity of the rule of law' and pointed out that they disregarded the requirement of an effective investigation under Article 2 of the ECHR.[64]

A representative of the Ballymurphy families, whose relatives were shot dead by the British Army in 1971 and who were cleared of any wrongdoing at an inquest in 2020, said: 'We see this as the British Government's cynical attempt to bring in an amnesty and a plan to bury its war crimes'.[65] A group of lawyers in Queen's University Belfast and CAJ, who had worked to find human rights compliant solutions to the legal and political challenges regarding dealing with the past in Northern Ireland, produced a devastating critique of the proposals.[66]

The legacy command paper contained two spurious claims. It noted that 'Security Forces were responsible for around 10 per cent of Troubles-related deaths – the vast majority of which were lawful'.[67] The 10 per cent figure, however, only refers to those directly killed by the security forces. As more evidence emerges of the involvement of state agents in killings, this figure needs to be revised. Instead of the responsibility for the deaths being attributed to the paramilitaries, they should be primarily or wholly attributed to the security forces. If, for example, the 171 suspected murders and conspiracies to murder in which the four state agents and informers Nelson, Haggarty and Haddock, and Scappaticci are believed to have been involved (Chapter 22), are allocated to the security forces, the 10 per cent figure would increase to 14.8 per cent.[68]

This percentage would increase still further if the 120 people killed by the Glenanne gang, which involved members of the RUC and UDR,[69] and the 70 murders arising from the importation of arms involving the collusive help of state actors, are also included.[70] This reworking of the statistics, as Brendan O'Leary has pointed out, will be seen as republican revisionism by unionists, and an effort to rewrite history, but 'what are at issue to any reasonable observer are the scale and depth of collusion between the security forces and loyalist militias, not its existence'.[71]

Second, the claim that the 'vast majority' of deaths at the hands of the security forces were 'lawful', is simply not true.[72] The 23 people killed by the British Army in Ballymurphy in 1971 and on Bloody Sunday in 1972 were all proven to be innocent, indicating a *prima facie* case that they were killed unlawfully.

Similarly, it cannot be claimed that all of the 186 children under sixteen who were killed by the security forces during the Troubles were killed lawfully.[73] In any event, no such claim that any of these deaths were lawful can be made in the absence of a robust Article 2 investigation and there are still many investigations outstanding.

Northern Ireland Troubles (Legacy and Reconciliation) Act, 2023

On 16 May 2022, late in the evening, the SoS for Northern Ireland announced that he would introduce legislation to enact the government's proposals on legacy. The very next day the Northern Ireland Troubles (Legacy and Reconciliation) Bill was given its first reading. The Bill contained an extraordinary provision, of which any dictator would have been proud, retrospectively nullifying any civil action which began on or after the first reading of the Bill on 17 May 2022. In other words, before the Bill even became law.[74]

The group of lawyers from Queen's University and CAJ continued to be highly critical of the proposed legislation, arguing that it was 'unworkable, in breach of the Good Friday Agreement and binding international law, and that it will not deliver for victims and survivors'.[75] In particular, the group was highly critical of the direct government control over the establishment and operation of all the proposed mechanisms. It was also universally condemned by victims' groups and politicians. Stephen Farry MP, Alliance Party deputy leader, described the legislation as 'irredeemable and fatally flawed'.[76]

On 18 September 2023, the bill received the Royal Assent. It constitutes one of the most egregious and pernicious pieces of legislation ever enacted in peacetime. It effectively abolishes the rule of law for the period of the conflict and is an assault on the administration of justice and the human rights of victims. It bans all further police and Ombudsman investigations. As well as stopping all civil actions, it bans all future inquests. Among hundreds of affected inquests, it will prevent the inquests into the six men killed in the three incidents investigated by Stalker. Within days, sixteen legal challenges had been lodged against the legislation.[77] In December, the Irish government initiated an inter-state case against the UK government at the ECtHR. It was particularly concerned about the provisions which grant immunity and which shut down existing avenues for truth and justice recovery. It considered that the provisions were incompatible with the UK's obligations under the ECHR which is, of course, enshrined in the Good Friday Agreement.[78]

The British government has put forward several different reasons for rejecting the legacy proposals agreed in the SHA: to produce better outcomes for victims;[79] the need to focus on reconciliation; ending the cycle of investigations;[80] and preventing 'divisive' legal processes from driving a wedge between the two communities[81] – as if they were not already divided. The dominant explanation, however, became the need for equal treatment of veterans who served in Northern Ireland with those who served overseas and to stop 'vexatious claims' against soldiers arising from police investigations. Stephen Farry, MP, challenged ministers to cite examples of what they meant by 'vexatious', but they failed to do so. He pointed out that the Northern Ireland criminal justice system was rigorous and self-polices any vexatious cases.[82] Johnny Mercer, a former British Army officer who was appointed Minister for Veteran Affairs in 2022, became the strongest advocate of this explanation for the NI legacy legislation: 'My point has always been that I don't want veterans' lives completely ruined and interminably investigated and exposed to trying to get to a truth that I think is almost impossible to get to now, 50 years later'.[83]

The much stronger explanation for the legislation, however, is that government, and MI5 in particular, wished to cover-up the Security Service and the security forces collusion with paramilitaries and the possibility that a whole range of public servants, many of them in senior ranks, could be prosecuted for offences committed in the out-workings of the MI5/Walker counter-insurgency strategy. Police inquiries, PONI investigations, inquests and civil legal actions, were slowly producing more evidence of the 'dirty war'. While enormous efforts have been made and continue to be made to restrict the amount of information in the public domain, judges were becoming increasingly critical of the delays in the production of documentation by the authorities.

The legislation establishes a so-called Independent Commission for Reconciliation and Information Recovery (ICRIR) with two principal positions: a Chief Commissioner and a Commissioner for Investigations. It is tasked with six main functions: to 'review' deaths and other harmful conduct during the conflict; to produce reports and determine whether to grant persons immunity from prosecution; to refer deaths, if necessary, to the prosecution authorities; and to produce a historical record of deaths. Despite its title, it will do little to help reconciliation and it is far from independent as the SoS has powers to control all aspects of the Commission's work.

Although the Commissioner for Investigations may decide that a criminal investigation is to form part of a review, it is significant that criminal investigations are not listed as one of the six functions. The emphasis throughout is on reviews. This is no accident. It will be recalled that Stalker had been expected to 'review' the material on the six killings but instead carried out detailed criminal investigations. He uncovered extensive criminality by state officials, causing considerable embarrassment. In preventing any further embarrassing revelations, the government appears to have learnt from the Stalker affair.

The ICRIR will have the power to grant immunity. It must do so if (a) a person has requested such immunity, (b) it relates to conduct during the conflict and is true to the best of the person's knowledge and belief, and (c) the immunity panel is satisfied that the disclosed conduct would expose the person to criminal investigation or prosecution. Professor Louise Mallinder, a legal expert on amnesties, pointed out that the proposals amount to an amnesty far wider than the one introduced by Augusto Pinochet in Chile.[84] The requirement that an applicant has only to believe their account is true sets an incredibly low bar for immunity and provides a convenient route for state agents, their handlers and those who devised the MI5/Walker counter-insurgency strategy to avoid prosecution for a range of offences.[85]

Another highly contentious feature of the Act pertains to disclosure. While it makes obligatory for the relevant authority to make available to the ICRIR information, documents and other material 'reasonably' required for the ICRIR to carry out its review and immunity functions, this obligation is nullified by a series of prohibitions on disclosure. The main prohibition concerns 'sensitive material'. This covers information held by MI5, MI6, GCHQ, the Ministry of Defence, the army, PSNI and GB police forces. Other prohibitions relate to data protection and international information. These extensive prohibitions undermine the stated purpose of the legislation, namely, to provide information to families about the circumstances of the deaths of their loved ones.

The Act contains a complicated schedule dealing with disclosure. The first part details disclosures that are permitted and the second part covers decisions to prohibit disclosure of sensitive information in the final reports. At every stage, the SoS is involved in the decision, making a mockery of the independence of the ICRIR. The disclosure of information to a family is only permitted if the ICRIR has notified the SoS and he or she has approved the disclosure. In making a decision to deny release of 'sensitive information' in a family report, the SoS must consider whether it 'would risk prejudicing, or would prejudice, the national security interest of the United Kingdom'.[86] These decisions cannot be taken without the advice of MI5 which will therefore become central in determining what can or cannot enter the public domain about the secret, illegal and counter-insurgency strategy which it introduced in 1981.

Four months before the legislation became law, the government announced that the former Lord Chief Justice of Northern Ireland, Sir Declan Morgan, had been appointed Chief Commissioner.[87] It left victims' groups and others incredulous as to how a Lord Chief Justice could accept a post which effectively abolished the rule of law. Crucially, he was now in a position to grant impunity to state actors which made a mockery of the constitutional distinction between the judiciary, legislature and executive branches of government.

The controversial body's independence was further undermined with the appointment of Peter Sheridan, a retired Assistant Chief Constable of the RUC as Commissioner of Investigations. Many viewed his appointment as the RUC investigating the RUC.[88] But concerns went much deeper. When Sheridan was Assistant Chief Constable, he worked with MI5 to develop principles designed to ensure the sharing of information between the two organisations.[89] With this background, columnist Brian Feeney asked, 'how can he be seen to meet the essential elementary requirement that an investigator must be independent from everyone under investigation when he could be investigating former comrades' actions?'[90]

In an interview Sheridan posed the question whether the legislation was morally justified.[91] He pointed to difficult decisions which had been taken in the past. He mentioned the release of paramilitary prisoners under the GFA, the decommissioning of weapons without being forensically examined, the end of all extradition cases and the remains of the disappeared not being tested, as if these decisions justified the legislation and his participation in it. All these decisions, however, related to the paramilitaries. The legacy legislation, crucially, covers state actors as well as non-state actors and raises the fundamental question in a democracy: *Quis custodiet ipsos custodes*? – Who guards the guards? As has been argued throughout this book, the state has an obligation to protect its citizens and uphold the rule of law. It must be accountable. This legislation will destroy every mode of accountability.

In October 2023, Jon Boutcher became interim head of the PSNI after the resignation of Simon Bryne. He was subsequently appointed Chief Constable. It was another crucial appointment in relation to the legacy legislation. He will now be the final arbiter of what information is released in the new legacy structures. There have been numerous examples in the past of the PSNI refusing, or taking an inordinate amount of time, to release information. One recent example is the case of Sean Brown.

On 12 May1997, Brown was murdered by the LVF. He was abducted as he was locking up the gates at Bellaghy Wolfe Tone GAC and shot. It was strongly suspected that there had been collusion or that one of the assassins was a state agent.[92] No one has ever been charged with his murder. In the 26 years since his death, there have been almost 40 linked inquest hearings. Deadlines for compliance and disclosure have been ignored by the MOD and the PSNI. At an inquest in early December 2023, a letter from the Crown Solicitor's Office was read out. It said that the PSNI had 'encountered issues arising from what can broadly be described as intelligence coverage' and that the issues required a closed hearing, which was not part of the coronial system. The letter then announced that the PSNI's position was that: 'an inquest is not the appropriate vehicle for the continuation of the investigation into the death of Mr Brown'.[93] Des Fahy, KC, the family's barrister, argued that the responsibility rested solely with the state parties and it was a public shame and disgrace.[94] At a more recent hearing, it was reported that state agents were among 25 individuals linked to Brown's murder.[95]

Nuala O'Loan, the Northern Ireland Police Ombudsman, who carried out an investigation into Brown's murder in 2004 and found that the police investigation was incomplete and inadequate, but there was no evidence of collusion, was asked about the latest development in the inquest.[96] She described the new information as 'shocking', pointing out that if she had had the new information, 'I would have had a different report'. She went on to say that she thought that it was 'outrageous that it has taken this long, and the Brown family have had to sit through hearing after hearing when material hasn't been produced'.[97]

The following week it emerged that the surveillance on a leading suspect in the murder, Mark Fulton, was lifted the night before the murder, adding to the family's suspicion that there was collusion. Following further demands for PIICs from state agencies for multiple redactions of sensitive files, the coroner abandoned the inquest. Niall Murphy, the solicitor for the family asked: 'What is it that MI5 have to hide from the family and indeed wider society?' He also asked: 'Who was it that decided that the surveillance on Mark Fulton be lifted the day before Sean Brown's murder?'[98] The coroner criticised how the state parties had handled disclosure, branding the repeated delays as 'deplorable and frankly inexcusable'. He said that he would write to the Secretary of State and ask for a public inquiry. Boutcher, now Chief Constable, said he recognised the continuing distress for families and acknowledged that they had a right to answers. His comments, however, will do little to encourage nationalists to join the PSNI after it was seen, along with MI5, to sabotage the inquest in the murder of a well-known and highly respected GAA official. The silence on Britain's dirty war is likely to affect policing for years to come.

On 24 February 2024, the High Court declared that the immunity provisions of the Legacy Act were incompatible with the ECHR and should be disapplied.[99] It further declared that stopping civil claims relating to the Troubles, the prohibition of criminal enforcement action, and sections of powers relating to interim custody orders were all incompatible with ECHR. However, there were two highly controversial declarations.

First, the court declared that the ICRIR was sufficiently independent given the statutory arrangements together with the published policy documents. This was unsurprising as it would have been very difficult for a High Court judge to argue that the head of the ICRIR, a former Lord Chief Justice, was not sufficiently independent. Perhaps there was even some 'judicial collusion' on the content of the policy documents to guarantee that they were compliant. In relation to Peter Sheridan, the ex RUC/PSNI officer who was appointed head of investigation, the court noted that he must recuse himself from any review involving an incident in which he was involved as a 'former RUC/PSNI officer, or in respect of which there is a personal conflict of interest'. But there will be a conflict of interest in any case in which a state agent was involved because he worked with MI5 on sharing of intelligence but he would not know in advance if a state agent was providing intelligence and therefore if there was a conflict of interest.

Second, the court concluded that, as the relevant authority must make available to ICRIR such information that may reasonably be required, the powers of disclosure are compliant with Art 2/3 of ECHR. Yet, the history of police investigations, civil actions and inquests over the last fifty years have all been characterised by the continual failure of the authorities, particularly MI5, to disclose information. They have used PIICs, closed hearings and or legislation pertaining to the vague notion of 'national security' to deny or delay access to information. The inquests in relation to the six killings investigated by Stalker all collapsed because of the failure to disclose information. Only in 2024, 27 years after the murder of Sean Brown, have MI5 released information that 'several state agents' were linked to the suspects, but withheld other crucial information. To expect MI5, an organisation which has consistently ignored the rule of law, to disclose information as a result of the insertion of the word 'must' shows a profound naivety. In any event, the inclusion in the legislation of the notion 'sensitive information', provides ample opportunity to retain details, particularly about the crucial role of state agents in murder and other crimes.

Disdain for the law

The legacy legislation was enacted against a background of recent Conservative governments moving to the right and showing a general disdain for international law, democratic principles and the rule of law. It was introduced in parliament by Brandon Lewis, SoS for Northern Ireland, who in March 2020 announced that the British government was shelving Irish Sea checks agreed with the EU. Although challenged by Hilary Benn to spell out what part of the Northern Ireland Protocol provided the power to take such unilateral action, he failed to do so. Lewis merely reiterated it was lawful and consistent with the progressive and good-faith implementation of the Protocol.[100] In 2023, he was knighted for public and political service.

Lewis is not alone in his disdain for the rule of law and democratic principles. On 28 August 2019, Prime Minister Boris Johnson requested the Queen to prorogue parliament in order to ensure that the UK left the European Union. The Supreme Court ruled that his government had acted unlawfully. During the Covid pandemic, the government rushed through emergency legislation which permitted the introduction, without debate, of many contradictory and confusing laws, forensically analysed by Adam Wagner.[101]

In June 2020, the government introduced a bill aimed at unilaterally changing trade, tax and governance arrangements in the 2019 Protocol deal with the EU. It was accompanied by a policy paper which claimed that it was legal, arguing that the doctrine of necessity in international law provided 'a clear basis' from which to justify non-performance of its international legal obligations.[102] The European Commission immediately announced that it would take legal action. Maroš Šefčovič, European Commission vice-president, said there was 'no legal or political justification whatsoever for unilaterally changing an international agreement'.[103]

In April 2022, the government announced a new immigration policy which allows the UK to deport asylum seekers to Rwanda, where their claims for asylum will be made to the Rwandan government for settlement in Rwanda. In November 2023, the Supreme Court declared unanimously that the scheme was unlawful. The government then introduced a bill which established for the purposes of UK law that Rwanda was a safe country. Of considerable concern, the Act disapplies certain sections of the Human Rights Act 1998 which allows the government to ignore emergency orders from the ECHR in breach of its international legal obligations.

At the same time, there has been much talk within government of withdrawing from the ECHR. If it did, the UK would join Russia, which withdrew just a month after it carried out its illegal invasion of Ukraine, and Belarus, which has never been a signatory. Greece withdrew in the 1960s after a military dictatorship abolished democracy. It rejoined later on a return to democracy. There has been little understanding among those who argue for ECHR withdrawal that the Good Friday Agreement commits to the protection and vindication of human rights for all, underwritten by a commitment to the ECHR.

All of these concerning developments have been accompanied by constant criticisms of those in the legal profession. On 4 November 2016, *The Daily Mail*, whose 1930s owner, Viscount Rothermere, supported Hitler,[104] infamously carried the headline, 'Enemies of the People' under a picture of three judges. More recently, criticisms have been directed at 'leftie lawyers' involved in immigration cases. In October 2020 over 800 judges, lawyers and legal academics signed a letter arguing that the prime minister and home secretary had endangered the personal safety of lawyers through their attacks on the profession. It was to no avail. In July 2023, Conservative Party officials circulated criticism of the Labour Party for having links to lawyer Jacqueline McKenzie, who had challenged an asylum seeker deportation to Rwanda. She was then subject to all sorts of threats and abuse.[105] The murder of Pat Finucane illustrates the danger of politicians making accusations against lawyers and judges. We live in dangerous times.

A final word

This book has examined the state and its institutions – the police, the military and the intelligence services and their role during the Troubles in Northern Ireland. One of the primary functions of any state is to protect its citizens from harm. Yet hundreds of innocent victims were killed by people employed as agents and informers by the state following the introduction by MI5 of the secret counter-insurgency strategy in 1981. As argued, it transformed policing from one principally based on the prosecution and detection of crime to one based on intelligence. Using a variety of methods, every opportunity was taken to recruit state agents and informers from within both loyalist and republican organisations. These individuals were then allowed to commit crimes, including murder, with impunity. Policing became an antinomian system effectively free of control and accountability. Deceit was hard-wired into the strategy.

The lies and cover-up stories discovered by Stalker were principally constructed to hide the methods of surveillance used and, to a lesser extent, the need to protect those who supplied intelligence. Following a killing by the police, a high-level group of RUC officers would meet to plan a cover story. Incidents were fabricated, documents altered, tapes destroyed, and key information withheld from the CID and DPPNI. Stalker was frustrated at every turn. There is little doubt that the difficulties and problems he faced in his investigation into the six killings stemmed directly from the counter-insurgency strategy. In all probability, it was also the direct cause of a conspiracy, most likely by MI5 and the highest levels of government, to remove him from leading the Northern Ireland investigation. He was threatening to undermine the strategy by demanding access to intelligence and methods of surveillance. He was also prepared to recommend the prosecution of the criminality of state actors associated with the strategy.

There was further deceit and cover-up of this deadly counter-insurgency strategy in 1988 when the Attorney General, Sir Patrick Mayhew, and senior government officials decided to stop all the prosecutions recommended by Stalker – and subsequently by Sampson – claiming that it was not in the public interest. It was never explained how granting impunity to those who perverted the course of justice was in the public interest. Throughout the period of the conflict, an egregious appeal to the notion of public interest was constantly made with the issue of Public Interest Immunity Certificates to prevent documents entering the public domain in an inquest or legal action. At other times, the authorities either denied that there were any relevant documents or simply delayed their production. The powers under the misnamed Public Records and Freedom of Information Acts are still being used to withhold from the National Archive thousands of files relating to the conflict in Northern Ireland.

There was further cover-up in Northern Ireland with the constant refusal to establish an inquiry into the murder of Belfast solicitor, Pat Finucane. Despite an international agreement with the Irish government, successive British governments have used a variety of methods to delay establishing an inquiry. When eventually de Silva revealed that there was no legal framework for running informers and state agents, there was further deceit, as we have shown. MI5 and government officials devised the system of authorisations, which David Cameron, the then Prime Minister, approved in secret. Authorisations were eventually legislated for in the Covert Human Intelligence Sources (Criminal Conduct) Act, 2021 – an act which extended the use of spies by government agencies.

In Manchester, the level of deceit was extensive. The GMP clumsily carried out a secret police investigation into its own Deputy Chief Constable. It then constructed a crime against Taylor, a Manchester businessman with no criminal record, in order to support a vague disciplinary charge against Stalker of associating with known criminals. Officers failed to sign and date documents, at least one document was forged, and others were changed or doctored. Files, police diaries and other records were hidden, lost or destroyed. Lies were told under oath. Huge pressure was put on witnesses in the criminal prosecution of Taylor for fraud and the police even attempted to disrupt the sale of Taylor's properties. Untrue and absurd statements were made by the Chief Constable, Sir James Anderton, such as Taylor 'was a central figure in the criminal life of Manchester and had connections with organised crime', and 'it could well be said by some that he [Stalker] has reasons to be sympathetic to the IRA'.

The legacy of the Stalker affair lives on. The families of those who lost loved ones during the Troubles struggle on an almost daily basis to seek truth and/or justice. Many have died but the determination to ascertain the truth continues with their next generation. While some may hope that they will be able to discover from the new legacy structures what happened to their loved ones and whether there was collusion, many more are united in their opposition to the ban on all Troubles-era police and ombudsman investigations, inquests and civil actions. Justice removed is justice denied.

Acknowledgements

THE RESEARCH for this book began nearly 30 years ago when I first met Kevin Taylor at the start of his civil action against the Greater Manchester Police. I subsequently met him and his wife, Beryl, on many occasions. The more I read, the more questions I wished to ask. They were both very willing to answer all my questions. Kevin subsequently gave me access to his personal papers, which proved invaluable in piecing the story together. Without Beryl and Kevin's help, the book would have been impossible. I am therefore deeply indebted to them. Since their untimely deaths, I have had the help of their two daughters Emma and Kate, and I thank them for their continuing support for a project which stretched out over so many years.

The book would also have been impossible without the help of David Hood, who was Kevin Taylor's barrister in the criminal trial and part of the legal team in the civil action. He encouraged my work from the outset and patiently listened as I tried to make sense of the contradictory and inconsistent reports and documentation. I was extremely fortunate to have had the help and advice of someone with an encyclopaedic memory who could recall names and details many years later.

While at Bristol University during the 1990s, I received a great deal of support and encouragement from several colleagues. I would like to thank, in particular: Brian Caddick, David Gordon, Hilary Land, Lois Bibbings, Chris Pantazis, Andrew Sanders, Peter Townsend and Sophie Watson. After moving back to Northern Ireland in 1999, I am most grateful to many colleagues at Queen's University and the University of Ulster. I would like to thank: Kieran McEvoy, Monica McWilliams, Louise Mallinder, Fionnuala Ní Aoláin, Bill Rolston, Phil Scraton and Mike Tomlinson.

Over the years, I have had intellectual inspiration and research assistance from chats, correspondence and interviews with many people, some of whom sadly, are no longer with us. I would especially like to thank: Frank Bannon, Jonty Brown, Maggie Beirne, Charles Buckley, Stephen Bullock, Tony Bunyan, Derek Burgess, Vicky Canning, Chris Jones, Dave Cox, Duayne J. Dillon, Jimmy Donnelly, Richard Dunley, Luis Fa, Michael Farrell, Pete Gill, Didi Gipser, Francis Green, Bill Greenslade, Tom Griffin, Brian Gormally, Adam Harkens, Stephen Hayes, Daniel Holder, Peter Jackson, Jeri Johnson, Seamus Kearns, Amanda Klapish, Barra McGrory, Gemma McKeown, Rob McLoughlin, Paul Lashmar, Micky Martin, Jennifer Miles, Chris Moore, John Moore, David Murphy, Chris Newstead, Maurice O'Connor, Paul O'Connor, Mary O'Rawe, Ian Palmer, Rodger Pannone, Sam Pollock, Ann Singleton, Steve Tombs, Brian Rowan, Chris Ryder, Patrick Speight, Mark Thompson, Mari Ward, Jane Winter, Scott White, Steve Wright and Heiner Zilmer.

Several people have read various drafts or the full manuscript and made many edits and suggestions. My considerable thanks to: Ann Cadwallader, Alan Brecknell, Martin Finucane, Paul Nolan, Carolyn Reading, Mike Ritchie, Dawn Sherratt-Bado, Joe Sim, Sophie Watson and Margaret Urwin. Over the years, I have been involved in four human rights NGOs: the National Council for Civil Liberties, Statewatch, the Committee on the Administration of Justice and the Pat Finucane Centre. I have benefited greatly from the insights and discussions with both staff and board members. I would like to thank them all.

The introduction of scanners allowed me to develop a database of material on my computer and provided the opportunity to research the documentation and to to write for periods in both northern and southern Italy. I would like to thank all my Italian friends who made these visits so productive and enjoyable: La famiglia Andreola, Grazia and Michele Angelini, Lello Calianno, Erminio Sertorelli, Sergio Sertorelli, la famiglia Comfortola, Roberto Bardhok, Beppe Mosconi, Massimo Simeone, Teresa and Pino Lapis, Anna, Nicola and Teresa Loparco, and all at Vetrère cantina. Other friends have given much encouragement along the way: to my Easy Rider buddies – Mari and Niall Fitzduff, John O'Neill and Paul Nolan; Maggie Feeley and Ann Hegarty; Krysia Piotrovska and Mike; many thanks.

Considerable thanks to Rachael Dickson who provided research support through funding from a Leverhulme Foundation Emeritus Fellowship. The Fellowship provided the resources and impetus to bring the research to completion. Their small grants encourage intellectual endeavour long after the normal retirement age of 65. My grateful thanks to all the grant assessors at the Leverhulme Foundation.

A very special thanks to Robbie McVeigh, Bill Rolston and Mike Tomlinson at Beyond the Pale Books for accepting my long manuscript. I owe considerable thanks to Mike for his numerous improvements, careful editing and support throughout the project. The final version of the book is considerably better than the original draft. Any errors which remain are mine.

Finally, I cannot express enough how indebted I am to my partner and wife, Margaret Ward, for her patience, support and love. Our two children, Fintan and Medbh, lived with the book from its inception. As it has been so long in the making, our family has expanded to include Gavin and three wonderful grandsons, Rory, Finn and Rowan. My thanks to all of them for their love and support.

When young, our son, Fintan, once retorted to a slight telling-off with the comment: 'I thought you believed in justice'. Hopefully, despite this minor lapse, the book confirms my long-standing commitment to justice and the rule of law. With unbearable sadness, Fintan died of cancer age 29 in 2014. The book is dedicated to him.

APPENDIX

Timeline of Key Events

Key: d.u. = [exact] date unknown; entries in italics refer to events centred on Manchester. Major events relevant to the Stalker affair are in bold.

1980

2 Jan   John Hermon is appointed Chief Constable of the RUC.

1 Apr   John Stalker is promoted to Assistant Chief Constable, GMP.

28 Nov GMP Chief Constable James Anderton signs Kevin Taylor's senior officers' mess programme: 'Best wishes, Jim'.

1981

26 Jan Klapish's premises, Cut Price (FG), Kent St, Belfast, is destroyed by firebombs.

3 Feb   Kevin Taylor purchases yacht, Diogenes, in Miami.

4 Feb   Two-day meeting in Belfast between RUC and GMP to discuss firebombing of Kent Street and the long firm fraud (LFF) involved. Chaired by Drew (RUC). Born, Patterson and Burgess (GMP) attend.

23 Feb MI5/Walker secret strategy is implemented. Transforms policing in Northern Ireland from detention and prosecution of crime to intelligence gathering, permitting informers and agents to commit crimes, including murder.

8 Jul   Start of the Moss Side disturbances in Manchester.

24 Aug MI5 report that the UDA are 'keen' to carry out assassinations of a number of individuals including Finucane. Meeting of MI5 and RUC SB decides no action be taken because intervention would compromise the security of the agent. Described by one as a 'courageous decision'.

3 Dec   Stalker goes on nine-day holiday on board Taylor's yacht, Diogenes, in Florida.

1982

2 Jan   Taylor's 50th birthday party at his home, Wood Mill, Summerseat.

4 Jan   British Army establishes secret Force Research Unit (FRU) to run agents and informers.

26 Feb American Express report notes links between criminals in Liverpool and Manchester, and criminals in London.

18 Mar DI Wilson, No. 1 RCS, makes the case for Operation City to investigate four alleged suspects of the LFF in Belfast – Monaghan and Schiavo brothers, but not Klapish.

19 Mar GMP senior officers' spring ball, Tyldesley Suite, Lancashire County Cricket Club.

21 Apr Operation City begins, ending 19 October 1983 and generating 203 pages of logs.

30 May Diogenes *leaves Miami for England, skippered by Colin Faulkner. Refuels in Cork.*

8 Jun Diogenes *arrives in Liverpool and then onto Salford Docks, Manchester. Faulkner declares guns, purchased for protection against pirates when cruising in the Caribbean, to Customs and Excise and insists they take possession of them.*

21 Jul Diogenes *leaves Manchester bound for Spain with Taylor, Kevin Shaw, Steve Hayes and Howard Tebay on board.*

2 Aug Diogenes *arrives in Spain.*

27 Oct DSgt Sean Quinn and PCs Paul Hamilton and Alan McCloy killed by an IRA landmine at Kinnego Embankment, Lurgan.

29 Oct GMP's officers' mess dinner at Manchester University. Mr and Mrs Taylor are guests of Stalker.

11 Nov Sean Burns, Gervaise McKerr and Eugene Toman shot dead by RUC HMSU officers.

24 Nov Michael Tighe shot dead and Martin McCauley badly injured in hayshed by RUC HMSU officers. The hayshed is bugged and there is a tape recording of the shooting. McCauley was mentioned by an informer in connection with the Kinnego explosion of 27 October.

d.u. Nov Deputy Head of RUC SB gives instructions that the hayshed tape and the monitor logs must be destroyed.

12 Dec Roddy Carroll and Seamus Grew shot dead by RUC HMSU officers.

15 Dec Klapish appears at Belfast Magistrates' Court. Outcome unknown.

1983

1 Jan Stalker attends twelve-month Royal College of Defence Studies course.

31 Jan Informer Burton granted bail after a successful application to judge in chambers.

18 Mar CC Anderton invites Taylor to lunch at GMP HQ.

4 May Meeting held in Belfast to discuss the three shooting incidents by RUC HMSUs. Present: Sir Michael Havers, Attorney General, the DPPNI, the CC, an ACC and staff from the offices of the DPPNI and AG.

10 May Vincent Schiavo arrested and bailed to appear Salford Magistrates Court on 9 June.

17 May Arrest of Joseph Monaghan, Mark Klapish, Jack Trickett, James Monaghan and Louis Schiavo. Klapish and Joseph Monaghan charged with conspiracy to defraud. Trickett with handling clock and fridge freezer.

19 May Burton arrested for his part in LFF

31 May Burton, alias Barbara Codd, supplies information on QSG to American Express.

d.u. Jun DPPNI orders a reinvestigation into all three shooting incidents. Hermon asks DCC McAtamney to carry out the task.

9 Jun Vincent Schiavo fails to appear at Salford Magistrate's court. He has fled to Spain.

15 Jun DSgt Reynolds records false information that Vincent Schiavo obtained a 6.52-ton yacht named Moriarty from Taylor in payment of a debt.

21 Jun The Deputy Head of RUC SB attends a meeting at the DPPNI's office in which he misleads the DPPNI by concealing the hayshed bugging operation.

27 Jun Interpol report that Sherama *is moored at Pier 1 and* Diogenes *at Pier 2, Puerto Banus.*

12 Aug MI5 informs the DPPNI that there was a listening device in the hayshed. Nothing is said about any recording or transcription.

28 Sep   Klapish, Burton and Monaghan committed for trial by Salford Magistrates for conspiracy to obtain goods by deception. Klapish and Monaghan remanded in custody. Burton bailed.

19 Oct   Operation City ends.

1984

11 Jan   Taylor makes his first visit to the Co-operative Bank seeking loan facilities.

2 Feb   Taylor makes an application for £2m in order to pay off existing borrowings. Loan was not taken up.

24 Feb   Stalker appointed Deputy Chief Constable GMP.

19 Mar   PC John Robinson appears in court charged only with the murder of Seamus Grew in the Mullacreevie Park shooting.

3 Apr   PC John Robinson is acquitted of murder of Seamus Grew.

11 Apr   DPPNI formally initiates a request for an independent investigation of the events at the hayshed.

24 Apr   GMP senior officers' mess St George's Day dinner. Taylor is Stalker's guest. CC Anderton notes on Taylor's programme: 'Good luck, Jim'.

1 May   Nelson contacts the Army to offer his services. Army task him to join the UDA. He becomes a state agent run by FRU.

20 May Stalker is asked to head inquiry into the six killings by RUC HMSU officers in the three separate 'shoot-to-kill' incidents in Northern Ireland.

22 May   Taylor sells the Moulton Street Precinct for £2.75 million.

24 May   Stalker meets CC Hermon and agrees draft terms of reference for his investigation into the six killings by the RUC HMSUs.

29 May   DSgt Montgomery and PCs Brannigan and Frederick Robinson appear in Belfast Crown Court in front of Judge Gibson, charged with the murder of Eugene Toman.

30 May   First visit of Flying Squad to Spain concerning the Security Express HQ robbery on Easter Monday 1983 when £6 million in bank notes were stolen.

30 May   DS Topping and DS Grant interview Donovan in Leyhill prison allegedly about police corruption.

4 Jun   CC Hermon writes to NIPA to say that Stocker (sic) has been appointed to carry out an inquiry into the six killings.

4 Jun   DSgt Montgomery and PCs Brannigan and Frederick Robinson acquitted of murdering Eugene Toman and commended by Judge Gibson 'for their courage and determination in bringing the three deceased men to justice, in this case to the final court of justice'.

9 Jun   Golf course conversation between DS McGourlay, Wareing and Lawlor.

11 Jun   Late morning, DS McGourlay informs CS Topping of the golf course conversation.

11 Jun   Sherama arrives in Gibraltar from Puerto Banus with 15 people on board including Ronnie Knight, Vincent Schiavo, and Jack Trickett.

11 Jun   2.30 p.m. DI Richardson claims he receives a call from Burton who says he has met Donnelly who told him that Stalker has a corrupt link with Taylor and James Monaghan, a.k.a. Jimmy Swords. No note in Richardson's police notebook of any communication from Burton.

14 Jun   No 1. RCS report on Taylor prepared for DS McGourlay.

15 Jun *DI Richardson claims he spoke with McGourlay on the phone. DS McGourlay insisted that he had not mentioned Stalker to Burton. No note in Richardson's police notebook of any communication with DS McGourlay.*

20 Jun *Taylor transfers BMW FDK 821W to Mohammad Hanif, Richmond Street, Ashton under Lyne, in lieu of a gambling debt.*

20 Jun *Claimed that ACC Lees meets CC Anderton and informs him of intelligence on Stalker and Taylor.*

22 Jun *CS Topping and DI Richardson meet Burton in Heaton Park.*

24 Jun *The offices of the Manchester Police Monitoring Unit are illegally entered. Nothing is taken but files are disturbed.*

28 Jun *Information from Burton re Kwok Man. Free meals for police total £20-30k. Claims DCC Stalker and other police officers have been going there for years without paying.*

12 Jul *Claimed CS Topping is informed that one of Taylor's cars is of interest to the Drugs Squad.*

17 Jul *Claimed first report on Taylor/Stalker inquiry by CS Topping. It is also claimed that it is passed to ACC Lees and on to CC Anderton.*

9 Aug *Burton is interviewed by a police officer at Belmont Public House.*

22 Aug Coroner for Armagh, Gerry Curran, resigns over irregularities in the RUC files on the deaths of McKerr, Burns and Toman.

d.u. Sep *DSgt Burgess retires from GMP.*

2 Sep *Burton is interviewed at Belmont Public House by DS Elder, Solicitors and Counsel.*

3 Sep *Start of trial of Burton, Klapish and Joseph Monaghan for their part in the Belfast LFF.*

4 Sep *Burton and Klapish convicted and sentenced to 30 months and four years respectively. Burton sent to Leeds Prison then to Kirkham Prison.*

5 Sep *Unsigned alleged memorandum from CC Anderton noting details of the reorganisation of the CID. DCC Stalker claims he never saw it.*

13Sep *DI Clarke interviews Burton in Kirkham prison.*

d.u. Oct *Flying Squad visit Spain. One task was to obtain a list of the passengers who had left Spain for Gibraltar on board Sherama on 11 June 1984.*

4 Oct *CS Topping interviews Burton in prison in the first of five interviews.*

12 Oct IRA blows up the Grand Hotel, Brighton during Conservative Party annual conference. Five die including one MP and 32 seriously injured.

24 Oct *CS Topping and DI Richardson interview Burton in Leeds Prison.*

29 Oct *DI Richardson and DI Russell interview Burton in Leeds prison.*

d.u. Nov Stalker learns of the existence of MI5 tape recording of the hayshed shooting of Tighe and McCauley.

3 Nov *It is disclosed that conversations in GMP HQ were being recorded to trap 'a top-level mole'.*

14 Nov *CS Topping and DI Richardson interview Burton in Lancaster Prison.*

30 Nov *Flying Squad visits GMP for three days.*

7 Dec *CS Topping and DI Richardson interview Burton in Lancaster prison*

17 Dec DCC Stalker and DCS Thorburn visit Myers, HMIC.

1985

d.u. CC Anderton makes CS Topping deputy to DCS Foster, head of Crime ('V') Department. Subsequently, the post divided. CS Topping appointed head of operations. DCS Foster demoted to head of administration.

d.u. Jan CS Topping interviews Sgt Burgess re Burton's 'I have found your rat' conversation of May 1983.

3 Jan CS Topping and DI Richardson interview Burton in Lancaster prison.

10 Jan Taylor obtains planning permission for Poynton site.

11 Jan DI Richardson interviews Burton in Lancaster prison.

25 Jan DI Richardson interviews Burton in Lancaster prison.

28 Jan Stalker meets MI5 in London. It agrees to co-operate fully. The senior legal advisor to MI5 does not inform Stalker that MI5 has its own copy of the hayshed tape.

d.u. Feb Stalker learns that he is being targeted by a terrorist group.

3 Feb Diogenes *arrives in Dartmouth. Suspected that drugs were unloaded at Blackpool Sands, Devon.*

4 Feb **Drugs Intelligence Unit is established in secret within GMP.** It is headed by DCI Born and staffed by DI Richardson, DI Murray, DI Waterworth, Sgt Fiddler and Sgt Ware (from 1.4.85).

6 Feb GMP policy review meeting chaired by Stalker. No mention of the DIU.

7 Feb DI Richardson and DI Murray interview Burton in Lancaster prison. First of five taped interviews.

14 Feb DI Murray and DI Richardson interview Burton in Lancaster prison. Second taped interview.

15 Feb McCauley is convicted of unlawful possession of firearms. Sentenced to two years imprisonment suspended for three years.

17 Feb CC Hermon and his wife spend the weekend with Myers, HMIC, and his wife in their home in Colwyn Bay.

18 Feb Taylor and Angelo Dundee guests of Stalker at GMP senior officers' mess.

20 Feb Stalker writes to RUC SB asking for the hayshed tape and information on informers. Receives telephone reply refusing request.

21 Feb DI Richardson and DI Murray interview Burton in Leeds prison. Third taped interview.

26 Feb DI Ricardson and DI Murray interview Burton in Lancaster prison. Fourth taped interview.

d.u. Mar Sampson report into Stalker's alleged misconduct subsequently claims that since March 1985, CC Anderton had kept Myers, HMIC, informed of the allegations against Stalker. Home Secretary claims HMIC only informed in October.

1 Mar GMP uses force to remove students during a protest against the visit of Leon Brittan, the Home Secretary, to Manchester University. Became known as the Battle of Brittan.

d.u. Mar Stalker interviews a very senior RUC officer under caution as a criminal suspect.

3 Mar The Miners' Strike ends.

4 Mar **Stalker sends Myers, HMIC, a report which spells out in 'very graphic and detailed form' the position that his NI enquiry has reached.**

5 Mar **Stalker writes to CC Hermon asking for the hayshed tape and the identity of witnesses to the hayshed shooting.**

7 Mar *DI Ricardson and DI Murray interview Burton in Lancaster Prison. Fifth taped interview.*

7 Mar *Taylor applies for a loan to the Co-operative Bank based on valuations of three of his sites: Poynton, Tottington and Trafford Park.*

9 Mar *Claimed second report on investigation into Taylor/Stalker by CS Topping. Letter to Lees: 'Brief notes to up-date you in relation to Taylor and Febb'.*

13 Mar **Stalker receives a reply from CC Hermon refusing request for tape and identity of witnesses to the recording of hayshed shooting.**

14 Mar *Claimed that Lees drafts a letter which CC Anderton sends to Myers, HMIC, informing him about Taylor's alleged link with the IRA, noting that developments may cause 'considerable embarrassment'.*

14 Mar *Burton dies in prison.*

21 Mar From Belfast, Stalker telephones CC Anderton to seek his advice on the problems he is experiencing with investigating the HMSU killings. The call is taped and transcribed but both records later go missing.

22 Mar *Claimed that Myers, HMIC, telephones CC Anderton in response to 14 March letter and that the call was taped and transcribed with copies kept in the DIU, but which later disappear.*

1 Apr *Sgt Ware joins the DIU.*

1 Apr *Taylor sells* Diogenes *to Brooks for £90,000.*

9 Apr Stalker writes to CC Hermon asking him to reconsider the decision not to supply the hayshed tape or details of witnesses.

9 Apr **Stalker writes to DCC Michael McAtamney requesting the suspension from duty of two RUC SB Superintendents but receives no response.**

18 Apr *Stalker picks up Taylor, Derek Britton (his accountant) and Vincent McCann, in a police car from Taylor's office and takes them to the Maine Road luncheon club at Manchester City Football club.*

21 Apr *DCS Foster retires from GMP with a sense of injustice.*

22 Apr **Stalker writes again to Sir John Hermon asking for access to the hayshed tape and requesting suspension of police officers. Both requests refused.**

24 Apr *DI Murray and DI Waterworth visit CII and CDIU at Scotland Yard.*

25 Apr Diogenes *arrives in Villamurra. False information from Customs and Excise to DIU that Taylor met the boat along with Whittaker and a number of 'heavies'.*

25 Apr **Buxton, NIO, writes to Stephens, NIO, informing him that DPPNI is very concerned about the outcome of Stalker's inquiry.**

26 Apr Stalker writes to DPPNI concerning the impasse over access to information.

29 Apr Stalker writes to CC Hermon asking to be released from his responsibility to report to the RUC and asking for access to DPPNI.

2 May *Sgt Ware talks to Sgt Green CDIU on the phone. Richardson also calls CDIU and speaks to Atkinson.*

7 May *Taylor's application to the Co-operative Bank for a loan of £240,000 is approved and drawn down.*

9 May *Vincent Schiavo returns to England.*

9 May Stalker meets CC Hermon in Belfast. Hermon promises to 'reconsider' his refusals.

10 May *Sgt Ware visits Inland Revenue at Chorlton.*

10 May *Vincent Schiavo arrested.*

13 May DPPNI and Home Office are informed of Stalker's lack of progress.

13 May Stalker meets CC Hermon.

13 May CC Hermon informs SoS about 'the difficulties he was having with Mr Stocker (sic)'.

14 May Stalker meets DPPNI.

15 May Stalker meets CC Hermon. Joined by an MI5 officer. Stalker asked to leave. Returns after 20 minutes. Hermon agrees to release the tape, 'if it exists', subject to approval of MI5.

16 May Diogenes *arrives in Guernsey crewed by Whittaker and Worswick.*

16 May *Manchester City Football Club luncheon. Taylor tells Anderton that he thinks his boat,* Diogenes, *has been used for drug smuggling. Anderton makes extensive note of the conversation. No police officer interviews Taylor.*

17 May MI5 assures CC Hermon that there was no objection to Mr Stocker (sic) being given access to certain equipment and to an individual RUC officer who could give evidence about it.

23 May MI5 reports that it will make the necessary investigations into the equipment which is at issue and interview the RUC officer involved, and then inform Mr Stocker (sic).

d.u. May *Myers and Anderton support Stalker's applications in May and June for senior police posts.*

d.u. Jun MI5 notes that the UDA plan another attempt to murder Pat Finucane. No action is taken by MI5.

6 Jun **DCS Thorburn delivers a further letter from Stalker to CC Hermon during ACPO conference in Bristol. It specifically asks who gave authority for the listening device to be placed in the hayshed.**

7 Jun *CC Anderton delivers a paper at the ACPO conference in Bristol entitled 'Community Self Help in Crime Prevention'.*

14 Jun **Meeting called by MI5 in London. CC Hermon refuses to release the hayshed tape unless it is 'in the public interest to do so'.**

18 Jun *DI Richardson and Sgt Ware interview Kim Berry concerning an incident in 1983 about which she made no complaint to the police.*

18 Jun CC Hermon telephones Stalker refusing access to informer details.

19 Jun MI5 agent reports that a leading loyalist paramilitary group was interested in Pat Finucane as a priority target.

20 Jun Myers, HMIC, informs Stalker that he cannot assist him further.

25 Jun *Eric Worswick, drug smuggler, appears in Preston Crown Court.*

26 Jun *Typed report by DI Richardson of an interview with Kim Berry.*

26 Jun Stalker writes to Hermon informing him of fresh evidence of unlawful killings by RUC officers.

28 Jun *DIU officers interview Neil Westbrook, Managing Director of Trafford Park Estates.*

28 Jun *DI Waterworth and Sgt Ware visit Lloyds Bank, Kings Street, Manchester, with whom Taylor has an American Express card.*

1 Jul **Stalker prepares his interim report on the HMSU killings.**

2 Jul *DCI Born and CI Murray interview drug smuggler Worswick.*

3 Jul *Vincent Schiavo appears in Salford Magistrates' court. Pleads guilty.*

4 Jul *DIU officers interview Westbrook. Second DIU interview.*

5 Jul *Sgt Ware visits Waterhouse, Taylor's brother-in-law.*

d.u. **MI5 destroy the only remaining copy of the hayshed tape.**

15 Jul *DI Waterworth and DI Richardson interview Ann Carroll – political opponent of Taylor in MCA.*

15 Jul *DI Murray interviews Worswick who agrees to become a police informer. Provides information that Blackpool Sands, Devon, was a drop point for drugs.*

22 Jul *DIU officers interview Victor Roberts, a one-time friend and colleague of Taylor, at the suggestion of Carroll. Roberts had fallen out with Taylor several years previously. First DIU interview.*

22 Jul *DCI Born and DI Murray interview drug smuggler Worswick again.*

23 Jul *CS Topping, DCI Born meet with DPP concerning the recruitment of drug smuggler Worswick as a participating informant. Mention was made of the QSG, a businessman, the IRA, and possible police connections.*

24 Jul **British Army's FRU pays for Nelson, now the UDA's intelligence officer, to go to South Africa to procure arms for the UDA.**

24 Jul *DSgt Ware spends two hours at Barclays Bank, Ashton-in-Makerfield, where Taylor has an account.*

25 Jul *DSgt Ware spends at least an hour at Barclays Bank, Aston in Makerfield.*

26 Jul *DSgt Ware interviews Roberts for two hours and makes no notes. Second DIU interview.*

28 Jul *ACC Lees, CS Topping and DCI Born attend meeting at New Scotland Yard seeking cooperation and involvement with drug smuggler Worswick.*

31 Jul *DI Richardson interviews Roberts. Third DIU interview.*

d.u. Aug *Taylor's businesses are near to collapse as a result of the police investigation. He ceases to pay the mortgage on his home.*

7 Aug *CC Anderton makes unprecedented visit to meet with the Deputy Head of Customs and Excise to assist the investigation into Taylor.*

7 Aug *The Taylors' 20th wedding anniversary at the Mason's Arms, Nangreaves, Bury.*

8 Aug A Sinn Féin councillor is identified as a target by the UDA. Councillor not warned by either RUC SB or Army.

9 Aug ***Robson, Taylor's solicitor, writes to CC Anderton asking if GMP are investigating Taylor.***

14 Aug *Vincent Schiavo appears in Crown Court. Changes plea to not guilty. Claims Magistrates' Court has no jurisdiction. Remitted back to determine jurisdiction.*

22 Aug *DIU officers meet with Customs & Excise.*

26 Aug *DI Richardson and DSgt Ware interview Victor Roberts. Fourth DIU interview.*

27 Aug *DSgt Ware interviews Victor Roberts. Fifth DIU interview.*

28 Aug *DI Richardson and DSgt Ware interview Victor Roberts. Sixth DIU interview.*

31 Aug *Stalker uses official car to attend retirement event of a GMP officer at Masons Arms Dukinfield.*

5 Sep *Taylor offered £1.6 million for Trafford Park site.*

6 Sep *DS Ryan replies to Robson saying that he can't help but the correspondence has been passed to CID command at HQ.*

6 Sep *DI Richardson interviews Victor Roberts. Seventh DIU interview.*

8 Sep *DI Richardson and DSgt Ware interview Sheppard, head of security at Co-operative Bank.*

10 Sep *DIU interview Westbrook. Third DIU interview.*

11 Sep *DS Machent writes to Robson to say that enquiries have not revealed officer involved.*

18 Sep **Stalker's interim report is delivered to RUC HQ.**

19 Sep *DI Richardson interviews police informer Bernard Rushton, who alleges that Taylor's Moulton Street Precinct has been used to store guns and other property.*

20 Sep *DI Murray receives information from Customs and Excise that an informer has said Taylor has no connection with drug dealing.*

23 Sep *Vincent Schiavo convicted at Salford Magistrates' Court and remitted to Crown Court for sentence.*

25 Sep ***Operation Kaluki begins. Intensive daily surveillance of Taylor's offices.*** *Lasts 114 days and utilises GMP's only surveillance squad. Ended March 1986.*

25 Sep *CC Anderton informed by ACC Lees that Taylor paid for airline ticket for Stalker to travel to Miami. CC Anderton writes note: 'very disturbing'.*

26 Sep *DSgt Ware to Travelmaster Ltd. Speaks to Alan Derbyshire re airline tickets.*

26 Sep *CC Anderton has secret session with ACC Lees. Writes note that it will be very damaging to Stalker even 'if no personal corruption or crime is proved'.*

26 Sep *CC Anderton requests urgent progress report on Taylor/Stalker investigation. DIU provides third report.*

26 Sep *History of MV Diogenes report implies erroneously that yacht was under constant surveillance. Author unknown.*

27 Sep *CC Anderton attends Alexian Brothers' dinner dance, Belfry Hotel, Wilmslow and later writes note that Stalker looked 'uncomfortable'.*

27 Sep Nelson is involved in the attempted murder of an individual in Northern Ireland.

27 Sep Nelson reports to his handlers that the South African deal has fallen through due to the inability of the UDA to raise the necessary funds.

30 Sep *DIU receive more information from Roberts.*

d.u. Sep *Taylor tells Stalker that CID have made enquires at his bank.*

1 Oct *DS Simons tells Stalker that Taylor is not under police investigation.*

3 Oct *DI Richardson and DSgt Ware interview Mr Virani, who bought the Moulton Street Precinct from Taylor.*

4 Oct *DSgt Ware visits Belfry Hotel, Wilmslow, to interview Mr Beech.*

8 Oct *DSgt Ware and DI Richardson interview Sheppard in the Co-operative Bank.*

12 Oct *Taylor and Stalker and their wives attend a function at Belle Vue dog track.*

16 Oct *DSgt Ware makes observations at Taylor's home, Wood Mill, Summerseat.*

18 Oct *DSgt Ware interviews Mr Virani in Piccadilly Hotel, Manchester.*

28 Oct   Taylor rings CC Anderton's office inviting him to the Conservative Party Ball. Anderton declines.

6 Nov   Stalker asks CC Anderton's advice about attending the Conservative Party Ball. Anderton later writes note: 'quite improper' for himself to attend.

8 Nov   DSgt Ware visits Tottington site to see if demolition has taken place.

11 Nov   DI Stephenson seconded to DIU.

12 Nov   DSgt Ware visits Tottington site again.

15 Nov   Vincent Schiavo sentenced in Crown Court to nine months under Theft Act and six months under Bail Act.

15 Nov   Anglo-Irish Agreement is signed by British and Irish governments.

15 Nov   Sarah Hollis' flat in Manchester is burgled. Believed that police arranged it to intimidate her because of her evidence in relation to the Battle of Brittan.

20 Nov   BBC 'Out of Court' programme on Battle of Brittan broadcast.

23 Nov   Conservative Party Association autumn ball, Hotel Piccadilly, Manchester.

24 Nov   DI Stephenson and DSgt Ware visit D&D Manchester to make enquiries re foreign companies.

26 Nov   DSgt Ware 'introduces' DI Stephenson to Sheppard, Co-operative Bank.

26 Nov   DSgt Ware interviews Mr Groves at the Piccadilly Hotel about the Conservative Party's Autumn Ball.

d.u. Dec MI5 assesses that 85% of the UDA's 'intelligence' originates from sources within the security forces.

2 Dec   DI Stephenson and DSgt Ware interview Arthur Bowen-Gotham in Poole about Diogenes.

3 Dec   DI Stephenson has contacted First Interstate Bank in America where Taylor has an account. Their solicitors write to Taylor informing him.

3 Dec   Kidnapping and robbery of postmistress in Tallaght, Dublin.

10 Dec   DI Stephenson and DSgt Ware liaise with the planning officer in Bury Town Hall re Taylor.

11 Dec   DSgt Ware visits Inland Revenue, Chorlton re Taylor.

12 Dec   Robson speaks with DS Simons and is told that the enquiry has gone past Taylor.

14 Dec   DI Stephenson and DSgt Ware visit Co-operative Bank.

16 Dec   DI Stephenson and DSgt Ware visit Sheppard in Co-operative Bank.

17 Dec   CS Topping, DI Stephenson DSgt Ware visit Sheppard in Co-operative Bank.

23 Dec   DI Stephenson visits Sheppard in Co-operative Bank for over three hours.

1986

6 Jan   Meeting involving Robson, Taylor and DS Simons. Taylor makes secret recording.

7 Jan   DI Stephenson and DSgt Ware visit Tottington site and then Bury Planning Department.

9 Jan   DI Stephenson and DSgt Ware visit Sheppard in Co-operative Bank.

13 Jan   Robson writes to CC Anderton to complain about Taylor's treatment, which Stalker opens in CC Anderton's absence.

15 Jan   Stalker hands Robson's opened letter of 13.1.86 to CC Anderton, who writes a note about the 'delicate situation' it placed him in.

15 Jan   MI5 record that Nelson could provide it with 'top level access' to UDA re: 'increasing political links between unionists and paramilitaries'.

17 Jan   Robson receives two letters from CC Anderton, dated 3.1.86 and 4.1.86. Latter states that he will neither confirm nor deny that enquiries are being undertaken into Taylor.

27 Jan   DI Stephenson and DSgt Ware go to the Co-operative Bank.

28 Jan   DSgt Ware visits Royal Bank of Scotland.

30 Jan   DI Stephenson and DSgt Ware visit Barclays Bank Inspections Dept.

3 Feb   CC Anderton suggests to Stalker that he distance himself from Taylor and says that he does not wish to be too closely involved in the investigation.

3 Feb   Robson writes to CC Anderton demanding an answer to previous correspondence.

8 Feb   DI Stephenson and DSgt Ware visit American Express Limited, London and liaise with a Miss Simpson and Mr. Chapman. They collect documents for both green and gold accounts of Taylor.

10 Feb   DSgt Ware visits Trafford Wharf Road site and makes observations re demolition work.

12 Feb   DSgt Ware liaises with DI Baythorpe.

13 Feb   CC Hermon sends Stalker's interim report to the DPPNI.

17 Feb   DI Stephenson and DSgt Ware visit British Airways for third time.

25 Feb   DCS Thorburn sends memorandum to CC Anderton saying that he felt humiliated and may have been deliberately misled – intense acrimony towards CS Topping and ACC Lees. DCS Thorburn receives no reply.

27 Feb   DI Stephenson applies for access orders to Taylor's bank accounts. Affidavit stated, inter alia, that Taylor was involved in drugs.

28 Feb   Taylor attends annual dinner dance of Variety Club of Ireland. He informs CC Anderton, who was present, of the problems he was experiencing as a result of the police investigation.

4 Mar   DPPNI writes to CC Hermon 'in absolutely stark terms' to provide the information requested by Stalker.

4 Mar   Myers, HMIC, asks Stalker for clandestine copy of his interim report.

12 Mar   Access orders are granted to Taylor's banks.

21 Mar   End of continuous 114-day surveillance of Taylor's offices.

21 Mar   Stalker and his wife are driven in police car to Old Trafford football ground for a Senior Officers' Mess ladies night event.

24 Mar   Robson writes to CC Anderton, concerned that the access order application was ex parte.

24 Mar   Anderton gives humorous speech about police committees at the silver jubilee dinner of Police Federation of Motor Clubs headed by Hermon, providing an opportunity for the two men to discuss the investigation into Stalker.

26 Mar   DSgt Ware drives a senior RUC Officer to Manchester Airport. Name of the officer and the purpose of visit unknown.

18 Apr   DI Stephenson and DSgt Ware interview Ann Carroll.

23 Apr   Stalker attends the senior officers' mess St George's Day function at GMP HQ. Taken there by police car.

28 Apr   Anderton replies to Robson, Taylor's solicitor, informing him that it is not GMP's policy to disclose information and that his persistence in writing is unprecedented.

28 Apr *DSgt Ware collects accounts of the MCA from Ann Carroll.*

30 Apr Hermon fails to keep appointment with DCC Stalker and DCS Thorburn. RUC SB records handed over, but no hayshed tape or transcript.

8 May *Taylor employs new solicitor, Ian Burton, to represent him.*

8 May *Extra two days of surveillance of Taylor's offices.*

9 May *Search warrants are executed on Taylor's home and offices, solicitors' offices, accountants' offices and elsewhere.*

9 May *Search of Taylor's house. Photograph albums taken in a perfunctory search.*

11 May *DIU prepare fourth report on Taylor/Stalker investigation for CC Anderton. Conjecture that the report from DIU may have been briefed up.*

12 May *CC Anderton travels to Colwyn Bay and meets Myers to give him DIU's claimed fourth report on Taylor and Stalker. Contains statement: 'it could well be said by some that he [Stalker] has reasons to be sympathetic to the IRA'.*

12 May CC Hermon writes to Stalker asking to see him before enquiries are recommenced. Appointment made for 19 May.

14 May Myers, HMIC, tells Stalker to cancel the Belfast appointment. No explanation is given. Arrangements made for him to return on 26 May.

15 May *CS Roberts speaks to CS Topping re a conversation he had with Ian Burton, Taylor's solicitor. CS Topping's minute of conversation disputed by Roberts.*

18 May Myers, HMIC, telephones Hermon and mentioned 'a C.C. seeing B.S. R.A. T.K. and that D.H. was "au fait" with developments'.

19 May Meeting held in Scarborough to discuss misconduct allegations against Stalker. Decision taken to appoint Sampson to investigate them and to compete the NI investigation. Present: Sir Lawrence Byford, Chief Inspector of HMIC, Myers, CC Anderton, Colin Sampson, CC of West Yorkshire and others. There is a rumour that CC Hermon also attended.

20 May Myers, HMIC, and CC Sampson visit CC Hermon at police headquarters and reveal that Stalker had been under investigation by GMP for several months.

21 May *First of at least ten meetings between GMP and DPP to discuss the prosecution of Taylor.*

21 May MI5 and FRU officers go to Germany to persuade Brian Nelson to return to Northern Ireland as an agent. No success.

22 May Myers, HMIC, writes to Andrew, NIO, recording previous day's conversation in which Andrew was informed of an investigation into Stalker. This appears to be the first occasion in which the NIO is informed.

23 May Myers, HMIC, again instructs Stalker to cancel his visit to Belfast. Arrangements made for his return on 2 June.

27 May *'Poison chalice' dinner at Moss Rock restaurant, Manchester with CC Anderton, Stalker, Colin Cameron and Peter Taylor from BBC TV.*

28 May *Mr Rees, GMPA, telephones Stalker to tell him he is suspected of disciplinary offences, and he is to take extended leave.*

29 May Stalker informed that he is removed from the Northern Ireland inquiry 'for ever'.

30 May *GMPA meeting followed by press statement noting that DCC Stalker is on extended leave pending investigation of alleged disciplinary offences.*

3 Jun *CS Topping writes to CC Sampson enclosing documents and implying that the information was brand-new.*

5 Jun   *Manchester Evening News carries story of Taylor's friendship with Stalker. Claimed this was released by Ian Burton, Taylor's solicitor.*

9 Jun   First disciplinary interview with Stalker. CC Sampson provides no details on charges.

10 Jun   *DSgt Ware liaises with Ann Carroll.*

11 Jun   *DI Stephenson, DSgt Ware and a police photographer visit Tottington and Trafford Wharf sites to take photographs.*

12 Jun   *DI Stephenson, DSgt Ware and a police photographer visit Poynton site to take photographs.*

16 Jun   *DI Stephenson and DSgt Ware visit Britannia Building Society, Cross Street, tasked by Sampson's inquiry into Stalker's alleged misconduct.*

16 Jun   *DSgts Caldwell and Knowles, and PC Hogg seconded to DIU to investigate Taylor's commercial affairs.*

16 Jun   'Stalker: Coincidence or Conspiracy', BBC Panorama programme broadcast.

17 Jun   Anglo-Irish Intergovernmental Conference at Stormont. Tom King, the SoS for Northern Ireland informs Peter Barry, Ireland's Foreign Affairs Minister, that Stalker's report was the final one when, in fact, it was an interim report.

19 Jun   *Meeting with DPP to discuss prosecution of Taylor. Present: CS Topping and DI Stephenson, Worthington, DPP. CS Topping wants early charge but DPP wants evidence.*

19 Jun   *DSgt Knowles makes enquiries about Taylor's move from his house and from his offices at 2 St. John Street.*

23 Jun   Second disciplinary interview with Stalker. CC Sampson serves him with a Regulation 6 Notice, detailing allegations. *Questions asked about Taylor's 50th birthday party five years earlier.*

30 Jun   Stalker is formally suspended from duty.

2 Jul   *DSgt Caldwell interviews Kim Berry.*

9 Jul   *CS Topping, DI Stephenson and DSgt Ware visit Co-operative Bank.*

10 Jul   *DI Stephenson, DSgts Knowles and Caldwell visit Co-operative Bank and interview Chadwick.*

11 Jul   *PC Hogg spends next six days analysing Taylor's Amex transactions and preparing statements.*

12 Jul   *DSgt Knowles visits Poynton site and makes enquiries with the local residents re tipping on the site*

12 Jul   CC Hermon suspends the two Superintendents, 15 months after the request by Stalker.

15 Jul   *PC Hogg visits Angela Simpson, American Express, in London and takes statement.*

15 Jul   *DSgts Caldwell and Knowles take Terence Bowley from the Co-operative Bank in Blandford Street, Newcastle to Bootle Street Police Station, Manchester and interview him from 11.00 a.m. to 8.10 p.m.*

16 Jul   *Meeting with DPP to discuss prosecution of Taylor. Present: CS Topping, CI Born DSgt Caldwell, Waring and Worthington. CS Topping is recorded as 'being anxious' that Taylor is charged quickly.*

16 Jul   *DSgt Knowles and PC Hogg visit Bishopsgate Police Station, Wakefield and deliver American Express statements for Sampson's disciplinary inquiry.*

17 Jul *Third disciplinary interview with Stalker. CC Sampson asks about 1981 holiday with Taylor in Florida, Hotel Piccadilly Ball in November 1985 and use of police cars.*

18 Jul *Trustee Savings Bank commences repossession proceedings against Taylor and agrees a series of payments.*

19 Jul **'MI5 Smear Scandal Exposed'. Morning Star claims that a meeting was held to 'cover-up' the mess that MI5 had caused by trying to smear Stalker.**

24 Jul *DSgts Ware and Corfield visit Mr. Fairhurst at Barclays Bank.*

24 Jul *Meeting with DPP to discuss prosecution of Taylor. Present Myers, HMIC, CC Anderton, CS Topping and DI Stephenson. CC Anderton and Myers make personal pleas that Taylor is charged immediately. DPP is informed that GMP has set up a special operation to challenge adverse media coverage.*

29 Jul *Fourth disciplinary interview with Stalker. Sampson asks more about police cars.*

30 Jul *DSgt Ware flies to London and delivers documents to the DPP.*

6 Aug ***CC Sampson completes investigation into disciplinary charges against Stalker.***

7 Aug *DSgt Caldwell interviews Stephen Wood, Co-operative bank employee.*

10 Aug *Meeting with DPP to discuss prosecution of Taylor: CS Topping, DCI Born, DI Stephenson, Corkery, and Worthington present.*

12 Aug *DSgt Knowles and DSgt Caldwell visit Poynton site re proposed tip. Find no movement of vehicles and no disturbance of site.*

d.u. Aug ***Unlawful leaking of the Sampson Report on Stalker to the press.***

15 Aug *DSgt Knowles learns that two men have visited the Planning Department to look at the Trafford Park site file. Obtains description of them and their vehicle registration numbers.*

19 Aug **'Stalker and Company', BBC Panorama programme broadcast.**

22 Aug ***GMPA vote to reinstate Stalker to post of Deputy Chief Constable.***

26 Aug ***CC Anderton tells DCC Stalker there was no inquiry into Taylor in October 1985 and no investigation into himself until April 1986. Both statements are untrue.***

26 Aug *DSgts Corfield and PC Hogg fly to New York, re separate case, but visit NYPD and make enquiries in relation to Operation Kaluki and Angelo Dundee and Taylor.*

26 Aug *CC Anderton tells Stalker that 'anything done was with his full authority and knowledge'.*

1 Sep *Press release from CC Anderton denying a conspiracy against his DCC Stalker.*

3 Sep *DSgt Knowles picks up Wood from Co-operative Bank and takes him to Collyhurst Police Station for further interview.*

5 Sep *DSgt Caldwell interviews Wood at Co-operative Bank.*

8 Sep *PC Hogg interviews Davenport and Wood at Co-operative Bank.*

8 Sep **CC Sampson, now completing Stalker's Northern Ireland inquiry, interviews CC Hermon under caution after supplying him with written questions.**

10 Sep *DSgt Caldwell and PC Hogg see Martin Edwards, Chairman of Manchester United re site at Trafford Park.*

12 Sep *CC Anderton appointed President of Association of Chief Police Officers.*

12 Sep *DSgt Caldwell visits Martin Edwards again.*

16 Sep *Meeting with DPP to discuss prosecution of Taylor. Present: CS Topping, DI Stephenson, DSgt Ware and PC Hogg, Waring, Worthington and Williams.*

17 Sep   *DSgt Knowles makes further enquiries at the Poynton site.*

18 Sep   First anniversary of delivery to RUC of Stalker's interim report. Still no prosecutorial decisions.

23 Sep   *DSgt Ware makes enquiries about motor vehicles owned by Taylor.*

23 Sep   **Taylor issues summons against CC Anderton and GMP Authority, for disclosure of documents used to obtain search warrants .**

25 Sep   *DSgt Knowles visits Taylor's home, Wood Mill, Summerseat, to ascertain whether the property is for sale.*

26 Sep   *Stalker receives legal bill of £21,980 for defending himself in the disciplinary case.*

30 Sep   *DSgt Caldwell and DSgt Knowles visit Co-operative Bank and ask Woods to accompany them to a police station. Not cautioned.*

6 Oct   *DSgt Ware visits Sheppard in Co-operative Bank re the statements of Davenport and Wood.*

10 Oct   *DSgt Ware visits Poynton site re imminent sale.*

13 Oct   *DSgt Knowles and PC Hogg visit Manchester Airport and meet two officers from the NYPD.*

14 Oct   **Criminal summons issued by Beryl Taylor, acting for Rangelark, against CC Anderton, CS Topping and DI Stephenson on a charge of conspiracy to pervert the course of justice.**

15 Oct   *Application for disclosure of documents used to obtain search warrants refused by Mr Justice Scott.*

17 Oct   *Meeting with DPP to discuss prosecution of Taylor. CS Topping, DI Stephenson, DSgts Ware and Caldwell informed by DPP that there is still insufficient evidence to proceed against Taylor.*

17 Oct   *GMPA refuses to contribute towards Stalker's legal costs. Public donations begin to arrive.*

22 Oct   **CC Sampson delivers first of three reports on the six RUC HMSU killings to CC Hermon and DPPNI.**

24 Oct   *Douglas Hogg, Parliamentary Under-SoS at the Home Office, informs Parliament that HMIC was advised in October 1985 of police enquiries into Taylor/Stalker.*

4 Nov   *DSgt Ware interviews Butterworth, estates manager, re sale of the access to the site at Trafford Park.*

5 Nov   *DSgt Caldwell visits Peter Harrison, ex-works Manager at Poynton site.*

6 Nov   *Home Office has no objections to public donations for DCC Stalker, subject to GMPA approval.*

16 Nov   *Meeting with DPP to discuss prosecution of Taylor. Present: CS Topping, DCI Born and DI Stephenson and Worthington.*

21 Nov   *DSgt Ware interviews Wilkinson, a tenant on the GEC site which Taylor wished to purchase.*

24 Nov   *CC Anderton granted application for judicial review of criminal summons brought against him, CS Topping and DI Stephenson on 14 October.*

24 Nov   *DSgt Ware has long interview with Wilkinson,*

26 Nov   *DS Thorburn leaves the police.*

26 Nov *DSgt Ware and DCI Born visit Saddleworth Moor to liaise with CS Topping where he is searching for the bodies of victims from the Moors Murders.*

5 Dec *DSgt Caldwell and DSgt Knowles visit Elliot Partnership re distress warrants issued on Taylor, as rent is owing at St John Street.*

5 Dec *DI Stephenson and DSgt Ware visit Reeds Rains estate agency re Wood Mill, Summerseat.*

8 Dec *DSgt Knowles visits bailiffs re distress warrants.*

9 Dec *DSgt Knowles visits Elliott Partnership re distress warrants.*

11 Dec *CC Anderton makes controversial AIDS 'cesspit' speech.*

15 Dec *DSgt Knowles visits Elliot Partnership.*

16 Dec *CC Topping arranges for Myra Hindley to be taken to Saddleworth Moor. DCC Stalker not told.*

19 Dec **Stalker decides to resign from GMP.**

20 Dec *Moors Murders search is called off for the winter.*

20 Dec FRU invites Nelson to return to Northern Ireland at their expense.

1987

d.u. The 2012 de Silva Report analysed security leaks and discovered 270 separate instances of assistance provided by members of the security forces to loyalist paramilitaries during the period 1987 to September 1989 – 'likely to represent only a small sample of a wider problem'.

7 Jan *HMIC luncheon. Present: Sir Lawrence Byford, Douglas Hurd, Sir Robert Armstrong, Sir Robert Andrew, Sir Philip Myers, Mr Vessey and Mr Partridge among others.*

14 Jan Nelson is met by MI5 and FRU officers at Heathrow Airport. Aim according to de Silva: 'tempt him [Nelson] to return permanently' to Northern Ireland.

16 Jan *DSgt Knowles visits Elliott Partnership to ask about the current rent position on 2 St. John Street.*

18 Jan *CC Anderton gives BBC interview, saying he is a prophet of the Lord and that 'God speaks through him'.*

30 Jan *DSgt Knowles visits Elliott Partnership for update on 2 St. John Street.*

13 Feb FRU operatives set off to Germany to meet Nelson but meeting cancelled following strong objections from MI5. They wanted to be involved. Patrick Walker, the then Head of Counter-terrorism in MI5 is very angry about the FRU's actions.

19 Feb Nelson is re-recruited by FRU after an offer of £7,000 and £200 monthly payments.

26 Feb Hearing of judicial review of criminal summons (14/10/1986) in front of Lord Justice May and Mr Justice Nolan.

27 Feb *GMP admit in court that there is no suggestion that Taylor is involved in drugs.*

9 Mar *DSgt Knowles to Elliot Partnership.*

13 Mar **DCC Stalker leaves the police.**

13 Mar The first high-level meeting to discuss new guidelines for informers takes place between NIO officials and senior RUC officers.

13 Mar CC Sampson delivered 2nd of three reports to CC Hermon and DPPNI.

23 Mar CC Sampson delivers final section of Northern Ireland report to CC Hermon and DPPNI.

31 Mar Meeting with DPP to discuss prosecution of Taylor. Present: DCI Born and DI Stephenson, DSgt Caldwell, Waring and Worthington.

d.u. Apr AG, Sir Michael Havers, tells SDLP leader John Hume that there would be 'shocks felt throughout the force' over the Stalker inquiry.

3 Apr Criminal summonses brought against CC Anderton, CS Topping and DI Stephenson (14/10/86) on a charge of conspiracy to pervert the course of justice quashed in judicial review.

8 Apr DSgt Knowles received call from bailiff at home 'Wishing to give information on Taylor'.

1 May DSgt Knowles to Elliot Partnership.

4 May Nelson reports that he is targeting Target E and Target F. They are not warned.

16 May NIO Internal memo wanting 'slow progress' on the development of informer/agent guidelines.

20 May Meeting with DPP to discuss prosecution of Taylor. Still no decision.

29 May Nelson reports that Target G is being targeted. No prior warning appears to have been given by the RUC.

3 June Trustee Savings Bank issues warrant for repossession of Wood Mill, Summerseat. Taylor issues counterclaim in relation to the bank's failure to uphold their obligation to confidentiality.

16 June DSgt Knowles and PC Hogg visit Wood Mill, Summerseat, to ascertain if there was any evidence of the Taylors moving out.

18 June DSgts Caldwell and DSgt Knowles visit Wood Mill, Summerseat to check if it is vacated.

18 June DSgt Caldwell to Bury to make enquiries at estate agents re sale of Wood Mill.

18 June DSgt Caldwell makes enquiries at the Elliott Partnership re St. John Street tenancy.

19 June DSgt Caldwell to Pickfords re pending Taylor's removal from Wood Mill, Summerseat.

23 June DSgts Caldwell and Knowles collect binoculars for observations on Wood Mill, Summerseat.

26 June DSgts Caldwell and Knowles observe removal van at Wood Mill, Summerseat with binoculars. They note seeing Mrs Taylor leaving house with a pile of clothes and driving off.

13 July Leave to appeal to the House of Lords refused following quashing of the summonses brought against CC Anderton, CS Topping and DI Stephenson (14/10/86) on a charge of conspiracy to pervert the course of justice.

17 July DSgt Knowles to Poynton re recent workings.

17 July DSgt Knowles visits Elliott Partnership re: present position of 2 St. John Street.

20 July DSgts Caldwell and Knowles visit Poynton site to see if there is any activity on site.

21 July DSgt Knowles and DI Waterworth to city re. "activity around St. John Street re. current inquiry", then visiting Tottington "re current inquiry", and then visiting Summerseat "to check that K.T. still resident in family house, Wood Mill".

1 Aug During August to October Nelson disseminates FRU targeting material extensively.

7 Aug NIO memo to RUC re developing informer guidelines. Suggestions to special inspection team led by Charles McLachlan, HMIC.

10 Aug Meeting with DPP to discuss prosecution of Taylor. Present: CS Topping, DCI Born, DI Stephenson and DSgt Caldwell, Corkery, Slade, Worthington.

14 Aug DSgt Knowles to Elliot Partnership.

20 Aug DSgt Knowles and PC Hogg visit Trafford Park site.

25 Aug A full-time serving member of the UDR returns to Palace Barracks in Holywood, asks for and given keys to the armoury. Drives off with 18 assorted guns and gives them to the UDA. One of the weapons was later used to kill Pat Finucane.

27 Aug DSgt Knowles and DI Waterworth visit Elliott Partnership.

28 Aug Meeting with Corkery. Present: DSgt Caldwell and others.

4 Sep FRU handlers give Nelson photocopied lists of nationalist suspect terrorists, including maps and aerial photographs. RUC considered to be the source of the documents.

11 Sep DSgt Knowles visits Poynton site re development or sale.

15 Sep Bowley is arrested and charged.

15 Sep DSgt Knowles visits Elliot Partnership.

17 Sep DSgt Knowles observes house of John Kennedy, builder, who had lent money to Taylor.

17 Sep DI Caldwell, DI Waterworth and DSgt Knowles make observations at Wood Mill.

22 Sep DI Caldwell, DSgt Knowles and PC Hogg make observations at Wood Mill, Summerseat, re movements of Taylor.

23 Sep FRU aware that Nelson is targeting Declan McDaid. He was given no warning by the RUC before his brother was mistakenly assassinated on 10 May 1988.

30 Sep Taylor and Britton arrested on conspiracy charge. GMP object to bail in respect to Taylor.

d.u. Oct RUC SB fully informed of the most serious example of Nelson's dissemination of targeting information. It takes no action.

5 Oct Vincent McCann arrested on conspiracy charge.

4 Nov Leave for judicial review of the decision of Manchester Recorder, Judge Presst, to grant access orders, granted.

25 Nov Gibraltar authorities are warned by telex of the danger of an attack by a IRA ASU.

d.u. Dec UDA, UVF and UR import a large consignment of firearms from Beirut. Nelson not involved. According to a PONI report (1994): 'This shipment was subsequently used in at least seventy murders and numerous other attempted murders'.

1988

8 Jan Patrick Walker appointed Director General of MI5.

25 Jan AG, Sir Patrick Mayhew, announces in Parliament that DPPNI has concluded that it is not in the public interest to prosecute anyone relating to the three incidents investigated by DCC Stalker and CC Sampson.

9 Feb   *Hearing of judicial review of the decision of the Recorder of Manchester, Judge Presst, to grant access orders refused.*

15 Feb   A high level meeting in Gibraltar agrees that the IRA ASU should be allowed to travel with their explosives so they could be caught red-handed. In attendance: The Governor, Director General of Counter Terrorism, and a JIC representative.

3 Mar   NIO writes to Home Office noting that Stalker/Sampson raised issue of guidelines for informers, which was then considered by McLachlan, HMIC. He concludes that they were not appropriate for the RUC and other forces engaged in counter-terrorist operations.

4 Mar   IRA ASU, Mairead Farrell, Danny McCann and Sean Savage, seen meeting at Malaga airport.

6 Mar   The SAS shoot dead Mairead Farrell, Danny McCann and Sean Savage, in Gibraltar.

d.u. Apr DIU closed down.

13 May   DG MI5 raises issue of need for agent handling guidelines with Prime Minister Margaret Thatcher.

6 Jun   *CC Anderton receives a report from DI Simons on aspects of Stalker's conduct of the Northern Ireland inquiry.*

10 Jul   FRU receive information about the targeting of Target O, a solicitor. He was never informed.

31 Jul   *CS Topping retires from GMP.*

18 Sep   Start of 'old style' committal hearing against Taylor, Britton, McCann and Bowley. Ends 8 November 1988.

23 Sep   Nelson plays key role in the murder of Gerard Slane by the UDA.

d.u. Nov MI5 circulates information relating to Pat Finucane that, according to de Silva, 'effectively involved fanning the rumours and speculation linking him to the IRA'.

9 Nov   Tom King, SoS for Northern Ireland, issues PIICs preventing the inquest into the death of McKerr and others from examining evidence about the role of the HMSUs, surveillance and intelligence which led to the operation.

14 Nov   Inquest opens into McKerr and others. Coroner James Elliott admits unsworn statements and refuses request by Pat Finucane, Eleanor McKerr's solicitor, to adjourn, so he could seek judicial review of the decision.

15 Nov   Finucane applies for leave to judicially review the decision of the coroner to admit unsworn statements. Case eventually decided in the House of Lords.

22 Nov   Justice Carswell in the High Court rules that the coroner in the McKerr case has discretion to admit unsworn statements but was wrong to refuse an adjournment.

24 Nov   Douglas Hogg, Home Office Minister, attends a briefing with CC Hermon and other senior officers of the RUC at which he is told, according to de Silva, that half a dozen or so solicitors were 'effectively in the pockets of terrorists'.

d.u. Dec MI5 receive intelligence indicating that a meeting of UDA military commanders is going to discuss plans to kill three solicitors.

8 Dec   RUC officer/s propose Finucane (along with at least one other man) as UDA targets when speaking to a loyalist paramilitary in Castlereagh.

20 Dec   Court of Appeal reverses the decision of Justice Carswell to allow unsworn statements in inquests.

1989

13 Jan   Douglas Hogg, Home Office Minister, is provided with 'profiles' of solicitors Finucane and Kelly produced by the RUC.

17 Jan   Douglas Hogg, Home Office Minister, informs Parliament: 'I have to state as a fact, but with great regret, that there are in Northern Ireland a number of solicitors who are unduly sympathetic to the cause of the IRA'.

12 Feb   Finucane is shot dead in front of his family by members of the UDA.

14 Feb   ACC Monahan tells DCI Alan Simpson, the CID officer tasked with investigating Finucane's murder: 'If I were you, I would not get too deeply involved in this one'.

31 May   CC Hermon retires from RUC.

10 Jul   FRU learns that a UDA member had passed on to Nelson that Mr McGrory, a Belfast solicitor, visited the Kitchen Bar every Sunday with his son. Information was not passed onto RUC SB.

25 Aug   Loyalists paste state intelligence documents on walls across Belfast.

1 Sep   Disappearance of confidential material from Ballykinlar Army camp.

14 Sep   Stevens inquiry established by the RUC CC, Hugh Annesley to investigate the theft of state intelligence material. (Stevens One).

22 Sep   Army orders the seizure of Nelson's intelligence dump by the FRU.

2 Oct   ***Trial of Taylor, Britton, McCann and Bowley commenced in Manchester Crown Court.***

2 Oct   NIO sets up Working Group to develop guidelines on the use of informers in NI.

10 Oct   Intelligence received by RUC that UVF are aware of McGrory's home and work addresses and plan to kill him because of his role in the Gibraltar inquest.

1990

5 Jan   *The car of Taylor's barrister, David Hood, is stolen and discovered the following morning, burnt out.*

10 Jan   Fire at Carrickfergus office of the Stevens' enquiry team, the night before they planned to arrest Brian Nelson. The team suspects the fire was organised by FRU. Fire alarms and telephones had been disabled.

12 Jan   Arrest of Brian Nelson

18 Jan   ***Prosecution counsel offers no evidence against Taylor, Britton, McCann and Bowley on all charges since 'in the circumstances of this case, it would not be proper that the prosecution should seek an adverse verdict against these four defendants'.***

8 Mar   House of Lords rules Court of Appeal wrong and unsworn statements *are* admissible in inquests.

3 Jun   Shoot to Kill, Yorkshire TV drama documentary broadcast.

10 Jul   Brian Fitzsimmons, Head of RUC SB gives a positive testimonial on Brian Nelson.

19 Jul   ***The PCA announces that CS Rothwell of the Merseyside police has been appointed to conduct an investigation into the collapse of the Taylor trial.***

1 Sep   Meeting between GOCNI and CC: 'The CC had decided that the Stevens inquiry would have no access to intelligence documents or information, nor the units supplying them'.

26 Sep	Tom King advised by the MOD that the prosecution of Nelson would feed speculation that the security forces were involved in a 'dirty tricks campaign' and are in collusion with loyalist paramilitary groups.

9 Oct	Martin Gerard McCaughey and Desmond Gerard Grew shot dead by the SAS near Loughgall. The killings have all the hallmarks of another shoot-to-kill operation. Desmond Grew was the brother of Seamus Grew shot dead by the RUC in 1982.

1991

13 Mar	Sir Patrick Walker, the DG of MI5, writes to the Home Office outlining his concerns in relation to the prosecution of Nelson, copied to the AG's Office.

*27 Mar	Taylor issues a writ against Anderton claiming damages for misfeasance in public office as Chief Constable, malicious prosecution and conspiracy.*

24 Apr	Sir Patrick Walker meets AG. He argues that the prosecution of Nelson would damage the morale of agents and cites the risk of kidnap that might face MI5 officials who give evidence, though he noted that he 'did not wish to exaggerate the concern'.

25 Apr	Sir Patrick Mayhew, AG, writes to Tom King setting out the reasons for his view that it would be in the public interest to prosecute Nelson noting: 'that Nelson furthered to the point of fruition the murderous criminality which the Army are in the Province to forestall'.

26 Apr	Sir Robin Butler, the Cabinet Secretary, writes to Prime Minister opposing the prosecution of Nelson on grounds that it would do lasting harm to intelligence operations in NI.

14 Jun	Stalker: The Final Chapter, BBC Public Eye programme broadcast.

*30 Jun	CC Anderton retires from GMP.*

3 Oct	Ken Barrett makes a hypothetical admission to DSgt Johnston Brown that he was involved in the murder of Finucane.

1992

3 Feb	Nelson is sentenced to 10 years imprisonment for five conspiracies to murder.

25 Mar	Sir John Blelloch, a former permanent secretary at the NIO, is asked to conduct a review of agent handling.

**5 May	A new inquest opens into the deaths of McKerr and others with third coroner, John Leckey.**

1993

*20 Sep	It is discovered that DCI Born has had a relationship with informer Burton's girlfriend and that papers relating to the investigation into Taylor are lost.*

1994

**8 Mar	John Leckey, the coroner, issues three subpoenas on RUC to disclose the Stalker and Sampson reports.**

22 Mar	New inquests into all six killings examined by Stalker/Sampson formally open. Adjourned so that Crown can consider PIIC position.

5 May	Sir Patrick Mayhew, SoS for Northern Ireland, issues PIIC protecting Sampson and Stalker reports from disclosure.

11 Jul   Justice Nicolson sets aside the subpoenas for the Stalker and Sampson reports requested by Leckey.

8 Sep   Coroner Leckey abandons the inquests into the six killings examined by Stalker and Sampson.

1995

9 May   PIIC applied for in relation to the evidence which Stalker will give in the civil action brought by Taylor and others against GMP for malicious prosecution.

16 May   Start of the civil action brought by Taylor and others against GMP for malicious prosecution.

17 May   Former DCC Stalker takes the stand in the civil action.

19 Jun   End of civil action brought by Taylor and others against GMP. An award to Taylor of £2.4 million agreed in settlement.

1997 to 2024

1997

d.u. Jan   RUC introduces new rules for the handling and management of informers. Chief officers decide that these rules should not apply to RUC SB.

1999

d.u. Mar   Stevens inquiry begins investigation into, among other things, the circumstances surrounding the murder of Pat Finucane (Stevens Three).

15 Mar   Rosemary Nelson, a Lurgan solicitor, is murdered by Red Hand Defenders.

27 May   DSgt. Johnston Brown is interviewed by Stevens inquiry concerning the tape of Barrett's confession of his involvement in the murder of Finucane. The original tape of the confession had been replaced by RUC SB with a tape not recording the confession.

27 Jul   The Stevens inquiry team arrest Barrett on suspicion of the murder of Finucane. He is released without charge.

2001

1 Aug   Weston Park Agreement. A joint statement issued by the UK and Irish governments.

2002

1 May   The government appoints retired Canadian judge, Peter Cory, to examine six controversial murders during the Troubles, including that of Finucane. The government is committed to establishing public inquiries if recommended by the judge.

2003

25 Mar   Ombudsman informs the Chief Constable of her concerns re informer handling.

2012

27 Nov   Prime Minister David Cameron writes to Sir Mark Waller, Investigative Powers Commissioner, informing him of the secret policy that MI5 handlers permit informers to participate in crime and for him not to provide a view on the cases.

2015

14 **Jan   DPPNI requests investigation into destruction of evidence by RUC and MI5, seeking 'full investigations into the actions of former RUC and MI5 personnel in relation to the withholding, concealment and destruction of surveillance evidence'.**

2018

1 Mar   Prime Minister Theresa May issues statement in the House of Commons on the 'Third Direction', which permits state agents to commit crimes.

8 Jun   A heavily redacted copy of the 'Guidelines on the use of Agents who participate in Criminality (Official Guidance)' is made available to the claimants in a civil action.

2019

27 Feb The Supreme Court issues judgement in the judicial review brought by Geraldine Finucane. It confirms that there has been no Article 2 compliant inquiry into Pat Finucane's death but argues that it does not follow that a public inquiry should be ordered. It is up to the state to decide what action to take to meet its procedural obligations.

20 Dec Investigatory Powers Tribunal decide by a majority of three to two that the Security Service Act 1989 has an implied power for MI5 to run agents who engage in criminal activities.

2020

18 Mar Brandon Lewis, SoS for Northern Ireland, announces 'a new approach' to dealing with the past.

20 Sep The government publish the Covert Human Intelligence Sources (CHIS) Bill to provide 'a clear and consistent statutory basis for a limited number of public authorities to continue to authorise participation in criminality, in carefully managed circumstances'.

30 Nov Brandon Lewis, SoS for Northern Ireland, informs parliament that the government will establish a public inquiry into the murder of Pat Finucane 'to look at any potential failings by government or State bodies'. However, he announces that he has decided 'not to establish a public inquiry at this time'.

2021

14 Jul Government publishes a command paper proposing a statute of limitations on all Troubles-related cases.

2022

17 May Publication of the Northern Ireland Troubles (Legacy and Reconciliation) Bill.

2023

18 Sep Legacy Act receives Royal Assent.

2024

24 Feb High court declares that the impunity provisions in the Legacy Act are incompatible with the ECHR and should be disapplied. It further declares that stopping civil claims and prohibition of criminal enforcement actions are also incompatible with the ECHR.

24 Feb PPS announces decisions on final Operation Kenova files. As a result, not one person has been prosecuted arising from the Kenova investigation costing £40 million.

8 Mar   Publication of the Kenova Report.

Notes

Chapter 1: Introduction (pages 1 to 10)

1 Stalker, John. *Stalker* (London: Harrap, 1988), p. 67 and p. 285.
2 Civil Action, 13 June 1995, pp. 32-54.
3 *Private Eye*, No. 684, 3 March 1988.
4 Hansard, House of Commons, 'Senior Police Officers (Meeting)' Vol. 127, 10 February 1988.
5 UK National Archives, File note of a meeting held at 1.30 p.m. on Monday 9th May 1986, in the Queen Alexander Room of the Royal Hotel, Scarborough, 6 January 1994, CJ4/6279; Civil Action, 16 May 1995, p. 22.
6 For an insider view of the QSG see: Donnelly, James. *Jimmy the Weed: Inside the Quality Street Gang* (Wrea Green, Lancs.: Milo Books, 2011). He denied it was a gang and described it as 'a web of interlocking and mutually beneficial friendships between men from poor backgrounds who were trying to make something of themselves', p. 91. See also: Walsh, Peter. *Gang War: the Inside Story of the Manchester Gangs* (Wrea Green, Lancs.: Milo Books, 2003), p. 11. For a critique of the notion of a gang, see: Hallsworth, Simon and Tara Young. 'Gang talk and gang talkers: A critique.' *Crime, Media, Culture: An International Journal*, 4:2 (2008) pp. 175-195. Hallsworth, Simon. *The Gang and Beyond: Interpreting Violent Street Worlds* (London: Palgrave MacMillan, 2013).
7 Tracks entitled: 'Johnny the Fox Meets Jimmy the Weed' and 'The boys are back in town'.
8 In 2019, a developer announced plans to turn an old commercial pub into the 'Quality Street Hotel'. See: 'Outrage over "tacky" plans to "honour" infamous Quality Street Gang.' *Manchester Evening News*, 27 April 2019.
9 Civil Action, 16 May 1995, p 22.
10 Greater Manchester Police Authority, Press Statement, 29 May 1986.
11 Horrocks, Paul. 'Stalker to hit back with his own report.' *Manchester Evening News*, 8 September 1986.
12 For a detailed and excellent analysis of the way the press covered the story see: Murphy, David. *The Stalker Affair and the Press* (London: Unwin Hyman, 1991).
13 Leigh, D., N. Davies and J. Foster. 'High-level order to silence Stalker.' *The Observer*, 6 July 1986.
14 *Ibid.*
15 Shannon, William. 'Only a conspiracy could explain it.' *Manchester Evening News*, 17 July 1986.
16 The Security Service was only formally established in 1989. Prior to this date, the existence of MI5 remained an open secret. For an official and selected history, see: Andrew, Christopher M. *The Defence of the Realm: The Authorized History of MI5* (London: Allen Lane, 2009). For an earlier critical analysis see: Bunyan, Tony. *The History and Practice of the Political Police in Britain* (London: Quartet Books, 1977), Chapter 4. As the term security services, with an 's', includes the army the police and the Security Service, to avoid confusion, the Security Service is referred to throughout the book as MI5.
17 *Private Eye*, No. 639, 13 June 1986.
18 Wallis, Neill. 'Stalker Affair: MI5 Smear Scandal Exposed.' *The Star*, 19 July 1986.
19 Doherty, Frank. *The Stalker Affair* (Dublin: Mercier Press, 1986).
20 Taylor, Kevin. *The Poisoned Tree: The Untold Truth about the Police Conspiracy to Discredit John Stalker and Destroy me* (London: Sidgwick & Jackson, 1990), p. 208.
21 Stalker, 1988, *op. cit.* pp. 263-264.
22 *Ibid.* p. 265.
23 The Leader, 'Stalker's Irish Jungle.' *The Guardian*, 2 February 1988.
24 PRONI, Stalker, CENT-3-20A, 1986.
25 Ryder, Chris. *The RUC 1922-2000: A Force Under Fire* (London: Arrow Books, 2000), p. 348.
26 See: Topping, Peter. *Topping: The Autobiography of the Police Chief in the Moors Murder Case* (London: Angus & Robertson Publishers, 1989), Chapter 22.
27 He has written numerous books on the subject. See: Taylor, Peter. *Beating the terrorists? Interrogation at Omagh, Gough and Castlereagh* (Harmondsworth: Penguin, 1980); *States of Terror: Democracy and political violence* (London: Penguin, 1994); *Provos: The IRA and Sinn Fein* (London: Bloomsbury, 1997); *Loyalists* (London: Bloomsbury, 2000); *Brits: the war against the IRA* (London: Bloomsbury, 2001); *Operation Chiffon: The Secret Story of MI5 and MI6 and the Road to Peace in Ireland* (London: Bloomsbury, 2023).

28 'Peter Taylor honoured with RTS Lifetime Achievement Award for outstanding contribution to journalism,' BBC, Media Centre, 20 February 2014. https://www.bbc.co.uk/mediacentre/latestnews/2014/peter-taylor-rts.html (Accessed, 3 July 2019).

29 *Inhuman and Degrading Treatment,* Thames TV, This week, 27 October 1977.

30 Taylor, Peter, 1980, *op. cit.* p. 222.

31 *Stalker: Coincidence or Conspiracy?* BBC Panorama Programme, 16 June 1986 and *Stalker & Company*, BBC Panorama Programme, 19 August 1986.

32 *Stalker & Company, ibid.*

33 Taylor, Peter. *Stalker: The Search for the Truth* (London: Faber and Faber, 1987), p. 136.

34 *Ibid.* p. 123.

35 *Ibid.* p. 190.

36 *Ibid.* p. 136.

37 *Ibid.* p. 123.

38 Murtagh, Peter. 'Stalker's Edge of Darkness.' *The Guardian,* 12 February, 1988.

39 *Ibid.*

40 Murtagh, Peter. 'Stalker: the Jury stays out.' *Fortnight,* No. 252, June 1987, p. 16.

41 Letter from Peter Taylor, *Fortnight,* No. 253, July-August 1987.

42 *Ibid.*

43 Taylor, Peter, 2001, *op. cit.* p. 252. Andrew, in his official history of MI5, uses this quote from Peter Taylor to contradict 'the ill-founded conspiracy theories'. See: Andrew, 2009, p. 739 and footnote 26.

44 Brooks, Richard. 'IBA board demands preview of "Shoot to Kill" docu-drama'. *The Observer,* 13 May 1990.

45 Herbert, Hugh. 'Stalking truth among the dead men'. *The Guardian*, 24 May 1990.

46 Horner, Rosalie. 'Drama behind the shooting of the Stalker Affair.' *The Observer,* 27 May 1990.

47 *Stalker: The Final Chapter,* BBC Public Eye,14 June 1991.

48 *Ibid.*

49 *Ibid.*

50 See for example: Boyd, Andrew. *The Informers: A Chilling Account of the Supergrasses in Northern Ireland*, (Dublin: Mercier Press, 1984), Chapter 1.

51 Informers are typically recruited by CID and given a small payment for each item of information they supply. State agents are mainly recruited, controlled and paid a retainer by RUC SB to provide information on 'subversive organisations'. The British Army and MI5 also recruited and controlled their own agents.

Chapter 2: Conspiracies in Death (pages 11 to 28)

1 Ballynery in books and documents in the Taylor/Stalker affair is sometimes spelt Ballynerry or Ballyneery. The correct spelling is Ballynery.

2 O'Leary, Brendan and John McGarry. *The Politics of Antagonism: Understanding Northern Ireland* (London: Athlone Press, 1993), p. 13.

3 See, for example: Beresford, David. *Ten Men Dead* (London: Grafton, 1987).

4 Cusack, Jim. 'Wounded man contradicts RUC version of killing.' *The Irish Times*, 26 November 1982.

5 Pollak, Andy. 'Man shot dead by RUC patrol.' *The Irish Times*, 25 November 1982.

6 *Ibid.*

7 Cusack, 26 November 1982, *op. cit.*

8 Stalker, 1988, op. cit. p. 41.

9 Cusack, Jim. 'Inquiry urged into the shooting.' *The Irish Times*, 13 November 1982.

10 *Ibid.*

11 Cusack, Jim. 'RUC version of roadblock killings queried by Councillor.' *The Irish Times*, 17 November 1982.

12 Pollak, Andy. 'RUC shoot two dead after chase in Armagh.' *The Irish Times*, 13 December 1982.

13 See: Faul, Denis and Raymond Murray. *British Army and Special Branch R.U.C. brutalities December 1971-February 1972* (Cavan: D. Faul, 1972). Faul, Denis and Raymond Murray. *The triangle of death: sectarian assassinations in the Dungannon-Moy-Portadown area* (Dungannon: The Authors, 1975). Faul, Denis and Raymond Murray. *The Castlereagh file: Allegations of RUC brutality 1976/1977* (Armagh: D. Faul, 1978).

14 Pollak, 13 December 1982, *op. cit.*

15 Leslie MacFarlane asked the same question in relation to the killing of Mairead Farrell, Danny McCann and Sean Savage in Gibraltar in March 1988. See MacFarlane, Lesley. 'Human Rights and the fight against terrorism in Northern Ireland.' *Terrorism and Political Violence,* 4:1 (1992) p. 94.

16 Deputy Chief Constable Michael McAtamney's evidence in the Robinson trial, see: Taylor, Peter. 1987, *op. cit.* p. 41.

17 *Ibid.* p. 39.

18 Moloney, Ed. 'The Hidden Force.' *The Irish Times,* 21 January 1985.

19 McKittrick, David, Seamus Kelters, Brian Feeney, Chris Thornton and David McVea. *Lost Lives: The stories of the men, women and children who died as a result of the Northern Ireland troubles* (Edinburgh: Mainstream Publishing, 2001), Table 1.

20 Taylor, Peter. 2001, *op. cit.* p. 249.

21 See: Cobain, Ian. 'Northern Ireland: when Britain fought terror with terror.' *The Guardian,* 9 July 2015.

22 Rolston, Bill. *Unfinished Business: State Killings and the Quest for Truth* (Belfast: Beyond the Pale, 2000), p. 91.

23 'Court told two men fired shots at car.' *The Irish Times,* 22 March 1984.

24 '3 RUC men face charge of murdering unarmed man.' *The Irish Times,* 30 May 1984.

25 Diplock, Lord, *Report of the Commission to consider legal procedures to deal with terrorist activities in Northern Ireland,* Cmnd. 5185 (London: HMSO, 1972).

26 *Ibid.* para. 90.

27 For detailed analyses of the Diplock Courts see: Boyle, Kevin, Tom Hadden and Paddy Hillyard. *Law and state: the case of Northern Ireland* (London: Robertson, 1975); Boyle, Kevin, Tom Hadden and Paddy Hillyard. *Ten years on in Northern Ireland: The legal control of political violence* (London: Cobden Trust, 1980); Walsh, Dermot, J P. *The Use and Abuse of Emergency Legislation in Northern Ireland* (London: Cobden Trust, 1983); and Hogan, Gerard and Clive Walker. *Political violence and the law in Ireland* (Manchester: Manchester University Press, 1989).

28 Kitson, Frank. *Low intensity operations. Subversion, Insurgency and Peace-keeping* (London: Faber & Faber, 1971). See also: Faligot, Roger. *Britain's Military Strategy in Ireland: The Kitson Experiment* (Dingle: Brandon Book Publishers, 1983); Newsinger, John. *British Counterinsurgency: From Palestine to Northern Ireland* (Basingstoke: Palgrave MacMillan, 2002); Hughes, James. 'Frank Kitson in Northern Ireland and the "British way" of counter insurgency.' *History Ireland,* 22:1 (2014).

29 See in particular: Urwin, Margaret. *A State in Denial: British Collaboration with Loyalist Paramilitaries* (Cork: Mercier Press, 2016) and McGovern, Mark. *Counterinsurgency and Collusion in Northern Ireland* (London: Pluto Press, 2019), Chapter 1.

30 McGlinchey claims to have killed 30 people. See: Taylor, Peter, 2002, *op. cit.* p. 244.

31 This account is from Stalker, 1988, *op. cit.* pp. 52-53. Peter Taylor provides an account, which differs in a number of key aspects. See: Taylor, Peter, 2001, *op. cit.* pp. 245-247.

32 'Accused RUC man tells of cover-up.' *The Irish Times,* 29 March 1984.

33 Doherty, 1986, *op. cit.* p. 19.

34 Cusack, Jim. 'Nationalist anger over the Grew killing verdict.' *The Irish Times,* 4 April 1984.

35 Holroyd, Fred and Nick Burbridge. *War Without Honour: Military Intelligence in Northern Ireland* (Hull: Medium Publishing, 1989), pp. 73-74.

36 *Ibid.*

37 See the excellent analysis: BIRW. *Complaint concerning the death of Gervaise McKerr,* (Belfast: British and Irish Rights Watch, October 1995). Also see: Stalker, 1988, *op. cit.* p. 41. He mentions that 108 shots were fired whereas in fact it was 109.

38 Saville, Rt Hon Lord. *Independent Report, Report of the Bloody Sunday Inquiry,* HC 29 (London: HMSO, 2010), Vol. VIII, para. 165.85.

39 See: Leigh, D., J. Foster and P. Lashmar. 'Ulster death squad secrets exposed.' *The Observer.* 12 October 1986; Stalker,1988, *op. cit.* p. 41; Murray, Raymond. *The SAS in Ireland* (Dublin: Mercier Press, 1990), p. 271.

40 Nine years later David Brannigan was found dead. It is believed he had shot himself. The NIPB challenged an assessment that his widow should qualify for a special pension award. 'Widow of RUC man to face pension challenge.' *Belfast Telegraph,* 20 October 2009.

41 R v William James Montgomery, David Brannigan and Frederick Nigel Robinson, Judgment of Lord Justice Gibson, Belfast Crown Court, 5 June 1984.

42 *Ibid.* p. 3.

43   *Ibid.* p. 4.
44   *Ibid.*
45   *Ibid.* p. 7.
46   *Ibid.* p. 9.
47   *Ibid.* p. 10.
48   *Ibid.* p. 8.
49   *Ibid.* p. 16.
50   *Ibid..*
51   Peter Barry, Speech in Cork, 9 June 1984. See: Coghlan, Denis, 'Barry seeks controls on NI forces'. *The Irish Times*, 11 June 1984.
52   'Top judge defends RUC men's acquittal.' *The Irish Press,* 7 June 1984.
53   See: Mullin, Chris. *Error of Judgement: The Truth about the Birmingham Bombings* (Swords, Co. Dublin: Poolbeg Press, 1987); Callaghan, Hugh. *Cruel Fate: One Man's Triumph Over Injustice*, (Swords, Co. Dublin: Poolbeg, 1993).
54   Widgery, Rt Hon. Lord. *Report of the Tribunal appointed to inquire into the events on Sunday, 30 January 1972, which led to the loss of life in connection with the procession in Londonderry on that day* HL 101, HC 220 (London: HMSO, 1972).
55   Mullin, 1987, *op. cit.* p. 216.
56   Woffinden, Bob. *Miscarriages of Justice* (London: Hodder and Stoughton, 1987).
57   As well as the Birmingham Six there have been other notorious miscarriages of justice cases. For example: Judith Ward, the Guildford 4 and the Maguire Seven. For a legal analysis see: Walker, Clive and Keir Starmer (Eds.). *Miscarriages of Justice: A Review of Justice in Error* (London: Blackstone Press, 1999). For their personal stories see: Ward, Judith. *Ambushed* (London: Vermillion, 1993); Armstrong, Paddy. *Life after Life: A Guildford Four Memoir* (Dublin: Gill Books, 2017); Conlon, Gerry. *Proved Innocent: The Story of Gerry Conlon of the Guildford Four* (London: Hamish Hamilton, 1990); Hill, Paul and Ronan Bennett. *Stolen years: Before and after Guildford* (London: Doubleday, 1990).
58   UK National Archives, Letter from Mr Angel, NIO, Whitehall to Mr Steel, 7 June 1984. CJ 4/5603.
59   This information was revealed by Chris Moore in a television broadcast in 1988. See: 'Shoot to kill car was bugged.' *The Irish Times*, 9 February 1988.
60   Dillon, Martin. *The Dirty War* (London: Arrow, 1991), pp. 400-401.
61   R v McCauley, Belfast Crown Court, 15-25 January 1985.
62   *Ibid.*
63   'Man gets suspended sentence as RUC evidence thrown out.' *The Irish Times*. 16 February 1985.
64   The Queen v McCauley [2014] NICA 60, para. 23.
65   See: Jennings, Anthony. 'Shoot to Kill: The Final Court of Justice' in A. Jennings (ed.) *Justive Under Fire: The Abuse of Civil Liberties in Northern Ireland.* (London: Pluto Press, 1988) pp. 64-130; Amnesty International. *Political Killings in Northern Ireland* (London: Amnesty International British Section, 1994).
66   Field Notes.
67   Asmal, Kadar. *Shoot to Kill? International Lawyers' Inquiry into the Lethal Use of Firearms by the Security Forces in Northern Ireland* (Dublin: Mercier Press, 1985), p.134.
68   Ní Aoláin, Fionnuala. *The Politics of Force: Conflict Management and State Violence in Northern Ireland*, (Belfast: Blackstaff Press, 2000). See also: Walsh, Dermot P J. *Bloody Sunday and the Rule of Law in Northern Ireland*, (Dublin: Gill & Macmillan, 2000), Chapter 6.
69   Ní Aoláin, 2000, *op. cit.* p. 96.
70   *Ibid.* p. 118
71   Jennings, 1986, *op. cit.* pp. 104-114.
72   Ní Aoláin, 2000, *op. cit.* p.125.
73   McKittrick, 2001, *op. cit.* Table 1, p. 1552.
74   Visit to RUC HQ, Knock, 1980.
75   Hermon, John C. *An Autobiography: Holding the Line* (Dublin: Gill and Macmillan, 1997), pp. 152-153.
76   *Ibid.* p. 153.
77   *Ibid.* p. 154.
78   *Ibid.* p. 138.
79   See: Urban, Mark. *Big Boys' Rules: The SAS and the Secret Struggle against the IRA* (London:

Faber and Faber, 1992), p. 153.
80 Hermon, 1997, *op. cit.* pp. 154-155.
81 Hansard, House of Commons, Debates, 25 January 1988 Vol. 126 Cols. 1-35.
82 Hermon, 1997, *op. cit.* p. 157.
83 UK National Archives, Memorandum to the Secretary of State for Northern Ireland from Mr Angel, NIO, 23 May 1984, CJ4/5603.
84 *Ibid.*
85 Hermon, 1997, *op. cit.* p. 158.
86 Ford, Richard. 'Inquiry into "cover-up" by RUC.' *The Times*, 31 May 1984.

Chapter 3: Recruiting Spies, Transforming Policing (pages 29 to 40)

1 Oxford University Calendar, 1954, p. 234.
2 Walker, Patrick. *Towards Independence in Africa: A District Officer in Uganda at the End of Empire* (London: I B Tauris, 2009).
3 Foucault, Michel. *Society Must be Defended: Lectures at the College de France, 1975-6* (London: Allen Lane, 2003), p. 103. See also: Bloch, Jonathan and Patrick Fitzgerald. *British Intelligence and Covert Action* (Dingle: Brandon, 1983). For an analysis of the impact of colonial thinking on successive security strategies in Northern Ireland, see: McGovern, 2019, *op. cit.* pp. 7-22. How colonialism historically structured relations in Ireland and continues to do so, see: McVeigh, Robbie and Bill Rolston. *Ireland, Colonialism and the Unfinished Revolution* (Belfast: Beyond the Pale Books, 2021).
4 Historical Institutional Abuse Inquiry. *Kincora Boys' Home (Part 2)* Chapter 28 (Belfast: HIAI, 2017), para. 34.
Chapter 28 - Module 15 - Kincora Boys' Home (Part 2)_0.pdf (hiainquiry.org) (Accessed 2 October 2020)
5 Urban, Mark. *UK Eyes Alpha: The Inside Story of British Intelligence* (London: Faber and Faber, 1996), p. 50.
6 *Ibid.*
7 *Ibid.* pp. 4-5.
8 But see: Dorril, Stephen. *The Silent Conspiracy: Inside the Intelligence Agencies in the 1990s* (London: Mandarin, 1994), Chapter 4.
9 Griffin, Tom. *British Intelligence Officers in Ireland: A spotter's guide for archival researachers,* (2017). http://www.patreon.com/tcgriffin
10 UK National Archives, Letter from Michael Alexander to Stephen Boy Smith, 27 May 1981, PREM 19/505.
11 UK National Archives, Letter from Robert Armstrong to Michael Alexander, 17 June 1981, PREM 19/505.
12 Milne, Seumas. *The Enemy Within: The Secret War Against the Miners* (London: Pan Books, 1995), p. 387.
13 'Sir Patrick Walker, Director General of MI5 who led the way as the agency shifted focus at the end of the Cold War,' *The Daily Telegraph,* 20 October 2021.
14 'Sir Patrick Walker,' *The Times,* 20 October 2021.
15 Andrew, 2009, *op. cit.* p. 700.
16 Urban, Mark, 1996, *op. cit.* p. 84.
17 Holland, Jack and Henry McDonald. *INLA: Deadly Divisions, The Story of one of Ireland's most ruthless terrorist organisations* (Dublin: Poolbeg, 1994), pp. 138-139.
18 Wharton, Ken. *Wasted Years, Wasted Lives: The British Army in Northern Ireland* (London: Helion and Company, 2013), p. 164.
19 Maume, Christopher. 'Countess Mountbatten of Burma, obituary: Survivor of IRA bomb and known for her work with bereavement charities.' *The Independent.* 16 June 2017.
20 Taylor, Peter, 2001, *op. cit.* pp. 221-222.
21 See for example: McClean, Raymond. *The Road to Bloody Sunday* (Swords, Co. Dublin: Ward River Press Ltd, 1983). McCann, Eamonn, Maureen Shiels and Bridie Hannigan. *Bloody Sunday in Derry: What Really Happened* (Dingle, Co Kerry: Brandon Book Publishers 1992).
22 Taylor, Peter, 1997, p. 228.
23 Dorril, 1994, *op. cit.* p. 56.
24 For more detail see Pat Finucane Centre archive:
https://www.patfinucanecentre.org/archive?search_api_fulltext=waterboarding (Accessed 5 January 2024)

25 In early 1980, there were rumours that Oldfield might be gay and could pose a security risk. MI5 investigated and found that he had failed to declare his sexual orientation in his positive vetting but had not compromised security. He retired after only a few months in post. Historical Institutional Abuse Inquiry, KIN-4076.
    https://www.hiainquiry.org/sites/hiainquiry/files/media-files/M15-D219-MI5-Officer-9004-Rev-RO.pdf (Accessed 2 October 2020)
26 Walker, Patrick. *Report on the Interchange of Intelligence between Special Branch and C.I.D. and the R.U.C. Units Involved, including those in the Crime Branch C1(1)*(1980).
27 Lashmar, Paul. *Spies, Spin and the Fourth Estate: British Intelligence and the Media* (Edinburgh: Edinburgh University Press, 2020), p. 4.
28 *Policing the Police*, UTV Insight Programme, June 2001. See: O'Brien, Justin. *Killing Finucane: Murder in Defence of the Realm* (Dublin: Gill & Macmillan, 2005), Appendix 1.
29 In the matter of an appeal to the First-Tier Tribunal (Information Rights) under Section 57 of the Freedom of Information Act, 2000 between CAJ, Information Commissioner and PSNI. Case No. EA/2017/0219. Skelton Argument on Behalf of the Commissioner. For Hearing 1-2 May 2018.
30 Walker, Patrick, 1980, *op. cit.*
31 *Ibid* para. 3. For an analysis of informers in 'normal' policing see for example: Billingsley, Roger, Philip Bean and Teresa Nemitz. *Informers: policing, policy, practice* (London: Routledge, 2005); Dunningham, Colin and Clive Norris. 'Some ethical dilemmas in the handling of police informers.' *Public Money & Management*, 21:5 (1998), pp. 21-25. There is very little literature on the use of state agents in conflict situations. See: Dudai, Ron. *The IRA and the shadow of the informer: punishment, governance, and dealing with the past*, PhD. School of Law (Belfast: Queen's University Belfast, 2013) and 'Informers and the Transition in Northern Ireland.' *British Journal of Criminology*, 52:1 (2012) pp. 32–54; Cochrane, Mark and Rachel Monaghan. 'Countering terrorism through the use of informants: the Northern Ireland experience.' *Behavioral Sciences of Terrorism and Political Aggression,* 4: 1 (2012) pp. 26-4; Sarma, Kiran. 'Informers and the Battle Against Republican Terrorism: A Review of 30 Years of Conflict.' *Police Practice and Research: An International Journal*, 6:2 (2005) pp. 165-180.
32 Walker, Patrick, 1980, *op. cit*. para. 10.
33 *Ibid.* para. 8.
34 *Ibid.* para. 11
35 *Ibid.* para. 12.
36 *Ibid.* para. 16.
37 See: Hillyard, Paddy. *Suspect community: People's experience of the Prevention of Terrorism Acts in Britain* (London: Pluto Press in association with Liberty, 1993).
38 Walker, Patrick, 1980, *op. cit.* para. 24-25.
39 *Ibid.* para. 54.
40 *Ibid.* para. 62.
41 Clarke, Liam. 'MI5 spy funding is under scrutiny.' *The Sunday Times*, 28 January 2007.
42 See for example: PONI. *Public statement by the Police Ombudsman for Northern Ireland, on her investigation into the circumstances surrounding the death of Raymond McCord Junior and related matter,* Operation Ballast, (Belfast: Police Ombudsman for Northern Ireland, 2007).
43 See for example: Morland, Michael, Valerie Strachan, and Anthony Burden. *The Rosemary Nelson Inquiry Report*, HC 947, (London: HMSO, 2011), para. 5.92.
44 Walker, Patrick, 1980, *op. cit.* para. 28.
45 Cobain, Ian. 'How many murders can a police informer get away with?' *The Guardian*, 8 March 2018.
46 Andrew, 2009, *op. cit.* p. 698.
47 'Tout' is a popular description of an informer.
48 For a discussion of some of wider moral and legal implications of intelligence gathering see: Bamford, Bradley. 'The Role and Effectiveness of Intelligence in Northern Ireland.' *Intelligence and National Security,* 20: 4 (2005) pp. 581–607; Cochrane, Mark and Rachel Monaghan. 2012, *op. cit.* pp. 26-40.
49 PONI. *The Murders at the Heights Bar, Loughinisland, 18 June 1994* (Belfast: Police Ombudsman for Northern Ireland, 1994), paras. 5.11.
50 Home Office, *Guidelines for the Police in the Use of Informants* (London: HMSO, 1969).
51 De Silva, Rt. Hon. Sir Desmond. *Pat Finucane Review: An independent review into any State involvement in the murder of Pat Finucane*, Vol. 1 and Vol. 2 (London: HMSO, 2012), para. 23.

52 *Ibid.* para. 4.16.
53 *Ibid.* para. 4.87.
54 McGovern, 2019, *op. cit.* p. 49.
55 *Spotlight on the Troubles: A Secret History*, BBC, 1 October 2019. See also: McClements, Freya. 'Documentary claims Stakeknife carried out IRA's Loughgall investigation.' *The Irish Times*, 1 October 2019.
56 Jamieson and McEvoy, in a comprehensive analysis of the outsourcing of state crime, argue that collusion is one element in a phenomenon of what they describe as 'juridical otherings', see: Jamieson, Ruth and Kieran McEvoy. 'State Crime by Proxy and Juridical Othering.' *British Journal of Criminology,* 45:4 (2005) pp. 504-527.
57 Elkins, Caroline. *Legacy of Violence: A History of the British Empire* (London: The Bodley Head, 2022), p. 15.
58 *Just News*, July-August 2018, p. 2.
59 O'Brien, Justin, 2005, *op. cit.* pp. 150-159.
60 For more details see: Larkin, Paul. *A Very British Jihad: Collusion, Conspiracy and Cover-Up in Northern Ireland* (Belfast: Beyond the Pale, 2004), p. 44.
61 Urban, Mark. 1992, *op. cit.* p. 109.
62 Jane Winter, British and Irish Rights Watch, commenting on the Walker Report. See Pat Finucane Centre: http://www.patfinucanecentre.org/index.php/policing/walker-report-internal-ruc-instructions-governing-interchange-intelligence-between-ruc (Accessed 2 October 2020)
63 Punch, Maurice. *State Violence, Collusion and the Troubles: Counter Insurgency, Government Deviance and Northern Ireland* (London: Pluto Press, 2012), p. 57.
64 See: Rolston, Bill. '"An effective mask for terror": Democracy, death squads and Northern Ireland.' *Crime, Law & Social Change,* 44:2 (2006) pp. 181-203.

Chapter 4: Conspiracies in Life (pages 41 to 55)

1 See: Levi, Michael. *The Phantom Capitalists: The organisation and control of long-firm fraud* (London: Heinemann, 1981), Chapter 2.
2 See: Levi, Michael. 'The Craft of the Long-Firm Fraudster: Criminal Skills and Commercial Responses' in M. Gill (Ed.). *Men at Work* (London: Palgrave, 1998).
3 'Market Trader gave dud cheques.' *Liverpool Echo and Express*, 23 July 1963.
4 'Man stole mother's cheques.' *Manchester Evening News*, 19 November 1968.
5 '£1,156 charge.' *Manchester Evening News*, 6 April 1972.
6 Civil Action, 14 June 1995, p. 25. For an excellent analysis of the Kray Twins' lives, see: Pearson, John. *The profession of violence: the rise and fall of the Kray twins* (London: Granada, 1984).
7 Field Notes. See also: Panter, Steve. 'Stalker and a Mitty liar.' *Manchester Evening News*, 22 August 1986.
8 'A plausible rogue jailed for six years.' *Manchester Evening News*, 23 March 1976.
9 *Ibid.*
10 Murtagh, Peter. 'RUC officer in Stalker link to province: Allegations by informer David Bertlestein involving Greater Manchester deputy chief constable.' *The Guardian*, 29 September 1986.
11 The CCF was set up in 1970 to compensate people who were victims of the Troubles. Individuals who were injured in bomb attacks or people whose businesses were attacked, could make claims for compensation. Throughout the 1970s it allocated around £50 million in compensation.
12 'Probe into "RUC grass link".' *Manchester Evening News*, 29 September 1986.
13 O'Clery, Conor. 'Contract-bombing' claim by MP.' *The Irish Times*, 23 June 1977.
14 Civil Action, 14 June 1995, p. 14.
15 Leigh, David, Paul Lashmar and Jonathan Foster. 'Lying Pest behind the Stalker Probe.' *The Observer*, 28 September 1986.
16 *Ibid.*
17 Civil Action, 22 May 1995, p. 26.
18 Civil Action, 14 June 1995, p. 25, and p. 34.
19 Stewart, James, 'Firebombs in Belfast Jewellers.' *Belfast Telegraph*, 26 January 1981. 'Ex-Lord Mayor held at gunpoint in attack.' *News Letter*, 27 January 1981.
20 Murphy, 1991, *op. cit.* p. 185.
21 Field Notes.

22 'Bombers go on a rampage across Ulster.' *Belfast Telegraph*, 27 January 1981.
23 Field Notes.
24 Civil Action, 14 June 1985, p. 26.
25 Civil Action, 22 May 1995, p. 26 and p. 28.
26 *Ibid*. p. 26.
27 *Ibid*. p. 28.
28 *Ibid*.
29 'Man on £81,000 fraud charges is granted bail.' *Belfast Telegraph*, 15 December 1982.
30 Sampson, Colin. *Report of the investigation by Chief Constable Colin Sampson, Q.P.M* (Wakefield: West Yorkshire Police, 1986), para. 198.
31 Field Notes.
32 Civil Action, 25 May 1995, p. 30.
33 Field Notes.
34 Civil Action, 18 May 1995, pp. 72-73.
35 Civil Action, 14 June 1995, p. 37.
36 Field Notes.
37 Sampson, 1986, *op. cit.* para. 185(a).
38 Civil Action, 22 May 1995, pp. 41-42.
39 Civil Action, 1 June 1995, p. 1.
40 Civil Action, 14 June 1995, pp. 16-17.
41 Civil Action, 18 May 1995, p. 53.
42 Civil Action, 14 June 1995, p. 18.
43 Civil Action, 18 May 1995, p. 51.
44 Civil Action, 14 June 1995, p. 18.
45 Civil Action, 24 May 1995, p. 24.
46 *Ibid*. p. 23.
47 Civil Action, 1 June 1995, p. 2.
48 Civil Action, 14 June 1995, p. 25.
49 *Ibid*. pp. 13-14.
50 Civil Action, 22 May 1995, p. 27.
51 Field Notes.
52 Panter, 22 August 1986, *op. cit.*
53 Civil Action, 25 May 1995, p. 31.
54 Field Notes.
55 Donnelly, 2011, *op. cit.* p. 193.
56 Civil Action, 14 June 1995, p. 28.
57 Civil Action, 19 May 1995, pp. 31-32.
58 Burgess, Derek. *Get Stalker: Fraud Squad officer accused senior investigating officers of Deceipt* (sic), (Manchester: n.d.), pp. 4-5.
59 Field Notes.
60 Field Notes.
61 Leigh, *et al.* 28 September 1986, *op. cit.*
62 'Jail for £1/2m fraud plotter.' *Manchester Evening News*, 5 September 1984.
63 Taylor, Peter, 1987, *op. cit.* p. 132.
64 Leigh, *et al.* 28 September 1986, *op. cit.* Monaghan pleaded not guilty and the jury could not reach a verdict. He was re-tried and again there was no agreed verdict.
65 Information supplied by DPPNI, 1 June 2017.
66 'Official Secrets'. *The Phoenix*, 24 October 1986.
67 Field Notes.

Chapter 5: Stalker in the Jungle (pages 56 to 76)

1 Stalker, 1988, *op. cit.* p. 25.
2 Field Notes.
3 DCS. Thorburn, DCI. Simons, DCI. Jim Smellie, DI. Brian Jackson, DI. Ron Gaffey, Sgts. Farrington and Eileen Hurt.
4 Stalker, 1988, *op. cit.* p. 28.
5 Civil Action, 17 May 1995, p. 25.

6   Leigh, David, Paul Lashmar and Jonathan Foster. 'Nosy police chief who refused to give up.' *The Observer*, 20 July 1986.
7   Hermon, 1997, *op. cit.* p. 154.
8   Stalker, 1988, *op. cit.* p. 27.
9   *Ibid.* p. 23. Greer too considered that there was doubt over its formal status, see Greer, Steven (1988) Book review of Stalker in *Journal of Law and Society*, 3:3 p. 317.
10   Stalker, 1988, *op. cit.* p. 69.
11   *Ibid.* p. 29.
12   *Ibid.* p. 30.
13   *Ibid.*
14   Hermon, 1997, *op. cit.* pp. 159-160.
15   Stalker, 1988, *op. cit.* p.30.
16   *Private Eye*, No. 683, 19 February 1988, p. 5.
17   Hermon, *op. cit.* p. 158. Hermon's continued misspelling is odd. Stalker had met him a week earlier and Hermon would now have been aware of his initial error unless he misheard his name during introductions and hence, understandably, repeated his initial error in his note to the Police Authority.
18   Doherty, Richard. *The thin green line: the history of the Royal Ulster Constabulary GC, 1922-2001* (Barnsley: Pen & Sword Military, 2004) p. 171.
19   Field Notes.
20   *A Pawn in the Game*, Granada Television, Open Eye, 30 April 1990.
21   Stalker, 1988, *op. cit.* p. 30.
22   *Ibid.* pp. 33-34.
23   *Ibid.* p. 49.
24   *Ibid.* p. 57.
25   *Ibid.* p. 93.
26   *Ibid.* pp. 57-58.
27   Hermon, 1997, *op. cit.* p. 160.
28   *Ibid.*
29   Civil Action, 31 May 1995, p. 83.
30   Stalker, 1988, *op. cit.* p. 66. As dates are so important in understanding what happened, it is unfortunate that he did not provide a precise date. It has been assumed that 'the early winter 1984' probably referred to sometime in November 1984.
31   *Ibid.* p. 66.
32   *Stalker: Coincidence or Conspiracy?* BBC Panorama programme, 16 June 1986.
33   Taylor, Peter, 1987, *op. cit.* p. 106.
34   *Ibid.* pp. 106-107 and Taylor, Peter, 2001, op cit. pp. 247-250.
35   Taylor, Peter, 2001, *op. cit.* p. 248.
36   Stalker, 1988, *op. cit.* p. 72.
37   Taylor, Peter, 1987, *op. cit.* p. 63.
38   Hermon,1997, *op. cit.* p. 161.
39   Stalker, 1988, *op. cit.* pp. 35-37.
40   *Ibid.* p. 75.
41   *Ibid.* p. 35.
42   Hermon, 1997, *op. cit.* p. 160.
43   Stalker, 1988, *op. cit.* p. 67.
44   The Queen v. Martin McCauley, No. [2014] NICA 60, para. 14.
45   Civil Action, 22 May 1995, p. 26.
46   *Ibid.* p. 28.
47   Stalker, 1988, *op. cit.* p. 42.
48   *Ibid.* p. 43.
49   R v McCauley, 1995, *op. cit.* para. 15.
50   Stalker, 1988, *op. cit.* p. 61.
51   *Ibid.* p. 62.
52   *Ibid.* p. 43.
53   *Ibid.* p. 54.
54   *Ibid.* p. 40.
55   *Ibid.* p. 99.
56   *Ibid.* p. 39.

57   Cadwallader, Anne. *Lethal Allies: British collusion in Ireland* (Cork: Mercier Press, 2013), p. 203. See also: Craig, Paddy. *Undercover cop: One man's true story of undercover policing in Ireland, the UK and Europe* (Dublin: Gill & Macmillan, 2008), p.13.
58   Steven Dorril. 'Stalker, Conspiracy?' *Lobster,* 23 (1992).
59   Stalker, 1988, *op. cit.* pp. 56-57.
60   For a broader sociological analysis of policing in Northern Ireland, see: Ellison, Graham and Jim Smyth. *The crowned harp: Policing Northern Ireland*, (London: Pluto Press, 2000).
61   National Archives Ireland, 2017/10/47 TAOIS - Complaints against the RUC (Jan-Apl 1987). My thanks to Margaret Urwin for this reference.
62   *Ibid.*
63   Stalker, 1988, *op. cit.* p. 69.
64   Hermon, 1997, *op. cit.* p. 162.
65   'Obituaries, Bernard Sheldon.' *The Times*, 27 February 2008.
66   Stalker, 1988, *op. cit.* p. 70.
67   *Ibid.* pp. 70-71.
68   Hermon, 1997, *op. cit.* p. 216.
69   Stalker, 1988, *op. cit.* p. 72.
70   Civil Action, 23 May 1995, p. 34.
71   Civil Action, 5 June 1995, p. 11.
72   Stalker, 1988, *op. cit.* p. 72.
73   *Ibid.* p. 73.
74   *Ibid.*
75   *Ibid.* p. 74.
76   *Ibid.*
77   *Ibid.*
78   *Ibid.* pp. 74-75.
79   *Ibid.* p. 76.
80   Hermon, 1997, *op. cit.* p. 162.
81   Civil Action 9 June 1995, p. 42.
82   *Ibid.* p. 43.
83   Stalker, 1988, pp. 80-81.
84   *Ibid.* p. 85.
85   *Ibid.* p. 86.
86   *Ibid.*
87   *Ibid.* p. 87.
88   *Ibid.* p. 92.
89   UK National Archives, Incidents in Armagh, PS/PUS (L), 8 March 1985, NIO London. CJ 4/5609.
90   *Ibid.*
91   UK National Archives, Buxton to Hermon, 21 March 1985, PB/85/3/2413/MD, CJ4/5603.
92   UK National Archives, Letter from Buxton to PS/PUS (B&L), 25 April 1985, PB/85/4/2488/MD, CJ4/5603.
93   UK National Archives, Letter from Buxton to Stephens, 16 May 1985, PB/85/5/2522/MD, CJ 4/5603.
94   *Ibid.*
95   *Ibid.*
96   UK National Archives, Minute by Buxton, 17 May 1985, PB/85/5/2529/MD, CJ4/5603.
97   UK National Archives, Minute by Buxton, 22 May 1985, PB/85/5/2531/MD, CJ4/5603.
98   *Ibid.*
99   UK National Archives, Letter from Andrew to Stephens, 1 July 1985. PUS/L/20/MLR, CJ 4/5609.
100 UK National Archives, Minute by Buxton, 2 July 1985, PB/85/7/2608/MD, CJ4/5609
101 *Ibid.*
102 *Ibid.*
103 Unger, Michael. 'Stalker Diary: When the rumour mill ground out tales of free meals in Chinatown.' *The Guardian*, 28 January 1988.
104 Civil Action 12 June 1995, pp. 4-5.
105 *A Pawn in the Game*, Granada Television, Open Eye, 30 April 1990.
106 Field Notes.

107 UK National Archives, Stephens to PS/Secretary of State, 15 May 1986, CJ4/6285.
108 Stalker, 1988, *op. cit.* p. 254.
109 *Ibid.* p. 94.
110 O'Clery, Conor. 'RUC shooting of youth in hayshed was tape-recorded by MI5.' *The Irish Times*, 20 June 1986.
111 O'Clery, Conor. 'King tells Barry that Stalker report is not final.' *The Irish Times*, 21 June 1986.
112 Hermon, 1997, *op. cit.* p.183.
113 PRONI, Stalker/Sampson Enquiry, CENT 1986, 1/15/40A, 1986.
114 Hermon, 1997, *op. cit.* p. 184.
115 Stalker, 1988, *op. cit.* p. 103.
116 Field Notes.
117 The Queen v. Martin McCauley, *op. cit.* para. 10.
118 *Ibid.*
119 *Ibid.*
120 *Ibid.*
121 *Ibid.* para. 21.

Chapter 6: Friendships and Policing Problems in Manchester (pages 77 to 92)

1 Civil Action, 23 May 1995, p. 37.
2 Unger, 28 January 1988, *op. cit.*
3 For a detailed synopsis of his career see: Stalker, 1988, *op. cit.* pp. 14-18.
4 *Ibid.* p. 15.
5 Civil Action, 17 May 1995, p. 18.
6 *Ibid.*
7 *Ibid.* p. 19.
8 *Ibid.*
9 Stalker, 1988, *op. cit.* p. 16.
10 Leigh, *et al.* 20 July 1986, *op. cit.*; Civil Action, 23 May1995, p. 33. The RUC described supergrasses as 'Converted Terrorists'. See: *Chief Constable's Annual Report 1983*, (Belfast: Royal Ulster Constabulary, 1984), p. xiii. See also: Hillyard, Paddy and Janie Percy-Smith. 'Converting Terrorists: The Use of Supergrasses in Northern Ireland.' *Journal of Law and Society,* 11:3 (1984) pp. 335-355; Greer, Steven. *Supergrasses: A study in Anti-Terrorist Law Enforcement in Northern Ireland* (Oxford: Clarendon Press, 1995).
11 See: Taylor, Peter. 1980, *op. cit.* A number of former RUC interrogators described how Mooney would fire up his interrogators and expect confessions. See also: Bennett, H. G. His Honour Judge, *Report of the Committee of Inquiry into Police Interrogation Procedures in Northern Ireland*, Cmnd 7479 (London: HMSO, 1979) and Cobain, Ian. 'Special report: Castlereagh: Terrifying centre where abuses were blamed on a few "rotten apples".' *The Guardian*, 12 October 2010.
12 Sampson, 1986, *op. cit.* para. 281.
13 Murtagh, Peter. 'RUC Officer in Stalker link to the Province.' *The Guardian*, 29 September 1986.
14 Civil Action, 17 May 1995, p. 20.
15 *Ibid.*
16 Unger, Michael. 'Stalker Diary (Part 2): The luxury yacht that sailed from Salford to centre of controversy.' *The Guardian*, 29 January 1988.
17 *Ibid.*
18 Stalker, 1988, *op. cit.* p. 20.
19 *Ibid.*
20 *Ibid.* p.184.
21 Luncheon club at Manchester City Football Club and a funding event in the evening at Swinton Rugby Club, 18 April 1985; Inspector's retirement evening in a Masonic Hall in Dukinfield, 31 August 1985; Senior Officers' Mess Ladies night event, 21 March 1986; and Senior Officers' Mess, St George's Day function at GMP headquarters, 23 April 1986. See: Sampson, 1986, *op. cit.* para. 303-305.
22 Police and Constabulary Almanac, Official Register for 1984.
23 This description of Taylor's life is based on his book – *The Poisoned Tree* – and numerous interviews.
24 See: Mullin, Chris, 1987, *op. cit.* pp. 9-14.

25 Taylor, Kevin, 1990, *op. cit.* p. 18.
26 Field Notes.
27 See for example: Hampton, Mark P. and Jason P. Abbotts. (Eds.). *Offshore Finance Centres and Tax Havens:* (Basingstoke: Macmillan Press, 1999).
28 Taylor, Kevin, 1990, *op. cit.* p. 20.
29 *Ibid.* p. 21.
30 Tipping rights were granted on 10 January 1985. See: Criminal Trial, 6 November 1989, p. 141.
31 See: https://www.zoopla.co.uk/property/pool-house-farm/pool-house-road/poynton/stockport/sk12-1ty/28245309 (Accessed 2 October 2020)
32 Criminal Trial, 15 January 1990, p. 17.
33 See: 'Dividing line for police policy: Difficulties between police authorities and chief constables,' *The Guardian,* 10 December 1984.
34 Field Notes.
35 *Ibid.*
36 Criminal Trial, 15 January 1990, p. 17.
37 Sampson Report, 1986, *op. cit.* para. 58.
38 *Ibid.* para. 32.
39 Cox, Gabrielle. 1988. 'The Irresistible Rise of a Folk Hero, Book review of *Stalker,* by John Stalker and *Stalker: The Search for the Truth,* by Peter Taylor.' *London Review of Books,* 3 March 1988.
40 *Ibid.*
41 See obituaries: Sir James Anderton, *The Times,* 9 May 2022; *The Guardian,* 10 May 2022.
42 Walker, Martin. *With Extreme Prejudice: An Investigation into Police Vigilantism in Manchester* (Guildford: Canary Press, 1986), p. 8.
43 Prince, Michael. *God's Cop: The Biography of James Anderton* (London: Frederick Muller, 1988), p. 40.
44 *Ibid.* p. 48.
45 Mortimer, John. 'The Creed of a Devout Copper: Interview with James Anderton.' *Sunday Times Magazine.* 2 November 1980.
46 Ó Siochrú, Micheál. *God's Executioner* (London: Faber and Faber, 2009).
47 Prince,1986, *op. cit.* p. 58.
48 Field Notes.
49 Kettle, Martin. 'Anderton's Way'. *New Society,* 8 March 1979.
50 GMP Annual Report, 1977, p. viii.
51 GMP Annual Report, 1985, p. 83.
52 McLaughlin, Eugene. *Community Policing and Accountability: A Case Study of Manchester 1981-1988,* PhD. Faculty of Law, (Sheffield: Sheffield University, 1990), p. 142.
53 'Anderton Race Speech blasted.' *Manchester Evening News,* 27 September 1980.
54 Horrocks, Paul. 'Picketline terrorism.' *Manchester Evening News,* 28 June 1984.
55 'Fight to suspend Jim in gay row.' *Manchester Evening News,* 4 February 1988.
56 'Jim faces a crunch: quiz will put his career in the balance.' *Manchester Evening News,* 10 February 1988.
57 Prince, 1986, *op. cit.* p.10.
58 'Wild words in a Wild Debate.' *The Guardian* 17 March 1982; Greig, Gordon. 'Enemy within – by a police chief.' *Daily Mail,* 16 March 1982.
59 Anderton, James 'Community Self-help in Crime Prevention', an address to ACPO, Summer Conference, Bristol, 7 June 1985.
60 McLaughlin, 1990, *op. cit.* p. 114.
61 *Ibid.*
62 *Ibid.*
63 Civil Action, 23 May 1995, p. 37.
64 Civil Action, 19 May 1995, p. 33.
65 Civil Action, 23 May 1995, p. 35.
66 Civil Action, 17 May 1995, p. 45.
67 *Ibid.* p. 47.
68 *Ibid.* p. 48.
69 Criminal Statistics for England and Wales, 1989, Table s3.1. and CIPFA Population Statistics.
70 Civil Action, 14 June 1995, p. 40.

71 Topping, 1989, *op. cit.* pp. 268-269.
72 Civil Action, 18 May 1995, p. 34.
73 Towner, Eric. 'Rogue Police Sold Away Duty – QC.' *Manchester Evening News*, 15 March 1983. See also: Civil Action, 31 May 1995, p. 37.
74 Fagin was one of the villains in *Oliver Twist* who taught the boys to pick pockets and he would then fence the goods.
75 Sharratt, Tom. '"Female Fagin" ensnared detective.' *The Guardian*, 15 March 1983.
76 'Inspector took bribe.' *The Times*, 30 March 1983.
77 For a detailed analysis of the wrongful conviction of Robert Brown by GMP, see: O'Neill, Eamonn. 'When time won't heal.' *The Herald*, 18 September 2004.
78 *Ibid.*
79 Civil Action, 18 May 1995, p. 71.
80 *Ibid.* p. 65.
81 Civil Action, 19 May 1995, p. 25.
82 *Ibid.* p. 27.
83 *Ibid.* p. 29.
84 Campbell, Duncan. 'Why the secret handshake between police and Freemasons should worry us.' *The Guardian*. 2 January 2018.
85 Civil Action, 8 June 1995, p. 55.
86 Cusick, James. 'The Masonic connection'. *Manchester Evening News*, 25 June 1986.
87 See in particular: Blomley, Nicholas K. *Law, Space and the Geographies of Power* (London: Guildford Press, 1994), Chapter 5.
88 See: Hillyard, Paddy and Janie Percy-Smith. 'Miners in the Arms of the Law: A Statistical Analysis.' *Journal of Law and Society*, 12:3 (1985) pp. 345-354.
89 The defeat of the miners fundamentally altered the power balance between workers and capital by weakening the power of trade unions in Britain. It increased inequality, with the share of income going to wages compared with profits declining over the next 15 years by some six per cent or £90 billion less. See: Lansley, Stewart and Joanna Mack. *Breadline Britain: The Rise of Mass Poverty* (London: Oneworld Publications, 2015), p. 103. See also: Atkinson, Anthony B. *Inequality: What can be done?* (London: Harvard University Press, 2015).
90 Walker, 1986, *op. cit.* p. 34; Pallister, David. 'Police chief denies having "hit squad".' *The Guardian*, 26 March 1986.
91 Walker, 1986. *op. cit.* p. 35.
92 *Ibid.* pp. 129-133.
93 *Ibid.* p. 119.
94 Unger, 28 January, 1988, *op. cit.*
95 Civil Action, 13 June 1995, p. 54.

Chapter 7: Documents of Deceit (pages 93 to 108)

1   Civil Action, 14 June 1995, p. 3.
2   *Ibid.*
3   *Ibid.*
4   Taylor, Peter, 1987, *op. cit.* p. 134.
5   Civil Action, 15 June 1995, p. 2.
6   Civil Action, 14 June 1995, p. 4.
7   *Ibid.* p. 64.
8   *Ibid.*
9   *Ibid.* p. 36.
10 *Ibid.*
11 *Ibid.*
12 *Ibid.*
13 *Ibid.*
14 *Ibid.* p. 39.
15 *Ibid.* p. 38.
16 *Ibid.* p. 36.
17 *Ibid.* p. 37.
18 Civil Action, 15 June 1995, p. 3.
19 Peter Taylor, 1987, *op. cit.* p. 134.

20 Civil Action, 18 May 1995, p. 68.
21 Civil Action, 13 June 1995, p. 20. While parts of the transcript are unclear, there is no doubt that it does not include mention of a call from Burton.
22 Civil Action, 13 June 1995, p. 21.
23 *Ibid.*
24 Civil Action, 15 June 1995, p. 12.
25 *Ibid.*
26 Field Notes.
27 Civil Action, 13 June 1995, p.17.
28 *Stalker: The Final Chapter*, BBC Public Eye programme, 14 June 1991.
29 *Ibid.*
30 Civil Action, 18 May 1995, p. 69.
31 Civil Action, 14 June 1995, p. 53.
32 *Ibid.* p. 52.
33 Topping, 1989, *op. cit.* p. 281.
34 Civil Action, 14 June 1995, p. 54.
35 *Ibid.* p. 12.
36 *Ibid.* p. 56.
37 Civil Action, 18 May 1995, p. 68.
38 *Ibid.* p. 74
39 *Ibid.* p. 75.
40 Civil Action, 14 June 1995, p. 5.
41 *Ibid.* p. 53.
42 *Ibid.* p. 5.
43 *Ibid.* p. 53.
44 *Ibid.* p. 54.
45 See: Foreman, Freddie. *Brown Bread Fred:The Autobiography of the Godfather of British Crime* (London: John Blake Publishing, 2007); Knight, Ronnie. *Memoirs and Confession* (London: John Blake Publishing, 1998); Knight, Ronnie, John Knight, Peter Wilton and Peter Sawyer. *Gotcha! The Untold Story of Britain's Biggest Cash Robbery* (London: Pan, 2003). It was the biggest heist in the UK until the Northern Bank in Belfast was robbed of £26.5 million in December 2004. See: Boycott, Owen and Ted Oliver. '£20m stolen in UK's biggest bank robbery – was it paramilitaries or common criminals?' *The Guardian*, 22 December 2004.
46 See: O'Connor, Maurice. *The Dealer: Drug Smuggling on the Costa Del Crime* (Wrea Green, Lancs: Milo Books, 2012).
47 Burrell, Ian and Adrian Levy. 'Men who run UK Crime.' *The Sunday Times*, 15 January 1995.
48 Civil Action, 19 May 1995, p. 6.
49 O'Connor, 2012, *op. cit.* pp. 45-52.
50 Infoclimat.
   https://www.infoclimat.fr/observations-meteo/archives/28/janvier/1984/gibraltar/08495.html (Accessed 2 October 2020)
51 Payas was charged with theft, false accounting and attempting to pervert the course of justice. His defence barrister was De Silva, who later carried out a desk review of the murder of Belfast Solicitor, Pat Finucane. In another coincidence reflecting the closeness of the UK and Gibraltar's law enforcement bodies, Payas was replaced by a police officer from GMP.
52 Field Notes.
53 Topping, 1989, *op. cit.* p. 280.
54 *Ibid.* p. 278.
55 Sampson, 1986, *op. cit.* para. 186.
56 Topping, 1989, op cit. p. 281.
57 *Ibid.*

Chapter 8: Criminal Intelligence (pages 109 to 119)

1 Sampson, 1986, *op. cit.* paras. 252-258.
2 *Ibid.* para. 252.
3 *Ibid.* para. 253.
4 Field Notes.
5 Sampson, 1986, *op. cit.* para. 254.

6   *Ibid.* para. 255.
7   *Ibid.* para. 256.
8   *Ibid.* para. 257.
9   *Ibid.* para. 258.
10 Civil Action, 23 May 1995, p. 20.
11 Sampson, 1986, *op. cit.* para. 259.
12 Field Notes.
13 Civil Action, 18 May 1995, p. 77.
14 *Ibid.* p. 78.
15 *Ibid.* pp. 79-85.
16 Field Notes.
17 Civil Action, 18 May 1995, p. 78.
18 Civil Action, 13 June 1995, p. 44.
19 Civil Action, 14 June 1995, p. 4.
20 *Ibid.* p. 47.
21 *Ibid.* p. 48.
22 Civil Action, 19 May 1995, p. 2.
23 Civil Action, 14 June 1995, pp. 47-48.
24 Civil Action, 15 June 1995, p. 5.
25 Civil Action, 14 June 1995, p. 68.
26 *Ibid.* p. 51.
27 Civil Action, 19 May 1995, p. 1.
28 Civil Action, 14 June 1995, p. 48.
29 *Ibid.* p. 50.
30 Civil Action, 19 May 1995, pp. 1-2.
31 Civil Action, 14 June 1995 p. 63.
32 *Ibid.*
33 *Stalker: The Final Chapter*, BBC Public Eye, 14 June 1991.
34 Topping, 1989, *op. cit.* p. 281.
35 *Ibid.*
36 Civil Action, 19 May 1995, p. 7.
37 Civil Action, 18 May 1995, p. 14.
38 *Ibid.*
39 *Ibid.*
40 Sampson, 1986, para. 360.
41 Civil Action, 13 June 1995, p. 46.

Chapter 9: A Point of Disbelief (pages 120 to 132)

1   Civil Action, 18 May 1995, p. 85.
2   *Ibid.*
3   *Ibid.* p. 86.
4   Civil Action, 15 June 1995, p. 38.
5   *Ibid.* pp. 38-40.
6   Taylor, Peter. 1987, *op. cit.* p. 135.
7   Leigh, *et al.* 28 September 1986, *op. cit.*
8   *Ibid.* p. 12.
9   *Ibid.*
10 *Ibid.* p. 13.
11 *Ibid.* p. 16.
12 *Ibid.* p. 17.
13 Civil Action, 19 May 1995, pp. 17-18.
14 *Ibid.* pp. 19-20.
15 *Ibid.* p. 20.
16 *Ibid.*
17 *Ibid.*
18 Civil Action, 19 May 1995, p. 22.
19 *Ibid.* p. 23.

20   *Ibid.* p. 22.
21   *Stalker: The Final Chapter*, BBC Public Eye, 14 June 1991.
22   Civil Action, 13 June 1995, p. 18.
23   Civil Action, 24 May 1995, pp. 6-7.
24   Stalker, 1988, *op. cit.* p. 66.
25   Duffy, Michael, 'Police chief's "phone trap"', *Manchester Evening News*, 3 November 1984.
26   Civil Action, 19 May 1995, p. 29.
27   *Ibid.* p. 28.
28   Burgess, n.d. *op. cit.* p. 8.
29   *Ibid.* p. 7.
30   Police and Criminal Evidence Act, 1984 (Commencement No. 2) Order 1985. Statutory Instrument 1985, No. 623 (C.9).
31   PACE, 1984, Section 86 and The Police (Discipline) (Senior Officers) Regulations 1985 and Part IX of PACE 1984.

Chapter 10: Secret Developments (pages 133 to 142)

1   Civil Action, 18 May 1995, p. 48.
2   Field Notes.
3   Stalker, 1988, *op. cit.* p. 212.
4   Her Majesty's Chief Inspector of Constabulary, *Annual Report, 1996/97*, Cm 246 (London: Stationery Office), p. 87.
5   Civil Action, 31 May 1995, p. 22.
6   Civil Action, 8 June 1995, p. 55; Civil Action, 13 June 1995, p. 26.
7   *Ibid.*
8   *Ibid.* Burgess had prepared the LFF case single-handedly and had retired in 1983 (See chapter 4).
9   Civil Action, 9 June 1995, p. 53.
10   Civil Action, 6 June 1995, p. 7.
11   Civil Action, 19 May 1995, p. 39.
12   *Ibid.* p. 35.
13   *Ibid.*
14   *Ibid.*
15   *Ibid.* p. 36.
16   Civil Action, 16 May 1995, p. 12.
17   Civil Action, 15 June 1995, p. 29.
18   Civil Action, 18 May 1995, p. 15.
19   Civil Action, 22 May 1995, p. 3.
20   Civil Action, 15 June 1995, p. 28
21   Police recorded crime in GMP increased between 1983 and 1984 from 234,747 offences to 252,682 – an increase of 17,935 or 7.6 per cent. Burglary was up by 14.4 per cent, overall theft by 5.2 per cent and unauthorised taking of a vehicle by 10 per cent. See: GMP Annual Reports for 1983 and 1984.
22   Civil Action, 12 June 1995, p. 35.
23   Civil Action, 18 May 1995, p. 15.
24   Criminal Trial, 9 January 1990, p. 28.
25   Civil Action, 18 May 1995, p. 7.
26   Field Notes.
27   Civil Action, 15 June 1995, p. 25.
28   *Ibid.* p. 27.
29   Civil Action, 16 May 1995, p. 10.
30   Civil Action, 15 June 1995, p. 27.
31   Reiner, Robert. *Chief Constables: Bobbies, bosses, or bureaucrats?* (Oxford: Oxford University Press, 1991), p. 191.
32   Civil Action, 18 May 1995, p. 7.
33   Civil Action, 22 May 1995, p. 2.
34   *Ibid.* p. 4.
35   *Ibid.* p. 2; Civil Action, 31 May 1995, p. 72.
36   Civil Action, 22 May 1995, p. 6.

37 *Ibid.*
38 Civil Action, 31 May 1995, p. 70.
39 *Ibid.*
40 GMP Annual Report, 1985, p. 17.

Chapter 11: Death of the Informer (pages 143 to 158)

1   Civil Action, 22 May 1995, p. 25.
2   Field Notes.
3   See: Sanders, Andrew and Richard Young. *Criminal Justice*, (London: Butterworths, 2000), pp. 171-176.
4   Philips, Sir Cyril. *Royal Commission on Criminal Procedure,* Cmnd. 8092 (London: HMSO, 1981).
5   Civil Action, 23 May 1995, p. 1.
6   Field Notes.
7   Field Notes.
8   Civil Action, 22 May 1995, p. 31.
9   *Ibid.*
10 *Ibid.* p. 33.
11 Civil Action, 13 June 1995, p. 16.
12 Civil Action, 14 June 1995, p. 53.
13 Civil Action, 22 May 1995, p. 56.
14 Sampson, 1986, *op. cit.* para 184 (a).
15 *Ibid.* para 186.
16 Stalker, 1988, *op. cit.* p. 35.
17 Civil Action, 23 May 1995, p. 34.
18 *Ibid.* p. 15; Civil Action, 13 June 1995, p. 29.
19 Civil Action, 13 June 1995, p. 28.
20 The origin of the codename Febb is unknown, but it has been suggested that it was short for February, the month in which GMP began to investigate Stalker with the establishment of the DIU.
21 Civil Action, 23 May 1995, p. 15.
22 Civil Action, 13 June 1995, pp. 28-29.
23 Civil Action, 19 May 1995, p. 22.
24 Civil Action, 13 June 1995, p. 28.
25 The numbering sequence in the items relating to Kevin Taylor was not continuous and jumped from item 19 to item 21 as shown in Table 11.2.
26 Civil Action, 23 May 1995, pp. 16-20.
27 *Ibid.* pp. 20-28.
28 Field Notes.
29 Civil Action, 23 May 1995, p. 23.
30 *Ibid.* p. 25.
31 Civil Action, 22 May 1995, p. 35.
32 Civil Action, 23 May 1995, p. 55-56.
33 Field Notes.
34 David Burton's death certificate.
35 Field Notes.
36 Field Notes.
37 Civil Action, 23 May 1995, pp. 32-33. Square brackets represent guessed text and the dots indicate that an unknown portion of the letter was not read out to court.
38 Civil Action, 23 May 1995, p. 34.
39 *Ibid.* p. 32.
40 Civil Action, 14 June 1995, p. 16.
41 Civil Action, 23 May 1995, p. 32.
42 *Ibid.* pp. 35.
43 Field Notes.
44 Field Notes.
45 Hansard, House of Commons, Vol. 102, Col. 1022W, 24 October 1986.
46 Civil Action, 15 June 1995, p. 58.

47   Civil Action, 23 May 1995, p. 34.
48   *Ibid.* pp. 34-38.
49   Civil Action, 13 June 1995, p. 59.

Chapter 12: Digging for Dirt (pages 159 to 172)

1   This is police jargon to describe someone who is suspected of engaging in criminality. Taylor admitted that he had some 'tasty' friends. See: Murphy, 1991, *op. cit.* p. 122.
2   Criminal Trial, 3 January 1990, pp. 61-64.
3   Criminal Trial, 9 January 1990, p. 10.
4   Criminal Trial, 8 November 1989, p. 14.
5   Criminal Trial, 9 January 1990, p. 14.
6   *Ibid.*
7   There are two further criteria: there is a duty to the public to disclose and the interests of the bank require disclosure. See: *Tournier v National Provincial and Union Bank of England* [1924] 1 KB 461 at 473, [1923] All ER Rep 550 at 554.
8   The legal position changed radically after the introduction of PACE in 1984 and, subsequently, under drugs and terrorism legislation. See Levi, Michael. 'Regulating Money Laundering: The Death of Bank Secrecy in the UK.' *The British Journal of Criminology* 31: 2 (1991), pp. 109-125.
9   Criminal Trial, 9 January 1990, p. 17.
10   *Ibid.* p. 18.
11   *Ibid.* pp. 24-25.
12   *Ibid.* pp. 22-23.
13   *Ibid.* p. 27.
14   *Ibid.* pp. 33-34.
15   *Ibid.* p. 19.
16   Civil Action, 24 May 1995 p. 39.
17   Henfield, Margaret and Alan Qualtrough. 'The date Stalker will remember forever.' *Daily Mail*, 11 August 1986.
18   Civil Action, 24 May 1995, p. 43.
19   *Ibid.* See also the Sampson, 1986, *op. cit.* paras. 159-164.
20   *Ibid.*
21   Civil Action, 24 May 1995, pp. 40-41.
22   *Ibid.* p. 17.
23   *Ibid.*
24   *Ibid.* p. 18.
25   Waddington opposed the reopening of the Birmingham Six case, but following new revelations, he referred the case to the Court of Appeal which recommended their release. He was the first Home Secretary for 20 years who was pro-hanging. See: Kavanagh, Dennis. 'Lord Waddington obituary: Chief Whip and former Home Secretary was loyal supporter of Margaret Thatcher.' *The Independent*. 26 February 2017.
26   Civil Action, 24 May 1995, pp. 18-19.
27   Taylor, Kevin, 1990, *op. cit.* pp. 43-44.
28   *Ibid.* p. 46.
29   Civil Action, 23 May 1995, p. 65.
30   *Ibid.*
31   Taylor, 1990, *op. cit.* pp. 43-44.
32   Civil Action, 23 May 1995, p. 62.
33   *Ibid.* p. 69.
34   *Ibid.* p. 70.
35   *Ibid.* p. 71.
36   *Ibid.*
37   *Ibid.* p. 74.
38   *Ibid.*
39   *Ibid.*
40   *Ibid.* p. 72.
41   *Ibid.* p. 74.

42 Field Notes.
43 Criminal Trial, 9 January 1990, p. 15.
44 Criminal Trial, 18 January 1990, p. 26.
45 *Ibid.*
46 *Ibid.* p. 27.
47 *Ibid.* p. 28.
48 Taylor, Kevin, 1990, *op. cit.* p. 62.
49 Criminal Trial, 18 January 1990, p. 29.
50 Sergeant John Speed. https://thepolicememorialtrust.org/sergeant-john-speed/ (Accessed 2 October 2020)
51 Kilday, Laurence. 'Leeds Police quiz man on Dublin Raid.' *Evening Press*, 19 December 1985.
52 Civil Action, 6 June 1995, p. 66.
53 See: Williams, Paul. *The General: Godfather of crime* (Dublin: O'Brien Press, 1995).
54 Civil Action, 6 June 1995, p. 75.
55 *Ibid.*
56 *Ibid.* p. 76.
57 *Ibid.*
58 https://crimewatch-uk.fandom.com/wiki/Sgt._John_Speed (Accessed 2 October 2020)

Chapter 13: *Diogenes*, Drugs and Dead Ends (pages 173 to 184)

1 Criminal Trial, 10 January 1990, p. 12.
2 Taylor, 1990, p. 39.
3 Field Notes.
4 *Ibid.*
5 Civil Action, 25 May 1995, p. 14.
6 *Ibid.* p. 15.
7 Field Notes.
8 Civil Action, 24 May 1995, p. 59.
9 Field Notes.
10 Police and Constabulary Almanac, p. 24.
11 Civil Action, 24 May 1995, p. 50.
12 *Ibid.* p. 51.
13 *Ibid.*
14 Civil Action, 24 May 1995, p. 52.
15 *Ibid.* pp. 48-49.
16 *Ibid.* pp. 51-52.
17 *Ibid.* p. 52.
18 *Ibid.*
19 Criminal Trial, 11 December 1989, p. 9.
20 Civil Action, 25 May 1995, p. 53.
21 Civil Action, 24 May 1995, p. 53.
22 Civil Action, 24 May 1995, p. 56.
23 Civil Action, 5 June 1995, p. 57.
24 Civil Action, 24 May 1995, p. 59.
25 Civil Action, 13 June 1995, p. 32.
26 *Ibid.*
27 Civil Action, 24 May 1995, p. 38.
28 *Ibid.*
29 Taylor, Kevin, 1990, *op. cit.* p. 60 and Civil Action, 25 May 1995, pp. 23-29.
30 Civil Action, 25 May 1995, pp. 23-29.
31 *Ibid.* p. 25.
32 *Ibid.* p. 26.
33 *Ibid.*
34 Taylor, Kevin, 1990, *op. cit.* p. 60.
35 Civil Action, 16 May 1995, p. 15.
36 Civil Action, 14 June 1995, p. 65.
37 Civil Action, 25 May 1995, p. 31.

38   *Ibid.*
39   Brooks, described as Mr Big in a massive drug smuggling ring, was arrested in Spain in 1989. It was reported that the Spanish police had been watching his luxury yacht, *Diogenes*, which he had brought from Taylor. See: Roland, Lisa. 'Police seize drug baron.' *Manchester Evening News*, 4 April 1989.
40   Civil Action, 25 May 1995, p. 36.
41   *Ibid.* p. 37.
42   *Ibid.* p. 40.
43   Taylor, Peter, 1987, *op. cit.* p. 146.
44   In the 1980s, there was no legal basis covering the use of police informers, only a set of Home Office Guidelines drawn up by the police at a conference. The Guidelines state that where an informer gives the police information about the intention of others to commit crime, in which they intend to play a part, they are only allowed to do so under three conditions. First, they do not actively engage in the planning or the committing of the crime. Second, they play only a minor role. Third, their role is 'essential to enable the police to frustrate the principal criminals and to arrest them'.
45   Civil Action, 25 May 1995, p. 41.
46   Civil Action, 6 June 1995, p. 12.
47   Civil Action, 24 May 1995, p. 40.
48   Civil Action, 22 May 1995, p. 6.
49   Civil Action, 25 May 1995, pp. 37-38.
50   Clarkson, Wensley. *Costa Del Crime* (London: John Blake Publishing, 2006), pp. 162-163.
51   Civil Action, 25 May 1995, p. 38.
52   *Ibid.*
53   *Ibid.* p. 42.
54   *Ibid.* p. 58.
55   *Ibid.* p. 46.
56   *Ibid.*
57   *Ibid.* p. 52.
58   *Ibid.* p. 47.
59   Committal Proceedings, 18 October 1988, p. 8.
60   *Ibid.* p. 8.

Chapter 14: Operation Kaluki (pages 185 to 193)

1   Civil Action, 6 June 1995, p. 40.
2   Criminal Trial, 16 January 1990, p. 71.
3   Civil Action, 16 May 1995, p. 16.
4   *Ibid.*
5   *Ibid.* p.17.
6   Criminal Trial, 9 January 1990, pp. 28-29.
7   Sparrow, Malcolm K. 'The application of network analysis to criminal intelligence: An assessment of the prospects.' *Social Networks*, 13 (1991) pp. 251-274, at p. 254.
8   Civil Action, 23 May 1995, pp. 46-54.
9   Civil Action, 18 May 1995, p. 14.
10   Civil Action, 25 May 1995, p. 51.
11   *Ibid.* p. 53.
12   'It's all change at the Film Exchange.' *Manchester Evening News*, 6 March 1985.
13   Civil Action, 24 May 1995, p. 15.
14   Civil Action, 23 May 1995, p. 61.
15   *Ibid.*
16   *Ibid.*
17   *Ibid.* p. 58.
18   *Ibid.*
19   Criminal Trial, 9 January 1990, p. 46.
20   Murtagh, P. 'DPP meeting over Taylor investigation: Report on Manchester Police inquiry into friendship between businessman and deputy chief constable Stalker.' *The Guardian.* 20 June 1986.
21   Criminal Trial, 16 January 1990, p. 66.

22 Field Notes.
23 Civil Action, 6 June 1995, pp. 40-41.
24 Taylor, Kevin, 1990, *op. cit.* p. 62.
25 Criminal Trial, 10 January 1990, p. 45.
26 Stalker, 1988, *op. cit.* p. 162.
27 Flackes, W.D. and S. Elliott. *Northern Ireland: A Political Directory, 1968-1993* (Dublin: Blackstaff Press, 1994), p. 84.
28 Ryder, C. 2000, *op. cit.* pp. 317-318.

Chapter 15: Banks, Banquets and Boats (pages 194 to 210)

1   Criminal Trial, 9 January 1990, p. 10.
2   Civil Action, 15 January 1990, p. 78
3   Criminal Trial, 9 January 1990, p. 37.
4   *Ibid.*
5   *Ibid.* p. 38.
6   Criminal Trial, 10 January 1990, p. 4.
7   *Ibid.* p. 5.
8   *Ibid.* pp. 5-6.
9   *Ibid.* p. 26.
10 *Ibid.* p. 30.
11 *Ibid.* pp. 30-31.
12 Criminal Trial, 15 January 1990, p. 76.
13 *Ibid.* p. 80.
14 *Ibid.* p. 81.
15 Field notes.
16 Criminal Trial, 3 January 1990, p. 43.
17 Criminal Trial, 4 January 1990, p. 50.
18 Criminal Trial, 18 January 1990, p. 29.
19 Criminal Trial, 15 January 1990, p. 26.
20 The full letter is reproduced in Taylor, Kevin, 1987, *op. cit.* p. 68.
21 Civil Action 16 May 1995, p. 13.
22 *Ibid.*
23 Committal Proceedings, 18 October 1988, pp. 21-22.
24 Criminal Trial, 18 January 1990, p. 32.
25 *Ibid.* p. 36.
26 Field Notes.
27 *Ibid.*
28 Taylor, Kevin, 1990, *op. cit.* p. 72.
29 *Ibid.* pp.72-73.
30 Criminal Trial, 10 January 1990, p.60.
31 Committal Proceedings 18 October 1989, p. 34.
32 Field Notes.
33 Civil Action, 7 June 1995, p. 31.
34 Criminal Trial, 9 January 1990, p. 35.
35 Criminal Trial, 10 January 1990, pp. 65-66.
36 Civil Action, 6 June 1995, p. 76.
37 Stalker, 1988, *op. cit.* p. 135.
38 Civil Action, 7 June 1995, p. 37.
39 *Ibid.*
40 *Ibid.* p. 34.
41 Criminal Trial, 10 January 1990, p. 9.
42 *Ibid.* p. 12.
43 *Ibid.* p. 13.
44 Criminal Trial, 9 January 1900, p. 35.
45 *Ibid.*
46 *Ibid.* p. 43.
47 *Ibid.* p. 48.

48 Criminal Trial, 10 January 1990, p. 18.
49 Civil Action, 17 May 1995, p. 25.
50 Criminal Trial, 15 January 1990, pp. 25-26.
51 Criminal Trial, 18 January 1995, p. 34.
52 Civil Action, 7 June 1995, p. 8.
53 *Ibid.*
54 Civil Action, 9 June 1995, p. 56.
55 Civil Action, 7 June 1995, p. 9.
56 *Ibid.* p. 10.
57 *Ibid.* p. 11.
58 *Ibid.* p. 12.
59 Stalker, 1988, pp. 187-188.

Chapter 16: Accessing the Inaccessible (pages 211 to 230)

1   Stalker, 1988, *op. cit.* p. 95.
2   Hermon, 1997, *op. cit.* p. 183.
3   Stalker, 1988, *op. cit.* p. 96.
4   Field Notes.
5   PACE, (Commencement No. 3) Order 1985. Statutory Instrument, 1985, No.1934 (C. 48).
6   PACE, Section 166(6)(e)(f).
7   PACE Schedule 1, Section 2(a).
8   PACE Schedule 1, Section 2(c).
9   Criminal Trial, 16 January 1995, p. 21.
10 *Ibid.* p. 38.
11 *Ibid.* p. 22.
12 Committal Proceedings, 18 October 1988, p. 7.
13 Criminal Trial, 10 January 1990, p. 53.
14 Committal Proceedings, 18 October 1988, p. 28.
15 Criminal Law Act, 1977, Section 1.
16 Theft Act 1968, Section 16(1).
17 Committal Proceedings, 18 October 1988, p. 27.
18 *Ibid.*
19 Criminal Trial, 16 January 1990, p. 21.
20 *Ibid.*
21 *Ibid.* p. 57.
22 Committal Proceedings, 18 October 1988, p. 9.
23 *Ibid.*
24 *Ibid.* p. 10.
25 Criminal Trial, 16 January 1990, p. 65.
26 *Ibid.* p. 66.
27 Committal Proceedings, 18 October 1988, p. 10.
28 *Ibid.*
29 *Ibid.* p. 11.
30 Criminal Trial, 16 January 1990, p. 69.
31 Committal Proceedings, 18 October 1988, p. 13.
32 *Ibid.* p. 12.
33 *Ibid.* p. 13.
34 *Ibid.*
35 Criminal Trial, 16 January 1990, p. 22.
36 *Ibid.* p. 23.
37 *Ibid.* p. 41.
38 *Ibid.* p. 25.
39 *Ibid.* p. 23.
40 Taylor, Kevin, 1990, *op. cit.* p. 70.
41 *Ibid.*
42 Criminal Trial, 16 January 1990, pp. 30-31.
43 *Ibid.* p. 41.

44 *Ibid.* p. 33.
45 Criminal Trial, 17 January 1990, p. 34.
46 *Ibid.*
47 *Ibid.*
48 Committal Proceedings, 18 October 1988, p. 16.
49 Criminal Trial, 16 January 1990, p. 35.
50 Criminal Trial, 18 January 1990, p. 24.
51 *Ibid.* p. 23.
52 Civil Action, 7 June 1995, p. 25.
53 See: R v Crown Court at Manchester, ex parte Taylor [1988] 2 All ER 796.
54 See: Barclays Bank plc v Taylor, [1989] 3 All ER 563.
55 Criminal Trial, 10 January 1990 p. 68.
56 PACE Section 14.
57 See: R v Guildhall Magistrates' Court, ex p Primlaks Holdings Co (Panama) Inc [1990] 1 QB 261, [1989] 2 WLR 841, 89 Cr App Rep 215, [1989] Crim LR 448, 133 Sol Jo 628, (1988) Times, 30 December.
58 PACE Section 8.
59 PACE Section 16 (8) (9) and section 19 (2).
60 PACE Section 16.
61 Civil Action, 6 June 1995, p. 57.
62 *Ibid.* p. 3.
63 PACE, Section 8(3)(c) and (d).
64 Committal Proceedings, 20 October 1988, p. 37-38.
65 Committal Proceedings, 18 October 1988, p. 2.
66 Taylor, Kevin, 1990, *op. cit.* p. 75.
67 PACE, Section 16(5).
68 Civil Action, 23 May 1995, p. 6.
69 Criminal Trial, 11 January 1990, p. 7.
70 *Ibid.* p. 11.
71 *Ibid.* p. 3.
72 *Ibid.* p. 19.
73 *Ibid.* p. 24.
74 *Ibid.* p. 9.
75 Criminal Trial, 10 January 1990, p. 70.
76 Criminal Trial, 11 January 1990, p. 24.
77 Committal Proceedings, 20 October 1988, p. 43.
78 *Ibid.*
79 Philips, Sir Cyril, 1981, *op. cit.*
80 For a critique of the Report see: Hillyard, Paddy. 'From Belfast to Britain: some critical comments on the Royal Commission on Criminal Procedure' in A. Hunt (Ed.). *Politics and Power,* (London: Routledge and Kegan Paul, 1981).
81 The relevant special provisions as to access became law on 1 January 1986. See: The Police and Criminal Evidence Act (Commencement No. 3) Order 1985, Statutory Instrument, 1985 No 1934 (c.48).
82 Civil Action, 8 June 1995, p. 49.
83 Civil Action, 16 May 1995, p. 19.
84 *Ibid.*
85 *Ibid.*
86 Civil Action, 16 May 1995, p. 20.
87 *Ibid.* p. 18.
88 Civil Action, 6 June 1995, p. 77.
89 *Ibid.* p. 96.
90 *Ibid.* p. 77.
91 *Ibid.* p. 94.
92 *Ibid.* p. 97.
93 *Ibid.* p. 96.
94 *Ibid.* pp. 93-94.
95 *Ibid.* p. 63.

96   *Ibid.*
97   Civil Action, 8 June 1995, p. 19.
98   Civil Action, 7 June 1995, p. 17.
99   Civil Action, 6 June 1995, p. 51.
100 International Consortium of Investigative Journalists, The Panama Papers: Exposing the Rogue
     Offshore Finance Industry. https://www.icij.org/investigations/panama-papers/ (Accessed 8
     January 2024)
101 Civil Action, 6 June 1995, p. 51.
102 *Ibid.* p. 52.
103 *Ibid.*
104 Bottomley, Robert. 'Call for inquiry after £5m trial collapse.' *Manchester Evening News*, 17 June 2003.
105 'Teaching job for cop in murder trial probe.' *Manchester Evening News*, 15 September 2003.

Chapter 17: Scarborough Fair (pages 231 to 250)

1   His move caused considerable controversy. See: Stalker, 1988, *op. cit.* p. 27.
2   Hermon, 1997, *op. cit.* p. 184.
3   Stalker, 1988, *op. cit.* p. 106.
4   Hermon, 1997, *op. cit.* p. 185
5   Civil Action, 16 May 1995, p. 21.
6   UK National Archives, File note of a meeting held at 1.30 p.m. on Monday 9th May 1986, in
     the Queen Alexander Room of the Royal Hotel, Scarborough, 6 January 1994, CJ4/6279; Civil
     Action, 16 May 1995, p. 22.
7   UK National Archive, Burns to Chilcot, 23 December 1993, CJ4/6297.
8   Civil Action, 16 May 1995 p. 22.
9   *Ibid.*
10   *Ibid.* p. 36.
11   Taylor, Peter, 1987, *op. cit.* p. 161.
12   Civil Action, 13 June 1995, p. 37.
13   *Ibid.*
14   *Ibid.* p. 39.
15   *Ibid.* p. 40.
16   *Ibid.*
17   *Ibid.* p. 44.
18   *Ibid.* p. 42.
19   *Ibid.*
20   *Ibid.* p. 52.
21   *Ibid.* p. 53.
22   *Ibid.* p. 51-52.
23   *Ibid.* p. 52.
24   *Ibid.* p. 39.
25   *Ibid.* pp. 14-15.
26   *Ibid.* p. 40.
27   *Ibid.* p. 44.
28   *Ibid.* p. 43.
29   *Ibid.*
30   *Ibid.* p. 49.
31   *Ibid.* p. 50.
32   *Ibid.* p. 36.
33   *Ibid.* p. 43.
34   Criminal Trial, 17 January 1990, p. 5.
35   Civil Action, 13 June 1995, pp. 44-45.
36   *Ibid.* p. 48.
37   *Ibid.* p. 50.
38   *Ibid.* p. 53.
39   *Ibid.*
40   *Ibid.* p. 51.
41   Stalker, 1988, *op. cit.* pp. 104-105.

42 *Private Eye*, No. 684, 4 March 1988.

43 Taylor, Kevin, 1990, *op. cit.* p. 154.

44 Hermon, 1997, *op. cit.* p. 185.

45 *Ibid.*

46 *Ibid.*

47 'Chief blue Comedian', *Manchester Evening News*, 24 March 1986.

48 Civil Action, 13 June 1995, p. 54.

49 Hermon, 1997, *op. cit.* p. 187.

50 Tendler, Stewart and Richard Ford. 'Inquiry starts into complaint against senior police officer'. *The Times*, 31 May 1986.

51 *Ibid.*

52 Civil Action, 16 May 1995, p. 25.

53 *Ibid.* p. 26.

54 Heather Mills. 'Stalker document promises new turmoil.' *The Independent*. 20 January 1990.

55 Tendler, Stewart, Philip Webster and Richard Ford. 'Home Office denies validity of 'evidence'.' *The Times*, 26 January 1990.

56 *Ibid.*

57 Hermon, 1997, *op. cit.* p. 185.

58 Hansard, House of Commons, Vol. 170, Col. 640, 4 April 1990.

59 Hansard, House of Commons, 4 April 1990, *op. cit.*

60 *Ibid.*

61 *Ibid.*

62 Byford, Sir Lawrence. 'Stalker and the RUC inquiry.' Letters to the Editor, *The Times*, 8 June 1990.

63 'Lightening the shadows around Stalker's removal.' Letters to the Editor, *The Times*, 12 June 1990.

64 *Stalker: The Final Chapter*, BBC Public Eye, 14 June 1991.

65 *Private Eye*, No. 735, 16 February 1990.

66 Hansard, House of Commons, John stalker, Vol. 100, Col. 267, 28 June 1986.

67 Norton-Taylor, Richard. 'For their eyes only: the secret stories ministers don't want you to read.' *The Guardian*. 29 December 2017; Norton-Taylor, Richard. 'I've worked for decades to reveal the truth about the "Wilson plot". But the cover-up continues.' *The Guardian*, 29 December 2023.

68 Andrew, 2009, *op. cit.* p. 632.

69 Hansard, House of Commons, 4 April 1990, *op. cit.*

70 Hermon, 1997, *op. cit.* pp. 186-187.

71 *Ibid.* p. 187.

72 Public Records Act 1958, Section 3(4).

73 See in particular: Cobain, Ian. *The History Thieves: Secrets, Lies and the Shaping of a Modern Nation,* (London: Portobello Books, 2016).

74 UK National Archives, Stalker, Minute from Stephens to PS/Secretary of State, 15 May 1986, CJ4/6285.

75 *Ibid.*

76 UK National Archives, Letter from Myers to Andrew, 22 May 1986, CJ4/7464.

77 *Ibid.*

78 *Ibid.*

79 Stalker, 1988, *op. cit.* p. 106.

80 *Ibid.*

81 UK National Archive, The Stalker Report, Minute, Andrew to SoS, 30 May 1986, CJ4/6285.

82 *Ibid.*

83 Hermon, 1997, *op. cit.* p. 186.

84 *Ibid.*

85 UK National Archives, Minute, Stephens to Innes, 4 June 1986, CJ4/6285.

86 Statement issued by the RUC on Friday, 6 June 1986.

Chapter 18 Sampson's Inquiry in Manchester (pages 251 to 266)

1 'Ulster Link on Stalker.' *The Times*, 29 September 1986.

2 Sampson, 1986, *op. cit.* para. 4.

3 See: Murphy, 1991, *op. cit.*

4   Terms of Reference notified to GMPA, by R.C. Rees, 29 May 1986.
5   'Roland Moyle, Labour minister for Northern Ireland – obituary.' *The Telegraph*, 29 August 2017.
6   See: Campbell, D. 'Inquiry finds disbanded West Midlands serious crime squad was "out of control".' *The Guardian*, 2 November 1991.
7   Stalker, 1988, *op. cit.* p. 114.
8   Civil Action, 8 June 1995, p. 9.
9   Stalker, 1988, *op. cit.* p. 126.
10   Sampson, 1986, *op. cit.* para. 1.
11   Farrington, David, P. 'The Prevalence of Convictions.' *British Journal of Criminology,* 21:2 (1981) pp. 173-175. For more recent data see: Ministry of Justice. *Conviction histories of Offenders between the ages of 10 and 52 England and Wales*, Statistics Bulletin (London: Ministry of Justice, 2010).
12   Sampson, 1986, *op. cit.* para. 3-10.
13   *Ibid.* para. 451.
14   *Ibid.* para. 31.
15   *Ibid.* para. 38.
16   Criminal Trial, 11 January 1990, p. 31.
17   Civil Action, 18 May 1985, p. 18.
18   Criminal Trial, 5 January 1990, p. 41.
19   Stalker, 1988, *op. cit.* p. 199.
20   Sampson, 1986, *op. cit.* para. 36.
21   *Ibid.*
22   *Ibid.* paras. 206-210.
23   *Ibid.* para. 183.
24   This claim was fictitious. Burton had only once given the Krays a lift. (See chapter 4).
25   Civil action, 22 May 1995, p. 25.
26   Sampson, 1986, *op. cit.* para. 184.
27   *Ibid.*
28   *Ibid.* para. 186.
29   *Ibid.* para. 198.
30   *Ibid.* para. 199.
31   *Ibid.* para. 205.
32   *Ibid.*
33   Murphy, 1991, *op. cit.* p. 77.
34   See for example: Leigh, D. *et al.* 7 September 1986, *op. cit.* and Leigh, D. *et al.* 'Witnesses deny Stalker report.' *The Observer*. 14 September 1986.
35   Murtagh, P. 'Officer claims Stalker report distortion.' *The Guardian*, 17 September 1986.
36   Sampson, 1986, *op. cit.* para. 130.
37   Field Notes.
38   Sampson, 1986, *op. cit.* para. 26.
39   Murtagh, 17 September 1986, *op. cit.*
40   Sampson, 1986, *op. cit.* para. 438.
41   *Ibid.* para 185(a).
42   *Ibid.* para. 201.
43   *Ibid.* para. 8.
44   *Ibid.* para. 42.
45   *Ibid.* para 446. See Stalker, 1988, op cit. p. 201.
46   Sampson, 1986, *op. cit.* para 201.
47   *Ibid.* para. 204.
48   *Ibid.* para. 87.
49   Civil Action, 6 June 1995, p. 75.
50   Sampson, 1986, *op. cit.* para. 234.
51   Murtagh, P. 'No file on Stalker friend, say drug investigators: US agency asked for information in case against Manchester deputy chief constable.' *The Guardian*, 2 August 1986.
52   Sampson, 1986, *op. cit.* para. 15.
53   *Ibid.* para. 16.
54   See for example Stalker's opinion on the QSG, Civil Action, 23 May 1995, p. 28.
55   Murphy, 1991, *op. cit.* p. 72.

56 Sampson, 1986, *op. cit.* para. 25.
57 *Ibid.*
58 Taylor, Kevin, 1990, p. 130.
59 Sampson, 1986, *op. cit.* para. 17.
60 Civil Action, 15 June 1995, p. 27. (See chapter 10)
61 Murphy, 1991, *op. cit.* p. 74.
62 Sampson, 1986, *op. cit.* para. 267.
63 *Ibid.* para. 28.
64 *Ibid.* para. 233.
65 MacLean, Rt. Hon. Lord., Coyle, Andrew., and Oliver, John. *The Billy Wright Inquiry Report, HC 431*, (London: Publisher, 2011), Para. 5.141.
66 Burgess, n.d. *op. cit.* p. 8.
67 Sampson, 1986, *op. cit.* para. 259.
68 Leigh, *et al.* 28 September 1986, *op. cit.*
69 Taylor, Peter, 1987, *op. cit.* p. 135.
70 *Private Eye.* No. 646, 19 September 1986.
71 Criminal Trial, 10 January 1990, p. 17.
72 Sampson, 1986, *op. cit.* para. 411.
73 *Ibid.* para. 459.
74 Davenport, Peter. 'I did my duty over the Stalker inquiry, says Anderton.' *The Times*, 2 September 1986; Davenport, Peter. 'Officials act to boost morale after Stalker case'. *The Times*, 3 September 1986.
75 Civil Action, 18 May 1995, p. 9.
76 Foster, J. 'Stalker frozen out of office by Anderton.' *The Observer*, 21 December 1986.
77 Stalker, 1988, *op. cit.* p. 233.
78 *Ibid.* p. 235.

Chapter 19: Sampson's Inquiry in Northern Ireland (pages 267 to 276)

1 UK National Archive, Stalker/Sampson, Minute, Andrew to Saunders, 17 October 1986, CJ4/6278.
2 UK National Archive, Stalker/Sampson, Letter, Cubbon to Andrew, 21 October 1986, CJ4/6953.
3 UK National Archive, Meeting with Sir Philip Myers: 9 February 1987, Jonathan Stephen to A.W. Stephens, 9 February 1987, CJ4/695.
4 UK National Archive, Minute, Andrew to PS/Secretary of State, 24 March 1987, CJ4/6953.
5 *Ibid*
6 *Ibid.*
7 Hermon, 1997, *op. cit.* p. 188.
8 UK National Archive, Minute, Andrew to PS/Secretary of State, 25 September 1986, CJ4/6277.
9 Hermon, 1997, *op. cit.* p. 188.
10 UK National Archive, Minute, Andrew to PS/Secretary of State, 25 September 1986, *op. cit.*
11 *Ibid.*
12 UK National Archive, Letter, Sampson to Andrew, 21 October 1986, CJ4/6278.
13 UK National Archive, Stalker/Sampson, Letter, Andrew to Saunders, 5 November 1986, CJ4/6279.
14 UK National Archive, Minute, Andrew to PS/Secretary of State, 23 September 1986, CJ4/6277.
15 Field Notes.
16 Taylor, Peter. 2001, *op. cit.* p. 252.
17 Cobain, Ian, 9 July 2015, *op. cit.*
18 UK National Archive, Letter, Sampson to Andrew, 21 October 1986, CJ4/6278.
19 Taylor, Peter. 2001, *op. cit.* p. 252.
20 Field Notes.
21 Davenport, Peter. 'Stalker who became the prey.' *The Times*, 8 February 1988.
22 UK National Archive, Letter, Sampson to Andrew, 21 October 1986, *op. cit.*
23 *Ibid.*
24 UK National Archive, Stalker/Sampson, Letter, Cubbon to Andrew, 21 October 1986, CJ4/6953.

25 UK National Archive, Letter, Andrew to Hermon, 5 November 1986, *op. cit.*
26 UK National Archive, Letter, Hermon to Andrew, 28 November 1986, CJ4/6953.
27 UK National Archives, Stalker/Sampson: Handling the Irish, Minute, Bell to Blackwell, 7 November 1986, CJ4/6279.
28 UK National Archives, Stalker/Sampson: Handling the Irish, Minute, Bell to PS/PUS, 15 December 1986, CJ4/6279.
29 UK National Archives, Stalker/Sampson: Handling the Irish, Minute, Bell to Blackwell, 7 November 1986, CJ4/6279.
30 *Ibid.*
31 UK National Archives, Letter, Hermon to Andrew, 20 June 1986, CJ4/6285.
32 *Ibid.*
33 UK National Archive, Minute, Stalker Report: Conversations with the Chief Constable, 23 June 1986, CJ4/6285.
34 UK National Archive, Letter, Hermon to Andrew, 18 July 1986, CJ4/6285.
35 UK National Archive, Letter, Hermon to Andrew, 20 August 1986, CJ4/6276.
36 *Ibid.*
37 UK National Archive, Conversation with the Chief Constable – 6 April 1987, Minute, Andrew to Stephens, 7 April 1987, CJ4/6953
38 *Ibid.*
39 UK National Archive, Letter, Hurd to Kinnock, 21 October 1986, CJ4/6279.

Chapter 20: Perverting the Course of Justice (pages 277 to 290)

1   Civil Action, 16 May 1995, pp. 23-24.
2   'Report on Stalker's friend with DPP.' *The Times*, 19 June 1986.
3   Civil Action, 16 May 1995, p. 23.
4   Civil Action, 8 June 1995, p. 64-65.
5   Civil Action, 16 May 1995, p. 25.
6   *Ibid.*
7   Civil Action, 8 June 1995, p. 63.
8   Civil Action, 16 May 1995, p. 26.
9   Henfield, Margaret and Peter Burden. 'Holiday allegation against police chief.' *Daily Mail*, 5 June 1986. See also: Stalker, 1988, *op. cit.* p. 121.
10 Foster, J., D. Leigh and M. Holland. 'Stalker 'smear' hinges on old photograph.' *The Observer*, 15 June 1986.
11 *Ibid.*
12 Murtagh, Peter. 1987, *op. cit.* p. 16.
13 *Ibid.*
14 *Stalker: Coincidence or Conspiracy*, BBC Panorama Programme, 16 June 1986.
15 *Ibid.*
16 *Ibid.*
17 *Stalker and Company*, BBC Panorama Programme, 19 August 1986.
18 *Ibid.*
19 Criminal Trial, 11 January 1990, p. 64.
20 Levin, Bernard. 'Let the moors keep their grisly secrets.' *The Times*, 22 December 1986.
21 *Ibid.*
22 UK National Archive, Stalker, Cubbon to SoS Home office, 30 September 1986. CJ4/6277.
23 *Ibid.*
24 UK National Archive, A note of a Meeting by Boys Smith, 2 October 1986, CJ4/6277.
25 Stern, Chester. 'Stalker case tycoon may now be charged'. *The Mail on Sunday*, 9 August 1987.
26 Hansard, House of Commons, Statement by the Attorney General, Sir Patrick Mayhew, 'Royal Ulster Constabulary (Stalker-Sampson Investigations)', Vol. 126, Col. 21-35, 25 January 1988.
27 PRONI, Report of Informal Ministerial Meeting, London, 10 February 1988, NIO 25/1/92, para 2.
28 *Ibid.* para 15.
29 *Ibid.*
30 Taylor, Peter. 'Secrets and lies.' *The Guardian*, 23 May 2000.
31 Ryder, Chris. 'No trial for security-risk RUC.' *Sunday Times*, 31 January 1988.

32   Phillips, Melanie. 'Commentary: Rule of law yields to the rule of war.' *The Guardian*, 15 June 1990.
33   Field Notes.
34   Hansard, House of Commons, Statement by Tom King, Secretary of State for Northern Ireland, Vol. 127, Col. 977, 17 February 1988.
35   *Ibid.*
36   *Ibid.*
37   De Silva, 2012, *op. cit.* para. 4.43.
38   *Ibid.* para. 4.44.
39   *Ibid.* para. 4.50.
40   Moloney, Ed. 'The cover-up goes on.' *Sunday Tribune*, 3 July 1988.
41   Pyle, Fergus. '20 RUC men face discipline over cover-up.' *The Irish Times*, 5 July 1988.
42   'Two RUC officers expected to retire.' *The Irish Times*, 6 August 1988.
43   Pyle, Fergus. 'RUC officers given 'lowest' disciplinary punishment.' *The Irish Times*, 15 March 1989.
44   Pyle, Fergus. 'RUC reprimands 'outrageous' Mallon.' *The Irish Times*, 16 March 1989.
45   'Coroner's court adjourned.' *The Irish Times*, 13 September 1984.
46   Moloney, Ed. 'Coroner says police files differ from trial evidence.' *The Irish Times*, 4 September 1984.
47   'RUC inquiry delays inquest.' *The Irish Times*, 31 August 1984. The misspelling of Stalker may have been a mishearing by the reporter. Alternatively, the RUC continued to believe that this was the correct spelling.
48   'Judge to rule on inquest move.' *The Irish Times*, 16 November 1988.
49   PIIC issued by the Secretary of State for Northern Ireland, 9 November 1988.
50   'Judge rules inquest can hear unsworn statements.' *The Irish Times*, 23 November 1988.
51   Pyle, Fergus. 'Crown may fight ruling on North inquest.' *The Irish Times*, 21 December 1988.
52   McKerr v Armagh Coroner [1990] 1 All ER 865.
53   O'Halloran, Marie. 'Lord's ruling affects inquests into 21 deaths.' *The Irish Times*, 10 March 1990.
54   For a summary of the inquest saga see: BIRW, 1995, *op. cit.*

Chapter 21: Arrests and Committal Proceedings (pages 291 to 298)

1   Field Notes.
2   The Building Societies Act, 1986.
3   Criminal Trial, 18 October 1989, p. 82.
4   Civil action, 19 June 1995, p. 7-8.
5   Criminal Trial, 11 January 1989, p. 41.
6   Criminal Trial, 2 November 1989, p.19.
7   This type of proceeding was abolished in 2013 with cases going straight to the Crown Court.
8   Taylor, Kevin, 1990, op cit. p. 133-134.
9   See for example: Gillespie, Raymond. *Conspiracy: Ulster plots and plotters in 1615* (Belfast: The Ulster Society for Irish Historical Studies, 1987).
10   According to one authority, it represents one of the greatest threats to civil liberties in English criminal law. Hazell, Robert. *Conspiracies and Civil Liberties*, (London: The Social Administration Research Trust, 1974), p. 9. See also: Spicer, Robert. *Conspiracy: Law, Class and Society* (London: Lawrence and Wishart, 1981). Hain sees the law of conspiracy as an agent of government. See: Hain, Peter. *Political Trials in Britain: From the Past to the Present Day* (Harmondsworth: Penguin Books Ltd, 1984), Chapter 7.
11   Hansard, House of Lords, Vol. 393, Col. 1118, 24 July 1972.
12   Taylor's lawyers used the law to try to challenge GMP's investigation. On 23 September 1986, they made an application for discovery in the Chancery Division of the High Court. It was rejected by Justice Scott. On 14 October, they brought a charge of conspiracy to pervert the course of justice against Anderton. Following a judicial review in front of Lord Justice May and Mr Justice Nolan the summons was quashed. In July 1987, they applied for a judicial review in relation to Judge Prestt's decision to grant access orders. It was heard in front of Lord Justice Glidewell, and Mr Justice French and the application was rejected. See: Taylor, Kevin. 1990, *op. cit.* pp. 113-132.
13   Committal Proceedings, 18 October 1988, pp. 5-6.

14   Taylor, Kevin, 1990, *op. cit.* p. 142.
15   Committal Proceedings, 18 October 1988, p. 1.
16   *Ibid.*
17   Committal Proceedings, 20 October 1988, p. 39.
18   Taylor, Kevin, 1990, *op. cit.* p. 144.
19   *Ibid.* p. 169.
20   Horrock, Paul. 'My blueprint for society.' *Manchester Evening News*, 26 July 1989.
21   *Ibid.*
22   *Ibid.*
23   Henfield, Margaret. 'Excuse me, waiter, there's a chief constable in my soup'. *Daily Mail*, 27 July 1989.
24   Topping, 1989, *.op. cit.*
25   Richie, Jean. *Myra Hindley: Inside the mind of a murderess*, (London: Angus Robinson, 1988).
26   Topping, 1989, *op. cit.* p. 282.
27   *Ibid.* p. 283-284.
28   *Ibid.* p. 279.
29   Hackworth, Fred. 'Hindley takes Topping to court.' *Manchester Evening News*, 30 August 1989.
30   Wylie, Ian. 'Topping faces jail threat for contempt.' *Manchester Evening News*, 9 February 1990.
31   Tendler, Stewart and Robin Stacey. 'Moors murder case detective served with writ over book.' *The Times*, 5 September 1989.

Chapter 22: Murder of a Solicitor (pages 299 to 326)

1   Alan Simpson. *Duplicity and Deception: Policing the Twilight Zone of the Troubles* (Dingle, Co. Kerry, Ireland: Brandon, 2010), p. 29.
2   Doherty, Fiona and Meg Satterthwaite. *Beyond Collusion: The UK Security Forces and the Murder of Patrick Finucane.* (New York: Lawyers Committee for Human Rights, 2002), Chapter 3. In 1999, the Macpherson report into the death of Stephen Lawrence, who was murdered in a racist attack in 1993, argued that 'institutional racism' can be defined in terms of the collective failure of an organisation to address policies, leadership and culture leading to discrimination on the basis of race rather than the attitudes and behaviour of individual officers. See: Macpherson, Sir William, Tom Cook, John Sentamu and Richard Stone. *The Stephen Lawrence Inquiry*, Cm. 4262-1. (London: HMSO, 1999).
3   McGovern, 2019, *op. cit.* also concludes from his extensive analysis that collusion was 'institutional in character', p. 167. See also: McGovern, Mark. 'Legacy, truth and collusion in the North of Ireland.' *Race and Class,* 64: 3 (2022) pp. 59-89.
4   Lawyers Committee for Human Rights, 2003, *op. cit.* p. 5.
5   *Ibid.* p. 3.
6   De Silva, 2012, *op. cit.* para. 67.
7   *Ibid.*
8   Hansard, House of Commons, Standing Committee B debate, Vol. 145, Col. 508, 17 January 1989.
9   *Ibid.* Col. 509.
10   Davies, Nicholas. *Dead Men Talking: Collusion, Cover-up and Murder in Northern Ireland's Dirty War* (Edinburgh: Mainstream Publishing, 2005), p. 16.
11   Stevens, Sir John. *Stevens Enquiry: Overview and Recommendations* (London: Unknown, 2003), para 1.5-1.6.
12   The montages were A4-sized posters containing information and photos about suspects used for briefing patrols. See: Stevens, John. *Not for the Faint-hearted: My Life Fighting Crime* (London: Weidenfeld & Nicolson, 2005), p. 176.
13   *Ibid.* p. 200.
14   Stevens, Sir John, 2003, *op. cit.*
15   Implementation Plan issued by the British and Irish governments on 1 August 2001, para. 19. https://cain.ulster.ac.uk/events/peace/docs/bi010801.htm (Accessed 2 November 2020)
16   Cory, Peter. *Cory Collusion Inquiry Report: Patrick Finucane* HC 470, (London: HMSO, 2004). http://cain.ulst.ac.uk/issues/collusion/cory/cory03finucane.pdf (Accessed 2 November 2020)
17   Article 2 states: 'Everyone's right to life shall be protected by law. No one shall be deprived

of his life intentionally save in the execution of a sentence of a court following his conviction of a crime for which this penalty is provided by law.'

18 Finucane v. the United Kingdom, no. 29178/95, judgment of 1 July 2003.

19 McKittrick, David. 'Finucane widow rails at 'insult' as David Cameron rejects inquiry.' *The Independent*, 12 October 2011.

20 McCann, Eamonn. 'Finucane case offers glimpse of ongoing MI5 role in North.' *The Irish Times*, 25 June 2015.

21 For an early and detailed analysis of the role of Nelson, See: Davies, Nicholas. *Ten-Thirty-Three: The Inside Story of Britain's Secret Killing Machine in Northern Ireland* (Edinburgh: Mainstream Publishing, 1999). He notes that 1033 was Nelson's 'code number'. However, de Silva records his 'source number' throughout his report as 6137. See: De Silva, 2012, *op. cit.* para. 6.80. It is not known what the difference is between a code and a source number.

22 For more details see: BIRW, *Response to Stevens 3* (London: British and Irish Rights Watch, 2003).

23 Stevens, 2003, *op. cit.* para 2.8.

24 See: De Silva, 2012, *op. cit.* para. 6.6. However, Cory records that he approached the Army in 1985. See: Cory, 2004, para. 1.45. Ian Hurst, aka Martin Ingram, who worked for the FRU, is of the opinion that he was recruited in 1979. See: Ingram, Martin and Greg Harkin. *Stakeknife: Britain's Secret Agents in Ireland*, (Dublin: The O'Brien Press, 2004), p. 179.

25 See: PPS, *Operation Kenova – Summary of decisions not to prosecute*, (Belfast: Public Prosecution Service, 29 February 2024) para. 71.

26 De Silva, 2012, *op. cit.* para. 6.7.

27 Stevens, 2005, *op. cit.* p. 191.

28 Larkin, 2004, *op. cit.* p. 57.

29 Ingram and Harkin, 2004, p. 182.

30 *Spotlight on the Troubles: A Secret History,* 1 October 2019.

31 De Silva, 2012, para. 5.17.

32 *Spotlight on the Troubles: A Secret History,* 1 October 2019.

33 Stevens, 2005, *op. cit.* p. 179.

34 Stevens, 2003, *op. cit.* paras 3.3-3.5.

35 Stevens, 2005, *op. cit.* p. 177.

36 *Ibid.* But in the Spotlight programme he relates the same detail, but the suggestion was his office should be based in army headquarters in Lisburn not in Holywood.

37 *Ibid.*

38 It is, of course, possible that a CME team started the fire in the wastepaper basket using a cigarette to shift the responsibility to the Stevens' team. Moreover, Simpson does not comment on the failure of the fire alarms, telephones, heat sensors and intruder alarms.

39 Stevens, 2005, *op. cit.* Chapter 1.

40 For more details see: Dillon, Martin. *The Trigger Men* (Edinburgh: Mainstream Publishing, 2003, pp. 265-366

41 De Silva, 2012, *op. cit.* para. 24.102.

42 *Ibid.* para. 24.153.

43 *Ibid.* para. 24.162.

44 For his background and role in Northern Ireland see for example: MacKay, Neil. 'The secret wars of a spymaster.' *Sunday Herald*, 28 November 2000.

45 BBC Newsline, 17 April 2003.

46 De Silva, 2012, *op. cit.* para. 4.65.

47 Taylor, Peter, 2023, *op. cit.* p. 213.

48 Hansard, House of Commons, Vol. 407, Col. 33, Written Answers, 16 June 2003.

49 De Silva, *op. cit.* 2012, para. 4.71.

50 See PONI, 1994, *op. cit.* paras. 9.20-9.22.

51 Brown, Johnston. *Into the Dark: 30 Years in the RUC* (Dublin: Gill & Macmillan, 2006), p. 160.

52 *Ibid.* p. 176.

53 *Ibid.*

54 *Ibid.* pp. 245-247.

55 The deceit was first revealed in a UTV *Insight* programme broadcast on 1 May 2001 in which Jonty Brown was interviewed. A full transcript of the programme is available from the Pat Finucane Centre. (www.patfinucanecentre.org)

56 De Silva, 2012, *op. cit.* para. 97.

57 *Spotlight on the Troubles: A Secret History*, BBC, 8 October 2019.
58 Cory, 2004, *op. cit.* para 1.146.
59 *Ibid.* para 1.178.
60 *Ibid.* para 1.252. A similar disproportionate bias was found in the prosecution process in the early days of the Troubles. For similar illegal acts, people from the Catholic community were charged with more serious offences than people from the Protestant community. See: Hadden, Tom and Paddy Hillyard. *Justice in Northern Ireland: a study in social confidence* (London: Cobden Trust, 1973).
61 Cory, 2004, *op. cit.* para 1.292.
62 *Ibid.* para 1.25.
63 *Ibid.* para. 1.53.
64 De Silva, 2012, *op. cit.* para 6.41.
65 *Ibid.* para. 6.40.
66 *Spotlight on the Troubles: A Secret History,* 8 October 2019.
67 Ulster Resistance, a citizens' army, was formed in 1986 to defend 'Ulster in her latest hour of crisis.' See: Taylor, Peter, 2000, *op. cit.* pp. 184-192.
68 See: Cobain, Ian, 2016, pp. 188-189.
69 McKittrick, *et al.* 2001, *op. cit.* Table 2, p. 1553. See also: McGovern, 2022, *op. cit.* Chapters 4 and 5.
70 PONI, 1994, *op. cit.* para. 42.
71 *Ibid.* p. 5.
72 Cowan, Rosie. 'How three sharply dressed robbers walked into Belfast's intelligence hub: New evidence that raid was planned down to the last detail.' *The Guardian*, 23 March 2002.
73 *Ibid.*
74 Clarke, Liam. 'Spy HQ raid puts informants and officers at risk.' *Sunday Times*, 24 March 2002.
75 Hinsliff, Gaby and Henry McDonald. 'Arrests put Ulster deal in jeopardy.' *The Observer*, 31 March 2002.
76 Hansard, House of Commons Debates, Vol. 409, Col. 40, Written Answers, 16 July 2003,
77 See: Hillyard, Paddy and Margaret Urwin. 'Shining a light on deadly informers: The de Silva report on the murder of Pat Finucane.' *Statewatch,* 23:2 (2013) pp. 8-15.
78 De Silva, 2012, para. 115.
79 *Ibid.* para. 4.89.
80 McGovern, *op. cit.* p. 22.
81 De Silva, 2012, *op. cit.* para. 4.38.
82 *Ibid.* paras 11.23 and 11.24.
83 *Ibid.* para, 11.43.
84 *Ibid.* para 8.86.
85 *Ibid.* para. 8.87.
86 Hansard, House of Commons, Statement by Prime Minister, David Cameron, on Patrick Finucane, Vol. 555, Col. 295, 12 December 2012.
87 Joint Committee on the Draft Detention of Terrorist Suspects (Temporary Extension) Bill, Oral and associated written Evidence, 3 May 2011, Q317. In his book, however, he notes that, 'in all we had arrested ninety-eight people and convicted sixty of them'. Stevens, 2005, p. 200.
88 Cobain, Ian, 8 March 2018, *op. cit.*
89 PONI. *Public statement by the Police Ombudsman for Northern Ireland, on her investigation into the circumstances surrounding the death of Raymond McCord Junior and related matters, (Operation Ballast)*, (Belfast: Police Ombudsman for Northern Ireland, 2007), para. 6.9.
90 McCord, Raymond. *Justice for Raymond*, (Dublin: Gill & Macmillan, 2008), p. 116.
91 *Ibid.* p. 121.
92 PONI, 2007, *op. cit.* para. 12.
93 Thompson, Mark. 'Haddock on the bottom rung of collusion ladder.' *North Belfast News*, 19 January 2007.
94 *Ibid.*
95 Two recently published PONI reports investigated loyalist murders in South Belfast (1991-2003) and the North West (1989-1993). They contained very similar criticisms of the MI5/Walker strategy that Stalker and Sampson had made in 1985/1986: the protection of state agents and informers dominated all decision-making; victims were not warned; and intelligence was withheld from the CID investigating the murders amounting to collusion.

See: PONI. *Investigation into police handing of certain loyalist paramilitary murders and attempted murders in the North West of Northern Ireland during the period 1989 to 1993* (Belfast: Police Ombudsman for Northern Ireland, 2022). PONI. *Investigation into police handling of loyalist paramilitary murders and attempted murders in south Belfast in period 1990-1998* (Belfast: Police Ombudsman for Northern Ireland, 2022).

96 For a detailed account Scappaticci's murderous activities see: Ingram and Harkin, 2004, *op. cit.* Chapter 4.

97 Cowan, Rosie. 'He did the IRA's dirty work for 25 years – and was paid £80,000 a year by the government.' *The Guardian*, 12 May 2003.

98 For more detail and Scappaticci's involvement see: Collins, Eamon and Mick McGovern. *Killing Rage* (London: Granta Books, 1997), pp. 216-217 and Chapter 18.

99 'What secrets were buried with Stakeknife, Britain's IRA spy?', *The Sunday Times*, 16 April 2023.

100 Stevens, 2005, *op. cit.* p. 206.

101 Ingram and Harkin, 2004, *op. cit.* p. 83. The Belfast Telegraph noted a figure of 40 murders. See: 'Stakeknife could have murdered 40 people - probe "potentially bigger than UDA Brian Nelson case"', *Belfast Telegraph*, 22 October 2015.

102 This figure is based on information from McKittrick, *et al.* 2001.

103 *Ibid.* p.1093.

104 Carlin, Willie. *Thatcher's Spy: My Life as an MI5 Agent Inside Sinn Féin* (Dublin: Mercier Press, 2019), Chapter 8.

105 Quoted in: Rowan, Brian. *Living with ghosts: The inside story from a 'Troubles' Mind,* (Newbridge, Co. Kildare: Merrion Press, 2022), p. 155.

106 For a detailed account of Gregory Burns' role as an informer, see: Ingram and Harkin, 2004, *op. cit.* pp. 122-135.

107 For a detailed account see: Taylor, Peter, 1994, *op. cit.* Chapter 8.

108 Ingram and Harkin, 2004, *op. cit.* p. 130.

109 *Ibid.*

110 The report has never been published but see: Moore, Chris. 'They played God: The Lost Souls of North Armagh.' *Sunday World*, 6 September 2009.

111 *Ibid.*

112 Lynch, Conor. 'Operation Kenova costs police over £37m since its launch.' *Belfast Telegraph*, 11 June 2023.

113 See: Operation Kenova. https://www.opkenova.co.uk/ (Accessed 12 September 2021)

114 For a detailed forensic analysis of these murders, see: Cadwallader, *op. cit.* 2013.

115 O'Rawe, Richard. *Stakeknife's Dirty War: The Inside Story of Scappaticci, The IRA's Nutting Squad, and the British Spooks who ran the War.* (Newbridge, Co Kildare: Merrion Press, 2023), Chapter 15.

116 O'Leary, Jennifer. 'The spy who got away with murder.' BBC News. 30 May 2023.

117 See: PPS. *Operation Kenova – Summary of Decisions not to Prosecute. Statement of Public Prosecution Service*, (Public Prosecution Service, 6 December 2023) para. 2.1.

118 McDonald, Henry. 'Stakeknife scandal: Freddie Scappaticci avoids perjury charge.' *The Guardian*, 29 October 2020.

119 Rowan, 2022, *op. cit.* p. 176.

120 'Man believed to be Stakeknife dies.' *Irish News*, 12 April 2023.

121 PPS. *PPS issues four decisions in connection with Operation Kenova* (Public Prosecution Prosecution Service, 29 October 2020).

122 Morris, Allison. 'More than 30 families of Freddie Scappaticci's victims set to sue estate of decreased informer.' *Belfast Telegraph*, 17 April 2023.

123 PPS, 6 December 2023, *op. cit.*

124 PPS. *PPS issues further decisions on files submitted by Operation Kenova* (Public Prosecution Service, 6 February 2024).

125 PPS. *PPS issues decisions on final Operation Kenova files* (Public Prosecution Service, 29 February 2024).

126 De Silva, 2012, *op. cit.* para. 8.173.

127 PPS, 29 February 2024, *op. cit.* para. 13.

128 De Silva, 2012, *op. cit.* para. 3.19.

129 PPS, 29 February 2024, *op. cit.* para. 13.

130 https://www.kenova.co.uk/kenova-report-set-for-new-year-after-release-protocol-finalised (Accessed 12 January 2024)

131 Boutcher, Jon. *Operation Kenova Northern Ireland Stakeknife Legacy Investigation Interim Report by Jon Boutcher*, QPM. 8 March 2024, p. 36.
132 *Ibid*. para. 63.9.
133 *Ibid*.
134 *Ibid*. para. 41.1.
135 *Ibid*. p. 28.
136 *Ibid*. para. 60.7.
137 *Ibid*. para. 60.8.
138 *Ibid*. para 41.2
139 In the matter of an application by Geraldine Finucane for Judicial Review (Northern Ireland), [2019] UKSC 7, para. 153.
140 *Ibid*. para. 118.
141 *Ibid*.
142 Hansard, House of Commons, Statement by SoS for Northern Ireland, Brandon Lewis, on the murder of Pat Finucane, Vol. 685, Col. 54, 30 November 2020.
143 In the matter of an application by Geraldine Finucane for Judicial Review and in the matter of a decision of the Secretary of State for Northern Ireland, The High Court Northern Ireland, [2022] NIKB, 21.12.2022, para 66.
144 *Ibid*. para 79.
145 *Ibid*. para 78.
146 'Northern Secretary to pay £7,500 in damages to Pat Finucane's widow', *The Irish Times*, 21 December 2020.
147 'Widow of murdered Belfast solicitor Pat Finucane to seek damages against UK government.' *The Irish Times*, 6 January 2023
148 'Secretary of State to pay further damages to Finucane's widow for 'culpable delay', *Irish News,* 31 March 2023.
149 'Judge went too far in declaring British actions unlawful', *The Irish News*, 19 September 2023.

Chapter 23: Taylor's Trial (pages 327 to 347)

1   Field Notes.
2   Criminal Trial, 17 October 1989, p. 32.
3   Criminal Trial, 3 November 1989, p. 81.
4   Criminal Trial, 16 October 1989, p. 9.
5   *Ibid.* p.11.
6   *Ibid.* p.10
7   Criminal Trial, 2 January 1990, p. 52.
8   *Ibid.* pp. 55-56.
9   *Ibid.* p. 64.
10   Criminal Trial, 24 October 1989, p. 58.
11   Criminal Trial, 15 December 1989, p. 9.
12   Birkett made a mistake over the date. The holiday was in 1986.
13   Criminal Trial, 12 January 1990, pp. 10-11.
14   *Ibid.* p. 10.
15   *Ibid.* pp. 54.
16   *Ibid.* pp. 54-55.
17   Criminal Trial, 28 November 1989, p. 1.
18   Criminal Trial, 4 December 1989, pp. 34-35.
19   Criminal Trial, 19 December 1989, p. 38.
20   Criminal Trial, 2 January 1990, p. 50.
21   Criminal Trial, 27 October 1989, p. 19.
22   Criminal Trial, 18 December 1989, p.1.
23   Criminal Trial, 21 December 1989, p.18
24   *Ibid.* pp. 14-15
25   Morton, James. 'Sir Michael Sachs: First solicitor on high court bench.' *The Guardian*, 2 October 2003.
26   Greer, 1995, *op. cit.* p. 121. See also: 'Defendant in plea over lawyer.' *The Irish Times*, 9 March 1984.
27   Obituary. *The Daily Telegraph*, 10 August 2009.

28   Taylor, Kevin, 1990, *op. cit.* p. 169.
29   *Ibid.* p. 173.
30   Civil Action, 19 June 1995, p. 11.
31   *Ibid.* p. 28.
32   Taylor, Kevin, 1990, *op. cit.* p. 175.
33   Criminal Trial, 16 October 1989, p. 47.
34   Criminal Trial, 2 January 1990, p.50
35   See: Salter, Alan. 'Police were getting at Stalker QC.' *Manchester Evening News*, 16 October 1989.
36   Criminal Trial, 9 January 1990, p. 11.
37   Criminal Trial, 10 January 1990, p. 31.
38   Criminal Trial, 11 January 1990, p. 5.
39   *Ibid.* p. 6.
40   Criminal Trial, 9 January 1990, p. 35.
41   Criminal Trial, 10 January 1990, p. 7.
42   *Ibid.* p. 65.
43   *Ibid.* p. 9.
44   Criminal Trial, 11 January 1990, p. 30.
45   *Ibid.* p. 80.
46   Criminal Trial, 10 January 1990, p. 56.
47   *Ibid.* pp. 54-56.
48   *Ibid.* pp. 56-59.
49   Criminal Trial, 2 January 1990, p. 62.
50   *Ibid.* p. 67.
51   Criminal Trial, 11 January 190, p. 65.
52   Criminal Trial, 4 January 1990, p. 71.
53   *Ibid.* p. 35.
54   Criminal Trial, 8 January 1990, p. 11.
55   *Ibid.* p. 36.
56   *Ibid.* p. 1.
57   Criminal Trial, 16 January 1990, p. 56.
58   *Ibid.* p. 57.
59   Stalker, 1988, *op. cit.* p. 162.
60   Criminal Trial, 15 January 1990, p. 37.
61   Criminal Trial, 16 January 1990, p. 14.
62   *Ibid.* p. 24
63   *Ibid.*
64   *Ibid.*
65   Criminal Trial, 16 January 1990, p. 25.
66   *Ibid.* p. 27.
67   *Ibid.* pp. 28-29.
68   *Ibid.* p. 40.
69   *Ibid.* p. 48.
70   *Ibid.* p. 57.
71   Criminal Trial, 17 January 1990, p. 6.
72   *Ibid.* p. 13.
73   *Ibid.* p. 16.
74   *Ibid.* p. 31.
75   Criminal Trial, 18 January 1990, p. 20.
76   The report was disclosed during the civil action.
77   Criminal Trial, 18 January 1990, p. 31.
78   *Ibid.* p. 39.
79   *Ibid.* p.40.
80   *Ibid.*
81   *Ibid.* p. 43.
82   Norton-Taylor, Richard. 'Home Office denies Stalker decision role.' *The Guardian*, 20 January 1990.
83   *A Pawn in the Game*, Granada Television, Open Eye, 30 April 1990.

84   *Stalker: The Final Chapter*, BBC Public Eye Programme, 14 June 1991.
85   Hansard, House of Commons, Debates, Vol. 177, Col. 25, 23 July 1990.

Chapter 24: Civil Action (pages 348 to 360)

1   It changed its name to the Government Legal Department on 24 February 2015.
2   Woolf, Lord. *Access to Justice, Final Report*, (London: Department of Constitutional Affairs, 2006).
3   Civil Action, 11 May 1995, p. 9.
4   See: Scraton, Phil. *Hillsborough: The Truth*, (Edinburgh: Mainstream Publishing, 2016), Chapter 10.
5   Panter, Steve. 'Taylor file papers lost: Top detective lover fury.' *Manchester Evening News*, 20 September 1993.
6   *Ibid.*
7   *Ibid.*
8   The others were: Sampson's inquiry into the allegations against Stalker; the Mullet inquiry into the leaking of the Sampson report; and the Rothwell inquiry following the collapse of the criminal trial.
9   Under Section 69 of the Supreme Court Act 1981, if a court is satisfied that the case is either a fraud or a claim of libel, slander, malicious prosecution or false imprisonment, it can allow a trial by jury. There is one proviso, namely: 'Unless the court is of the opinion that the trial requires prolonged examination of documents or accounts or any scientific or local investigation, which cannot conveniently be made before a jury.'
10   See: Beta Construction v Channel 4 Television [1992] All England Reports, p. 1012.
11   In the High Court of Justice (Queen's Bench Division) Liverpool District, Kevin Taylor and Sir James Anderton, The Chief Constable of GMP, 20 December 1994.
12   For an excellent analysis, see: Norton-Taylor, Richard. *The State of Secrecy: Spies and the media in Britain* (London: Bloomsbury, 2020).
13   Sharratt, Tom and Richard Norton-Taylor. 'Mayhew in court move to gag Stalker: Ex-police chief faces court ban.' *The Guardian*, 10 May 1995.
14   Lashmar, Paul. 'The Stalker Affair.' *Charter 88 Unlocking Democracy Violations of Rights in Britain Series 3,* No. 27 (2003), p. 1.
15   Panter, Steve and Gerard Henderson. 'Taylor may appeal over Stalker Gag.' *Manchester Evening News*, 11 May 1995.
16   Panter, Steve and Gerard Henderson. 'Govt. Bid to Gag Stalker.' *Manchester Evening News*, 9 May 1995.
17   Sharratt, Tom and Richard Norton-Taylor. 'Judge upholds Minister's attempts to "gag" Stalker.' *The Guardian*, 12 May 1995.
18   *Ibid.*
19   For example: Civil Action, 16 May 1995, p. 36.
20   Sharratt, Tom and Richard Norton-Taylor, 1995, *op. cit.*
21   Civil Action, 31 May 1995, p. 24.
22   Civil Action, 5 June 1995, p. 20.
23   Civil Action, 16 May 1995, p. 2.
24   Civil Action, 11 May 1995, p. 15.
25   *Ibid.* p. 7.
26   *Ibid.* p. 9.
27   *Ibid.* p. 10.
28   Civil Action, 16 May 1995, p. 4.
29   *Ibid.* p. 5.
30   *Ibid.* p. 7.
31   *Ibid.* p. 8.
32   *Ibid.*
33   *Ibid.* p.15.
34   Civil Action, 16 May 1995, p. 17.
35   *Ibid.* p. 28.
36   Civil Action, 17 May 1995, p. 5.
37   *Ibid.* p. 13.
38   See for example, Civil Action, 25 May 1995, pp. 18-20, 15 June 1995, p. 51.

39   Civil Action, 22 May 1995, p. 58-59.
40   *Ibid.* pp. 60-61.
41   Civil Action, 23 May 1995, p. 37.
42   Civil Action, 31 May 1995, p. 23.
43   *Ibid.* p. 24.
44   Civil Action, 6 June 1995, p. 24.
45   *Ibid.* p. 19.
46   Civil Action, 6 June 1995, p. 20.
47   Civil Action, 31 May 1995, p. 94.
48   *Ibid.* p. 89.
49   Civil Action, 31 May 1995, pp. 94-95.
50   Civil Action, 14 June 1995, p. 32.
51   Civil Action, 31 May 1995, p. 64.
52   Civil Action, 5 June 1995, p. 63 and 15 June 1995, p. 51.
53   Civil Action, 25 May 1995, p. 19.
54   Civil Action, 19 May 1995, p. 7.
55   Civil Action, 23 May 1995, p. 75.
56   Duncan Campbell, 'Stalker's friend offered £625,000 to settle case against police.' *The Guardian*, 12 January 1995.
57   Field Notes.
58   '"Stalker Affair" case settled out of court.' *The Guardian*, 27 June 1995.
59   *Ibid.*
60   Select Committee on Home Affairs. 'Confidentiality of police settlements of civil claims.' Second Report, *Session 1997-1998* (London: House of Commons, 1998) para. 12.
61   *The Guardian*. 27 June 1995, *op. cit.*
62   Select Committee on Home Affairs, 1998, *op. cit.* para. 14.
63   *Ibid.*

Chapter 25: Coincidences, Conspiracies and Consequences (pages 361 to 390)

1   Field Notes.
2   Civil Action, 23 May 1995, p. 19 and 6 June 1995, p. 75.
3   Field Notes.
4   Civil Action, 14 June 1995, p. 12.
5   Field Notes.
6   Dorril, Stephen. 'Stalker, Conspiracy?' *Lobster* 23 (1992). See also: Dorril, Stephen. 1994, *op. cit.* p. 94.
7   Stalker, 1988, *op. cit.* p. 35.
8   Stalker, 1988, *op. cit.* p. 47.
9   Civil Action, 22 May 1995, p. 59.
10   Civil Action, 14 June 1995, p. 51.
11   A recent study explored the role of MI5 from the end of the Second World War to 1964. It concluded that it acted neither with statutory authority nor statutory powers, and with no obvious forms of statutory accountability. See: Ewing, Keith, Joan Mahoney and Andrew Moretta. *MI5, the Cold War, the Rule of Law*, (Oxford: Oxford University Press, 2020).
12   De Silva, 2012, para, 54 and 55.
13   *Spotlight on the Troubles: A Secret History,* 8 October 2019.
14   See: Moore, Chris. *The Kincora Scandal: Political Cover-up and Intrigue in Northern Ireland* (Dublin: Marino Books, 1996).
15   Hart, Sir Anthony. *Historical Institutional Abuse Inquiry.* Volume 1, Chapter 3, Findings (Belfast: HIAI, 2017), para. 413.
16   *Lost Boys*, Directed by Des Henderson and Produced by Ed Stobart, World Premiere, Odeon Cinema, Belfast, 28 September 2023.
17   'Lost Boys', *The Irish News*, 29 September 2023.
18   Historical Institutional Abuse Inquiry. *Kincora Boys Home (Part 2),* Chapter 28 (Belfast: HIAI, 2017), para. 636.
19   Hansard, House of Commons, 13 March 2006, Vol. 443, Col. 1185.
20   'Force of Freemasons', Letters, *The Guardian*, 19 April 1988.

21 Clarke, Liam and John Hunter. 'Who's Who in Northern Ireland Freemasonry.' *Fortnight,* No. 203 (1984) pp. 4-7.

22 Patten, Christopher. *A New Beginning: Policing in Northern Ireland, Report of the Independent Commission on Policing for Northern Ireland* (London: HMSO, 1999).

23 Cusick, James. 'The Masonic connection'. *Manchester Evening News,* 25 July 1986.

24 Short, Martin. *Inside the brotherhood: further secrets of the freemasons* (London: Grafton, 1989), p. 244.

25 Dorril, 1992, *op. cit.*

26 Field Notes.

27 Ellicott, Claire. 'Thatcher's legal chief wanted to send the police into Downing Street over shoot-to-kill policy he feared was being covered up "by MI5 and the cabinet".' *Mail Online,* 28 December 2018.

28 NIO letter, 31 October 2019, Reference FOI 19/133.

29 NIO letter, 20 January 2020, Reference FOI 19/133.

30 NIO letter, 30 April 2021, Reference FOI/21/52.

31 *Ibid.*

32 NIO letter, 7 June 2021, Ref AP/21/6.

33 ICO letter, 7 July 2021, Reference IC-114433-W9H8.

34 McBride, Sam. 'Thousands of NIO files have been quietly hidden – and lots of them are acutely sensitive.' *The Belfast Telegraph.* 24 June 2023.

35 McCaffrey, B. 'Government destroyed Stalker Sampson files weeks before "Shoot to Kill" inquest was due to open.' *The Detail,* 19 September 2014.

36 Cobain, Ian. 'Revealed: the bonfire of papers at the end of Empire.' *The Guardian,* 29 November 2013. See also: Cobain, 2016, *op. cit.*

37 Murtagh, Peter. 'Mourners told of courageous officer who led shoot-to-kill inquiry in North.' *The Irish Times,* 2 March 2019.

38 Murtagh, Peter. 'Man whose faith was broken.' *The Guardian,* 20 December 1986.

39 See for example: Hamill, Desmond. *Pig in the middle: the army in Northern Ireland 1969-1984* (London: Methuen, 1985).

Chapter 26: Justice Removed is Justice Denied (pages 391 to 415)

1 See: Moloney, Ed. *A Secret History of the IRA* (London: Allen Lane, 2002). Holland, Jack and Susan Phoenix, *Policing the Shadows: The Secret War Against Terrorism in Northern Ireland* (London: Hodder & Staughton, 1996). See also: Frampton, Martyn. 'Agents and Ambushes: Britain's 'Dirty War' in Northern Ireland' in S. Cohen (Ed.). *Democracies at War against Terrorism* (Basingstoke: Palgrave MacMillan, 2008).

2 See for example: Matchett, *William. Secret victory: The Intelligence War that Beat the IRA,* (Belfast: Self Publication, 2016); Edwards, Aaron. *Agents of Influence: Britain's Secret Intelligence War against the IRA* (Dublin: Merrion Press, 2021).

3 Leahy, Thomas. *The Intelligence War Against the IRA* (Cambridge: Cambridge University Press, 2020).

4 Matchett, 2006. *op. cit.* pp. 100-101. He based his calculation on two bland assertions without any supporting evidence: first, that at any one time there were fifteen well-placed agents in the IRA; second, each agent saved on average 37 lives per year. Thus, adding up to 16,650 lives in a 30-year period.

5 Sarma, Kiran. 2005, *op. cit.*

6 Matchett, 2016, *op. cit.* pp. 47-59.

7 Taylor, Peter. 2023, *op. cit.*

8 See: Hillyard, 1993, *op. cit.* p. 1.

9 De Silva, 2012, *op. cit.* para. 4.38. (See chapter 21).

10 *Ibid.* para. 4.55.

11 *Ibid.* para. 4.61.

12 *Ibid.* para. 4.56.

13 *Ibid.* para. 4.88.

14 Hansard, House of Commons Debates, Stevens Inquiry, Vol. 405, Col. 89WH, 14 May 2003.

15 For information on the action, see: https://privacyinternational.org/legal-action/third-direction-challenge (Accessed 3 January 2021)

16 It was replaced by the Investigatory Powers Commissioner under the Investigatory Powers Act 2016.

17 Hansard, House of Commons, Prime Minister's written statement, Vol. 636, Col. 34WS, 1 March 2018.

18 *Ibid.*

19 Investigatory Powers Tribunal, Case Nos. IPT/17/86 & 87CH. Privacy International, Reprieve, CAJ, PFC v. SoS for Foreign and Commonwealth Affairs, SoS for the Home Department, GVHQ, Security Service, and Secret Intelligence Service. Re-Amended Statement of Grounds, 29 March 2019.

20 Security Service Guidelines on the use of Agents who participate in Criminality, March 2011. (See https://www.privacyinternational.org)

21 *Ibid.* para 3.

22 *Ibid.* para 5.

23 *Ibid.* para. 6.

24 *Ibid.* para. 9.

25 Investigatory Powers Tribunal, Case Nos. IPT/17/86 & 87CH, *op. cit.*

26 See: Security Service Act 1989, Section 1.

27 Boycott, Owen. 'MI5 provides immunity for agents' criminal acts, tribunal told.' *The Guardian.* 4 October 2019.

28 Cabinet Secretary. *Lessons learnt by government departments from Sir Desmond de Silva's Report of the Patrick Finucane Review*, (London: ND). https://assets.publishing.service.gov.uk/government/uploads/system/uploads/attachment_dat a/file/396046/de_Silva_report_of_patrick_finucane_review_-_report.pdf (Accessed 3 January 2020)

29 Investigatory Powers Tribunal, Case Nos. IPT/17/86 & 87CH. *Op. cit.*

30 The Investigatory Powers Tribunal, Judgment, 20 December 2019, [2019] UKIPTrib IPT_17_186_CH. Para. 60.

31 De Silva, 2012, *op. cit.* para. 112.

32 *Ibid.*

33 Privacy International and others v Secretary of State for Foreign and Commonwealth Affairs and others, [2021] EWCA Civ 330.

34 Judgment, 20 December 2019, *op. cit.* para. 61.

35 Privacy International and others v Secretary of State for Foreign and Commonwealth Affairs and others, *op. cit.* para. 20.

36 *Ibid.* para. 22.

37 *Ibid.* para. 57(2).

38 For an excellent critique of the Act see: Scott, Paul F. 'Authorising Crime: The Covert Human Intelligence Sources (Criminal Conduct) Act 2021.' *Modern Law Review,* 85:5 (2022) pp. 1245-1260.

39 Her Majesty's Revenue and Customs, Department of Health and Social Care, Home Office, Ministry of Justice, Competition and Markets Authority, Environment Agency, Financial Conduct Authority, Food Standards Agency, and Gambling Commission. The Covert Human Intelligence Sources (Criminal Conduct) Act 2021, Section 4, Part A1.

40 Grainne Teggart, Amnesty's Northern Ireland campaigns manager, quoted in: 'Undercover police and MI5 agents to be permitted to commit crimes.' *Scottish Legal News*, 20 September 2020.

41 McGurk, Tom. 'Who will pay for mass murder?' *Sunday Business Post*, 28 January 2007.

42 Home Secretary announces terms of reference for undercover policing inquiry, 16 July 2015. https://www.gov.uk/government/news/home-secretary-announces-terms-of-reference-for-undercover-policing-inquiry (Accessed June 2021)

43 Ellison, Mark and Alison Morgan. *Review of possible miscarriages of Justice: Impact of Undisclosed Undercover Police Activity on the Safety of Convictions. Report to the Attorney General,* HC 291. (London: Home Office, 2015).

44 Operation Turma. https://www.opturma.co.uk (Accessed 14 June 2022)

45 PPS, 6 December 2023, *op. cit.*

46 Ní Aoláin, 2000, *op. cit.* p. 96.

47 PPS, 29 October 2020, *op. cit.*

48 Howard, Harry. 'Britain's top IRA spy Stakeknife, two MI5 officers and prosecutor will not face charges after probe into Northern Ireland killings.' *Mail Online*, 29 October 2020.

49 Ware, John. 'Boris Johnson's handling of the troubled Anglo-Irish past is reckless'. *The Article*, 10 May 2021. https://www.thearticle.com/boris-johnsons-handling-of-the-troubled-anglo-irish-past-is-reckless (Accessed 27 November 2021)

50   Black, Rebecca and David Young. '"This is how to do legacy": Operation Kenova set benchmark for investigations says new Chief Constable.' *The Irish News*, 8 December 2023.

51   For a detailed analysis of limitations of post-Agreement investigative mechanisms see: CAJ. *The Apparatus of Impunity: Human Rights Violations and the Northern Ireland Conflict* (Belfast: Committee on the Administration of Justice, 2015).

52   Stormont House Agreement, 23 December 2014.

53   New Decade, New Approach, 9 January 2020.

54   Hansard, House of Commons, Addressing Northern Ireland Legacy Issues, 18 March 2020, HCWS168.

55   *Ibid.*

56   Joint Committee on Human Rights. Legislative Scrutiny: The Overseas Operations (Service Personnel and Veterans) Bill, 2020, para. 54.

57   Hansard, House of Commons, Addressing Northern Ireland Legacy Issues, 18 March 2020, *op. cit.*

58   Interim Resolution CM/ResDH(2020)367, Execution of the judgments of the European Court of Human Rights, McKerr and other seven cases against the United Kingdom, Adopted by the Committee of Ministers on 3 December 2020 at the 1390th meeting of the Ministers' Deputies.

59   The right to life. In the case of *McCann and other v United Kingdom*, arising out of the Gibraltar killings, states must conduct a full, open and transparent investigations into the death and refrain from unlawful killing.

60   Queen's Speech, 19 December 2020.

61   Secretary of State for Northern Ireland. *Addressing the legacy of Northern Ireland's past*, CP 498, July 2021.

62   PFC/JFF. *Dealing with the Legacy of the Past* (Derry: Pat Finucane Centre/Justice for the Forgotten, 2021), p. 4.

63   Archer, Bimpe. 'Legality of "shocking proposal" to abolish the right to inquests questionable – former DPP.' *The Irish News*, 16 July 2021.

64   McCambridge, Jonathan. 'Legacy plans raise "profound issues" about rule of law – human rights chief.' *Belfast Telegraph*, 16 July 2021.

65   UTV News. 'Northern Ireland Troubles Legacy: Government to introduce statute of limitations on prosecutions'. 21 July 2021. https://www.itv.com/news/utv/2021-07-14/northern-ireland-troubles-legacy-government-to-introduce-statute-of-limitations-on-prosecutions (Accessed 22 July 2021)

66   See: Bryson, Anna, Brian Gormally, Daniel Holder, Louise Mallinder, Kieran McEvoy and Gemma McKeown. *Addressing the Legacy of Northern Ireland's Past, The Model Bill Team's Response to the Northern Ireland Proposals* (Belfast: Queen's University Belfast and CAJ, 2021).

67   Secretary of State for Northern Ireland, 2021, *op. cit.* p. 20.

68   McKittrick, *et al.*, *op. cit.* 2001, attribute 367 of 3631 deaths to the army and RUC, and 3264 to Republicans and Loyalists. i.e. 10 per cent and 90 per cent respectively. Attributing the 171 murders and conspiracies to murder, in which the four state agents and informers are believed to have been involved, to the army and RUC increases the percentage to 14.8 per cent.

69   See Cadwallader, *op. cit.* 2013.

70   PONI. 1994, *op. cit.* para. 4.195.

71   Brendan O'Leary. *A Treatise on Northern Ireland, Volume 3: Consociation and Confederation* (Oxford: Oxford University Press, 2019c), p. 288.

72   See Bryson, *et al.* 2021, pp. 32-34.

73   Duffy, Joe and Freya McClements. *Children of the Troubles: The untold story of the Children Killed in the Northern Ireland Conflict* (Dublin: Hatchette Books Ireland, 2019), p. xx.

74   Northern Ireland Troubles (Legacy and Reconciliation) Bill, 17 May 2022, Clause 38.

75   McEvoy, Kieran, Anna Bryson, Louise Mallinder, Daniel Holder, Gemma McKeown and Brian Gormally. *Model Bill Team initial response to Northern Ireland Troubles (Legacy and Reconciliation) Bill* (Belfast: Queen's University Belfast and CAJ, 2022).

76   Hansard, House of Commons, Northern Ireland (Legacy and Reconciliation) Bill, Vol. 715, Col. 231. 24 May 2022.

77   McCambridge, Jonathan. 'Legacy Act has sparked 16 legal bids so far court hears.' *Irish News*, 21 September 2023.

78   'Ireland had "no option" but to take case against UK over Northern Ireland Troubles legacy Act, says Taoiseach.' *The Irish Times*, 20 December 2023.

79   Queen's Speech, 19 December 2019, *op. cit.*

80 Hansard, House of Commons, Addressing Northern Ireland Legacy Issues, 18 March 2020, *op. cit.*

81 Secretary of State for Northern Ireland. Addressing the legacy of Northern Ireland's past, CP 498, July 2021.

82 Hansard, House of Commons, 24 May 2022, *op. cit.*

83 Ward, James. 'Former veterans minister "does not have confidence" in Brandon Lewis.' *Belfast Telegraph*, 3 July 2021.

84 Bryson, *et al. op. cit.* Chapter 1

85 See: CAJ. *Briefing from the Committee on the Administration of Justice on the Northern Ireland Troubles (Legacy and Reconciliation) Bill, House of Lords Report Stage, Government Amendments* (Belfast: Committee on the Administration of Justice, 2023), p. 2.

86 Northern Ireland Troubles (Legacy and Reconciliation) Act, 2023, Section 4 (3).

87 SoS announces ICRIR Chief Commissioner. 11 May 2023. https://www.gov.uk/government/news/secretary-of-state-announces-icrir-chief-commissioner (Accessed 12 May 2023)

88 See for example the views of Christine Duffy whose 15-year-old brother Seamus was killed by a plastic bullet fired by an RUC officer in 1989. 'Victims voice concern about appointment of former police officer Peter Sheridan to legacy body.' *ITV News*, 14 September 2023. See also: PFC Press Statement on the appointment of the Commissioner of Investigations to the ICRIR, 14 September 2023.

89 SDLP. *Protecting the People, Patten and Politics: SDLP Response to MI5 paper.* (Belfast: Social, Democratic and Labour Party, 2006). https://www.patfinucanecentre.org/sites/default/files/2016-11/0610sdlp.pdf (Accessed 26 September 2023)

90 Feeney, Brian, 'British Bad Faith belies season of goodwill.' *The Irish News*, 27 December 2023.

91 Young, Connla. 'New legacy investigations chief reveals he consulted republicans and loyalists before going for the post.' *The Irish News*, 16 October 2023.

92 See: PONI. *The investigation by police of the murder of Mr. Sean Brown on 12 May 1997* (Belfast: Police Ombudsmen for Northern Ireland, 2004). The Ombudsman concluded that the 'investigation was not efficiently and properly carried out, and no earnest effort made to identify those who carried out the murder'. She found no evidence of police collusion, but the current problem over intelligence suggests some MI5 involvement.

93 Young, Connla. 'Family of Sean Brown say treatment at hands of state agencies "cruel, inhumane and degrading".' *The Irish News*, 23 November 2023.

94 Young, Connla. 'Lawyer: Brown inquest delays a "public shame and disgrace".' *The Irish News*, 2 December 2023.

95 'State agents among 25 linked to Brown murder.' *The Irish News*, 28 February 2024.

96 PONI. *The investigation by police of the murder of Mr. Sean Brown on 12 May 1997* (Belfast: Police Ombudsmen for Northern Ireland, 2004).

97 Young, Connla. 'Sean Brown murder: Nuala O'Loan might have "produced a very different report" if she'd known about state agent links.' *The Irish News*, 28 February 2024.

98 Young, Connla. 'RUC carried out surveillance op lifted before Brown murder.' *The Irish News*, 6 March 2024.

99 Judicial Communications Office, Summary of Judgment, 24 February 2024.

100 Hansard, House of Commons, Vol. 690, Col. 878, 10 March 2021.

101 Wagner, Adam. *Emergency State: How We Lost Our Freedoms in the Pandemic and Why It Matters* (London: Bodley Head, 2022).

102 Northern Ireland Protocol Bill: UK government legal position, Foreign, Commonwealth & Development Office Policy Paper, 13 June 2022.

103 EU takes new legal action against UK over post-Brexit deal changes, BBC News, 15 June 2022.

104 O'Brien, James. *How they broke Britain* (London: WH Allen, 2023), p. 99.

105 Mason, Rowen and Aletha Adu. 'Government attacks on lawyers degrading, say former Tory law officers.' *The Guardian*, 11 August 2023.

Index